THE RENAISSANCE SPEAKS HEBREW

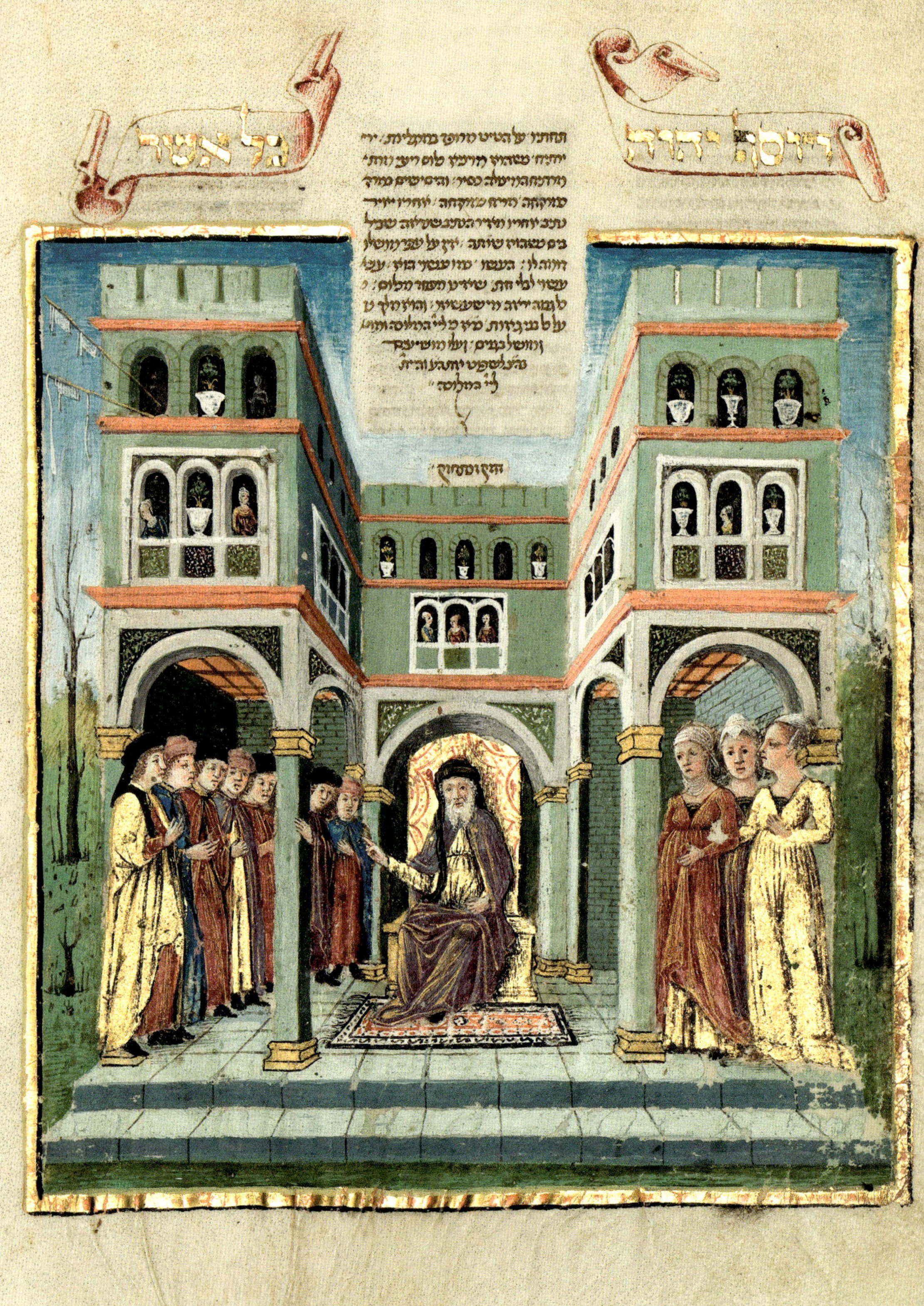

כל אשר

ויקם יהוה

תחתנו על הטיט הרוקע מוכלים יחיה
יחיה מהוזי הריבץ שום ריב נותי
מרה המריטה כסיר והסיסים מרה
מריקה מרה מזוקקה יוחרו יחיר
נתב יוחרין וצירי הטעב נשטרוה שבל
בם שבוותי שוותב יחין על שברו מ
הוזה לו העשו מזו עשרי הזי עשי
עשרי ומלי חת שידיע המוד מלום
לגבוה ירוה ורי שעטיאו והוזי ת
על ט מגזיות מיז כי לי הזולוס
נוושלכנים ועל מושיעב
מה לשפט יחתבהעו זהית
לי מלוכה

חזיומתוק

THE RENAISSANCE SPEAKS
HEBREW

edited by
Giulio Busi and Silvana Greco

SilvanaEditoriale

Medal of the President
of the Italian Republic

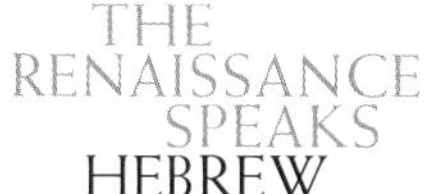

THE RENAISSANCE SPEAKS HEBREW

An Exhibition by
The National Museum
of Italian Judaism
and the Shoah

Under the Patronage of

*Ministero per i beni
e le attività culturali
Regione Emilia-Romagna
Comune di Ferrara
Unione delle Comunità
Ebraiche Italiane
Comunità Ebraica di Ferrara*

Ferrara, MEIS
April 12 – September 15, 2019

Exhibition Curators
Giulio Busi and Silvana Greco

*Museum and Exhibition
Design*
Studio GTRF
Giovanni Tortelli
Roberto Frassoni
Architetti Associati

*Works and Coordination
Management*
Giovanni Tortelli
with Francesca Ferlinghetti,
Erika Oliboni, Davide Piazza

*Graphic Design,
Reconstructive Drawings,
Re-compositions*
Studio GTRF
Giovanni Tortelli
Roberto Frassoni
Architetti Associati
with Daniele De Santis, Rocco
Pagnoni, Alessandro Polo

*Design and Creation of
Multimedia Installations*
Umberto Saraceni
Amalia Zeffiro

Brand Design
Teikna Design
Claudia Neri
with Elisa Stagnoli

Translations
Vicky Franzinetti

Press Office and Marketing
Studio Esseci

Shipping
Montenovi

Insurance
Assicurazioni Generali

Installation and Supplies
Amisura s.r.l.
Apice Venezia s.r.l.
Permasteelisa Group
Archi&Media s.r.l.
Graphic Report
Bosi Alessandro
Italvideo Service s.r.l.

Technical Assistance
Andrea Conci

Security Manager
Stefano Bergagnin

Legal Advice
Maria Letizia Govoni

With the support of

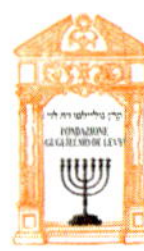

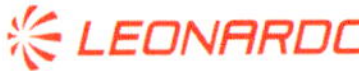

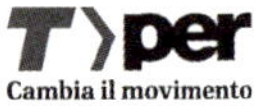

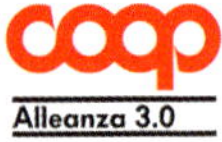

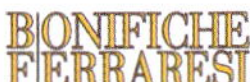

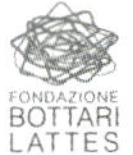

The exhibition was made possible thanks to the generous contribution of Ambassador Giulio Prigioni

and of:
Norsa Pesaro Family
Dr. Alessandro Treves
Comitato Nazionale per le celebrazioni del centenario della nascita di Giorgio Bassani

Lenders

Accademia Carrara, Bergamo
Archivio di Stato di Ferrara
Archivio di Stato di Firenze
Archivio di Stato di Modena
Archivio di Stato di Palermo
Archivio di Stato di Pesaro e Urbino
Archivio di Stato di Venezia
Basilica di Sant'Andrea – Diocesi di Mantova
Biblioteca Apostolica Vaticana
Biblioteca Ariostea, Ferrara
Biblioteca Civica "Vincenzo Joppi", Udine
Biblioteca Estense – Gallerie Estensi, Modena
Biblioteca Mediceo-Laurenziana, Florence
Biblioteca Palatina – Complesso Monumentale della Pilotta, Parma
Biblioteca Queriniana, Brescia
Biblioteca Teresiana, Mantova
Catedral de Mallorca, Palma de Mallorca
Civici Musei d'Arte Antica – Museo della Cattedrale, Ferrara
Civici Musei d'Arte Antica – Palazzo Schifanoia, Ferrara
Comunità Ebraica di Ferrara
Comunità Ebraica di Vercelli
Direzione Generale Archivi, MiBAC, Roma
Fondazione Palazzo Bondoni Pastorio, Castiglione delle Stiviere
Galleria Doria Pamphilj, Rome
Musée d'art et d'histoire du Judaïsme – long-term loan from the Musée de Cluny, Musée National du Moyen âge, Paris
Museo Diocesano Tridentino, Trento
Pinacoteca Nazionale di Siena – Polo Museale della Toscana
Staatliche Museen zu Berlin – Gemäldegalerie

Catalogue edited by
Giulio Busi and Silvana Greco

With the support of
Fondazione De Lévy

Essays by
Guido Bartolucci
Giulio Busi
Donatella Calabi
Saverio Campanini
J. H. Chajes
Andreina Contessa
Miriam Davide
Silvana Greco
Maria Giuseppina Muzzarelli
Mauro Perani
David B. Ruderman
Angela Scandaliato
Salvatore Settis
Giacomo Todeschini
Francesca Trivellato
Giuseppe Veltri
Gianni Venturi
Joanna Weinberg

Catalogue of exhibited works by
Giulio Busi

page 2
Job seated on a chair of honor, from the *Rothschild Miscellany*, Italy, c. 1479. Israel Museum, Jerusalem

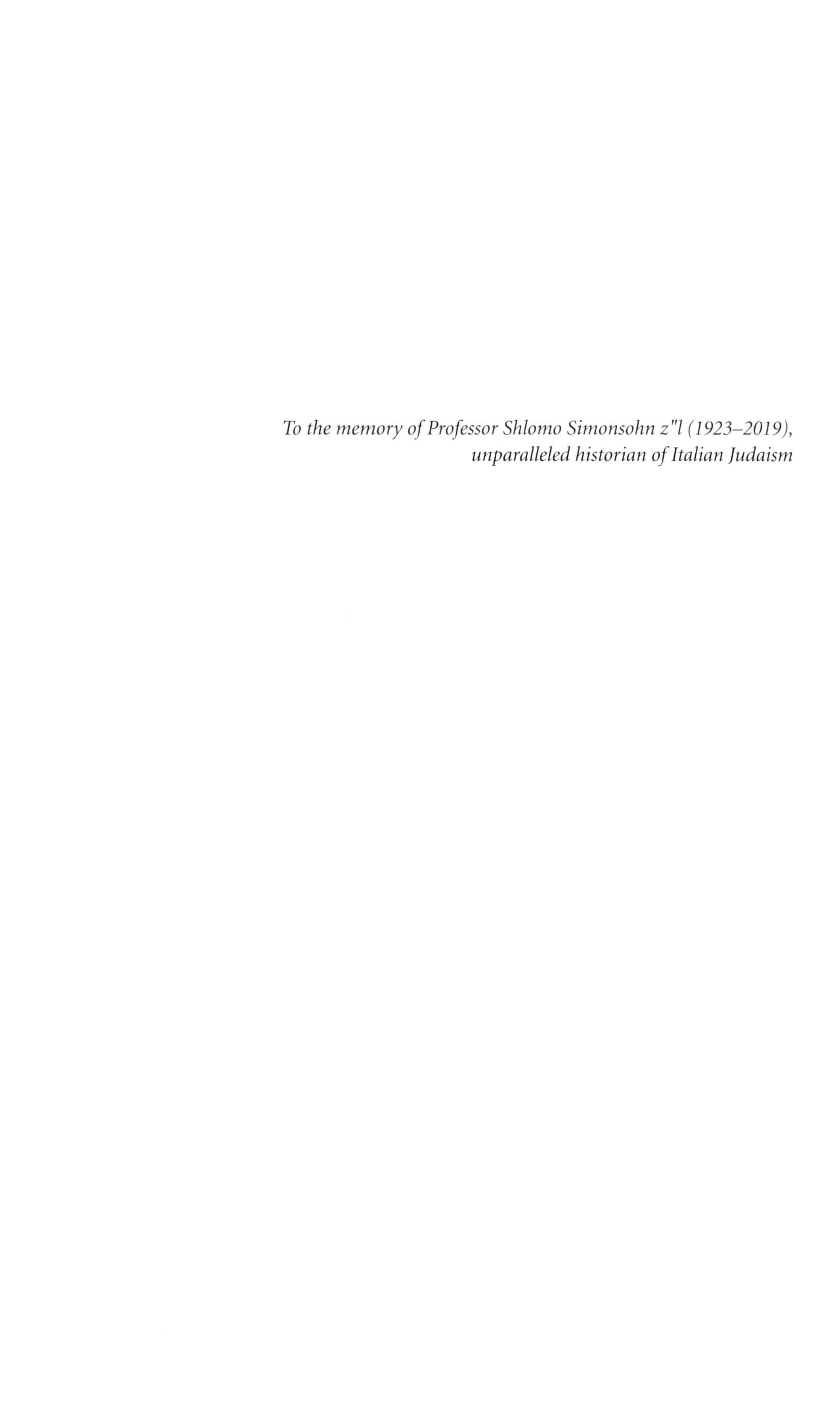

*To the memory of Professor Shlomo Simonsohn z"l (1923–2019),
unparalleled historian of Italian Judaism*

Contents

Jews, an Italian Story:
A Fascinating New Chapter

Dario Disegni
President
The National Museum of Italian Judaism and the Shoah

Following the success of *Jews, An Italian Story. The First Thousand Years*, with which in December 2017 it launched its new exhibition space, inaugurated by the President of the Italian Republic, Sergio Mattarella, The National Museum of Italian Judaism and the Shoah (MEIS) now presents *The Renaissance Speaks Hebrew*. Curated by Giulio Busi and Silvana Greco, this major new exhibition offers a fascinating preview of the museum's second section of permanent exhibits, providing an opportunity to verify the communication, display, and narrative solutions chosen to present the collection to the public.

The exhibition, which was awarded the prestigious Medal of the President of the Italian Republic, explores one of the richest and most varied periods in the history of the Italian peninsula—one responsible for the emergence of an Italian cultural identity—through the prism of the interactions between Italian Jews and the Christian-majority society that surrounded them; a prolific and productive dialogue founded on the universal values of Humanism. Designed by the Studio GTRF Giovanni Tortelli Roberto Frassoni, *The Renaissance Speaks Hebrew* offers visitors from Italy and elsewhere a unique opportunity to experience that wondrous age for themselves, leading them on a journey from Venice to Ferrara, and on to Pisa, Genoa, and Rome across the arc of the fifteenth to the mid-sixteenth centuries. It describes the Renaissance cities in which the Jewish communities lived and worked, the synagogues where they gathered to pray, the crafts and professions that provided their livelihoods, and the art in which they sought to express their culture, including the esoteric discipline of Kabbalah.

The exhibits include paintings by Mantegna, Carpaccio, Mazzolino and Sassetta—never presented before, all together, to the wider public—all testament to a fascination with Judaism and the Hebrew language. There are also examples of the Renaissance finest Jewish art, from painting, sculpture and carving to the written word. These include: the oldest extant wooden synagogue furnishings in Italy, a 1472 *Aron ha-qodesh* (Holy Ark) and a *Bimah* (pulpit) originally from Modena, which are making their first return to Italy from Paris; the oldest Torah scroll in the world still in use by a Jewish community, the thirteenth-century *Sefer Torah* of Biella; the so-called *Maimonides's codex*, a manuscript of the *Guide for the Perplexed* by the celebrated Jewish physician and philosopher Moses Maimonides (1138–1204) that was conserved for centuries by the Norsa family of Mantua before its very recent acquisition and restoration by the Italian Ministry of Cultural Heritage and

Activities; and, on loan from the Vatican Library and the British Library, Giovanni Pico della Mirandola's translations of Kabbalistic texts.

On behalf of the MEIS, and myself, I wish to thank our distinguished curators, the institutions that have loaned exhibits, the exhibition designers, the conservators, those who have contributed to the catalogue, our publisher, and all of the creative and skilled professionals who have made *The Renaissance Speaks Hebrew* such a unique experience for our visitors.

I also wish to express profound gratitude for the support provided by the MiBAC (Italian Ministry of Cultural Heritage and Activities), which has provided the MEIS with the essential resources it needs to fulfill its constitutional objectives of promoting awareness of the history and culture of Italy's Jewish people, and dialogue between the different communities that make up Italian society.

Our warmest thanks also to the Ferrara City Council and the Emilia-Romagna Regional Authority, not only for their generous backing, but also the practical and moral support they have provided throughout the museum's testing, but increasingly inspiring, journey to date.

The MEIS enjoys an equally close relationship with the UCEI (Union of Italian Jewish Communities), which has provided active and positive input on the role of the museum and how it can engage with the issues of greatest interest to Italian Jews; the same applies to the network of major Jewish and memorial museums around the world.

This exhibition would not have been possible without the contribution of key private partners. I would particularly like to thank Intesa Sanpaolo, which was involved in our inaugural exhibition, and which we have again been able to count on for support. The same is true, of course, for our individual donors, none more than Ambassador Giulio Prigioni; the museum's teaching room will be dedicated in memory of his daughter Francesca, who tragically passed away at a young age in Israel.

There only remains for me to express a final wish: that this significant new exhibition—which is as original as it is important in the cultural education of the Italian and European people—may help the MEIS to consolidate its progress and increase its profile and popularity in Italy and further afield; all this as it pursues a path that is undoubtedly challenging but more essential than ever to the promotion of the fundamental values of civilization at this complex moment in history.

Let Us Draw a Lesson
for Today from Our Past

Simonetta Della Seta

Director
The National Museum of Italian Judaism and the Shoah

Showcasing the Renaissance at The National Museum of Italian Judaism and the Shoah (MEIS) marks a critical step in the museum's growth. Not only because this beautiful exhibition, curated by Giulio Busi and Silvana Greco, and designed by Studio GTRF Giovanni Tortelli Roberto Frassoni, adds another building block to the museum's permanent content, but also because the Renaissance chapter of Jewish history, and in particular that of the Italian Renaissance, touches the heart of the museum's mission in all senses. It tells the story of a dialogue between a majority and a minority: complex but possible; not always free of darkness, but practicable; sometimes fruitful and often enriching. This is an invaluable lesson that Italy learns from its past and offers to the present, in particular to Europe. Spreading this lesson is the primary role that has been entrusted to MEIS by its institutional supporters, understood as a commitment by those building its content, and recognized by its visitors.

During the Italian Renaissance, Jews intertwined with the life around them and were active players, taking on leading roles and serving as true interlocutors. As we first learned from Roberto Bonfil (*Gli ebrei in Italia all'epoca del rinascimento* 1991), the diversity/contrast represented by Jewish identity had "even a positive function." In terms of historiography, we have fortunately moved well away from what the great American historian, Salo W. Baron (1895–1989), termed, a "lachrymose conception of Jewish history." Jews shaped their own lives and were in a position to participate in the great cultural revolution that was underway during the Renaissance. At times, they were fully a part of it, deep in its workings, inspiring movements and productive mechanisms. To again cite Roberto Bonfil, "It is the story of gaining new self-awareness through specular reflection of the other, which is to say, reflecting the Other as if in a mirror."

The British historian Cecil Roth, a staunch supporter of the Italian Jewish cause, was so intrigued by the role of Jews during the Renaissance that he published the volume *The Jews in the Renaissance* in 1959. It was the first study to reveal the originality and extent of this cultural embrace, as well as its effects on both the dominant culture and, in an almost mirror-like way, that of the Jews. Indeed, Judaism had a critical impact on Renaissance society, entering it fully, enriched by it and at the same time contributing to its growth. A society that engages in dialogue, is today as well, a society more capable of development.

Another great strength of the exhibition *The Renaissance Speaks Hebrew* is the close connection that it creates between MEIS and the city of Ferrara, which was a linchpin of and hothouse for dialogue between Jews and Christians during the age of Humanism. Visitors can end their time at MEIS and continue to immerse themselves in the Renaissance city, as well as in Jewish Ferrara, which was of course, the source of several of the exhibition's key objects and some of its most engaging stories.

In short, the Renaissance represented a turning point in history, just as it does today in the museum. It ushered in the unexpected rebirth of Jewish culture after suffering a trauma nearly equal to that of the destruction of the Temple of Jerusalem by Emperor Titus in 70 CE: the expulsion of the Jews from all of the Spanish territories—southern Italy included—following the Alhambra Decree in 1492. After they were brutally driven out of all of Italy's southern cities, where in some cases they comprised 10% of the population and contributed to its cultural and economic fabric, some of the Jews headed to Ottoman territory, while others moved north up the peninsula. They streamed not only into Rome, but also Florence, Mantua, Ferrara, Venice, Genoa, Pisa, and more. These were also the cities where Jews arrived fleeing from Spain and Portugal. And so, while the south was emptying itself of a Jewish culture that had been present there for more than fifteen centuries, the north was encountering a new Jewish culture, the Sephardic one (which takes its name from the Hebrew term for Spain).

This was when Jews with different origins began to coexist in Italian cities: they came from the Holy Land and Rome (their rite by this time designated as "Italian"), from Sicily, Catalonia, Castile, and Portugal (the Sephardic rite) and from Central Europe (the Ashkenazic rite, from the Hebrew word for Germany). This was especially true in Venice and Ferrara, generating positive effects on both Jewish culture and the world around it, before being hit again by a severe wave of anti-Semitism.

The exhibition also explains how the embrace between cultures can sometimes give rise to hostile prejudice. This is an extremely modern and important aspect of the exhibition's narrative. In brief, the story of anti-Semitism creates a link, in the museum, to the part of its permanent content that tells of the more recent persecutions and, in particular, the Shoah. After having seen the degree to which the Jews were truly part of the life, culture, and history of Italy, their discrimination, both old and new, comes as even more of a shock to the visitors. They are profoundly struck by the tragedy that it has wrought, not only for the Jews, but for everyone.

It is remarkable that MEIS can offer visitors, young and old, such a range of content only a year and a half after its opening. For this, we have to thank the museum's institutional supporters, the attention and constant stimulus provided by its leadership and administration, the passion and devotion of those who work there, the skill and helpfulness of all of the experts involved, the extraordinary professionalism of the curators, the unfailing creativity of the designers, the vision and generosity of the donors and the positive response from its tens of thousands of visitors. I would like to express my deepest gratitude to all of these wonderful people, who contribute greatly to building MEIS. Giving shape and breathing life into a project that is significant for our time is an unparalleled opportunity and a true privilege.

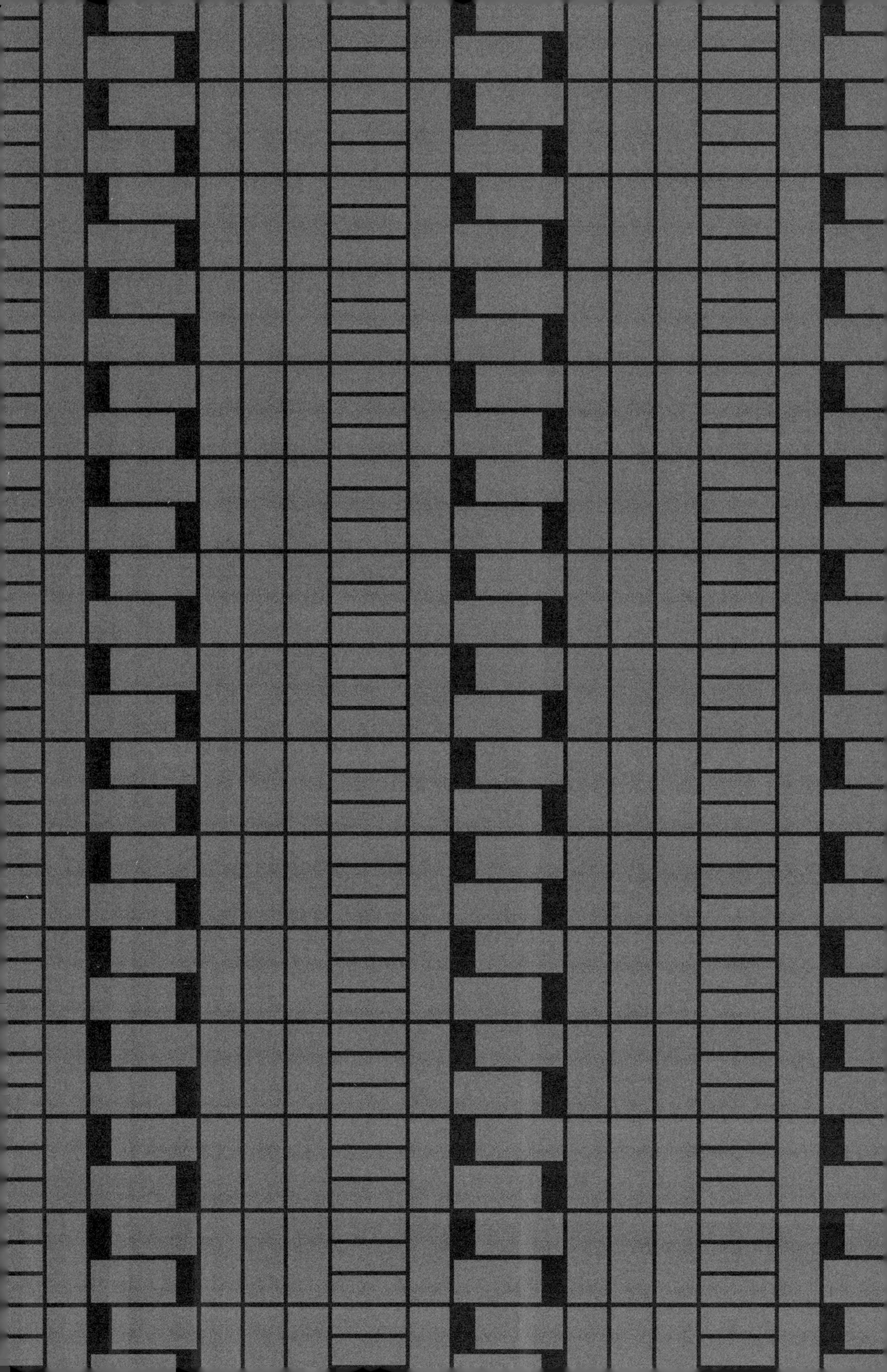

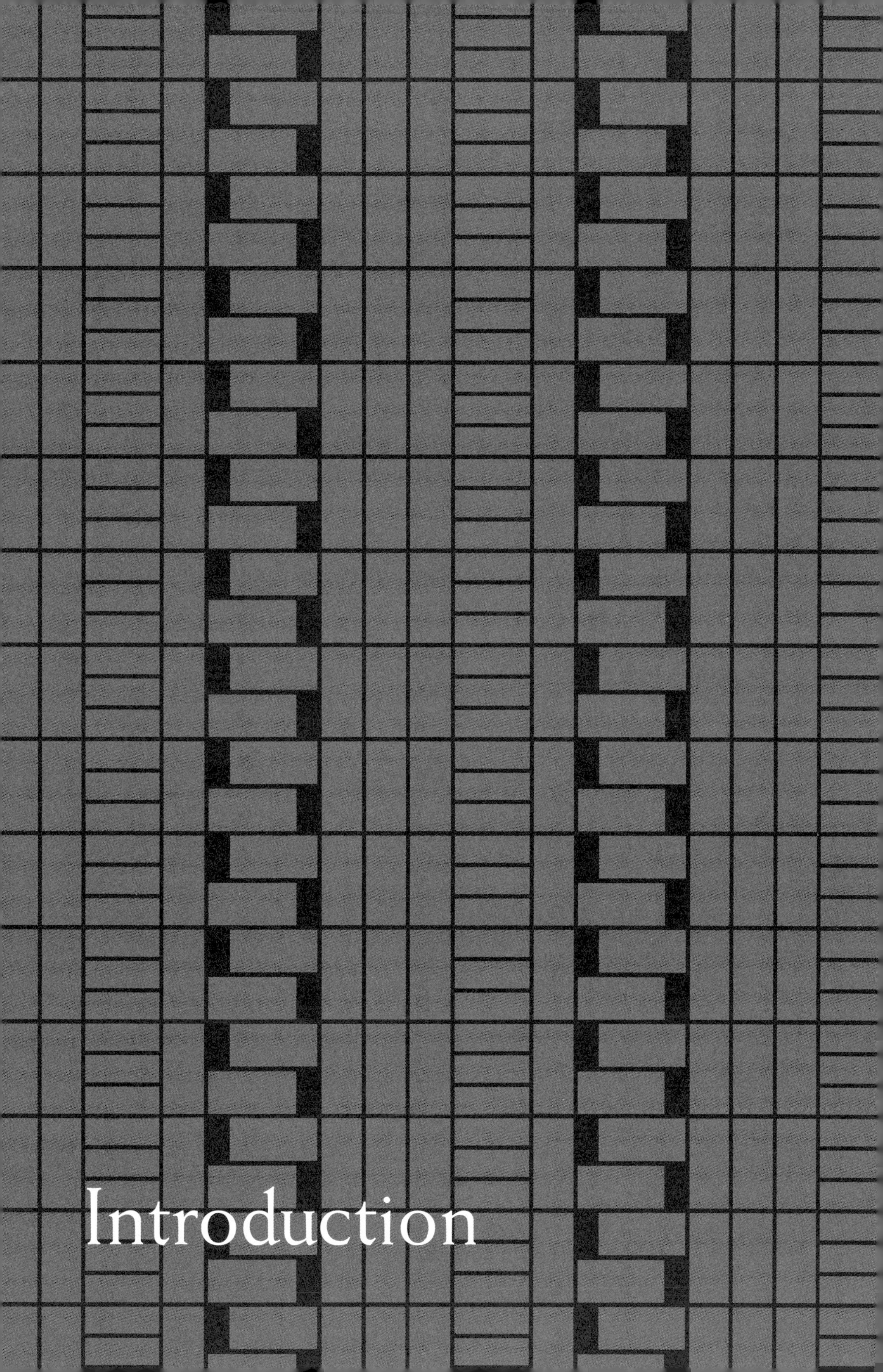

Introduction

The Renaissance Speaks Hebrew
Giulio Busi

The Plural Renaissance

Following the inaugural exhibition *Jews, An Italian Story. The First Thousand Years* (*Ebrei* 2017), MEIS (The National Museum of Italian Judaism and the Shoah) is now turning to one of the most important periods in the cultural history of Italy with the exhibition *The Renaissance Speaks Hebrew*. Given its unmatched artistic creativity, its symbolic value, and the influence it exerted over the entire historical and intellectual edifice both north and south of the Alps, the period of the Renaissance was clearly decisive in the creation of Italian identity.

It was also a time of widely-varying, even contradictory, events: encounters, clashes, peaceful moments and sudden ruptures. Not by chance, in recent historiography there has been talk of "Renaissances" (Crouzet-Pavan 2013) to highlight these multiple facets of intellectual life on the threshold of modernity. Indeed, the plural experimentation of the Renaissance has much to teach us today in our increasingly multicultural world. This is not because History repeats itself or because the past can be imitated, but rather because an open society should explore the myriad roots of its vitality.

The Renaissance Speaks Hebrew recounts this extraordinary period in the form of a dialogue. On the one hand, we hear the voice of the Christian-majority society, with its rich network of cities, courts, and territorial states in fierce competition among themselves for political, economic, and artistic supremacy; on the other hand, we listen to the powerful and expressive voice of the Italian Jews. At the beginning of the Renaissance, the Jews in Italy had a long history behind them and a widespread presence throughout the country, with strong autonomy and an urgent desire to participate in a shared impetus toward revitalization. The message that *The Renaissance Speaks Hebrew* transmits to the Italian and international society of today is clear and affirmative: Jews were present during the Renaissance, on the frontlines, active and resourceful. Of course they took, imitated, and reproduced. But they also gave, influenced, and inspired.

Although Judaism represented an integral part of the Renaissance world, the complex nature of the interaction between the renewed Christian tradition and Jewish identity in Italy has not yet been adequately studied. While clearly the majority culture disseminated many of its own formal models, Judaism nonetheless managed to penetrate the citadels of art, literature and humanistic philosophy, giving the Italian Renaissance certain unique and novel inflections.

In the interest of reconstructing a similar commingling of experiences today, first of all the debt of Italian culture to Judaism must be recognized and the Jewish premises of Renaissance culture explored. Without hyperbole, without rhetoric. Creativity does not always mean harmony, nor acceptance always devoid of trauma. Thus episodes of intolerance, contradictions, social exclusion, and violence will also emerge. The Renaissance must be understood through its shadows as well as its many lights. This type of critical approach is even more necessary when dealing with the history of the Jewish people, committed as they are to the strenuous defence of their own specificity.

The Renaissance speaks Hebrew, with its dark corners and contradictions as well as its exceptional creative power.

A shared space

The exhibition is grounded in a shared space, a zone of confrontation, of encounters and conflicts between Judaism and Christian society. It is a material space, with historic documents and artistic creations, but also a virtual stage for representation of the self and the other (see also Greco's essay in this volume). Through the constant mirroring of physical dimensions and mental images, the visitor is able to measure the incursion of Renaissance elements into Jewish culture and, conversely, to appreciate the reverberation of Judaism in Renaissance thought and art forms.

The exhibition is divided into four thematic centers, each representing an area of interest and bringing together artistic and literary expressions with documentary testimony. On display are everyday objects and evidence of the liturgical and literary life of Jews, synagogue furnishings, illuminated manuscripts and even a sample of numerous archival documents that anchor the Jewish heritage in the historic memory of Italy. The perception of Judaism in the Renaissance is revealed in the writings of Christian scholars of Hebrew and Jewish studies and, even more so, in several masterpieces of painting in which the Hebrew language and the visual signs of Judaism are incorporated as structural elements of the artistic vocabulary.

Chronological, geographic, and thematic criteria

The sections are articulated according to the three-fold criteria of chronology, geographic distribution, and intellectual synergy. Chronologically speaking, the exhibition examines the period between the early fifteenth century and the middle of the sixteenth, which is to say, from the full flowering of Humanism to the conclusion of the Council of Trent. While the first decades of the fifteenth century were marked by the emergence of a philological interest in Hebrew, documented, for example, by the studies of Marco Lippomano (Busi

Sera damnato ale pungiente spine,
Se sancta humilita non li fa schermo. finis

Non dico fra li hebrei ma fra christiani
qualunque sia, e prima amiser cino,
E guido caualchante, e lbuo sabino,
Miser colucio, e uoi nestor pisani,
Facio degluberti et passo fra zumani,
El poeta laurento fiorentino
Chinqueste rime fece ilsuo camino
Damor scriuendo in cose alte esoprani.
El stile suo quantumq alto ezentile
Fosse amico mio suppbo et antico
Non preterisse iltuo p quel chio sento
Maturo, graue, Alto, esignorile,

Ed ognj' uil parlar crudel nemico
Ne loro piu che mi fa contento   finis.

Responsiua salomonis hebrei ad antedictum

Gli antiqui gesti ho lecto di Romani
 Quel dale Historie antique, patauino
 Salustio generoso epelegrino
 Valerio ch Adopro le sacre mani
Codici ho lecto non sol di pagani
 Ma deli sacri: elsuo scriuer diuino
 Lantiquo Firmiano et Augustino
 Egli deuoti grandi de Ambrosani
Versi Anchor prose di cieschun guentile
 Ben ch que'l studio Ame sia nemico
 Za mai legendo lor no fui contento
Non ch Ingiegno loro Fusse ville
 Ma di ti Ferarino claro io dico
 Ch ognaltro auanza il tuo bel sentimeto

and Campanini 2004), humanist and high-ranking dignitary of the Republic of Venice, the 1560s, with the definitive advent of the Counter Reformation, brought an irreversible caesura in Jewish social life and in Italy's cultural climate.

Within these two time limits, the exhibition is divided by geographic clusters, reflecting the specific dynamics of the Jewish-Christian interaction topographically. This geography is largely determined by cultural circles and courts: the Florence of the Medici, the Marches of the Montefeltro and Venice's dominions, then Milan and Genoa, and finally Rome with its papal patronage. In the background lies the south, where the ancient, strong Jewish presence would be eliminated by expulsions between the late fifteenth century and the early decades of the sixteenth. Special attention is devoted to Mantua under the Gonzaga and Ferrara under the Este, full-fledged hothouse of interconnections between humanistic culture and Jewish tradition. In each case, the exhibition illustrates the situation of the Jews as well as Christians' exploration of Judaism, finding there material for theoretical and artistic inspiration.

Given that the history of Renaissance culture is first and foremost a story of intellectual circles and personal relationships between members of the elite, the exhibition also offers a third level of representation—a cross-section view of the complex web of interpersonal contacts, most of which are specifically documented or can at least be inferred from the material evidence.

The historical context

At the end of the thirteenth century, at the dawn of the humanist movement, the Jewish communities in Italy were in a phase of profound transformation. While, for centuries, the Jews of Rome represented the strong core of Italian Judaism, their progressive migration northwards now brought moneylenders of Roman origin into central Italy and subsequently into Romagna and the Po Valley. At the same time, a good number of Jews from French and German territories were migrating toward the south, settling principally in the regions of Veneto and Piedmont (Colorni 1983, pp. 229–42; Toaff 1987). Thus Jews became an increasingly vital part of Italy's dynamic economic life in the fourteenth and fifteenth centuries.

Indeed, it is thanks not least to the contribution of Jewish capital that the cities and courts of Italy were in a position to expand their sphere of investments, enabling the intense social and artistic ferment that transformed the peninsula into an unparalleled intellectual laboratory. While maintaining their own distinct identity, Italian Jews entered into increasingly close contact with the Christian majority in daily life. Until the very end of the fifteenth century, Italy was only marginally affected by the traumatic persecutions that afflicted Judaism in the rest of Europe, and even church-based anti-Judaism was balanced by considerations of the economic utility of the Jewish communities, which, in any event, were almost always small and relatively elite. Thus, in addition to brisk economic interactions, Jewish literary and artistic expression also had room to flourish, in the spirit of re-awakening intrinsic to the Renaissance.

Some learned Christians began to turn their attention to Judaism as an as yet unexplored, but fundamental source of knowledge. In the general trend of re-evaluation of the ancient sources typical of humanist ideals, Hebrew gradually acquired its own prestige, alongside Latin and Greek. It was in Italy, in fact, that Christian Hebraism first appeared, thanks to scholars who not only collected books but also sought to acquire the rudiments of the language and a general notion of Jewish culture through direct relations with Jews themselves. While such studies frequently took place in an ecclesiastical context, there were many lay intellectuals interested in exploring Jewish wisdom as well.

The exhibition itinerary

The exhibition is divided into four sections, within which relevant thematic groupings highlight phases of special cultural intensity.

Over the course of two hundred years, from the late thirteenth to the late fifteenth century, Judaism in Italy underwent a profound transformation as Jews settled in countless different localities. Sometimes, these were revivals of ancient or early medieval communities, but more often, such a growth was a new and surprising phenomenon, though not always a positive one. The Po Valley, where the Jewish presence was once so sparse, blossomed with enclaves that penetrated deep into the territory, permeating local economic activity, social life, and culture.

Southern Italy, on the other hand, had a more complex, disconnected situation and in fact, the overall Renaissance dynamics there have yet to be fully understood. While Naples had abundant Jewish cultural activity throughout the fifteenth century (Lacerenza 2002) and was, for a number of years, a safe haven for Jews exiled from Spain and Portugal, important initiatives also flourished in other regions. A telling example is the commentary on the Torah written by Salomon ben Isaac and published in Reggio Calabria in 1475 (Iakerson 2012). Meanwhile, however, although Jews were expanding their presence throughout central and northern Italy in the period covered by the exhibition, they were being expelled from Sicily and Sardinia and later from the entire peninsular south, which until then had been demographically crucial for Italian Judaism. This was a drastic upheaval, with a total reversal in populations and places.

While the expulsion decree of 1492, and subsequently those of 1510, 1514, and 1541, grew out of the harsh anti-Jewish policy reigning in the Iberian peninsula, the success of settlements in the new territories east and north of Rome was achieved thanks to the initiative of Italian Jews. At first concurrent with loans from Christians, then with a distinct superiority, and finally holding a virtual monopoly, financiers from Rome conquered a role of great importance. They operated with city authorizations and, beginning with the papacy of Martin V (1417–31), by papal exemption as well (Papal Bull *Sicut Judeis* of January 31, 1419 in Simonsohn 1988–91, vol. 2, no. 596), granting loans secured by pledges (Toaff 1996, pp. 268–69).

Around the moneylenders and their families, and on the basis of well-defined term contracts with local authorities—the so-called *condotte*—small, mobile, enterprising groups of Jews began to gather in localities large and small. It has been calculated that while representing less than one percent of the population, between the fourteenth and sixteenth centuries Jews settled in approximately fifteen percent of the existing towns of central and northern Italy (Luzzati 1996, p. 212). As Christians gradually withdrew from providing consumer loans in the late fourteenth and early fifteenth centuries, Jewish bankers were able to jump into the resulting financial vacuum. Clearly advantageous for the Christian elites, who in this way obtained financing for their economic activities and consumption, the Jewish bank by pledge also served to control passive interest rates for the less well-off classes, or to "help the poor," as the *condotte* often specified.

The benefits brought by this financial activity were mutual. While the myth that all Jews were rich reflects anti-Jewish stereotypes (see Todeschini's essay in this volume), contradicted by the sources, it is true that the most successful Jewish bankers achieved a socioeconomic level largely comparable to that of the Christian nobility and upper classes. As a matter of fact, during the Renaissance, Jews in Italy enjoyed a level of prosperity that elsewhere would only be reached after emancipation (Luzzati 1996, p. 213).

Such wellbeing attracted new blood from the rest of Europe and overseas, making Italy the most important demographic center of the diaspora. Sustained by trade and energized by cultural projects, Jewish Italy of the Renaissance was easy to idealize as a happy oasis in the long and tormented history of the Jews. This idealization, however, which predominated in the nineteenth- and much of twentieth-century historiography, must also take into account the destructive dynamics of prejudice and persecution. Even the limpid skies of Renaissance prosperity darken at times, and not only due to the expulsions in the south. With the bank being the fulcrum upon which expansion was based, it is no surprise that loans became the chosen object of many anti-Jewish attacks, especially in the fifteenth century. For preachers of the mendicant orders—Franciscans in particular, who promoted the Monti di Pietà (non-profit lending institutions)—Jews were enemies to be segregated, denied their economic and social influence, and, in the end, expelled (see Muzzarelli's essay in this volume).

Spaces, scenes, backdrops

Cities, homes and synagogues were the main spaces in which Jews operated. In the cities, we see them sometimes on the fringes and sometimes in the center of the urban scene. We see them in their homes, in the intimacy of their families, or busy at work, or in places of worship and collective identity. The Jewish presence in the cities of Italy was diverse and changing, just as was the face of the urban and political scene of the entire peninsula. In some centers, there is evidence of an almost uninterrupted presence of Jews for hundreds and hundreds of years; in others, Jews are recorded in documents and then fade away. They often lived grouped closely together in predominately Jewish streets or blocks, although there is also ample evidence of Jewish homes interspersed among the rest of the population. It was almost always their own choice to live together, however, as a way to keep the bonds within the group strong, ensure a more effective defense against anti-Jewish attacks, and pursue a full religious life of praying together, ritual slaughter, and religious instruction.

In one of the rare cases of Jews being corralled into a specific area of the city, in the thirteenth century Jews in Pisa were obliged to live in their own alleyway, called the "*classus Iudeorum*," similar to but not quite a genuine ghetto (Luzzati 1994, p. 514). The Jewish streets had their own colors, sounds, and customs, an intimate microcosm where Jewish identity was reinforced and the spaces and rhythms of daily life were shared. In the fourteenth century, Roman Jews, who lived dispersed in various areas of the city, were required to wear a distinguishing badge when among Christians but not when in largely or exclusively Jewish streets (Milano 1963, p. 149).

The situation in Ferrara during that same period was quite different. An oath of loyalty to Pope Clement V vowed by the citizens of Ferrara in 1310 (Fontana 1887, pp. 132–33; Colorni 1983, pp. 167–68; Franceschini 2007, p. 30 no. 46; Graziani Secchieri 2012, pp. 163–66) reveals a relatively large Jewish nucleus in the "Centum Vassurarum" district, living in close proximity with Christians. This contiguity almost certainly entailed daily exchanges and interaction—indeed, overall, a shared life experience (see Greco's essay in this volume, also as regards the contemporaneous persecution of Jews by the Ferrara inquisitor).

This is all still far, however, from the forced, discriminatory living arrangements that would be imposed almost everywhere in Italy as of the sixteenth century. The first to institute such residential restrictions was Venice, in 1516, when Jews were confined to an area in the Cannaregio district called *ghetto*, which became the definitive name for this contemptible form of segregation (see Calabi's essay in this volume). In theory, no synagogues could be built, and yet old ones could be restored as long as they were not too lavish or obtrusive. For centuries and centuries, since Christianity became the predominant religion, the existence of Jewish places of worship was tolerated under condition of rigid restrictions—rigid and inflexible at least on paper. Their enforcement varied widely and exceptions abounded. Thus here and there new synagogues appeared beside the older ones. While, as far as we know, the exteriors were always rather plain, the interiors were often ornate and carefully maintained. Almost the only traces that remain of medieval and early Renaissance synagogues take the form of iconographic testimony in illustrated manuscripts, and various rare artifacts. The heart of the synagogue is the *aron ha-qodesh*, the Holy Ark where the scrolls of the Torah are kept, embellished with silver finials and Hebrew script on parchment in black ink. The ancient holy words were read aloud during services, for which Jewish law required a quorum of at least ten adult men.

Professions and trades: real and imagined lives

The second section of the exhibition deals with the most common activities among Italian Jews of the time as well as their spiritual world. The itinerary is divided by exemplary types that defined the world of men and that of women. Outstanding Jewish intellectuals of this period often had the expertise to operate in a variety of fields. Not infrequently, men working as doctors were bankers as well, but also philosophers and poets capable of sophisticated theoretical reflection.

Jewish women were no less competent. Although their traditional roles as wives and mothers revolved around the home and family, we repeatedly find them involved in business. Many were moneylenders, on their own (see Davide's essay in this volume) or representing their husbands or sons; others were midwives or doctors. Such was the case of Virdimura, the Jewish Sicilian wife of a certain doctor Pasquale from Catania, who requested and obtained permission to practice medicine in 1376 (see cat. 10). She was certainly not the only woman with medical expertise, which, on the contrary, was probably not uncommon. This area, however, needs to be explored in future research.

In 1460, in Fano, we have documentation regarding Perna, a Jewess perhaps from Urbino, who was also granted her request to practice medicine (Luzzatto 1902, p. 27). There were also manuscript copyists, such as Paola, daughter of the Roman Jewish scribe Abraham ben Joab. The four codices she copied between 1288 and 1306 and the short personal references she included therein speak of a cultured and enterprising woman, able to tackle the challenging, complicated texts of rabbinical tradition (Busi 1990, pp. 45–47; Sabar 1990). In fifteenth-century Sicily there were even women managing taverns or working as matchmakers or auctioneers (Simonsohn 2011, p. 446 and 1997–2010, no. 7784, 4911).

The lives of Jews—as male and female dance teachers (see cat. 23), synagogue cantors, musicians, gamblers, coppersmiths, blacksmiths, silversmiths, jewelers, painters, tanners, fabric manufacturers and merchants—played out amongst themselves and with Christians, within the walls of their native cities and beyond distant seas. They traveled, came back again, dreamed of a pilgrimage to Jerusalem or actually settled there permanently. Or from Jerusalem, they moved back to Italy with the intention of staying there for as long as they could, for as long as possible.

A famous example of Aliyah, or emigration to the land of Israel, by an Italian Jew of the late fifteenth century was that of Obadiah of Bertinoro, rabbi and exegete. He set out from Città di Castello in 1486, stopped in Palermo for several months, and then continued on to Messina, Rhodes, Alexandria and Cairo. He eventually reached Jerusalem, where he remained until his death. Obadiah sent lengthy, vivid, inspired letters to Italy, which manifest the strong bond between Italian Judaism during the Renaissance and Jerusalem and the Holy Land ('Ovadiah da Bertinoro 1991).

Clashes

While it is true that Italian Jews enjoyed a fair degree of tolerance in this period, there continued to be episodes of persecution, which grew especially intense beginning in the second half of the fifteenth century and continuing into the sixteenth. The third section of the exhibition is devoted to this ongoing ordeal of antagonism, threats, abuse, and violence.

Anti-Judaism was expressed with varying degrees of intensity over the long history of Italy. In many cases, different levels of intolerance existed simultaneously in different geographical areas or even within a single city. There was no single, consistent policy or attitude that lasted from the fourteenth through the sixteenth century, the period under consideration here. There were often quite substantial divergences between actual social and political policies and Church theology, which sought to convert Jews, whom they tolerated while, nonetheless, relegating them to a distinctly inferior social condition. Not infrequently, popes and sovereigns first prohibited and harassed Jewish life within their dominions only to turn around and allow or even encourage it later. To give one of many possible examples, on May 3, 1427 Giovanna II d'Angiò Durazzo, Queen of Naples, abolished all privileges previously recognized for her Jewish subjects and forbid them to loan money, but then simply reversed her own decree on the following August 20. Ten days later, she re-authorized loans, at the enormous interest rate of 45%, no less, a totally unprecedented percentage (Milano 1963, pp. 188–89).

A volatile queen, one might say, were it not that the fate of Jews in the period we are considering was so volatile and discontinuous in general, forever teetering between co-existence and intolerance. While there is no question that they represented a significant

commistio

[Item postea dicto anno Indictionis et die … … abbatis … presentibus testibus …]

[…]

[Joseph olim magistri … ex una parte, et Franciscus olim domini … ex altera parte …]

[…]

finis

[Item postea dicto anno Indictionis et die et loco … testibus …]

[Johannes filius …]

component of the economic life of the era, thanks to their initiative and mobility, it is also evident that these very same qualities of entrepreneurship made them anathema to potential rivals and an easy target for social resentment. Long ingrained religious prejudices—Jews were accused of deicide for killing Jesus and of "perfidy" for their persistent refusal to adhere to the Christian faith—intertwined with denunciation of alleged Jewish "usurers."

During the fifteenth century, sermons condemning usury frequently sparked protest, violence, and assaults on Jewish property and people. One of the most sensational cases of persecution was a trial held in Trent during the reign of Prince-Bishop Johann Hinderbach, which resulted in the condemnation and execution of fifteen Jews from the local community accused of killing a Christian child named Simon Unferdorben on Easter of 1475. Veneration of the child, known as Simon of Trent, was officially approved in 1588 and only suppressed by the church in 1965 (see cat. 24).

Encounters: lived, painted, and written

Encounters between Jews and Christians—the subject of the fourth section of the exhibition—took place primarily in daily life, out of mutual curiosity. At times, this interest proved controversial while, at others, collaboration seems to have overcome the barriers of faith and identity. The accounts of clashes, anti-Judaism and discrimination are true; nonetheless, there was another side of Jewish life in Italy from the thirteenth to the sixteenth century with a different flavor, much less bitter, involving reciprocal curiosity, daily contact and even friendship.

It would be wrong to overestimate this brighter side and envision late medieval and Renaissance Italy as a blissful oasis, yet it is equally partial to negate the interpenetration between Jewish and Christian cultures. In fact, it is almost impossible not to recognize that interaction upon even cursory examination. One need simply browse through paintings of the great Italian masters of the period to realize that Jewish subjects, and their holy language, were in full view, even appearing in the foreground—and not in minor works.

It was the leading artists who presented this ancient, distinguished Judaism—almost always taken as a respected model—to the faithful in their churches and rich patrons in their palaces and castles. Giotto, Beato Angelico, Cosmè Tura, Ghirlandaio, Mantegna, Carpaccio, Michelangelo, and Raphael are only some of those among the ranks of artists drawn to Jewish themes in their paintings or sculptures, but surely this short list is enough to communicate whom we are dealing with here. Between the late thirteenth century and the early sixteenth, Judaism penetrated into the heart of artistic creativity in some of Italy's most important intellectual centers. Christians and Jews in Florence, Ferrara, Mantua, Venice, and Rome explored each other's traditions, as humanist Christians collected Hebrew books and studied the holy language, often with the help and friendship of learned Jews.

Art, however, was merely the outward sign—albeit a magnificent one—of what was happening in the studies of scholars and the courts of the great powers of the Renaissance. These courts, in fact, were the point of encounter *par excellence*, where Jews were generally welcomed and appreciated. Jewish moneylenders, doctors, and merchants were valued for their economic support, advice and even entertainment. Would you like another list—this time of princes, philosophers and men of letters? Lorenzo de' Medici, Federico da Montefeltro, Isabella d'Este, Giovanni Pico della Mirandola, and Angelo Poliziano were all patrons,

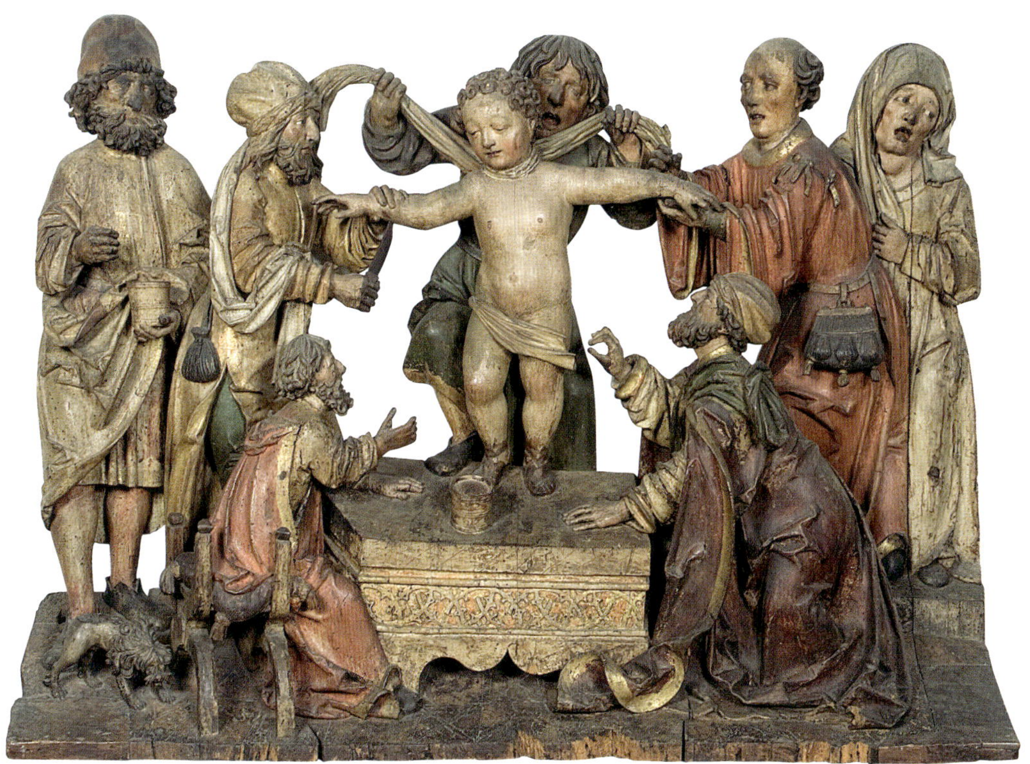

collectors, scholars and enthusiasts of Jewish culture. It was Pico who was responsible for the discovery of Jewish mysticism and its inclusion in the canon of humanistic knowledge.

Of course not everyone was in favor of this embrace of Jewish traditions. The *Conclusiones*, published by Giovanni Pico in 1486 and replete with the mysteries of the Jewish Kabbalah, were first banned and then burned by order of Pope Innocent VIII (Busi and Ebgi 2014, pp. VII-XLIX; see cat. 31), while the Christian Kabbalah was viewed as heresy almost as soon as it appeared. Nor did this period of exchange, discussion and dispute born of mutual curiosity last very long. By 1517, the furor of the Reformation was unleashed by Luther, nurtured not least by his Jewish studies, including translating the Bible from Hebrew into German.

The Church became more vigilant. Arguably, Luther's translation of the Bible would have been impossible without the scholarly Christian interest in Hebrew studies. And the Jews, free to come and go, to study with Christians and be their teachers, were they not a hotbed of doctrinal confusion and insubordination? Even before launching the counter-attack on the Protestants of northern Europe, test runs of the repression of dissent began right at home, and needless to say, the Jews were the ones to pay the price. In 1553, Julius

III ordered the first massive burning of Jewish books. In 1555, in the Papal Bull *Cum nimis absurdum*, Pope Paul IV ordained that Jews must live in specific areas separate from the rest of the population.

It was a time of bitter crisis, not only for Judaism. The entire culture and society of Italy suffered the repercussions of the authoritarian backlash of the Counter-Reformation, accompanied by the loss of political autonomy in vast areas of the peninsula. For Italy, the long twilight of foreign domination and political and economic decadence had begun. The age of interaction and exchange faded away, to the detriment of everyone, on both sides of the ghetto walls.

Jewish teachers, Jewish students

It was not only Jewish books that influenced Christian culture of the time, but many Jewish individuals as well. The interests of Christian humanists for Hebrew language and culture and that of learned Jews for humanist thought are presented in the exhibition through a number of highly significant documents, coming from actual experience and not only from literary culture. In the 1430s, the Florentine humanist and linguist Giannozzo Manetti (1396–1459) took up Hebrew. Manetti was no ordinary scholar. Born into a prosperous family of merchants, he was also a public man involved in the civic life of Florence who held many high-level diplomatic positions with honor and demonstrated great skill as an orator. He left Florence in 1454, for reasons that are still unclear but include unspecified financial problems. After a period of time in Rome, he moved to Naples, where he entered into the service of Alfonso d'Aragona, who granted him the extremely generous stipend of 900 florins per year (Foà 2007). Our Florentine humanist had quite innovative ideas about language study, including a full immersion approach that seems surprisingly modern. Vespasiano da Bisticci offers this account in his *Life* of Manetti:

> He had in his home two Greeks and one Jew who had become Christian, and he wanted the Greek to speak to him only in Greek and the Jew likewise only in Hebrew. Of the two Greeks, one I know was named Demetrius. I sometimes saw [Manetti] have them recite the same Psalm in Greek, Hebrew and Latin for his enjoyment. Such were the pleasures he took at times. Having read the Bible, as said, he wanted them to read him authoritative commentary such as by Rabbi Moysi and other comments on the Bible. The Jew read all these works to Messer Giovannozzo, just to do as he wished. Messer Giovannozzo read to the Jew all the natural and moral philosophy, and when the Jew had read, Messer Giovannozzo read him the philosophy lesson (Vespasiano da Bisticci 1892–93, vol. 2, p. 91).

This first-hand account serves as a representative glimpse of the many scholarly relationships between Christians and Jews in the humanist era. The Jew with whom Manetti practiced his Hebrew was actually a convert to Christianity, and in effect, Manetti wrote and used his ability to speak and understand Hebrew primarily to aid in conversion efforts: he hoped to convince Jews, in their own language, of the truth of Christianity. In this and other cases, the asymmetrical relationship should be recognized as a more or less direct imposition of the majority vision and faith on members of the Jewish minority. The fifteenth-century text also speaks to us, however, of everyday experiences and the exchange of knowledge. The convert reads and explains Hebrew works to Manetti, and Manetti corresponds by giving him lessons in "natural and moral philosophy." Overall, the era of Renaissance encounters can be understood as moving between these two poles of asymmetry and reciprocity.

More complex and elusive is the relationship between Giovanni Pico della Mirandola and Flavius Mithridates, a converted Jew who, over the course of only a few months, translated a considerable number of kabbalistic texts for the learned count. In 1486, Pico, who was working at the time on his ambitious project of universal knowledge that took shape in his 900 *Conclusiones*, entrusted Mithridates with the truly challenging task of revealing to him a remote, intricate, and still unexplored wisdom. As far as we know, no Christian by birth had ever ventured before into the labyrinth of texts of the Jewish mystical tradition, written in Hebrew and Aramaic and jealously guarded among small circles of scholars.

Born into a Jewish family in Sicily and converted in his youth, Mithridates was the man for the mission. Not only did he know Hebrew, Aramaic, and at least some Arabic, but he also mastered Latin and Greek and was a frequent presence in humanistic circles. Pico probably met him through Marsilio Ficino, the most celebrated philosopher of the Medici circle. Along with his undeniable talents, however, Mithridates had more than a small dose of unscrupulousness. If his patrons, Pico above all, were seeking traces of the mysterious wisdom of the Jews and Chaldeans, Mithradites came up with obviously invented, outrageous works for the count and his acquaintances, in addition to his authentic translations (Busi and Ebgi 2014, pp. XXVII–XXX). Not surprisingly, given such frauds and biographical pirouettes, the inventive, talented Mithridates ended up in prison, in 1489, after which we know nothing about him. Nonetheless, his inventions, talent, and cultural idiosyncrasies left their mark in the form of Pico's epic discovery of Jewish mysticism, whose influence resonated throughout European culture in the sixteenth and seventeenth centuries.

Painted and written encounters: in Tuscany, from Giotto to Michelangelo
The first traces of iconographic interest in Hebrew in Italy seem to emerge in ecclesiastic circles and specifically among the Tuscan monastic painters (Lorenzo Monaco and Beato Angelico) in Florence and Siena. Santa Maria Novella in Florence was one of the principle centers of Dominican study at the time. Teaching there, from the late thirteenth into the early fourteenth century, were both the Arabist Ricoldo di Montecroce and Giordano da Pisa, whose associations with Jews are well documented. It is also there that Giotto created a trilingual *titulus crucis*, whose first line is written in good Hebrew (Sarfatti, Pontani and Zamponi 2001).

After a fourteenth-century phase of apparent regression in knowledge of Semitic languages (when we find instead pseudo-Hebrew and pseudo-Kufic), interest in Hebrew and Jewish culture and religion began to grow in the first half of the fifteenth century, in both painting (Sassetta, Beato Angelico, and Benozzo Gozzoli) and humanist scholarship (Ambrogio Traversari and Giannozzo Manetti). Specifically, in paintings with Christian themes, the presence of Hebrew signaled an Old Testament setting. In the more general humanist scheme of a return to original sources, historical accuracy, and a philological approach to the past, the holy language became one of the best ways to show the Jewish nature of Jesus and his environment, as part of the antiquarian revival of the stories of the Bible and evangelical preaching.

It matters little that the majority of those admiring the works of art were unable to read Hebrew. Patrons, learned inspirers of the iconography, and painters—a copy of the alphabet in hand—endeavored to show that the *hebraica veritas* was integral to the rebirth of the ancient and a renewed declaration of the Christian faith. Not by chance, one of the most widespread icons of Renaissance Christian trilingualism was the so-called *titulus crucis*, the inscription attached to the cross, according to the Gospels, and described by John (19:20) as being written in Hebrew, Latin, and Greek. Beginning with Giotto's *titulus* on the crucifix for Santa Maria Novella, the trilingual symbol manifests a precocious appearance of the Hebraism that would emerge fully in the fifteenth and early sixteenth centuries.

Giovanni Pico della Mirandola and the humanist discovery of the Kabbalah
With the arrival of Giovanni Pico della Mirandola in Florence in September–October 1484 (Busi 2007, p. 38, note 46), Tuscany became the international center of a new cultural trend, which saw Hebrew, and in particular the mystical tradition of the Kabbalah, as an essential key to ancient wisdom. From the labors of translation carried out for Pico, mostly, as we said, by Flavius Mithridates, the Hebrew trend worked its way into art. The interest in Hebrew on the part of the Medici circle is reflected artistically in works by Cosimo Rosselli and Domenico Ghirlandaio and in the trilingual *titulus* placed by the young Michelangelo on his wooden crucifx in the church of Santo Spirito in Florence (Busi 2017b, pp. 41, 265–66).

Saint Jerome, as painted by Ghirlandaio in a fresco in the Florentine church of Ognissanti, represents the other major symbol of the trilingualism of this period. While the *titulus crucis* links Hebrew, Greek, and Latin to the messianic destiny of Jesus, Jerome rose to become the model of the linguistic skills required to understand and vivify the message of the Scriptures, mostly due to his Latin version of the Bible, the Vulgate, translated from the original Hebrew and Greek. The Hebrew scroll in Ghirlandaio's painting that hangs from the shelf in Jerome's study is in itself a mark of erudition and intense study (Busi and Ebgi 2014, pp. LXVI–LXIX for an interpretation and contextualization of the Hebrew writings in Ghirlandaio's work).

Federico da Montefeltro: an unscrupulous collector
In the second half of the fifteenth century, Hebrew had become a fundamental part of the humanistic ideal of perfect erudition. This is visible, for one, in the representations of Moses and Solomon painted by Justus van Gent (Joos van Wassenhove) and Pedro Berreguete for Federico da Montefeltro (Cheles 1986; *Lo studiolo* 2015). Montefeltro, one of the most respected *condottieri* of his time and a great expert in military affairs, had a remarkable interest in Hebrew studies, mirroring what was by then a widespread conviction among the most sophisticated intellectual circles of the era. No curriculum of study was complete without a substantial presence of Hebrew texts. And if the Jews did not want to let go of their bibliographic treasures—even for an exorbitant price—then the answer was to simply take them as the spoils of war, as happened to the libraries of the Jews of Volterra.

Federico da Montefeltro was a compulsive and unscrupulous collector. Witness the Hebrew manuscripts he hoarded after the fall of Volterra in 1472, where he led the troops sent by the Florentines to seize the rebellious city. These precious works were taken by Montefeltro in the anguished days of the defeat of Volterra and carted away to Urbino to enrich his celebrated library (Busi 2016b, pp. 91–92). Needless to say, Federico did not know how to read Hebrew, but he was obviously able to recognize its prestige and symbolic value. That was enough for him, war or no war.

Ferrara: the Este family
Between about 1475 and 1528, Ferrara under the Este was the home of a prolonged commingling of art and Jewish doctrine. This episode—whose longevity may make it unique in the history of culture, and not only Italian culture—resulted from a variety of factors. First of all, there was the openness of the ruling Este to the Jews, and in particular to the moneylenders and entrepreneurs who revolved around the court. But the inclusion

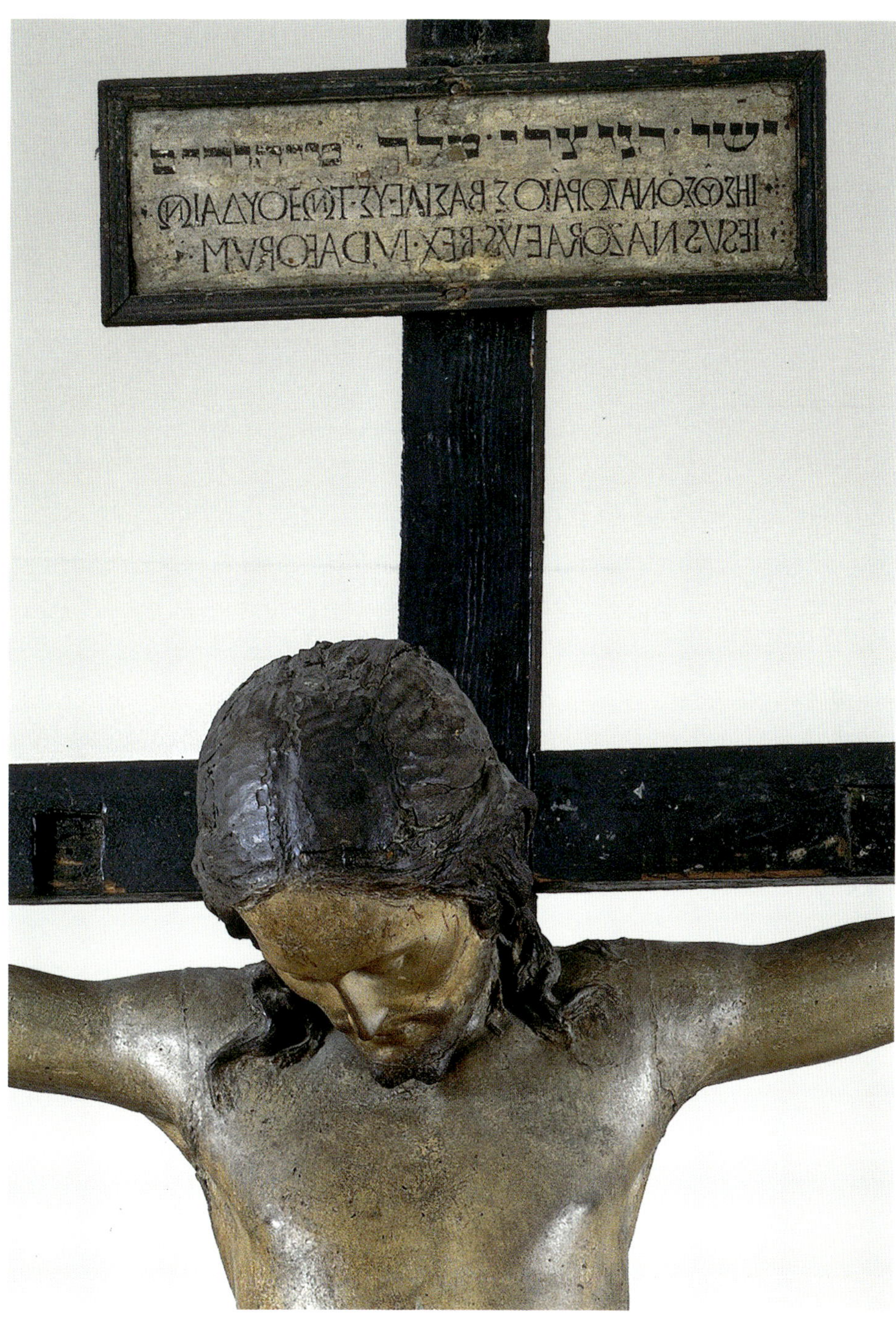

4. Michelangelo Buonarroti, wooden *Crucifix*,
detail, c. 1493, Florence, church of Santo Spirito

of Hebrew in a number of the major works of art produced in Ferrara in the late fifteenth and first decades of the sixteenth century was also the result of certain personal relationships. The most well-documented such bond is the friendship between Abraham Farissol, a learned Jew living in Ferrara, and two leading Christian intellectuals, Pellegrino Prisciani and Celio Calcagnini (Busi 2007, pp. 72–97: Busi and Ebgi 2014, pp. LVIII–LXIII). Of their encounters, spread out over several decades, we have detailed literary testimony revealing their mutual respect and their ability to communicate in the same intellectual language (see Greco's essay in this volume).

Even more importantly, the attention paid to Jewish themes, born from Prisciani and Calcagnini's humanistic interests, found formal expression in the paintings of the city's great artists. Already around 1474, Hebrew figures noticeably in the *Virgin and Child Enthroned* by Cosmè Tura, where it appears on the tablets on either side of the Virgin. The design of the tablets links them unquestionably to Pellegrino Prisciani, who used identical shapes in those same years on the sarcophagus he designed for his father Prisciano (see cat. 44). On the other hand, the painting's succinct version of the Ten Commandments—in perfect Hebrew—points to the involvement of Abraham Farissol, a skillful scribe, great expert of Jewish texts, and observant and respected presence in Christian circles (Cassuto 1918, pp. 325–26; Ruderman 1981; Busi 2016b, p. 328).

The holy language is also quite visible in the works of Ercole de' Roberti and Lorenzo Costa, evidence of the durability of interest in Hebrew in Ferrara. Costa went so far as to sign his *Saint Sebastian*, now at the Gemäldegalerie in Dresden, in Hebrew script (but Latin words) (Busi 2007, pp. 91–92), so great was the reputation of these arcane alphabetical symbols in the sophisticated circles of his patrons. It was the Renaissance painter Ludovico Mazzolino, however, who more than any other made the inclusion of Hebrew letters part of his personal style. The exhibition proposes two versions from Mazzolino's wide Hebrew repertoire. The two *Christ Disputing with the Doctors in the Temple*, one in Rome and one in Berlin (see cat. 41 and 42), strike the viewer visually with a vivid, alive Judaism, though presented in its dialectical tension with Christianity that is embodied here by the astonishing wisdom of the twelve-year-old Jesus (Haitovsky 1999; Busi 2007, p. 93).

Mantua: the Gonzaga family
As early as the 1470s, Mantua was home to the school of Jewish Humanism of Judah Messer Leon, where the principles of Renaissance rhetoric were taught to students through examples from Biblical culture (Busi 2007, pp. 47–51). Messer Leon's instruction was accompanied by the publications of Abraham Conat and the contribution of intellectuals such as Johanan Alemanno, schooled in Latin culture as well as Jewish philosophy and mysticism (Busi 2017a). With the arrival of Isabella d'Este, the artistic scene in the city was energized, including by a newfound curiosity about Jewish culture. Isabella's mentor in this field and the inspiration for Hebrew iconography was the aristocrat Paride da Ceresara, an unusual character, at once courtier, humanist, and man of letters. It was probably upon his suggestion, at least in part, that Hebrew references appeared in the work of Andrea Mantegna, the greatest, most respected artist in Mantua in the late fifteenth century. *Minerva Chasing the Vices from the Garden of Virtue*, Mantegna's enigmatic masterpiece, was painted for

5. Ludovico Mazzolino, *Christ and the Doctors*,
c. 1519. Galleria Doria Pamphilj, Rome (cat. 41)

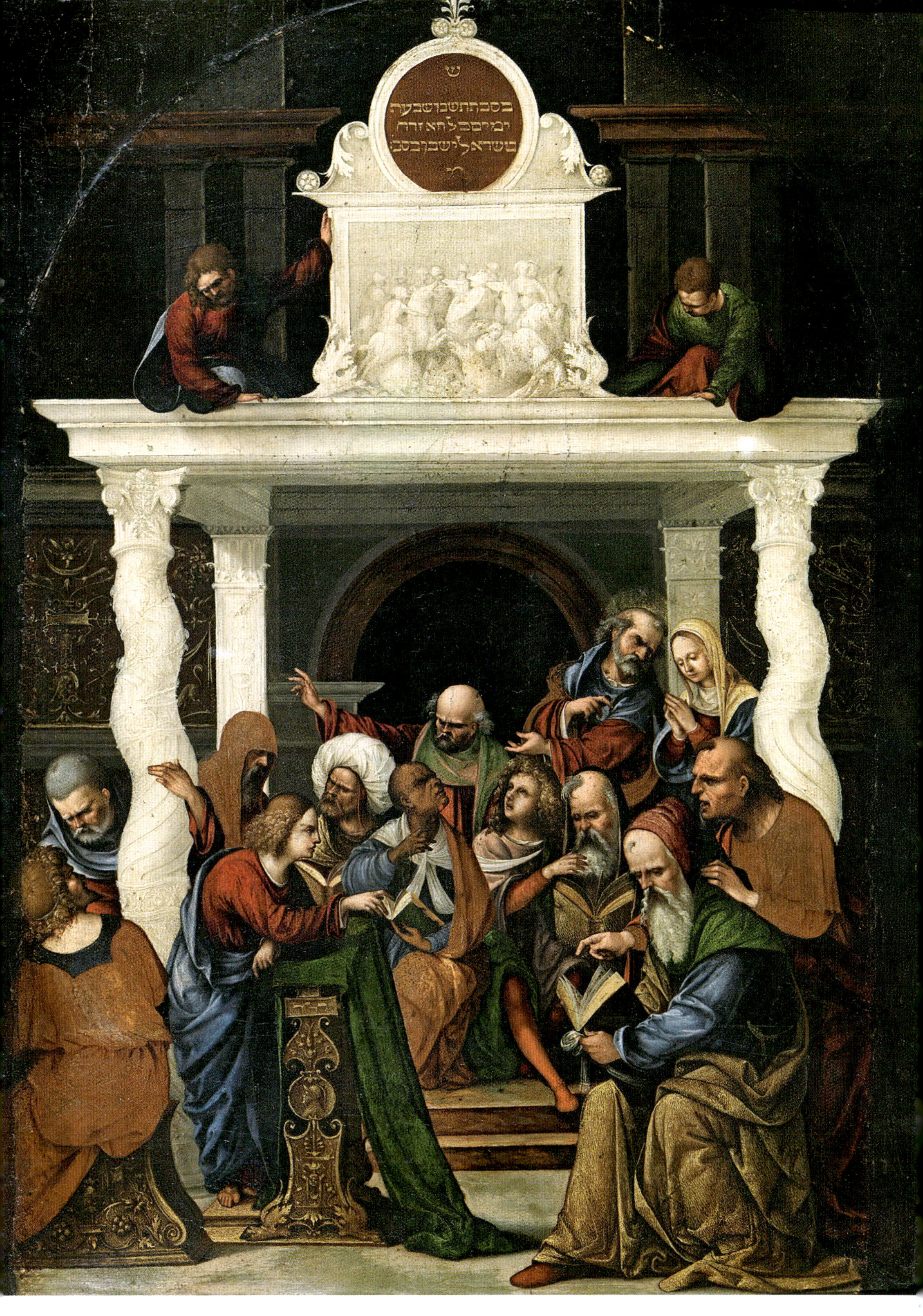
ש
בסבתתשבושבערה
ימיסבלחאזדה
ישראלישבורסב
ן

the *studiolo* of Isabella d'Este between 1499 and 1502. On the left stands a Daphne-tree: the nymph has just begun her transformation into a laurel tree to escape the clutches of Apollo, as narrated by Ovid in his *Metamorphoses*. Around her body, already caught in the oblivious tree trunk, winds a scroll featuring strange, twisted characters. The alphabetic sequence seems to be rising up from the roots in a trilingual succession of Hebrew, Greek, and Latin. But it is just an optical trick: the Hebrew is indecipherable. Yes, there are some "real" Hebrew consonants, but others have spurious shapes and appear to be invented figures of undefined origin. The Greek has no better fate, being not Greek but a series of squiggles harboring Latin letters and suggesting the same phrase, which is finally legible in the authentic Latin in the topmost swirl: *Agite pellite sedibus nostris | foeda haec vicioru[m] monstra | virtutum coelitus adnos red[e]u[n]tium divae comites* (Oh come, companions of the Goddess of Virtues, returning to us from the Heavens, expel from our homes these shameful monsters of vice). Why so much subterfuge and alphabetical masquerades? Why is the Hebrew falsified and the Greek disguised? It helps to know that, in the medieval tradition of a moralizing interpretation of Ovid, which Mantegna certainly had in mind (Busi 2007, pp. 102–3), Daphne's laurel tree is seen as a prefiguration of the wood of the cross. Just as the cross bears the trilingual *titulus* at the top, so we believe the Daphne-tree, in Mantegna's painted version, is decorated with a sort of *titulus* in the process of becoming. It is as if the non-Latin languages participated in the process of metamorphosis that

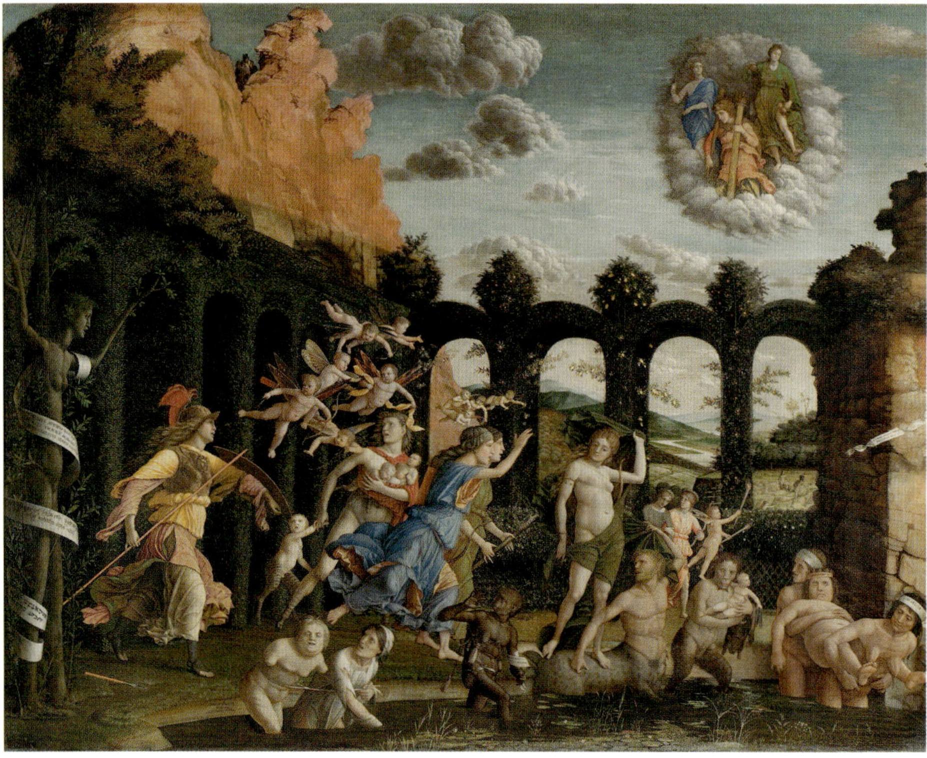

6. Andrea Mantegna, *Minerva Chasing the Vices from the Garden of Virtue*, 1499–1502. Musée du Louvre, Paris

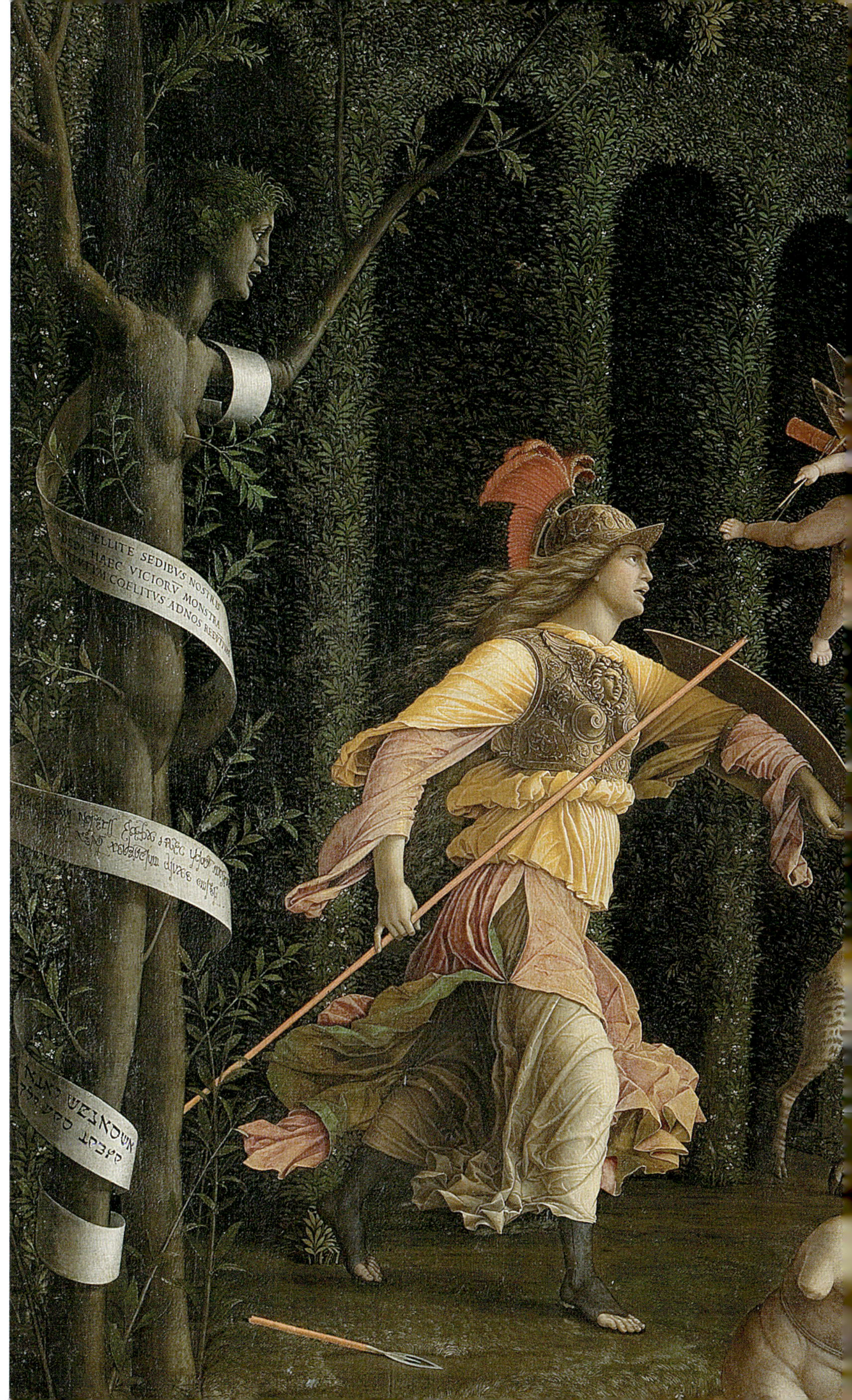
...ELLITE SEDIBVS NOSTRIS
...HAEC VICIORV MONSTRA
...M COELITVS ADNOS REDIT...

strikes the nymph, transforming her forever. The words on the scroll seem to emerge from Daphne's mouth, open in an apparent cry. As she gradually turns into a tree, even her voice cracks and stiffens. If this were the case, the pseudo-Hebrew would signal the increasing subtlety of her words, ending in an arboreal silence. Add to this the fact that Isabella insisted on ever-new inventions that would be impenetrable to the common observer, all the mysterious linguistics of the *Minerva* in the Louvre is perhaps explained.

The function of Hebrew in Mantegna's *The Holy Family and the Family of Saint John the Baptist* is completely different. This painting, on loan to the exhibition from the church of Sant'Andrea in Mantua (cat. 33), shows Joseph on the extreme left wearing a band around his head with Hebrew letters. Two central letters combine to make the word *av*, or "father," as if to emphasize the meaning of the figure for those who can read them. We know that the painting was made by Mantegna for his own funeral chapel, where it has remained to this day. It is pleasing to think that the Hebraist arc of this master artist, after wading through pseudo-Hebrew, finally reached the shores—in the looming presence of death—of a serene legibility, devoid of all anti-Jewish or overly arcane connotations.

Venice: erudition, tolerance, and ghetto
There are clear signs in Venice of a deep interest in Jewish culture beginning in the early fifteenth century, when the noble lord Marco Lippomano engaged in an exchange of letters in Hebrew with the erudite Crescas Meir who was living in Puglia at the time (Busi and Campanini 2004). Fueled by scholars such as Francesco Zorzi, an aristocrat with important positions in the Franciscan order and a distinct predilection for the Kabbalah (Busi 1997a; Busi 2007, pp. 161–86; S. Campanini in Zorzi 2010, *passim*; also see the essays by Campanini

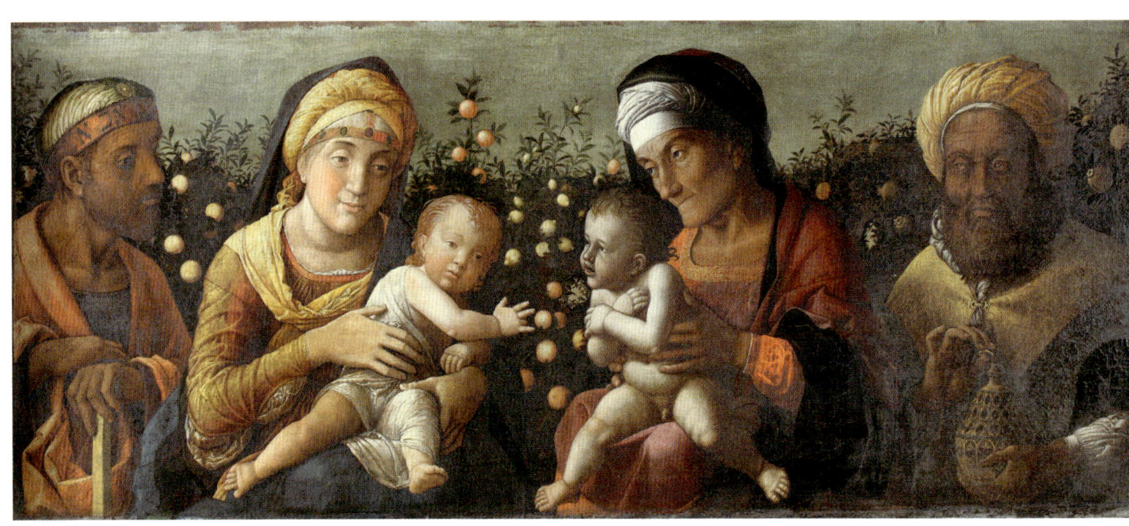

7. Andrea Mantegna, *The Holy Family and the Family of Saint John the Baptist*, c. 1504–6. Basilica of Sant'Andrea, Mantua, Chapel of Saint John the Baptist (cat. 33)

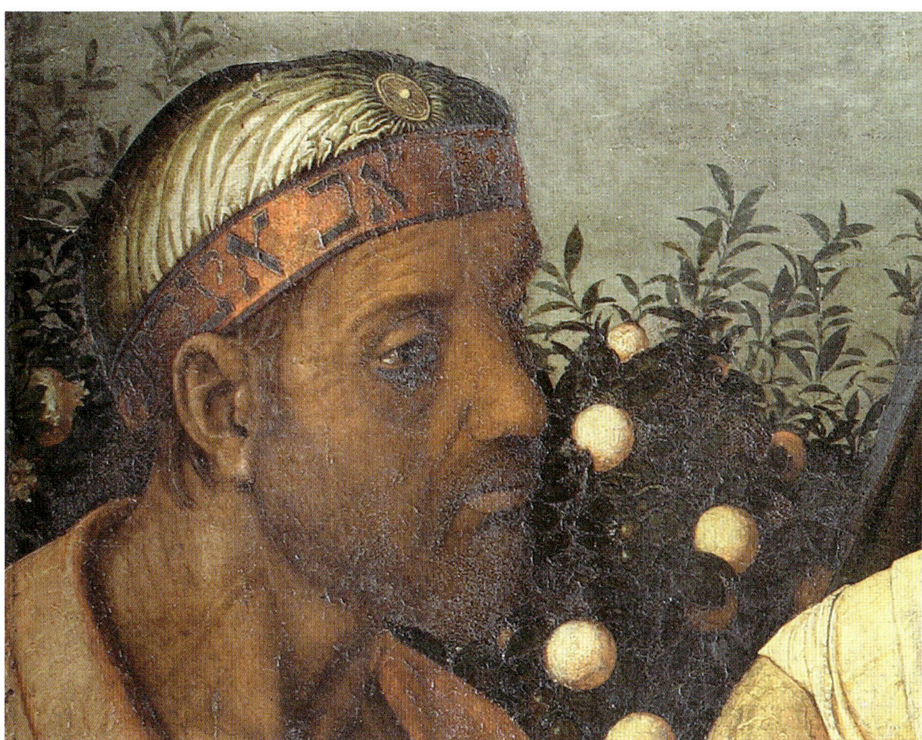

and Bartolucci in this volume), this Jewish-related scholarship made its mark on the visual arts in Veneto as well. The *Hypnerotomachia Poliphili*, printed by Aldus Manutius in 1499 and recognized as the most important illustrated book of the fifteenth century, features engravings with phrases wherein the Hebrew evokes a sense of mystery (Busi 2007, pp. 131–32).

For a brief but intense period, Manutius's circle included the learned publisher Gershom Soncino, who began his publishing work in the Lombard town of Soncino and then moved to Venice, perhaps as early as 1498, seeking new opportunities for collaboration. He was probably involved with Manutius in the ambitious project of printing a trilingual edition of the Bible but unfortunately, all that remains of this enterprise, which required such massive sums of capital and the involvement of a number of skilled Jewish printers, is a single test folio (Bibliothèque nationale de France, Paris, MS graec. 3064, fols. 86–87; Renouard 1834, pp. 388–99). It is possible that Manutius and Soncino did not get along personally, or disagreed about the financial arrangements of the work. Regardless, in the middle of 1501 Soncino had to leave Venice, just before Manutius began printing a brief *Introduction* to the Hebrew language, written in Latin by Soncino himself. The fact that the edition was released without the name of the author, and that years later Soncino lamented this omission in a reprinted version, suggests that the relationship between the two had somehow degenerated (Busi 2007, p. 135).

Other than a bitter ending, another outcome of Gershom Soncino's stay in Venice can be glimpsed in the elegant painting by Vittore Carpaccio created for the Scuola degli Albanesi in the city. While the exact date is still debated, it is most probably between 1502 and 1507. Presently in the Accademia Carrara in Bergamo, the painting depicts an interior scene sugges-

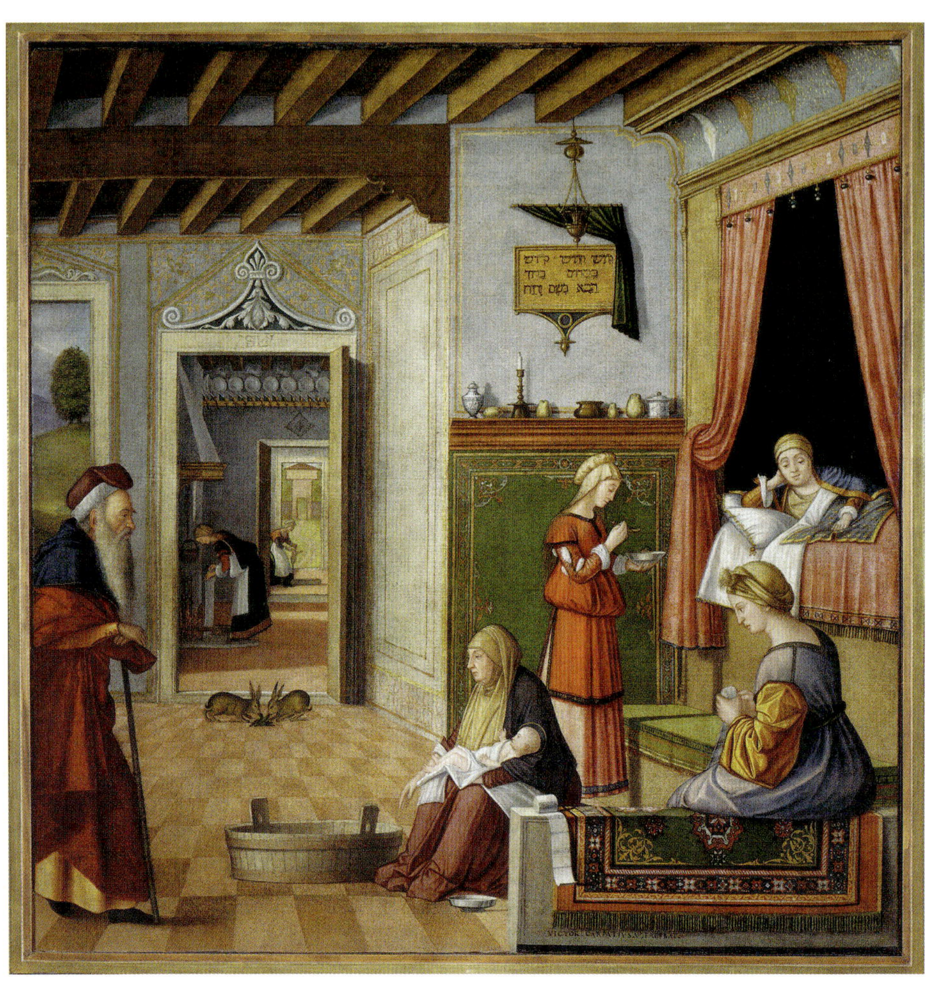

8. Vittore Carpaccio and workshop, *Birth of the Virgin*, c. 1502–7. Accademia Carrara, Bergamo (cat. 35)

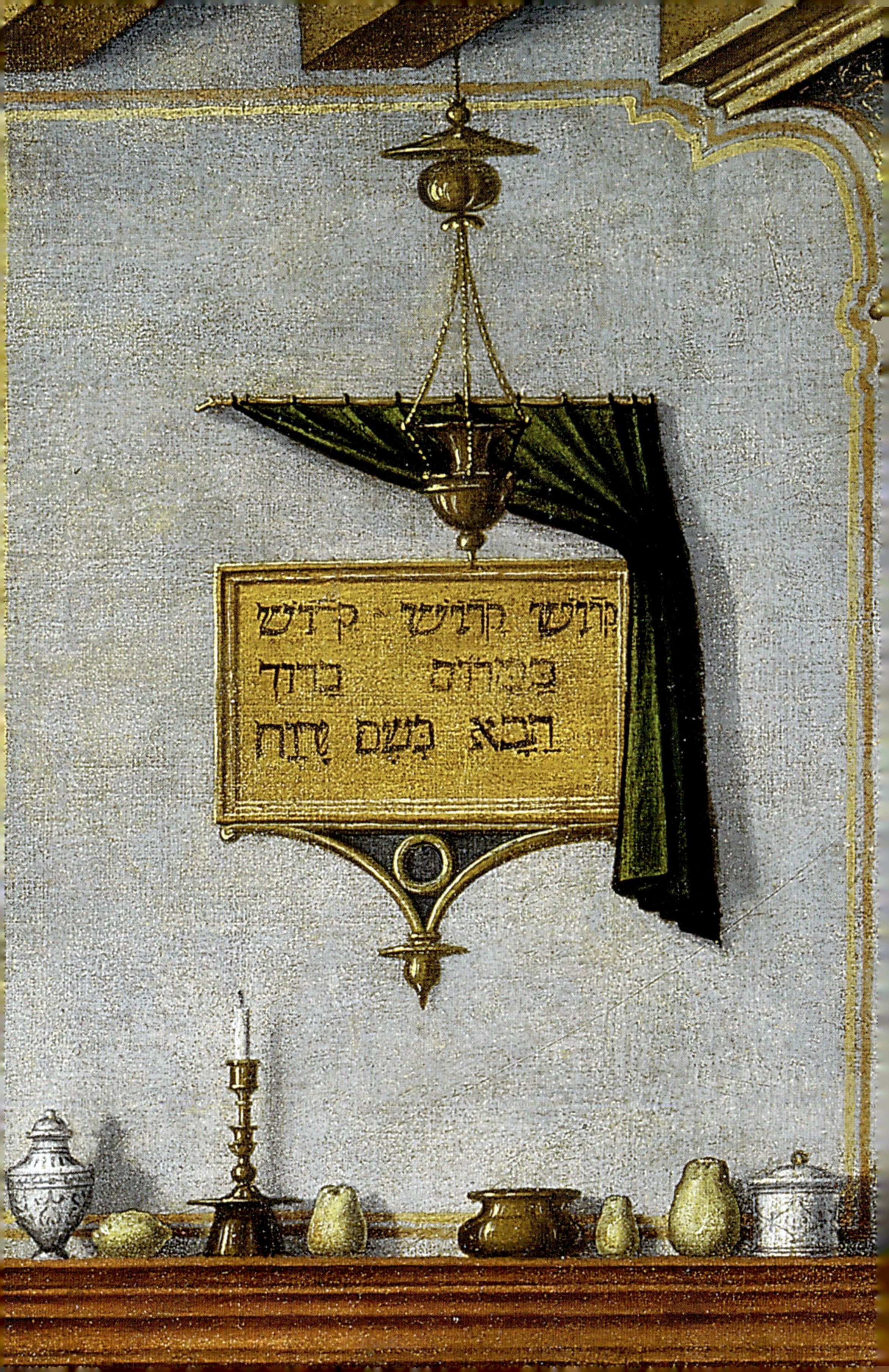

קדוש · קדוש · קדוש
בהדר במרום
רבא משם שזה

tive of a warm, intimate daily life. On the middle wall hangs a panel with Hebrew writing: it's the *Sanctus* of Christian liturgy, a succession of two Biblical quotations (Isaiah 6:3 and Psalms 118:26): "Holy, holy, holy. Hosanna in the Highest. Blessed who comes in the Name of Lord."

We do not know who inspired Carpaccio to include this Hebrew feature, although one aspect can help clarify at least part of the mystery. The word "Lord" corresponds in the original to the Tetragrammaton, the four-letter name of God that Jews are not allowed to pronounce or to write in profane contexts. The lines used by Carpaccio to render the Tetragrammaton are the same as those found in Soncino's *Introduction* to the Hebrew, where the same formula of the *Sanctus* appears. The letters are arranged in such a way as not to reproduce the holy name precisely; this is surely a precaution that no Christian would have taken, but is easily understandable on the part of an erudite Jew (Busi 2007, pp. 136–38). Thus, whether Carpaccio's painting incorporates specific advice from Soncino or whether the *Introduction* served as the model for the form of the letters, Carpaccio's *The Birth of the Virgin* actually "speaks Hebrew," in the manner and with the accents dictated by Jewish culture of the Renaissance.

Only a few years after Soncino's brief sojourn in Venice, the situation of the Jews in the city had changed radically. In 1509, with the League of Cambrai threatening its very existence, Venice allowed Jews living on the mainland to seek refuge in the city. After several years of adjustment, however, in 1516, the bulging Jewish population was forced to reside in a specifically designated area of the Cannaregio district (see cat. 3 and Calabi's essay in this volume).

It might be expected that the Jews, choked and relegated to the edge of the city, would soon settle into a minor, submissive role. And yet, with this supposed marginalization began a new, long-lasting social and cultural phase, marked by abundant commerce and a more or less peaceful co-existence, though not without sudden restrictions and episodes of discrimination (see Trivellato's essay in this volume). Just as the institution of the ghetto was being consolidated, Daniel Bomberg, an entrepreneur from Antwerp, launched an extraordinary publishing venture, which printed Hebrew books that made their way throughout the entire diaspora (Habermann 1978b; see also Campanini's essay in this volume). Thanks to Bomberg, along with a number of other Christian publishers who relied on the city's network of Jewish scholars and typographers, Venice exceeded all other cities in the production of Hebrew books (Busi 2016).

The Duchy of Milan and the uneasy refuge of Genoa
The pro-Jewish policies of the Visconti encouraged the settlement of Jews in the Duchy territory in the closing years of the fourteenth century, fostering the emergence of a rich network of Jewish culture. Jews there continued to flourish into the epoch of the Sforza, at least until 1489, when Ludovico il Moro ordered their expulsion from the Duchy after a trial against a number of Jews (Antoniazzi Villa 1986). The edict, however, was never applied widely (Simonsohn 1982–86, pp. XXIV–XXV).

Jewish intellectual production in Lombard territories is documented, for example, by the dynamic typographic work of the Soncino family, one of whose members was the Gershom whom we saw in Venice. The Lombard Canon Regular Teseo Ambrogio Albonesi was a pioneer of Semitic studies and collector of Hebrew texts and testimonies (see cat. 37). It is likely that the various appearances of Hebrew in painting, such as the trilingual *titulus* in the *Crucifixion* painted by Bramantino around 1510 (*Crocifissione* 1992), can also be attributed to ecclesiastical inspiration.

While Genoa had political bonds with Milan, it held a different attitude toward Jews. Jealous of its commercial prerogatives, the city tried to limit the stable Jewish presence, even if close examination of the documents reveals, again and again, flourishing Jewish business activities in the city and region during the fifteenth century (Urbani and Zazzu 1999, vol. 1). Genoa became a major stop of the Sephardic diaspora after 1492. At least for a short time, the city was home to Judah Leon Abravanel, also known as Leone Ebreo (Pflaum 1926, pp. 78–80; Leone Ebreo 1929, pp. 1–18 no. 8), whose *Dialogues of Love* offered the most successful synthesis of Jewish-humanist Neo-Platonism of the sixteenth century (see cat. 38). Also from Genoa was Agostino Giustiniani (1470–1536), one of the most distinguished Christian students of Hebrew culture of his time. Of his projected polyglot edition of the Bible, only the *Psalter* was completed: it was printed by Giustiniani, at his own expense, in the house of his brother Nicolò in Genoa in 1516 by the Milanese typographer Pietro Paolo Porro (see cat. 40).

As had happened in the case of Aldus Manutius some years earlier, it turned out that a multilingual edition of the Bible was simply not feasible, at least in Italy. In fact, the first successful multilingual edition appeared in Spain, at Alcalá de Henares, near Madrid. Known as the *Complutensian Polyglot Bible* (Complutum was the Latin name for Alcalá), it was begun in 1502 and published in 1520 (*Una Biblia* 2014). This transfer of the humanist Bible project outside of Italy—a project that required the new knowledge of Jewish culture and language developed in the late fifteenth and early sixteenth centuries—is a mark of the transformation taking place in the larger culture of the time. Christian interest in Jewish studies, first nurtured in the intellectual dynamism of the cities of Italy, had now spread to become a more generalized European legacy.

The precarious protection of the popes
The Jewish community of Rome is the most ancient in Italy and the only one that can boast of an uninterrupted presence going back two thousand years. Bound by a particular and often assiduous relationship to the papal court, Roman Jewry at the beginning of the fourteenth century had achieved a certain level of importance in the economic and cultural life of the city. Despite the decline during the Avignon Papacy, the Jews of Rome were involved in the humanistic movement and influenced the interest in Semitic scholarship among the popes, as documented beginning with Nicholas V. Between 1469 and approximately 1475, as many as eight Hebrew incunables were printed in Rome, the oldest of which are considered to be the first books in Hebrew to appear with the new printing process recently introduced in Italy—right in Lazio, in Subiaco and Rome—by German artisans (Offenberg 1999).

Also in Rome, in 1498, appeared the influential but fictitious work packed with Semitic references, almost all invented or distorted, by the Dominican Giovanni Nanni, better known as Annius of Viterbo (*Commentaria* 1498; see Weinberg's essay in this volume and cat. 41). The book was a virtual monument to the humanistic interest in the Hebrew and Aramaic worlds. On closer inspection, however, this "monument" is a spurious one in which the author, who enjoyed the respected role of Alexander VI's official theologian, claims to have found "Chaldean" roots in Italy's primordial history, not without fabricating false documents and distorting languages and etymologies for his pseudo-scholarly purposes.

During the papacies of Julius II and Leo X, the fascination with Judaism powerfully informed the artistic and literary scene in Rome. Not least thanks to the work of Cardinal Giles of Viterbo, general of the Augustinians and ardent student of Hebrew culture (Weil

1963; see the essays by Campanini and Bartolucci in this volume), Jewish themes have a significant presence in paintings by Raphael. While the only Hebrew inscription attributable to Michelangelo Buonarroti appears in the aforementioned *titulus crucis* on the Santo Spirito crucifix in Florence, probably datable to 1493, Raphael would include both pseudo-Hebrew and correct Hebrew script in his paintings.

While Moses in the *Disputation of the Holy Sacrament* (Stanza della Segnatura, Vatican Museums) displays a Biblical text written with pseudo-Hebrew letters, the vigorous figure of *Isaiah* in the Roman church of Sant'Agostino displays a scroll written with correct, though slightly confusing Hebrew letters, saying "Open the gates that the righteous nation may enter, the nation that keeps faith. Whose mind is steadfast" (Is. 26:2–3). It has been suggested that Giles of Viterbo, a highly influential theologian under the papacies of Julius II and Leo X, was involved in both the insertion of this Hebrew phrase and the Stanza della Segnatura iconography (Pfeiffer 1975, p. 299).

In fact, Giles pursued Jewish studies with great seriousness, probably not unrelated to his friendship with the highly learned Jew Elia Levita, who was a guest in Giles's home in Rome for a considerable length of time. It can be surmised that, if Giles—such a high-ranking figure in the ecclesiastical hierarchy—was interested in Judaism and in contact with learned Jews in the early sixteenth century, the general attitude of the Catholic

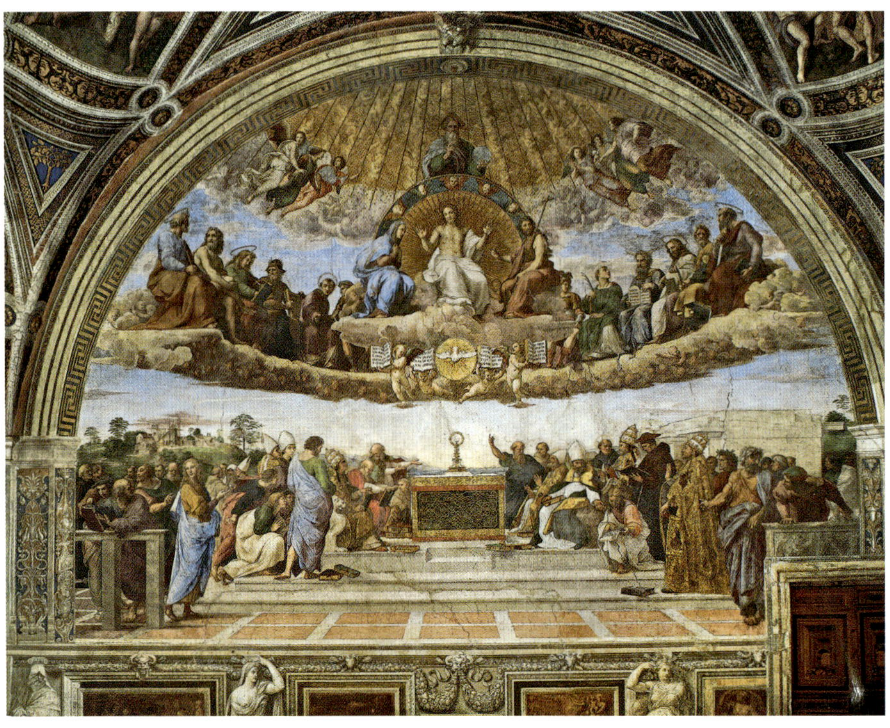

9. Raphael, *Disputation of the Holy Sacrament*, 1509. Apostolic Palace, Vatican City, Stanza della Segnatura

Church toward Jewish culture suffered a significant degeneration by the middle of the century. In 1553, Pope Julius III ordered the confiscation and destruction of the Talmud, an act with grave consequences for the entire heritage of Hebrew books (Sonne 1954; Busi 2007, pp. 111–12). It was not only the books to suffer: the very principle of co-existence—which had managed to survive for hundreds and hundreds of years, in fact if not in legislation— was now being re-considered, tightened, and drastically limited by the Counter-Reformation church. With forced residence, harsh enforcement of norms regarding identity badges, limitations on lawful trades, and abolition of all honorific titles (Stow 2007, p. 398), a new era of trials and humiliation had begun for the Jews of Rome, and the many others living in central and northern Italy.

Adding to these restrictions the fact that the Jewish communities in southern Italy and the islands had been wiped out by expulsions in the meantime, it becomes clear that, by the mid-sixteenth century, the Renaissance season of contradictions, encounters, and creativity was truly closing. Of course, there were important exceptions in the subsequent decades and centuries: in Leghorn and, to a certain extent, still in Venice and also elsewhere Italian Judaism showed tenacious resilience. That, however, is a different chapter of history, which would need another exhibition to be recounted. Clearly, MEIS still has much to do and say.

Translated by Lauren Sunstein

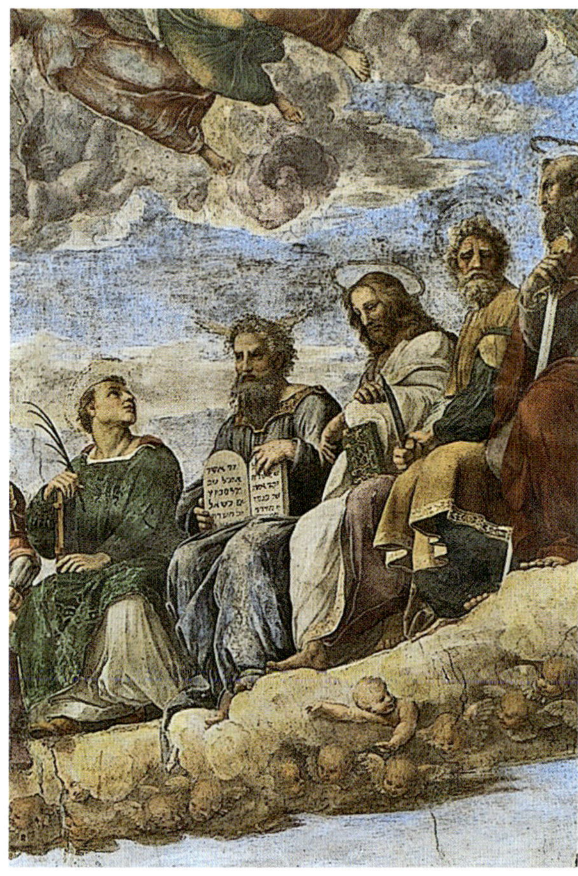

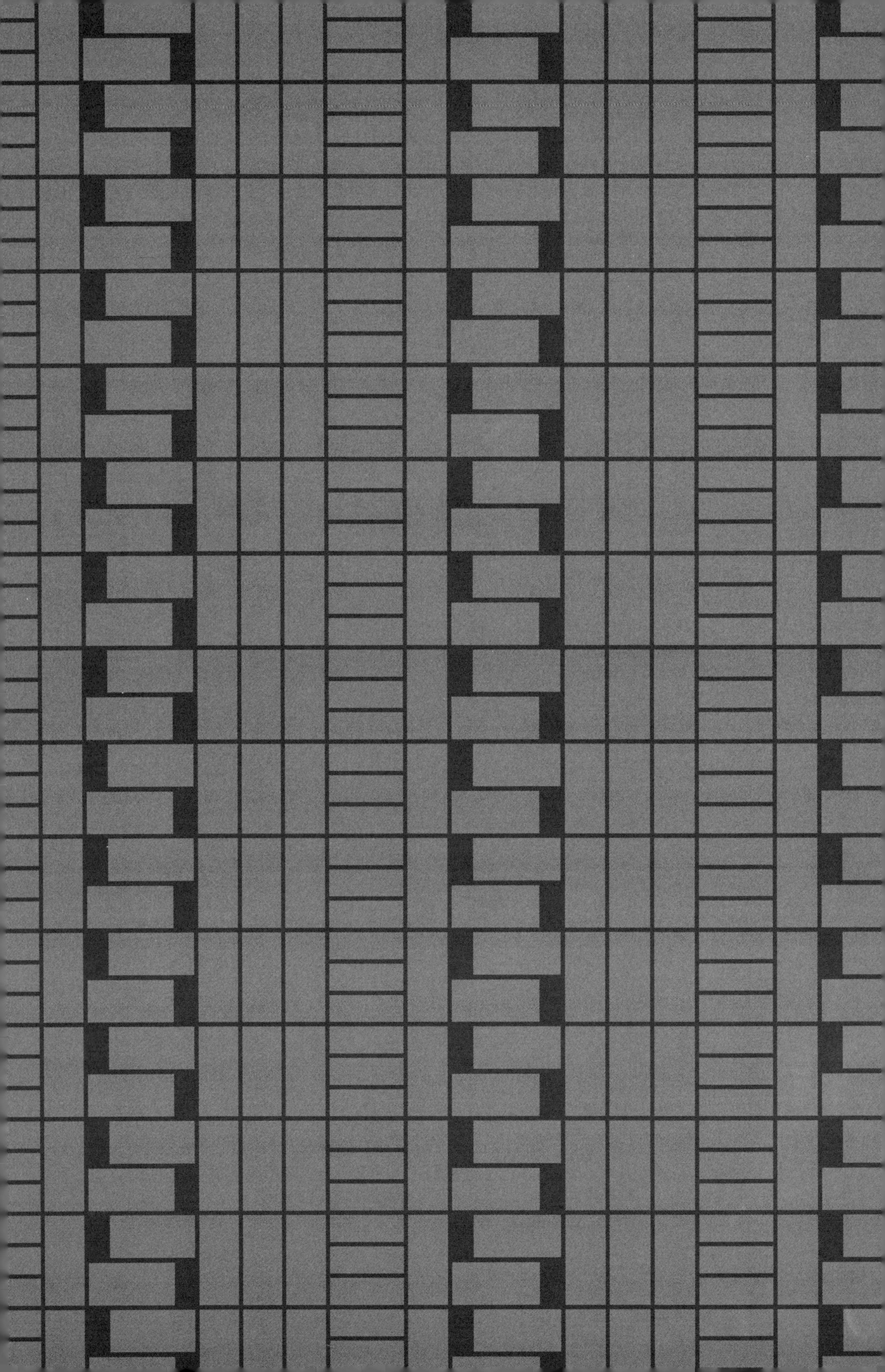

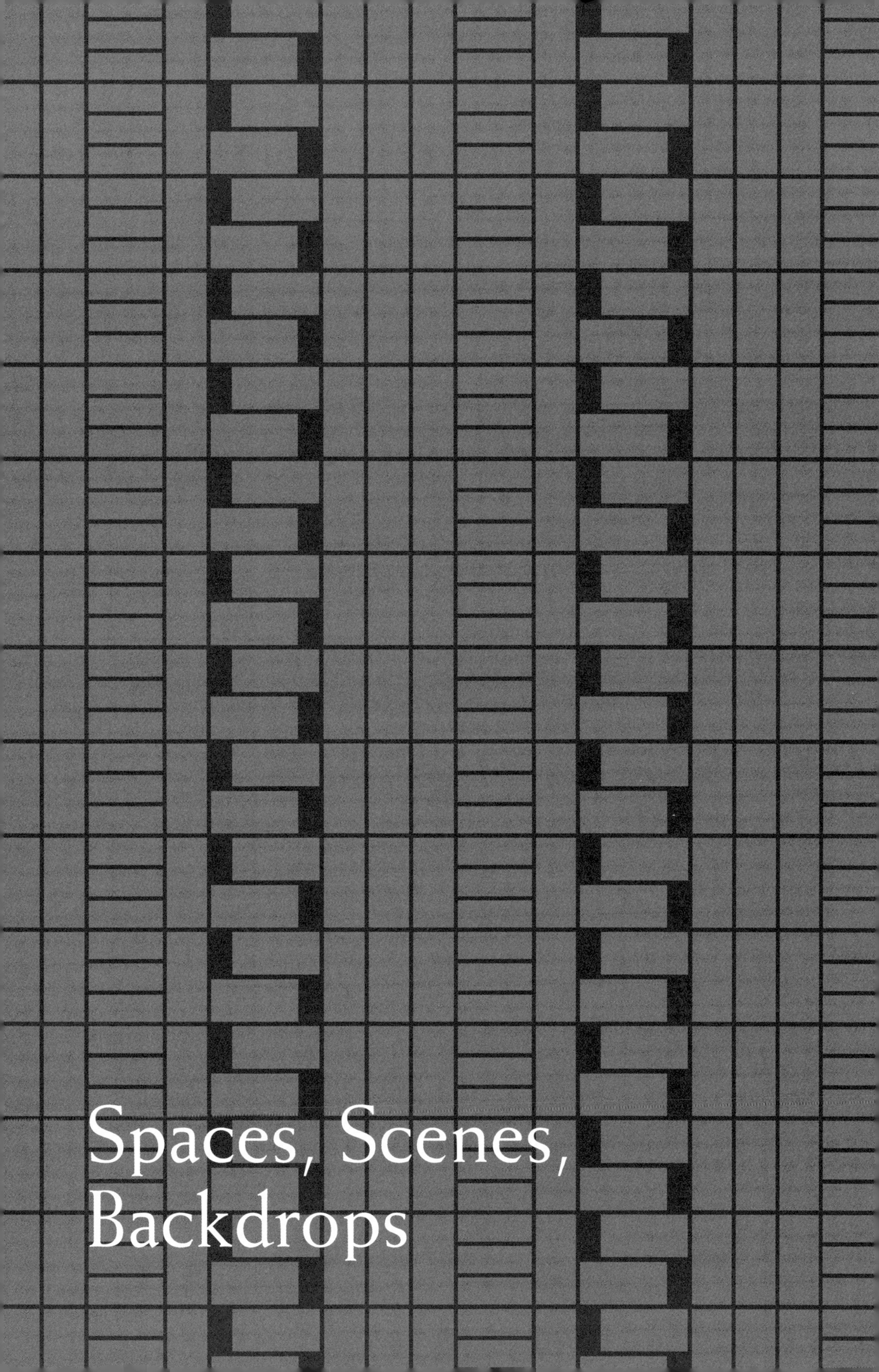
Spaces, Scenes,
Backdrops

Jews in Italy in the Renaissance:
A Sociological Perspective, with Ferrarese Examples
Silvana Greco

Cohesion, relationships, social dynamics

"Renaissance society" is a topic that is only rarely addressed, and it is even less frequent that a sociological perspective is applied to the Renaissance world. The traditional prism through which to interpret the Renaissance is a cultural one; it was a movement of styles, literature, art. That the extraordinary intellectual vitality of the fifteenth and sixteenth centuries was played out against the backdrop of a society—in other words, a relational structure—is a fact that has been fully perceived and analyzed by the most attentive of academics (Brucker 1971; Burke 1987; Martin 2016 [1932]). But it is, precisely, a backdrop, onto which attention has been focused only occasionally. The decisive battles fought by the Renaissance man concerned his self-expression. Not by chance, the most enduring image evoked by Jacob Burckhardt, in his pioneering work *Die Cultur der Renaissance in Italien: Ein Versuch* (1860), is that of the Renaissance as the time of individualism. Individuals doing all sorts of things, and in the best cases "making" art of unrivaled quality, while still affirming their own identities. They do it, they finance it, they admire it, they theorize it, each in search of their own route. Singular, exclusive, unmistakable (Martin 2004; see also Campanini's essay in this volume).

To focus on the Jewish experience in Italy is to come up immediately against the limits of a Renaissance interpreted purely as a cultural product in the strictest sense—i.e., as the fruit of the genius of the single artist or intellectual. By its very nature, Judaism should be read in terms of cohesion, relationships, and social dynamics. As ancient and persistent as it may be, Jewish culture is but one of the forces at play. The identity-giving strategy of the Jewish minority passed through the cultural—expressive—dimension, but it did not stop there. It was the group as a whole, in its shared values, beliefs, and practices that would take on a fundamental role. And it is the group, with its confines sometimes clear-cut and other times fluid, that constitutes the main subject of this exhibition. Certainly, the group is made up of individuals. But, at least in the context of our investigation, the group does not correspond to the arithmetical total of the individuals within it. The *minyan*, the quorum for the validity of synagogal liturgy, requires a minimum of ten male Jewish adults. Given that it is accurate to talk about the Renaissance as the period in which individualism was asserted, the Jews of that period were there to demonstrate to us that the relational dimension is unavoidable and essential; and also that culture and society are both cut from the same intertwined, durable, surprising historical cloth (Greco 2016a and 2016b).

Studying the Jews in Italy during the Renaissance is, then, an opportunity to re-think the entire representation of this period, which was so fundamental for the Italian and wider European consciousness. It involves seeing the season of the Renaissance also as a tangle of relationships between groups, with limits that are overstepped, transgressed, on a temporary or definitive basis. By definition, an exhibition displays objects, seeking the attention of the visitor through what is visible, tangible, audible. But it inevitably also showcases the social relationships that are crystallized in those works, and explores the relationships that made such material expressions possible—those and not others, then and not now.

A painting, a network of relationships

To better illustrate this dual register—at once extrinsic and intrinsic—that binds together culture and society, let us look at the exemplary case of the so-called *Madonna Roverella* (also known as *The Virgin and Child Enthroned*) by Cosmè Tura, now at the National Gallery in London. What we have in front of us is a magnificent example of Ferrarese art of the 1470s, in which two large tablets with Hebrew letters can be seen. Even those who cannot decipher the Hebrew lettering can still see them and can perceive their impact on the composition. The shrewdest of observers, who realize that they are looking at the Mosaic Decalog, will think quite correctly that those letters serve to recall the law of the Old Testament, right on the throne on which Mary sits together with her son who, according to the Christian message, brought to the world the announcement of the New Testament. No one, though, neither visitors not fluent in Hebrew nor those that are, can chart simply by looking at the painting the network of relations that made the work possible. Bringing back to light that network is the task of historiography.

Historical and philological research tells us that the tablets painted by Tura are the result of the encounter between Christian and Jewish erudition, and that their conception very probably involved two individuals who were familiar with each other—the Jew Abraham Farissol and the Christian Pellegrino Prisciani (Busi 2007, pp. 79–88). As well as sharing the space of the urban setting of Ferrara and the Este court, Farissol and Prisciani evidently had a shared language in which to communicate. By "language" we mean naturally not just the instrument of direct exchange—the vernacular in use in the city at that time—or even Latin, Hebrew or some other idiom. The language we are referring to here is a system of norms and values that, at least in part, the two men shared. Behind the *Madonna Roverella* it is possible to discern a "humanistic platform" in which the ancient and venerable Jewish knowledge has a recognized value, and is an object of consent, beyond the divisions of faith that distinguish the Jew from the Christian. And it is at this point that the sociological perspective comes into play. It is precisely the duty of the scholar of society to frame these shared values within a relational dynamic, implicit in Tura's painting but still all to be rendered explicit at the cognitive level. The Renaissance, this unreachable object of historiographic desire, was also—indeed, above all—a relational space, in which the Jews who were living in Italy (and had often been for hundreds of years), were sometimes "inside" and other times "outside."

Farissol and Prisciani were both "inside" Hebrew, whereas observers who did not know the language remained "outside." At the same time, Tura, Prisciani and the faithful Christians who admired the Altar were "inside" the faith in Mary and her son, whereas Farissol and the other Ferrarese Jews were "outside" that shared religion, and this was based on a non-negotiable choice on their part. The continual attempts to convert the Jews represented one of the possible alterations of the relational boundaries, to the benefit of Christianity and to the detriment of the Jewish minority. In this sense, the practices, the shared historical memory, the dietary laws, and endogamy all represented the protection of the identity-giving boundaries, to which Jewish laws and traditions have dedicated, for thousands of years, so much effort, so much devotion, and so much lucid awareness.

What is the substance of this space of interrelation, which is so important for getting a handle on the role of the Jews in Italy during the Renaissance?

The Ferrarese urban continuum

Let us stay in Ferrara, but move from the late fifteenth century of Tura, Prisciani, and Farissol back to the early fourteenth. In March 1310, the city's inhabitants were called upon to swear their allegiance to Pope Clement V. The ceremony aimed to undermine the dominion of the Este family, imposing direct pontifical authority (Fontana 1886, pp. 8–10; Colorni 1983, pp. 167–68; see Busi's

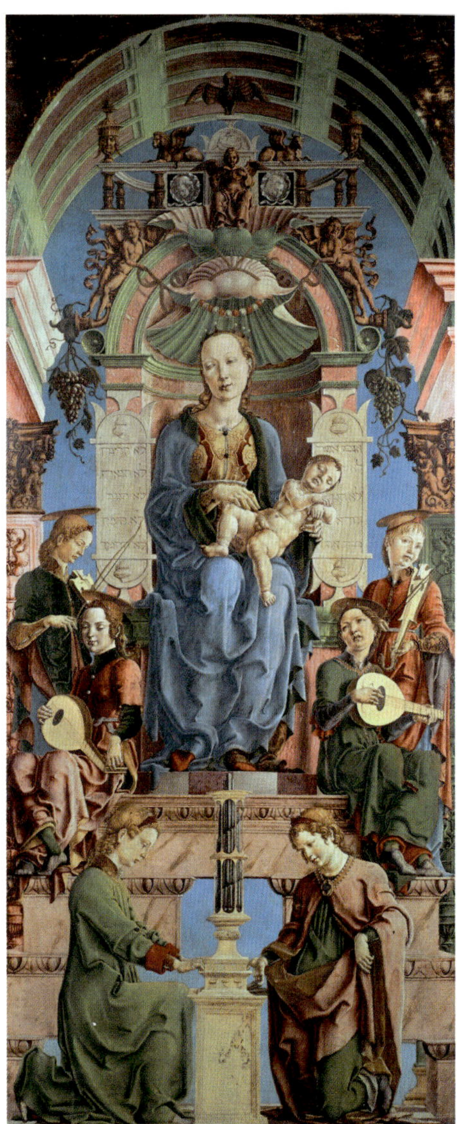

1. Cosmè Tura, *The Virgin and Child Enthroned* (*Madonna Roverella*), c. 1475. National Gallery, London

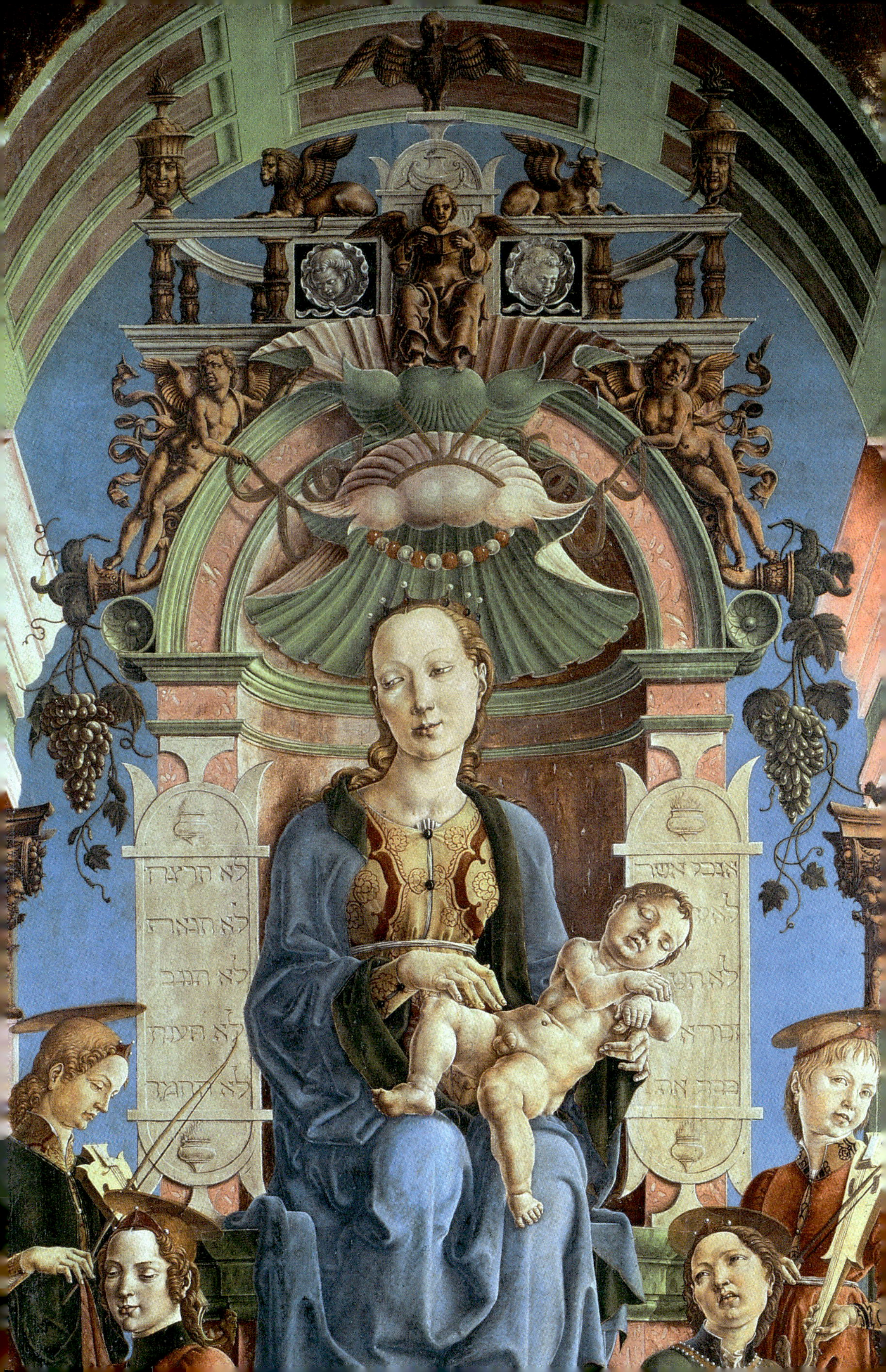

essay in this volume). Actually, the oath had no long-lasting effect—the Este soon reaffirmed their supremacy—but it is of interest to us here for the perspective that it opens up on the Jewish settlement in the city. From March 5 to 28, around 3,500 people appeared in front of notaries and witnesses, district by district, after giving their names. The Christians swore on the Bible, while the Jews did so on the "Law that God gave to Moses on Mount Sinai." If we are not wrong, this procedure of the collective swearing of Christians and Jews together had no parallel in Italy at the time, and it makes clear their co-existence, cheek by jowl, within the same urban space. The list of those taking the oath—which is conserved as a manuscript in the Vatican Library—in the "Centum Vassurarum" district, modern-day Via Centoversuri, records a small Jewish group. There were 17 households, accounting for a total of around 70–80 Jews out of a population of around 16,000–20,000 citizens (Colorni 1983), who lived in close contact with the Christian inhabitants. For the Pope, who longed for legitimization, the Jewish faith was as valid in this instance as the Christian. It is said that Jewish consent was sought in an instrumental fashion, in an operation that appears to have been politically motivated. But then, if those Jews standing in line with the others were not part of a Ferrarese *continuum*, it would have made no sense to involve them. For those looking for relationship networks, in daily life rather than in abstract theoretical reconstructions, the 1310 document is very telling. The difference in faith was reflected in the different oath taken. This marked the frontier in terms of regulations and religious practices, albeit against the backdrop of a clear residential proximity and the shared status of oath takers. We are at the dawn of the humanist era, well before the fifteenth-century unfolding of the Renaissance, but this inter-confessional topography seems to have lasted, in Ferrara and elsewhere, until the age of the ghettoes—more or less tolerated, sometimes fought against by anti-Jewish preachers, yet tangibly appreciable. Amid highs and lows, naturally. And the fact that the "lows"—the phases of bitter discrimination and persecution—could take shape at any moment is evinced by the very history of the early fourteenth century. The echo of the declaration of faith had still not died out, and in 1310 the inquisitor monk Giovanni Pizzigotis imposed very severe punishments on 12 Ferrarese Jews, probably considering them guilty of "usury." Pizzigotis was so diligent as to demand that the Jews should wear the distinctive sign of the yellow cloth badge. Later, in July 1313, the same monk initiated a trial against the Jew Elisha, which tragically ended with the burning at the stake, only to then resort in private, as the documents attest, to the services of these same pawnbrokers that he pursued in public (Colorni 1983, pp. 168–71). It was a glaring example of duplicity, in a social fabric in which prejudices oscillated, caught fire, and were then attenuated based on circumstance and convenience.

Moreover, in the real-life experience of which the Ferrarese documents speak, the stereotype of economic specialization—where Jews were always money-lenders and, for this reason, separate, isolated and disagreeable to the majority—was contradicted by the facts of more than one case. If we flash forward to 1370, we find a decree issued by Marquis Niccolò II d'Este that grants exclusive rights to money-lending in the city, for five years, to six lenders. The first two were Jews—Bonaventura Simoneti and Bonaventura Consilii— whereas the remaining four were not. The gentiles were Iacobo de Baidis de Parma, alongside three Tuscans: Ioannis Bondi del Chaca de Florentia, Baronus Balducii de Montecatino and Corda de Florentia (Franceschini 2007, pp. 36–37 no. 64). Of course, a sociological perspective cannot be constructed with isolated examples; but even just a handful of cases may suffice to deconstruct overly certain hypotheses on insurmountable boundaries. Seen through the eyes of an inhabitant of Ferrara in the late fourteenth century, the symbolic relation between lender and borrower should not be read purely in terms of Jew/non-Jew.

2. *The people of Ferrara swear allegiance to Pope Clement V*, thirteenth–fourteenth century. Vatican Library, Vatican City (cat. 1)

(Un) prohibited games

It is worth concentrating for a moment longer on the Ferrarese documents, in an effort to find other examples of the minority Jewish group interacting with the majority Christian context at different levels of proximity. We are well aware that the case of the Este is far from representative of Italy as a whole. Indeed, in the period covered by our exhibition, the mosaic of local situations—each with its own political, administrative, and economic specificities—surely makes it impossible to point to such a thing as a typical case. If Italian society was highly heterogeneous, the Jewish experience by its very nature was even more fluid. On the other hand, restricting ourselves to the confines of a single community, or a single city and its inhabitants, does make it possible to measure instances of containment and trespassing, and it enables us to explore what "being there as a Jew" meant, deeply inserted into the local dimension, as well as what "not being there as a Jew" meant, either due to exclusion or discrimination, or through one's own specific identity-defining choices.

If we scroll through the hundreds of archive documents and accounts concerning, directly or indirectly, the Jews in the city of Ferrara and its district, we are struck first and foremost by the remarkable dynamism, the ongoing aggregation and redistribution of family units, the ductility of biographical trajectories, and the general precariousness of the equilibriums, forever on the edge of change. If the Renaissance was the period of rapid fortunes and equally rapid falls from grace, the Jews lived in a temporal dimension that was even more accelerated. Their wellbeing and the effectiveness of their interrelations were subject to the mutable favors of the dominant class, and they were often destined to fall upon hard times, both economic and existential, on timescales that were on occasion very short indeed. It is true that the House of Este maintained, from the fourteenth right through the sixteenth century, a generally favorable attitude to the Jewish elite, who were considered a precious economic resource for the State's coffers and for the prosperity of the dynasty, but this benevolence was usually expressed in a politics of "privileges," that is, special dispensations vis-à-vis the current regulations and administrative customs. For each privilege accorded, and for every space of interaction opened up, there was a non-privileged—or rather, highly discriminatory—normality. This very special Jewish condition, of doubling between the legitimate—for some and for a short time—and the illegitimate, between recognition and negation, applied to Renaissance Italy as it did to any ancient regime society prior to Emancipation. Added to that was the proverbial Jewish mobility, which transcended any territorial Italian limit of the time and produced an effect of further dynamic intensification. For such a mobile minority, the spheres of aggregation and breakdown were geographically extended, with families and individuals structuring their business affairs and their bonds of marriage, as well as their experiences of study and of acculturation, across exceptionally wide stages. We referred above to Abraham Farissol, the erudite interlocutor of the Christian Pellegrino Prisciani. While Prisciani's family owed its fortunes to the favor of the Este dynasty and endeavored to expand its possessions and its influence behind the Este boundaries, Farissol came from a family that had been active for many years in southern France (Avignon, Montpellier, Perpignan) and maintained intellectual links with various hubs of the European diaspora, moving, for a certain period, between Mantua, Bologna, and Florence.

It is possible to imagine the structural relationships involving Italian Renaissance Jews as being like crystals that combine and dissolve very rapidly. Sometimes, the aggregations are brilliant, luminous. Other times, the breakdowns are unexpected and produce prolonged damage. On certain occasions, the Jews were acknowledged as playing an extremely favorable role, which differentiated them from the common Christian populace. For example, few people today would expect to discover for the Jews an exceptional access to the gambling table. Is this a minor, frivolous issue? We do not think so, since any mapping of society must also include the greatest possible number of dynamics of socialization, even those that are "irregular." Identity through play? You decide, we are just dealing cards.

On November 18, 1473 "Ercole I d'Este, Duke of Ferrara, received a petition from Lazzaro, Vitale, Noè, and Deodato da Norcia (Jews and lenders at the Riva, or Ripa, pawnshop) and from Bonaiuto, Isach and Daniel (Jews and lenders at the Sabbioni pawnshop), and permitted them to gamble, and even to play prohibited games, when the occasions arose, both with local people and with strangers, only for recreational purposes and in their own homes, regardless of statutory dispositions to the contrary" (Franceschini 2007, p. 320 no. 868). In short, this was a license to run a gambling house, even if only in a domestic context and only "for pleasure," exempting the bankers from the rules that applied to others. While here "local people and strangers" were allowed to take part, in another document dating from just a month before, the Duke himself authorized "Isach of the late Vitale" to "run in Ferrara and its villages games of all types, be they card or board games, even prohibited games, in their own homes or rented or leased to them, for payment or free of charge, and any Jew may play in them at any game, on condition that no Christian take part with other Christians or with Jews, or Isach and companions must pay a penalty of 25 gold ducats for each Christian found playing and each time, with the Christian in question being subject to the penalties imposed in the proclamations on the game" (Franceschini 2007, p. 315 no. 849). Inclusion and exclusion, then, but with a sign opposite to that used habitually. The Jewish home assumed the traits of a privileged space, where there was permission to do what the Christians were barred from doing. In Jewish houses, during the Renaissance, the domestic liturgy was observed, such as that of the Shabbat. Here, the dietary rules (*kashrut*) were applied, and people would study and teach, and in certain cases everyone came together for the collective prayer (in fourteenth- and fifteenth-century Italy, oratories were frequently found in private homes). Within the four walls of the home, though, it was even possible—at least for the privileged Ferrarese bankers—to engage in pastimes that would have been illegal in other places. In this case, we can imagine that many non-Jews with a passion for gambling would have happily transgressed the denominational boundaries in order to indulge in a session in peace. Jews and Christians could not play together? As for every Renaissance rule, here, too, there was an immediate exception—and it was a sensational transgression, given the individuals involved:

> The most illustrious Duke of ours distributed his offices. He had not given them during the feasts of past Christmases, as was customary, since he spent every day [to] play with a certain Jew named Abbram, who has much money, and the Duke emerged the winner (*Diario ferrarese* 1933, p. 45)

It is obvious that the Duke considered himself exempt from his own edicts. And moreover, the prolonged gambling was staged at the court and not at the home of the Jew… The "Abbram," who seems to have lost out to a considerable extent, was a figure who reappears frequently in the Ferrarese archives. His full name was Abramo di Mandolino da Cittadella di Padova, but he is often referred to, rather more eloquently, as "Abraam Zugadore" (the player). A professional gambler, he was also involved in other commercial and business operations. At court and in the city he was also given the nickname "Tusebec"

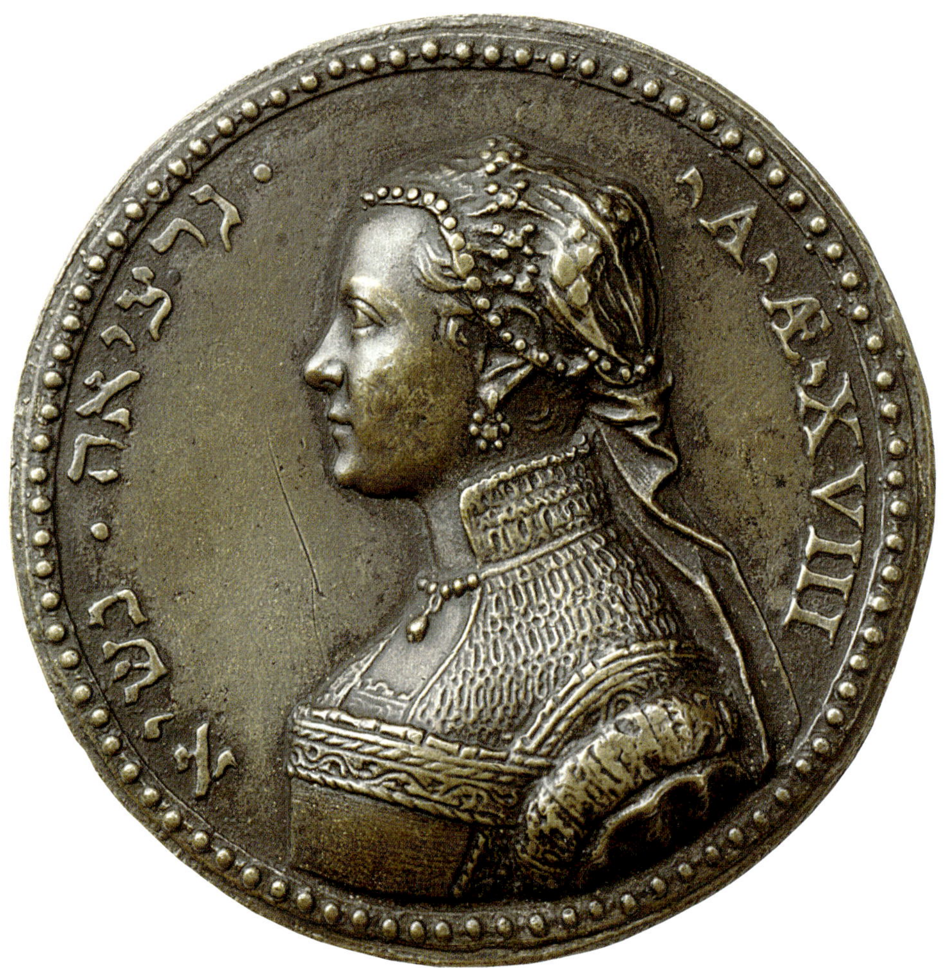

("Tu sei becco," meaning "You are hooked"), which was probably a scornful anti-Jewish reference to his pronounced nose (Ortalli 1996, p. 191). He was, then, a well-known character, who would have attracted the attention (i.e. curiosity, envy, and malevolence) of the wider Christian general public. That Ferrara's Jews were keen gamblers is also confirmed by another document, which even reveals the name of one of the gambling games that was in vogue in the fifteenth century.

On October 2, 1461, "Deodato di Sabbato, a Jew from Norcia, explained to the Giudice dei XII Savi [one of the officials responsible for effecting ducal policy in matters of tax] that in the current year he had given to the Jew Angelo dal Chitarrino a precious fabric and a number of valuables as collateral were he, Angelo, to win the gambling game called *sbaramò*" (Franceschini 2007, p. 267 no. 708). Once the game was over, Deodato wanted his collateral back, but Angelo denied ever having received anything from him. More than the decision of the judge, of which there is no trace in the document, we would like to know the rules of the game, in part because the Angelo in question, known as a musician and called Mordecai in Hebrew, was none other than the father of the scholar Abraham Farissol, to whom we have already referred above.

The duke or the princess?

More subdued but nevertheless discernible and significant in the Ferrarese documentation are the voices of Jewish women. Here, too, the relational structures changed and were redefined relatively rapidly. Marriage, dowries, and inheritances were, naturally, the thresholds through which the female world entered most markedly into the accounts and notarial deeds of the period. Exercising the rights of fiancées, married women, and widows is revealed to have been a challenging task. On more than one occasion, we find ourselves facing rather strong-willed characters who made their mark on what was predominantly a male preserve—the world of business and of patrimonies. It is safe to say that there are portions of the documents given over partially or fully to women. On October 19, 1479, the Jewish woman "Consola, tutor of Stella and Rosa, her daughters and pupils" acted "to recover her dowry from the assets of her late husband Israel, which are invested in the Banco di Campo in the district of Vicenza, together with the dowries" of two other Jewish women, Sara and Fresca (Franceschini 2007, doc. 988). It was a complex back-and-forth of reciprocal compensations, involving the transfer of considerable sums of money, which ended with a peaceful agreement between the women—the sign of a bargaining power parallel to that of men, with women appearing, consenting, opposing, and sometimes disappearing. In 1453, the Bishop of Ferrara, Francesco de Lignanime, made the Jew Salomone, lender at the Ripa pawnshop in Ferrara (on its location, see Graziani Secchieri 2017, pp. 53–54), promise that he would make known any reappearance of his two granddaughters, Anna and Consula, who had vanished after converting to Christianity. Should he fail to do so, Salomone would have to pay a fine of 200 gold ducats. This was a substantial sum for these unreachable converts, who had probably regretted the step they had taken and gone into hiding. We could call it a relational field *manqué*, with the Jewish female protagonists removing themselves from the ever-watchful attention of the ecclesiastical authorities, to re-emerge who knows where, protected by the family network (Franceschini 2007, p. 216 no. 564).

And since we have entered the female side of Jewish Ferrara, we cannot neglect its strongest, most celebrated and most widely discussed figure—Beatriz de Luna, alias Gracia Nasi, who in December 1548 (Leoni 2011, p. 360) appeared like a meteorite in the city of the Este. She did not stay for long, but she left an indelible historiographic record. Born in Lisbon around 1510 into a Jewish family that had been forced to convert to Christianity, in 1528 she married Francisco Mendes, one of the period's most important traders in spices and silver. Ten years later, having been widowed, she found herself, together with her brother-in-law, Diogo Mendes, at the helm of a *bona fide* business empire, with interests spanning not only half of Europe but also South America. In 1543, Diogo himself—who had in the meantime married Brianda, Beatriz's sister—promptly died. The Inquisition, and Mary of Austria, sister of the Holy Roman Emperor Charles V, had their eye on the fortunes of the Mendes; Beatrice thus fled to the more tolerant surroundings of Venice, together with her daughter, her sister Brianda and Brianda's daughter (Grunebaum-Ballin 1968; Brooks

2002). Certainly, around the group of women there was a whole host of agents, advisors, assistants, and suitors, but they were the heroines, in good times and bad. They operated at the highest level of society, fawned over by the government of Venice, sought out by ambassadors and sovereigns, flattered by writers and adventurers. Many different people wanted to get their hands on their money, and it mattered little that they had remained Jewish, behind the facade of conversion. Their true affiliation was a wide-open secret, and one that was politely brushed under the carpet, at least amongst the high-society contingent.

Brianda and Beatriz serve to show us, in the most eloquent way, another sphere of Renaissance interrelation—that of the *conversos* (see Ruderman's essay in this volume), or as they were disparagingly called at the time, *marranos* (converts), who had come to Italy from Spain and Portugal. Having fled persecution, these reluctant Christians, on the borderline between the societal majority and minority, found themselves perennially in limbo, caught between a sense of belonging and a sense of exclusion. Yet for this very reason, they were transversal and enterprising, revered by Italian states and statelets on the lookout for economic relief whenever the markets turned tough. The Mendes women were heroines, and of a very litigious type at that. They were riven apart by the family's assets, over which Beatriz tended to assert unilateral control. Brianda opposed her, staking her own claim, and flagged up the conflict to the Venetian authorities. It was the umpteenth dispute with her sister that led Beatriz to arrange a nighttime flit from the lagoon and head for Ferrara (*Processi del S. Uffizio di Venezia* 1987–99, vol. 1, p. 342). She was welcomed with open arms—in this instance the metaphor should be taken literally—by Duke Ercole II, who was known to be a friend of the *conversos* (even if he did "dispose" of those who had immigrated more recently, during the plague of 1549; see Leoni 2011). It goes without saying that he was particularly fond of their great commercial nous. In Ferrara, Beatriz—who had begun to use the name Gracia Nasi—managed international affairs, lived in grand style, and protected the press and writers. Under her patronage there appeared an epochal translation of the Jewish Bible in Spanish (or, more accurately, in Ladino, which is Judeo-Spanish), variously reprinted (M. Lazar in *Biblia de Ferrara* 1996, *passim*; see cat. 43), one with a dedication to Ercole II d'Este and one dedicated to her, "la muy magnifica Señora Doña Gracia Naci." Together with a handful of other books issued by the printing presses of the *conversos* in Ferrara, and promoted by Beatriz/Gracia, the 1533 Bible contains within its pages universes of new, secret, surprising interrelations. In Hebrew, *naśi* means "prince," and this begs the question, who was calling the shots—the duke or the princess? They were paired up in the dedication, but remained one step away from each other. They were, however, also combined in the Jewish imagination, as esteemed authority figures, with the latter even more highly thought of than the former. In 1553—calculated as 5313–14 since the creation of the world—Ferrarese society may well have had two patrons and protectors, one male and the other female, one Christian, the other Jewish. In its own way, this, too— indeed, this very phenomenon itself—encapsulates the Renaissance.

Translated by Gordon Fisher

4. *Biblia en lengua española traduzida palabra por palabra dela verdad Hebrayca por muy excelentes letrados vista y examinada por el officio dela Inquisicion.* Printed in Ferrara by Abraham Usque in 1553. Biblioteca Ariostea, Ferrara (cat. 43)

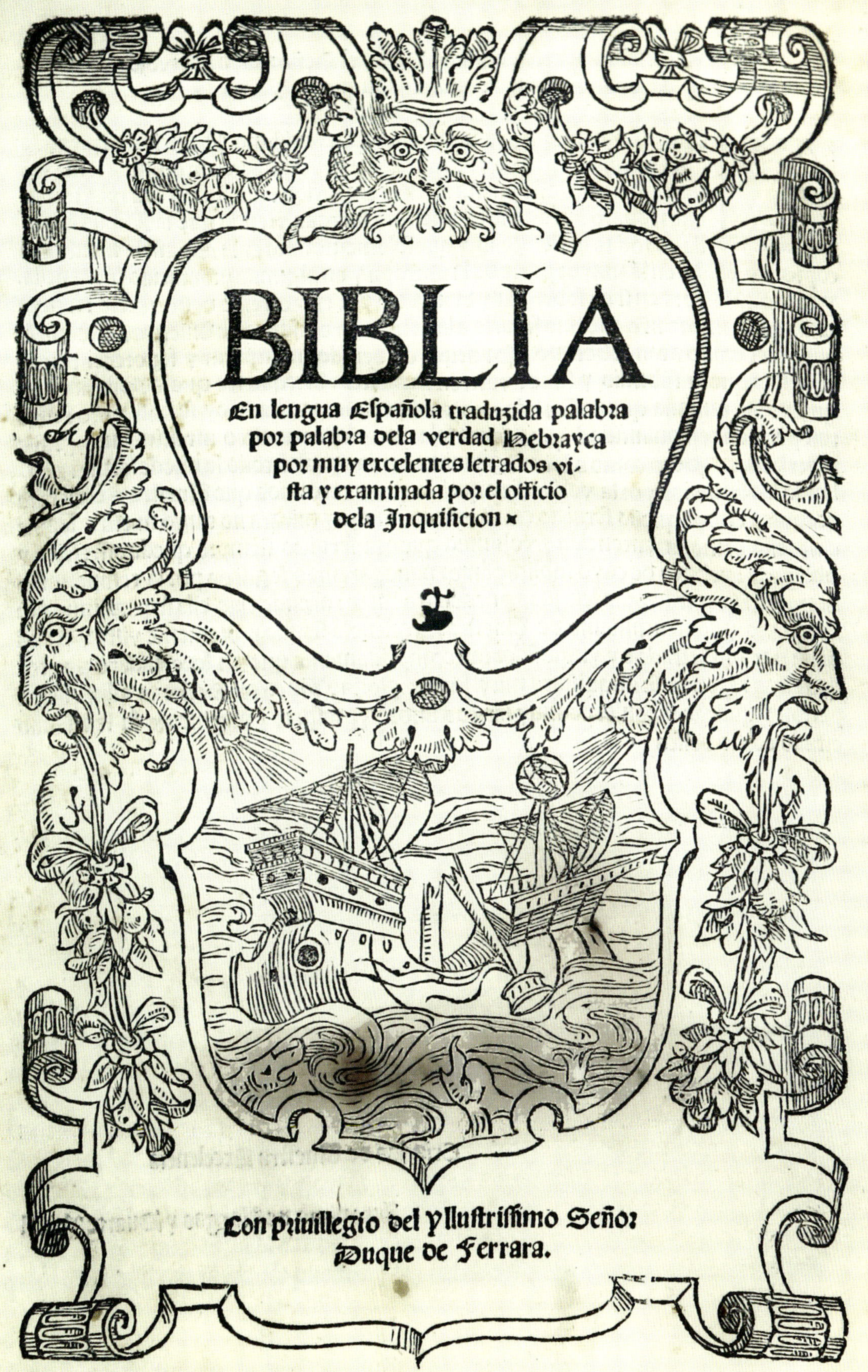

BIBLIA
En lengua Española traduzida palabra
por palabra dela verdad Hebrayca
por muy excelentes letrados vista y examinada por el officio
dela Inquisicion ⁂

Con priuillegio del Ylluftriſſimo Señor
Duque de Ferrara.

Sicilian Jews from the Fourteenth to the Sixteenth Century
Angela Scandaliato

In his *Sefer Ha-Ot* (The Book of the Sign), Abraham Abulafia, the thirteenth-century Spanish mystic who lived in Sicily for a decade, assumed the theophoric name of Zechariahu, "the Lord remembers," the messenger sent to the people of the "Island of the mirror" or "of power"—Sicily. Indeed, the Hebrew terms *ha-re'i* (mirror) and *gevurah* (power) equate to 216, a number that indicates the divine name of 72 letters, like the word *Sitziliyah* (Natan ben Sa'adyah Har'ar 2001, p. 42). On the island, Abulafia composed around two-thirds of his kabbalistic output, which would even go on to influence the Christian culture of the Renaissance. The Jewish presence in Sicily was an important one:a school encompassing students of medicine and astrology, men of letters such as Ahitub ben Isaac (the Doctor of Palermo) rooted in Judeo-Arabic culture, and famous kabbalists such as Nathan ben Saadia Har'ar, author of the *Sefer sha'are tzedeq* (The Book of the Gates of Justice), in which appear the Sufic notion of *'alam al-mithal* (the world of imagination) and the Sufic technique of *dhikr*, a concentration method of Islamic mysticism. These intellectuals made their mark on the history of Sicilian Judaism, with an influence that was heterodox with respect to traditional *halachic*-rabbinical hermeneutics. Since the time of the Swabian emperor Frederick II, the tradition of the *maqama* (literally, in Arabic, assembly) had become consolidated in Sicily, sparking dialog between the learned of different cultures and religions. The learned Sicilian Jews, however limited in number they may have been, brought with them a plurality of interests, from exegesis to mysticism, poetry, philosophy and mathematics, as well as scientific, astronomical-astrological, and kabbalistic studies. Indeed, the Sicilian Jews found themselves on the borderline between the Islamic and the Christian world; out of this liminal space there arose a diachronic dialogue with Islam, supported by a cultural identity/heritage that distinguished them from the peninsula's other communities. Their peculiarity lay in their use of Judeo-Arabic, which they would retain until the expulsion of 1492 (Perani 2005; Mandalà 2011). Their knowledge of Arabic afforded them access to the philosophical and scientific texts of Islam, and through them to Greek culture, and it is here that we can perhaps identify the conduit for the transmission of new knowledge to Italy and Renaissance Europe. Notwistanding the opinion according to which "los judíos no tienen don innato de lenguas" (Romano, 1991–92, pp. 212–13), it is a fact that geography and circumstance made them polyglots, *turgimans* (interpreters), ambassadors, intermediaries in the Mediterranean world, and translators of texts of Greek, Arabic, and Jewish culture. The historical-geographical context always conditioned their culture, both in their continuity with respect to the world of Sefarad and in the elements of discontinuity and specificity determined by geography and their particular history. As an island refuge of travelers, exiles, merchants, wayfarers, and pilgrims from North Africa, the

Near East and the Iberian peninsula, Sicily was a veritable paradigm of experimentation. Learned Mediterranean Jews passed through or stayed on the island: the intellectuals fleeing Aragon following the wave of anti-Jewish massacres of 1391 included Isaac al-Ahdab, who crossed the island from Siracusa to Palermo, where he gave rise to a dynasty of copyists and translators (Mandalà 2012).

The Jews deeply integrated into medieval Sicily, a "Mediterranean nation," and participated in the historical memory and the mystery-secret of the origins of its population. Bresc recalls the episode of the learned Jew of Palermo Isaac de Guillelmo, of Pisan origin, who—in a dialogue with the Dominican humanist Ranzano, to whom he presented the book *Sefer Yosippon* (an abbreviated version in Hebrew of the history of Flavius Iosephus, compiled in the tenth century in southern Italy)—declared as authentic a forged Kufic inscription engraved on the tower of Baich: the fruit of a brilliant deception, the inscription stated that the city had been founded by Sepho, son of Esau, a descendant of Abraham. The Jews in Sicily were, then, participants in a Pirandellian game of truth (Bresc 2001, pp. 62–64; Zeldes 2006).

The understanding of the culture of the Sicilian Jews has been enriched by research carried out over recent decades. In the fifteenth century, they were looking at the changes taking place on the Italian peninsula. Their intellectual development took many directions, but generally followed the flow of magical-astrological-astronomical and mystical currents, scientific in the widest sense. The debate amongst Italian humanist intellectuals on the political and religious renovation, the search for the *prisca theologia* (ancient theology) and the aspiration to reconcile Christianity and Judaism, rediscovering their shared origins, was played out in the fifteenth and sixteenth centuries, with significant input from Jews and Sicilian converts. Various clues lead us to think that they transferred to Sicily, together with the memory of their human experiences, a heritage of knowledge, yet to be investigated.

The Sicilian intellectual who had the greatest impact on Italian and, indeed, European Renaissance culture in the second half of the fifteenth century was, without doubt, the Jew Samuel Bulfarag (Samuel ben Nissim), who upon his conversion renamed himself Guglielmo Raimondo Moncada alias Flavius Mithridates from Caltabellotta (Cardillo Di Prima and Scandaliato 2014). At the nexus of several cultures, Samuel / Guglielmo / Flavius used his Jewish identity as the starting point for an existential adventure that was as ambitious as it was risky. He communicated to the world of the humanists the *arcana judeorum*, arousing curiosity on the mysterious *Vetus Talmud*. As Busi emphasized, "Jewish culture proved fascinating because it was an ancient civilization: Jewish studies were reconciled with the antiquarian passion for all of the millennial cultural expressions" (Busi 1992, pp. 10–11). In Germany, Rudolph Agricola defined Flavius as an "exceptionally learned man in all languages … he was also a theologian, philosopher, poet—in short, he was a true one-off." Sebastian Brant wrote a celebratory ode in his honour: "Ille Mithridates qui farmaca partica novit, qui vel ab Antycira detulis helleborum." An epigram was dedicated to him by the Florentine humanist Naldo Naldi, beginning with "Audieram patrem Musas" (Busi 2010b, notes 63–73). His father, Nissim Bulfarag, had been a student of Isaac al-Ahdab, the patriarch in Palermo of the Abenladeb or Belladeb family. Rabbi Nissim and his son Samuel appear in two manuscripts, the MS hebr. 246 of the Bayerische Staatsbibliothek in Munich, dated to between 1429 and 1431, which contains kabbalistic works and writings on astronomy by Ibn al-Ahdab, and the MS Sacerdote 202 of the Biblioteca Casanatense in Rome, copied by Nissim and dated 1445–56. The *colophons* feature dedications "to the venerated teacher" al-Ahdab. At the end of the MS hebr. 246, there is a note of ownership by Samuel, in which he states: "Of me, Samuel, the humble Abul-Farag, that he may live in eternity, and also his seed" (Mandalà 2012; Perani 2012a). The Cod. Urb. Lat. 1384, one of the jewels of the library of Duke Federico da Montefeltro of Urbino, is a testament to a crossroads of knowledge in which the wandering cleric-Jew Moncada/Mithridates was educated. He was cherished and detested by two popes, Sixtus IV and Innocent VIII, and was sought-after in the Renaissance courts for his stunning translation ability and for his wealth of knowledge on astrology, Kabbalah, and talismanic magic. He translated from Arabic to Latin the *Liber de Yimaginibus cœlestis* by Ibn al-Haytam, inserting a drawing of a magic square made of gold leaf with inscribed letters from the Hebrew alphabet. He respectfully recalled his father Rabbi Nissim, an expert in the fabrication of amulets (Starrabba 1878, p. 85; Campanini 2004). Illuminated by Franco de Russi, an artist at the service of Federico da Montefeltro, the manuscript is considered by Piemontese as "the most wonderful bilingual exemplar in Italy" (Piemontese 2002). In the preface, Moncada announces a tetraglot version of the Quran, of which in the same codex he translates suras 21 and 22 (Grévin 2018). The young Cardinal Alessandro Farnese became his friend and both frequented the circle of Lorenzo de' Medici in Florence. Flavius had requested protection from Farnese in 1489, when he found himself in prison in Viterbo—the result of a risky life and his involvement in the well-known adventures of Pico della Mirandola, of whom he was the controversial teacher of Hebrew and Kabbalah. In a letter, Mithridates stated that he was *conductus ad legendum*, that is, invited to teach in the city. He almost certainly collaborated with Annius of Viterbo (Scandaliato and Mandalà 2012), who in 1491 wrote a treatise entitled *De Viris Illustribus* dedicated to Ranuccio Farnese, in which he had the Farnese family descending from Osiris, and for which he was commended by the future pope Paul III. So, Annius and Moncada formed part of the circle of intellectuals of the Farnese court, alongside Gregorio da Spoleto, Demetrio Calcondila, Stefano d'Aquila, Pomponio Leto, Augusto Valdo, and Scipione Forteguerri.

A group of Jews from the Sciacca and Caltabellotta area moved to Rome and Terracina following their expulsion. The rabbi and physician Michael Zumat—of the Summato or Zumat family, which founded the Jewish hospital of Sciacca—integrated very successfully into the Sicilian community in Rome. Defined in sixteenth-century Jewish notarial

1. Pair of *rimmonim* (finials) from Cammarata
(Sicily), fifteenth century. Museo de la Catedral,
Palma de Mallorca (cat. 6)

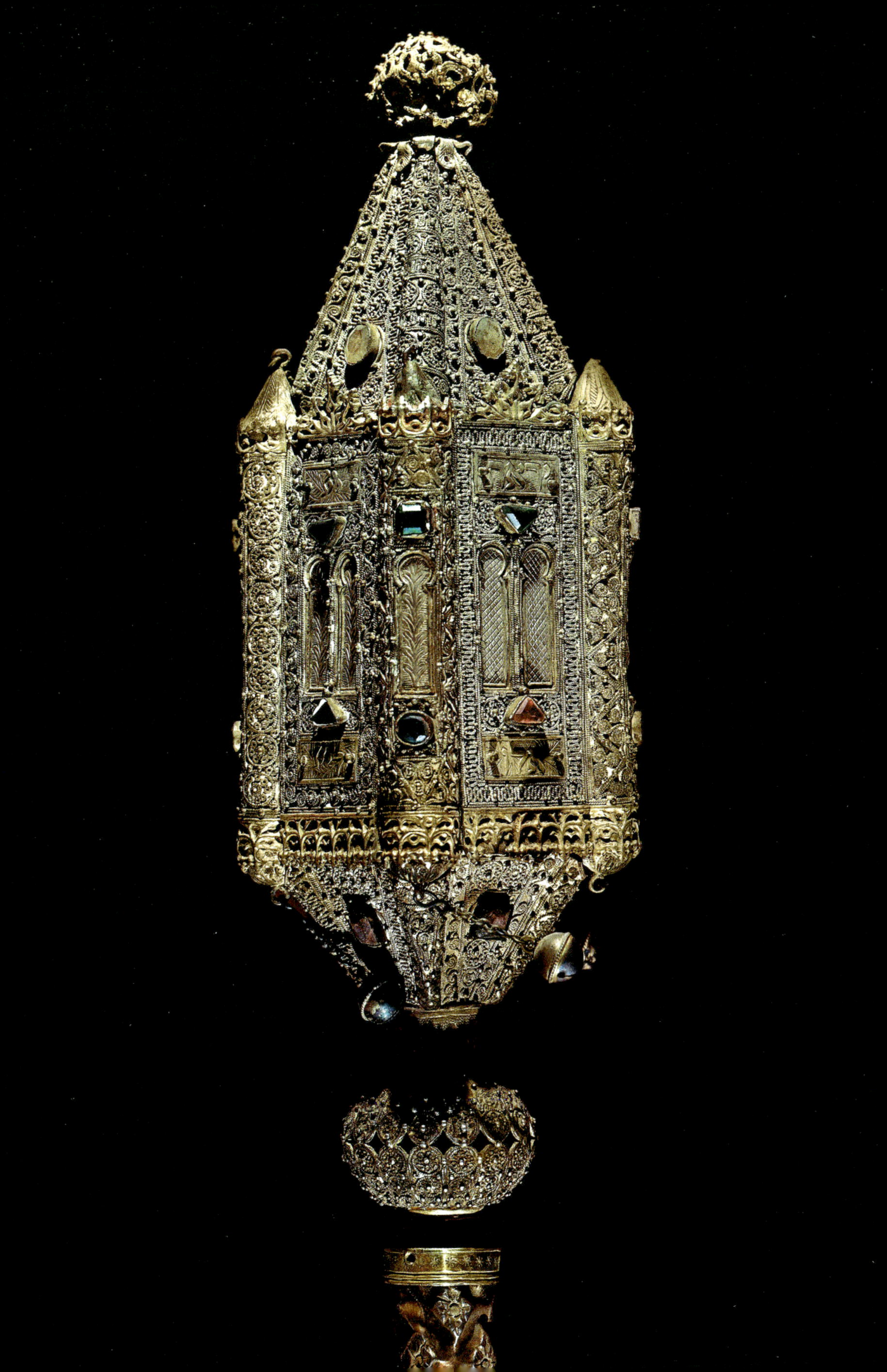

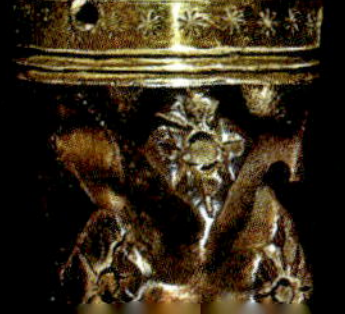

documents as the *hakam shalem*, he was a man of wisdom and a physician and became the Hebrew and Kabbalah teacher of the humanist Cardinal Giles of Viterbo and of Johann Albrecht Widmannstetter. Pope Paul III Farnese granted important privileges to Zumat: exemption for him and his family from the payment of taxes and the obligation to wear the distinctive badge, as well as authorization to practice as a banker. Michael Zumat was thought of very highly also by the Universitas hebreorum forensium et ultramontanorum in Urbe, which requested his input on ritualistic matters. He kept a kabbalistic library, and employed young copyists whom he recompensed by teaching them the Torah (Scandaliato 2013).

All of this points toward a collaboration between Jewish and Christian intellectuals in fifteenth-century Sciacca, with effects throughout Italy and in the Rome of the Medici and Farnese popes during the sixteenth century. Contact between the Sciacca and Caltabellotta area and the papal court was ongoing through the fifteenth and sixteenth centuries: the Sciacca painter Riccardo Quartararo was in the service of Pope Alexander VI (Rodrigo Borgia); Tommaso Fazello, the historian of sixteenth-century Sicily, was a friend of Paolo Giovio; a nephew of Pope Leo X and of Lorenzo il Magnifico, Aloisia Salviati, married Sigismondo de Luna, Count of Caltabellotta. Last but not least, an intellectual humanist physician of Jewish origin, Ferdinando Balami of the Balam family of Sciacca, known as Ferrante Siciliano, would become the primary physician of popes Leo X and Clement VII. At the behest of Clement VII, he translated and published in 1535 the rediscovered text of Galen's *De Ossibus* (with refined anatomical engravings) and other treatises by the same author. In the dedication, he commends himself to the new Pope Paul III, whom he got to know when he was still Cardinal Alessandro Farnese. He also provided Latin verses for various characters in Paolo Giovio's *Elogia* (1548). In Rome, Ferdinando Balami owed his career both to his talent and to the Balam family's links with the counts De Luna and the Medici popes. Mastro Ferrante would also enter into business with the counts of Mirandola, descendants of Pico, and would become a member of the Accademia dei Vignaioli together with Giovio, Bembo, Castiglione, Annibal Caro, and Giorgio Vasari. His beautiful palazzo, frescoed with the labors of Hercules (today's Palazzo Balami-Galitzin, on Via della Scrofa in Rome), had been built by Giovan Francesco Sangallo, cousin of the well-known Roman architect (Mandalà and Scandaliato 2015). From these fragments, I believe we can start to explore the culture of the Sicilian Jews and the contributions they made to the history of the Renaissance in Italy and throughout Europe.

Translated by Gordon Fisher

2. *Licence to practice medicine*, granted to the Jewess Virdimura, Catania, Sicily, November 7, 1376. Archivio di Stato, Palermo (cat. 10)

offert est p[ro] p[re]sens l[itte]ras b[e]n[e]uisas offi[ci]alib[us] p[ro] tota cur[i]a ꝯ[con]firmino
et ꝯ[con]firmo[n]s, ac p[ro]pon[er]e aliqs ta ꝑ[rese]nt qd pu[n]o, offi[ci]ar l[itte]ras i[n]spicu
r[e]s fideli[ter] o[mn]iu[m] r[e]s[er]

Cu[m] ad humile[m] supp[li]ca[ti]on[e]m pl[e]rra[m] q[uo]nd[am] excoll[entie] n[ost]re ꝑ b[ene]d[i]ma[ri]a Judea
d[e]xore p[ro]pt[er]alis de medic[in]o d[e] cat[h]er[in]a Judey [con]am n[ost]re d[e] t[er]ra[r]ia p[re]a
tical a vn[i]a medic[in]e arca ouras phys[i]cas ꝯ[con]p[or]e humana[s] in p[ar]t[e]
p[ar]t[i]u[m] quib[us] d[e]firit[ur] cons[er]u[er] mesa phys[i]c[or]um et medic[or]um salaria ꝑ
tu[r] d[e]l[e]g[ere] cor[or]e d[omino]m r[e]g[is] h[ab]et ord[in]at[er] co h[ab]et q[uo]d h[a]p[ro]m b[ene]d[i]m[ari]a
examinacio diligt[er] form[am] ꝑ phys[i]cos n[ost]ros i p[re]n[o]ta disp[osi]ta qu[o]
ead[em] b[ene]d[i]m[ari]a p[rese]n[ti]a examina[r]et ꝑ[rese]n[t]a ut n[u]ad[r]e p[er]ma tan[t]
d[a]tib, et exp[er]t[ur]a g[e]d[a]b[i]l[e]r co[m]mendat[ur] et approbat[ur] est adm[m]e[n]da
i p[re]n[n]e[r] phys[i]ca[s] fer[e] ꝯ[con]u[en]q[ue] d[isp]b[er] i[n]te[n]da
d[a]t[um] f[it] m[m] q[uo]d ꝑ[rese]n[t]a b[ene]d[i]m[ari]a p[re]an[ud]e i b[ene]d[i]m[on] vn[i]a medic[in]e
d[e]xat[ur] d[e]l[e]g[ere] anu[er]mu[m] t[er]a[m] r[eb]oco[r] d[omino]m r[e]g[is] q[uo]d ord[in]e b[is]g[ere]
fer n[ost]re ar[e]ta[r]e[m] ꝑ t[er]ta[m] p[er]n[er]r[er] d[e] g[e]p[re]r aud[ro] ꝑ[rese]nu[m] p[ro] g[e]r[er]os
obp[ra]m[u]tu[r] i p[er]nano, d[a]t[um] r[e]s

Venice and the Jews: A Cosmopolitan Ghetto in the "Centre of the World's Economy"

Donatella Calabi

What was the context in which the Venice of the early sixteenth century "spoke Hebrew," that is, when the earliest attempts were made by Aldus Manutius at trilingual printing (Greek, Latin, and Hebrew) alongside the Hebrew publishing undertaken by the Antwerp-born businessman Daniel Bomberg? It is well known that the working conditions in the Venetian printing industry were changing rapidly when, in 1515, the Senate of the Venetian Republic issued a privilege to the Flemish entrepreneur and when, over the subsequent decades, other Venetian printers of noble origin, such as Marcantonio Giustinian and then Alvise Bragadin elected to undertake a similar path (Busi 2016a, pp. 194–96). Jews—not just converts like Felice da Prato, who helped Bomberg on the use of difficult-to-decipher characters, but also potential new customers interested in the publications—were by now becoming established in the city: from March 1516, the Campo di Ghetto Nuovo was the acknowledged hub of one of Venice's most culturally active and valuable minorities (Archivio di Stato, Venice [henceforth: ASV], *Senato Terra* 1516; see cat. 3).

Indeed, some of those volumes had been requested by geographically distant Jewish communities in Thessaloniki, Aleppo, and Istanbul, which were presumably in contact with Venice. Others were sent to Eastern Europe (Krakow) and to Amsterdam: an important testament to the close cultural relations extending even beyond the Mediterranean basin (Ruderman 2010, pp. 99–102). A number of years later, Hebrew writing also appeared on the Istrian marble facade of one of the city's most significant Renaissance monuments, Jacopo Sansovino's church of San Zulian, in two scrolls between pairs of Doric fluted semi-columns that flank the portal.

In the climate of cosmopolitan syncretism of that *bona fide* center of the world economy that was Venice (Braudel 1953), peopled by humanists, Christian scholars, converted Jews, and orthodox Jews, cultural circles and academies were set up by individuals for the dissemination and exploration of Jewish culture and its sacred texts (*Venezia e le sue lagune* 1847, Appendix, p. 105; Bonfil 1987). In this context emerged the figure of Sara Coppio Sullam, who was renowned as an expert on history, philosophy, classical literature, and Jewish traditions. Blonde and very beautiful, she composed music and poetry and her guardians and friends included Leon Modena who—together with the gentiles—assiduously frequented her cultural salon (Busetto 1983).

How, in the meantime, was changing that peripheral area of the Cannaregio district, already known as "the ghetto," which the Senate of the Republic had designated on March 29, 1516 as a *ghetto dei zudei*? It was a "courtyard of houses," surrounded by a canal where from the very outset, alongside the homes, there had been a number of butcher's counters, an inn, and a bakery (ASV, *Senato Terra* 1516; Calabi 2016).

Starting from the second half of the century, the district that had by now been expanded with the addition of the homes and gardens of the Ghetto Vecchio (old ghetto) appeared fully structured. Artisanal workshops were opened up, even for trades officially banned but practiced nonetheless (such as that of the *sartor* or tailor), along with grocery stores and *strazzerie* (premises selling clothes, fabrics, and second-hand items of all types). The units were small (similar to those on the Rialto bridge) and looked out over the piazza or the street. They were cobbled with squares of Trevisan cotto tiles and had a grated window, a counter of bare stone, and walls with wooden shelving (ASV, *Notarile*, Atti 1582, 1607).

The Camera dei Guardiani was an office overlooking the square, with an entrance hall and adjacent warehouse (ASV, *Savi alle Decime* 1582). For the day-to-day water supply, they used four public wells (the three in Campo di Ghetto Nuovo and one in the old ghetto); the water-carriers sold it by the pail, but there were also a good number of private wells within the buildings (ASV, *Inquisitori agli Ebrei* 1638).

In terms of civilized living, the Jews were not slow to get themselves organized. Between 1541 (the year of the establishment of the Ghetto Vecchio, in addition to the existing Ghetto Nuovo) and 1590, Rabbi Cain Baruch concerned himself fully with the safety and maintenance of the houses, the paving of the roads, the fitness for use of certain facilities (a wine store, a grocery store, new butcher's "hooks"), as well as guaranteeing greater freedom of movement for his people and simplified access to designated places (sea customs post, duties on the Rialto bridge) (ASV, *Inquisitori agli Ebrei* 1590).

Equally complex were the decisions relating to business activities: while some were permitted to work in the print shops of Christians or to stage performances with their own musicians and dancers in the homes of Venetian gentlemen, others had requested and obtained a license to live and ply their trade outside the enclosure as "inventors" of sublimate, the hazardous nature of which made it advisable to limit production to occupied warehouses (ASV, *Ufficiali al Cattaver* 1586; *Compilazione Leggi* 1655; *Senato Terra* 1650). Still others needed convenient units for the unloading of goods being imported into areas of the city such as Giudecca, which were more suited to storage and artisanal production.

Daily life became enriched by retailers selling essential goods and by workplaces and shops: a bakery producing bread and azymes in Ghetto Nuovo and one in Ghetto Vecchio; numerous sellers of vegetables and fruit, wine, meat, cheese, pasta and wax candles; a barber, a hatmaker, a darner, a godmother figure to bring up Jewish girls, a tailor, a bookseller (often with his own print shop and bookbinding premises next door); a workshop for the fabrication of alchemical material; a hostelry for foreign Jews; an engraver; a timber store;

Pro Hebreis.

1516. Die 29 Mensis Martij In Rogatis.

È stà proviso per diverse leze del Cons.o de Pregadi, et del ma-
gor Cons.o che li Zudei non possano star in questa Città Nostra, sal-
che zorni quindeze intervelladi in tutto il tempo de l'an-
sono etiam stà posti diversi altri ordini Catolici, e necessar[ij]
obviar alla perfidia hebraica Che per esser à dett[i] volt[e] sup-
flua è comemoraoli Unde ancor per la necessità et urgentis-
condicion di tempi sia stà permesso che i prefati Zudei se
ducano ad habitar in Venetia, Il che principaliter successe
acciò le facultà de Cristiani ch'erano in man loro fussero pr-
serviade, Tamen non de esser de voler de cadaun del stato N-
che dividevo viver con timor de Dio che da poi reducti i sono and-
parzendose per tutta la Terra standi in aze cum Cristiani,
nadino Zorni, e Notte dove ghe piaceno facendo tanti mancam[enti]
et cum detestandi, et abominevoli come per tutto è divulgà
che è cosa vergognosa de cristioli cum offension graviss[i]ma dilla
Maiestà divina, et non vulgar nota d'questa ben instituto
Repub[lic]a; Alcle essend omnino necessario far opportuna, et utile
provisione.

L'andarà parte che per obviar à tanti disordini, et inconvenie-

Venice and the Jews: A Cosmopolitan Ghetto in the "Centre of the World's Economy"   **67**

a majolica store; and a coffin depository (ASV, *Procuratori di San Marco de Ultra* 1574; *Notarile* 1656; *Savi alle Decime* 1661).

As in the main European trading centers (Antwerp, Nuremberg, Amsterdam), the city's widespread specialization by districts appears congruent with a long-standing desire, reconfirmed many times, to welcome to the lagoon people from far-off countries who spoke different languages, practiced other religions and had distinct customs. Little by little, the foreign communities specialized in certain specific services that involved a diversified articulation of the urban fabric: the trade in fustians and woollen cloth was entrusted to the Germans; that in gold to the subjects of the Ottoman Empire; silk became the prerogative of the Florentines, whereas typography and printing were concentrated in the hands of the Armenians.

Traditionally, Jews were mostly bankers and pawnbrokers, while also dealing in used items. Over time, various authorizations from the Senate reaffirmed these activities as their main functions in the city. In any case, between the mid-sixteenth and the mid-nineteenth century, the jobs done in Venice, both within and outside the ghettoes changed considerably, influencing relationships between the residential quarter subject to restrictions, intended for one part of the population, and the rest of the city. Trade, along with the linguistic and cultural exchanges in the Mediterranean basin, involved a network of relationships with, for example, Madrid, and with a number of fairs such as those of Piacenza and Besançon. These interactions are verified by the strongly international nature of certain seventeenth-century female wills, in which monies were left to Jewish brotherhoods, or Venetian charitable organizations such as the Hospitals, or the "poor" of the ghetto or, more often than not, family members.

The socio-economic stratification of the various nations represented in the ghetto is confirmed by the jobs done by the inhabitants, but also by the varying quality of the homes. Along with pawnbroking, as we have seen there were other occupations such as the buying and selling of used goods (the so-called *strazzaria*) alongside more humble domestic services and other low-level forms of employment. In addition, there was a series of maritime trades with wide-ranging, profitable outlets in the markets of the Levant (Calabi 2016).

"Out of the liberal professions … they only had access to medicine," affirmed Marin Sanudo. At the practice in Padua, famous Jewish physicians would run courses and give lessons, including Elias del Medigo, of Cretan origin, who had Pico della Mirandola among his students; Abraham de Balmes, from Naples, whose followers and students of Hebrew included Cardinal Domenico Grimani (a noble collector of ancient sculptures); others emigrated to the lagoon from Spain or Portugal; and some were entrusted with special tasks, even including the poisoning, at the behest of the Council of Ten, of Hieronimo Adorno—a figure who had become politically inconvenient. On July 29, 1516 Jewish physicians obtained permission from the Senate to go out at night to participate in scientific meetings or to look after the sick (Sanudo 1879–1903). Their knowledge of the healing power of herbs and water, of ways to prevent the plague, of the importance of aeration, of the living conditions in the city and the country, and of the risk of famine was universally recognized and appears well documented in the literature of a number of travelers (Vanzan Marchini 1979; Oliveri 1987).

In one way or another, all of the Jews who resided in the ghettoes were concerned with trade, but they did so using diverse methods, benefitting from inconsistent privileges and paying duties at varying percentages. The criteria on which they used the space as-

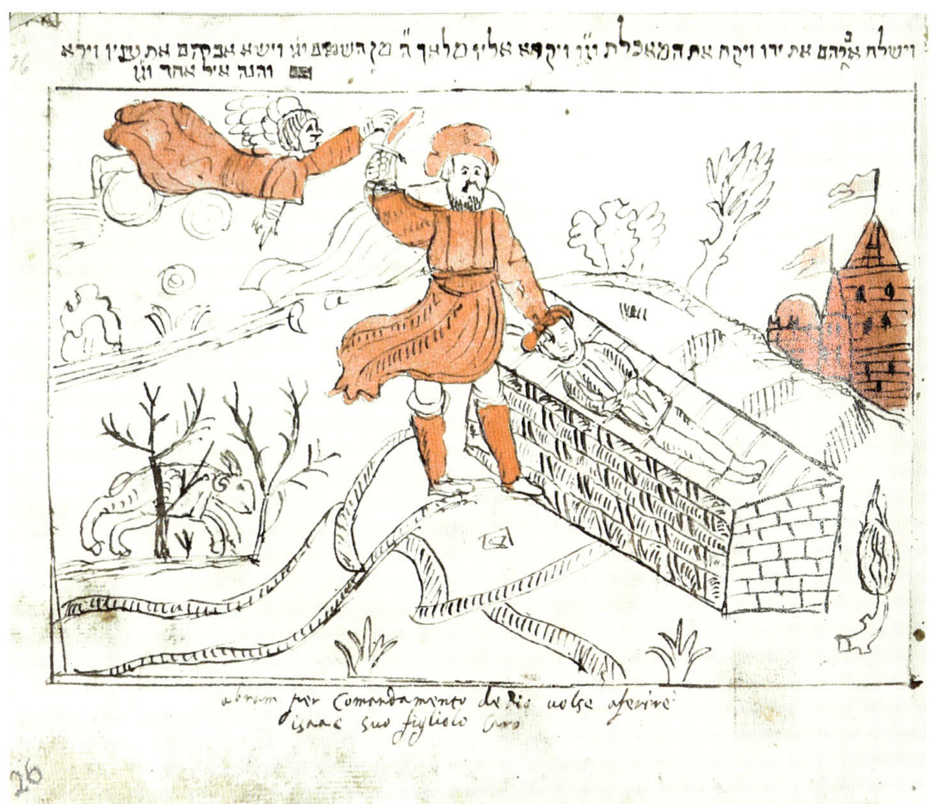

2. Illustrations for the *Pentateuch*, with captions
in Hebrew and Latin script, copied from Moses
da Castellazzo's originals, Venice, sixteenth
century. The National Museum of Italian Judaism
and the Shoah, Ferrara. Anastatic reprint: Vienna,
1986 (cat. 34)

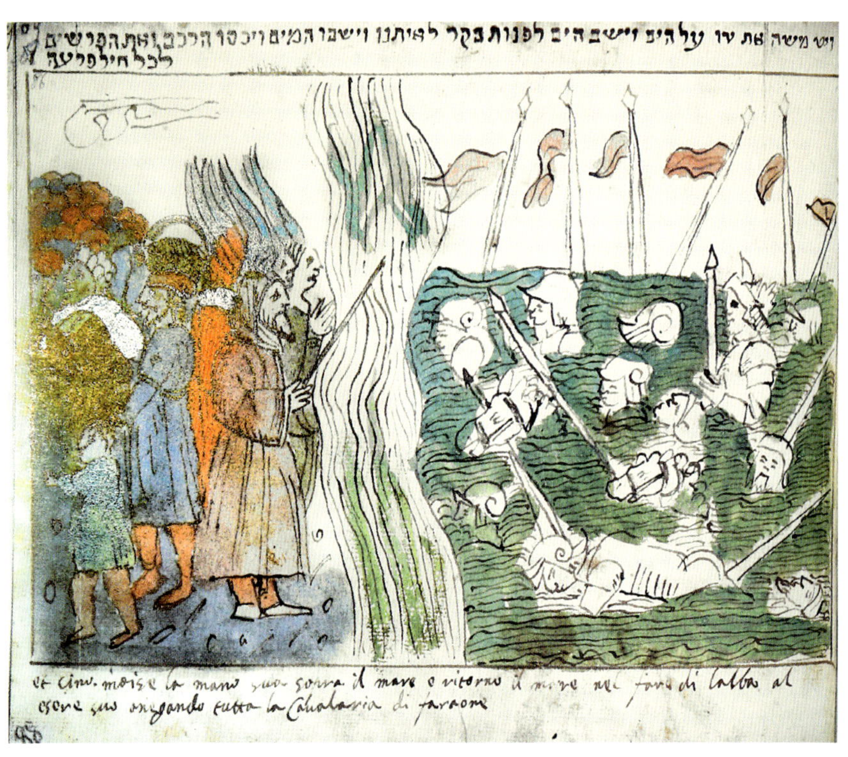
ויט משה את ידו על הים וישב הים לפנות בקר לאיתנו וישבו המים ויכסו הרכב ואת הפרשים לכל חיל פרעה
et Cinq. moise la mano sua sopra il mare e ritorno il mare nel fare di l'alba al essere suo anegando tutta la Cavalaria di faraone

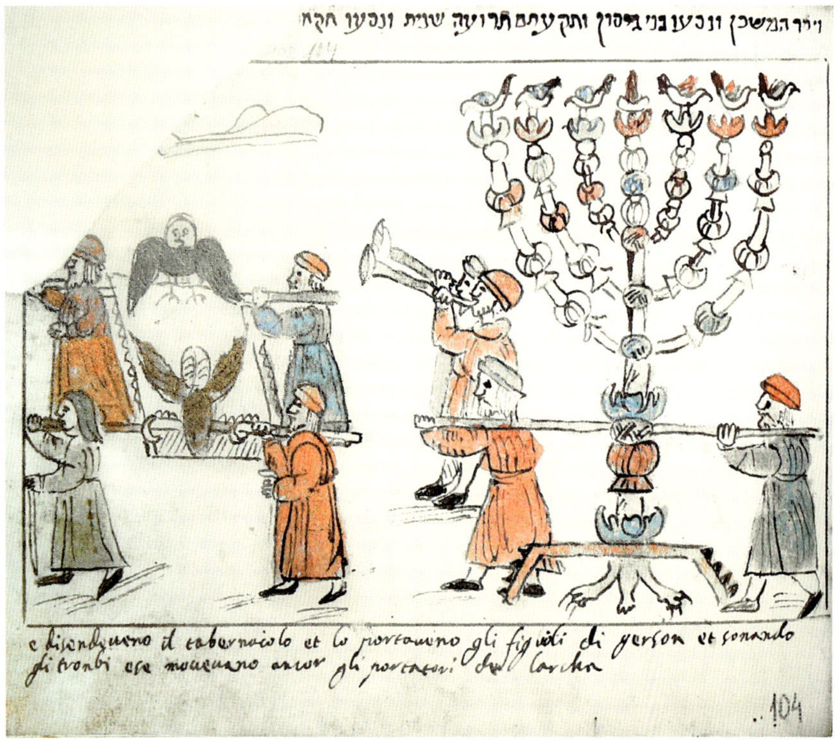
ויורד המשכן ונכעו בני בסון ותקעתם תרועה שוית ונסעו חקא
e disandauano il tabernaculo et lo portauano gli figlioli di gerson et sonando li trombi ese moueuano ancor gli portatori dell larche
·104

signed to them also differed, creating a subjective relationship with the city and with the frequentation of its physical space (Calabi 2016).

The administrative, economic, and even judicial role of the Jewish merchants, or those who spoke Greek or had Byzantine origins, had become crucial in the relationships between the commercial hubs of the Mediterranean and the Ottoman Empire. Venice constituted one of the primary centers: the Venetian Jews were changing both the structure of the commercial links with the Levant and the attitudes of the Venetian nobles, who were perfectly happy to delegate the trade with Eastern Europe to the Jews. The Jews were charged with the responsibility of ensuring a constant flow of money to the capital—so much so, in fact, that they often settled in the Adriatic area with the consent and complicity of the Republic.

Translated by Gordon Fisher

Documents
Archivio di Stato, Venice

Compilazione leggi, May 16, 1655, b. 189, fol. 219.
Consiglio de X, Misti 1516, Reg. 41, fol. 4r.
Inquisitori agli Ebrei, September 17, 1638, b. 25, fol. 466; March 14, 1590, b. 19, fols. 371r–374v.
Notarile, Atti, July 11, 1582. b. 8869, fols. 104–105v; *Notarile, Atti*, February 25, 1607, b. 10117/1227; A. Calzavara, February 29, 1656 (m.v. 1655), b. 2970, fol. 981r.
Procuratori di San Marco de ultra, February 10, 1574 (m. v. 1573), b. 55, fasc. 4, doc. 11, fols. n.n.
Provveditori alla Sanità 1516, Capitolare II, b. 3, fol. 14r.
Savi alle Decime, June 4, 1546, Reg. 1238, fol. 100v; *Savi alle Decime* 1582, bb. 161, Castello, 858; 162, Cannaregio 323, 146; 163, Cannaregio, 586; 164, Cannaregio, 1241; 171, DD, 1178, 834; 169, DD, 84; 1661, b. 426, *Condizion aggiunte* 1589, 2, b. 181, n. 3416, registered adì March 18, 1598.
Senato Terra, Deliberazioni, March 29, 1516, Reg. 19, fol. 96r; January 31, 1597 (m.v. 1596), Reg. 66, fols. 165v–172v; June 13, 1650.
Ufficiali al Cattaver, June 13, 1586, b. 242, Reg. 3, fols. 53v–54r; November 23, 1590, b. 243, Reg, 3, fol. 190v; September 9, 1593, b. 244, reg. 5, fol. 101v; February 18, 1595 (m.v. 1594), b. 244, reg. 5, fol. 137v; October 21, 1631, b. 242, fol. 155.

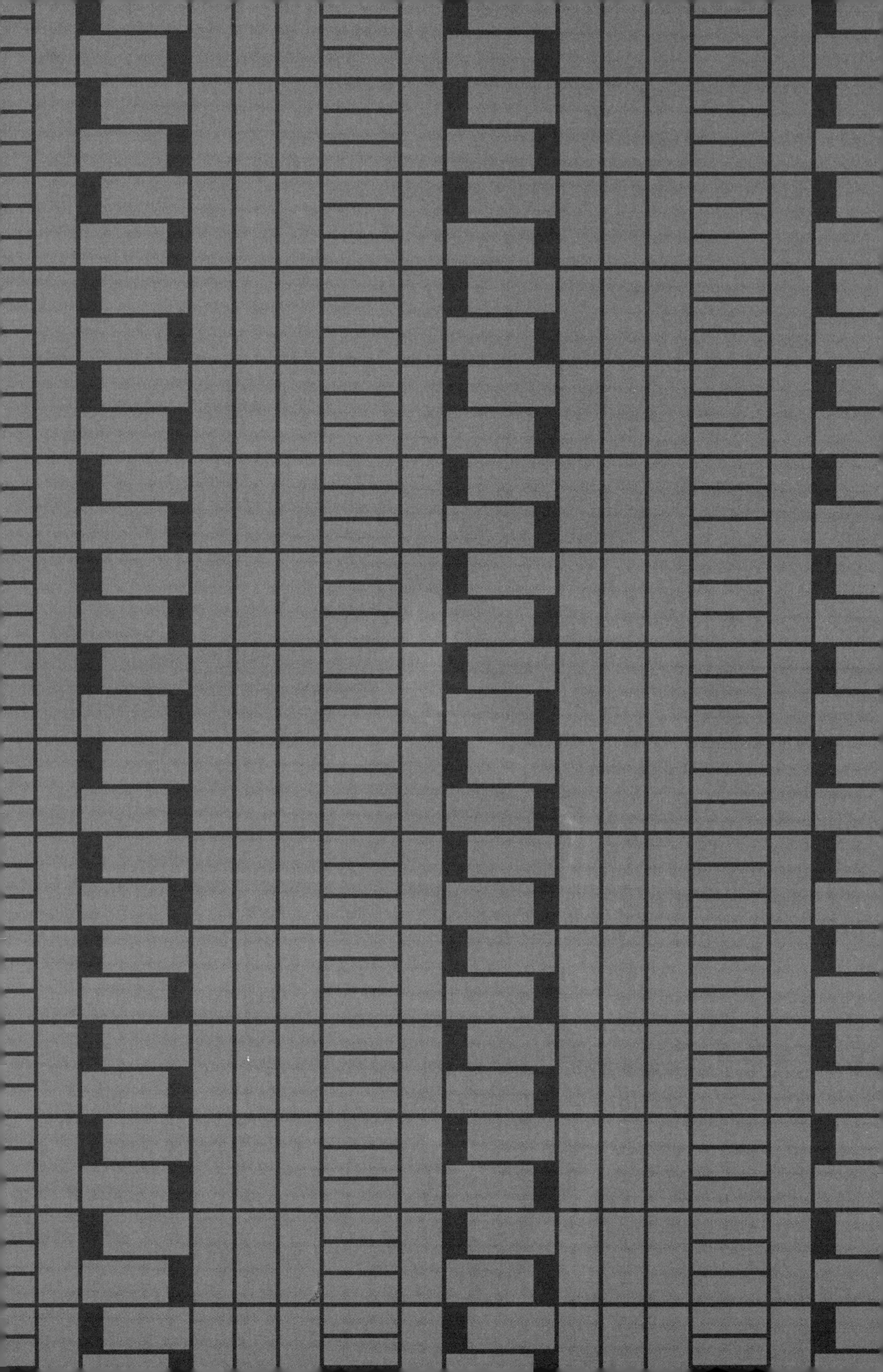

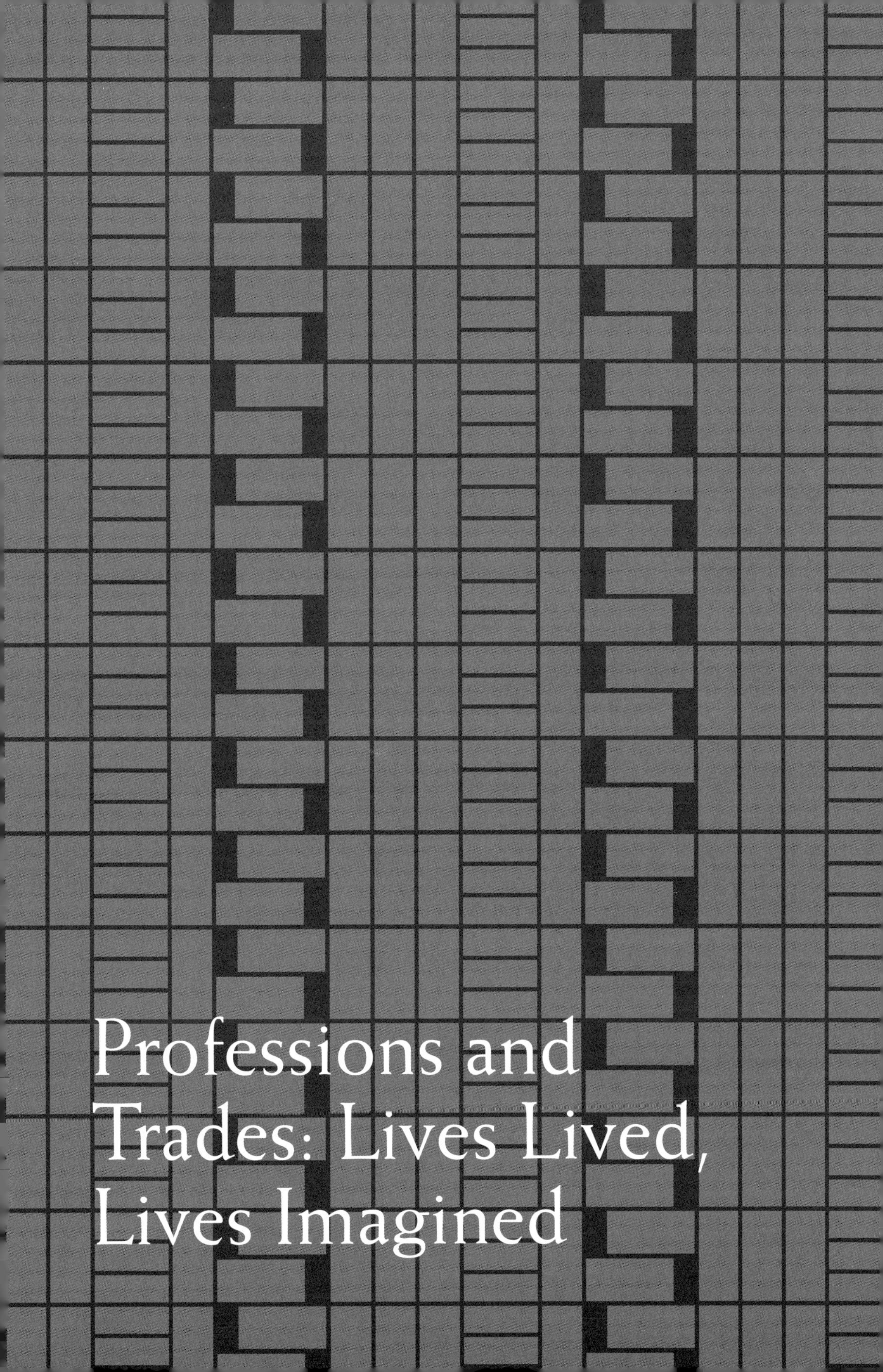

Professions and Trades: Lives Lived, Lives Imagined

Female Jewish Lenders in Northeastern Italy
Miriam Davide

In the late Middle Ages, numerous female lenders, mostly of Ashkenazi origin, operated in northeastern Italy. Managing a loan bank alongside their husbands or in total autonomy, relying on partners and agents, was common practice in the homelands of the Jewish communities that had begun to form in the second half of the thirteenth century in the Patriarchate of Aquileia (Bato 1956; Toaff 1991; *Geschichte der Juden* 2002; Jörg 2008). Indeed, there is considerable evidence of female lenders in German and Austrian Ashkenazi communities operating in a segment of credit that was not limited to just consumer loans (Keil 2004 and 2008), as was the case with the female banker Zorline, who drew up numerous loan contracts with the Frankfurt authorities before moving to the Jewish community in Treviso (Möschter 2008).

It should be kept in mind that female lenders could control, through the practice of their profession, the ways in which the dowry was invested in their family businesses. The resulting profits were divided into three parts, with wives having the right to use one third of them as they saw fit. This income was added to the personal wealth of the female usurers, who customarily used it to balance unshared financial decisions made by their husbands in favor of their children. In general, female lenders tried to favor their daughters, fated to receive only dowries as their inheritance, or, more generally, children seen to be weak in comparison to the rest of the family and so incapable of finding professional fulfillment without assistance.

The earliest cases of female lenders are documented in Cividale, where a community formed, complete with a rabbinical court, that served all of the small- and medium-sized Jewish enclaves in Friuli, the Veneto, and Istria (Zenarola Pastore 1993; Mentgen 2008). The activity of these women is documented in numerous notarial acts that mostly concern interest-bearing loans and highly speculative credit sales of wine and grain. Their clients were for the most part city-dwelling artisans and numerous rural farmers, two groups in need of consumer loans that could meet the incidental needs typical of developing areas. Female lenders were able to slip with little difficulty into a credit market where other non-local operators (mostly from Lombardy and Tuscany) were working, to the point that their activity ensured them a prominent role in their communities during the periods of their husbands' absence. Lenders' wives almost always handled the family business during the last six months before their *condotte* (contracts) expired, replacing their husbands who

1. *Iron safe*, Italy, sixteenth century?
Jewish community, Ferrara (cat. 12)

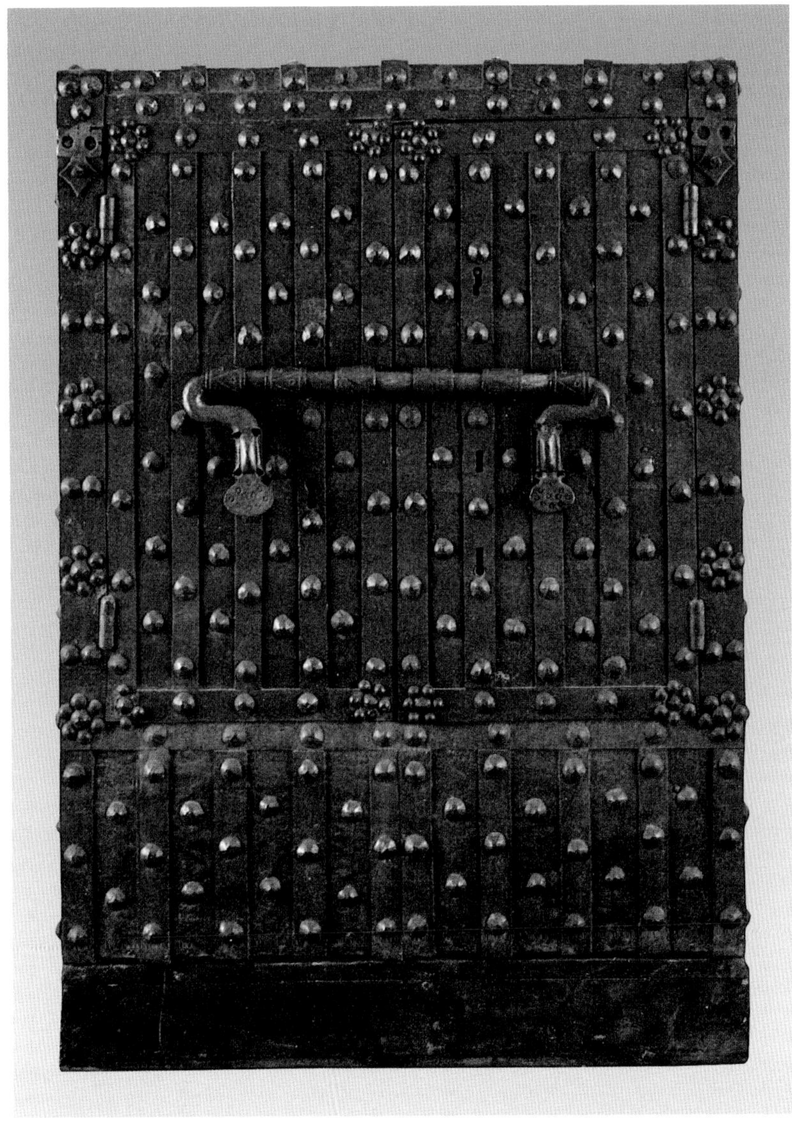

were out looking for new places where they could practice moneylending. During these periods, wives concentrated primarily on collecting outstanding loan payments and supervising auctions of unclaimed pawned goods, which were periodically organized by the public authorities.

In most cases, the husband's death does not seem to have questioned the management and administration of the loan banks, in particular in the case of young heirs who had been expressly put in the care of the female lenders by their husbands. Widows generally continued to manage the family business until their sons came of age. In Trieste, the city with the highest documented number of female lenders, it is clear that they tended not to share the administration of their loan banks with new partners, preferring instead to rely on the experience of agents, preferably ones who had already worked with them when their husbands were still alive, or even appointing proxies on a case-by-case basis for individual operations (Durissini 1997; Davide 2005, 2012, and 2016).

The most extraordinary case of a woman deciding to continue her lending activity independently is that of Mina di Aydelbach and her under-age sons Bonomo and Joseph di Garlacht, to whom the municipality of Gemona granted *condotte* in 1388 (Billiani 1895; Davide 2009). She chose to manage the bank with just the help of agents, and without looking for a new partner, after successfully initiating and concluding negotiations with the municipality.

The deep knowledge of the credit market was not limited to direct experience with running loan banks, but is also evident in the decision to invest and deposit sums of money in the network of loan banks run by fellow Jews, both in the lender's city of residence and in other parts of the region, the Veneto, and Istria. Many female lenders from Trieste were, for example, accustomed to simultaneously managing multiple loan banks in the city and on the Istrian coast. Careful management of investments ensured high earnings for them, which were used almost exclusively to improve their daughters' financial position through the establishment of bequests in their favor. Female testators almost always opted to have their last will and testament drawn up by a Christian notary in order to protect their daughters (the primary beneficiaries of maternal assets), who would have thus had extra legal backing in case they needed to defend themselves against claims to the maternal inheritance brought by their brothers. In the case of only male children, it seems that female lenders in Trieste divided their inheritances in a discretionary manner (Davide 2010). There were fewer women directly managing loan banks in the Veneto, including the Ashkenazi community in Treviso, which became the most important Jewish centre in northeastern Italy during the fifteenth century. With few exceptions, women generally entrusted the purchase of shares and management of deposits to proxies, who could be either family members or trade professionals.

Translated by Sarah Elizabeth Cree

2. *Rental contract for the pawnshop formerly run by Moses Norsa in Mantua,* Mantua, December 17, 1517. Archivio di Stato, Modena (cat. 13)

351.2

200 05

351

The Illuminated Hebrew Manuscript in Renaissance Italy

Mauro Perani

Italy and the Hebrew manuscript

Before describing the fine art of the decorated Hebrew manuscript produced in Italy between the fifteenth and early sixteenth centuries, we need consider the cultural and historical context of Italian Judaism during that period in order to understand how the Italian peninsula became, through a series of fortunate historical synergies, the cradle and most fecund source of the Hebrew manuscripts that now enrich libraries and collections all over the world. How is it possible that more than half of all of the Hebrew manuscripts preserved today worldwide came from Italy, either because produced there or copied in Ashkenazi and Sephardic areas a century or so earlier and brought there? Why did Benjamin Richler, one of the greatest scholars of the history of Hebrew manuscript collections, their movements and travels, define Italy the "breadbasket" of the world's Hebrew manuscripts? And how can this have happened, considering that, although Jews have been present in Italy longer than anywhere else in the West and boast more than two thousand years of history there, the number of Jews in Italy over this long chronological period never exceeded forty or fifty thousand?

Benjamin Richler's explanation

Of particular use is the quantitative analysis carried out by Richler drawing on demographic calculations and data relative to manuscripts either produced in Italy or that came to Italy, within a research he conducted at the Institute of Microfilmed Hebrew Manuscripts, an annex of the National Library of Israel. Through the Ktiv Project, the Institute's microfilms have been replaced by the digital reproduction of manuscripts, which can now be consulted with incomparable clarity with respect to microfilms. Richler writes that "any broad survey of Medieval Hebrew Manuscripts will reveal that a disproportionately large number of the manuscripts were written in Italy or show signs of Italian provenance" (Richler 2013, p. 137).

Umberto Cassuto was already aware in 1929 of the astonishing disproportion between the number of Jews and the number of Hebrew manuscripts in Italy, writing that "the many thousands of Italian manuscripts that reached our day … can not but appear … surprising to us also in relation to the number of Hebrew manuscripts coming from other countries. Indeed, I believe that one can assert that a large proportion, if not the majority, of the Hebrew manuscripts now preserved in libraries throughout the world are of Italian origin" (Cassuto 1931, p. 69), either because produced in Italy or because brought there by immigrating Jews.

Malachi Beit-Arié also carried out calculations of considerable interest. According to him, the Hebrew manuscripts produced in Italy between the late fourteenth and late fifteenth century represent around two-thirds of all dated and surviving Hebrew codices produced in Italy up to 1500, and 40% of all of the dated and surviving Hebrew manuscripts that were copied in the world, during that period, in Sephardic or Ashkenazi—but not Italian—Jewish scripts (Beit-Arié 2018, preprint edition).

After the expulsion, the number of Jews who resided in Italy was two times that of those residing in eastern Europe and equal to the number living in Europe outside the Italian peninsula. Which is to say that in the sixteenth century, half of the European Jews were living in Italy and, as a consequence, the same quantity (half) of the Jewish manuscripts existing at the time were in this country (Richler 2013, pp. 140–41).

The systematic destruction of Hebrew manuscripts

Due to a series of particular historical and religious circumstances, we can estimate that only a very small proportion, around 5%, of the medieval Hebrew manuscripts produced in Europe during the Middle Ages have survived. The two most important reasons for such a high percentage of loss are the following.

First, the books of the Jews, and in particular the Talmud, which was considered the reason for the Jews' stubborn refusal to convert to the "true" religion, were destroyed in vast numbers by the various Inquisitions, especially the one that started in the middle of the sixteenth century, which began eliminating the books of the Jews following a papal bull issued by Julius III in 1553 ordering the confiscation and the mass burning of the Talmud in Rome and in the other cities ruled by Christian princes.

The second reason is linked to the Jewish preoccupation with avoiding the profanation of the holy tongue and in particular the Tetragram, the holy name of God, which appears in the Bible 6,828 times, 1,419 of which in the Pentateuch alone. Ritual law therefore prescribed that any Hebrew text, whether a manuscript or printed book, that was no longer being used or was deteriorated from use must be placed in a temporary storage area, called a Genizah, before being buried in a cemetery.

Further reasons can be added to these two main ones. For example, there was a widespread practice of taking apart Hebrew codices made of parchment, especially from the middle of the sixteenth century through the entire seventeenth and beyond, in order to reuse the sheets as binding. This practice, which not only concerned Hebrew parchment

1. *Sefer Torah* (Torah scroll),
northern France, c. 1250.
Jewish community, Vercelli (cat. 9)

משכן העדת אשר פקד על פי משה עבדה
הלוים ביד איתמר בן אהרן הכהן ובצלאל
בן אורי בן חור למטה יהודה עשה את כל
אשר צוה יהוה את משה ואתו אהליאב
בן אחיסמך למטה דן חרש וחשב ורקם
בתכלת ובארגמן ובתולעת השני ובשש
כל הזהב העשוי למלאכה
בכל מלאכת הקדש ויהי זהב התנופה תשע
ועשרים ככר ושבע מאות ושלשים שקל
בשקל הקדש וכסף פקודי העדה מאת ככר
ואלף ושבע מאות וחמשה ושבעים שקל
בשקל הקדש בקע לגלגלת מחצית השקל
בשקל הקדש לכל העבר על הפקדים מבן
עשרים שנה ומעלה לשש מאות אלף
ושלשת אלפים וחמש מאות וחמשים ויהי
מאת ככר הכסף לצקת את אדני הקדש
ואת אדני הפרכת מאת אדנים למאת הככר
ככר לאדן ואת האלף ושבע המאות
וחמשה ושבעים עשה ווים לעמודים וצפה
ראשיהם וחשק אתם ונחשת התנופה
שבעים ככר ואלפים וארבע מאות שקל
ויעש בה את אדני פתח אהל מועד ואת מזבח
הנחשת ואת מכבר הנחשת אשר לו ואת
כל כלי המזבח ואת אדני החצר סביב ואת
אדני שער החצר ואת כל יתדת המשכן
ואת כל יתדת החצר סביב ומן התכלת
והארגמן ותולעת השני עשו בגדי שרד
לשרת בקדש ויעשו את בגדי הקדש
אשר לאהרן כאשר צוה יהוה את משה

ויעש את האפד זהב תכלת וארגמן ותולעת
שני ושש משזר וירקעו את פחי הזהב
וקצץ פתילם לעשות בתוך התכלת ובתוך
הארגמן ובתוך תולעת השני ובתוך השש
מעשה חשב כתפת עשו לו חברת על
שני קצוותיו חבר וחשב אפדתו אשר עליו
ממנו הוא כמעשהו זהב תכלת וארגמן
ותולעת שני ושש משזר כאשר צוה יהוה
את משה
ויעשו את אבני השהם
מסבת משבצת זהב מפתחת פתוחי חותם
על שמות בני ישראל וישם אתם על כתפת
האפד אבני זכרון לבני ישראל כאשר

צוה יהוה את משה ויעש את
החשן מעשה חשב כמעשה אפד זהב
תכלת וארגמן ותולעת שני ושש משזר
רביע היה כפול עשו את החשן זרת ארכו
וזרת רחבו כפול וימלאו בו ארבעה טורי
אבן טור אדם פטרה וברקת הטור האחד
והטור השני נפך ספיר ויהלם והטור
השלישי לשם שבו ואחלמה והטור
הרביעי תרשיש שהם וישפה מוסבת
משבצות זהב במלאתם והאבנים על שמת
בני ישראל הנה שתים עשרה על שמתם
פתוחי חתם איש על שמו לשנים עשר
שבט ויעשו על החשן שרשרת גבלת
מעשה עבת זהב טהור ויעשו שתי משבצת
זהב ושתי טבעת זהב ויתנו את שתי הטבעת
על שני קצות החשן ויתנו שתי העבתת
הזהב על שתי הטבעת על קצות החשן
ואת שתי קצות שתי העבתת נתנו על שתי
המשבצת ויתנם על כתפת האפד אל מול
פניו ויעשו שתי טבעת זהב וישימו על
שני קצות החשן על שפתו אשר אל עבר
האפד ביתה ויעשו שתי טבעת זהב ויתנו
על שתי כתפת האפד מלמטה ממול פניו
לעמת מחברתו ממעל לחשב האפד
וירכסו את החשן מטבעתיו אל טבעת
האפד בפתיל תכלת להית על חשב האפד
ולא יזח החשן מעל האפד כאשר צוה
יהוה את משה
ויעש את מעיל האפד מעשה ארג
כליל תכלת ופי המעיל בתוכו כפי
תחרא שפה לפיו סביב לא יקרע ויעשו
על שולי המעיל רמני תכלת וארגמן
ותולעת שני משזר ויעשו פעמני זהב
טהור ויתנו את הפעמנים בתוך הרמנים
על שולי המעיל סביב בתוך הרמנים
פעמן ורמן פעמן ורמן על שולי המעיל
סביב לשרת כאשר צוה יהוה את
משה
ויעשו את הכתנת שש מעשה ארג
לאהרן ולבניו ואת המצנפת שש ואת
פארי המגבעת שש ואת מכנסי הבד
שש משזר ואת האבנט שש משזר

ויעש את
החשן מעשה חשב כמעשה אפד זהב
תכלת וארגמן ותולעת שני ושש משזר
כאשר צוה יהוה את משה
ויעש את ציץ נזר הקדש זהב טהור ויכתב
עליו מכתב פתוחי חותם קדש ליהוה ויתן
עליו פתיל תכלת לתת על המצנפת
מלמעלה כאשר צוה יהוה את משה
ותכל כל עבדת משכן אהל מועד
ויעשו בני ישראל ככל אשר
צוה יהוה את משה כן עשו
ויביאו את המשכן אל משה את האהל
ואת כל כליו קרסיו קרשיו בריחו ועמדיו
ואדניו ואת מכסה עורת האילם המ
ואת מכסה ערת התחשים ואת פרכת
המסך את ארון העדת ואת בדיו ואת
הכפרת את השלחן את כל כליו ואת
לחם הפנים את המנרה הטהרה את נרתיה נ
נרת המערכה ואת כל כליה ואת שמן המאור
ואת מזבח הזהב ואת שמן המשחה ואת
קטרת הסמים ואת מסך פתח האהל ואת
מזבח הנחשת ואת מכבר הנחשת אשר לו את
בדיו ואת כל כליו את הכיר ואת כנו את קלעי
החצר את עמדיה ואת אדניה ואת המסך לשער
החצר את מיתריו ויתדתיה ואת כל כלי
עבדת המשכן לאהל מועד את בגדי השרד
לשרת בקדש את בגדי הקדש לאהרן הכהן
ואת בגדי בניו לכהן ככל אשר צוה יהוה
את משה כן עשו בני ישראל את כל העבדה
וירא משה את כל המלאכה והנה עשו אתה
כאשר צוה יהוה כן עשו ויברך אתם משה

וידבר יהוה אל משה לאמר ביום החדש
הראשון באחד לחדש תקים את משכן
אהל מועד ושמת שם את ארון העדות
וסכת על הארן את הפרכת והבאת את
השלחן וערכת את ערכו והבאת את המנרה
והעלית את נרתיה ונתתה את
מזבח הזהב לקטרת לפני הארן ושמת
את מסך הפתח למשכן ונתתה את
מזבח העלה לפני פתח משכן אהל
מועד ונתת את הכיר בין אהל מועד וב

manuscripts but all manuscripts irrespective of language, including Christian ones, was triggered by the spread of printed books, which were relatively inexpensive in comparison to the extremely costly manuscripts, thus creating fierce competition for the latter and leading to their disappearance from the book market (Perani 2008).

And then there was a whole series of other reasons, among which the intense daily use of manuscripts for study (a religious duty for Jews) and the poor conditions for keeping books at home and during travel, which left them exposed to the elements and at risk of theft and damage, unlike Christian codices, which were preserved for centuries protected in the great religious institutions.

The tragic result of the combination of all of these factors, in particular the first two, although for different reasons, was the destruction of a very large proportion of the valuable Hebrew manuscripts produced in the Middle Ages.

The surviving manuscripts

The surviving manuscripts, including those from the early modern period, number around 70,000, and are scattered throughout libraries and collections all over the world. Of these, 40,000 are medieval, to which we need to add around 210,000 fragments discovered at the end of the nineteenth century in the renowned Genizah (as noted above, a repository created for ritual reasons to avoid the profanation of the name of God) of the Ben Ezra synagogue in Old Cairo. Texts were stored in this deposit for 800 years, from the twelfth century, i.e. the time of Maimonides (1138–1204), to the nineteenth (Hoffman and Cole 2011). Most of the manuscripts found there were copied between the years 1000 and 1400. And then there are around 100,000 fragments of Hebrew manuscripts from other Genizot (Sirat 2002, pp. 8–9; Richler 1990, "Introduction").

In the last forty years, the only source of newly discovered manuscripts has been the unearthing—in archives in Italy and other European countries—of tens of thousands of folios and bifolios from manuscripts that were taken apart to be used as binding.

Returning to the 40,000 surviving medieval manuscripts, we can estimate that around 3,000 of these, and so just 7.5%, are dated, while the percentage of those for which the places of their copying are also known is only 3%. Among the 40,000, there are around 4,200 *colophons*, the oldest of which dates to the year 903–4. This of course means that only slightly more than 10% of the surviving Hebrew manuscripts have a colophon (Perani 2015c, pp. 347–82). The *colophons* mention the names of around 4,500 scribes, some of whom were famous scribes who produced dozens of manuscripts, others illustrious unknowns.

The chronological phases of the Hebrew manuscript in Italy

The Jewish community in Rome is the oldest known in Europe, tracing back, without interruption, to antiquity. Indeed, there was already a Jewish settlement in Rome in the first century BCE, composed of prisoners of war deported by Pompey to the capital after he conquered Jerusalem in 63 BCE, when Palestine became a province of the Roman Empire.

The Italian peninsula was thus home to Europe's first Jews, and was then the garden into which the whole legacy of the Land of Israel was transplanted in the first half of the fifth century CE. From this heritage, after the end of the Patriarchate, a flourishing Judaic culture blossomed in the area of Puglia and Basilicata accompanied by the re-emergence of Hebrew language in the West, manifested in the epitaphs of the catacombs of Venosa in the eighth century, while the first works written in Hebrew in the Western world appeared in the ninth century in southern Italy. Umberto Cassuto wrote:

> Hebrew was all but forgotten by the Jews who settled in Europe and was first revived in Apulian communities, where, starting at the beginning of the ninth century, it became a literary language, used instead of the previously customary Greek or Latin to engrave the tomb inscriptions of Apulian Jews (Cassuto 1938, p. 66).

Indeed, if we set aside the southern-Italian Hebrew epitaphs inscribed in stone in the seventh and eighth century, we have to wait until the ninth century to talk about written literary sources again, when a literary tradition began that boasts more than a thousand years of history and is the oldest of Western Judaism.

The oldest Italian and European Jewish manuscripts were produced by the Otranto scribal school between the eleventh and twelfth centuries CE. Around ten of these have come down to us intact, and a handful of sheets provide evidence of around ten more, which were taken apart and discovered in archives in northern Italy, where they were re-used as binding (Perani and Grazi 2006, pp. 13–41).

Puglia was the first region in which Western Hebrew literary production emerged. From there, this production shifted to Rome and then Lucca, continuing on toward France and the Rhineland in Germany.

In the thirteenth century, the three types of Western script—Italian, Sephardic, and Ashkenazi—began to become distinguished and emerge as such, differentiating themselves from the shared model of square Eastern script, in particular that of the north-east (Babylonian) and south-west (Palestinian), from which they all derived.

In the thirteenth century, one of the most important centers of Hebrew manuscript production was Rome and its environs. This century marks a turn in the history of Hebrew literary production in Italy, which was manifested in the intense manuscript creation of Roman Jews; this was the Roman Hebrew manuscript's brightest and most fervent period (Busi 1990, pp. 28–29; Perani 2016, vol. I, pp. 377–409).

Looking at Hebrew manuscript production in Rome, we find 22 scribes, 14 patrons and around a dozen illuminated manuscripts, while, in regard to the place where the copies were made, 16 manuscripts were copied in Rome and more than 30 in its environs (Perani 2015b, pp. 89–123; see cat. 16). Since all of these manuscripts were copied— and many of them stunningly illuminated and decorated—between the thirteenth and first half of the fourteenth century, they fall outside of our present chronological range. But, even so, they merited at least a mention.

The golden age of the Hebrew manuscript in Renaissance Italy

Having completed this introduction, without which it would not have been possible to understand the important role played by Italian Judaism in the production, concentration, and preservation of Hebrew manuscripts—and, incidentally, in the production of printed Hebrew books as well, starting with the first Roman incunabula of the late

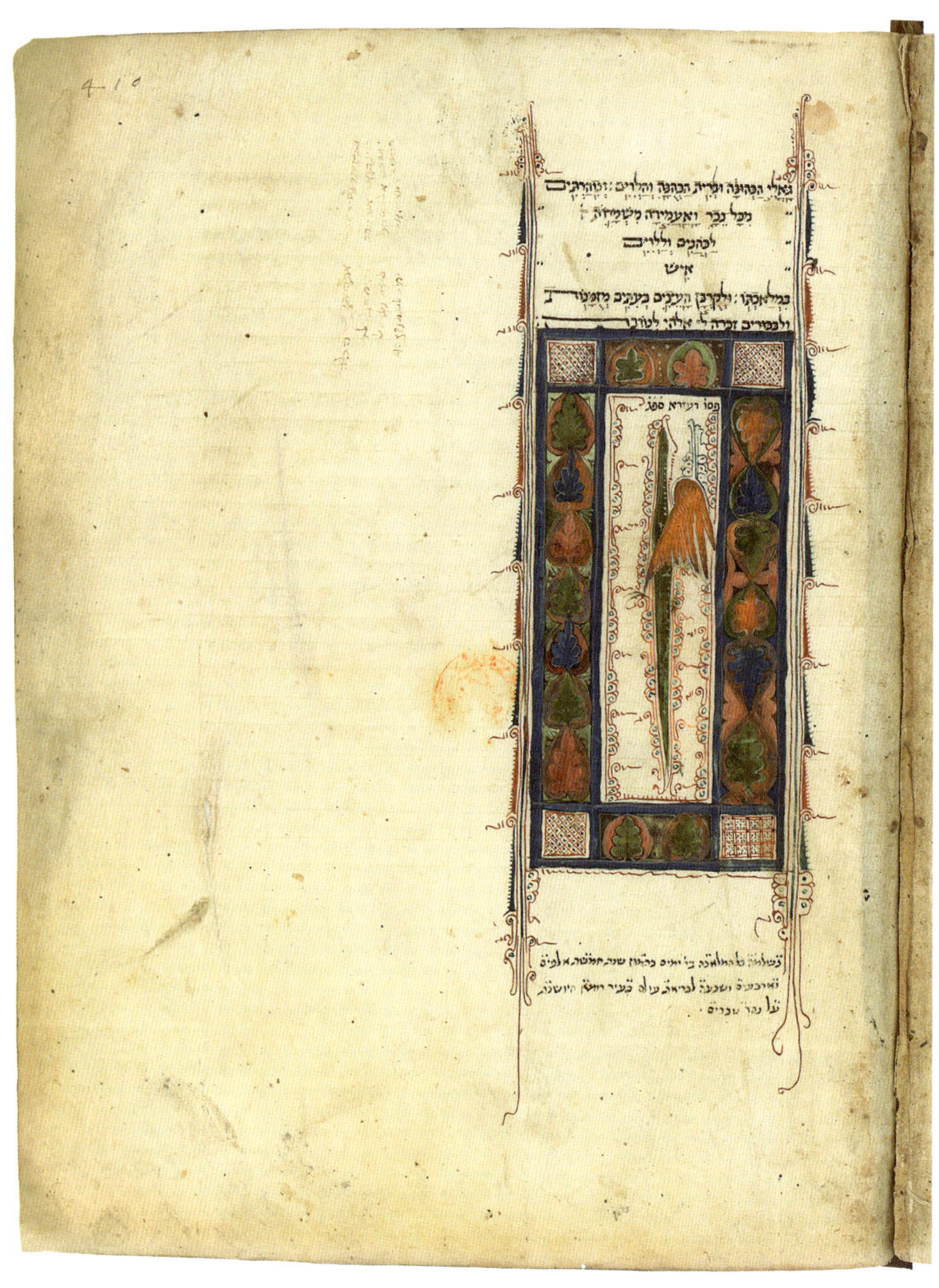

2. *Hebrew Bible*, with vowel-points and accents.
Excerpts from the *Masora parva* and *magna*,
Rome, 1287. Vatican Library, Vatican City (cat. 16)

fifteenth century and in the subsequent centuries—we can shift our attention to the specific theme of this study, focused on the Renaissance and the first half of the sixteenth century.

The golden age of the Hebrew manuscript is generally identified with the fourteenth and fifteenth centuries, and we can certainly consider the Renaissance as the apex, the culmination and highest peak in terms of the beauty, completeness and decoration of manuscripts, not just Hebrew ones. Indeed, toward the middle of the subsequent century, specifically 1540, which scholars consider the watershed year, after reaching the apex of its splendor, the manuscript began to decline, gradually losing its importance until it totally disappeared, replaced by the printed book. After the first printing of the Latin Vulgate Bible in Mainz in 1455 by Johannes Gutenberg, print gradually spread bringing with it price competition, being tens if not hundreds of times less expensive, as well as representing the modern and the new, to the utter disadvantage of the work of scribes.

In the fifteenth century, driven by persecution and massacres (Cassuto 2017, pp. 47–70, in English, originally published in Hebrew in 1942), the Jews from the southern regions of Italy flowed north, first toward the central regions of the peninsula and then the northern ones. A few cities hosted hundreds of Jews, like Mantua, Bologna, and Ferrara, but most of the settlements were limited to just Jewish lenders and bankers and their entourage—so, small groups of around a dozen people. And it is precisely this type of population that is important for the study of the Hebrew manuscript and its splendid illumination. The lenders and their entourage, who were usually well educated, often copied manuscripts for their own use and then commissioned the illuminations from Christian artists and artisans.

Here, one should keep in mind that in the Jewish world, unlike that of the Christian majority, there were never any true *scriptoria*. Instead, the work was entrusted to individual scribes, who worked on commission, at most at the family level or working with other scribes, who shared the work of copying, which is called *'avodat ha-qodesh'* in Hebrew, "holy work."

It was not until the Renaissance that Italian Jews began to also commission illuminations and decorations for their *ketubbot* (an official nuptial agreement script), for which Italy became the largest and most outstanding center of production, in terms of both quality and quantity.

It will be clear that the Jews who commissioned splendid manuscripts from the best Jewish scribes and the best artists (for the most part Christian) were very wealthy and very well educated, meaning often rich moneylenders and bankers. This was undoubtedly a small, upper middle-class cultural elite, probably no more than 5 or 10% of the Jewish population. The cost of a manuscript was of course very high, involving preparing the parchment and folded sheets, copying the work onto loose bifolios, creating the illuminations and assembling the completed work. In some appraisals of dowries and inheritances, it appears that a fine manuscript was worth as much as a home.

In this case as well, history has been reconstructed based on documentation left by a small group of the rich and powerful. Like the vast majority of Christians, the vast majority of Jews were not rich and, just like their Christian counterparts, did not leave us documents. That's why it's so difficult to reconstruct their history: it's only possible to trace back over events partially and with great effort.

The miniature in Hebrew manuscripts

We know that there are decorations in tenth-century Islamic manuscripts from which the Jewish miniature might have drawn its models and themes. The Jews commissioned miniatures from Jewish artists and artisans as well as, more frequently, Christian illuminators. The earliest traces of decorations in the Hebrew manuscripts in our possession date to the tenth and eleventh centuries, but we are unable to determine whether they were founded on an already strong tradition. In the thirteenth century, there was a prohibition on representing the human form in Germany, especially in the Pietist circles of the *Ḥaside Ashkenaz*, influenced by the Christian asceticism of southern Germany and northern Italy in the twelfth and thirteenth centuries. Rabbi Meir from Rothenburg, the undisputed leader of the rigorist spirituality of the Ashkenazi Jewish communities, took a negative view of the representation of figures, in part because they could be a distraction from prayer.

Many fundamentally important studies have been devoted to the Jewish miniature, demonstrating, among other things, that the decoration of the Hebrew manuscript, often carried out by non-Jewish artists, seamlessly adhered to the changing styles and tastes of the Christian world between the thirteenth and the sixteenth century. The most recent study, carried out by Silvia Maddalo with the collaboration of Eva Ponzi and published in two volumes in 2016, is focused on Rome and very rich in information, also containing an essay by the present writer on Hebrew codices (*Il libro miniato* 2016, pp. 377–409 and color plates: vol. II, plates 59, 143, 144, 145, 146, 147, 148, and 149). For further literature, see D'Ancona 1914; Bandera Bistoletti 1977; Mariani Canova 1978; Conti 1981; Garzelli 1985; Mortara Ottolenghi 1993–94; Mariani Canova 1995; Mortara Ottolenghi 1997; Pace 2011.

The splendor of Hebrew codices illuminated in Bologna and Florence

The members of the Italian Jewish middle class living in Tuscany, Emilia Romagna, Lombardy, Veneto, and Piedmont favored personal libraries stocked with books for which they had commissioned decorations from the most celebrated artists. These regions were home to a wealth of manuscripts of rare quality, not only produced in Italy but also in the Franco-German and Sephardic areas, which were brought to Italy (from the former after the fourteenth century and from the latter after the year 1500) in large quantities by the Jews expelled by the Aragon Catholic monarchs in 1492.

One example is the splendid Miscellany now preserved at the British Library in London, MS Add. 11639, which was copied and decorated in the Franco-German area around 1280, but was in Treviso in 1431 and Venice in 1479 (Mortara Ottolenghi 1997, p. 981).

Bologna was an important center for the production of copies of manuscripts, often magnificently illuminated. In the last three decades of the fourteenth century, 10 manuscripts were copied in Bologna, followed by 21 in the fifteenth century and 16 between the beginning of the sixteenth century and 1574. We will list only a few, including some kabbalistic works.

3. *Hebrew Bible, Psalms,* with vowel-points and accents, northern Italy (Emilia?), late thirteenth century. Biblioteca Palatina, Parma (cat. 4)

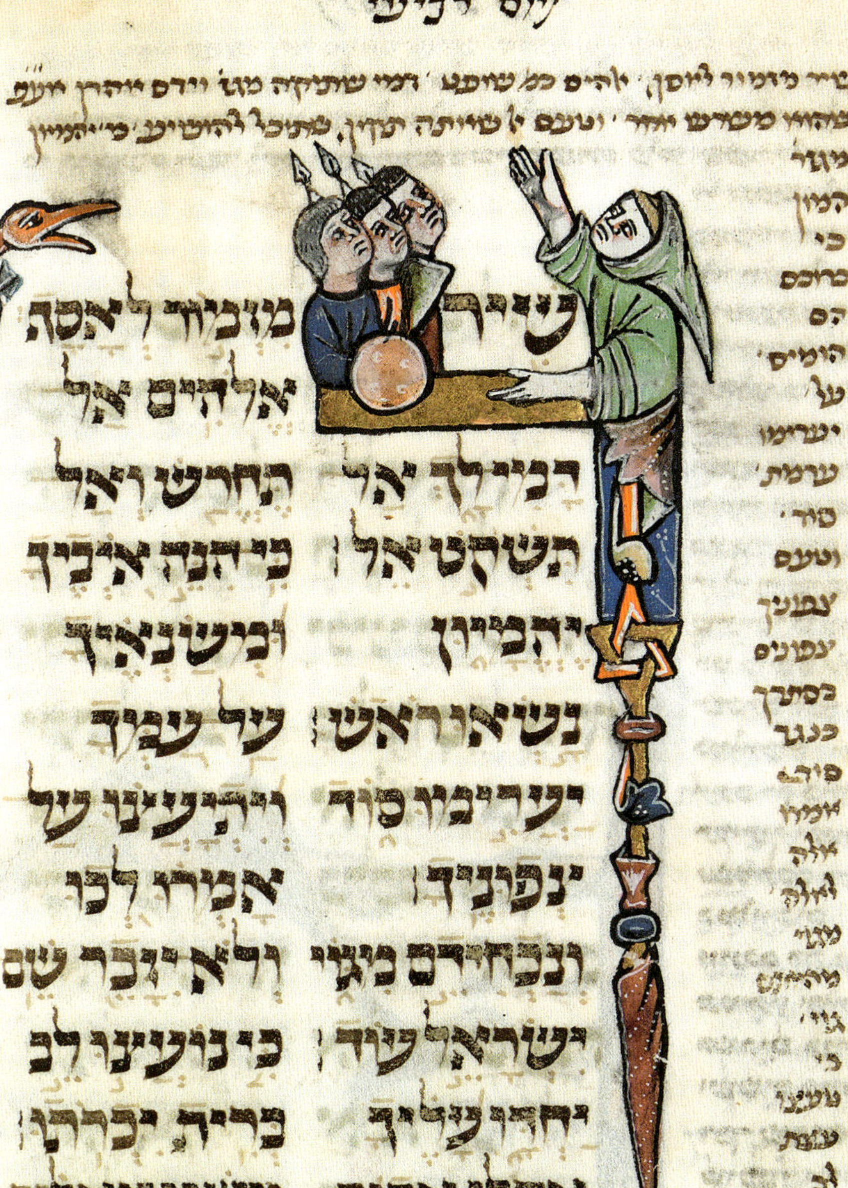

מזמור לאסף

אלהים אל דמי לך אל

תחרש ואל תשקט אל כי הנה אליך

כי הנה אויביך יהמיון ומשנאיך

נשאו ראש על עמך

יערימו סוד ויתיעצו על

אמרו לכו ינפניך

ונכחידם מגוי ולא יזכר שם

ישראל עוד כי נועצו לב

יחדו עליך ברית יכרתו

אהלי אדום וישמעאלים

In 1398–99, an unknown scribe copied the commentary to the *Sefer Yetzirah* erroneously attributed to Nachmanides but actually the work of Azriel from Gerona (State Library, Moscow, MS Guenzburg 133).

In 1400, the scribe Shem Tov ben Samuel Baruk produced a parchment copy in Sephardic script of Abraham ibn Ezra's *Commentary to the Torah* for Joel ben Isaac (Biblioteca Palatina, Parma, MS parm. 3116; *Hebrew Manuscripts* 2001, pp. 100–1 no. 533).

In 1403, the scribe Benjamin ben Joab made a copy, while in prison in Bologna, of Joseph ben Abraham Giqatilla's *Sefer ha-orah* (Bibliothèque nationale de France, Paris, MS hébr. 814).

In 1423, at the venerable age of 79, the scribe Ben Levi made a copy in Bologna of the Hebrew translation in rhymed prose of the Arabic version of Abraham ben Hasday's story of Barlaam and Josaphat, titled *Ben ha-melek we-ha-Nazir* (The Prince and the Monk). His age is revealed in the *colophon*:

> The month of Nisan in the year of the Blessed God of Eternal Life (*la-'ed* = 1344) was that of my birth, and yet my eye has not weakened, since this is my art … and I completed it here, in the city of Bologna, in the month of Tevet in the year 1423 … I, Ben Levi.

The manuscript is preserved in the Bibliothèque nationale of Paris, MS hébr. 1283/1.

In Florence, besides what we have already noted, in 1441 Joseph ben Abraham from Tivoli commissioned a *Maḥazor* from the scribe Moses ben Abraham that is now found in the Schoken Library in Jerusalem, MS 13873.

Still in Florence in 1467, Jacob son of Guglielmo (or Beniamino) di Dattilo of Abraham da Montalcini commissioned a scribe to produce two splendid manuscripts containing the Psalms, Job and Proverbs, with stunning miniatures by Mariano del Buono, now in New Haven at the Yale University Library, MS 409.

In 1492, the year of the expulsion of the Jews from the Kingdom of Aragon, Abraham ben Judah ben Jehiel from Camerino copied a splendid *Maḥazor* in Florence that was commissioned by Elijah ben Joab from Vigevano of the Galli family (see cat. 19), a richly illuminated manuscript now preserved in New York at the Library of the Jewish Theological Seminary (MS Mic. 8892).

In 1494, Attavante degli Attavanti, one of the greatest Florentine artists, decorated and illuminated a Hebrew Bible that had been copied by the scribe Shimshon Zarfati ben Eliezer Halfon and was commissioned by Menahem ben Meshullam from Terracina; the codex is now in the Biblioteca Palatina in Parma, MS parm. 2162 (*Hebrew Manuscripts* 2001, p. 37 no. 153; Mortara Ottolenghi 1993–94).

An unicum: the "illuminated Avicenna" in the Biblioteca Universitaria of Bologna

We cannot fail to mention the illuminated Avicenna, a celebrated manuscript considered an unicum for its illustrations and decorations, including six brightly-painted full-page miniatures embellished with gold. Miniature specialists disagree over the school to which illuminations of this fifteenth-century masterpiece should be attributed, arguing for the Florentine, Lombard, Ferrara, Venetian and even French milieus. Although there are some incomplete miniatures and decorations in the second part, this codex is, regardless, truly exceptional. Its full-page miniatures include the representation of the physician teaching medicine to his followers (fol. 2); a splendid table of contents (fols. 2*v*–6*r*); the signs of the zodiac alternating with various kinds of work and a urine examination (fols. 6*r* and 7*v*); the cure of madness with ice-cold water and the gathering of medicinal herbs (fol. 78*r*); the medical school of Salerno, with the four ages of human life and a detail of the death of the queen (fol. 210*r*); the physician visiting the sick (fol. 402*r*), and the interior of a pharmacy stocked with medicine (fol. 492*r*) (see Tamani 1988).

A unique figure: Abraham Farissol, intellectual, writer, and scribe

Abraham Farissol was a prominent figure among the intellectuals of the Italian Jewish Renaissance. Born in Avignon in 1451, he moved to Italy at the end of the 1460s, first living in Mantua between 1469 and 1470, then around 1472 in Ferrara and later for a brief period in Florence, drawn by the splendor of the Italian Renaissance (see the essays by Busi and Greco in this volume). It seems that he died in Ferrara around 1528. Although he was a prolific writer, we shall not be discussing these works, as what interests us here is his production as a scribe. Around 53 manuscripts survive, copied by Farissol in Mantua, Sermide and, especially, Ferrara over the course of 59 years of scribal activity between 1469 and 1528 (Ruderman 1981; Engel 1992).

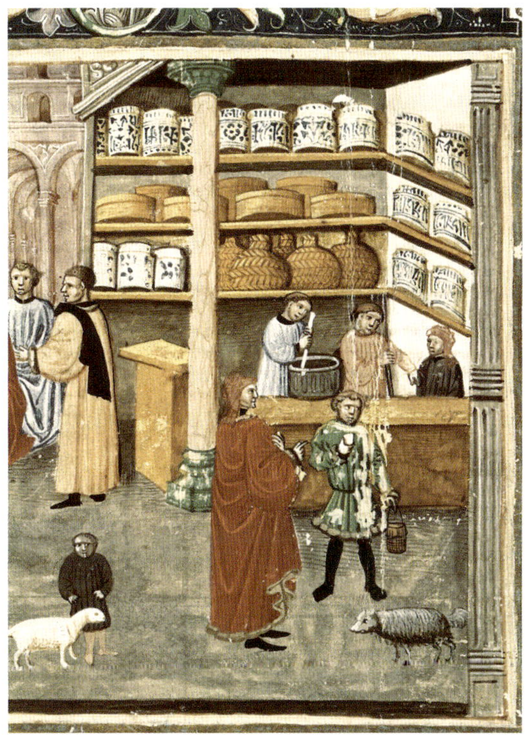

4. Avicenna, *Canon of Medicine*: interior of a pharmacy, fol. 492*r*. Biblioteca Universitaria, Bologna

He naturally started out copying codices in the Sephardic script that he learned in Provence, but, over time, he mastered the style typical of manuscript production in northern Italy and soon also perfected the Italian script, both the semi-cursive style, heavily influenced by the roundness of the Carolingian script, and the square style. During the latter part of his life in Italy, Farissol was therefore able to offer his clients the choice between a manuscript in square or rounded Italian or Sephardic script (Engel 1992).

In Mantua in 1484, he copied a *Mahazor* of the Italian rite, that is, a book of prayers for the entire year, for the Jewish printer from Bologna Abraham Caravita, who ran the first Jewish printshop in Bologna from 1477 to 1488. We have Caravita to thank for the *editio princeps* of the Torah, edited with vowels and accents by Abraham ben Hayyim dei Tintori from Pesaro and published on January 25, 1482. It was habitual for intellectuals and scribes to associate with members of the Jewish middle class. They were not only commissioned to copy codices for their patrons, but were also their guests, staying for even long periods in the homes of bankers and printers. In the *colophon* for Caravita's manuscript, Farissol confirms his familiarity with the cultural elite and the Jewish middle class—in this case, those of Bologna:

> Praise the benevolent Lord who helped me, his servant Abraham ben Mordecai Farissol from Avignon, giving me the strength and energy to finish this *Mahazor* complete with prayers for the whole year for His Excellency the illustrious Lord Joseph Caravita—may he always be protected and given vitality and vigor, here in the city of Bologna, in his home, Friday 16 Tammuz 1484.

The manuscript is preserved in Cincinnati, in the Hebrew Union College library, MS 331. In 1485 Farissol, still in Bologna and probably still Caravita's guest, produced a copy of the *Siddur* for the printer's daughter, Donnina Caravita, as we learn from the *colophon*:

> I, Abraham ben Mordecai Farissol from Avignon, completed this *Siddur* of the whole year for the honorable, gracious Lady Donnina, daughter of the illustrious and learned Master Joseph Caravita and wife of Lord Shemuel ben Isaac from Revere, on 28 Nisan 1485.

This manuscript remained in Italy and is preserved in the Biblioteca Medicea Laurenziana, Florence, MS Biscioni Or. 475 (Perani 2002).

The Jewish community in Mantua was among those that could boast a very large library with a great many kabbalistic (Busi 1996; Busi 1997b; Busi 2001) and scientific manuscripts (Tamani 2003). A part of them, along with early printed ones, were unfortunately sold to a bookseller in Vienna in 1925–26, although some were stopped at the Brennero customs office and returned to Mantua (Perani 2015a [2017], pp. 63–91).

The career of the exceptional scribe Isaac ben Obadiah from Forlì:
Bologna, Mantua, Florence

In 1427, the famed scribe Isaac ben Obadiah from Forlì, one of the best in Italy, is documented as active for the first time in Bologna, where he copied part of the *Seder Tahanunim*, a book of liturgical prayers containing supplications. In the *colophon*, he wrote:

Isaac ben Obadiah ben David from Forlì completed the *Tahanunim* here in Bologna in the year 1427, in the month of Elul, Thursday 13 Elul for Joseph Kohen ben Solomon Kohen…

This parchment manuscript was written in Italian script and might have been originally part of a *Maḥazor* of Roman rite, whereas it now constitutes sheets 383–418 of a codex in the British Library, London, MS Harley 5686.

A few years later, in 1435, the same Isaac ben Obadiah copied an exemplar of Jacob ben Asher's *Arba'a turim* (The Four Orders) in Mantua, commissioned by Mordecai ben Avigdor. This valuable manuscript is preserved in the Vatican Library (MS Ross. 555).

Six years later, in 1441, Isaac ben Obadiah was in Florence. The brothers Jacob and David from Perugia, sons of Solomon, had also moved there to run the Banco dei Quattro Pavoni as partners. The two wealthy brothers had probably had the opportunity to admire Isaac's work around 15 years earlier in Bologna and now, finding him in Tuscany, commissioned him in 1441 to produce a book with prayers for the whole year in two extremely fine volumes, the result being a masterpiece of the scribal art now in the British Library (MS Harley 5716).

Manuscripts copied by bankers for personal use

Three Hebrew manuscripts copied in Crevalcore (Bologna) between the fifteenth and sixteenth centuries by two bankers from the Finzi family, who ran a loan bank in that town at the Modena border, are preserved, respectively, in Oxford, Moscow, and Vienna. It is interesting to note that the name of the city of Crevalcore is written in Hebrew in the three *colophons* as *SMḤ LB*, or "Allegralcore" (Brighten the Heart), which was the name of the town for a period of time, recent enough for the moneylenders to have a memory of it.

The first manuscript contains Mosheh Narboni's commentary on the *Moreh Nevukim* (Guide for the Perplexed), and was copied by the banker Yekutiel, son of Solomon Finzi in 1428. This codex is now preserved in Oxford's Bodleian Library (MS Opp. 598, Neubauer no. 1260). Additional information is found in the *colophon*:

I, Yekutiel, son of Solomon Finzi, may he rest in Eden, completed this *Commentary to the Guide for the Perplexed*, here in the city of Allegralcore, located in the Province of Bologna, in year 5188 of the creation of the world in the month of Adar. I copied it in two months during the winter, and I wrote it for myself and for my descendants.

The second and third codices were copied around seventy years later by Osea Finzi, another banker from the same family based in Crevalcore. In 1504–5, Osea copied, for his personal use, a manuscript containing the Hebrew Pentateuch in an Italian square script, filling the outside margins of each page with the relative *Targum* or Aramaic version of the Hebrew text, written in semi-cursive Italian script. This manuscript is now kept in Moscow, Russian State Library, MS Guenzburg 786.

In the *colophon*, which is difficult to read in a few places due to faded ink, we read:

The work of the entire pure and perfect Torah is complete, together with the Targum and enriched by all of the Haftarot … May he who up until now has blessed me and rendered me worthy of beginning and completing this work [allow my children and me] to meditate on his

Torah until our deaths — I, the smallest of the lawgivers, Osea Finzi …. Here in Allegralcore Bolognese in the year 1504–5.

The third manuscript was copied in 1508 by the same banker-cum-scribe Osea Finzi, again for his own use, and contains the *Sefer ha-ḥinnuk* (Book of Education), a classic of medieval Jewish literature containing a summary of the Torah's 613 precepts and attributed to Aharon ha-Lewi of Barcelona (1230–1300). The manuscript is preserved today in Vienna at the Österreichische Nationalbibliothek, MS hebr. 189 (Schwarz 70). In the *colophon*, Osea tells us:

> The work of this *Ḥinnuk* was completed on Friday, 19 Iyyar 1508. I wrote it for myself, the youngest of my family, Osea Finzi, son of the venerated David, may he always be remembered, here in Allegralcore Bolognese. May the Lord render me worthy of meditating on this and the other holy books, myself and my descendants and the children of my children, until the end of all of the generations.

 In these cases, the copyists were therefore not professional scribes, but two moneylenders or bankers, living in Crevalcore, capable of carefully written script—as was the norm for this elite—and for whom, on the long, cold winter evenings near the Panaro River, there was nothing better than copying manuscripts for their personal use.

We have seen the quantity and fine quality of the Hebrew codices, many of which illuminated, which were produced in Italy during the Renaissance. They are not only important for the text they contain and their miniatures, but are also a valuable historical resource, for the history of the transitions from one owner to another and from one library to another, as well as for the notes of ownership and sale and comments made by censors (Perani 2004). For the story of the provenance of the manuscripts, a fundamental resource is the second edition of the *Guide to Hebrew Manuscript Collections* (Richler 2014).

This survey, which is quite brief with respect to the available material, nevertheless reveals the abundance of splendid Hebrew codices produced in Italy and, later, acquired by the world's leading collections. This heritage of codices produced in or passing from Italy represents, as noted, more than half of all surviving Hebrew manuscripts.

During the Renaissance, the Jews paraphrased the name Italy with the Hebrew *I tal Yah*, meaning "Island of God's dew." Those living in Mantua wrote the city name in their *colophons* as *Man tovah*, "Good manna," and those living in Bologna, *Bo lan Yah*, or "Where God stays the night." As we have seen, they had a true abundance of reasons for word play of this kind.

Translated by Sarah Elizabeth Cree

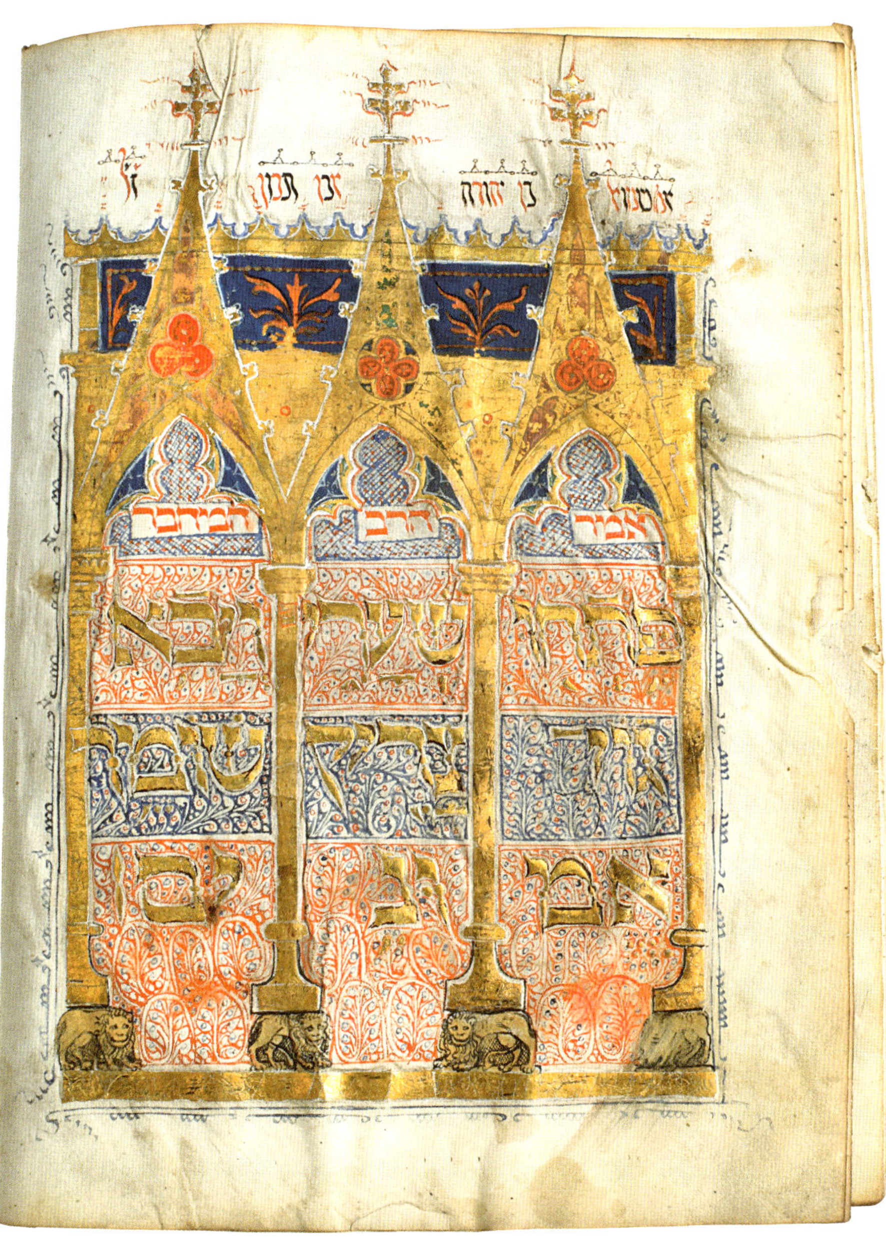

this and following pages

5. Moses Maimonides, *Moreh nevukim*
(Guide for the Perplexed), Ashkenazi area, 1349.
MiBAC, Direzione Generale Archivi, Rome (cat. 14)

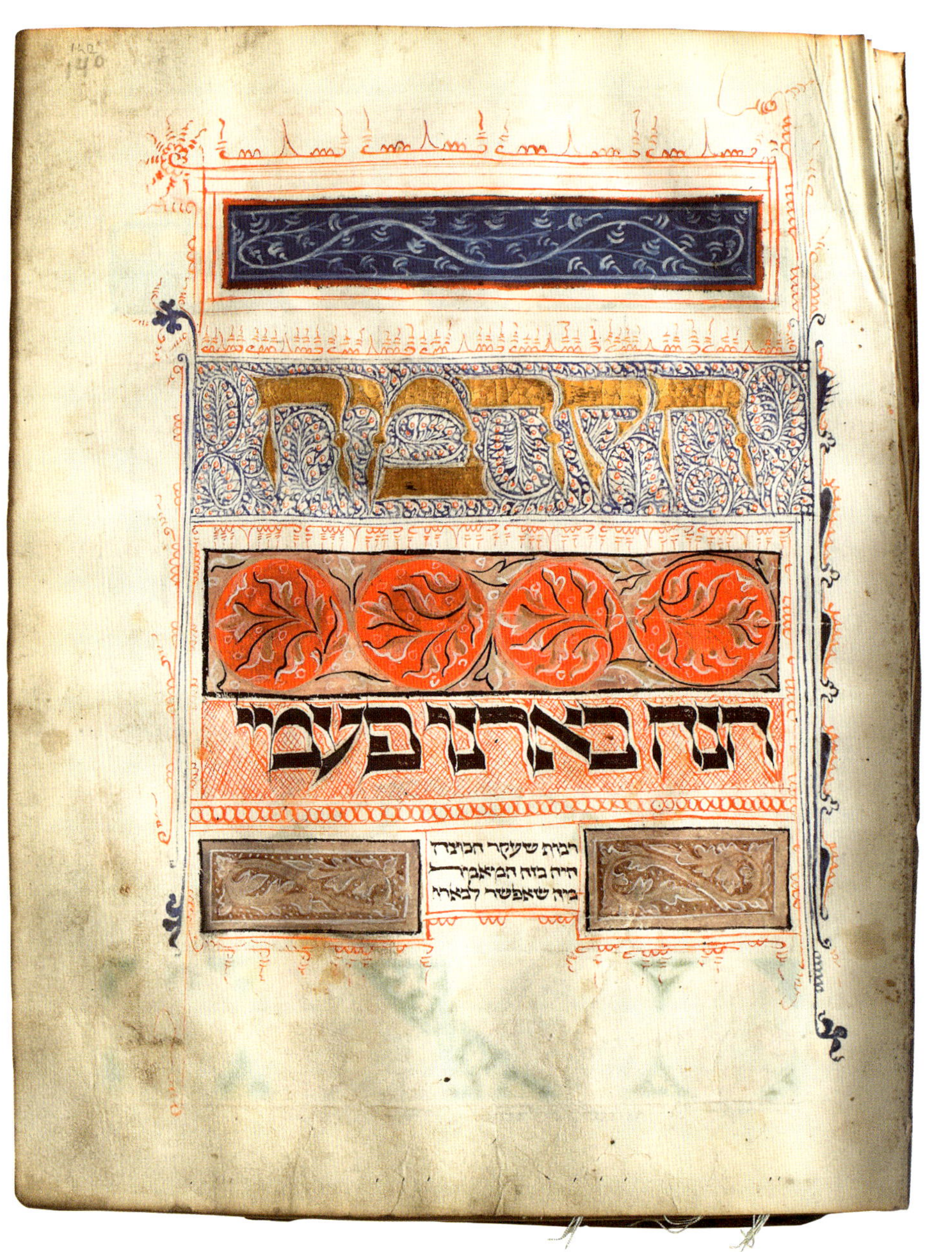

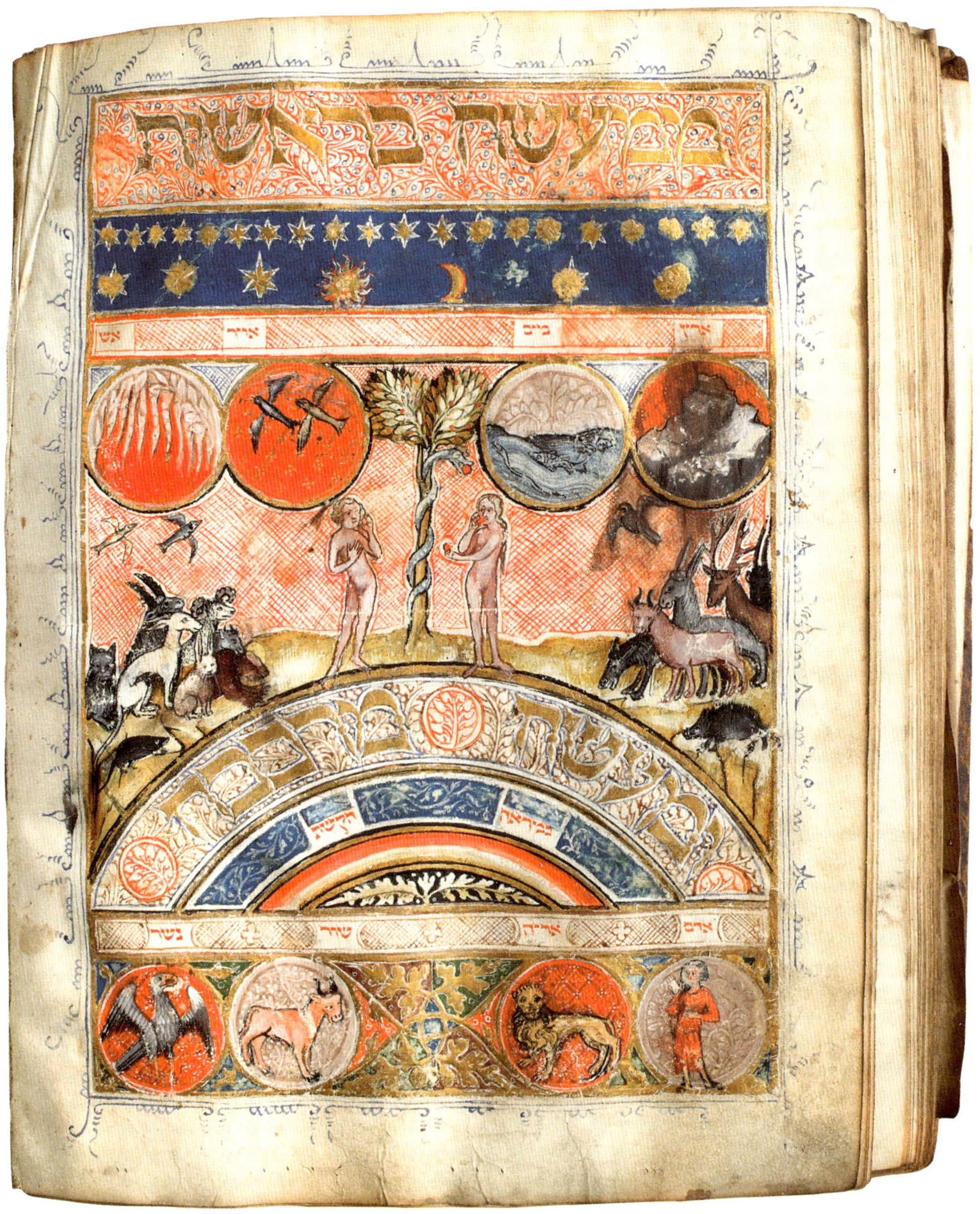

Jewish Merchants in Renaissance Italy
Francesca Trivellato

In Shakespeare's *Merchant of Venice*, Bassanio, a noble Venetian, visits Shylock the Jew to ask for a loan of 3,000 ducats, which he intends to pay back in three months. The loan is to be secured by his dear friend Antonio, a generous, if a bit ingenuous soul, who is, however, most importantly a Catholic merchant based in Venice who ably directs sizable overseas shipments. In deciding whether or not to grant the loan and at what interest rate, Shylock reflects on the nature of Antonio's business:

> He hath an argosy bound to Tripolis, another to the Indies, I understand moreover upon the Rialto, he hath a third at Mexico, a fourth for England, and other ventures he hath squand'red abroad, —but ships are but boards, sailors but men, there be land-rats and water-rats, water-thieves and land-thieves, (I mean pirates), and then there is the peril of waters, winds, and rocks" (Act I, Scene 3).

When he evaluates Antonio's solvency, Shylock therefore proceeds in the way customary at the time: he does not ask the Venetian merchant for a deposit, instead using the tools at his disposal (experience and circulating information rather than statistical data) to calculate the probability that the guarantor's investments would survive the risks of the sea, pirates and shipwrecks included. I would add, incidentally and for accuracy's sake, that the Jewish lender's calculations did not account for the fact that Venetian merchants from that period were in the habit of insuring both ships and goods, although insurance policies never provided full coverage. In any case, after completing his calculations, Shylock concluded: "the man is notwithstanding sufficient—three thousand ducats—I think I may take his bond."

Up to this point, the celebrated play is realistic in many ways, and indeed a few historians have even searched the archives looking for the names of merchants who really lived in the Venice ghetto during the sixteenth century who might have served as a model for Shakespeare, although of course the English playwright's genius is not to be measured in terms of his adherence to reality. However, the next step in the story is utterly unrealistic and yet has fascinated theater-goers, readers and scholars alike: the infamous pound of flesh that Shylock requires as a security. This is, of course, a paroxysmal literary strategy, which draws on and at the same time pushes to the extreme an anti-Semitic tradition according to which the Jewish merchant was always and only bent on bringing his Christian debtors to ruin. Shylock himself recognizes its paroxysmal nature, describing it as a "merry bond" when he arranges with Antonio to draw up the agreement at a notary's.

In the figure of Shylock, the late-medieval stereotype of the Jewish pawnbroker, caricatured to the extreme, is therefore projected onto the sociological figure of the early-modern Jewish merchant, who built up dense networks of commercial credit with merchants of every religious denomination without requiring material security for their bonds, instead undertaking the meticulous examination, as Shylock did at first, of the information available concerning the reliability of the contracting party. The figure of the early-modern Jewish merchant was new when the first edition of Shakespeare's *The Merchant of Venice* appeared (it was published in 1600), and indeed originated in Italy, or more specifically, in Venice and Leghorn.

Between the late thirteenth and late fifteenth centuries, small Jewish communities were established in cities of various size in central-northern Italy, in the wake of agreements (*condotte*) negotiated between Jewish bankers and local authorities. In exchange for opening a pawnshop at the disposal of the city's poor, and sometimes special moneylending services for the prince or the town coffers, the *condotte* granted a few assurances necessary to Jewish life, including minimal freedom of cult and religious education, the right to bury their dead and practice kosher butchery, and the physical safety and inviolability of the proprietary rights of the bankers themselves. This model for the control and regulation of Jewish communities in late-medieval Italy corresponded to the norms and premises of the fourth Lateran Council (1215), which had forced Jews to wear distinguishing dress in order to minimize mixing with Christians and render their subordination visible. Moreover, Constitution 67 of the same Council maintained that the Church, the owner of vast expanses of land and enmeshed in broad credit networks, was a victim of excessive interest rates (*graves et immoderatae usurae*) charged by Jews who managed their tithes. In the late fifteenth century, the Franciscan friars founded mounts of piety (an institution recognized by Rome in 1515) that offered consumer loans at extremely low interest rates, sending the Jewish banks into crisis (Milano 1963; Todeschini 2018).

The progressive decline of the Jewish pawnshop in the late fifteenth century coincided chronologically with epochal transformations in Europe and the world. In 1492, sponsored by the crown of Castille and Aragon, Christopher Columbus reached the Caribbean and, in so doing, threw open the American continent for European conquest. The same year, the Spanish monarchs decreed the mass expulsion or forced conversion of the kingdom's Jews. Five years later, in 1497, the Jews who had left Spain to take refuge in Portugal, probably numbering around 80,000, were subjected to the same fate. Finally, in 1498, Vasco da Gama led a Portuguese fleet to India, rounding the Cape of Good Hope and thus opening up a sea route that created competition for the caravans that had for centuries

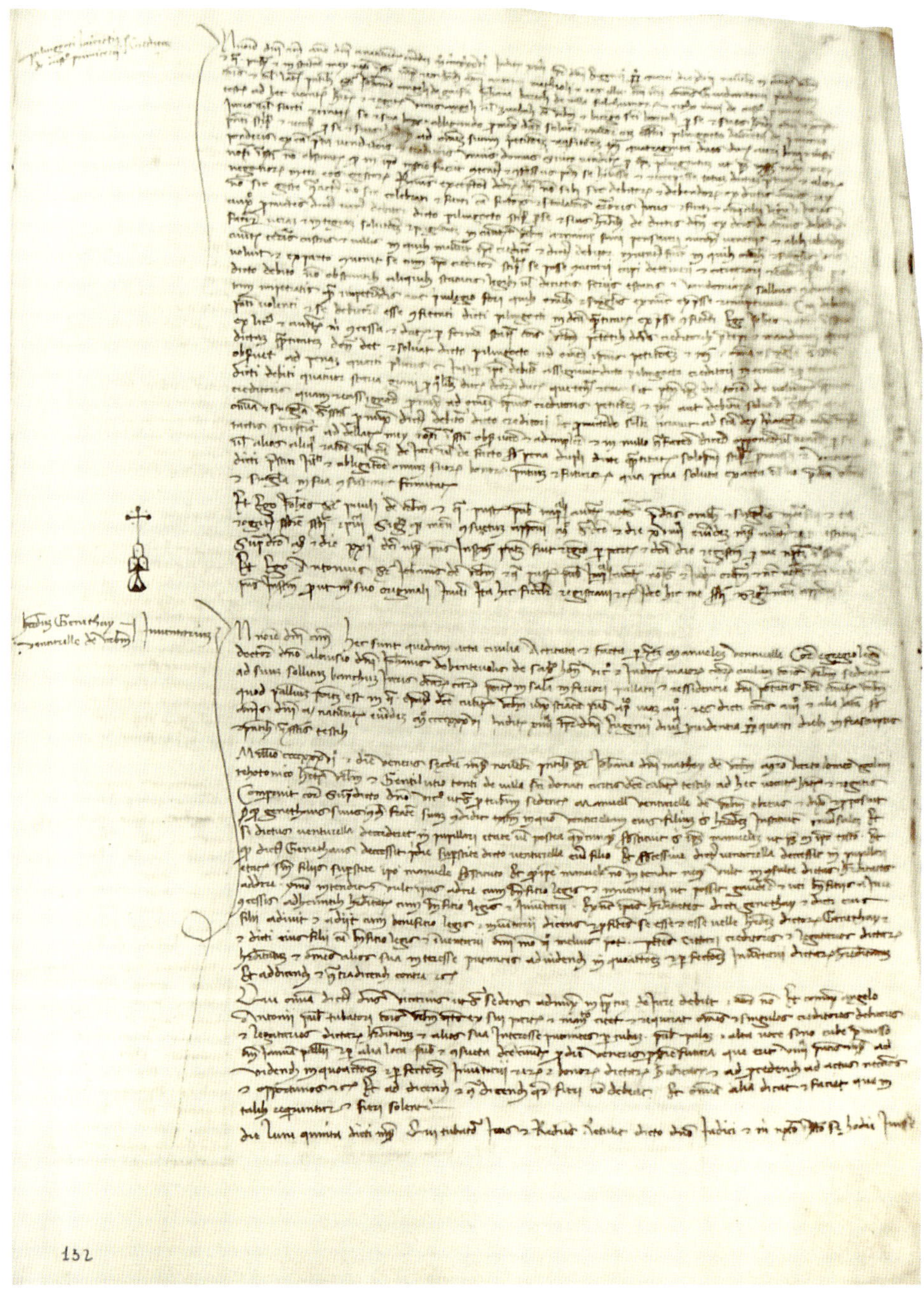

1. *List of debtors and inventory of assets belonging
to the banker Genatano di Ventura*, Urbino, 1436.
Archivio di Stato, Urbino (cat. 15)

brought spices and other Asian products to the coasts of the Middle East and Egypt, where contingents of savvy Venetian merchants awaited them.

These events had direct repercussions on the major trading powers of Italy, undermining their hard-won hegemony. In response to the changes in the axes of international trade, the Republic of Venice and the Grand Duchy of Tuscany implemented, among other things, new policies designed to attract the Jewish minority. The processes triggered by these policies led to the rise in the seventeenth century of a Sephardic oligarchy in Venice and Leghorn, which enjoyed unprecedented social recognition and ample legal rights. Meanwhile, the establishment of new economic hierarchies and new legal statutes within the Venetian Jewish community during the sixteenth century led to the marginalization of Italian and Ashkenazi Jews and the rise of a new figure, the Sephardic merchant. Who was, in many ways, more similar to Antonio than Shylock.

Until 1516, a small community of Jewish lenders had lived in Mestre and only worked in Venice during the day. The heavy financial burdens of the Italian Wars had led the government of the Republic to request sizeable contributions from various Jewish communities in the hinterland, in addition to the ones due in times of peace. For the same reason, in 1516 the Venetian Senate decided to grant the Jews a peripheral area of the city, in the parish of San Girolamo (Cannaregio), with two entrances that were to be closed every night. It seems that 700 Jews fleeing devastation and persecution in the neighboring regions immediately took refuge there. In accordance with the late-medieval model described above, these Ashkenazim were granted residence in Venice in exchange for heavy payments to the tax authorities but also for opening "banks for the poor" in a city that did not have a mount of piety (Milano 1963). As before, these pawnshops confined the Jews within a subsistence economy, alienating and antagonizing the economically weaker segments of the populations who relied on them.

While the Republic was creating the Venetian ghetto, the Ottoman Empire was readying itself to defeat the Mameluke sultan, extending its domain to Syria and Egypt, as well as to the sacred sites of Saudi Arabia (1517). Soon after, Suleiman the Magnificent spread his military might in the Balkans, pushing ahead to the gates of Vienna (1529). The Turkish presence was, in short, an increasing threat for Venice, both in its Friulian territories and the markets of the eastern Mediterranean. These events inspired a new Venetian policy concerning the "Levantini," that is, the Jews expelled from the Iberian peninsula who had taken refuge in the Ottoman Empire. In 1541, following the war of 1537–40 with the Sublime Porte, during which Venice lost the Peloponnese, the Senate of the Republic expanded the ghetto to include an area for the Levantini. It further specified that this group was prohibited from running pawnshops and selling used items: the Levantini were only allowed to work in trade (Ravid 1987). In an attempt to attract Jews with capital, expertise and contacts all over the Mediterranean and beyond, the Venetian government guaranteed them access to markets that up until that time had been the prerogative of patricians and citizens of the Republic, a choice that in turn contributed to creating distinct hierarchies within the ghetto.

Under growing pressure from its competitors in the Ottoman Empire and the Atlantic nations, in particular the English and the Dutch who were quickly establishing themselves in the eastern Mediterranean, Venice further expanded privileges for the Jews, this time those fleeing Spain and Portugal. These were in a position to mobilize even greater economic resources than the Levantini, but risked creating open conflict with the Church authorities since, by definition, anyone born on or living in the Iberian peninsula after

1497 had been baptized. The institution of the Roman Inquisition in 1542, with courts in every regional state in central-northern Italy, meant that the rulers of the Republic needed to exercise great caution in their relations with the Protestant and Jewish minorities. According to canon law, anyone who had been baptized could be condemned as an "apostate" if found to not be observing the precepts of the Church. Toward this end, the Inquisition launched widespread investigations to ascertain the Jewish origin of the so-called "New Christians" who had taken refuge in Ferrara, Florence, Venice, Ancona, and Rome or reveal their secret practice of Judaism.

In the 1570s, the Venetian Inquisition thus found itself working with the Roman prelates to determine the identity of a man named Righetto Marrano, who lived as a Jew in the Venetian ghetto but had taken on different guises in each of the many ports of the Mediterranean where he had been. After years of interrogations and investigations, the Venetian Church tribunal concluded that Righetto had been born in Lisbon and had therefore been unquestionably baptized. As a consequence, he was found guilty of apostasy. This episode was highly alarming to the Republic's ruling patricians, who rightly feared that convictions of this kind would discourage the New Christians from settling in Venice right when they were trying to attract Sephardic families that would revitalize its markets (Pullan 1985). To alleviate these fears, a new *condotta* was devised in 1589 that included guarantees specially designed for the "Ponentini," the Jews coming from the Iberian peninsula, such as an assurance that, should they decide to live as Jews in the ghetto, the Inquisition, which in principle did not have jurisdiction over Jews and Muslims, would not be able to investigate their past (Ravid 1976). The Republic thus found a way to protect the economic interests of the Ponentini merchants and become a nerve center for the Sephardic world. A few years later, in 1591–93, the Grand Duke of Tuscany followed the Venetian example and granted even greater privileges to Sephardic Jews, making a clear distinction between them and the Pisan bankers. Over the next two centuries, in part thanks to these privileges, the Jewish Nation became the dominant merchant community in Leghorn (Trivellato 2009).

The agility with which Shakespeare blended the image of the late-medieval Jewish usurer and that of the—probably Sephardic—merchant who lent large sums of money to the elite of the Catholic merchant class in sixteenth-century Venice confirms the persistence and malleability of anti-Semitic stereotypes. At the same time, one should recognize the improvements to the legal and social status of the Jewish merchants who worked in long-distance trade in Renaissance Italy. At least in Venice and Leghorn, new forms of tolerance, however consonant with societies that had no inkling of the concept of equality, were strengthened on the basis of the economic interest of both the State and its subjects. Indeed, Antonio intentionally speaks words in this regard that, although inflated, capture the meaning of the change that had taken place. In answer to Solanio, who reassures him saying that "I am sure the duke will never grant this forfeiture to hold," Antonio replies, voicing the pragmatism of reason of State: "The duke cannot deny the course of law: For the commodity that strangers have with us in Venice, if it be denied, will much impeach the justice of the state since that the trade and profit of the city consisteth of all nations."

Translated by Sarah Elizabeth Cree

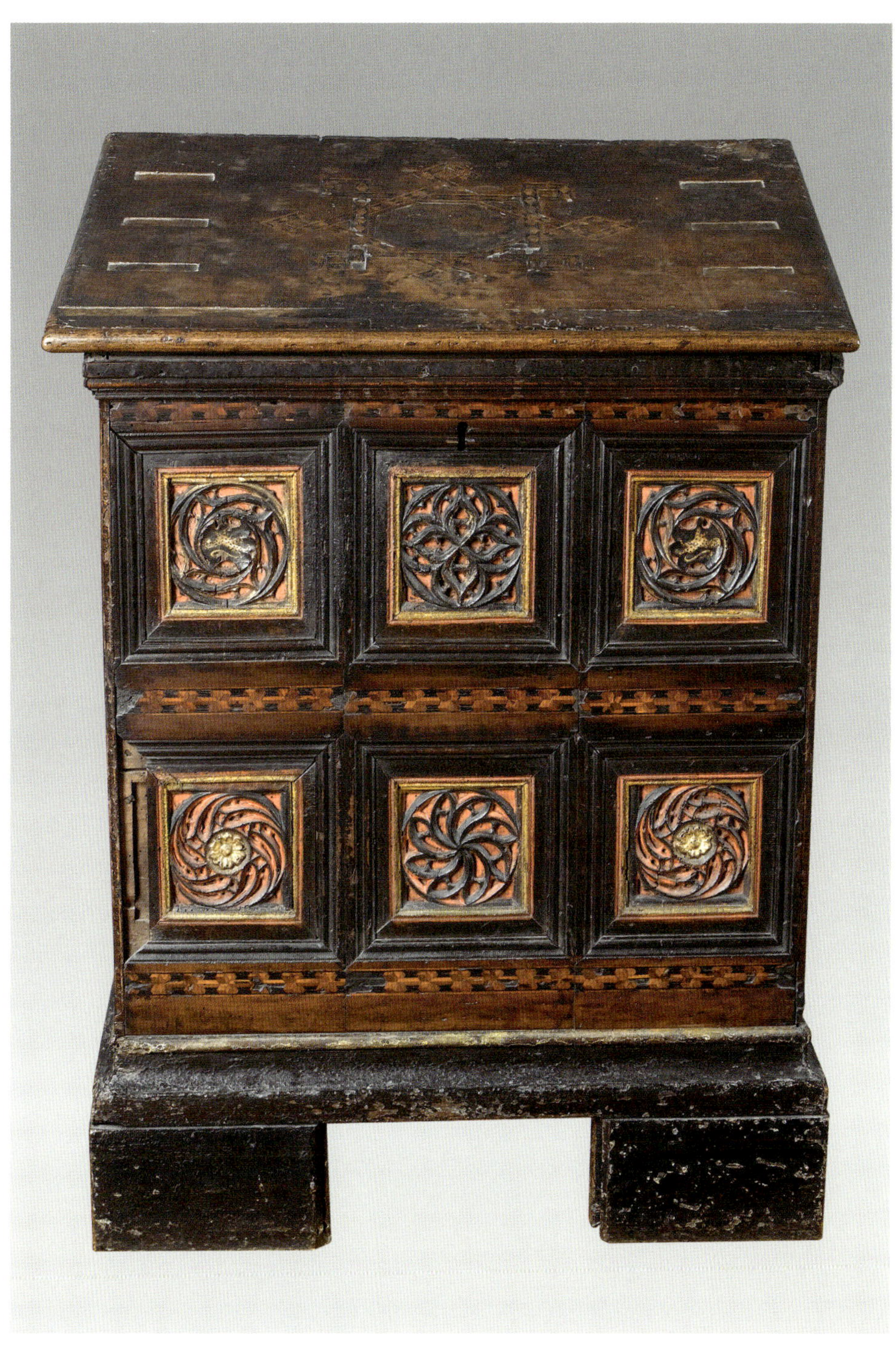

2. *Bimah* (pulpit), northern Italy,
c. 1440–75. Musée d'art et d'histoire
du Judaïsme, Paris (cat. 8)

Jewish Philosophy during the Renaissance
Giuseppe Veltri

The decisive historical turn in Western thought and philosophy was, without question, the Renaissance. Philosophical interests shifted from the study of the (meta)physical world, focused primarily on issues concerning the essence and existence of the sublunar and supralunar world, to problems of an epistemological nature that projected the Renaissance man into a "new" dimension. Jewish thought also underwent an abrupt change: from the philosophical search for the mystery of creation (*arcana mundi*) to the demythologization of the Jewish tradition. This historical contingency and consequential opening to new speculative horizons laid the bases for the birth of Jewish philosophy (*Philosophia Hebraeorum*) and the Jewish religion (*Religio Hebraeorum* or *Iudaeorum*).

First of all, we must consider an important question: is it really possible to talk about Jewish Humanism and a Jewish Renaissance? Looking at the classic definition of the Renaissance (Burckhardt 1860; Roth 1959), which stemmed from Enlightenment/Romantic ideology and saw the germ of individualism and origin of the sciences in the humanistic spirit of "freedom," we can say that the Judaism of the time was extraneous to these trends. The new spirit instead spawned a new class of intellectual Jews (Ruderman 1995) that developed out of intercultural exchange between Jewish communities and the Christian sphere.

But the Renaissance is not limited to Burckhardt's categories and includes all of the knowledge, discoveries, and scientific methods that enriched it. Jewish intellectuals did not just contribute to the circulation of the ideas that served as a prelude to the modern sciences—including a new definition of history and of historical truth, scientific and geographical discoveries—but also actively participated in debates on political philosophy, the immortality of the soul and the legal definition of religion and religious rituals.

Neoplatonism is the first philosophical current that can be traced within Renaissance philosophical literature. Judah Leon Abravanel, known as Leone Ebreo, was the leading figure of this initial phase of the reception of Plato in the Jewish Renaissance, which is why he can be considered the "one and only Jewish Renaissance philosopher" (Guttmann 1933). He was unquestionably one of the greatest exponents of Jewish thought in the sixteenth century. His best-known work, the *Dialoghi d'Amore*, first published in Rome in 1535, is a celebration of the cosmic love through which the relationship between God, the universe and man is revealed (see cat. 36).

Although some editions of the *Dialoghi d'Amore* (1541 and 1545) deliberately played on the ambiguity of a presumed conversion to Christianity ("Leone Medico, di Natione hebreo, et dipoi fatto Christiano"), Leone Ebreo himself never tried to conceal his roots or Jewish identity. Indeed, on the contrary, it is in the *Dialoghi* that the writer asserts that the origin of wisdom (*sophia*) is in the essence of the Mosaic religion.

His "identity" is also one of the distinctive elements of his style. In the *Dialoghi d'Amore*, Leone uses the possessive pronoun "our" with reference to all authorities from the Jewish tradition and culture. Among the commentators on Aristotle, he of course cites "our Rabbi Moses of Egypt," or Maimonides (*Dialoghi*, II, 69b). Among the interpreters of Plato's thought, we find Ibn Gabirol, who is referred to as "our Albenzubron," the name by which the author was known in Christian circles (*Dialoghi*, III, 51a). And Moses and Abraham are succinctly addressed as "our saints" (*Dialoghi*, III, 5b).

The harmonization of Plato and Aristotle can be considered to have been an ongoing process that began in antiquity and continued into the Middle Ages and Renaissance (*philosophia perennis*). Jewish thinkers, first and foremost Leone, had always seen Aristotle as the "bad disciple" of Plato, contributing to the corruption of wisdom among learned Greeks, who had received the key to "true" knowledge from wise Jews in Egypt.

This harmonization was actually nothing more than a kind of "correction" of Aristotle, a *reductio ad Platonem*. In light of this interpretation, Leone introduces the figures of Plato and Aristotle in the *Dialoghi d'Amore*, highlighting their different positions on the creation of the world and the origin of knowledge. Leone considered Divinity to be numerically one in essence, but triune in the prism of human perception, or rather in the process of knowledge. Marsilio Ficino used a similar expression in the preface to *Theologia Platonica*. But direct knowledge of Ficino's doctrine is evident in the third dialogue: in the argument used to demonstrate divine unity, Leone uses the sun, light, and the mirror as a metaphor. The same reference is found in Ficino's treatise *Orphica comparatio Solis ad Deum*, written in 1479,and later in *De Sole* (Kristeller 1953). This symbolic image plays an essential role in both Ficino's theodicy and Leone's gnoseology. For both philosophers, the incontrovertible similarity between God and the Sun stands at the foundation of the unity of knowledge and the relationship between the human and divine. In this context, Leone uses a formula that highlights the "triune" nature of God, that of lover, beloved, and love, which is also a clear reference to Ficino's doctrine.

The *Dialoghi d'Amore* are not so much a philosophical treatise as a vernacularization of a few ideas drawn from the classical Jewish tradition. Through his *Dialoghi*, Leone Ebreo made obscure philosophical doctrines accessible—a task that Ficino had utterly failed in the Christian sphere. Cosmic love, as an emanation of the world of creation, is nothing more than a kiss between love and beloved, a kiss that leads back to the divine essence upon man's death.

Plato is inextricably tied to the oldest Jewish traditions. According to Johanan Alemanno (c. 1435–1504), the Greek philosopher marked the end of the age of prophecy. But, at the same time, a new epoch began, that of the Kabbalah. Indeed, the most arcane secrets of the Kabbalah were revealed to Plato, the "theologian" or the "divine."

According to a tradition that became widespread in the Middle Ages, Plato was the disciple of the prophet Jeremiah, an idea that was introduced and repeated in the Renaissance through the works of Isaac Abrabanel, Leone Ebreo, Abraham Farissol, Johanan Alemanno, Jehiel da Pisa and David Messer Leon. The process of the "Judaization" of Plato was carried out in the context of the Jewish vision of *prisca theologia*, according to which the Mosaic religion was the foundation of Hermeticism and Platonism (Tirosh-Rothschild 1991).

Some Renaissance trends were in continuity with the classical medieval tradition, such as Aristotelianism and Averroism. In this case as well, the approach of thinkers and philosophers to specific issues—such as the immortality of the soul—opened the door to modern science.

Indeed, the Renaissance is also characterized by a phenomenon that can be described as "Jewish Scholasticism" (Zonta 2006). While, on the one hand, Aristotelianism survived in a few intellectual circles and universities (such as the University of Padua) without suffering any discontinuity with the medieval and scholastic tradition, we can also perceive a new way of thinking about Aristotle that can be defined as typically Renaissance (Bianchi 2007).

During the fifteenth and sixteenth centuries, many Jewish thinkers wrote philosophical treatises that concerned the exact same issues as those dealt with by their Christian contemporaries, using the same methods and the same literary genre (Zonta 2006). This trend was directly connected to Averroes's interpretation of Aristotle's thought, which characterized the entire medieval period. Jewish philosophers were, here as well, a bridge between the old philosophy and the new teachings (Ivry 1983).

In the Renaissance, the Jewish intellectual elite introduced a program into its educational system that was very similar to that of the Christian *curricula*. One case worthy of mention is that of the *yeshivah* of Judah ben Jehiel Messer Leon (c. 1422 – c. 1498), in which classical religious studies (halakah and aggadah) were joined by study of the seven liberal arts: the *trivium* (grammar, rhetoric, and logic) and the *quadrivium* (arithmetic, geometry, music, and astronomy). Judah Messer Leon is not only considered by the scientific community to have been one of the most important exponents of Jewish Scholasticism—as the author of an original treatise on rhetoric, *Sefer Nofet Tzufim* (Book of the Honeycomb's Flow)—but he also wrote numerous commentaries on logic and the natural sciences, such as the supercommentary on Averroes's middle commentary on the *Isagoge*, the *Categoriae*, the *Analytica* (*Priora* and *Posteriora*) and *De Interpretatione*. Messer Leon also wrote a commentary on the middle and long commentaries on the first three books of Aristotle's *Phyiscs*.

One of the most important activities that distinguished the Jewish intellectuals of the Renaissance was their special interest in the translation of classical works from the peripatetic tradition. The *Corpus Aristotelicum* of the medieval period was enriched by the gradual introduction of translations of Greek, Latin, and Arabic commentaries. Averroism retained its important significance in Renaissance philosophy, to the point that one can say

1. Isaac Alfasi, *Sefer halakot* (The Book of Laws),
with commentary, northern Italy, c. 1440–80.
Biblioteca Palatina, Parma (cat. 5)

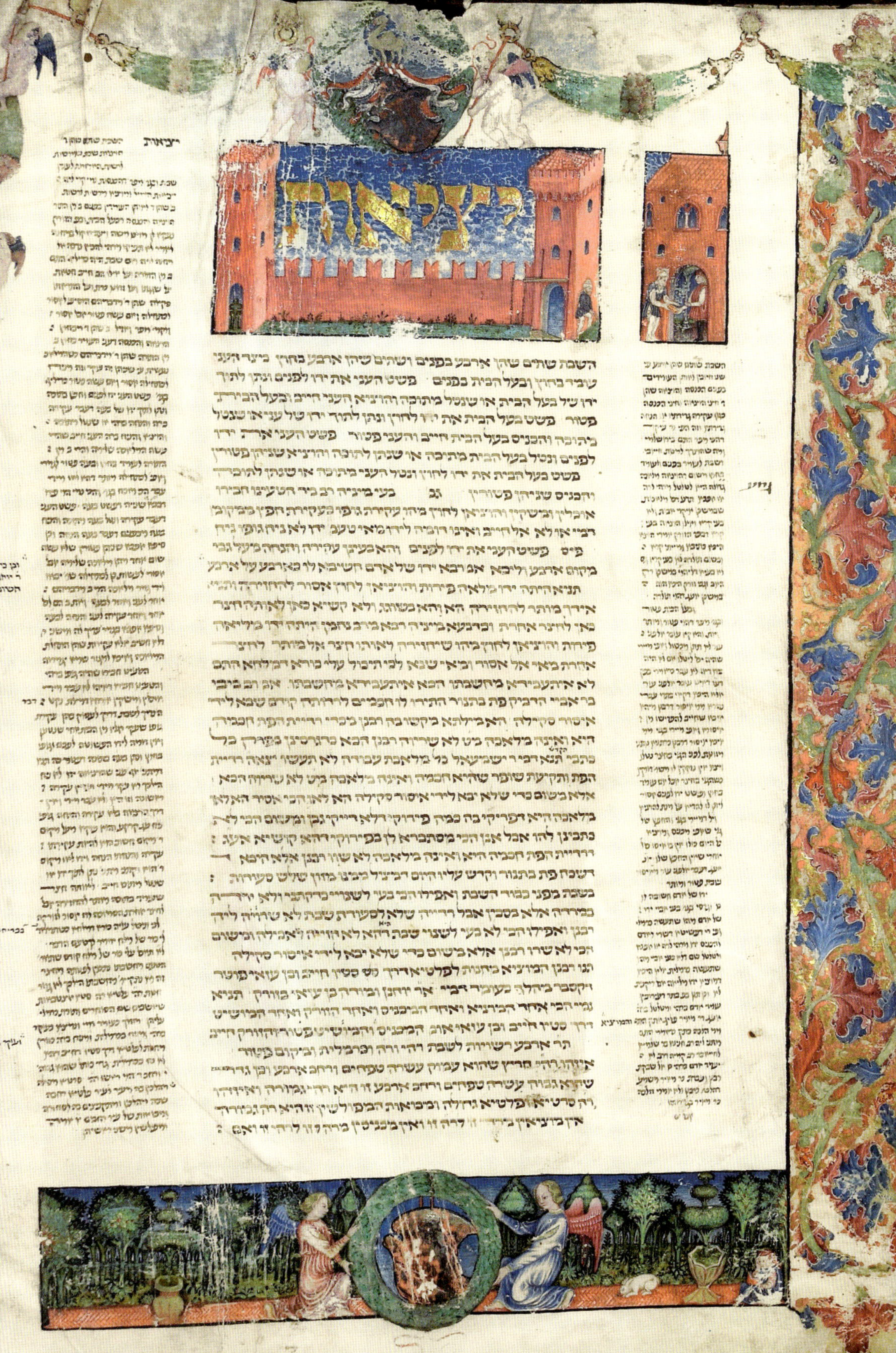

יציאות

that Jewish translators and intellectuals worked "in the shadow" of Averroes (Ivry 1983). Between the fifteenth and sixteenth centuries, many works were translated into Latin by Jewish thinkers: Elia del Medigo (d. 1493), Calonymos ben David, known as Calo Calonymos (c. 1476–1518), Abraham ben Meir de Balmes (c. 1460–1523), Jacopo Mantino (d. 1549), Moses Alatino (1529 – c. 1605), and Moses Finzi (active in 1558), among others.

As briefly noted, reflection on the issue of the immortality of the soul and on the nature of the human intellect are among the most important aspects of the Jewish Renaissance. In this context, Averroes's long commentary on *De Anima* played a fundamental role. Two new translations from Latin to Hebrew appeared in the sixteenth century: the Giunta edition by Mantino and De Balmes (1562) and a version by Abraham of Benevento (Zonta 2004). These two works replaced the older translation from Arabic to Hebrew by Zerahiah ben Shealtiel Hen (Zonta 2011). Calo Calonymos translated part of the *Libellus seu epistola de connexione intellectus abstracti cum homine* (1527), while Abraham de Balmes translated Al-Farabi's treatise *De intellectu et intellegibili* (c. 1522–23) and Averroes's *Summary* of *De Anima* (1552). Another version of the *Summary* was produced by Elia del Medigo for Giovanni Pico della Mirandola. Del Medigo can be considered one of the most important exponents of Jewish Averroism in Italy. He not only translated treatises on logic, physics, and metaphysics from Hebrew to Latin for Christian patrons (Engel 2017), but he also wrote two Averroist treatises on the soul (1482). Originally in Latin, they were later translated into Hebrew (Bland 1995). The first is on the concept of the unity between material intellect and possible intellect in their conjunction with the active intellect. The second concerns the immortality of the soul, highlighting incongruities between Averroes's position in the *Summary* and that in the commentary on *De Anima* III, 36.

Translated by Sarah Elizabeth Cree

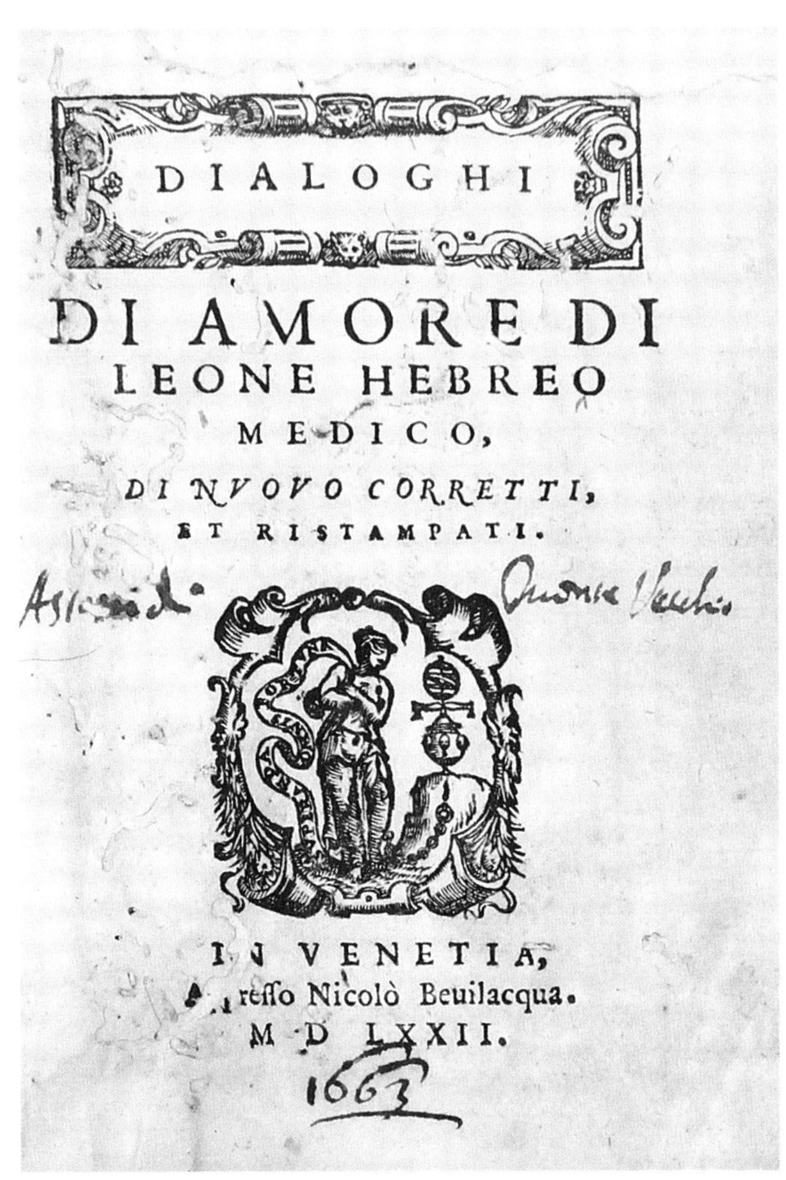

2. *Dialoghi di amore di Leone Hebreo medico,
di nuovo corretti et ristampati.* In Venetia, appresso
Nicolò Bevilacqua, 1572. The National Museum of
Italian Judaism and the Shoah, Ferrara (cat. 36)

Mingled Identities: *Conversos*, Hebraists, and Individual Converts

David B. Ruderman

On many grounds the rabbis of the early modern period had reason for concern. Along with the unmanageable explosion of knowledge triggered by printed books, the curtailment of their authority by lay leaders and governmental officials, they also witnessed with alarm another troubling phenomenon: the recurrent and conspicuous boundary crossings between Judaism and Christianity on the part of a small but conspicuous number of Jews and even Christians. My goal in this short essay is to describe succinctly the simultaneous appearance of some interrelated developments that emerge as discrete phenomena but ultimately converge to create a new complexity, an utter confusion of confessional loyalties and religious identities in early modern Europe.

I begin with the *converso* phenomenon, a primary factor in the erosion of social and religious boundaries that traditional Christian and Jewish authorities had erected for centuries. As several historians have argued, the religious and cultural ambiguity of Jewish self-definition first became an acute problem in early modern Europe with the reintegration of the *conversos* into Jewish life in Italy, northern Europe, and the Ottoman Empire (Yerushalmi 1971, p. 44; Kaplan 1994; Bonfil 1997; Kaplan 1997; Kaplan 2000, pp. 1–28). For New Christians who fully returned to Judaism their *rite de passage* was neither simple nor complete (Kaplan 1989; Graizbord 2004). Consciously or unconsciously, they retained deeply ingrained attitudes to and associations with their distant past, both religious notions and ethnic loyalties, which, in most cases, they could not dislodge. For New Christians who exited the Iberian Peninsula but hesitated to publicly acknowledge the Jewish faith, lingering in a transitional state between Judaism and Christianity, their religious and ethnic perceptions of themselves were even more complex. If one adds to this condition the highly secularized lifestyle of many of them, with their ever tenuous connections to ritual life and the synagogue, then it is easy to understand the genuine fears and anxieties of their religious leaders.

The new Jewish identity of the *conversos*, whether leaning to Jewish or back to Christian orthodoxy, or wavering between the two, was unique because it was based on choice, on personal autonomy. Neither the Catholic Church nor the Inquisition nor the rabbinic authorities could impose it from above. A *converso* strove and often succeeded, either publicly or clandestinely, in creating his or her self-definition. The returning New Christians also created their own communal structures and secured unique political arrangements with local authorities in Pisa, Leghorn, and then later in Amsterdam, or Hamburg, often uniquely different than those of the organized Jewish community (for Pisa and Leghorn see Bonfil 1992a; for Amsterdam, see Kaplan 1989, 1994, 1997, 2000, and Bodian 1997; for Hamburg see Studemund Halevy 1994–97). They were highly mobile, engaged in long distance trading, multi-lingual, with often competing cultural loyalties. But above all, they were the first Jews to determine their own religious identity, the various components of faith and praxis they would choose to accept or reject, and whether to believe in any form of monotheistic faith or not. The *conversos* had been victimized by a Catholic inquisition that could not tolerate their religious ambiguity. Rabbinic leaders faced with consternation this same ambiguity when these individuals attempted to return to the Jewish community. While they proclaimed themselves Jewish, many could not easily adjust to traditional norms and practices that were as obnoxious to them as those they had abandoned in Catholicism, or they remained indifferent to any religious ritual or doctrine whatever their origin. Others clung exclusively to a notion of ethnic or racial identity. Resembling notions of their own oppressors, they viewed themselves as members of the "Nação," distinguishable from their Ashkenazic counterparts and from those Jews who saw their identity as primarily or exclusively confessional.

Along with the phenomenon of the *conversos*, a new factor contributing to boundary crossings and religious intermingling was Christian Hebraism. Long before the early modern period, Christian scholars pursued Hebraic subjects especially related to biblical exegesis and medieval theology. But beginning in the Renaissance, and accelerated by the capacity of the printing press to reproduce Hebrew books efficiently and cheaply, the early modern era represented the high point of Christian study of Jewish texts. Individual Christian scholars mastered not only biblical studies but post-biblical as well. From the post-biblical library of Flavius Mithridates prepared for Pico della Mirandola (Ruderman 1987; Wirszubski 1989) in fifteenth-century Florence to the Hebraic scholarship of Johannes Reuchlin and Sebastian Münster in the respective fields of Kabbalah and rabbinics during the Protestant reformation, the Christian intellectual world took Judaism as a religious culture and intellectual legacy more seriously than ever before (Friedman 1983; Rummel 2002). And because of a rising market for Jewish books intended for Christian readers, the products of this new intellectual fascination were readily available. While the new Christian Hebraism could be labeled a form of philosemitism, it was certainly much more than the term denotes: an intellectual explosion fed by print and university learning; a Christian spiritual quest rooted in the essential notions of rebirth and reform propelling the intellectual and religious energies of the sixteenth century and beyond; and also an appropriation and aggrandizement of the Judaic element of Western civilization to be utilized and appreciated by Christians alone.

Was the new Christian Hebraist a syncretist? Did his intense preoccupation with Jewish texts attenuate his Christian loyalties while bringing him closer to the Jewish core of his

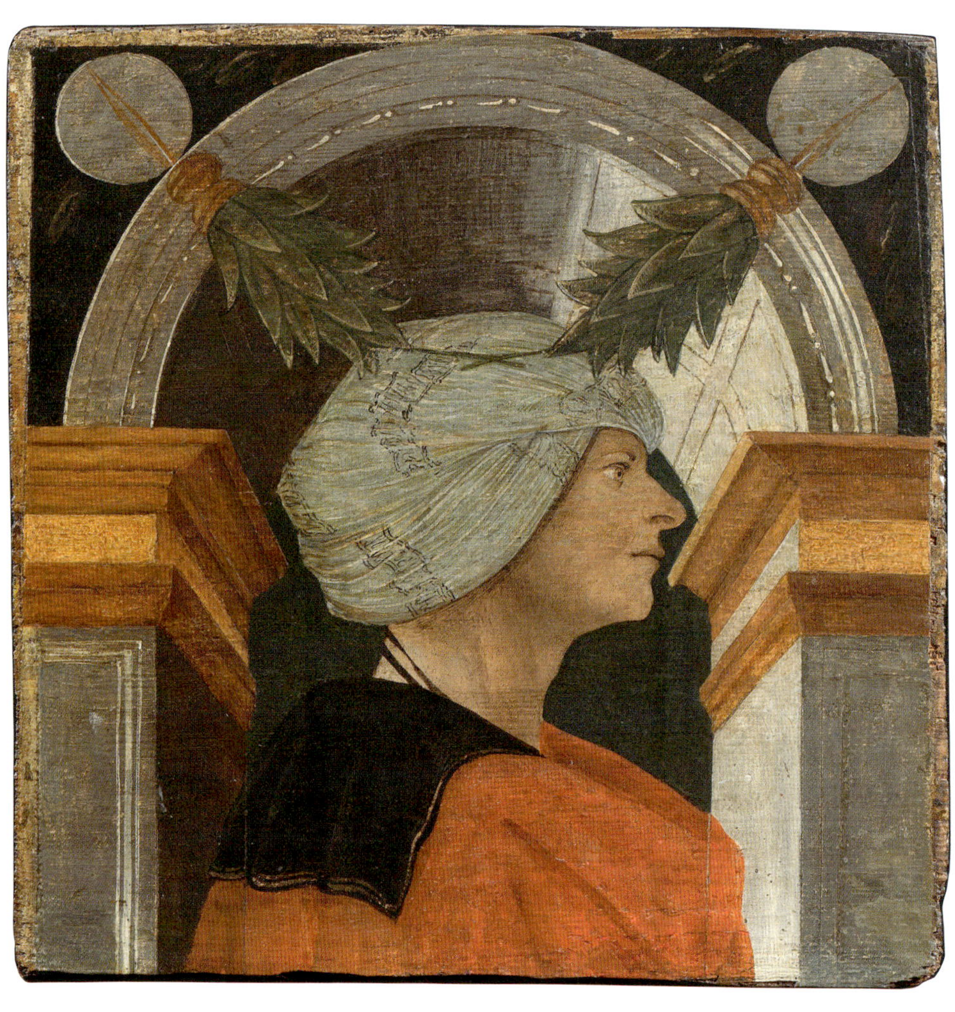

1–2. Lombard artist, *Profile of a man, with turban;*
Profile of a man, with Jewish-style headgear (?),
c. 1500–12. Private collection (cat. 21–22)

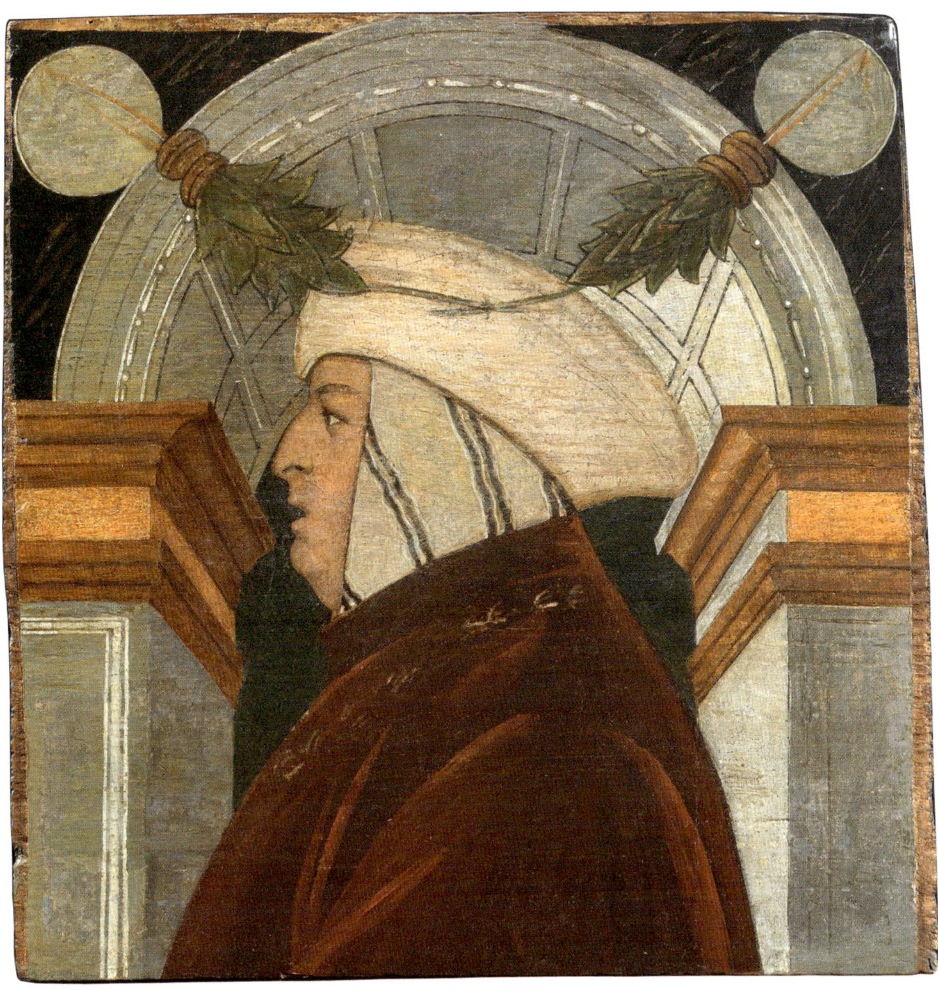

identity? There is no simple and unequivocal answer to such questions. Christian scholars who devoted their lifetimes to the study of Sacred Scriptures, Jewish languages, ancient Jewish history and literature, and even, in some cases, the ethnographic study of Jewish customs and ceremonies could hardly be motivated by intellectual reasons alone. Some indeed saw their responsibility to reclaim an authentic reading of the Hebrew Bible for Christians; others hoped to locate in their study the original, pure, and unpolluted version of Christianity practiced by Jesus; some were smitten by Jewish forms of esotericism which they hoped to appropriate to replenish the wells of Christian spirituality; while others even believed that early rabbinic Jewish culture and literature were the principal keys in deciphering New Testament prophecies. Whether the new breed of Christian Hebraists actually became more "Jewish" in the process of their prodigious Jewish learning or not, they were often perceived as such, as Judaizers whose seemingly excessive exposure to Jewish sources had brought them unwittingly closer to Jews and Judaism.

There was yet another group of highly complex individuals who were literally "boundary crossers," moving from Judaism to Christianity. These were the conspicuous numbers of Jews who chose to be baptized and joined, sometimes quite publicly, a Christian denomination, either Protestant or Catholic. The individual convert, unlike the *converso* who generally left Catholicism for some form of new Jewish identity, was usually engaged in the reverse crossing—from Judaism to Christianity. Whether motivated for economic, social, or religious reasons, or simply the victim of aggressive missionaries, the convert from Judaism had to encounter an uncertain future, where economic benefit or social acceptance or religious credibility in the newly acquired faith were often in doubt. The surest path was to become a so-called expert in Jewish affairs, a living testimony of the fallacies of the Jewish and the truths of the Christian faith. In assuming the role of Hebrew teacher and authority in Jewish texts, the convert often found himself in an uncertain and uneasy relationship with the Christian Hebraist who presumed to acquire a similar role by virtue of his consummate learning in Judaism (Carlebach 2001, pp. 200–21).

The primary evidence of the passage from Judaism to Christianity is the enormous literature of conversionist testimonies allegedly written by the converts themselves to document their separation from Judaism and to testify to the revelatory experience of their conversion. While many of these tracts eschew the personal and idiosyncratic for the conventional and expected narrative journey from spiritual degradation to inspired illumination, a few reveal the personal struggles, the complex ambivalence, and the hesitations and backslidings of the confused convert. Theirs was a life betwixt and between Judaism and Christianity. And for some, as soon as they had converted, there were misgivings and regret. For aggressive Protestant missionaries, the task was allegedly easier in that they could offer the potential convert a faith heavily drawn from the Old Testament, a faith based on *sola scriptura*, which superficially resembled their former one. But this was hardly a guarantee that the conversion would hold, and the convert would soon realize how the pain of separation from his family and friends and the uncertainty of economic and social security might make his new Christian self even more debilitating than his former Jewish one.

I present here but one example of the complex identities of the Jews who voluntarily converted to Catholicism (or Protestantism) but retained some persisting sense of their former Jewish identities. This example concerns an Italian Jew and is therefore particularly relevant in the context of the present exhibition.

In 1554, Ludovico Carretto, also known as Todros ben Joshua Ha-Cohen, published a testimony of his conversion to Catholicism in Latin and Hebrew for the sake of his former coreligionists. Todros was none other than the brother of Joseph Ha-Cohen, the well-known physician and Hebrew chronicler of Genoa. The work shares much with the many other surviving testimonies of conversion used to justify the act and to inspire others to apostatize. What is unique about this text is its publication in mid-sixteenth-century Paris, a place uninhabited by Jews; the prominence of the author within the Jewish community; and his creative use of prophecy and kabbalistic arguments to proselytize on behalf of Christianity utilizing the language and traditional sources of his former ancestral faith (Bonfil 1992b). It would be an exaggeration to speak of Todros's new religious identity as anything other than Christian. Nevertheless, the reader of his fascinating text in Hebrew is struck by how "Jewish" Todros actually appears, articulating his newly found faith in traditional Jewish language for his former coreligionists. This strange mingling of a simple faith in Christianity with the familiar patterns of religious expression for Jews suggests, at the very least, that Todros remained embedded in some way in his Jewish past. No doubt his printed tome was meant to manipulate and seduce Jews by describing Christianity in the intimate language of Jewish spirituality. But in so doing, I would contend, Todros betrayed, nonetheless, the vestiges of a Jewish faith he had still not fully overcome or erased.

While the confessional convert in early modern Europe was a phenomenon distinct from the *converso*, surely for both, their ambiguous and ambivalent statuses in Christian and Jewish societies were overlapping and intersected with each other. Add to this mix Christian Hebraists in pursuit of their pristine Jewish origins and you'll begin to appreciate the fascinating complexity of Jewish-Christian relations in early modern Europe and the appearance of what some have labeled Jewish Christians and Christian Jews. When Jewish identity became a matter of choice rather than imposed communal will; when a growing secular lifestyle for some severely attenuated religious commitments and the time they spent in either a synagogue or a church; when certain Christians attempted to recover a lost spiritual innocence through their intense study of Judaism while certain Jews found social and intellectual relations with Christians more attractive and satisfying than ever before, the possibilities for Jewish-Christian syncretistic thinking and praxis were unlimited. Surely these new configurations reflect the weakened and fragile state of Judaism and Christianity by the mid-sixteenth century and the prominent search for spiritual meaning in an unstable political and social climate. They also provide the relevant context for understanding the continued persistence of these expressions of mingled identity in the seventeenth and eighteenth centuries as well as the emergence of a profound new expression located among the followers of the messianic figure of Shabbetai Zevi (see *Sabbatian Heresy* 2017; Stuczynski 2019).

This essay draws heavily from Ruderman 2010, Chapter 5.

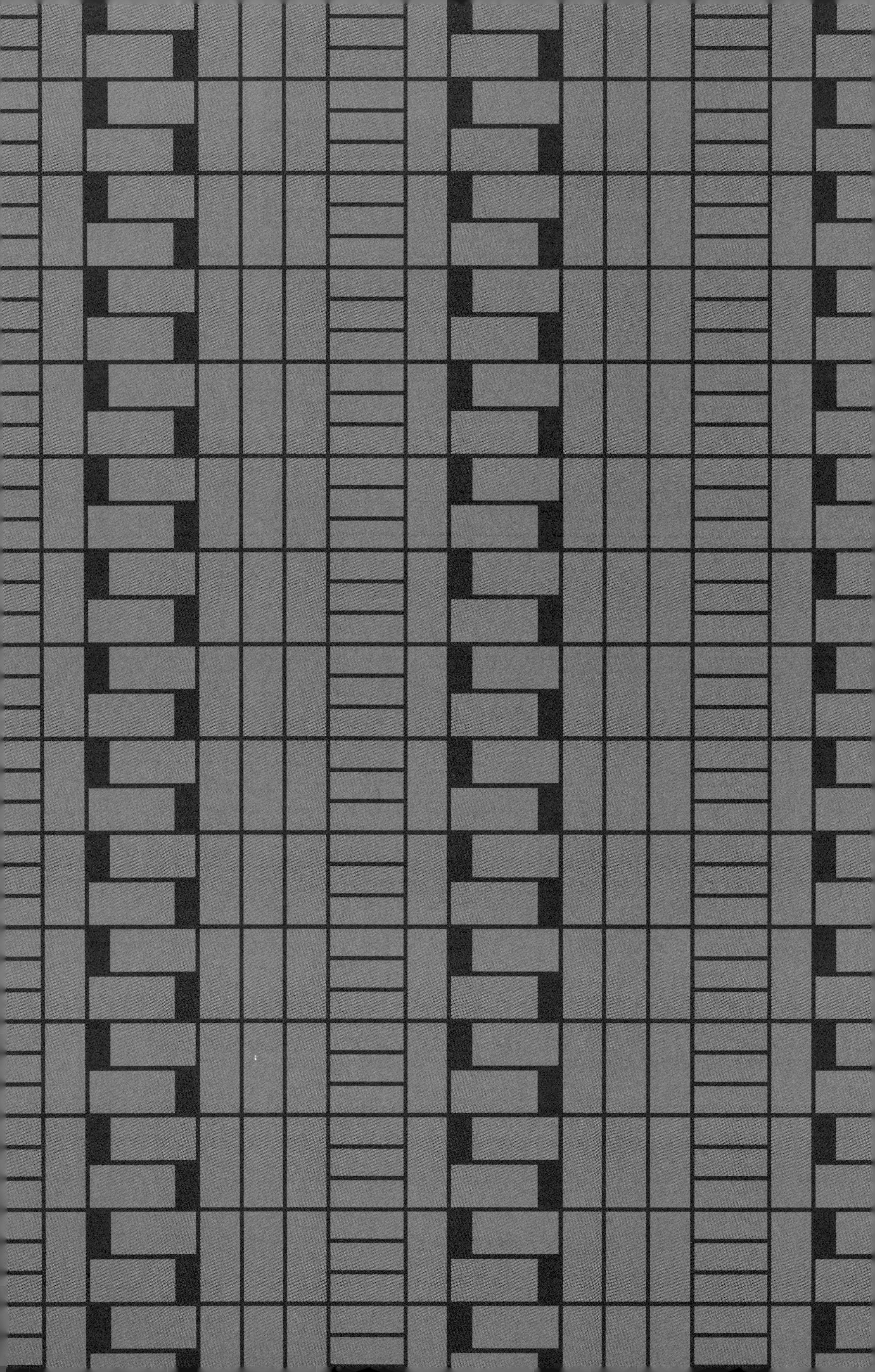

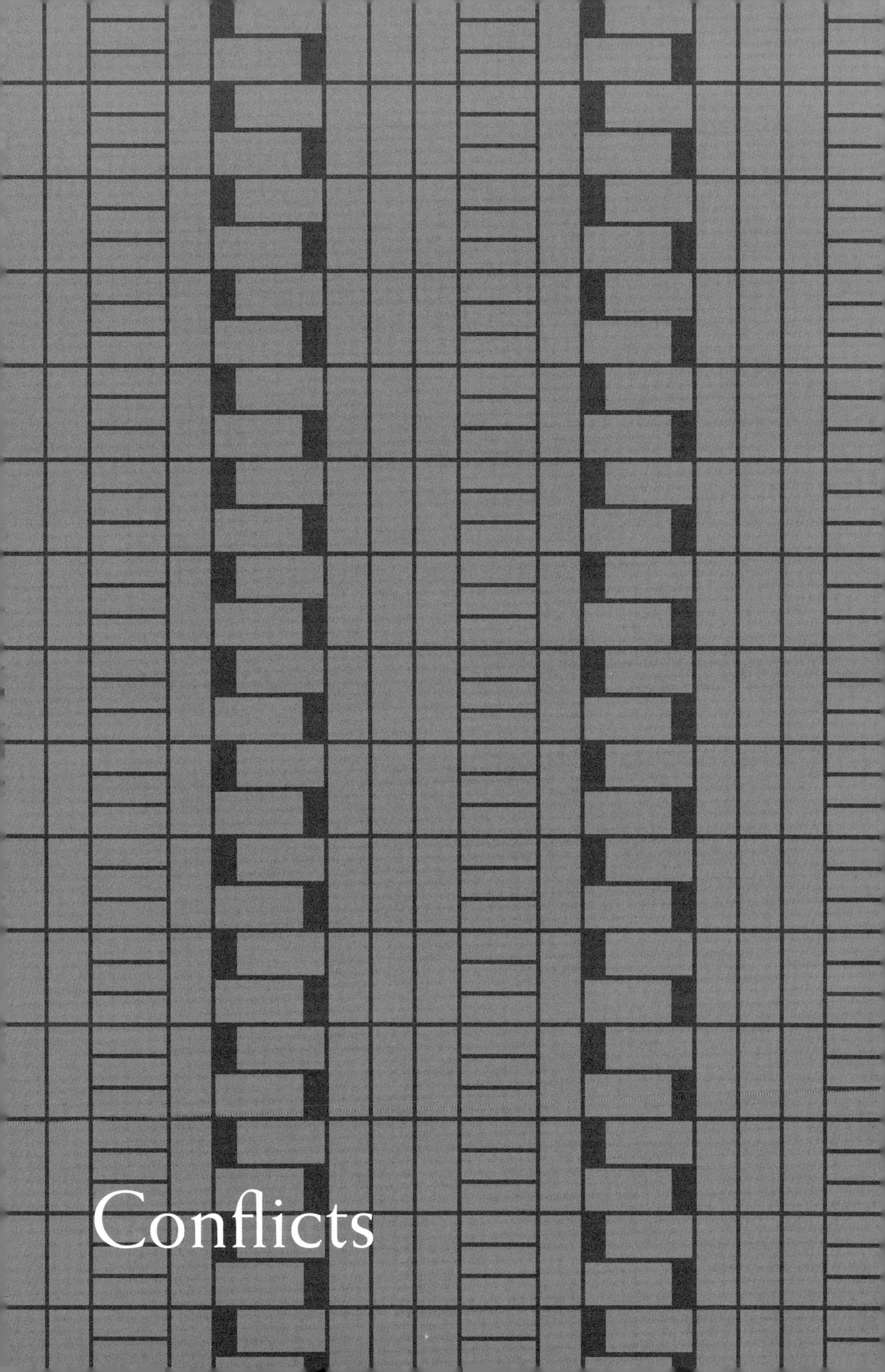
Conflicts

The Money Lending Benches of the Jews, the Christian Bank, and Anti-Semitic Stereotypes

Giacomo Todeschini

One of the most important inventions of the Italian Renaissance was the bank, understood as a credit institution managed directly by the State, or, during that era—between the fifteenth and sixteenth centuries—by the aristocrats in power or republican government of a territory (De Roover 1970; *L'alba della banca* 1982; Le Goff 2006; Melis 1987; *Banchi pubblici* 1991; Palermo 2008; Todeschini 2016). Given that we are speaking of an economic phenomenon directly related to political power, it was obviously a Christian invention. Indeed, the first Italian public banks drew their origins, in the sixteenth century, from credit and money lending experiences of the previous century, culminating in the founding of the Monti di Pietà (Mounts of Piety), beginning in 1462 (Muzzarelli 2001; Carboni 2008 and 2014).

Traditionally, historiography has portrayed the Monti di Pietà and their founding, for the most part proposed by Franciscan preachers of Primitive Observance, as an initiative aimed at providing economic assistance to citizens in need. At the same time, they have been described as a political-religious strategy employed by Christian governments to eliminate the need for the poor or impoverished to seek pledge loans with interest at banks run by Jews. Initially, in fact, the Monti di Pietà asked their debtors, in addition to pledges to secure the loan, for an apparently very modest interest (Montanari 2001). However, on careful examination, this reconstruction of the Monti's foundation and their relationship with those in need of money and with the Jewish lenders (*Monti di Pietà* 1999) seems to depend more on an accumulation of uncritically validated stereotypes than on an unbiased and detailed historical analysis. In fact, it is already quite clear on early examination of the data offered by the sources at our disposal that, on the one hand, the Monti di Pietà, not always founded by the Franciscans, were complex and more than simply charitable institutions, and on the other, the role that Italian Jews played in providing credit between the fourteenth and fifteenth centuries and their relationship with the Monti di Pietà were determined by the Christian policies that, in the meantime, were being organized from a banking point of view (Fornasari 1993; Carboni 2014). Between the fifteenth and sixteenth centuries, the Monti di Pietà paved the way for the creation of State Banks, while the credit activities delegated by the States to the wealthiest Jews between the fourteenth and fifteenth centuries were declassified as nefarious usury, of which Christianity had to rid itself.

To understand this sequence of events, however, we must go back a century and a half from the time when, at the end of the fifteenth century, the Monti di Pietà began to assist the Christian powers in realizing their political-religious and economic aspirations for direct control over various aspects of the finances and daily lives of those living in their subject territories.

From the first half of the fourteenth century, in Italy, we witness the singular phenomenon in which the existing regional authorities, municipalities or lordships entrusted the management of pledge loans with interest to Jewish "bankers," sometimes of Ashkenazi origin and sometimes of Roman or central Italian origin (Poliakov 1974; Luzzati 1996; Toaff 1996). Only uncritical acceptance of centuries-old stereotypes, such as the extraordinary wealth or exceptional economic acumen of the Jews, could lead to the belief, as with many historical reconstructions, even recent ones (Botticini and Eckstein 2012), that this phenomenon of delegating part of the credit relations in the Italian territories to the "Jews" was something natural and easily understandable in light of the Jews' long history. The contrary was true, however. Indeed, the appearance of Jewish money lenders in many large and small towns of central-northern Italy during the fourteenth century, far from being part of the natural historical development of Italian economics, and connected to an unprovable Jewish specialization in credit, reveals, on careful study, the complexity of the credit issue from the point of view of Christian politics and law (Todeschini 1989 and 2016). It also reveals an anti-Semitic economic stereotype developing and taking hold in Christian Italy between the fourteenth and fifteenth centuries, directly dependent on earlier and more ancient anti-Semitic theological-political arguments. In other words, the early Italian Renaissance was confining Jews, starting from medieval premises in turn based on an older baggage of stereotypes, to the role of moneylenders and credit experts in more or less explicit potential conflict with Christian credit institutions. The Monti di Pietà and later, the State Banks, would have been the morally acceptable protagonists in this conflict.

The accusation of avarice made by Christian theologians and jurists toward the Jews is very ancient. Originally, in the patristic and early medieval phase of the anti-Semitic discourse, between the fourth and ninth centuries, between East and West, from Ambrogio di Milano to Augustine of Hippo and Agobard de Lyon (Blumenkranz 1960; Schreckenberg 1999), it was not a reference to the financial attitude of the Jews among Christians. The term "avarice" (*tenacia, avaritia*) was instead used metaphorically to condemn and harshly denounce the Jews' "obstinate" attachment to their Truth and their stubbornness (*durities*), their refusal to abandon their Truth and convert to Christian religion and Law (Todeschini 2007 and 2018). The Jewish insistence on maintaining their own Law, their own interpretation of the Scriptures, and the set of customs and behaviors that defined Judaism, both before and after the definitive codification of the Talmudic treatises between the fifth (Jerusalem Talmud) and the seventh (Talmud of Babylon) centuries, had, since the fourth century, been viewed by Christians as a mental attitude similar to unproductive hoarding. The image, also metaphoric, of currency devalued to injuriously designate

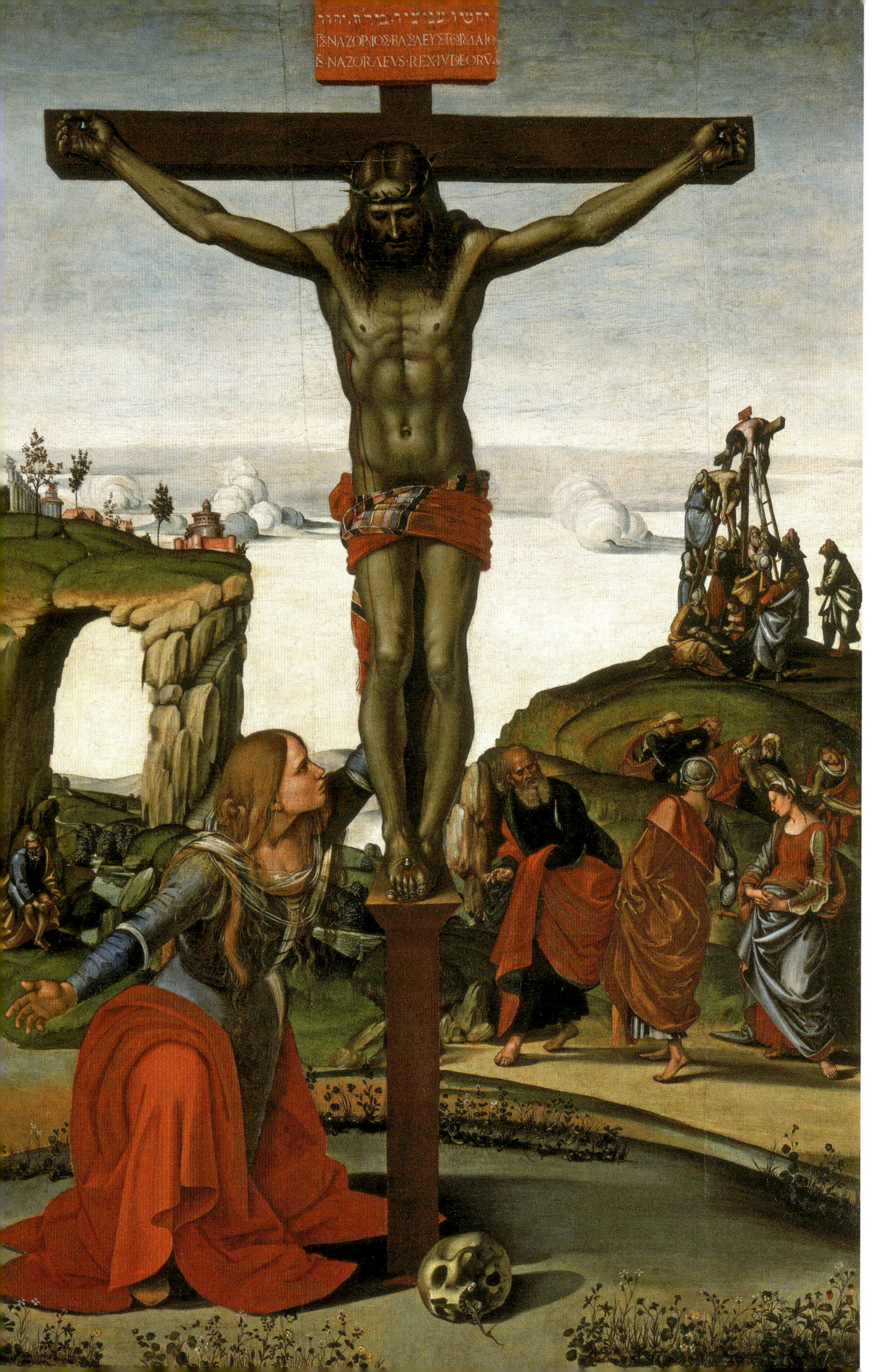
ישו עצריה מלכא דיהו
ΙΞ ΝΑΖΟΡΙΟΣ ΒΑΣΙΛΕΥΣ ΤΟ ΒΑΔΙΟ
IS · NAZORAEVS · REX · IVDEORV·

Jewish Law as being in opposition to Christian Law, is not a coincidence and was created in parallel with that of Jewish *avaritia*. The Jews were presented by the early-medieval Christian apologists and theologians as custodians of a patrimony (the Holy Scriptures) whose profound sense they did not understand, being avaricious hoarders of a heritage that, in their hands, was transformed into useless and sterile matter (Schreckenberg 1999; Todeschini 1989). The contrast between the "fertility" of the Christian interpretation of the Scriptures and the "sterility" of the Jewish interpretation, underlying the origin of the attribution of Jews as "avaricious" petty hoarders, opened up an ideological and political opportunity for a Christian portrayal of the Jews, founded on the notion of accumulated and ultimately, tenaciously guarded wealth, stolen from those who would have known how to use it better. In tandem with this debatable habit of representing Jews as greedy and stubborn was the tendency of the anti-Semitic Christian argument to describe the Jews with animal metaphors, resorting in particular to the image of the onager, the wild ass: an animal symbolizing the savage and, indeed, obstinate indomitability of those who refused to convert to Christianity (Todeschini 2003 and 2009).

However, although consigned to the arsenal of the anti-Jewish Christian argument in an early stage, the accusation that the Jews were spiritually *avaricious* did not assume a more specifically economic meaning for centuries. We must wait for the so-called "commercial revolution" of the Middle Ages, the acceleration and expansion of the markets, credit, and contractual relationships between the eleventh and twelfth centuries (Palermo 1997 and 2008; Cortonesi and Palermo 2009). Here we witness a transformation of the image of Jewish avarice into a more concrete imputation of a cupidity thought to economically threaten Christian society and the churches that embodied it. At this stage, emblematically represented by a famous letter to the king of France from Peter the Venerable, abbot of Cluny (Friedman 1978; Dahan 1990; Iogna Prat 1998), the Jews are not yet labeled as usurers, but their participation in the market economy is obsessively considered ambiguous, insinuating that their earnings are the result of illegal economic transactions detrimental to the Christian economy. As frequently noted, during this era, the fear experienced by the ecclesiastical institutions in the face of an economic and monetary reorganization that made credit transactions the pillar of much of the economy, putting churches and monasteries (and the papacy itself) at risk and into debt, tended to hold the Jews—strangers par excellence in the Christian land—responsible for a financial and commercial revolution that in reality was primarily managed by Christian businessmen and groups of authority. It is a fact that, between the twelfth and thirteenth centuries, in the climate generated by the conciliar legislation that, from the third to the fourth Lateran council (in 1179 and 1215) (Grayzel 1933; Pakter 1979 and 1988; Linder 1997), began to oppose the interest-bearing loan and, in general, the credit operations of Christian bankers and merchants, the Jews began to be singled out as those responsible for the economic instability of churches and sacred institutions. At this point, in all of Europe, in both the secular and ecclesiastical Christian juridical and legislative documentation, a very particular phenomenon occurs: while on the one hand the numerous economic activities of the Jews, from agriculture to crafts, medicine and trade, are poorly represented (although they are well described in private documents and chronicles), the interest-bearing loan, "usury," is increasingly portrayed as the preferred economic activity of the Jews (Mell 2017). Between the twelfth and fourteenth centuries, precisely when the civil and Christian canon law, but also the Scholastics' treatises, against the background of Roman law summarized by the Justinian Code, began to analyze the sphere of credit and financial investment in detail, establishing multiple ways of legitimizing the credit operations practiced by businessmen, money changers, and Christian bankers, the Christian legal and political culture was increasingly singling out the Jews as protagonists of what might be called the dark side or less bright side of credit: the consumer loan (Greilsammer 2007).

This is the definition that modern economists and economics historians use to designate the loan with interest, generally on collateral or pledge, whose aim is to meet a need for liquid money for the purchase of consumer goods or to manage household finances. It was therefore a form of credit aimed at the lower-middle segment of medieval society, usually those barely taken into account by the Christian commercial and banking companies that, rather, did business with their peers or with the political-institutional powers. The consumer loan, especially between the twelfth and thirteenth centuries, was instead managed, in Italy as in Europe, by entrepreneurs with little political importance (Bordone 1994; Kusman 2013), by merchants and currency changers known at the time as "lombardi" or also "caorsini" or "toscani" (in reference to their geographical areas of origin). These retail moneylenders had affiliations with the Christian religion and culture, but were often suspected of heresy and dishonesty. They remained on the margins of official economies at least until the fourteenth century, when they disappeared or became members of the more prominent economic and financial groups, entering the ruling classes (Giansante 2008; Milani 2017) and so erasing their reputations as public "usurers" (*usurarii manifesti*).

It is precisely at this stage, in Italy, but also in other parts of Europe, and therefore between the thirteenth and fourteenth centuries, that Jews began to be classified as usurers by definition, and unlike the "lombardi" or "caorsini," impossible to integrate into the respectable world of Christian finance. From the early fourteenth century, in Italy, many cities stipulated contracts with Jews which, in exchange for the opening of a loan or retail bank, defined the fixed-term right of residence for a group of Jews (Luzzati 1996). In other words: in the historical moment in which, on the eve of the Renaissance, and in a decisive phase of Christian commercial and financial civilization, Christian credit dynamics were becoming more and more specialized (there was a careful distinction, also legally, between the minutiae of consumer loan transactions and the politically significant major financial transactions), the Jews were blamed for being moneylenders, or entrusted with the role of public moneylender, the economic evil needed to meet ordinary people's daily needs for monetary liquidity, needs that the new Christian economy could not or did not intend to satisfy, and which it regarded as a morally ambiguous manifestation of managerial incapacity, of petty greed, of suspicious social decay.

From the Jewish point of view (Auerbach 1870; Weingort 1979 and 1998; *Oxford Handbook* 2010), the loan with interest was part of the large family of economic and commercial bond-based transactions that Talmudic and Rabbinic jurisprudence admitted as

2. Master of the Baptist Capital, *Capital with the Feast of Herod and Beheading of the Baptist*, Ferrara, c. 1200. Museo della Cattedrale, Ferrara (cat. 2)

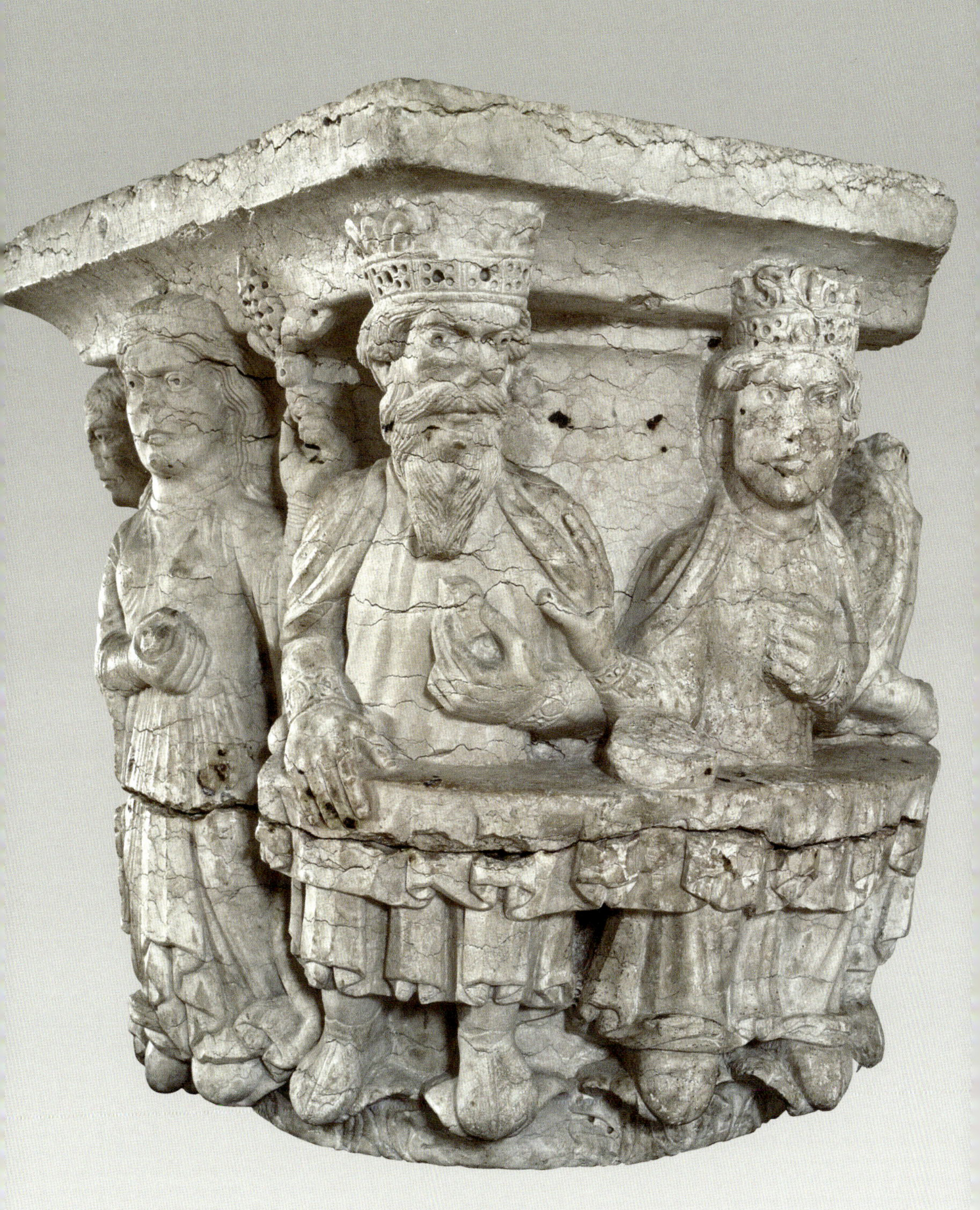

lawful, provided they did not harm the poor and did not become an instrument of social oppression and marginalization. Then, in the Jewish environment, precisely during the medieval "economic revolution," the Jews began to participate in the new forms of market organization with the different prospects offered by these realities. Between the twelfth and fourteenth centuries, the Jews, as traders, farmers, artisans, doctors or rabbis, became involved in the network of Jewish, Christian and Jewish-Christian economic relations in which credit, loans and financial dialectics took shape. No documentary source authorizes us to think that the Jews, or the Christians, preferred to devote themselves to money lending with interest during this period (*Wirtschaftsgeschichte* 2008; Toch 2013). Instead, like the Christians, they lent or borrowed money to the extent required by the economics of the lives they were living. As a normal practice, this eventually ceased or was altered when, in the fourteenth century, particularly in pre-Renaissance Italy, Christian cities preferred and sought out the money lending benches or banks managed by the Jews, or certain wealthier Jews. But what was the reason behind this rather sudden change?

As we have seen, the Christian political powers, especially in central-northern Italy, or in an area with heavy mercantile and financial development, entrusted to the Jews the management of a "minor" credit sector that local Christian economies were not adequately managing. Roman, German, or generically Italian Jews (Milano 1963; Poliakov 1974; Toaff 1987; Luzzati 1996) met this need and were rewarded with systematic citizenship rights for themselves, their families and the group, or the community to which they belonged. However, this explanation raises a broader question, namely the deep reason behind the Christian conviction that the Jews had available liquid money, and the reason the Christian municipalities and ruling aristocracy were willing to entrust the "Jews" with consumer credit management (Todeschini 2018). In this case too, no documentary evidence supports the hypothesis of outstanding Jewish monetary wealth (Toaff 1989; Todeschini 1989 and 1990) in the Italian economic environment that saw Jewish lending banks proliferate (an analysis of the dowries of girls from well-to-do families shows below-average wealth compared to dowries of wealthy Christians). Similarly, there are no traces of Jewish initiatives that originally promoted, favored or encouraged the establishment of lending benches in various localities. Once the contracts (the so-called *condotte*) between Jewish lenders and Italian city-states were stipulated, if the money lenders wished to renew their pacts, obviously so as not lose rights of citizenship and settlement that affected their whole community, there is nothing to confirm that the spread of Jewish money lending benches under the auspices of agreements between cities and the Jews derives from Jewish proposals. Close attention needs to be paid to both the previously mentioned economic situation—namely, growth in consumer loans and Christian economies too inadequate to deal with them—and the political-religious motivations that might explain the attitude of the Christian powers toward Jews and their hypothetical economic-credit resources. As a matter of fact, the professional "ghettoization" of a part of Jewish society dealing in consumer loans, as we see in Italy between the fourteenth and fifteenth centuries, appears to be a far more complex phenomenon than often described. It is as much a result of a stereotyped symbolic and religious portrayal of Jewish groups produced by the Christian powers, as it is a reflection of a problematic economic situation (the so-called "fourteenth-century crisis" in the market economy: see *Crescita economica* 2017) that involved both Jews and Christians, but that Christian policies and economies struggled to come to terms with.

In fact, the lack of liquidity in circulation, or the increased demand for credit (for purchasing power) that characterized the economic transition from the thirteenth to the fourteenth century throughout Europe and primarily Italy (Palermo 2008), and at the same time the local governments' entirely political-economic desire to control the cost of money (interest rates), a century before the foundation of the Monti di Pietà and two centuries before their conversion into state banks provoked the public authorities into seeking institutional, public, and controllable forms of consumer credit: the loan banks entrusted to Jews were a partial solution to the problem (Dorin 2016a). However, singling out the wealthy Jews among those better-known and "more familiar foreigners" (Trivellato 2009) to discover an excellent source of financing for local economies was not based on a "scientific" analysis of the local resources, anachronistic for the time. It depended instead on the Christian elite's negative preconception of the Jews based on centuries of anti-Semitic juridical and theological culture and layer upon layer of stereotypes that targeted the "Jews" as a potential economic/political threat to be avoided and managed. And, possibly, exploited. In this cultural arsenal, which local Christian governments primarily inherited through religious and political languages, the theme of Jewish *avaritia* and the ability of the "Jews" to appropriate Christian economic assets and, in particular, those of churches, prevailed. The notion, originally theological and then strongly controversial, of the ill-gotten fabulous wealth of the "Jews" (in the twelfth century, Peter the Venerable of Cluny defined it as the *male parta pinguedo*) helped to apparently rationalize the representation of the Jews as human coffers perennially available to Christian governments. Since the thirteenth century, Christian Europe and Italy were convinced, as treaties, letters and decrees bear witness (Dorin 2016b), of the government's right and duty to use fiscal and administrative means (Chester Jordan 1989) to tap into Jewish wealth, presumed in any case (and against any historical or documentary evidence) to be usurious in origin, or sinful if not malicious. It was not in vain that the fourth Lateran Council of 1215 (*Il lateranense* 2017), an epic event for the Catholic West, provided legislation on a separation between Jews and Christians, nor did their establishing the imposition of a distinguishing sign (Cassen 2017) for the Jews go unnoticed. It was also within this council that, for the first time, Jewish "usury" was officially condemned as a moneymaking technique that stripped Christians and their churches of their wealth.

In this climate, which, as often happens in history, dialectically interwove practical and pragmatic needs and reasonings with deeply rooted prejudices lacking both practicality and pragmatism, between Jewish "bankers" (Toaff 1996) and Italian city-states agreements were made, generating a widespread and local credit system that will be definitively sent into crisis at the end of the fifteenth century by the foundation of the Monti di Pietà, which were transformed into public banks in the sixteenth century (Todeschini 2016). This system of consumer lending banks, while establishing an opportunity for settlement and a form of citizenship sanctioned by law for Jewish inter-family groups and communities, also reaffirmed and violently publicized the stereotype of Jewish avarice, updating it to the professional term of "usury" understood as a useful but perverse financial activity. At this point, the Jews who were moneylenders, craftsmen, farmers, matchmakers, merchants, doctors, rabbis or in one of the thousand trades they practiced in Italy and Europe between the fourteenth and sixteenth centuries (*Ebrei in Italia* 2006; *The Cambridge History* 2018) could be officially classified, economically and politically, as experts in money and finance, namely as public moneylenders (*usurarii manifesti*) by definition. The contrast between the Jewish jurisprudential definition of money lending as an occupation, under certain conditions, legitimately and ethically practicable alongside other trades in the commercial field, and the complex and contradictory Christian definition of the money trade as a sometimes legal, sometimes suspicious and in any case assessable in relation to its political and public significance (Ceccarelli 2003 and 2012; Todeschini 2002 and 2016) made it paradoxically easier to codify and transmit, in a Christian environment, the stereotyped portrayal of Jews as usurers.

Starting in the early fifteenth century, when what is called Humanism was fully flourishing, and what would later be called scientific economic thought (Maifreda 2012) was developing, there was growing controversy both in local Italian governments, such as in Siena and Naples, and within theological-religious institutions such as the Franciscan Observance. There was debate that financial realities such as Jewish lending banks seemed to impoverish rather than enrich Italian economies (*Monti di Pietà* 1999; Melchiorre 2012; Capriotti 2014). The financial growth of Christian commercial enterprises, the increasingly clear definition of the proximity between these centers of economic power and the political powers of the city-states or kingdoms (De Roover 1970; Palermo 2008), banking's progressively closer ties to taxation and government, and the need to centralize credit mechanisms and have the public authorities directly take over the credit business were needs that emerged in the most diverse local situations. Banking gradually shifted from the delegation of money lending to Jewish "banks" to government and Christian management of the public bank. The rhetorical and propagandized portrayal of Jewish "usury" as a wrong and harmful form of credit and use of money proved to be crucial in this process, and the late fifteenth-century Monti di Pietà were an essential stage in it. The stereotype of the ill-gotten wealth of the Jews and its compliment, "usury," as their favorite activity (Mell 2017), allowed Christian governments and preachers to define the Christian credit and banking model in the ethical and solidaristic terms of the "Monte" (the future public savings "Cassa") through languages of "piety," or the strongest faction of society's love for its weakest faction. This point, and especially after 1515, marked the beginning of the gradual but increasingly clear distance between the credit managed by Jewish banks and Christian credit managed by public banks. From this moment on, public banks were able to manage both consumer credit and larger financial enterprises in direct contact with the policy-makers and government. The "usurious" Jewish stereotype was intensifying, degrading the Jewish economic presence to a tolerated and disturbing daily reality, a dark side to the Christian state economy celebrated by the banking institutions that originated with the Monti di Pietà. The age of the ghettos had begun.

Translated by Elizabeth Burke

this and following pages

3. Giovanni Mattia Tiberino, *Passio beati Simonis Tridentini* (*Passion of the Blessed Simon of Trento*), c. 1475–1500. Biblioteca Queriniana, Brescia (cat. 25)

m supplicio, & surdicto spiritu collapsis viribus deficiebat.
Attollens graues oculos in celum supos aduocare videbatur
mestos. Et inclinato capite sanctus dno reddidit spiritum.
Purpureus veluti cum flos succisus aratro. Languescit mo-
riens Lapsosque papauera collo, demisere caput, plumea cum
forte granantur; Et relinquentes illud corpus seruus prec-
perunt, ut sub adis uincens illud occulerent. Timebant
eis proclamationes ministris, et crebrescentis i cos magis atque
magis famam, ne furore populi capti, & cesi ad torturam
subito traherentur; Altera die que passionis dm concti
in Xpo credentis, ad memoriam renocat, restricis labentib[us]
in urbem fluuius, Parentes infantis una cum cohorte
storia ubicuque querentis no inuenere eum; Die autem
sabbati quem ienens i synagoga cunctis euentibus aduersa
super Almemor extenderunt. Est enim Almemor
mensa quedam ante altare, ubi psalmos, antyphonas
ymnos que decantant; Perfidis que oronibus suis, rursus
eodem in loco reposuerunt corpus; Terciam vero die que
sanctum pasca xpi fidelibus attulerat, ut postenserunt
sudei, cuius pene menbris in cos fore suspensas, mito consilio
libratis que plurimor opinionibus dixerunt; Proiciamus
corpus istud uestitum in flumen quod nostra domo pretterfluit.
Et eunctis ad pontificem dicamus, quod quoniam illud
in domum nostram aquam deduxit, & retrie fixo retentum
no potuit una cum flumine dilabi. Talibus eis dict, credat
nemo iudeos pueru extinxisse; Placuit omnibus sententia.
Et ascendens ad antistitem proditor, rerum seriem eo quo
fuerat institutus ordine pandidit; Lunc gauisus pontifex
Johannem de Salis storem, Et Jacobum de Sporro Ca-
pitaneum, sue tridente ciuitatis illuc ubi iacebat puer
secum iussit accedere; Et descendentes statim inuenerut
cadauer i aqua pannis inuolutum, quo protinus extracto,

eiusque vulneribus diligenter annotatis, illud in sacello sancti
petri collocauerunt. ubi maxima ptorum languentium que
confluente frequentia multis maximisque indies miraculis
fulget; Ecce xpiane iesum inter latrones rursum cruci
fixum, cere quid faerent sudei, si inter xpi fideles ha-
berent imperium. Gloriosus simon virgo martyr, et
innocens dix ablactatus, et cuius lingua nundum hu-
manu soluebat eloquium i ptemptum nostre fidei a
sudeis est extensus in crucie; Audi qui tam crudele hoius
genus tuus in viribus patris; Judei eterno statuto
decreuerut, ut diuine eucharistie boue que marie
semp virgini, gottidie maledicat[ur]. Poluta omnia que ba
petentiz asserentes pp illa que in contemptum romane
ecclesie agere dignoscuntur; Item in chieser idest in
tertio libro Talmut. hunc eis eciam proferunt sudei
libris moisi & prophetar[um]. Et ut magis credatur
Talmut fabulis addit fabulas dicentus: quod deus
strideat Talmut. ibi ppetua lege sanatur, ut ter
singulis diebus in orone quam efficaciorem cundis
fabus existimant: omnes xpi fideles deuouentur.
Hanc iam oronem stantes: et functis pedibus, ad
nullam rem mondi intentionem agentes euomunt:
uiri in hebreo. Mulieres ea lingua quam apud
omnes didicerunt. Solus leuita eam alta uoce decan-
tat. Alys omnibus respondentibus amen. Verba orontis
sic sonant: Conuersis non sit spes, & omnes repete
dissegant: In matribus minoretur paruuli: et amplius
non resurgant: Et omnes inimicia tue genus israel
destruantur: et regnum nostre xpianorum era
dicetur & consundat[ur]; Fac domine: fac impleas
quod petimus in diebus nostris velocit. quia tu es
deus benedictus fugans inimicos, & destruens

Impios, Et in chieser naasim i. in secundo talmut affirmat
quod dominus noster iesus xpus maxima in inferno tormeta
patiatur; Non est mirum xpiani: si nos bello: fame
siti: grandine: pruina xpus affligat: si nos populum
suum precioso sanguine suo redemptum p semper ad
dectiora labi sustineat. Cum patimini inter nos regnare
inimicos eius. Non est aliud quam sacrosancta fide despecta
sinis ppriis hostibus ad herere; Natus est die venis
sexto kal decembris anno a partu virginis salutifero
septuagessimo secundo: supra millesimz quaternarium
Ex andrea et Maria parentibus pauperrimis; dno Johanne
hinderbacch quarto pontifice: et domino tridentino
impante feliciz; Obquam rem sudei omnes a
matore usque ad minorem, in carceribus athenis que
conclusi sunt, no inde recessuri pasque debitas penas
luant.

Sayt hebreorum cuislaz presstor adhortus
Cuz sedet infelix, hic sibi somnus adest
Hunc locus impanes, miseruz desurbat i ignes
Auxilium querens carpit aena manu;
Tempora confestim feruentibus diruit undis
Et cute consompta lumine cossis eget
Terra rouevett miracula maxima lisstrans
Hanc sedem merito dat tibi sancte puer

Preachers and Jews
Maria Giuseppina Muzzarelli

The relationship between Christians and Jews, intense, enduring, multifaceted, in Italian cities between the Middle Ages and early modern times, also left traces in preaching. In the sermons, in fact, there is no lack of references to the Jews. Between the fifteenth and sixteenth centuries in particular, the preachers influenced, or at least tried to influence, that relationship, which in some cases was certainly conditioned by them. This was done through a vectorially-oriented action in a single or almost single direction, whereby the risks inherent in the relationship with the Jews, usurious or otherwise, and attachment to them, and therefore also all forms of spontaneous sociability, were denounced. This attack was unleashed with different degrees of intensity and for various reasons. Preachers' sermons tended to warn Christians of the dangers of continuing economic-credit relations with the Jews and, more generally, of allowing sand to get into the gears of cohabitation. By the mid-fifteenth century, Italy had had more than two centuries of experience in cohabitation, not always easy but as successful and fruitful for Christians as it had been for Jews.

One thing is undisputed: the usefulness of the services rendered by the Jews—something that undoubtedly facilitated acceptance, so much so that city authorities were persuaded to call upon them (hence the name *condotte* or "conducts" attributed to official acts that established the rules of cohabitation) even in smaller centers that were unfamiliar with religious positions and daily customs that differed from those of the majority. As long as many, if not all, were witness to their usefulness, preachers appeared to have rarely attacked them. Indeed, the preachers often dealt with issues of usury and trade that raised doubts, but almost exclusively referred to Christians involved in these activities.

From the second half of the fifteenth century, the preachers' view of the Jews who had dwelt in so many of these cities for so long appears to have changed dramatically. They focused on the alleged effects of their feneratitious activity, negative for both Christian economies and souls. The turning point is usually connected with the conception and foundation of the Monti di Pietà, an institution that owes much to the Friars Minor, a branch of Franciscanism that tirelessly preached to promote these civic credit centers with a function similar to the Jewish money lending benches or private banks dispensing pledge loans (Muzzarelli 2001). Actually, there were numerous differences between the Jewish lending banks and Christian banks, one over all: the Jews worked according to the *condotta* stipu-

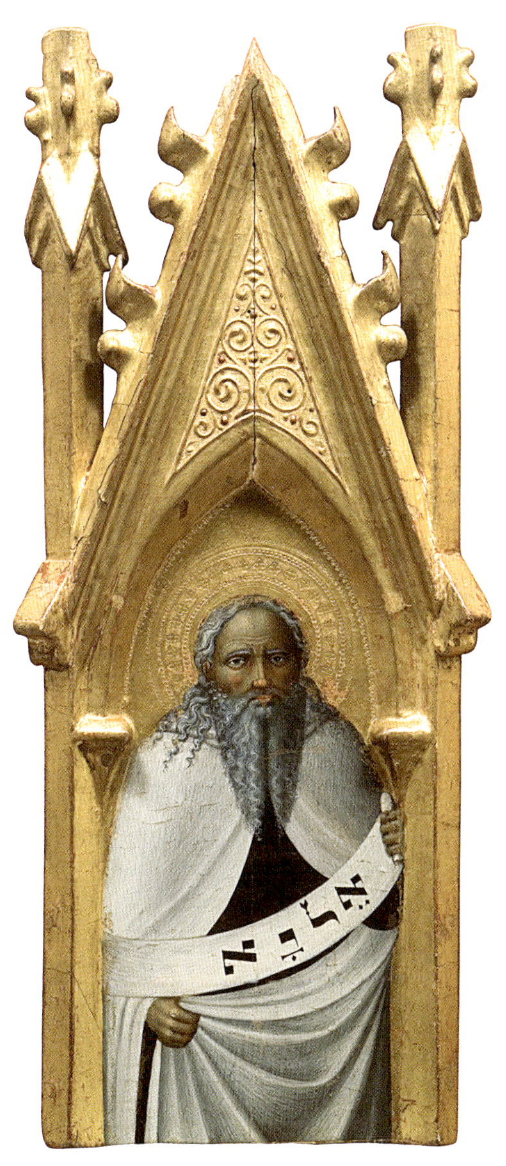
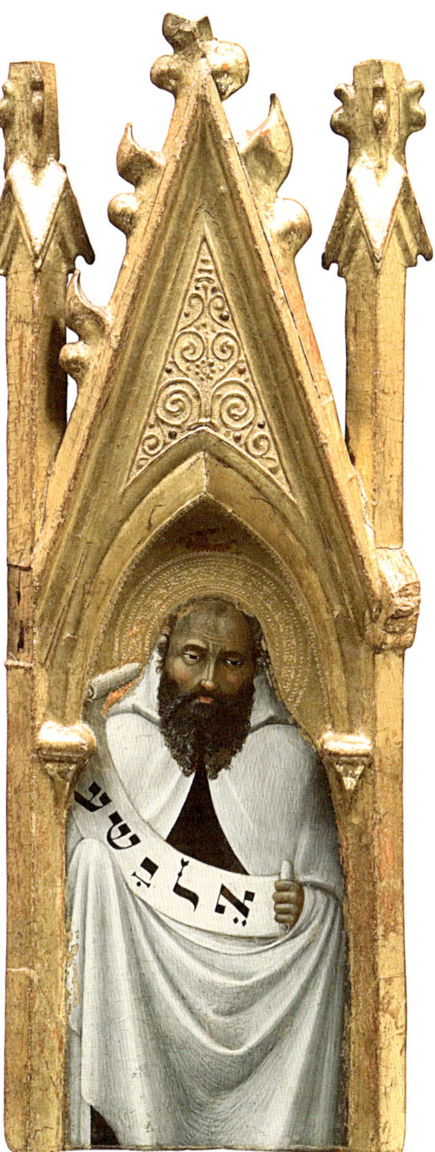

lated with the city authorities and according to known regulations and easily controllable methods, unlike private Christian lenders. Likewise, there were many differences between private pledge loan banks and the Monti di Pietà. The three main differences regarded the public nature of the Monte, which also affected the formation of capital available to customers; the identification of a type of needy person as its chosen customer, or rather, as the institution's only possible customer; and the request, when there was one, for an interest that in the Monti's case was a simple reimbursement of expenses, equal to about 5% per year, as opposed to interest at least seven, eight times higher, but legitimately requested, when it came to Jewish lenders who had made precise agreements with the city authorities.

So the Monte offered a service that was similar but distinct from that of private lenders, Jews or Christians. The Monte was unable to cover the same roles as private bankers, or satisfy the same customers. This would result in the possibility of coexistence and indeed the opportunity for a sort of support system. Things in most cities did not go that way, and in conjunction with the proposal to found a Monte, the relationship with Jews, lenders and non-lenders, became subject to reassessment. The intention to do without the Jews arose from the sermons aimed at proposing a Monte Pio (Bernardino Tomitano da Feltre 1964) while from the chronicles or advisory Acts, something can be gleaned of how the institution's foundation affected the Christian-Jewish relationship. There is a vast difference in the way the sermons viewed the Jews before and after the 1460s, and this has to do with the founding of the first Monti.

In the late Middle Ages, preachers habitually intervened in social life, even harshly criticizing behaviors deemed incompatible with the principles of Christianity. These were not generic observations or abstract reproaches. One only has to think of the frequent criticisms of luxury and vanity, the denunciation of illicit games or suspicious trades. Statutory revisions are known to have been made following a series of sermons aimed at raising doubts and reservations but primarily to eradicate behaviors that did not respect Christian morality (Montesano 1995). If and when preachers referred to Christian-Jewish cohabitation before the mid-fifteenth century, this was mostly related to the opportunity to distinguish the Jews with a special sign (see cat. 26). A possible example is that of the Blessed Matteo da Girgenti who took part in the Sumptuary Law of the cities of Agrigento and Palermo but also took and supported restrictive measures against the Jews, subject to prohibitions and limitations since the time of Frederick II (Mulè 2009). In the late 1420s, Matteo's sermons dealt not only with the theme of distinction but also with Jews being prohibited from living in close proximity to Christians, and this a century before the *Cum nimis absurdum* Bull (1555). The latter imposed "enclosure" of the Jews, all forced to live within the confines of the ghetto. When speaking of usury, Matteo targeted more Christians than Jews.

In the sermons held by Bernardino da Siena in Campo di Fiori in 1427 (Bernardino da Siena 1989) practically the only reference to the Jews is precisely in reference to the sign, an "O" on the chest, a means to appropriately recognize the Jews in accordance with what had been established for the first time in 1215 by the fourth Lateran Council. Bernardino speaks of it in a sermon on "taking sides" (XXIII) to condemn partisan leanings also by exhibiting specific signs ("those who wore signs distinguishing the Guelph or Ghibelline side"). Those distinctive signs that for the Sienese preacher were a source of tensions and violence became opportune when imposed on the Jews to avoid unwanted familiarity and mingling. On closer inspection, the sign that also distinguished the Jews was potentially and in some cases actually an instigator of violence against Jews. The ancient obligation

3. *Decree issued by Duke Ercole I d'Este requiring Jews to wear a distinctive yellow symbol*, Modena, March 13 and 17, 1498. Archivio di Stato, Modena (cat. 26)

was applied loosely over the centuries and with a certain patchiness, but proposed and imposed time and time again with varying intensity. This in a society that distinguished its ranks and members by external signs, by fabrics, colors and garment shapes, for different social affiliations (Muzzarelli 1996).

It is known that Bernardino inspired statutory revisions and repeatedly preached against waste, vanity, without or almost without referring to the Jews. The same Bernardino and other Franciscan confreres were called into question however, albeit indirectly, to justify the change in attitude toward the Jewish presence recorded in Orvieto at the end of the 1420s (Santilli 2017). In fact, in 1427, Christians were again warned that they were no longer to have relations with the Jews and to cancel immunities and privileges particularly related to money lending. This was happening in the first half of the fifteenth century, so totally unrelated to the proposal to create a Monte. In Orvieto, admonition developed into a vote in the Council where the motion to annul the relationship was approved by a very large majority. But the need for credit services that then arose prevailed over the emotion incited by the preachers: relationships were resumed but then called into question again after Bartolomeo di Colle Val d'Elsa's sermon in preparation for the establishment of a Monte. The *condotta* was cancelled and the Monte was founded. This is one of the many cases for consideration that bring us back to the connection between the attacks on Jews by preachers and the proposal for foundation of a Monte. There was talk of an open war between Jews and the preaching Observant friars, but there were also less fraught periods and cases of inter-socializing (Toaff 1989).

It is well known that the preachers played a role in spreading information and education, but this role must be emphasized. Prepared to convince, and therefore mastering the techniques required to be effective (Muzzarelli 2005), when they committed to supporting and spreading the public bank with its system of theoretical solidarity and *modus operandi* coherent with the nature of the institute called Monte Pio, they resorted to every possible argument and to various strategies that might achieve the goal. Singling out the Jews as responsible for a widespread state of poverty, emphasizing their diversity of faith and customs and their privileged connection with the ruling class as being harmful to the poorest was a choice that proved effective among the masses. The best-known preachers attracted great throngs in squares where thousands of people gathered many hours in advance, even coming from afar to get a good spot for watching a highly anticipated event. Suggesting to these crowds that the Monte was the solution and that the Jews were the enemy and should be fought became part of the method used to propose and support the new institution. This happened virtually everywhere with not quite identical outcomes. Some cities renounced their relationship with the Jews and others maintained it. In Bologna, where the Monte was founded in 1473, after a year of business the institute closed and the citizens continued to use the services of the Jews, maintaining the centuries-old relationship.

In 1462, Michele Carcano threatened excommunication in Perugia, where the first Monte Pio was founded, if agreements with the moneylenders were not terminated, thus hailing in an operating method destined to spread. The script included threats to the authorities, warnings to the citizens, promises in this life and the next one of rewards to those who supported the Monte, proposed as a solution for the credit needs of the "less poor poor." The fate of the extremely poor was separate, and entailed alms. There was no consideration of the fate of those who did not fall into the category of the "less poor poor." The Monte di Perugia, forefather of the series, effectively represents the contradiction inherent in the attack on the Jews, together with the need for their money to finance the founding of the Monte itself (Majarelli and Nicolini 1962).

In the reconstruction of the foundation of this or that Monte, one or another Franciscan preacher is attributed with, in many cases, forwarding the proposal in harsh and offensive tones directed at the feneratious Jews. It should be stated that aggressive attacks were recorded even before the second half of the fifteenth century. While we have mentioned the case of Orvieto, what specifically draws our attention is the regularity and intensity of the attacks after 1460.

In this regard, there is the illuminating case of Bernardino da Feltre, serial founder of Monti di Pietà, who dedicated the last ten years of his life (1484–94) to spreading and supporting the institutions. We have the text of some of his sermons about the Monti, in which the creation of the institution, recommended for an extensive series of reasons, is placed in correlation with the end of the relationship with the Jews: the sermons state that the Monti "ward off sins, save the soul, support the body, helps the poor, relieve the wealthy, and does away with the Jews" (sermon no. 55); that the Jews "devour the poor" and that for no reason it should be "allowed to keep usurers" (sermon no. 56). But as a whole, in four sermons strictly related to the creation of the Monti (sermons nos. 55, 56, 57, and 73) there are very few references to the Jews. A different picture emerges from the reading of the "Life of Blessed Bernardino da Feltre" (1439–1494), written in 1573 by Bernardino Guslino (Checcoli 2008), a text thickly punctuated with allusions to the Jews: about 25% of the edition's pages contain reference to them. Bernardino da Feltre's biographer tells us that he specifically addressed the Jews' lending practices, and did this in order to declare that it was ruinous for the Christians and heralded divine punishments such as the plague. According to him, the rulers should be responsible for returning the loans, cancelling the pacts made, and working to create a Monte. This was roughly the script, with some significant variations such as attacks on trust in regard to Jewish doctors or the blaming of those who had family connections with the Jews (Christians participating in Jewish feasts and in general "conversing with them"). These sermons were veritable "attacks on spontaneous sociability, especially playful sociability, aimed at erecting a wall of estrangement between Jews and Christians" of which Albano Biondi spoke (Biondi 1994). In an essay published in 2015 in *The Jewish-Christian Encounter in Medieval Preaching*, which is full of information and reflections on the Jews in the sermons, I investigated the practical consequences of Bernardino da Feltre's words for Jews (Muzzarelli 2015). He promised to "wipe" the cities clean of the Jews and many effects of his preaching can be gleaned from the biography, starting with the well-known case of the child, Simon of Trent ("whose case was discovered by the blessed Bernardino"). The Jews were accused of his death, with devastating consequences for the local community. In Pavia during the Lent of 1480 "he often spoke out against the Jews and their usury and the conversations that Christians had with them," to the extent that a commissioner of the Duke of Milan arrived with ducal letters which asked that the Jews be left alone, that "neither should one get heated up over their ruin" (p. 91). Preaching in Mantua in April 1484, he maintained that the princes should "be aware of the Jewish usury carried out in their cities" (p. 107) and said many other terrible things, concluding without giving the blessing, which "pleased the city and especially the people" but worried the nobility. The examples could go on, effectively emphasizing the preacher's attack on the Jews and the consequences of his words enjoyed by the masses but not by the nobility, nor, presumably, by the intellectuals. The nobility appreciated his moral preaching but not his political opposition to the Jews. In Assisi, his preaching provoked the expulsion of the Jews: the latter mostly suffered but sometimes resisted or reacted primarily by asking the authorities to respect the agreements stipulated. Certainly foremost in Bernardino's mind and preaching was the objective of founding the Monti di Pietà and the attack on the Jews appears to be mainly for this purpose. However, another more general declared objective was to end relations between Christians and Jews. In various cities he preached against those who had "conversation" with them, speaking of the damage caused by those who favored and supported them. On several occasions, he urged the people not to fall into the hands of Jewish doctors. For centuries they had enjoyed the trust of Christians in cities where they did not hesitate to stipulate specific *condotte* to practice medicine. From Guslino's reconstruction, which is perhaps affected by the deterioration in the relationship after the mid-sixteenth century, having been written in 1573, it is inferred that this preacher's persuasive power was truly remarkable and probably based largely on the involvement of the people in town squares. Historiography often attributes early-medieval preachers with the intention of reinforcing social cohesion and sees them as peacemakers in city conflicts, but this is only partly true for Bernardino da Feltre. His sermons about the Jews caused arguments, fear, created conflicts if not riots, and changed the banking landscape.

That the words of the preachers were and came to be considered effective indirectly proves the phenomenon of forced conversion through preaching—in other words, the obligation for Jews to attend sermons, one of the means identified to compel them to convert. According to Anna Foa, it was the most spectacular approach used in the conversionist movement of the early modern age (Foa 1992). This practice had a long tradition dating back to the late thirteenth century, when forced conversion through preaching was introduced in Spain by the Dominicans, and then vigorously resumed in the second half of the sixteenth century at the time of the so-called "Infamous papal bulls" (Milano 1963). In 1584, the Jews of Rome were obliged to listen to a sermon held every Saturday by the most famous converts who knew what subjects to use and how to make them attractive. But the results seem to have been modest.

The preacher's words could have sway and very much depended on the natural gifts of the individual, his preparation, the goal that he wished to achieve and the expectations of the public, but also the historical phase in which he was preaching. In the fifteenth and sixteenth centuries, an important redefinition of the Christian-Jewish relationship occurred in which the preachers, not only Franciscans but also Dominicans—one needs only to refer to Vincent Ferrer (Losada 2015)—played an important part. What took place with the Monti di Pietà appears emblematic and illuminating in terms of the role of communication, partially carried out by the preachers.

At the end of the sixteenth century, in many parts of Italy the Jewish-Christian relationship atrophied: preachers and Jews no longer spoke to each other. A fruitful cohabitation that had endured for centuries fell silent.

Translated by Elizabeth Burke

4. Luca Signorelli, *Crucifixion*, 1494.
Galleria Nazionale delle Marche, Palazzo
Ducale, Urbino

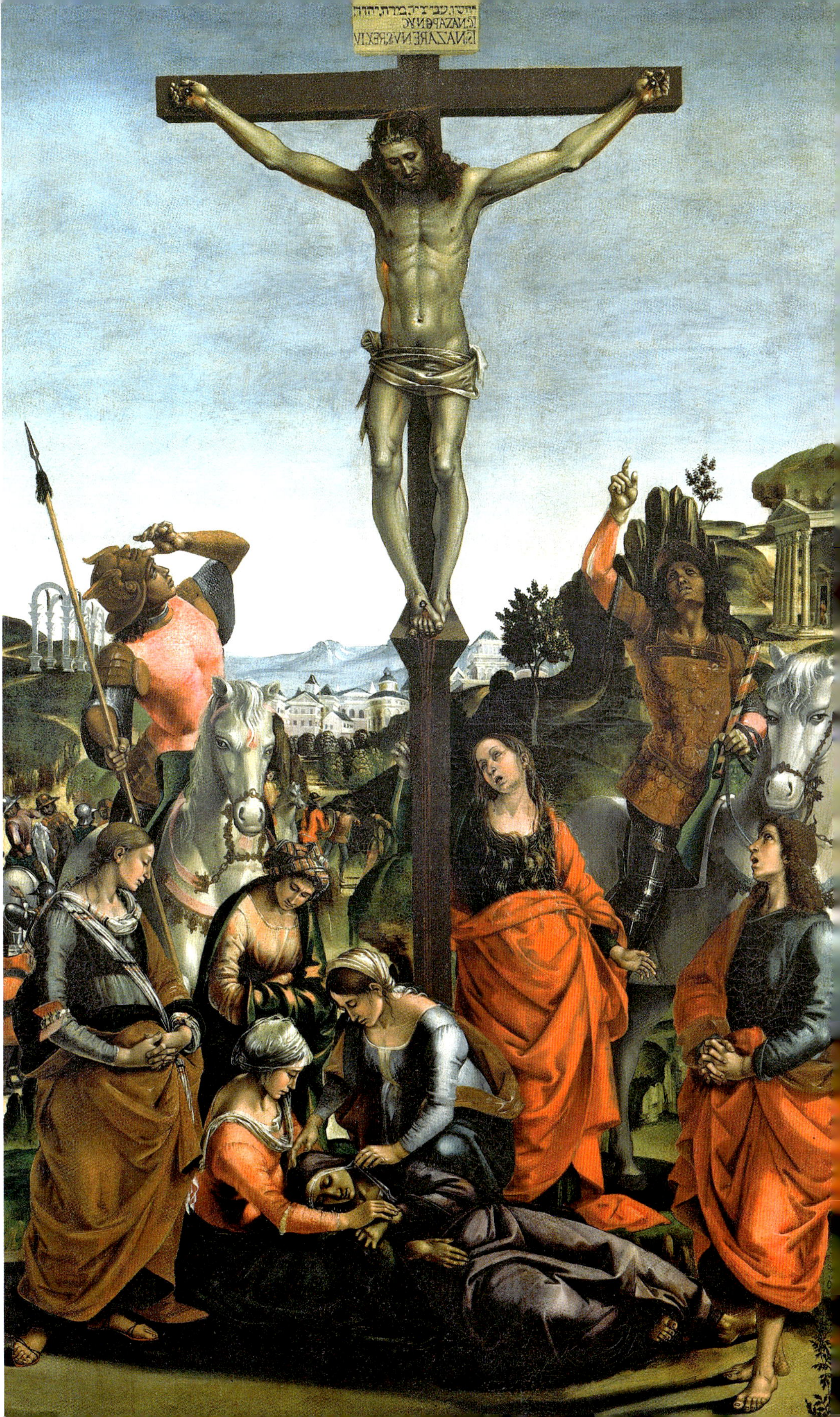
INRI
IGNAZARENVC
SNAZAREINVSREYA

Mantua 1495–1514: Three "Madonnas of the Jews"
Salvatore Settis

In memory of Michele Luzzati

1. The history behind Andrea Mantegna's *Madonna of Victory*, now in the Louvre (fig. 1), is an unusual one. It shows how and to what extent the initiative of the court and the ruler—the occasion and the "invention" of the picture—can be shaped by public concerns and forces, even some that are less praiseworthy. But it shows, too, how shaky our usual categories of judgment can be: anyone, looking at the painting today, would tend to identify the donor in the image of the soldier in armour, kneeling in prayer at the Virgin's feet. And in a certain sense this is true, but here we have a donor who did not shell out one cent for the picture, because he found a way of making someone else pay for it in cash: a Jewish merchant accused of sacrilege.

The celebration of the debatable, ephemeral victory that the Marquis of Mantua, Francesco II Gonzaga, achieved at Fornovo on July 6, 1495 at the head of the army of the anti-French Italic League against the troops of Charles VIII of France (Bourne 2008, pp. 65–99) gave the picture the name by which it is still known today, even on the walls of the Louvre. But this was not the only reason behind this outsized *ex voto*. Entwined with the military virtues of the Marquis in the events that led up to the commissioning and execution of the painting are the private troubles of Daniele Norsa (or "da Norsa"), son of Leone, who had moved to Mantua shortly before. In 1493 he had bought as his home a house in the city (Portioli 1882–84, pp. 58–59) and soon obtained from the bishop's vicar permission "to have taken down the images of saints" that were painted on the exterior or a wall of the vestibule (ibid., p. 75); "and I paid everything the lord vicar ordered me to," Norsa opportunely adds, recounting the background of the matter in a petition he addressed to the Marquis on May 29, 1495 (ibid., pp. 60–61). If he wanted to erase these Christian images from the outside wall of his home it was not only to remove the vivid sign of a religion he did not share, but also out of fear that others might damage the fresco and then wrongly accuse him because he was a Jew: "and worrying … that said figures might be ruined by someone other than me … the blame might fall on me" (ibid; see also Luzzati 1983, p. 867, note 25).

As Michele Luzzati rightly maintained, Daniele Norsa must have had in mind a precedent of a few years earlier, that is, the long negotiations for erasing two images of Saint Christopher (one on the exterior and the other in the interior of a house) that took place in Pisa in 1491. The protagonists were Isacco di Vitale da Pisa, a member of the richest and most influential family of Jewish bankers in Italy, and the civic and religious authorities of the city. It is not possible here to give a summary of these complex negotiations, which the documents enable us to follow closely as they unfolded, but it is worthwhile to note, with Luzzati, the contrast between what happened in Pisa and the very different outcome of Norsa's request in Mantua. The da Pisa family had lived in the house in question since 1408 (immediately after the conquest of Pisa by Florence), first as renters and then, from 1466, as owners, but they waited another twenty-five years before asking permission to remove the Christian images, and they asked both the archbishop's vicar and the civic authorities. After various site visits and notarized documents, the images were finally erased, almost a year after the request was made, in the presence of a notary who drew up a public document. And the whole matter ended there. Isacco da Pisa in turn probably had in mind another precedent, a similar episode that took place in Gubbio in 1471, concerning the Jew Samuele di Consiglio, who had family and business ties with Da Pisa (Luzzati 1983, p. 849 and note 6).

It was thus on the basis of earlier examples, in particular that of Pisa, which he must have known, that Daniele Norsa attempted to do the same. But he made two mistakes: the first mistake was that, after obtaining authorization from the bishop and paying what was asked of him, he did not ask permission from the Marquis's government; his second mistake was to proceed immediately to destroy the sacred image. Where the da Pisa family had lived with those Christian images for almost a century and had very prudently negotiated their destruction over a period of many months, documenting every step with notarized statements, Norsa wanted to do everything without delay and just a few short years after buying the house. Perhaps he was counting on Francesco II's tacit consent, given that the bishop of Mantua at the time was his uncle Ludovico Gonzaga; and perhaps he was not aware, or not aware enough, that the uncle and nephew did not get along (indeed, there was "fierce enmity"), in part because the uncle bishop aspired to a cardinal's hat, which Francesco II wanted (and ended up attaining) for his brother Sigismondo (Luzzati 1983, pp. 866–67, note 24).

Daniele Norsa paid dearly for these errors of judgment. Their consequences drove him back into all the vulnerability of his condition as a Jew subject to gratuitous abuses of power and oppression of every sort. On May 27, 1495 (two days before the above-mentioned petition to Francesco II), during a procession for the Feast of the Ascension, "certain images of saints were placed facing that house, where as the procession passed by everyone looked and many people shouted and threw rocks at the house." Norsa was not at home just then; only intervention by the Captain of the Guards Jacopo da Capua ended "such excess." By his very vagueness in describing the images ("certain images of saints") in his petition to the Marquis, the Jew Daniele seems to be distancing himself from his modest, negotiated, iconoclasm. But other sources tell us that the figures "taken down" from the exterior of his home were (at least) the Virgin and Child. The petition did not go unheeded: on June 11, 1495 Francesco II granted broad safe-conduct permissions to the Jews in his state, and Daniele Norsa was cited at the head of the list (Luzzati 1983, pp. 847 and 856, note 3; according to other scholars, for example Katz 2000, p. 475, the decree was issued by the marchioness Isabella in her husband's absence, but not necessarily without his knowledge). Seemingly this concluded the matter; but the worst was yet to come.

On July 6 of that same year Francesco II won his first military victory at Fornovo. His attempt to cut off the French army's progress was unsuccessful, but the Marquis had fought skilfully and valiantly, and the enemy's behavior after the battle—their precipitous flight and the advantageous terms offered by Philippe de Commynes on his king's behalf the next day—led the episode to be interpreted, in the next days and then in the echo that soon spread all over Italy, as a great victory (Mazzoldi 1961, vol. II, pp. 101 ff.; Bourne 2008, pp. 67–68). On July 31 the Marquis, who was besieging Duke Louis of Orléans holed up in Novara, seemed suddenly to recall the painting erased from Norsa's house and wrote to his brother Sigismondo (apostolic protonotary and not yet cardinal) in Mantua:

> We remember that on the corner of the house that used to belong to Scaldamazi toward San Simone there was painted the figure of Our Lady, and after the Jews bought it this appears to have been scraped away; and since it seems [that] an insult to the glorious mother and our most holy faith is a disgrace, arrange that, under whatever terms of punishment you deem proper, the Jews with all due speed have it remade as elaborate and beautiful as possible, and do this with such diligence that when we come home we can see it to our satisfaction (Kristeller 1902, p. 558 no. 134).

Francesco II evidently hand in mind putting the painting back on the wall where it had been. He remembered the figure before Norsa had had it "scraped away," but it almost seems as though he had just learned of the incident recently, even though he had been in residence in his state at the time it happened (just two months earlier), had received Norsa's petition about this matter, and indeed had reacted favorably, as we have said; nor did he fear annoying his uncle the bishop, who had given, upon payment, his permission to "scrape away" the image. Thus the process was set in motion that would result in the *Madonna of Victory* by Andrea Mantegna.

Sigismondo Gonzaga must have passed the assignment received from his brother on to the Augustinian hermit Fra Girolamo Redini. It was he who wrote to the Marquis on August 8, already revealing he had grander plans:

> I have urged up to today to see to it that the blessed image of Our Lady which was taken down by the Jews at their expense be remade, beautiful and very elaborate, as noble and devout as possible, to appease … Jesus Christ, who was too greatly offended by this … Our Father Marcho Antonio Da Porto says that certainly Your Lordship must build a church in that house, which will be called Saint Mary of Victory … In this month Mr. Andrea Mantegna, at the fervent urging of your brother the Most Reverend Monsignor, will do the picture of this image and you, armed as a victorious captain, will be along with your brothers [Francesco II had two brothers, Sigismondo, the future cardinal, and Giovanni] under the cloak on one side, and on the other your Most Illustrious spouse (Kristeller 1902, p. 558 no. 135).

The minimal act of devotion envisioned by the Marquis (to restore the image erased from Norsa's house in its original place and form, that is, a fresco on the exterior) was thus transformed, in his absence and by the actions of three churchmen, into a much more ambitious project: to turn the Jew's house into a church and to put a painting by Mantegna in it, with the intention of uniting the expiation of Norsa's sacrilege with celebration of the victory at Fornovo. Or, to put it more maliciously, to make the Jewish merchant pay the cost of the *Madonna of Victory*. These documents reveal that it was not Francesco II who took the initiative of a church and a picture to commemorate his endeavour and express his gratitude for the protection he received from Heaven. It appears that the idea was beginning to take shape in Mantua while Francesco was in Novara; along with Sigismondo

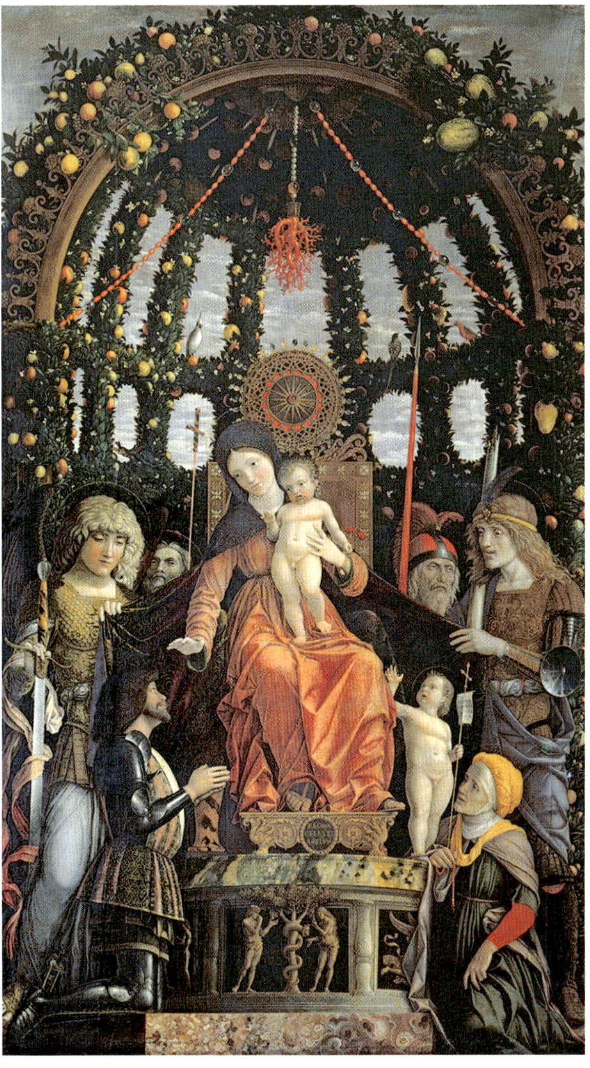

1. Andrea Mantegna, *Madonna of Victory*, 1495–96. Musée du Louvre, Paris

Gonzaga and Fra Redini, a third churchman seems to have played a major role, Marco Antonio Da Porto, at the time famous for his mystical visions (Togliani 2009, p. 163), who originally had the idea of turning the sacrilegious Jew's house into a church to be named after Our Lady of Victory. The Marquis's first intention (to restore the image "scraped away" by the Jew) grew into a completely different plan: an altarpiece in a new church to be built for this purpose. And the commission for the painting was given—for the "satisfaction" of the Marquis upon his return home—to none other than Andrea Mantegna, the artist who enjoyed the greatest prestige at the court of Mantua. To persuade Francesco II, Redini used specious and underhanded arguments in his letter: divine wrath, of which "God has shown great signs, which you will discern later"; the information (which we know to be false) that the house had been a church dedicated to Our Lady, "as later we shall give you to understand"; visions "of this blessed image" that were already circulating about the city, to the "great consolation" of all. These are vague impressions and claims, which are not substantiated by the known documents, but were used to argue in favor of the Jews doing "what was necessary with all due speed and at their expense."

It is easy to see that Francesco II found attractive the idea of transforming the new image of the Virgin into a celebration of his victory at Fornovo, and what is more, painted by Mantegna at zero expense for the Marquis's coffers. Redini was already submitting for his approval an early idea of the iconography: sheltered under the Virgin's cloak on one side Francesco II and his brothers and on the other his wife Isabella d'Este, as though this were a family *ex voto*. Only the fact that Francesco would be "armed like a victorious captain" alludes to his recent victory. The Marquis replied by return courier (August13), ordering his brother

> … that the Jew Daniele of Norsa have made in front of his house, in the spot where it was before, an image of the glorious Virgin Mary costing 110 gold ducats, made by the hand of Andrea Mantegna, and said Daniele must disburse this money within three days … and if he doesn't pay within that time … you will order him to be hanged in front of his house in the very spot where the image was painted … and his house be taken away from him (Kristeller 1902, p. 559 no. 136).

It is a rather curious sensation to read the alternative proposed by this letter to placate divine wrath: either paint another Madonna or hang the sacrilegious Jew on that same spot ("in front of his house"). But the enormity of the threatened punishment and the brevity of the time granted (three days) indicate that the Marquis had already made his decision and did not want to leave Norsa any choice. Nonetheless, Francesco II continued to speak of an image to be painted (albeit by Mantegna) exactly where it was before, that is to say on the exterior wall of the desecrated house; nor does he mention the idea of building a church there, as though he had absentmindedly skimmed Redini's letter of a few days before. Indeed, confiscation of Norsa's house is foreseen only—along with hanging—among the extreme consequences, in case he did not want to pay the prescribed sum immediately. Moreover, the letter does not mention the iconography but only the high cost of the painting, "which merits this price"; but perhaps such a high cost indicates that the figures to be painted would not be done in the fresco technique and may have been more than just the Virgin and Child. At any rate, a mechanism had been set in motion, to Norsa's detriment, which could not be reversed: everybody, from the Marquis to his brother Sigismondo, and Redini and Da Porto, all are clear on the advantages of a painting by Mantegna at the injudicious Jew's expense.

2. In the face of these threats (death, confiscation of property), Daniele Norsa handed over the sum of money on the same day he was told to (Kristeller 1902, p. 559 no. 137). And Redini soon resumed putting pressure on the Marquis with a new letter, dated August 29, in which he reiterated the terms of his earlier one, to which Francesco II had not properly replied:

> I wrote a few days ago and on behalf of my Father Marco Antonio that those houses should be made into a church, which will be Saint Mary of Victory. This same thing has been confirmed by your brother Monsignor. In this way: his Most Reverend Lordship will command, keeping your suggestion in mind, that Andrea Mantegna make two saints, one on either side of the Madonna, holding her cloak under which will be your Lordship in armor, that is Saint George and Saint Michael, which everybody likes very much, but especially I, for the words that he added wisely and I believe inspired by God, saying that these two saints were victorious, one for the body and the other for the soul, and that these two together with the Most Holy Mother of Christ, your devoted advocate and only hope, will give victory to your Most Illustrious Lordship; and he said in closing that he hoped to see a beautiful devotion in that place (Kristeller 1902, p. 560 no. 138).

The roles here are well distinguished: Marco Antonio Da Porto had the idea of building a church dedicated to Saint Mary of Victory, while the iconography of the altarpiece was the work of Sigismondo Gonzaga, who however, even though writing a letter to accompany Redini's, left to the friar the task of describing, for Francesco II's reference but also for Mantegna's, what should be in the painting.

In this second iconographical program some essential points have changed compared to the earlier one: the Virgin does not lift her cloak with her own hands, as was usual for the type of the Virgin of Mercy (Belting-Ihm 1976), but lets it be held by two warrior saints "victorious for the body and the soul," Saint George and Saint Michael the Archangel. Furthermore, the Marquis's brothers (including Sigismondo himself) and his wife have disappeared from the original plan which placed them under the Virgin's cloak: alongside the Virgin and saints, Francesco II remains alone. When this letter was written Mantegna had not yet set his hand to painting the picture, but "he wants to do an excellent job" (Sigismondo Gonzaga to his brother, in Kristeller 1902, p. 560 no. 138). The changes between the first and second versions of the program seem to have been made with the aim of exalting Francesco II by showing him armed and next to two warrior saints so as to highlight the allusion to a military victory. Was it Sigismondo (with his advisers Girolamo Redini and Marco Antonio Da Porto) who changed the plan for the painting? Maybe; in any case, it seems that this is what Redini is saying. But then, is it not strange that the Marquis's brother had arranged for his own image to be cancelled out in the passage from the first to the second program?

We must ask ourselves another question: what was (if there was) Francesco II's personal intervention in the painting? In the few months he spent in Mantua between the siege of Novara and the expedition to the Kingdom of Naples (from early November 1495 to February 22, 1496), he must have continued orally the conversation with his brother and with Redini (and probably also Da Porto) begun by letter. Indeed, it was only his absence from Mantua in the months when the program of the painting was taking shape that occasioned the correspondence we have reviewed in part, enabling us to recount the picture's back story before Mantegna set hand to brush. On the contrary, for the period when

Francesco II was in Mantua, no archive can ever give us the conversations held at court or in Mantegna's studio, where the artist was at work painting. And the personal influence of the Marquis, as well as any other changes suggested by his advisers or his artist, can only be read in the final results of the painting as we know it. What is certain is that already on 6 July 1496, on the first anniversary of the battle of Fornovo, not only Mantegna's painting but also the new church of Santa Maria della Vittoria were ready. The Marquis was in Campania on the day of the solemn consecration of the church and painting; this is why we can fortunately grasp an echo of it in the letters of his correspondents (Kristeller 1902, p. 560 no. 138; p. 561 no. 140, letter from Sigismondo Gonzaga of July 6; pp. 561–62 no. 141, letter from Antimaco of July 7; p. 562 no. 142, letter from Marchioness Isabella of July 12).

The "beautiful procession" that carried the painting through the city into the new church was "ordered," i.e., organized according to an appropriate ritual, by Sigismondo Gonzaga himself, who in fact gives the best description of it. Mantegna's painting was placed on a sort of triumphal litter, "most majestically adorned" and carried by twenty bearers; all around paraded "a young man dressed as God the Father," prophets, apostles, and angels "singing certain lauds." But above all,

> … Friar Petro da Caneto gave a beautiful speech in the vernacular to the people in praise of the glorious Virgin, urging them to hold her in devotion, reminding them that it was she who liberated Your Excellency on a similar day [i.e., the same date one year before] from many perils, and that we should all pray to her to keep you happy in the future. And in this manner truly everybody prayed with one voice: so that Your Lordship should draw great consolation from so much love and reverence as this entire people shows toward you, [they] who are not at all ungrateful for the good things that you do for them all the time … I believe that in a short time it [Mantegna's altarpiece] will attract very great devotion (Kristeller 1902, p. 560 no. 138).

Indeed, as his secretary Matteo Sacchetti (known as Antimaco) wrote to Francesco II, the exultant people could not "get enough of seeing such a worthy work [Mantegna's picture], especially—besides the image of the Virgin—that of Your Most Illustrious Lordship, which fills everyone with tenderness," while the Marchioness Isabella "stayed at the window … to see the show pass by" (Kristeller 1902, p. 562 no. 141).

In this episode in Mantua, private and public devotion combine with themes of personal and dynastic propaganda, while Norsa's financial contribution and the merciless threats to which he had been subjected had faded into oblivion. Besides, Sigismondo Gonzaga himself had predicted almost a year earlier the "great shared feeling of devotion" that he recounted to his brother in July 1496—or perhaps we should say, planned and fomented (ibid., p. 560 no. 138). "A great shared rush of devotion," "many Masses," and "many votive candles" to the new Madonna are mentioned in a letter from Benedetto Capilupi to the Marquis of August 3, 1496, less than a month after the solemn opening of the house of worship (ibid., p. 562 no. 143). But the matter was not yet closed: on June 16, 1497 Jacopo da Capua wrote to Francesco II, who was out of town, that the Norsa family, fearing that he, after having dinner "with Father Iheronimo [Redini] … and with Father Marco Antonio … might decide to expel the Jews from Mantua," were offering him as a gift what was left of their houses at Santa Maria della Vittoria, "and they will do whatever Your Excellency wishes" provided that "Father Iheronimo does not bother them any more," suggesting that it was Redini who wanted to take possession of their remaining property on that site. Four days later (June 20) the Marquis replied with satisfaction that "those Jews in the house at Santa Maria della Vittoria … very gladly and willingly" were open to giving him their house: "so you will thank them on our behalf for that house, and you will give them to understand … that they did not do this to someone with a short memory" (Bourne 2008, pp. 400–1 nos. 144 and 145). Thus it was that the little convent annexed to the church was built, "a little place for the residence of a good hermit named Girolamo Redini, that he may officiate it," according to the words of Ippolito Donesmondi (Donesmondi 1612–16, vol. II, pp. 85–86). Finally appeased, two months later (August 19, 1497) Francesco II once again assumed the role of the magnanimous ruler, granting the Jews in his state, Norsa first and foremost, a *Liberatio a singulis delictis, criminibus, facinoribus, flagitiis, debitis et obligationibus*, a sort of plenary absolution extended also "to the profanation of sacred images—a matter of which the Marquis had been made aware, but was not proved" (Luzzati 1983, pp. 855 ff. and p. 869, note 27). This is a highly unusual clause, as though the Marquis, somewhat absentmindedly, had forgotten that he had threatened Daniele Norsa with death just a year earlier, extorting from him the entire cost of an Andrea Mantegna painting. Or rather as though, mollified by that disbursement and the "voluntary" gift of the house, he just pretended not to remember what had actually happened.

3. Daniele Norsa's justifications, which had been brutally repressed, could no longer be heeded by this point, nor was it opportune to draw attention to his role as the sole financer of Mantegna's commission for the altarpiece. It had been all too convenient to channel the strong feelings expressed by the people on Ascension Eve of 1495 over the "scraped" image, but even more against the Jew, into a new object of worship: a brand new artwork. But in Mantegna's painting, now quite famous, in a significant and unpredictable departure with respect to the immediate occasion (reparations for sacrilege), the dominant theme becomes the special protection granted by the Virgin to the Marquis-captain: the easy victory over the Jew has given way to the questionable victory at Fornovo, and "devotion" for the Virgin is mixed with "reverence" for the lord of Mantua by his subjects.

In the meantime the church of Santa Maria della Vittoria had been built; it still stands there today, although desecrated and ruined by a floor slab that slices across the space, forming two separate floors. After the traumatic removal of Mantegna's altarpiece, the little church lost all of its dignity and later also its liturgical function; it was clumsily partitioned off and used as military storage space, a sculptor's workshop, and a nursery school. Recent restoration (2005–6) brought to light important remnants of the original fresco decoration, which should naturally be read concomitantly with Mantegna's altarpiece. And too, it would be an easy matter, by tearing down the nineteenth-century floor slab defacing the space, to recover its original volume. Thus in this church, "built according to Andrea's order and design" (an improbable attribution coming from Vasari), the *Madonna of Victory*, along with the Mantegnesque frescoes made to surround it (pilaster strips, candelabras, bunches of acanthus leaves, twelve saints in the webs), would be better able to tell its unusual story. (On the restoration of the church and the fresco remnants, see Agosti 2005, p. 223; Bazzotti 2006, pp. 200–19; Agosti 2008, pp. 297 ff.; Bazzotti 2010, pp. 669–86.)

Mantegna painted the figures adhering scrupulously to the second version of the iconographical program devised by Sigismondo Gonzaga and Girolamo Redini, even if (obviously) making it richer and more precise. Francesco II wearing armor and in a devout pose—the only one among all the figures to be presented with a slight *sott'in su* effect—is the only living person present. The Virgin, welcoming him under her cloak, looks his way, just leaning her head toward him and stretching out her right hand to protect him (Schleif 1993, pp. 1–32, esp. 23–28; it should be noted that this unusual gesture probably derives from the statue of Marcus Aurelius on the Capitoline Hill, represented as *pacator orbis*). Also the Christ Child looks at the Marquis and blesses him; on the other side of the throne are the infant Saint John the Baptist and his mother Elizabeth (whose name corresponds to that of the Marchioness Isabella). Joining the two warrior saints mentioned in the second iconographical program, dressed by Mantegna in fantastical gilded armor, are the two patron saints of Mantua, Andrew and Longinus, peeping over the edge of the cloak held by Saint Michael and Saint George. In the medallion on the Virgin's footstool is the inscription "Regina celi let[are] alleluia" (Queen of Heaven, rejoice, hallelujah), while around the base of the throne are three faux reliefs: in the center the original sin, with half-hidden panels on either side. In the first panel can be recognized God shaping Adam (Signorini 1996, pp. 303–4), therefore the winged figure in the last one, largely hidden by Saint Elizabeth's cloak, must be the angel who drove Adam and Eve out of the garden of Eden, even if it is modeled on a pagan winged victory, in any case appropriate in the context of the painting.

This little crowd of figures which, "wisely and I believe inspired by God," Sigismondo Gonzaga chose to gather around his kneeling brother does not just celebrate the victory over the French, which had already happened, but is aimed at guaranteeing future military glory for Francesco II: "Saint George and Saint Michael … with the Most Holy Mother of Christ, your advocate … will give victory to your Most Illustrious Lordship" (Kristeller 1902, p. 560 no. 138). Therefore, in this same church, Francesco II gave as a votive offering to the Virgin the armor he wore at Fornovo, as was the custom in the nearby shrine of the Madonna delle Grazie (Donesmondi 1612–16, vol. II, p. 85. According to Margonari and Zanca 1973, p. 41, one of the suits of armor in the wooden balcony lining the nave of the shrine is "curiously similar" to the one worn by Francesco II in Mantegna's painting). Thus the picture is certainly an *ex voto* but also a manifesto of Francesco II's ambitions: just six months before the battle of Fornovo, the Doge Agostino Barbarigo had refused to appoint him Captain General of the Venetian Republic, "since Your Excellency is not expert in the use of weapons nor has ever been on the field" (Mazzoldi 1961, vol. II, p. 101). Precisely because of his mediocre reputation as a military man, when shortly thereafter the allied armies were united under his command, forced by circumstances, it was crucial for him to affirm his fighting prowess, and so he prepared for combat "with such great zeal that a greater [zeal] cannot be described," certain "not only to resist the French, but exterminate them forever" (ibid., p. 102). After Fornovo, the Doge ended up writing to him, praising his "prudence and generosity… immortal glory" and promising him "not just personally, but equally all your posterity and descendants … all those benevolent signs of honor, comfort and argument that in any way they might desire." And a few days later his greatly desired appointment as Captain General of the Venetian army arrived (ibid., pp. 105–6). The new victories that the *ex voto* painted by Mantegna was supposed to accrue to the Marquis are thus the hopes (his own and those of his court) for his fortunes as a military commander. This is another reason why the initial motive for setting in motion the commission for the *Madonna of Victory*—reparation for the sacrilege of which Daniele Norsa was accused—is completely absent from the picture; perhaps an allusion, albeit faint, could be the connection between the original sin shown on the base and redemption referenced in the inscription on the standard held by the infant Saint John: "Ecce Agnus Dei ecce q[u]i tollit p[eccata] m[undi]" (Behold the Lamb of God, who takes away the sins of the world), which could be interpreted as the exclusion of the Jews from Christian salvation.

And the inscription that Saverio Bettinelli tells us (1774) ran along the frame limits the intent and meaning of the altarpiece to the Marquis's gratitude to the Virgin Mary for the victory she had enabled: "Victoriae memor Franciscus sacravit" (Lightbown 1986, p. 427). The painter Mantegna could not help but be aware of the fact that the person paying for his work was not the soldier shown in arms, but a Jew whose back was against the wall. We shall never know how the artist truly felt about this aspect of the story.

4. Daniele Norsa paid a high price, and paid it in full. Then disappeared into the shadows without leaving a trace of his passage in the glorious painting by Mantegna. But there was someone who could not resign himself to letting the episode of the Jew's sacrilege and the easy victory of the powerful lord of Mantua over Norsa (who was punished, fined, and expropriated) fall into oblivion. Not Francesco II, who indeed a year after his cruel imposition assumed the guise of generous guarantor of a degree of freedom for the Jews who were his subjects, as we have seen. Not Sigismondo Gonzaga, who a few years later (1505) obtained the desired cardinal's hat from Julius II. It was instead Girolamo Redini, the Augustinian hermit friar who had followed and promoted the entire project, furnishing specious excuses to justify the persecutory measures against Norsa, dreaming up iconographies for Mantegna, and writing and talking with the Marquis, his brother Sigismondo, and the visionary mystic Marco Antonio Da Porto.

On March 9, 1498 Francesco II entrusted the care of the little church of Santa Maria della Vittoria to Redini as perpetual rector (Portioli 1882–84, p. 75; Togliani 2009, p. 175; it is unclear whether the subsequent concession of the church to the Hieronymites, ibid., p. 176, severed all Redini's ties with it), with a "little place of residence" for him, as we have

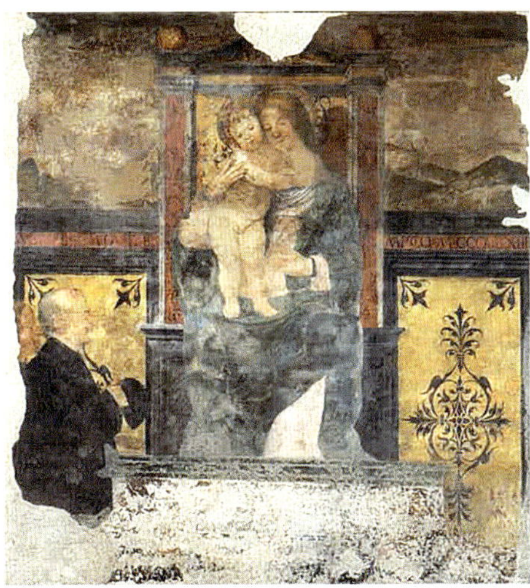

2. Mantuan fresco painter, "Madonna of the Jews," 1514. Palazzo di San Sebastiano, Mantua (from the storerooms of the Palazzo Ducale)

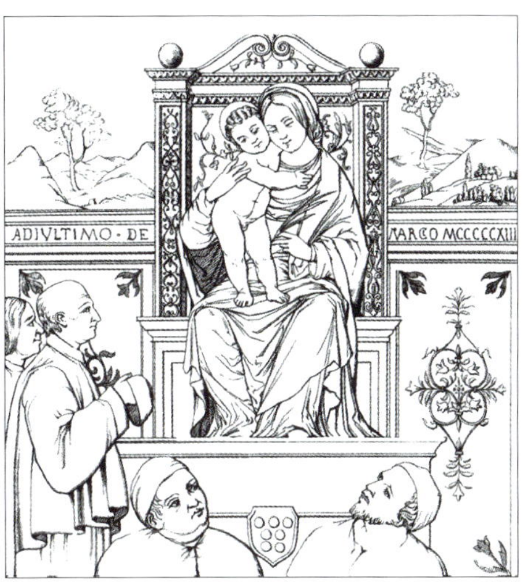

3. Drawing of the "Madonna of the Jews," fresco, c. 1857 (from C. D'Arco, *Delle arti e degli artefici di Mantova. Notizie illustrate con disegni e documenti*, Mantua, 1857–59, vol. I, plate 46)

seen (Donesmondi 1612, vol. II, pp. 85–86). And right in this church, just a short step away from Mantegna's canvas, were two other paintings in which Jews are included by full rights, as though to supplement Mantegna's insuperable masterpiece with additional information. We shall start with the first (because it is dated): a fresco now in Palazzo San Sebastiano (see fig. 2). It was originally on the church exterior, suggesting a position similar to that of the "figures of saints" erased by Norsa (L'Occaso 2011, pp. 142–44 no. 92 and plate XXXII), but also close to the Marquis's original intentions, as we have seen. Detached in 1852, the fresco is so faint now that in order to read it, especially its lower section, we must look to the only known drawing of it, made shortly after it was detached and fortunately included in a scholarly book by Carlo D'Arco (D'Arco 1857–59, vol. I, plate 46 and pp. 60–62) (see fig. 3). The inscription running along the edge of a sort of parapet furnishes a date, down to the day: "A dì ultimo de marcio MCCCCCXIIII" (the last day of March 1514). One numeral is cut off in the drawing but is still visible in the fresco; moreover, this fits perfectly with the slight enlargement of the church that we know (from Donesmondi and others: see below) was carried out in that very year 1514.

The Virgin enthroned with the Child is still easily seen in the center of the painting, and the drawing fully matches the remnant of fresco, where two landscape vistas can be barely distinguished on either side of the throne, beyond a parapet decorated, besides with the date, with broad vegetable motifs. On just one of the sides (to the Virgin's right), in front of the parapet, is a personage in ecclesiastical clothing; he has removed his hat and seems to look toward the Virgin in an attitude of prayer or submission. He is accompanied, just visible behind him and like him in profile, by an acolyte, who can be seen better in the drawing than in the fresco. Damaged to the point of illegibility are the figures in the lower section of the fresco, which the drawing shows clearly: they are two Jews who also look toward the Virgin but, as opposed to the devout donor, they keep their hats firmly on their heads. The fact that they are Jews and not someone else is shown, even more than by the drawing (whose perfect fidelity cannot be ascertained), also by other clues. First and foremost, the testimony of the erudite churchman Ippolito Donesmondi, who tells us that shortly after the church of Santa Maria della Vittoria was enlarged in 1514, "on the outside wall was painted the image of the glorious Virgin, with some kneeling people in it, holding a board with coins on it, and the inscription, or motto, 'Debellata Iudeorum perfidia'" (Donesmondi 1612, vol. II, p. 119; on his anti-Semitic hostility, see Bertolotti 2011, pp. 291–306: 300). This is not only early but also reliable evidence, given that Donesmondi was in the early seventeenth century secretary of the bishop of Mantua Francesco Gonzaga and, what is more, quite hostile to the Jews and therefore attentive to stories and images like this one. No less strong is a second argument: the precise iconographic parallel with the canvas (of which we shall soon speak), now in Sant'Andrea but originally in the refectory of Santa Maria della Vittoria, where four figures, certainly of Jews (the two men wear caps and yellow badges), are in front of the Virgin's throne, while above is the inscription, a perfect parallel to the one Donesmondi read in the fresco, "Debellata hebraeorum temeritate."

This interpretation must be tested against the fresco's most ambiguous detail, the "board with coins on it" that Donesmondi placed in close relation to the inscription on the perfidy of the Jews. It is useless to scrutinize what is left of the fresco, which has been entirely destroyed in this part. In the drawing presented by D'Arco, the "board" that Donesmondi saw has taken the form of a shield and the "coins" have become the heraldic device of balls, which D'Arco interprets as the Medici arms. D'Arco goes even further: he traces two painters, brothers, working in Mantua, Costantino and Gian Luigi Medici, and maintains that the arms are theirs—thus, the equivalent of a signature. This hypothesis is highly dubious, because it is hardly feasible that a painter, even if he were truly a Medici (but the Medici in Mantua came from Milan), would sign a painting with his own coat of arms and not that of his patron.

D'Arco was convinced that Donesmondi, in his description of the fresco (the earliest we have), had mistaken a "board with coins on it" for what he preferred to read as the Medici coat of arms, but the opposite seems to me much more probable. That is to say that D'Arco, convinced he had found in the two Medici painters in Mantua the authors of the fresco, had read as a coat of arms that "board with coins on it" (maybe even then hard to read), and had pointed the drawing in that direction. Even more so since as early as the middle of the eighteenth century Federico Amadei described the fresco (which he attributed to Mantegna) as "a most pious image of Our Lady, at whose feet are two half-figures of persons by now almost unreadable and ruined by weather, who are holding a board with money on it" (Amadei 1954–57, vol. II, p. 422). Yet there is not that much difference between one reading and the other (money or heraldic arms): in the language of Italian heraldry balls are more properly called *bisanti*, a term derived from the name of a Byzantine coin, and one of the most common explanations for the origin of this heraldic device is that it originates in the stylization of a gold coin and symbolizes riches, especially mercantile wealth. Finally, Donesmondi's description suggests a close tie between the "board with coins on it" and the "inscription or motto 'Debellata Iudeorum perfidia'"; the inscription could have been placed on the board or next to it. This reading is reinforced by identification of the donor to the Virgin's right as Fra Girolamo Redini, contained in one of the manuscript *zibaldoni* (notebooks) kept by Donesmondi himself (Togliani 2009, p. 181, note 343), where the correspondence of the habit of the Augustinian hermits with that worn by the donor of the fresco is pointed out. This identification is very likely, given

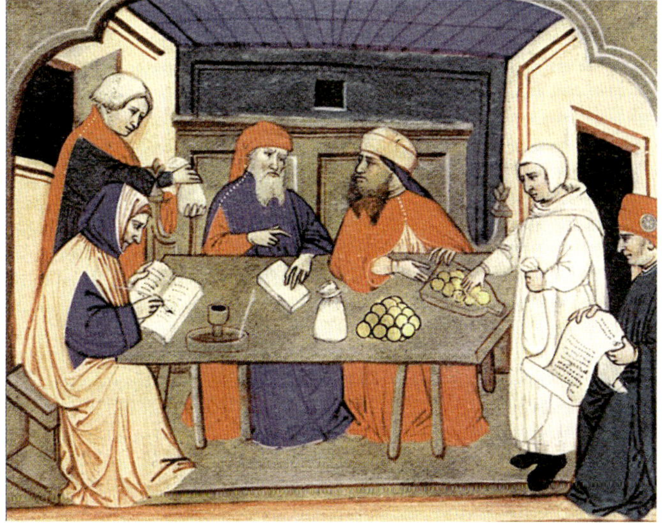

4. *Scene of a payment in the office of the Procuratori di San Marco in Venice*, c. 1390 (from the Cadaster of San Maffeo in Murano of the Camaldolese Benedictines, Biblioteca del Seminario Patriarcale, Venice)

Redini's role first as the instigator heeded by Francesco II, and then as the perpetual rector of Santa Maria della Vittoria (for the specific Augustinian congregation to which Redini belonged and which he had helped to found, see ibid., pp. 140 ff. and 147).

So then, just what was this board with coins that the two figures at the Virgin's feet were holding according to Donesmondi and Amadei, and which must have been connected with the inscription on Jewish perfidy? I think we should, in a virtual reconstruction of the part of the fresco by now lost, hypothesize that what the two Jews had in their hands was a *pala*, a sort of shovel or paddle once used to take up, count, and distribute money. We can see clearly the shape and use of these objects, for example, in a group of four miniatures, quite similar to each other, from the Cadaster of San Maffeo in Murano of the Camaldolese Benedictines (c. 1390), now in Venice in the Library of the Patriarchal Seminary (Luzzatto 1961, plates II–V). The one reproduced here (see fig. 4)shows, according to the descriptions of Reinhold C. Müller's and Vittorio Formentin, a room in the Procuratoria di San Marco, with, from left to right, the chamberlain, the treasurer (*camerarius*), two Procuratori, a lay brother from the monastery receiving a legacy, and a notary in the act of recording the operation (Lane and Müller 1985, p. 98; Müller 1977, p. 460, fig. 17; Formentin 2018, pp. 170–73, esp. p. 173 no. 12). According to Formentin, in Venice this instrument was called a *sèssola*, a sort of paddle with the sides slightly turned up, which could be used for bailing water from a boat but also for scooping up and moving grain, flour, etc. In this case, according to the description offered by an expert such as Reinhold C. Müller, the large side of the shovel was used to count the coins of a transaction—10, 50 or 100 *grossi* or *ducati*—and then was slightly lifted to allow the coins to fall into a bag.

It seems to me highly likely that something similar was used in Mantua (with a similar name, perhaps the variant *sássola*, or something else). A *sèssola* or paddle similar in shape to the one we see being used in Venice to count coins was therefore a wooden board pointed at one end to form a handle, as we see in the miniature (fig. 4). A shape of this sort, in a fresco by this point heavily "ruined by weather" as described by the sources already in the eighteenth century, could lead us to think of a heraldic shield, and thus explain the misunderstanding (or forced interpretation) made by D'Arco and the draughtsman he had assigned to transcribe on paper the little that could be seen. The two figures in the fresco held "in their hands" this "board with coins on it," offering in this way their tribute, in cash, to the Virgin Mary above them. If we trust the drawing, it is difficult to imagine in detail how the two men could hold an object like this in their hands; but once "decided" that it was a coat of arms, it is possible that it was designed with some further improperness. Nor is it clear in what pictorial and spatial relationship were the board with coins and the anti-Jewish inscription, as attested by Donesmondi in the early seventeenth century. That the two figures were really kneeling, as Donesmondi says, is also a dubious claim; perhaps it should be understood only in the sense that, since they are half-figures (as Amadei reports and like the ones in the other "Madonna of the Jews" of which we shall soon speak), they could appear, to the further consternation of the Jews, prostrate at the Virgin's feet. This is thus a very rare—if not unique—case where we can see "live" the money of a fine that was at the same time that of an artist's commission. The only, and imperfect, parallel I know of is a *Virgin and Child* by Andrea della Robbia in Empoli, dated 1518 (see fig. 5), which was paid for by a Jew accused of sacrilege. This is recorded in the inscription at the Virgin's feet: "Of the price [paid] by the Jews for their error the Eight had this made in God's praise. Sitting in 18 [was] Domenico Parigi praetor here" (Proto Pisani 2006, pp. 124–26). With regard to the text of the inscription, it should

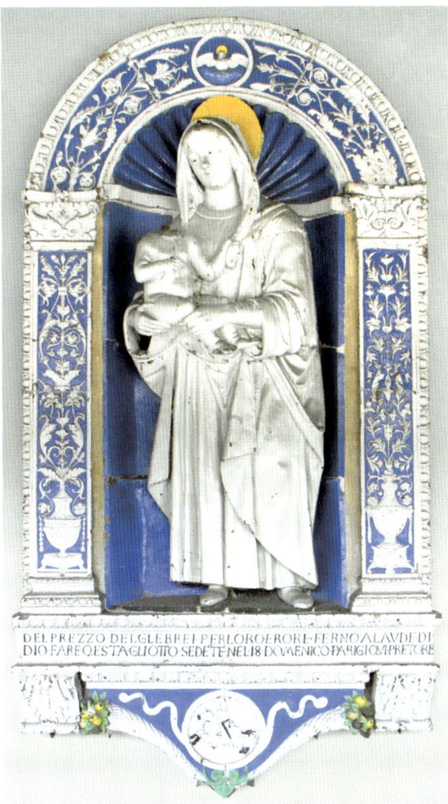

5. Andrea della Robbia, "Madonna of the Jews," 1518. Museo della Collegiata di Sant'Andrea, Empoli (from the Palazzo Pretorio)

be noted that: 1) in the original wording, the demands of meter would require *fare* (made) to be elided into *far*; 2) the number 18 gives us the date *ad annum*: 1518. So it was the Otto di Balia in Florence who inflicted the fine on the sacrilegious Jew, but the one who boasted of turning them in was the *podestà* (or *pretore*) of Empoli, Domenico Parigi.

What we can draw from this reading, in part conjecture but certainly not unfounded, is that in 1514 Girolamo Redini, grasping the opportunity of an enlargement of the little church which held Mantegna's *Madonna of Victory*, had a fresco painted on an outside wall celebrating the defeat (*debellatio*) of Jewish perfidy, showing two Jews at the Virgin's feet in the act of offering to her on a board a sum of money in cash (presumably gold). We cannot expect that one of the two was Daniele Norsa and the other, let's say, a brother of his; and yet it is certainly possible that the tribute money shown here alluded to the sum paid to Mantegna for his picture. But before comparing the famous canvas that was inside the church to the dark and faded fresco on its outside wall, we should look at a second "Madonna of the Jews" from Santa Maria della Vittoria.

5. This canvas, like the fresco, is rather low in quality, but is a bit better known, also because it is better preserved and more visible, having been taken from Santa Maria della Vittoria to Sant'Andrea some time ago. This one too (see fig. 6) shows the Virgin and Child, both of them intent on blessing the scale model of the new church that commem-

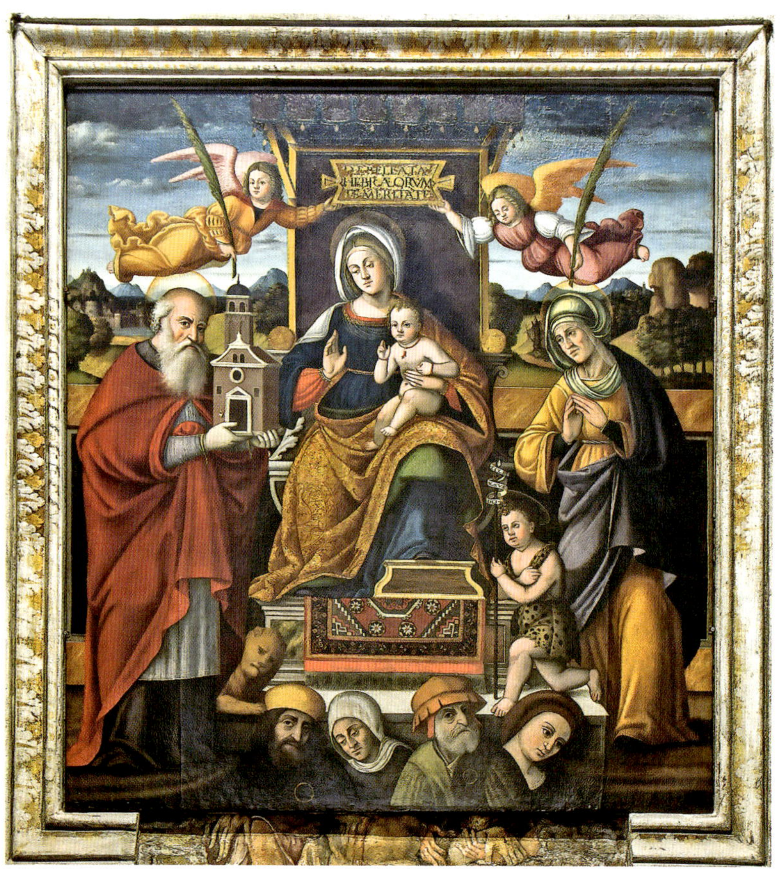

6. Painter active in Mantua, "Madonna of the Jews,"
c. 1514. Church of Sant'Andrea, Mantua

orates the victory, held by a bearded Saint Jerome with his usual lion; on the other side of the throne (just like in Mantegna's painting) stand Saint Elizabeth and the young Saint John the Baptist, his little knee bent in devotion. Above, two angels bearing palm fronds (the signs of victory) hold a cartouche inscribed: "Debellata hebraeorum temeritate." We mention it because it is almost identical to the one adorning the fresco with "Debellata Iudeorum perfidia" (see fig. 2); but at the bottom of the canvas can be easily seen four figures of Jews, two women and two men with covered heads and yellow badges on their clothes (Muzzarelli 1996, pp. 51–53). They are the defeated ones, and the mediocre artist wanted to have us view them as repentant and sorry (Lauts 1960, p. 14 and fig. 16; Katz 2000, pp. 483–98). According to D'Arco, the bearded churchman in the picture is "Fra Girolamo Redini offering the model of the church of the Victory" (D'Arco 1857–59, vol. II, p. 61); but this is undoubtedly Saint Jerome, perhaps chosen precisely because he is Redini's name saint, and a pleasing choice also for the Hieronymites who would later take over the church (Togliani 2009, pp. 176 ff). D'Arco's other misinterpretation is more serious: he mistakes the Jews under the Virgin's throne for "some of the faithful," a misunderstanding that is worth mentioning only because, in times closer to our own, some of the few scholars who have commented on the above-mentioned fresco fell into the same trap (see figs. 2 and 3).

We know from Donesmondi that the painting was originally, and at least until the early seventeenth century, in the refectory annexed to Santa Maria della Vittoria (Portioli 1882–84, p. 24). Three times, then, in this tiny church, the Madonna was meant to symbolize some *debellatio* or victory: that at Fornovo in the triumphal painting by Mantegna (paid for, however, by a Jewish merchant in expiation for a claimed sacrilege), and that against the Jews in general (and Daniele Norsa in particular) in the altarpiece in the refectory and in the fresco on the exterior wall. It is now time to compare these three paintings with each other, but before doing so we should discuss the date of the latter canvas, which in recent years has earned something of a reputation as a *Madonna of the Jews*, also because in 1998 it was the object of fierce debate over its possible removal (in that it was anti-Semitic), with the proposal to move it from its current location in the Basilica of Sant'Andrea into the Museo diocesano (Minervino 1998, p. 33).

At the time of my first version of this study, I had somewhat superficially supposed not only that the commission for this *Madonna of the Jews* came from Girolamo Redini, but also that it was painted slightly later than when Francesco II entrusted him with the care of Santa Maria della Vittoria (1498). In the second edition of his important work *Studi sul paesaggio*, Gianni Romano quite rightly observed (Romano 1990, p. XXXI) that the canvas had to be significantly later than the *Madonna of Victory*, and Giovanni Agosti later proposed 1514 as a plausible date (Agosti 2005, vol. I, pp. 232 and 479; *Storia di Mantova* 2005, vol. I, plate 9): the same date as the fresco (figs. 2 and 3). Romano's other observations were and remain unsubstantiated: it is not true that "the four figures at the Virgin's feet could hardly belong to the Jewish community" because "they do not present any of the characteristics of physiognomy and clothing of Jews" (Romano 1990, p. XXXI; see also Bertolotti 2011, p. 305, note 78). As we have seen, on the contrary, they are wearing a readily visible yellow badge, which Maria Giuseppina Muzzarelli considered to be exemplary in her study on the topic of clothes and ornaments. It is not true that "the church Jerome holds in his hands is not a specific building, but a recurrent iconographical attribute," not only because the model of a church is not at all a "recurrent iconographical attribute" of Saint Jerome and not only because the model imitates the appearance of Santa Maria della Vittoria, but also because the painting was located in the refectory of that very church (something of which Romano seems unaware). Rather, the double gesture of blessing, one from the Mother and the other from the Child, since it is addressed toward the saint holding the model of the church, obliges us to place the picture in relation to its foundation, even if this was some years before. Finally, it is not true that a date of ten or fifteen years later is a hindrance to linking the commission and intent of the painting with the very same events that resulted in the *Madonna of Victory* by Mantegna.

There is no doubt that Mantegna's masterpiece precedes the other two Madonnas at Santa Maria della Vittoria, not only because of its unparalleled quality but also because of its significantly earlier date. But which of the two more modest Madonnas of the Jews was painted first? And under what circumstances? The close affinity in layout (the Virgin enthroned, the defeated Jews at her feet) and the conceptual identity of the inscriptions are not the only points of contact. It should be noted that the supposed Girolamo Redini in the fresco and the certain Saint Jerome in the canvas both occupy the same position, at the Virgin's right (like Francesco II in Mantegna's painting), and that the eponymous saint holds the model for the church for which Redini had worked so hard and of which he had been rector. The fresco could thus be a simplified version of the canvas, or the canvas an expanded version of the fresco, but they substantially overlap, even if in one the Jews are four and in the other two, and Saint Elizabeth and the baby John are missing in the fresco. As for the difference (in words, not in concept) between the two inscriptions, this can be explained better in terms of a deliberate *variatio* than the passage of time; one could think that, while maintaining the key word *debellata*, the person who devised the phrases preferred to write "perfidy" in the inscription visible from the street, and the more erudite term *temeritas* on the canvas in the refectory; similarly, he chose "Iudaei" (closer to the Mantuan vernacular *zudeo*) for the street, reserving the more scholarly term "Hebraei" for the refectory. A date around 1514 for both paintings, then, not too far apart, seems to me to be the only conclusion possible; but this does not imply agreement with Romano's precipitous opinion that they must refer "to other events, for the moment unknown."

It seems to me, on the contrary, highly likely that these two "Madonnas of the Jews" are a later tribute to the harsh anti-Jewish campaign waged by Redini (who was no longer rector of the church, but still very much alive and active in 1514); nor does it matter so much if he was the one to commission them or if the Hieronymites, once they were settled in the church, decided to honor him by remembering the origins of the church in the sacrilege committed by Norsa, his forced donation of money, and the *debellatio* suffered by him and the Jewish community. Redini, as far as we know, continued to have authority and influence up to his death in 1524 (Togliani 2009, p. 200), and it was common knowledge that the very existence of the church (with its Mantegna over the altar) was due to him. And in those same years (from 1511 to 1521) the head of the diocese of Mantua was the very same Sigismondo Gonzaga (cardinal since 1505) who had been Redini's accomplice in the plans for Santa Maria della Vittoria (including Mantegna's picture) and the extortion of 110 gold ducats from Daniele Norsa.

6. Comparison of the three paintings, all three the result of analogous external causes, made in the same context, a few years apart, and for the same place, can shed light, conversely, on the meaning of each. To bring out their affinities of context despite the enormous differences in structure and quality, we can group them together as three different "Madonnas of the Jews," even if one of the three (the one by Mantegna) bears no trace of a Jewish presence. The other two Madonnas are fully focused on the devotional—and openly anti-Semitic—key of reparation for the sacrilege, and yet they borrow from Mantegna's picture elements that I might call military: the palm fronds, the Roman *tabula ansata* held by the angels, the very word *debellata* which places the unfortunate Jews among the Marquis's enemies, just as Charles VIII of France had been at Fornovo. A painting whose true intent was only to appease the divine wrath challenged by Norsa could easily have been made following a similar structure, even if entrusted to the much more skilled hand of Mantegna. On the contrary, the *Madonna of Victory* had hinged on the celebration of a success in war and on the hope for new laurels for the thirty-year-old ruler of Mantua, without any allusions to the Jew's misdeed. The different location of the three paintings partially explains the difference in their content and at the same time reveals a hierarchy of values: in the refectory (seen by very few) the modest *debellatio* of the Jews, which seems rather to recall the personal success of Girolamo Redini when he persuaded the Marquis to dedicate the church and the painting; in the church, for the *reverentia* of all the people, Francesco II's devotion to the Virgin, to guarantee for him in

perpetuity military virtue and fortune; and finally, on the street, in memory of the earlier image "scraped away" by Norsa, a sort of simplified projection of a story meant to be edifying, exhibiting on a special board (or *sèssola*) even the coins of the forced disbursement. The differences in content and structure among the three paintings (we shall not speak here of style), in short, can be explained by the difference in audience. "What had been subliminal in Mantegna's painting was re-evoked two decades later with didactic precision" (Bertolotti 2011, pp. 291–306, esp. p. 299). The two minor "Madonnas of the Jews" are, so to speak, compensation paintings. They are meant to give back to Redini his own due: the insistent condemnation of Daniele Norsa's sacrilege and the initiative of the votive church. But, in an unforeseen side effect, they bring Mantua's Jews onto the stage. Yes, they present them as perfidious and rash enemies defeated by Redini, but at the same time they show them to us face to face, with their caps, their badges, the humiliation to which they were subject, and even their money, which Mantegna collected in the end for having painted his masterpiece. Which therefore, in its own way, without spelling it out, is also a "Madonna of the Jews."

But the difference in the results and Redini's involvement next to the Marquis lead us to ask a more radical question: who was truly the donor of Mantegna's picture? Not, for once, "the one who pays"—not Daniele Norsa, who on his own initiative would never have commissioned a Christian picture. The devout posture of Francesco II, posed by Mantegna kneeling in prayer in accordance with the iconographic tradition for donors, indicates him as the painting's "real" donor, or rather the intentional one; and this indicates it not just to us, but above all to its contemporary audience. He was playing a role: in their letters to the Marquis, his brother Sigismondo and Redini declare to their lord, away at war, that the picture will be painted in accordance with "Your Excellency's idea," and "keeping in mind your intention" (Kristeller 1902, p. 559 no. 137; p. 560 no. 138). These expressions reflect the conviction of his correspondents that they were working according to his implicit or presumed intentions. In any case, in keeping with the conventions of the time, the *inventio* (concept) always fell, at the outset, to the donor, especially if he was a ruler. In those same years, which were also the years of Leonardo's *Last Supper*, Luca Pacioli attributed to Ludovico il Moro the choice of subject as well as of artist, and praised the duke for his "singular devotione" to the group of Jesus with his Apostles "for having it … arranged [fatto *disporre*] in the most sacred church of the Grazie by our … Leonardo with his graceful brush" (Pacioli 1956, p. 34). Elsewhere too in that same treatise, which was dedicated to Ludovico il Moro, Pacioli uses the same language in describing the *Last Supper*, "where by deeds and gestures [the Apostles] seem to speak with each other with vivid and heartfelt admiration, so worthily did our Leonardo arrange it [lo *dispose*] with his graceful hand" (ibid., p. 17). The language is that of rhetoric, which pervaded everything: even a sublime artist like Leonardo is assigned the *dispositio* (arrangement) of the painting, while the *inventio* fell, by invincible social convention, to the ruler, understood as the natural patron in that he was the absolute ruler over the site (Settis 2010, pp. 32–50).

The protonotary Sigismondo Gonzaga, Fra Girolamo Redini, and Fra Marco Antonio Da Porto conceived of a painting on Francesco II's behalf (in other words, in his place) and Andrea Mantegna painted it. But the advisers tend to disappear behind the patron; if Sigismondo cancelled himself out of the painting, it was so that it might correspond better with his brother's intention: a privileged presentation of his glory and destiny, without anyone else in it. The fact that in this role-playing there was no room left for Daniele Norsa, even though it was he who paid Mantegna's bill, must have seemed perfectly natural to everybody. Everybody, that is, but Norsa and the other Jews of Mantua on one side, and on the other Girolamo Redini, who could not claim even a minimal place for himself in Mantegna's picture but found a way to manifest his role a little less than twenty years later.

     7. There were other stories of Jews who had to pay significant fines or were otherwise severely punished for having wanted to "scrape away" Christian images from the walls of their houses, but none is so richly documented or tied to an artist as great as Mantegna. We have already mentioned the cases of Gubbio (1471) and Pisa (1491), but there were certainly others, for example Cesena in 1506 and Empoli in 1518, as we have seen (Agosti 2005, p. 232, note 4). Again in Mantua, expansion of a Jesuit church in 1584 would have entailed the (total or partial) destruction of the synagogue, which was warded off by payment of a voluntary tribute of a good 3,500 scudi (Bazzotti 2006, pp. 215 ff). Not to mention the much more serious events of 1602, when seven Jews here hanged by order of Duke Vincenzo Gonzaga, and another one lynched by the mob. This story, in some way connected with Rubens' *Holy Trinity* in Mantua, has been capably reconstructed by Maurizio Bertolotti (Bertolotti 2011, pp. 291–306; the popular engraving showing the seven Jews hanging upside down after being killed is reproduced as his fig. 22). It all started with a fiery sermon by Fra Bartholomaeus Cambi de Salutio. In a packed town square in the presence of the Duke, he had deplored the liberties enjoyed by the Jews in Mantua, exhorting Gonzaga to close them off in a ghetto, take away all their privileges, and force them to wear a yellow badge. In the afternoon "much anger against the Jews" exploded in the city, while seven Jews were making fun of the preacher by staging next to the synagogue a sort of parody of his passionate sermon. Increasingly enraged, the friar demanded immediate repressive measures, and after some resistance the Duke decided to protect himself from ecclesiastical censure by having the seven killed "and hang them all from a high scaffold with their feet up above [i.e. upside down], and with yellow caps … with this inscription in block letters: For having mocked the word of God in derision of the Christian religion." An engraving made that same year shows the horrendous scene, with three devils tormenting the poor wretches. Thinking he had done enough to merit the Church's favor, the Duke then attempted mediation by sending a trusted representative to the papal court; but Clement VIII replied with a letter ordering him to put an end "to the abuse and insolence of the Jews and the continued insults perpetrated by them, mostly because of the continuing excessive familiarity that the Jews have with the Christians in that city and the many privileges either given to them or tolerated or usurped by them." The friar was then shut up in a convent until his death in 1617, but the Duke gradually had to submit to limiting the freedom of the Jews, to the point of setting up a ghetto in 1610. As is clear from the documentation, the terrible punishment had been set in motion, more than by the mocking behavior of the seven, by the relatively advantageous conditions enjoyed by Jews in the duchy, indirectly proved also by the liberty a few of them had taken to make fun of the friar in public.

    Bertolotti maintains that "the friar's aggressive preaching and Clement VIII's pressure on Duke Vincenzo" were "the final, decisive attack on an equilibrium that had been established in Mantua for more than a century," to the point that in church circles in the city it was held "that the Jews of Mantua had been granted too much freedom." Francesco II too, faced with Daniele Norsa, wavered back and forth: one minute he showed him signs of benevolence (including exemption from having to wear the badge; ibid., p. 298), the next he threatened him with death. Therefore Bertolotti is convinced, perhaps slightly overdoing it, that the three churchmen who led the plan for the church and altarpiece of the *Madonna of Victory* (Sigismondo Gonzaga, Girolamo Redini, and Marco Antonio Da Porto) were not so much the Marquis's collaborators as his antagonists, and that their "punitive intent, fed by hostility toward the Jews," was in opposition to the tolerant attitude of the Marquis, who valued the contribution to the prosperity of his state made by Norsa and the Jewish community (Bourne 2008, pp. 73–74; Katz 2000). In short, "the extraordinary importance assumed by the Jews in the economic and cultural life of Mantua" could explain both the oscillations in the behavior of Marquis Francesco (and a century later of Duke Vincenzo) and the sudden deflagration of the crises of 1495 and 1602, both of them set off by churchmen with fierce anti-Jewish convictions. Even the self-representation in terms of faithful orthodoxy and devotion, for which Francesco II mobilized Mantegna and Vincenzo called on Rubens, may have been meant to balance the suspicion, in the curia of the bishop but also of the pope, of excessive concessions to the Jewish presence in the city.

These few pages do not aim at an adequate discussion of this conclusion. Suffice it however to mention that another Norsa residing in Mantua, Moshe, bought in 1513 the stunning fourteenth-century illuminated manuscript of the *Guide for the Perplexed* by Moses Maimonides (cat. 14), and that the list of his books now held in the Bibliothèque nationale in Paris shows at least another 62 manuscripts and printed books (Moscone 2018, pp. 36–49). The Maimonides manuscript remained the property of the Norsa family, always in Mantua, for 500 years, until in 2016 it was fortunately acquired for the patrimony of the Italian State. Together with the *Madonna of Victory* by Andrea Mantegna, this outstanding manuscript bears witness still today to the deep roots long sunk in Mantua (as elsewhere in Italy) by a cultured and active Jewish community, and the many traces, sometimes by their choice and sometimes forced by adverse circumstances, the Norsa family left in this—their and our—city. But among these traces, at times glorious like Mantegna's picture, we should not forget the other two "Madonnas of the Jews," a poor yet vivid testimony of ancient discriminations, sufferings, and injustices.

Translated by Susan Scott

An early version of this text was first published in Settis 1981, and later (with some revisions) in Settis 2010, pp. 3–88, esp. pp. 18–31. The section on the Madonna of Victory *was presented also in Settis 2018 (with an English translation). I offer here a new version of the text, expanded and revised on some essential points, but without systematically updating the bibliography. I am grateful to Giulia Ammannati, Vittorio Formentin, Chiara Frugoni, Stefano L'Occaso, Reinhold Müller, Daniela Sogliani, and Alfredo Stussi for their suggestions and help. The story was told, based on the main documents, for the first time in Portioli 1882–84. For the documents cited in the text as I go along, my reference is Kristeller 1902; reference is made to Portioli only for the documents not reported by Kristeller. Among the studies on the subject published after my essay, particularly important, even if usually ignored by art historians, is the excellent contribution by Michele Luzzati in 1983 (with a bibliography on the history of the Norsa family). I dedicate this new version, which owes so much to him, to Luzzati, my colleague at the Scuola Normale di Pisa during my tenure there.*

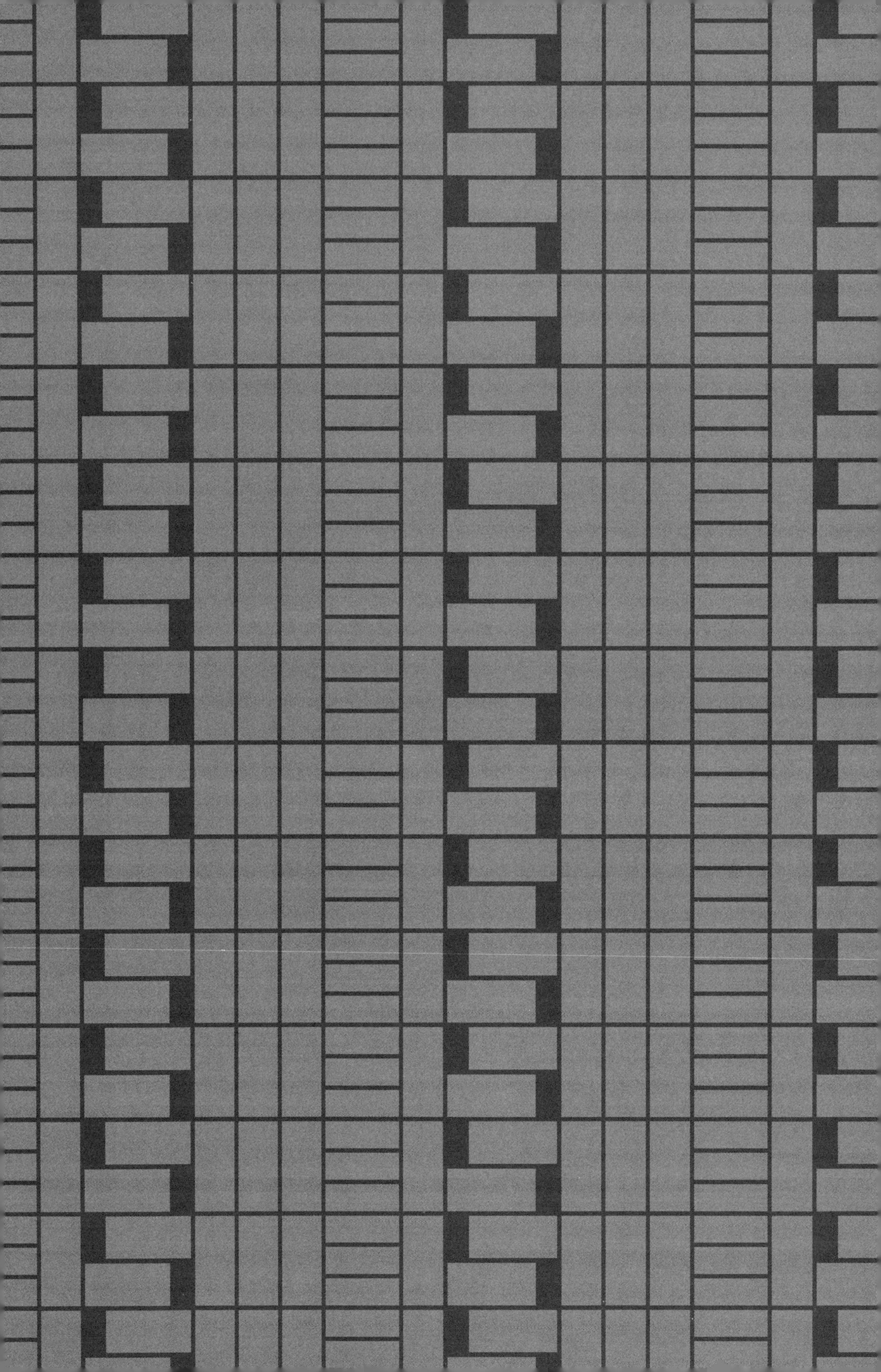

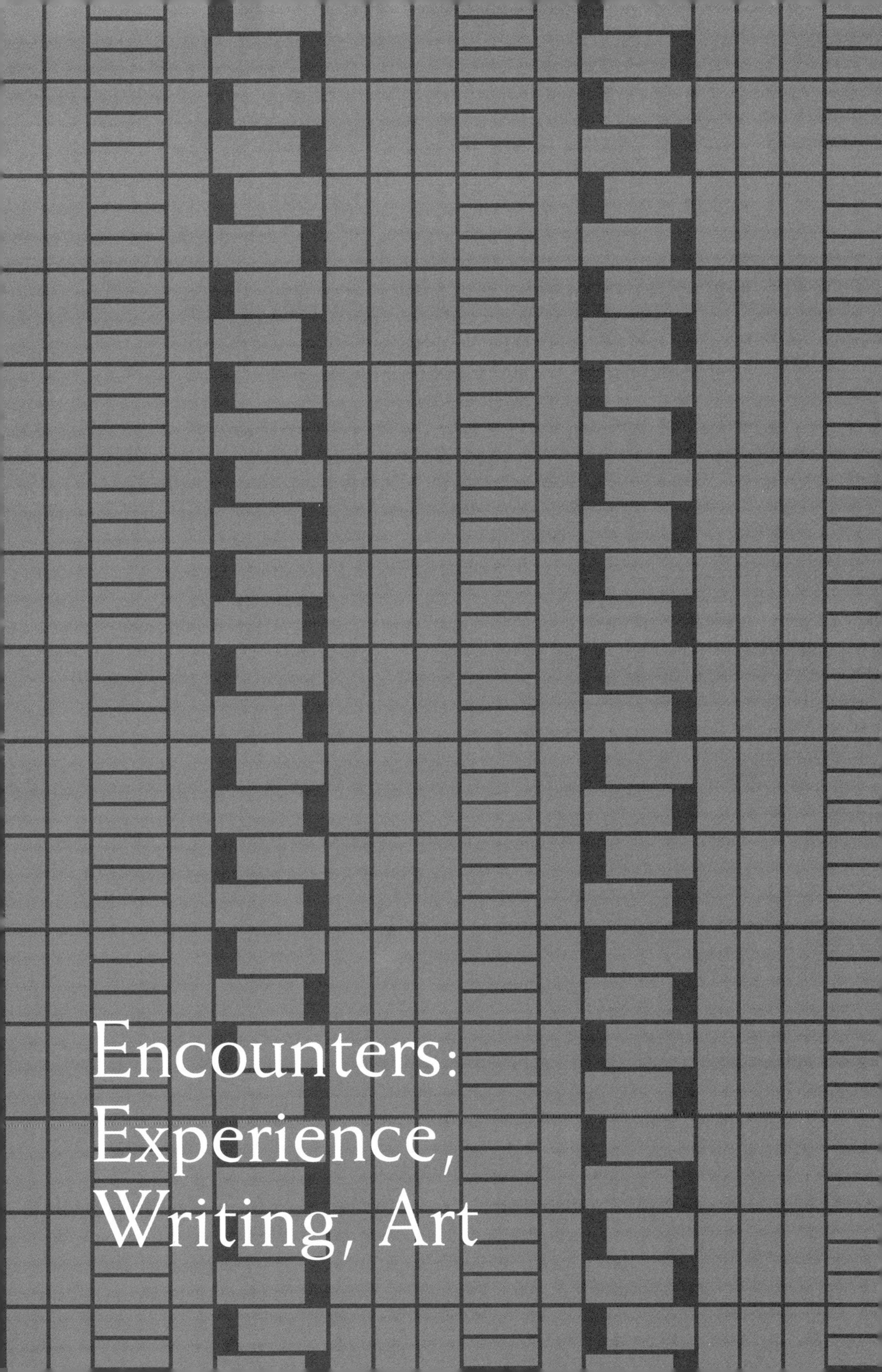

Encounters:
Experience,
Writing, Art

Art and Jewish Patronage in Renaissance Italy
Andreina Contessa

Judaism is linked to Italy by a history of cultural multiplicity. For centuries, the Italian peninsula was characterized by territorial fragmentation, a feature that is clearly reflected in its Jewish heritage. The Renaissance period was marked by an extraordinary parallel development of Jewish activity in the sphere of art, supported by generous patronage and distinguished by the production of liturgical objects and illuminated manuscripts of high artistic value. Italian Jews participated in the innovation and spirit of Renaissance art, creating a unique fusion between the artistic forms of the period and Jewish content.

The fifteenth and sixteenth centuries were an age of relative socio-economic prosperity for Jews, especially in small Renaissance cities such as Florence, Urbino, Mantua, and Ferrara, where the rulers encouraged Jewish settlement in the interest of promoting market development, private credit, and public finance. Jews worked in various professions, in particular trade and crafts like jewelry, textiles, and printing, and were deeply involved in court life and culture. However, since they could not belong to merchant or artisan guilds, many Jews concentrated their activity on loan banks and worked directly in the exchange markets and the field of bank loans, coming to play an important part in the economic affairs of cities in northern and central Italy. Following their expulsion from various European countries, Jews migrated from abroad, first from the Ashkenazi areas and then from the Sephardic ones. New communities were founded, while the oldest enclaves were in constant expansion. Moreover, in the fifteenth and sixteenth centuries, the city-states in central and northern Italy invited Jewish bankers from southern Italy, the German area, and the Iberian peninsula to live in their cities in order to attract capital and stimulate trade.

During this period of economic growth and overall prosperity, intellectual and artistic activity flourished: Humanism, intellectual curiosity, philosophical discussion, and the rebirth of culture were an important part of the Jewish world. This new way of thinking touched every side of it, having a creative influence on the thought and artistic production of the time. Many of the great Jewish merchant and banking families commissioned works of art and, in imitation of the Italian nobility, and even created crests, which we still see today imprinted on numerous objects and codices from the time. The great Jewish entrepreneurs conducted themselves identically to their non-Jewish counterparts. They were successful businessmen and members of the families that contributed to running the Italian Renaissance banking system, but also cultured scholars, men of letters, philosophers, art lovers and, often, patrons and collectors (Roth 1946, pp. 193–215; Bonfil 1988; Tirosh–Rothschild 1988; Tirosh–Samuelson 1990; Lesley 1992).

The bankers gave financial support to Jewish scholars and scribes, promoted the development of Jewish study and culture, provided money for clothing and feeding the poor and funded dowries for destitute brides. The areas in which these bankers channeled most of their investments were those of sumptuous furnishings for public and private synagogues and costly Hebrew manuscripts.

Both of these had complex social implications within the Jewish community. By investing part of their fortunes in support of their community, embellishing synagogues or producing liturgical books, the patrons redistributed part of their wealth and at the same time reinforced and confirmed their Jewish identity. While little survives, as we shall see, from the synagogue furnishings, manuscript production is a well-documented sphere of patronage and boasts an extraordinary quantity of exemplars, important for their originality, beauty, and richness.

Patronage of synagogue art

Throughout Italy, the exponents of the Jewish economic elite competed in the decoration of synagogues with valuable religious furnishings, with the intent of putting into practice the teaching of embellishing the precept. Synagogues, collective places of prayer and gathering as well as of study and learning the Torah, had been substituting the ancient Temple of Jerusalem for centuries and had become the fulcrum of the Jewish community and its institutions. Modest on the outside and often incorporated into private buildings, synagogues had carefully furnished interiors, filled with precious textiles, silver, and wooden inlay. Little material and artistic evidence of the religious decoration from the early Renaissance survives, but what does remain helps us to understand the level of refinement that all of the minor furnishings and religious objects must have had.

A central component of the Jewish cult was the Holy Ark (*aron ha-qodesh*), which contains the Torah scrolls and, together with the *bimah*, remains to this day one of the two cornerstones of synagogue space and prayer. The ark was initially a wooden repository that evoked the ancient Ark of the Covenant of the Temple of Jerusalem, which contained the Tablets of the Law given to Moses on Mount Sinai. This tie is particularly clear in the world's oldest securely dated (1472) wooden ark, which was originally in Modena and (now at the Musée d'art et d'histoire du Judaïsme in Paris; see cat. 7 and fig. 1). The ark has the appearance of a tall, narrow monumental chest, divided into two quadrangular sections carved and decorated with colorful geometric inlay and flanked on each side by

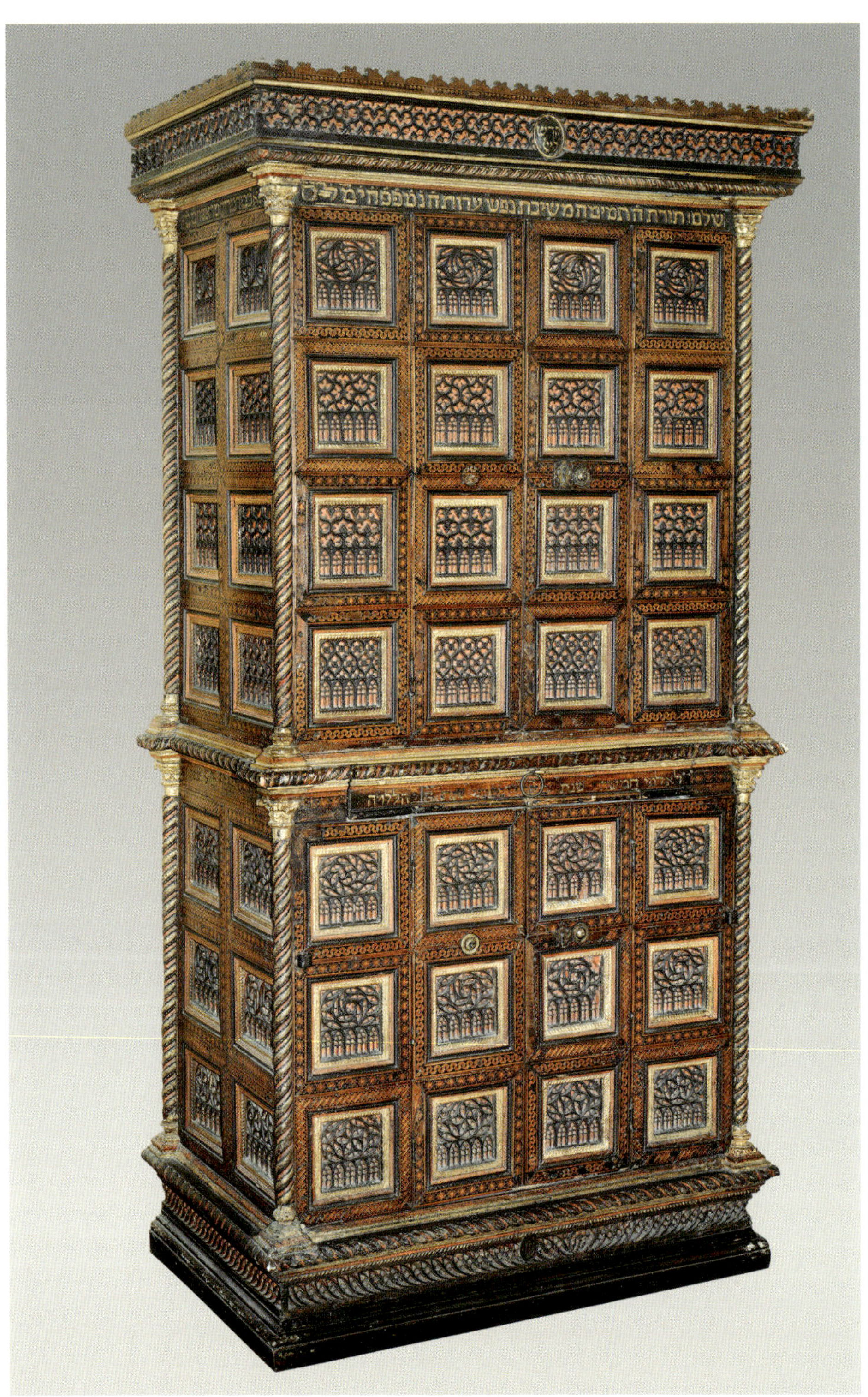

slender twisted columns. The crenelated decoration at the top of the structure gives it a tower-like appearance (Klagsbald 1981, pp. 94–96; Rodov 2010).

The inscriptions on the frieze of the Modena ark clearly associate it with the Biblical Ark of the Covenant (*aron ha-berit*) and the throne of God (*kisse ha-kavod*). The epithets of God, *ram ve-na'ssa* (high and lifted up), recall the description of the divine throne placed above the sanctuary (*Hekal*) in the Book of Isaiah (6:1). The concept of the worldly sanctuary, earthly base of the throne of God, is explicated in the inscription on the upper-left frieze of the Modena ark, which cites Jeremiah (17:12): "A glorious high throne from the beginning is the place of our sanctuary." Another inscription reveals the year in which the ark was made, 1472, and the name of the donor, Elhanan Rephael, son of Rabbi Daniel.

In this massive, fortress-like ark, the openings are difficult to detect since the structure is divided into multiple compartments. The uniform grid of square panels, 28 per row on the front and 14 per row on each of the two sides, conceals the openings on every level, so that when the ark is closed the compartments for the Torah scrolls are barely visible. The beautiful wood decoration has been attributed to the carvers Lorenzo and Cristoforo Canozzi, masters of the art of intarsia, which especially flourished during the Italian Renaissance.

There is an illustration of an ark similar to the one from Modena in the prayer book (*Maḥazor*) of Joab Immanuel, a manuscript produced in Reggio Emilia in 1466, with miniatures attributed to the workshop of one of the artists who worked on the magnificent Bible of Borso d'Este, possibly Giorgio d'Alemagna. One of the miniatures shows prayer in the synagogue on Shabbat and the ark in the middle appears like a Gothic tower topped by a spire, the tip of which seems to be surrounded by lamps (British Library, London, MS Harley 5686, fol. 28*v*).

An important component of the ark of Modena are the twisted colonnettes, which follow the symbolic model of the columns that, according to tradition, decorated the Temple of Jerusalem built by King Solomon.

The motif of the twisted columns was used to evoke the Temple in many holy arks, often featuring an architectural structure incorporating elements such as columns, Corinthian capitals, brackets, and gables.

The extraordinary ark of Mantua/Sermide has a shrine-like structure with an architrave supported by two side columns topped by Corinthian capitals and decorated with floral reliefs (see fig. 2). At the top of this symmetrical structure, like acroteria, sit two elegant decorative amphorae at the apex of which is a flame representing the perpetual light (*ner tamid*) dwelling in all synagogues. Between the two amphorae, in the middle, there is an elegant frieze of acanthus leaves and volutes in relief, similar to the ancient Roman decoration that was regularly imitated during the Italian Renaissance. The frieze contains the following inscriptions: "Crown of the Torah" and, below, "Prepare to meet thy God" (Amos 4:12).

The ark belonged to the Sinagoga Grande of Mantua and is dated 1543, as we learn from an inscription. This splendid example of Renaissance wooden sculpture includes

1. *Aron ha-qodesh* (Holy Ark), Modena, 1472, Musée d'art et d'histoire du Judaïsme, Paris (cat. 7)

all of the characteristics typical of the period: orthogonal and symmetrical articulation, simple, plain harmonious structure and a gilded bas-relief frieze decorated with racemes and other floral motifs.

The ark is flanked by two monumental cathedrae, also made of finely carved, sculpted and gilded wood, decorated with elegant and highly refined racemes and acanthus leaves. The ark and cathedrae were later brought to the little village of Sermide, near Mantua, where they remained for centuries. In 1955 they were transported to Jerusalem, to what is now the Umberto Nahon Museum of Italian Jewish Art (Nahon 1970; Cassuto 2004; Contessa 2015). On the inside of the ark's doors, there is a Hebrew inscription carved in gilded wood: a poetic song on the Decalogue, unique of its kind, which was specially composed for it. The ark is unique in that it was donated by a woman, the name of whom we know thanks to an inscription on one of the cathedrae. Indeed, this inscription tells us not only the date and place for which it was commissioned but also that the donor was Consilia Norsa, daughter of Shemuel da Pisa and wife of Isaac Norsa of Ferrara (Contessa 2016a). The recent discovery of a link between this donor and a splendid Hebrew prayer book from 1520, originally in Ferrara, has made it possible to shed new light on the role of women in Jewish culture during the Renaissance (Contessa 2017).

In sixteenth-century Italy, patronage was very common among Italian Jewish bankers, but much remains to be known about female Jewish patronage (Adelman 1991). Jewish women contributed to the community's various charitable institutions and to the decoration of the synagogue (Yaniv 1989; Weber 1997–98; Nashman Fraiman 2006). Female donations were typically linked to sewing and embroidering the textiles used for the synagogal rite, using fine fabrics embellished with silk embroidery: the curtain for the ark (*paroket*), the Torah binder (*avnet*) and the mantle (*meyl*) for the Torah scrolls and the cover (*mappah*) for the lectern (*bimah*). We must not forget that many women participated in family businesses tied to the textile trade and made a significant contribution to tailoring, embroidery, book production, and repair. The female involvement in the *strazzaria* (second-hand fabrics and garments) trade can be seen in synagogue items created by using highly valuable silk brocade and velvet second-hand fabrics to make covers for the Torah scroll or the Torah ark curtains (Contessa 2016a).

One interesting case of reuse is that of the Tedeschi Torah ark curtain, which is also quite old and securely dated. Considering its large size (198.5 x 23.3 cm), it would have been originally used as a tablecloth or desk cloth and was later converted into a Torah ark curtain (*paroket*). The fabric base is a burgundy velvet, embroidered with decorative motifs in silk, satin, and silver thread. Most of the ornamentation can no longer be seen, having been lost and consumed over the centuries. When the cover was transformed into an ark curtain, four inscriptions were added in four cartouches, so that they would be legible in the fabric's new orientation. Very little of the inscriptions remains, but fortunately the place, Venice, and the date, 1572, are still clearly visible.

The embroiderers' expert skill is revealed in the dedicatory inscriptions stitched along the borders of the textile furnishings used for cult purposes and preserved in the focal points of the synagogue, the ark and the *bimah* (Yaniv 2009). The embroidered dedications were used to commemorate important events in the life of a woman, like marriage and the birth of a child, or to honor the memory of a family member, generally the father or husband. An extremely long embroidered linen Torah binder from Padua, now preserved at the Nahon Museum in Jerusalem (fig. 3), with sixteenth-century bobbin-lace inserts, has an *à jours* inscription that was embroidered by Tamar, wife of Rabbi

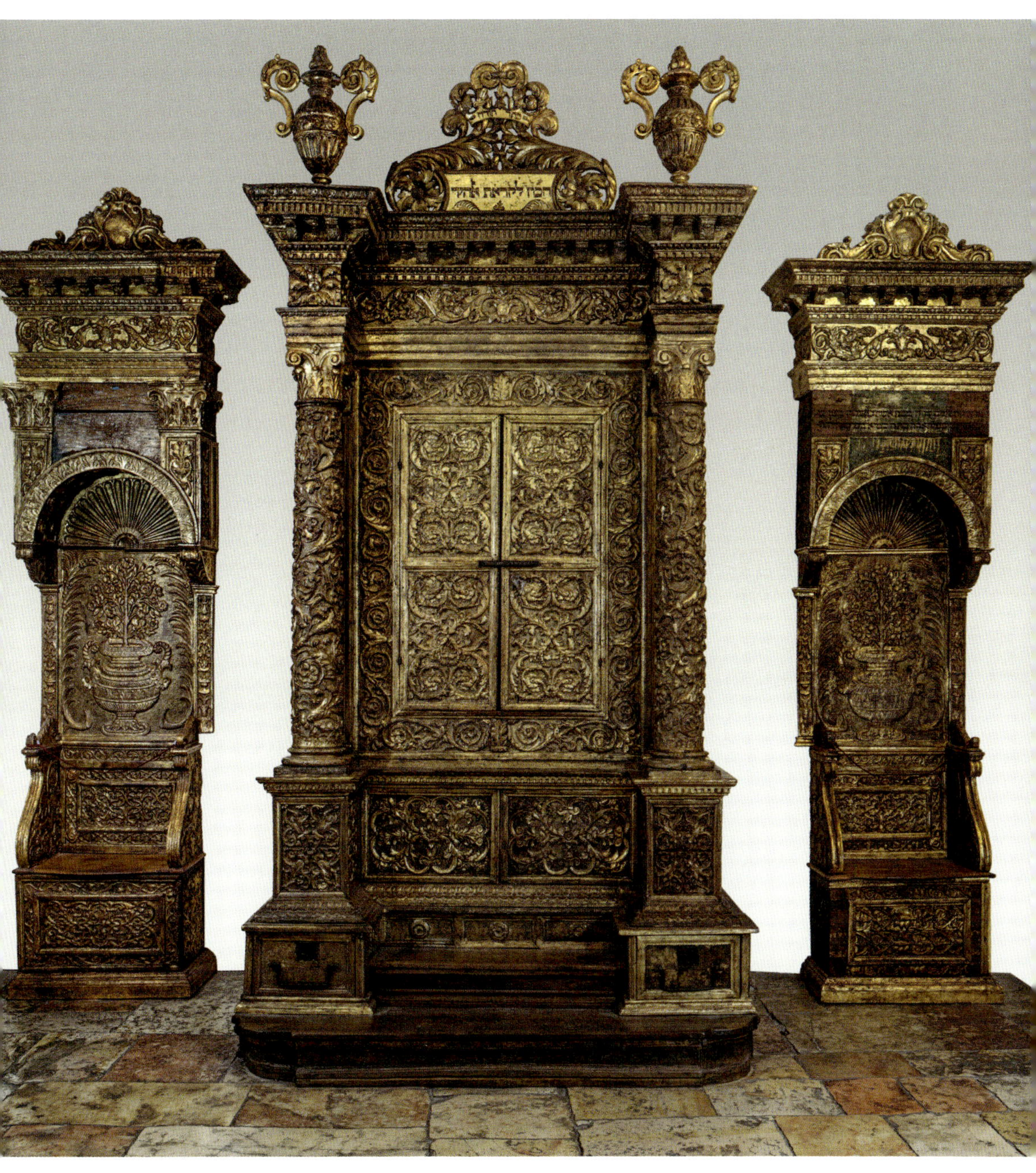

2. *Aron ha-qodesh* (Holy Ark) and *Cathedrae*,
Mantua, 1543 (later brought to Sermide). Umberto
Nahon Museum of Italian Jewish Art, Jerusalem

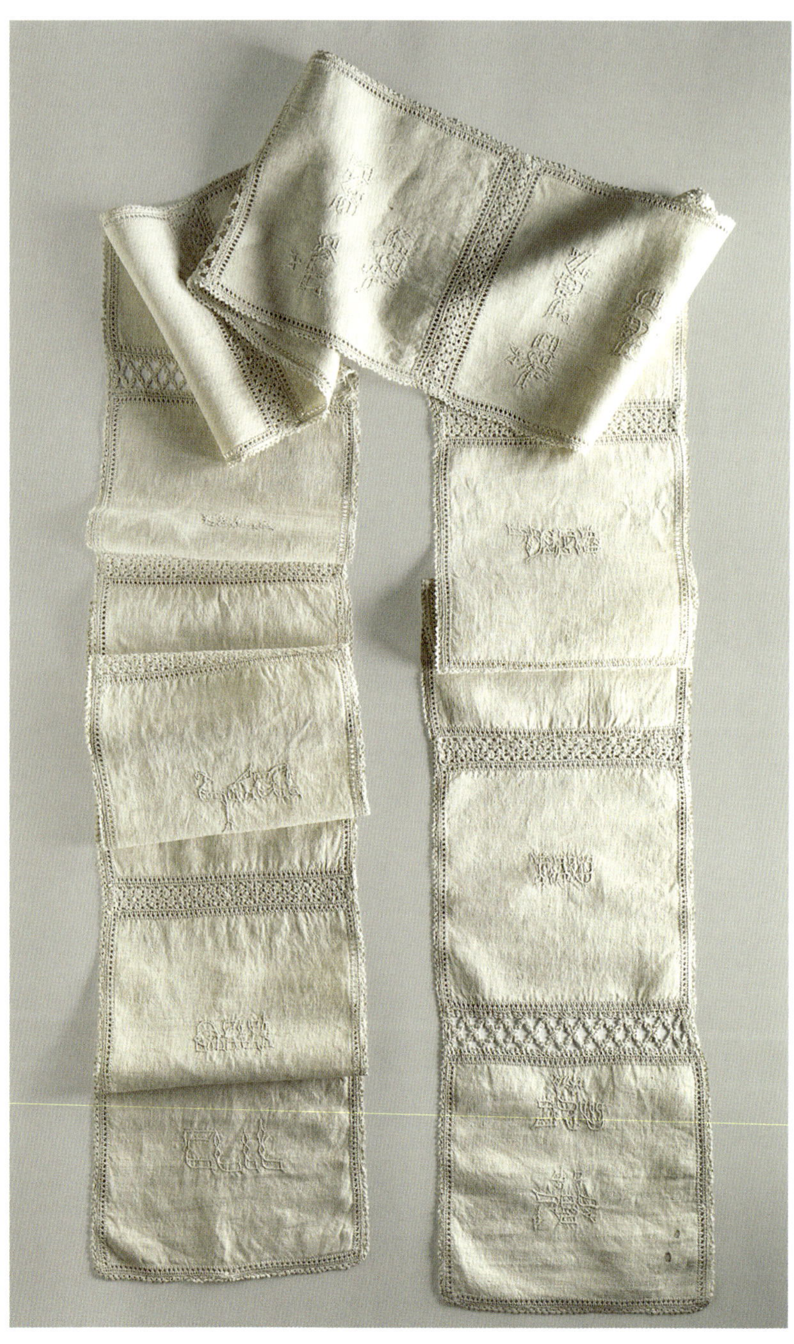

3. Linen Torah binder from Padua, 1572. Umberto
Nahon Museum of Italian Jewish Art, Jerusalem

Moses, to whom it dedicates various blessings that appear along with the date, again 1572 (Contessa 2016b).

Cases of public and recognized female patronage are rarer, one being that of the above mentioned Consilia-Sara Norsa, who commissioned and donated an extraordinary Torah ark to the Sinagoga Grande of Mantua in 1543.

Decorated book patronage

Most patrons of fine books were members of the major wealthy families, such as the da Pisa, Finzi, Norsa, Fano, del Banco, Rieti, Aggio, and Tivoli. The members of these banking dynasties also included intellectuals, poets, scribes, and rabbis, and it was important to them to invest considerable sums in this art, which played a key role in the self-promotion of the patrons (Contessa 2013; Richler 2013). Between the fifteenth and sixteenth centuries, this sphere of activity was marked by intense innovation and production. In Italy during this time, the layout and decoration of prayer books and Bibles was re-conceived and the illustration of the Passover Haggadah was given a contemporary overhaul, both in manuscripts and in prints (see the Haggadah printed in Mantua in 1560); but most importantly, this is probably when the illustration of the Esther scrolls was conceived and created. The richness of book production was also due to the fact that it was one of the arts that Jews were permitted to practice. The prohibition against Jews joining the guilds of the arts and professions did not in fact include the one for scribes and manuscript illuminators.

In some cases, we know the names of the scribes who produced these codices, but only rarely those of the artists who decorated and illustrated them, making them precious and unique. On the other hand, we quite often know the names of the patrons, noted by the scribe in the *colophon* accompanied by a praise and blessings. Many Jewish patrons of manuscripts were also book collectors and buyers of the Jewish codices brought to Italy by Jews expelled from Spain and Portugal (Contessa 2009). There are also a few women among the recipients and patrons, such as Brunetta, daughter of Elijah from Vigevano, a wealthy Florentine banker who was the recipient in 1490 of a prayer book, now in the Biblioteca Estense in Modena (MS aJ9.21), and Lady Maraviglia, the recipient of another prayer book, now in the British Library, London (MS Add. 26957).

The production of handwritten and decorated books in Italy between the fifteenth and sixteenth centuries is distinguished for an extremely high level of execution, seen in the quality of the parchment, the calligraphy, and the decorative technique. Copied by expert scribes (*soferim*), the codices were decorated by calligraphers and often illustrated in accordance with the style of the time. The innovative aspect was the addition of small, meticulously painted images of animals and enchanting landscapes, where nature was accurately described and the interiors depicted following the recent dictates of perspective. The content of the books was diverse and varied, ranging from religious and literary to medical and scientific, as were their illustrations (Narkiss 1969). A copy of the *Avicenna Codex* produced in Florence around 1440 was, for example, decorated with a series of images that describe medical case histories and practice, providing a lively and intriguing glimpse of everyday practice, customs, clothing, contemporary pharmacy, and domestic interiors (Biblioteca Universitaria, Bologna, MS 2197; see Perani's essay in this volume). On the other hand, some codices copied and decorated in Florence around 1470, such as

Joseph Albo's *Sefer ha-'iqqarim* (Book of Principles) (Biblioteca Silvestriana, Rovigo, MS 220) and Moses Nachmanides's *Commentary on the Pentateuch* (John Rylands Library, Manchester, MS heb. 8), were embellished with splendid "white vine stem" decoration, putti and animals with no connection whatsoever to the text.

The most interesting creative experiment with Jewish manuscript painting during the Renaissance was the Rothschild Miscellany (Israel Museum, Jerusalem), produced in the Veneto between 1460 and 1480. This 946-page manuscript was conceived as a unique collection of a large number of distinct texts selected by the patron: Biblical and liturgical books; rabbinical exegesis (*midrash*); texts on Jewish Law, on Jewish ethics and philosophy; and then astronomy, historical legends, and even literature. Almost all of its pages were decorated and illustrated with extremely fine miniatures: more than 200 detailed vignettes illustrating the text, dozens of golden decorated initials, and a variety of depictions of animals and flowers. The scenes represent prayer, feast preparations, weddings and funerals, as well as Biblical episodes, like Abraham receiving the three messengers, Jacob's struggle with the Angel, David playing the harp and the stories of Esther and Judith. The illustrated texts also include the *Meshal ha-qadmoni*, an ancient Hebrew version of Aesop's fables. This extremely fine masterpiece required the invention of numerous images for contents that had never been illustrated before and the creation of an enormous unique and exceptional decorative system, which necessitated considerable artistic originality and skill.

Also of special interest is a series of codices from Ferrara, a community that had welcomed the Jews expelled from Spain, Bohemia, eastern Europe and Milan. The works of the Ferrara school—which produced various Bibles for private use, prayer books and copies of philosophical works—feature decoration in fine black or gold filigree on a colorful background, pairs of symmetrical flowers painted in contrasting hues, and elegant medallions containing images of lively birds and animals against a naturalistic background. The palette of contrasting blues and reds was typical of the Ferrara school, its exponents including painters like Giorgio d'Alemagna and Antonio Maria Sforza, who both worked at the Este court. Artists like Martino da Modena and Marsilio di Bologna exported the style from Ferrara to Venice, Parma, and Bologna. At the end of the century, Ferrara's ornamental repertoire had spread throughout a large area of northern Italy. Decoration in the Ferrara style is found in almost all contemporary Hebrew manuscripts produced in that area, examples including a Bible produced in 1473 (now at the Bibliothèque nationale de France in Paris, MS hébr. 42), which is particularly close to the work of Giorgio d'Alemagna, and the frontispiece of Maimonides's *Guide for the Perplexed* (Bibliothèque nationale de France, Paris, ms hébr. 685), also from 1473 (Sed-Rajna 1994). The Jews who wanted richly decorated books almost certainly turned to non-Jewish local workshops, but it cannot be ruled out that there were also Jewish miniature painters.

Some of the codices decorated in the Italian Renaissance style are in Sephardic script, which means that the Italian patrons were commissioning new Jewish Bibles and prayer books in this script in spite of a long-standing tradition of using semi-cursive Hebrew Italian script. The number of manuscripts produced in Italy and written in Sephardic script by scribes from Spain and Portugal is surprisingly high with respect to the number of Hebrew codices produced on the Italian peninsula during those years (Beit-Arié 2003). One of these scribes was Moses ben Hayyim Aqris, a Sephardic Jew exiled from Spain, who lived in Ferrara between 1512 and 1527 and produced various codices

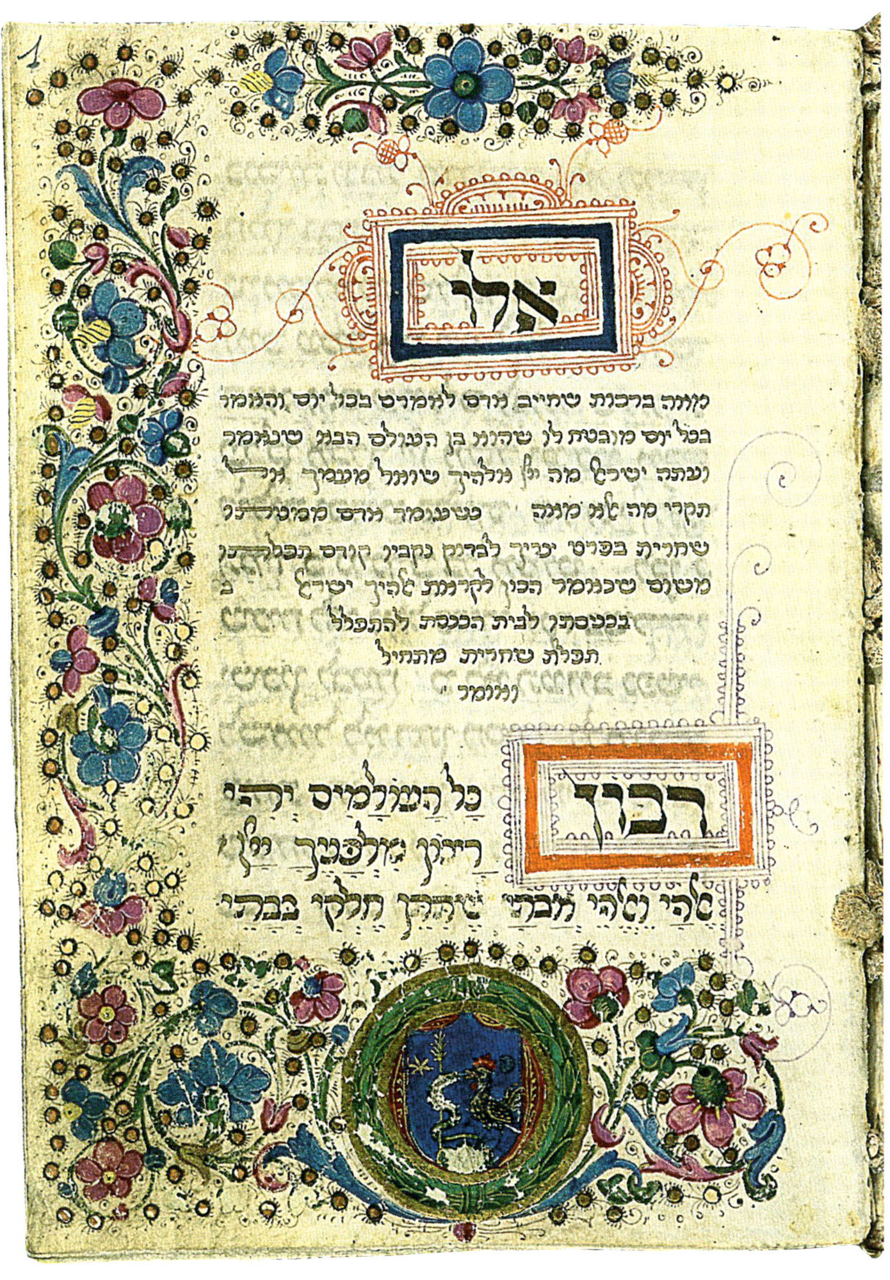

4. *Siddur* (Daily prayer book) according to the Italian or Roman rite Florence, 1490. Biblioteca Estense Universitaria, Modena (cat. 19)

(Contessa 2019). One of these is a splendid prayer book, a *Maḥazor*, that was copied in Ferrara in 1520 and is now at the Bibliothèque nationale de France in Paris (Fondation Smith Lesouef, MS 250). This fine codex was commissioned by a Ferrara banker, Isacco Norsa son of Emanuel, but the book was for his wife, Consilia-Sara, the donor mentioned above of the stunning Holy Ark of the Sinagoga Grande of Mantua (Contessa 2016a and 2017).

As we mentioned, the creation of the decorative cycle for the Esther scroll, which originated in Italy in the fifteenth and sixteenth centuries, is also of immense interest. It is worth noting that the Book of Esther belongs to the group of five scrolls that Jewish tradition prescribes are to be read in the synagogue. The parchment scroll, written by hand in Hebrew, is called a *megillah*. This scroll in particular occupies a place all of its own in the cultural history of Judaism. Since it is the only book in the Jewish Bible in which the name of God does not appear, it was therefore possible to develop a tradition of decorating its parchment with ornamentation and illustrations, a practice tacitly accepted, in this case, by most rabbis.

The oldest known version of a decorated Esther *megillah* seems to be an Italian scroll, very likely from the late fifteenth century, that opens with a decorated initial on a deep red background, with white floral motifs (Biblioteca Palatina, Parma, MS parm. 3304 – De Rossi 53). The first complete, securely dated and entirely decorated *megillah* seems to be a splendid Venetian scroll dated 1564 and now in the Braginsky Collection. What makes it extraordinary is the fact that it was copied by a woman, Stellina, the daughter of Menahem son of Yequtiel. There are a few known examples of medieval female scribes, but this is the only known Renaissance example of a parchment scroll produced by a woman, with her name featuring clearly. Although the family emblem placed next to the *colophon* cannot be identified with certainty, there is no doubt that both Stellina's father and her grandfather were prominent members of the Venetian Jewish community (*A Journey* 2009). In Stellina's *megillah*, the decoration above the columns of texts consists of a series of arches and green leaves, ornamented with human and animal masks painted in gouache. The columns of text are separated by monumental caryatids and satyrs balancing vases and oil lamps on their heads. The figures are unrelated to the story of Esther and are purely decorative.

It is no accident that the idea to decorate and illustrate the Esther scrolls emerged in northern Italy. This Italian Renaissance invention was most probably influenced by the popularity of the figure of Esther in various areas of contemporary culture—in particular, theatre, poetry, and the visual arts. Not forgetting that Venice and Mantua were the main theater centers at the time and the story of Esther was staged a number of times in Venice during the sixteenth and seventeenth centuries. These theatrical performances might have influenced the artists who decorated the Esther scrolls, and this would explain the sophisticated clothing and theatrical gestures of the figures depicted (Friedman 1988; Sabar 2012; Budzioch 2016).

It is worth noting that the first ever Hebrew play dedicated to Esther was written in 1558 on this very subject (it was entitled *Esther*) by Solomon ben Abraham Usque (c. 1530 – c. 1596) in Venice, and was staged in that same city in 1559 and 1592. And we must not forget that during the Renaissance, the theme of Esther was particularly frequent in Christian art, examples including the *cassoni* painted by Jacopo del Sellaio (1442–493) in the second half of the fifteenth century and the frescoes by Paolo Veronese (1528–1588) on the ceiling of the Venetian church of San Sebastiano.

As for printed illustrations of the Esther cycle, we know from written sources that, around 1560, a small press run by Giuseppe Ottolenghi in Riva di Trento printed an Esther scroll with sixteen sheets of parchment. None of the copies have survived, the rabbis having ruled that they needed to be destroyed since they had not been written by hand, as per synagogal requirement. Around ten years later, it was decided to print the illustrations, and so the first Esther scrolls were produced with handwritten text and printed border decoration that was then painted by hand. The earliest surviving examples are decorated with copper-plate engravings by Andrea Marelli, a Christian engraver active in Rome between 1567 and 1572, who produced a whole repertoire of Mannerist borders with garlands, masks, grotesque figures, and animals (Budzioch 2017).

This short excursus clearly shows that the artistic choices of Jewish patrons reflected their affiliation with the Renaissance milieu and acquaintance with Italian artists and humanists, with whom they had both financial and cultural exchanges. The Jewish humanists operated within the social context of their community, followed its precepts and honored its traditional customs and rabbinical studies. But at the same time they were also interested in various fields of humanist culture, including grammar, rhetoric, poetry, history, philosophy, and art; they generously supported Jewish scholars and artists and invested in luxury goods—whether textiles, silver or codices. They were thus in a position to foster the creation of a few works of great cultural interest, putting Italian Renaissance knowledge and creativity in the service of their own tradition, and bending the materiality of the objects to their own spiritual aspirations

Translated by Sarah Elizabeth Cree

Kabbalistic Trees (*Ilanot*) in Italy: Visualizing the Hierarchy of the Heavens
J. H. Chajes

The image of the Renaissance in scholarship has changed remarkably over the last generations. The seminal works of the late nineteenth and early twentieth centuries cast it as the precocious precursor of the rational, disenchanted outlook associated with modernity. From the mid-century, however, scholars increasingly turned their attention to the magical and mystical pursuits of the leading exponents and architects of the Renaissance, pursuits that were no less dear to them than their concomitant commitments to the advancement of Humanism—and that were often profoundly intertwined with them. Thus, for example, Pico della Mirandola's 1486 *De hominis dignitate*, the "manifesto of the Renaissance," was revealed in Brian Copenhaver's well-known study to be deeply indebted to the kabbalistic sources that Pico passionately studied (Copenhaver 2002). Pico's kabbalistic oeuvre has been systematically examined by Giulio Busi, who has also published critical editions of the Latin translations prepared for him by Flavius Mithridates. Of particular relevance to the current essay is the edition and commentary of the so-called "Great Parchment" (*The Great Parchment* 2004). Just as key Christian figures of the Renaissance took great interest in the Kabbalah, often studying privately with their local rabbis or engaging the services of Jews who had converted to Christianity to assist with the gathering, translation, and study of this esoteric lore, many Italian Jews quite naturally identified with the project of the Renaissance writ large. The "Renaissance style" literary productions of Italian rabbis—which continued well into the seventeenth century, long after the historical period is generally considered to have come to an end—has been extensively treated by social, intellectual, and art historians too numerous to mention. Like their counterparts specializing in Christian Renaissance culture, these scholars of Jewish culture first focused on "secular" expressions of this sensibility before embracing a more complex picture in which "rationalism" and Kabbalah were no longer cast as being in opposition to one another, but indeed frequently concurrent.

If the historical picture of the "Hebrew-speaking Renaissance" is now richly drawn, having attended to most fields of Jewish creativity, there remains at least one genre that has only recently received scholarly attention: that known as *ilanot*. *Ilanot*, the plural form of the Hebrew word *ilan* (tree), is a genre borne of the wedding of schema and medium. In its classical form, it is an arboreal diagram inscribed on a parchment sheet. By the sixteenth century, Guillaume Postel and Moses Cordovero articulated such a generic conception of these artifacts, but literary evidence reveals that this designation had already been in use for generations. If the generic term *ilanot* was a metonym for such a map of God on parchment by sometime in the fifteenth century, its arrival displaced an earlier metonym for these artifacts: *yeriot* (singular *yeriah*), meaning (parchment) sheet (Chajes 2019).

Ilanot are literally maps of God, which in a kabbalistic context means that they provide diagrammatic visualizations of the *sefirot*—the divine categories at the heart of this tradition. Given the generic appellation, the arboreal schema is, not surprisingly, dominant. Unlike the Porphyrian Trees associated with this figure, which made their debut in medieval natural philosophy in the eponymous commentary of Aristotle's *Categories* as a useful means of visualizing the scale of being, the kabbalistic tree is fully ontologized: it is understood, to borrow Gershom Scholem's phrase, as the true "mystical shape of the Godhead."

The use of the arboreal schema to represent the structure of the divine did not begin, however, with such dedicated parchments. The earliest extant kabbalistic manuscripts, copied in Rome in the late thirteenth century, include a number of diagrams (Busi 2005, pp. 125–36) among which a tree figure that looks rather more like Darwin's famous tree than Porphyry's. Early kabbalistic diagrams in codices that represent the sefirotic structure are generally modest from a graphical-aesthetic point of view, adumbrating or schematizing the arboreal form. The names of the *sefirot* are arrayed to suggest the tree, but the medallions and channels we commonly associate with the schema are omitted. These diagrams often accompany discussions of the "correct" structure of the Godhead, and present divergent views of the sefirotic constellation as found in the works of the early kabbalists.

It is not apparent that the authors of these early treatises regarded such diagrams as trees, despite their frequent use of arboreal metaphors in the adjacent texts. In fact, the tree was one of the two dominant metaphors for the shape of the divine in classical Kabbalah, the other being the human body. In the seminal thirteenth-century introduction to the *sefirot*, *Sha'arei orah* (Gates of Light), by the Spanish kabbalist Joseph Giqatilla (extant only in manuscripts from the fourteenth century and later), we thus find him drawing a "form" (*tzurah*) of the *sefirot* that could rightly be classified as an arboreal diagram, but which he clearly meant to suggest the human form. It is truly a "stick figure," as, for instance, in a mid-sixteenth-century Italian manuscript now preserved in the Bibliothèque nationale de France in Paris (MS hébr. 822, fol. 94*r*). There was no need to choose between the two metaphors, of course. The rabbinic tradition had for centuries insisted on the conflation, intentionally misreading Deuteronomy 20:19 as "man is like the tree of the field." I suspect that the rich mythologogomena associated with the tree in Jewish tradition—from the Tree of Life of Genesis, to the "Tree that is All" of the foundational kabbalistic *Bahir* of twelfth-century Provençal provenance, as well as the scientific prestige of the Porphyrian Tree, ultimately conspired to bring kabbalists to effect the conflation of metaphor and schema. And if these trends began with the emergence of Kabbalah in Provençe and Spain, and ultimately led to the production of *ilanot* wherever there were kabbalists, it is clear that the development and full flowering of this genre took place on Italian soil from the fourteenth to the sixteenth century and beyond.

Although no parchment-sheet *ilanot* have been found from the fourteenth century, we know they were in use—and in Italy. In that century, the Italian kabbalist Reuben Sarfatti composed the texts for two such artifacts. They have survived, almost exclusively, in text-only copies (*The Great Parchment* 2004, pp. 23–27). Known as "Commentary on the Great Parchment" and "Commentary on the Lesser Parchment," these works, as they have reached us, were copied from the *ilanot* (referred to still as *yeriot*) of which they were originally an integral component. Sarfatti's textual compositions were devoted to introducing the *sefirot* to those beginning the study of the Kabbalah. It was a commonplace of the time to refer to such introductions as "commentaries" on the *sefirot*, and the genre proved to be immensely popular. Gershom Scholem devoted an early publication to listing, catalogue-style, no less than 134 such treatises (Scholem 1933–34). As basic research on *ilanot* has advanced, the close connection between these two genres has become clear: in many cases, the texts we find inscribed in and around the sefirotic trees of *ilan* parchments can be identified with one of the "commentaries" in Scholem's catalogue. It is not always clear whether an *ilan*—as "iconotext" combining text and image—came first, or whether an existing text was subsequently re-presented by the maker of an *ilan*. Either way, the intimacy of these genres is highly significant and illuminates a central function of the *ilanot* of the era. Rather than representing kabbalistic knowledge in the linear mode of pure textuality, the *ilan* inscribes it *in loco*. Organized in and around the diagram, this knowledge is layered and patterned to reveal complex but ordered fields of meaning. Spatializing information is also critical to its recollection, a mnemonic function that we now know, thanks to the studies of Mary Carruthers and Lina Bolzoni among others, to be no less about generative creativity than about storage and retrieval. Using an *ilan* was thus an invitation to practice Kabbalah in a manner that combined textual study, visualization, and some form of mental manipulation or movement as suggested by the diagrammatic shape or structure. Pedagogy and theurgy thus went hand in hand. The medium may also have lent a certain performative impetus of its own, as parchment sheets (scrolls or rotuli) were, by this period, reserved exclusively for ritual use among Jews: Torah scrolls, phylacteries, doorpost scrolls (*mezuzot*), scrolls of Esther. One did not merely *study* a parchment but *perform* it.

Sarfatti's "Commentary on the Great Parchment" provides a fine example. It was listed by Scholem in his catalogue of sefirotic introductions (Scholem 1933–34, no. 28 and no. 52, under different titles). It was also studied by Giovanni Pico della Mirandola in the Latin translation prepared for him by Flavius Mithridates, again strictly as a text. These texts (Hebrew, Latin, and even a new English translation) were published not long ago in a critical edition produced under the direction of Giulio Busi—the pioneer of the study of "visual Kabbalah." Busi rightly noted the connection of a very amateurish sketch found in a manuscript now preserved in the Biblioteca Palatina in Parma (MS parm. 2419, fols *2v–3r*), as related to such a parchment, but this sketch contains little beyond basic captions. Only one fact escaped the attention of these preeminent scholars: the existence of a 1606 copy of a much older *ilan* that included Sarfatti's complete Hebrew text. The old, Italian *ilan* had been acquired by Cardinal Giles of Viterbo early in the sixteenth century. It would subsequently pass to the library of Caterina de' Medici, the Italian noblewoman who became the queen of France. The *ilan* was in such poor condition and so difficult to read that the great scholar Isaac Casaubon found it impossible to decipher upon discovering it among

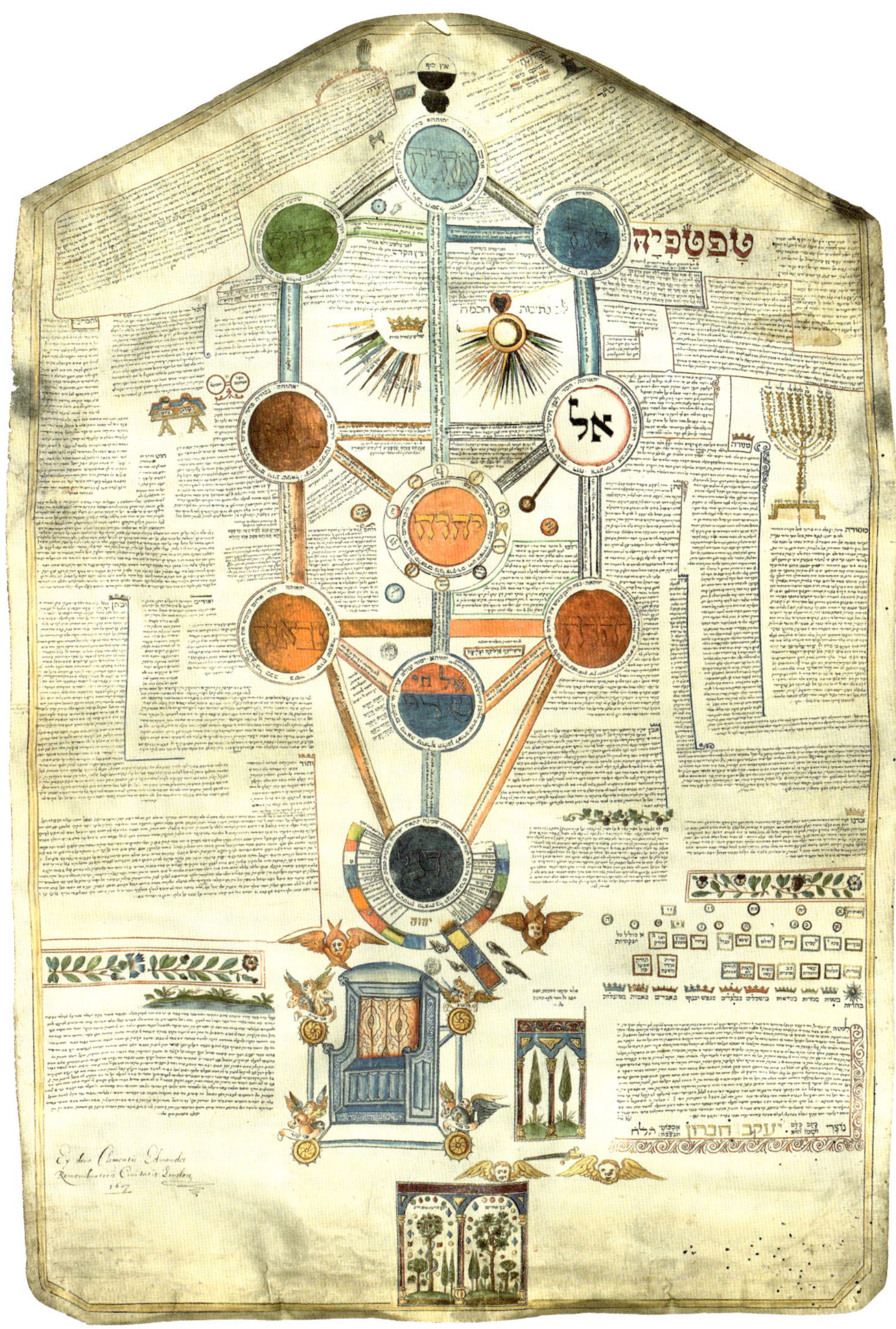

1. *Sefirotic tree featuring Sarfatti's Commentary on the Great Parchment,* copied by James Hepburn, 1606. Bodleian Library, Oxford, MS Hunt. Add. E

the manuscripts that arrived in the Bibliothèque royale of Paris from Caterina's collection. Casaubon thus commissioned the skilled Scottish Hebraist James Hepburn to undertake its reproduction (Grafton and Weinberg 2011). Hepburn was not merely a talented Hebraist, but a fine artist—as his famous "Virga Aurea" engraving, which he printed in Rome in 1616, amply demonstrates. Hepburn's copy of the old *ilan*, which includes a colophon in which he is called "Jacob Hebron," is today in the collection of the University of Oxford (Bodleian Library, Oxford, MS Hunt. Add. E.; Neubauer 1886–1908, no. 2429) (see fig. 1).

In addition to Sarfatti's text, this *ilan* displays many of the features found in early *ilanot*: above the arboreal diagram, a circle suspended with its bottom-half blackened and its top inscribed with *Ein Sof* (No End), representing the apophatic divine; the tree of *sefirot*, with large, inscribed medallions and channels; drawings of the candelabrum (*menorah*) and shewbread table (*shulhan*); a representation of the Chariot, with the four four-headed "beasts" (*kruvim*) carrying the Throne of Glory (Ezekiel 1); and a view of the Garden of Eden, and its Cherub-guarded gates. The candelabrum and shewbread table, each bearing a long history of symbolic and contemplative meaning, were arrayed to the right and left of the tree, in accordance with their placement in the southern and northern sides of the Temple. The Chariot with its four four-headed angelic beasts was the quintessential marker of the liminal zone between creation and creator; these beasts guarded the gates

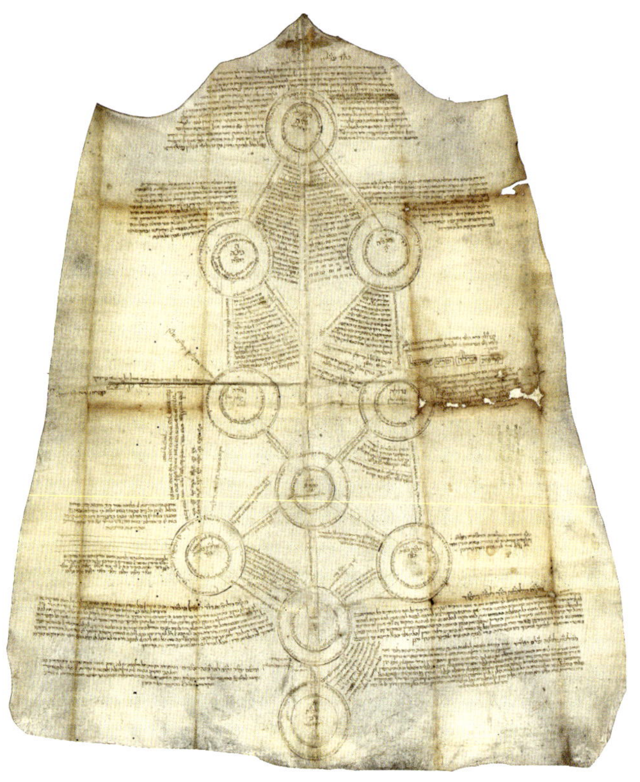

2. *Sefirotic tree*, Candia (Crete), 1451. Vatican Library, Vatican City, MS Vat. ebr. 530 III

of Eden (Genesis 3, 24) and appeared when the skies opened above Ezekiel's head to reveal the "Heaven of Heavens" (Ezekiel 1)—the latter being the direct inspiration for many diagrammatic kabbalistic renderings. They also adorned nearly every component of the Tabernacle—designed to create a portal to the divine—from the tent tapestries to the Ark of the Covenant. In a glance, therefore, we may already sense how the *ilan* invited the contemplative to explore and to integrate the symbolic systems of a variegated body of Jewish esoteric knowledge, represented in a map-like diagrammatic form.

Without the original parchment for comparison, it is hard to assess whether Hepburn was faithful to its aesthetics and merely recreated them, or whether he took the liberty to embellish as he copied. Hepburn's *ilan* is indeed a beauty, with its rich dyes (applied also in the sefirotic medallions so as to convey their respective color associations), floral decorative motifs, and cherubic angel figures. Its Throne of Glory recalls the "cabinet-style" throne chairs of Renaissance Italy, which could be found in the homes of Florentine nobility. Giuliano de' Medici had a particular broad one at his Palazzo Strozzi; more modest throne chairs resembling the one pictured in the *ilan* could be found in synagogues as well. Such a "synagogue throne" from Siena was in the Berliner Kunstgewerbemuseum at the beginning of the twentieth century (Bode 1902, p. 19). The Throne of Glory may also be compared to much earlier artifacts, such as the sixth-century Episcopal Throne of Archbishop Maximianus in Ravenna's Museo Arcivescovile. Unlike the rest of the figures of the *ilan*, the Throne of Glory is rendered to suggest three-dimensionality. The firmament upon which it sits is also drawn as a cube, with diagonals converging underneath it from each of four corners—a technique used in medieval treatises of geometry to convey three-dimensionality but indeed unusual to find in kabbalistic works, to say the least (for a cube represented in two dimensions using the same technique, see, e.g., Gerbert of Aurillac, *Geometria*, c. 980, Oxford, Bodleian Library, MS Selden supra 25, fol. 119*v*; English, Canterbury?, c. 1200).

It would seem that the basic graphic elements of *ilan* parchments we have noted were in place by around 1400. They provided the matrix for any number of texts—from singular compositions such as Sarfatti's to eclectic anthological collages. An examination of the latter reveals not only what was on the bookshelves of the kabbalists who extracted the passages for inscription in and around the diagrammatic elements, but what they thought particularly significant in each.

Of course, not all *ilanot* had the aesthetic ambitions of the Hepburn *ilan*—which too may have outstripped its long-lost model in this regard. Few *ilan* parchments from before 1500 have reached us, and those that have are truly austere. Like Hepburn's *ilan*, they avail themselves of an entire parchment sheet. Inscribed upon the sheet is a single, albeit large, arboreal figure that serves to visually organize a commentary on the *sefirot*. A Vatican parchment (Vatican Library, MS Vat. ebr. 530 III) is a striking example despite its visual austerity (see fig. 2). Its top edge cut in a manner that retains something of the natural contours of the animal skin while suggesting something like a clerestory roof, this intriguing *ilan* was drafted in 1451 according to the *colophon* on its verso. The text arrayed throughout is a commentary on the *sefirot* that was listed, in its two very similar forms, in Scholem's aforementioned index (Scholem 1933–34, nos. 76 and 115). A version of the same commentary appears on an *ilan* recently discovered in the Biblioteca Queriniana of Brescia (MS L FI 11; see cat. 30 and fig. 3). The schema of the Brescia *ilan* is somewhat unusual and clearly expresses a view of the sefirotic structure in which the central *Tiferet* is dominant. The "arrowhead" element atop *Keter* is also distinctive; might it be related to

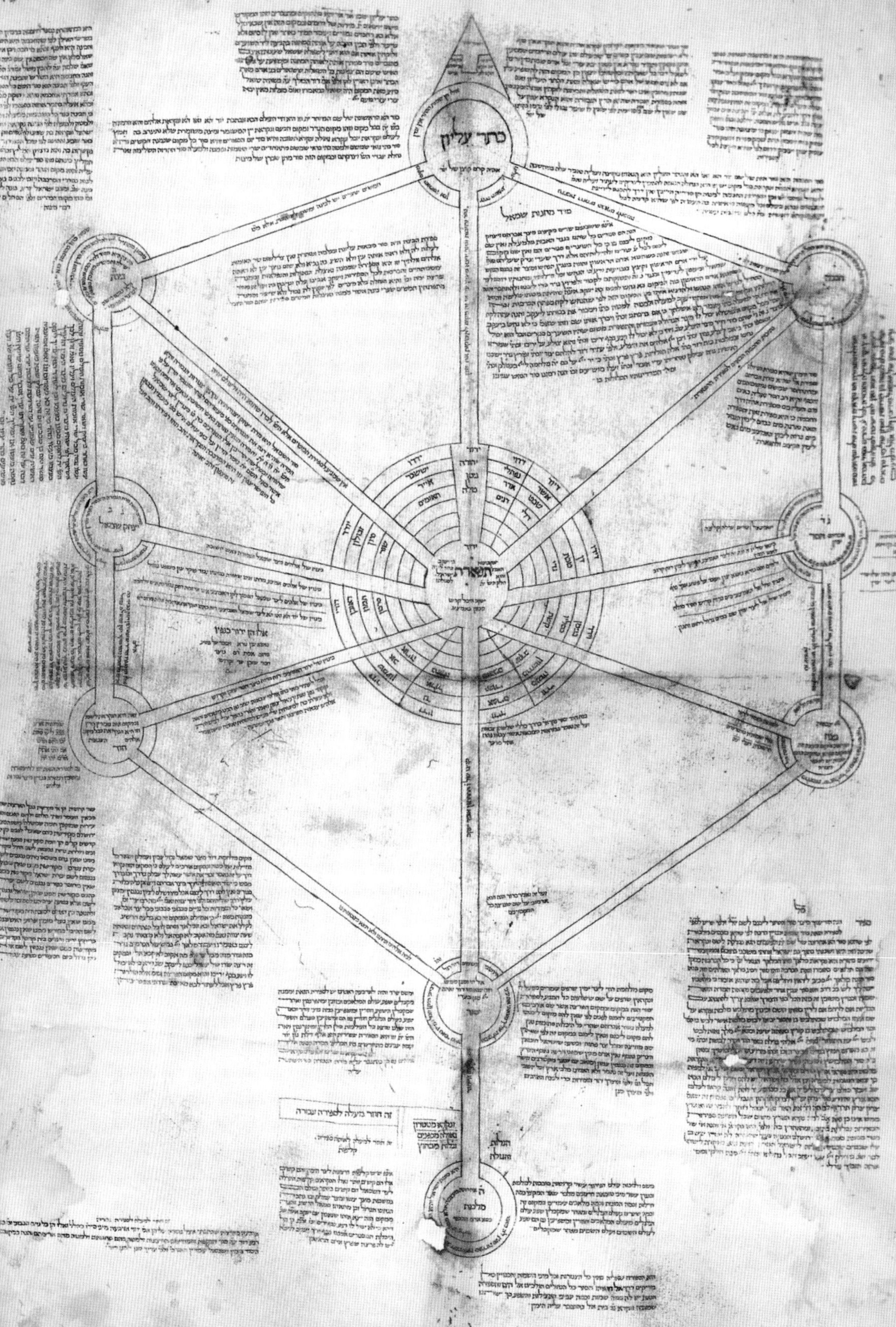

כתר עליון
תפארת
מלכות

the cut of the parchment found in MS Vat. ebr. 530 III? Neither of the two *ilanot* embed *Ein Sof* in shape of any kind, preferring instead to write of the Infinite in the upper background space of the parchment.

Not every *ilan* was committed to parchment. It is at times difficult to tell whether the more amateurish sketches drawn upon the opening or closing binding pages of old codices were fashioned by students on the basis of their own readings and for their personal use, whether they were preliminary studies for what might next be executed on parchment, or if they were copies quickly made of impressive *yeriot*. In this regard we may point to the very old codex that is today housed in Munich's Bayerische Staatsbibliothek, MS hebr. 119. It is a small miscellany and the compositions it contains were copied by different hands; one of the scribes, a certain "Shem Tov son of Jacob the Sefaradi," left a colophon attesting to his having created the work for himself in the city of "Modon on the Sea," today Methoni in Messenia (Peloponnese, Greece), once under Venetian rule. In 1404, Shem Tov, who wrote in a Spanish script, left a fascinating rota diagram of the *sefirot* with permutations of the Tetragrammaton inscribed around a central medallion in which *Tiferet*, the central *sefirah*, was inscribed. The rest of the miscellany, also dated to the fifteenth century, is written in an Italian script—and concludes with an arboreal diagram that shows just how established was the genre by this time. The template that we see in the "Great Parchment" is essentially the same: a denary tree occupies the large, central space of the double page, flanked on either side by candelabrum and shewbread table. The lowest *sefirah* of *malkhut*, identified with the most immanent expression of the Godhead, the divine presence called *Shekhinah*, appears as if it were docking atop the celestial spheres—the latter represented, not surprisingly, as concentric circles. By illustrating the created cosmos with this established astronomical schema, the *ilan* aligns itself with a prestigious scientific tradition and stakes its claim to a totalizing knowledge that literally goes beyond it. Arrayed in four squares around the meeting point between the divine and celestial spheres is the illustration of the Chariot, here rendered schematically rather than with the representational approach we have seen in Hepburn's copy of the Great Parchment. In this rather improvisational sketch—an impression confirmed by the scribe's attestations to elements in need of revision—we find texts written in every conceivable angle, in and around the diagrammatic elements. Among them are selections from the seminal thirteenth-century *Meirat Einayim* (Light of the Eyes), and, most prominently, from the Zohar commentary by the great early Italian kabbalist, Menachem Recanati. During the fourteenth and fifteenth centuries, most Italian kabbalists knew of the Zohar primarily through Recanati's commentary—and the Italian *ilanot* of this era rarely contain zoharic material that is not borrowed from his popular work.

Although the basic elements of *ilanot* in these centuries were stable and recurring, the range of kabbalistic positions on basic questions relating to the layout of the divine topography produced graphic variations. Some of these variations seem to reflect local preferences. To take a very easily discernable example, we may observe the array of the top three *sefirot* of any given *ilan*. In those we have adduced thus far, the arrangement is triangulated. Spanish kabbalists believed this layout to be the most accurate representation of the structure of the uppermost *sefirot*, made in keeping with the zoharic traditions they so revered.

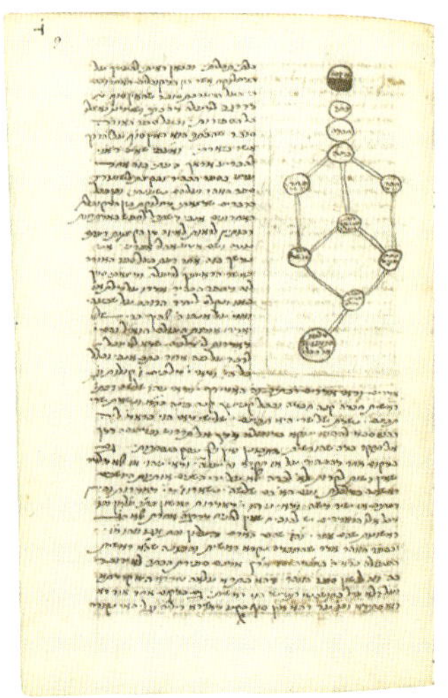

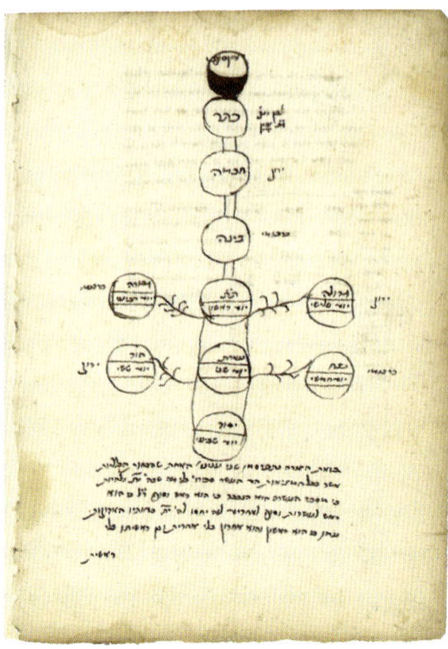

4. Elijah Hayyim of Genazzano, *Iggeret hamudot*, 1526. Bibliothèque nationale de France, Paris, MS hébr. 857, fol. 9*r*

5. *Sefirotic tree*, early sixteenth century. Vatican Library, Vatican City, MS Vat. ebr. 441, fol. 111*v*

In the mid-sixteenth century, R. Moses Cordovero, whose name bespeaks his family's Iberian origins and whose magnum opus, *Pardes Rimmonim*, both preserved and codified kabbalistic opinions in a manner recalling the halakhic oeuvre of his Safedian neighbor R. Joseph Karo, decided unequivocally in its favor. Cordovero refers to the overall schema as *segolta, segol, segol*: the names of particular paratextual symbols used in the cantillation and vocalization of the Torah that resemble *deltas* and *nablas*. The mnemonic had been coined by the kabbalist R. Judah Ḥayyat, a refugee of the 1492 Spanish expulsion, in his *Minhat Yehudah*, a work he composed in large measure to assert the authority of Iberian traditions in his new home, Italy. It seems that among Italian kabbalists, there was a certain preference for a different configuration of the uppermost *sefirot*, one in which they were centered one atop the other. Why? Because the spatial implications of right and left could not possibly apply to such sublime recesses of divinity—something of a philosophical concern, in keeping with the general character of so much Italian kabbalistic speculation. This tower-like configuration may be seen in many Italian codices of the period, with examples including the *Iggeret hamudot* of R. Elijah Hayyim of Genazzano from the late Quattrocento (Bibliothèque nationale de France, Paris, MS hébr. 857, fol. 9*r*, an Italian manuscript dated 1526. On this work, see Lelli 2002 and fig. 4 above), in the sefirotic diagrams included in *Seder ha-ilan* (Order of the Tree), an anonymous Italian work that may be compared to the emblem books of the period that feature symbolic images and accompanying explanations (e.g. in Vatican Library, Vatican City, MS Vat. ebr. 441, fols. 110*r*–117*v*, an Italian manuscript dated to the early sixteenth century (see fig. 5). Dr. Eliezer Baumgarten and I are nearing completion of a critical edition of this work, to be published in the Vatican's *Studi e testi* series). Of particular interest is the arboreal diagram displaying this configuration that also includes decorative botanical elaboration, something rarely found in kabbalistic trea-

6. Elijah Menahem Halfan, with the assistance of Abraham Sarfatti, *Sefirotic tree*, Venice, 1533, Biblioteca Medicea Laurenziana, Florence (cat. 29)

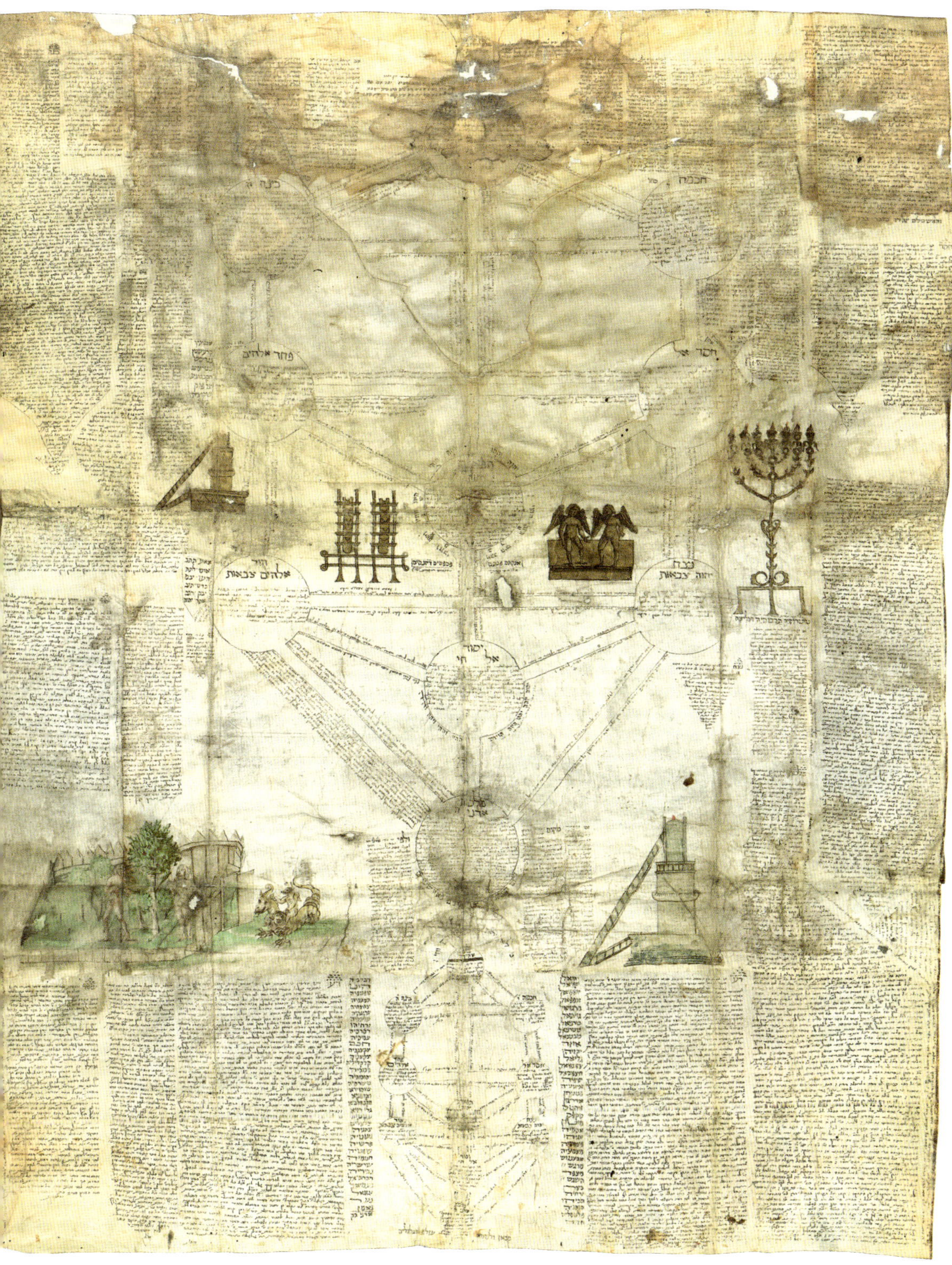

tises. As we shall soon see, the grandest of
all Renaissance *ilan* parchments, the anonymous creator of which drew extensively on
Seder ha-ilan, fashioned the dominant central figure of the imposing rotulus in this
"Italian" style.

Additional examples of variations
expressing conceptual differences could be
proffered, but let us suffice with two: the
representation of *Ein Sof*, the Infinite represented above the sefirotic tree, and what
might be called the overall perspective of a
given *ilan*. Regarding the former, the black
and white circle was widely used—generally with black below and white above (as
we have seen in Hepburn's *ilan* as well as in
the *Iggeret hamudot*). A white bottom and
black top might be used as well, however, as
in Munich, Bayerische Staatsbibliothek, MS
hebr. 119. These variations suggest differing
conceptions of the relationship between the
sefirot, which for all their sublimity retain
some degree of knowability, and the Infinite. The issue of perspective was hotly
debated in these centuries as well. Why was
the right side of the divine represented by
the vertical sequence of *sefirot* on the right
side of the arboreal diagram as we face it?
Would that not imply that they were on the
left of the divine? Would that not throw all
of kabbalistic symbolism, with its clear associations between right and mercy opposing left and judgment into disarray? Rather
than enter the thicket of such discussions, a
story will suffice: the aforementioned R. Judah Ḥayyat tells of having seen an *ilan* that
was the mirror image of the iconic tree. As
if spun 180° on its vertical axis, it expressed
the divine perspective: right and left as dex-
ter and sinister. "And I bear witness that I
saw in an Italian city called Reggio, in the
possession of a man of understanding, an

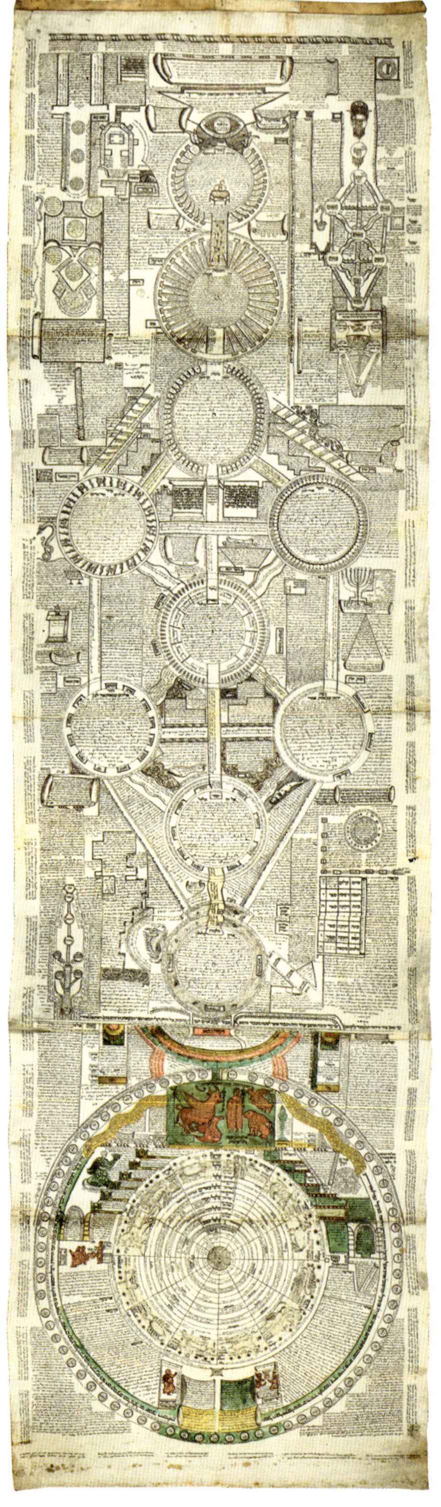

ilan that was drawn in this [inverted] manner. And they told me that a great man had made it." No *ilan* of this sort has reached us, although suggestive "misplacements" of Abraham (associated with the right but inscribed on the left) and Ishmael (vice-versa) are to be found, including in the Hepburn *ilan*.

No review of the Italian *ilanot* of the Renaissance would be complete with at least a brief discussion of two other artifacts—one, indeed, a *family* of manuscripts with some dozen extant witnesses. The other is a unique *ilan* crafted in 1533 by R. Elijah Menahem Halfan, in collaboration with his mentor, R. Abraham Sarfatti. Today in the Biblioteca Medicea Laurenziana in Florence (MS Firenze, Bibl. Medicea Laurenziana, Plut. XLIV.18; see cat. 29 and fig. 6), this *ilan* was discovered by Isaia Sonne (Sonne 1934) and then described by Giulio Busi (Busi 2005, pp. 385–86) and by Fabrizio Lelli (Lelli 2008). Let us begin with this latter scroll. Writ large, Halfan's *ilan* has quite a bit in common with Hepburn's: the large denary tree dominating its center, the candelabrum and shewbread table (supplemented by additional figures in this case), and an even more elaborate representation of the Garden of Eden. These elements are well-executed, the scene in Eden representing an attractive, smiling couple on either side of a tree with green leaves and red hanging fruit. In the background we see a section of the wall that is imagined having surrounded the garden, albeit with an open door. Approaching the happy couple is a satyr-like creature riding a dragon, reflecting kabbalistic traditions that cast the biblical snake as the demonic couple Samael and Lilith. Although neither the divine Chariot nor the celestial spheres are drawn, two Cherubs (as in Hepburn's *ilan*, of the "cherubic" rather than of either the beastly or the diagrammatic sort)—presumably representing those atop the Ark of the Covenant—are placed among the other Temple vessels, whereas the central, lower-most inscription declares that "from here and below is the World of the Spheres (*galgalim*)." Mention should also be made of the peculiar detail of the replicated but miniaturized arboreal diagram placed just below the central figure. This diminutive tree seems to represent the *sefirot* apprehensible by the human mind, as they are separated from the larger tree above them by an arching biblical inscription: "no person may see Me and live" (Exodus 33:20). Halfan's *ilan* is also densely inscribed with texts. Here again, the text is of the "Commentary on the Sefirot" genre, and is Halfan's own, who maintains to have followed the recommendations of the older Abraham Sarfatti (Scholem 1933–34, no. 10, attributed to Halfan; at no. 119 the text is mistakenly presumed to be anonymous). Halfan's responsibility for both the textual and graphic facets of his *ilan* shows us with unusual clarity the profound convergence of the two genres of *ilanot* and *sefirot* commentaries.

We conclude with the crowning achievement of Italian *ilan*-making in the Renaissance. Sometime in early to mid-sixteenth century, a still unidentified Italian kabbalist and scribal artist was inspired to create an *ilan* of unprecedented scale and beauty (Oxford, Bodleian Library, MS Hunt. Add. D). A broad, long parchment rotulus, illuminated, colorful, and intricately inscribed, it was a masterpiece by any standard. Over its multiple stitched membranes, this great parchment revealed a map of the heavens—and the "Heaven of Heavens"—stretched out, not *like* parchment, as in Psalm 104:4, but *upon* it. On parchment sheets stitched sequentially to form a long, vertical rotulus, he inscribed an iconotextual summa: an integrated presentation of the visual and textual Kabbalah as he knew and understood it, expressed in the exquisite conventions of representation that reigned in the Renaissance Italy of his day. Its aspirations to pansophy, or universal knowledge, is evident in its dedication of the bottom third of the rotulus to the presentation of a Ptolemaic scheme of the earth surrounded by the heavenly spheres (fig. 7).

The imposing vertical scroll is lushly filled with hundreds of discrete graphic elements, diagrammatic schemata, symbolic forms, and decorative embellishments, around and within which texts are inscribed. Finely wrought, its density is made possible by the elegant precision of its execution, impressive from afar for its grand scale and, when inspected closely, in the details of its minutiae. Although at present we cannot identify its author, his creation was clearly appreciated, as the many copies that remain with us five hundred years later attest. Copying this work was anything but a trivial matter: only scribes with a mastery of their craft—including complex draftsmanship and decorative illustration—could take on such a commission, and only the wealthiest patrons could have afforded to place an order. Unlike many *ilanot*, this was most certainly *not* made by kabbalists for themselves or their students. This luxury manuscript would have undoubtedly been commissioned by the individuals and families for whom illuminated festival prayer books, *hagadot*, *ketubot*, and the like were fashioned. Given the interest in Kabbalah in Renaissance Italy among non-Jewish elites, the acquisition need not have been limited to wealthy Jews alone. In all likelihood this was the "Tree of Kabbalah" to which Benedetto Blanis, a Florentine Jew of the early seventeenth century, referred in a letter to his patron Don Giovanni de' Medici (Goldberg 2011, pp. 120–21):

> I am delighted to have so important a Tree of Kabbalah here in Florence, brought from Lippiano at my request. I am having it copied on vellum with great diligence, so it will not be inferior to the original in any way but even better. I hope that this Tree will please Your Most Illustrious Excellency and that we will be able to enjoy it together.

The Tree was cultural capital: to possess it was literally to possess an all-encompassing picture of the cosmos in an age during which the distinction between a picture and the thing depicted, the sign and its referent, was often elided. It would have been presumed to be a powerful talisman as well, the divine structures it represented not being merely symbols but figures of divine reality itself.

Extracted from the schemata within and around which they are inscribed are texts that add up to over 30,000 words. A careful study of these texts is only now taking place. Indeed, the brief entry in no. 829 of the Margoliouth Catalogue (Margoliouth 1909–15) and the poetic lines in Giulio Busi's pioneering monograph are the only descriptions of the Tree ever published (Busi 2005, pp. 387–88). Hand-written notes in the archives of Gershom Scholem reveal that the legendary scholar had inspected the exemplars in the British Library and the Bodleian at the University of Oxford. Scholem wrote that they contain an "unknown gigantic text" (*unbekannter Riesentext*) and copied the *colophon* of MS Or. 6465 from the British Library in London (the note is found in file 92.4 of the Scholem archives, held by the National Library of Israel in Jerusalem). In this *colophon*—the only one found to date on a witness in this manuscript family—the itinerant Polish kabbalist David Darshan takes credit for having drafted the copy while in Modena in 1556.

Until all of the texts have been transcribed and sourced, we must be circumspect in our characterization of its authorial voice, but still, the Tree seems anything but the work of a neutral compiler. Its selections and the connective tissue that binds them reveal an author/editor who chose, introduced, adapted, and integrated a wide range of material—kabbalistic and scientific, philosophical and magical. In his world, these terms were fluid, complementary, and overlapping if not homologous. Initial surveying reveals an integrative, synthetic, even encyclopedic work, with selections drawn from the corpus of kabbalistic literature circulating in mid–fourteenth-century Italy, including passages from, among others, the *Bahir*, Nachmanides, the *'Iyun* circle, Joseph Giqatilla, *Ma'arekhet elohut*, Menachem Recanati, Abraham Abulafia, and Joseph ben Shalom Ashkenazi. The presence of Maimonides is also felt. The *absence* of texts from the zoharic literature (citations from Recanati aside) and of post-1450 materials more generally, provides a *terminus post quem* that is in full accord with the results of preliminary paleographic and aesthetic analysis, which reinforces the dating of the original to the late fifteenth century.

Just as the creator of the Tree assembled its texts from the corpus at hand, so too its images. Gazing from afar, two stand out: the large, decadal arboreal diagram that dominates the upper two-thirds of the long parchment, and the formidable representation of the concentric circles of the Ptolemaic heavens filling its bottom third. For a kabbalist c. 1500, these were the two authoritative schemata for mapping the structure of the *sefirot* and the spheres. The central *ilan* of the Tree adopts the tower-like array of the three uppermost *sefirot*. The image of the lower frame, with its spheres sliced into the twelve divisions of the zodiac, is in accordance with the Ptolemaic world-picture and would have been familiar to, and accepted as authoritative by, any scholar of the age.

Taking a closer look at the details of this great parchment, smaller images abound. There is the "Eye": atop the highest *sefirah*, the Infinite God ('*Ain Sof*) is figured as an open eye. There are dragons and snakes, bubbling springs and flowing rivers, altars and candelabra, and, most surprisingly, rabbis: Rabbi Akiva, one of the "four who entered *Pardes*," pictured to the left of the spheres. Akiva stands tall above the spheres as well, amidst the Chariot beasts that stand just below the concave, rainbow-like firmament upon which a pedestal is inscribed, the "figure of the Throne" (*dmut ha-kise*). Were we looking at a Christian cosmograph of the spheres—Jesus and the saints might have been pictured above them in the Empyrean. For our kabbalist, however, the figure of the Divine above the Chariot is visualized as the sefirotic tree.

The great Tree was not a huge textual anthology that happened to be inscribed alongside a myriad of images over a series of parchment sheets. To the contrary, in it, text and image are thoroughly interwoven. This kind of inseparable wedding of text and image has been called an "iconotext" by scholars and refers to an artifact in which the two elements cannot truly be separated. How was one to engage—we can hardly say "read"—with this *ilan*? This luxury manuscript is hardly representative of the genre, of course. It *can* be studied, navigated thoroughly and methodically, but it was likely perceived more as a talisman than a textbook. As it represents the totality of the cosmos, it is not necessary that every part be read and studied, because they convey the idea in its entirety. The sublime is characterized by the very fact that it is too much, too great to grasp.

My research on this topic is supported by the Israel Science Foundation (Grant 1568/18).

Jews and Christian Hebraists in Renaissance Italy
Saverio Campanini

In the autumn of 1528, in response to an appeal by the French ambassador Jean de Langeac, Bishop of Avranches, the Council of Ten in Venice decreed that the Jewish physician Jacob Mantino would be exempted from the rule that obliged Jewish residents of the Most Serene Republic to wear a yellow hat as a distinguishing, and vilifying, marker of identity. Mantino, a physician and philosopher of Spanish origin and translator of numerous medical and philosophical texts from Hebrew to Latin, was permitted to wear the black cap of a Doctor, a title which he took quite legitimately as a holder of a university degree and, especially, a former teacher of Medicine—with a special permit and stipend—at the Archiginnasio of Bologna. All the same, the magistrates insisted on two things: that the exemption was not indefinite, and that Mantino still had to reside in the ghetto, like all Jews had been required to do since 1516. That this exemption—always for just a few weeks at a time—was out of the ordinary is underlined by the fact that, over many years and multiple visits to Venice, Mantino was required to renew it over and again. This he achieved with the intercession of respected, influential figures including—besides the French ambassador—the Pontifical Legate, the Imperial ambassador Mendoza, the diplomatic representative of Henry VIII of England, and the Marshall of France Teodoro Trivulzio, whose variable health made Mantino's services as a doctor indispensable (Kaufmann 1893; Ravà 1903; Münster 1954). Such a concession, issued with apparent reluctance, and only to avoid displeasing "such worthy personages," can be viewed in many respects as being emblematic of the fortunes of Jews during the Renaissance.

In fact, the distinct standing of the Jews in the late-antique and medieval Christian world was nothing new. They were the only heterodox minority to be tolerated, albeit not always or in all places, and enjoyed, so to speak, a special status in Christian theology, and equally in civic law and statutes. When this had been experienced before by the Jewish people, prior to the advent of Humanism, it had always been as a collective; they were perceived as a separate group, a community with a unified identity, and not as a sum of individuals. The emergence of the individual, on the other hand, was one of the most characteristic phenomena of the Renaissance; it was certainly one of the most debated, at least since the publication of Burckhardt's admirable *The Civilization of the Renaissance in Italy* (1860), a work that, albeit of its time, still gleams like a mirror. Over the years, Burckhardt's interpretation has not been spared from critique or revision. Stephen Greenblatt (1980) and, more recently, John J. Martin (2004) have both highlighted an interesting if not unexpected paradox: the individualism of the Renaissance was essentially a social creation (see Greco's essays in this volume). This can be demonstrated by focusing on the experiences of a conspicuous selection of Jews who were involved in the development of Humanism and Renaissance values, especially in Italy, in the fifteenth and early sixteenth centuries: the sort of social mobility to which these Jewish intellectuals aspired was invariably an individual one—indeed, it could not have been otherwise. At the same time, the iron fetters against which this sort of emancipation *ad personam*, if we can call it that, was straining were invariably applied by the collective. The Jewish face of the Renaissance—so neglected by Burckhardt, who in private did not disguise his scant regard for Jews and Judaism—was in part restored by Ludwig Geiger, who authored the supplements and appendices to the third and later editions of *The Civilization* (1877–78; Herrmann 2003). All the same, it was only in the twentieth century that, having been underappreciated if not outright ignored for so long, the central role of Jews in the origin and development of Humanism and the Renaissance began to be recognized, especially in the work of Cassuto (1918), Roth (1959), Shulvass (1973), Ruderman (1981), Bonfil (1991), and Busi (1992, 2007). Yet, much remains to be done to rescue the place of Jewish people and the Hebrew language in the history and, more so, in the mythology of the Renaissance from this recurrent amnesia. Furthermore, as we will see in the final analysis, the very conditions that enabled the extraordinary proliferation of the Renaissance also, inversely, marked its dramatic decline.

The key moments in the Christian rediscovery of Hebrew—after centuries of neglect only interrupted by short, solitary episodes that were largely limited to single individuals or remote monasteries and did not lead to a unified significant movement or produce any form of material to aid study, if not on a localized level—generally coincided with moments of crisis and renewal in the Church, such as the medieval flourishing of interest in Hebrew (particularly in Spain and England) around the time of the emergence of the mendicant orders. These currents were consolidated and ratified in the period of the Avignon Papacy by a resolution of the Council of Vienne (1311), which solemnly provided for the establishment of chairs of Hebrew and Arabic at the universities of Oxford, Paris, Bologna, and Salamanca, though this provision remained effectively unfulfilled. Thus, it was not until the time of the Council of Constance (1414–18) that we see a new and distinctive intellectual "scene" emerge. Along with the humanistic enthusiasm that drove myriad churchmen and diplomats to convent libraries in search of Latin manuscripts—and, increasingly, Greek texts as well— we begin to find the first signals of a growing interest in the Hebrew language. An early example is provided by the use of Hebrew and Hebrew characters to draw up a note of ownership in two codices belonging to Giordano Orsini, who is associated with the figure of Nicholas of Cusa (Questa 1957). Joining Orsini at the Council of Constance was Poggio Bracciolini who, on his journey home, during a stay in Baden, decided to follow advice he had received more than once from Niccolò Niccoli and start learning Hebrew. In the same years, Marco Lippomano, an official of the Republic of Venice, was able to enjoy a fully-fledged correspondence in Hebrew with a Jewish physician named Crescas Meir, who was living in Apulia. In the first letters, Lippomano is proud to reveal his progress with the language; the correspondence goes on to deal largely with philosophical issues and, in good humanist fashion, the search for books, including both Jewish writing and, particularly, Hebrew versions of Arabic texts. Soon enough, the exchange moves on to the more familiar, if much more treacherous, terrain of religious polemic (Busi and Campanini 2004). Even in this early example we can identify a pattern that would characterize Renaissance Christians' investigation of Hebrew and Judaism: the encounter is always on an individual level, and originates in questions of science, technology, and other neutral subject matters before veering rapidly into the more well-trodden but ultimately barren territory of clashes of identity, in which loyalties to the collective regain the upper hand (Campanini 2004). As we will see, in the decades of the chaotic and tumultuous discovery of the Hebrew language and Jewish culture by Renaissance Christians, this model is repeated by numerous illustrious pairings. However, it is worth investigating, ultimately, whether despite the setbacks and sudden lurches and overturnings, these exchanges might have sown some seed whose fruit was gathered in a later age or, indeed, remains for us to reap (*L'hébreu* 1992; *Cultural Intermediaries* 2004).

From the very beginning, the spread of the study of Hebrew among humanist scholars, especially those in Florence, encountered robust opposition from positions of authority, an indication that the path of the Hebraist—which for theological reasons would often be disguised as literary investigation—was destined to be a rocky one. When Giovanni Cirignani announced to the great humanist and translator Leonardo Bruni that he had started learning Hebrew with a view to verifying Jerome's Latin translation of the Bible, Bruni responded with a famous letter in which he tried to dissuade his correspondent. He observed that nothing could be expected of the study of Hebrew in terms of new knowledge; he maintained that one need only observe the Jews themselves to see that knowledge of the language and literature had not profited them, before adding, provocatively, that if Aristotle had been translated by one such as Jerome, then he (Bruni) would not have needed to learn Greek (*Hebrew Study* 1999).

Nonetheless, notwithstanding these early indications of an opposition that was soon to become better organized, if we are to believe Vespasiano da Bisticci, it is around this time that Ambrogio Traversari also began to apply himself to the study of Hebrew. Among his students—at a time when, at least in Florence, knowledge of Hebrew was fast becoming a requirement of a complete humanistic education, in a foretaste of the trilingual ideal that saw Hebrew assume a place of honor alongside Latin and Greek—was Giannozzo Manetti, a figure whose work incorporated all of the most salient aspects of this first phase of the humanist Hebraism: the verification of the Vulgate through a return to the sources and the original language of what the Christians call the Old Testament, namely the Jewish Bible; taking the argument to the Jews on their own turf by acquiring the necessary competencies for an informed debate on Hebrew literature; the collection of Hebrew manuscripts, this in the years before the invention of the printing press, which would soon make available (for the first time, and at accessible cost) the sought-after treasures of Hebrew literature (Dröge 1987; Campanini 2006; see Busi's essay in this catalogue and cat. 18). The printing of Hebrew texts—a key development in the Western study of Hebrew and Jewish literature—was an activity that saw Christian Hebraists and typographers and Jewish intellectuals collaborate in a sort of "joint venture" that, through a fruitful combination of tangible and intangible assets, bore enduring results such as the publication of the Rabbinic Bible and Talmud in Venice and, some time later, that of the Zohar in Cremona and Mantua (*The Hebrew Book* 2011; Campanini 2012).

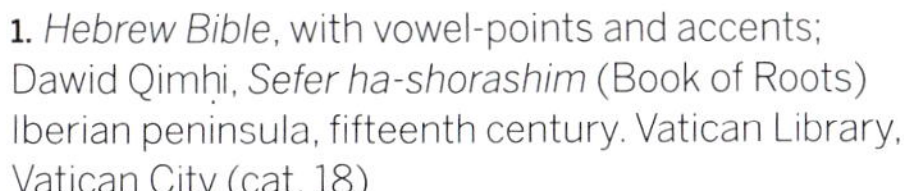

1. *Hebrew Bible*, with vowel-points and accents;
Dawid Qimḥi, *Sefer ha-shorashim* (Book of Roots)
Iberian peninsula, fifteenth century. Vatican Library,
Vatican City (cat. 18)

The picture that emerges—albeit from small, individual instances—shows a widespread study of Hebrew and increasingly regular relations between Jews and Christians, especially in Florence in the second half of the fifteenth century: it was a Florentine Jewish craftsman, for example, who bound for Federico da Montefeltro the splendid trilingual codex of the Psalms (Urb. Lat. 9), which was the jewel in a collection already greatly enriched by a haul of clearly much-prized Hebrew manuscripts taken during the sack of Volterra in 1472 (Alexander-Skipnes 2010; see Busi's essay in this volume). Still in Florence, we learn that, on his death, Diotifeci Ficino bequeathed a large quantity of Hebrew books to his son Marsilio. Marsilio was not to become a great Hebraist; his interests and contributions lay elsewhere, most notably in the Greek of Plato and his followers and the Hermetic tradition that, spurred by Cosimo the Elder, he was instrumental in disseminating in the West. All the same, as recent research has revealed, he was by no means detached from the study of Hebrew literature that flourished in the Medici Florence of the later fifteenth century and subsequently inspired a wider culture of Christian Hebraism throughout Europe. In particular—albeit he made his own contribution to the controversialist literature with the treatise *De christiana religione*, a vast compendium in which the writings of the convert Paul of Burgos feature prominently—Marsilio managed to cultivate a climate of dialogue, still on a strictly individual level, in which we find contributions from Jews, Christians, and converts alike (Bartolucci 2017). It is most likely in Florence that the nobleman Giovanni Pico della Mirandola met the converted Jew Guiglielmo Raimondo Moncada, who signed his texts with the name Flavius Mithridates (Flavio Mitridate), though his name at birth had been Samuel ben Nissim Abulfarag (Campanini 2008b; *Flavio Mitridate* 2012). However it came about, their meeting was an event of great importance. In 1486, while the young count, Pico, was working on his *Theses* in preparation for a public debate scheduled for the day of the Epiphany in January 1487, he discovered the Jewish Kabbalah. From then on, he set about assembling a library of associated texts—which became one of the most extensive and prestigious of its age—and engaged Mithridates to prepare translations of the Hebrew into Latin (*The Great Parchment* 2004; *Bahir* 2005; Menahem Recanati 2008; Giqatilla 2010; *The Gate of Heaven* 2012; see cat. 31). These translations, the first of the kabbalistic texts, which had hitherto been virtually unknown among non-Jews, formed the basis of the theses Pico elaborated in his own writings on the Kabbalah. These, in turn—not least for their extensive commentary—stimulated extraordinary interest, persuading many, and not only in Italy, that the obscure, esoteric doctrines of the Kabbalah might actually preserve mysteries of universal legitimacy, and even serve to confirm the truth of Christianity, explain the miracles, and unlock the meaning of creation and the Biblical revelation itself (Campanini 2014). A personal relationship with a Jew was already characteristic of his approach—he was keenly interested in Jewish philosophy and Hebrew translations of Arabic philosophical works and Hermetic and sapiential texts—as we can discern from the lively, if fragmentary, correspondence he maintained with Elia del Medigo, a Cretan Jew who lived in Venice (Perles 1884; Licata 2017). Partly for his impetuous character, and partly because, in his unbridled rush to rediscover the lost sources of an Ancient Wisdom—subsequently described as "perennial philosophy"—he had opened the Pandora's box of Jewish literature and learning, Pico provoked a rather uncoordinated reaction from the theologians of the Curia and Pope Innocent VIII himself, who found him guilty of contumacious heresy. It was only after Pico's death that the verdict—which had been mitigated by the protection of Lorenzo de' Medici, and by Pico's decision to live at the Dominican convent of San Marco in Florence—was annulled by Pope Alexander VI, and Pico was redeemed in the eyes of the church.

2. *Collection of kabbalistic texts* in the Latin
translation by Flavius Mithridates for Giovanni Pico
della Mirandola, c. 1486–87. Vatican Library,
Vatican City (cat. 31)

One of Pico's numerous readers, who even visited him in Florence to ask for clarifications on some of the obscure aspects of his dazzling but enigmatic ideas, was the Swabian scholar Johannes Reuchlin. Reuchlin was quick to understand that Christian Hebraism, of which he represents a sort of founding father, would not make much progress without equipping itself with the necessary instruments for educating a new generation of Hebraists, and that the Kabbalah, being intrinsically tied to the Hebrew language, would remain completely impenetrable to potential Christian readers unless they were provided with a grammar, a dictionary and—pending the emergence of Hebrew publications specifically designed for Christian readers, which only began to circulate from the 1520s onwards, in particular in Venice—also a bibliography of essential texts to guide what would be an anything but simple exploration of the vast world of Hebrew books, which were as obscure as they were precious, and often difficult to obtain. Reuchlin assumed the role of defender of Hebrew literature when, at the instigation of the convert Johannes Pfefferkorn, the Dominican Order endorsed far-reaching efforts to confiscate Hebrew texts accused of fostering blasphemies against Jesus, the Virgin, and Christians. Pfefferkorn's campaign, which managed even to secure the support of the Hapsburg Emperor Maximillian I, sought to destroy all Hebrew books save the Bible. Reuchlin, consulted as an expert on the matter, resolutely opposed this iniquitous scheme, advocating that before a book was burned, it should at least be read to ascertain whether it deserved such a fate, and adding that, based on those he had been able to read, it was possible to derive much benefit from them and, indeed, find doctrines of great value that had lain buried since time immemorial, and risked being lost forever.

In Reuchlin, the advocate and defender of Hebrew books, we can thus clearly discern a humanist collector with a passion for Hebrew literature and a commitment to unlocking a world that was so close and yet virtually inaccessible. Still, his beginnings were not easy: he was able to start his studies in Germany with the help of Jacob Jechiel Loans, physician to the Emperor Frederick III, but he had to face a series of set-backs as revealed in a Hebrew letter from the Rabbi of Regensburg, Jacob Margalit who, albeit very courteously, expressed his willingness to help Reuchlin with anything he needed except provide him with kabbalistic books, which the latter had been requesting with notable insistence (Campanini 1999). This is why—in another demonstration of the exceptional climate in which relationships between Jews and Christians had developed in Italy—on the recommendation of Cardinal Domenico Grimani and while on a diplomatic mission to the Vatican of Pope Alexander VI, Reuchlin recruited Obadiah Sforno—a young physician and philosopher from Cesena, and one of the most learned and eloquent Jewish scholars of his generation—to instruct him in Hebrew grammar (Campanini 1996). Furthermore, as we see from the notes of acquisition that are still conserved for a good part of his extraordinary library, in the summer of 1498 in Rome he was able, perhaps with Sforno's assistance, to procure a large quantity of Hebrew books that proved essential both for his personal study of the language and for the composition of his most successful works (Christ 1924; Reuchlin 1996; Von Abel and Leicht 2005). Invigorated by his experiences in Rome, in 1506 Reuchlin published the *De rudimentis Hebraicis*. Accompanied by a Hebrew-Latin dictionary, this was the first systematic Hebrew grammar (only a couple of modest introductions to the Hebrew alphabet had appeared shortly beforehand, one an anonymous volume published by Aldus Manutius in Venice in 1501, the other a Konrad Pellikan work of 1504) and has provided the model for Jewish studies in their historical development up to the present day. Before publishing, in 1518, a treatise dedicated exclusively to Masoretic accents, in 1517 he presented his true masterpiece, the *De arte cabalistica*, a summa of the Christian Kabbalah and anthology of kabbalistic texts that would nourish many generations of scholars of esoteric Hebrew literature (Dan 1997). Reuchlin's example, which established a formative journey to Italy as a necessary step for Christian scholars searching for new paths to the study of Hebrew, became famous around Europe as testified to by the French humanist François Tissard who, while in Ferrara, came into contact with Abraham Farissol—a synagogue cantor, tutor, and copyist of exquisite manuscripts employed by the Norsa family of bankers, as well as a "magnus cabalista"— which led to the publication in Paris, in 1508, of the first Hebrew grammar to be printed in France (Kessler and Mesguich 2013; see the essays by Busi, Greco, and Perani in this volume).

Besides this, in France, particularly during the reign of Francis I who encouraged the importation of Italian models in various areas of culture and the arts, the first decades in the development of a Christian Hebraist tradition relied entirely on prominent Italian scholars. A couple of these deserve particular mention, such as the Genoese Dominican cleric Augustine Giustiniani, who was called to Paris to teach Hebrew in the newly established Collège Royal, the forerunner to the Collège de France. Giustiniani—who had assembled an extraordinary library of Hebrew and Arabic books and had published, in addition to a small, exquisite volume of kabbalistic prayers (1513), a sumptuous polyglot Psalter complete with extensive kabbalistic scholia (1516; see cat. 38)—took advantage of his time in France to have a number of volumes published that were variously of interest to the Hebraists, from grammars and Hebrew bibles with a Latin translation for beginners to other essential texts such as the *editio princeps* in Latin of the *Guide for the Perplexed* by Maimonides (Campanini 2008). Giustiniani was not an isolated case, however. There was Sante Pagnini from Lucca, for instance, another Dominican who established himself in Lyon and who is known for his essential and highly erudite grammatical and lexicographical works as well as a literal translation of the Bible—actually, a philological challenge to the authority of the Vulgate—which featured prominently in the debate between the Catholic Church and Calvinist reformers (Centi 1945). Another brilliant Hebraist who deserves special mention is Agazio Guidacerio. Born in Calabria, he studied in Rome during the pontificate of Leo X but moved to Paris after the sack of Rome of 1527, in which he lost his admirable collection of Hebrew books. In addition to publishing a number of successful grammars, Guidacerio was Professor of Hebrew at the Collège de France until his death, and helped bring through an entire generation of Europe's finest Hebraists (Mulè 1990).

This model of pairings formed by a Christian clergyman or intellectual and a learned Jew (particularly experts in the Kabbalah) became widespread throughout the Italian peninsula in the early sixteenth century. We shall again mention only the most notable cases. The German-born grammarian Elia Levita lived for many years in Rome as a guest of Giles of Viterbo (Egidio da Viterbo), the Prior General of the Augustinians and later a cardinal, who is mentioned with great affection and respect in the forewords of Levita's numerous published texts. In truth, he was not alone, because Giles surrounded himself with numerous Jewish scholars whom he employed to translate a large quantity of Hebrew and Aramaic works, particularly kabbalistic texts; but none of the others was offered the same, distinctive arrangement as Levita: in the *Massoret ha-massoret*, a grammatical treatise that would be highly influential in the debate around the contested antiquity of the vowel-points accompanying the consonants of the Biblical Hebrew text, he outlines a sort of "trade" in which, in return for his assistance *in hebraicis*, he would receive lessons in Greek from Giles. Such an understanding is emblematic of the way Jews and Christians could occupy the same space in the humanistic tradition without either having to surrender any part of their religious identity (Weil 1963; see also the essays by Busi and Bartolucci in this volume and cat. 40).

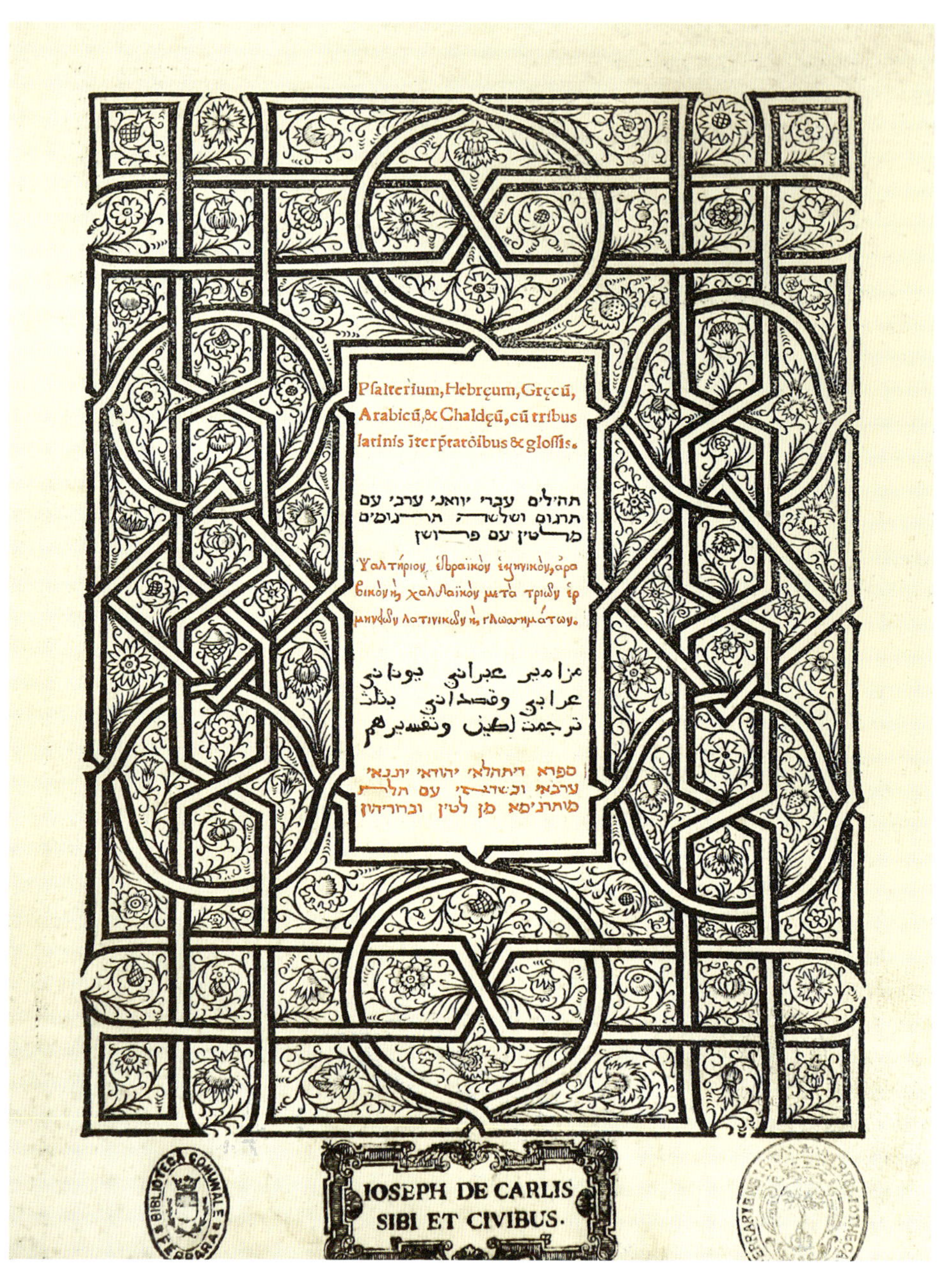

3. *Psalterium Hebraeum, Arabicum et Chaldaeum cum tribus Latinis interpraetationibus et glossis,* Genuae: Petrus Paulus Porrus, 1516. Biblioteca Ariostea, Ferrara (cat. 38)

That of Levita and Giles is perhaps the best known of these pairings, but the early decades of Christian Hebraism are populated by many other examples. We need only mention the collaboration between the Venetian Friar Minor Francesco Zorzi and the converted Jew Marco Raphael, who would help him procure books and establish contacts among the Jewish community. Raphael also copied for Zorzi numerous kabbalistic texts that provided the foundation for his voluminous works of Platonic philosophy and Biblical exegesis (Zorzi 2010; Campanini 2016).

Remaining in Venice, we also encounter the physician and philosopher Abraham de Balmes. A native of southern Italy, de Balmes became acquainted with the previously mentioned Cardinal Domenico Grimani, to whom he offered Latin translations of Hebrew texts—notably the works of Averroes—and became a much admired teacher of philosophy in Padua (so much so that, according to the chronicler Gedaliah ibn Yahya's *Sefer Shalshelet ha-qabbalah*, following his death in 1522 he received tributes from Christian students). He also established a good relationship, against the wishes of other Jews, with the printer Daniel Bomberg, who published for him a Hebrew grammar with a parallel Latin text titled, variously, *Miqneh Avram* or *Peculium Abrae*, which was clearly aimed at Christian Hebraists (Campanini 1997). Another cardinal with an enthusiasm for Hebraic studies was Federico Fregoso, who decorated his private chapel in Gubbio with monumental inscriptions in Hebrew. He, too, is known to have consulted with a "most eminent kabbalist," who has recently been identified as Leone di Salomone from Mantua (Campanini 2015–16).

In light of the above, an episode relayed with casual detachment in the autobiographical journal of the Cardinal Girolamo Aleandro takes on new and greater significance: Aleandro recounts, as though it were the most normal thing, that in 1498, in order to complete his education, his father Francesco brought to Motta di Livenza near Treviso, where they lived, a Spanish refugee named Moses Peretz. Peretz lived at the Aleandro home for a year, except for the period of Lent, which he thought it was appropriate to spend elsewhere. It is worth noting that during this period, he went to stay at Portobuffolé, a village that is unhappily associated with the violent persecution of Jews in 1480. In 1499, when Girolamo was already established in Venice where he was, himself, giving lessons in Hebrew—a sign both that he had made excellent progress, and that the demand for teachers among Venice's patrician and upper-mercantile classes was outstripping supply—he was called home by his father to be present at the formal ceremony of his former tutor's baptism (Omont 1896; Paquier 1900). In the incendiary climate of the disputes between Catholics, humanists and followers of Luther, Girolamo himself was accused of being a Jew, such was his competency in Hebrew. Indeed, even such a paladin of Humanism as Erasmus of Rotterdam was not above spreading rumors to this effect to stymie Aleandro's political ambitions in the German-speaking world. It is understandable, therefore, in an environment where Jewish origin was considered a mark of shame, that Aleandro would be at pains to refute such an accusation and document how he had learned Hebrew from a young age, and how his tutor had converted to the "true" faith (Campanini 2018).

Not that similar accusations were uncommon in the experience of many Christian Hebraists. The Franciscan Pietro Galatino, for instance, and the German Johann Böschenstein, who taught Hebrew to Philip Melanchthon, were also both accused of really being Jewish. Böschenstein went as far as to publish a pamphlet to refute this insinuation. These are the first signs of a radical shift in the climate. Once again, we find they coincide with an Ecumenical Council, the Council of Trent, which sought to bolster the Roman Catholic identity against the protestant schism. The Council, and the decidedly anti-Jewish papacies of Julius

III, Paul IV, and Sixtus V, resulted in a sort of doctrinal entrenchment and marked the end of an age in which it had appeared that the values of Humanism might open a pathway to the emancipation of the individual. Such vacillations are sadly all too familiar in Jewish history, but there is a unique aspect to the case of the Renaissance and Humanism that marks it out as exceptional in the experience of Jews in the Christian world: the Jews involved—whether they remained proudly Jewish or opted for the more practical and millennia-old path of conversion—had been accepted, listened to and respected not *in spite* of their origins, but *by virtue* of them. For once, their history, their sacred language and their rich literature were not destined to be consigned to oblivion or hidden away out of shame and embarrassment but, instead, to become their most precious gift. Christians regarded them with new—if in another sense "ancient"—eyes, in which they were restored to the status God had given the Jews in perpetuity: "to them belong the adoption, the glory, the covenants, the giving of the law, the worship, and the promises … the patriarchs" (Rom. 9:4–5).

Just as Hebraism was experiencing an unhappy decline in Italy, it began to flourish elsewhere, largely through the work of Lutheran and Calvinist pastors and professors such as the elder and younger Buxtorfs. Such work was often pursued in a spirit of superiority, and in an undisguised effort to seize the monopoly that the Jews had held over the study of Hebrew. It should be noted that Hebrew was considered purely as an instrument of scriptural study: post-biblical literature was demoted to the level of an auxiliary discipline that could help in the comprehension of Scripture, an area of frequent disagreement.

Jewish people, meanwhile, were the subject of an ethnographic curiosity, which heralded a new chapter in the history of Hebraist studies that, at least to our eyes, adds an unsettlingly modern veneer to an otherwise baroque canvas. What survived of the Renaissance, and the humanist project? Apart from the large collections of Hebrew manuscripts—in many cases dispersed to the four corners of the Earth and only now painstakingly reconstructed—and the early advances in Hebrew grammar and lexicography, very little remained of the fruits of an unrepeatable age that had been the envy of the early-nineteenth-century Wissenschaft des Judentums (Science of Judaism) movement in the north of Europe, which saw in Humanism, in Reuchlin's defence of Hebrew literature, in the polyglot Scriptures, and papal archiaters a precedent to the heady age of emancipation in which they were living. In years characterized by faith in an apparently unstoppable progress, less attention was given to the fact that, alongside the stories of individual advancement and promotion we have briefly summarized here, Jewish people were experiencing a severe harshening of their environment—the age of ghettoes and exclusion, as a collective, from public discourse. Exchanges yielded rich results, but they were always between individuals; conflicts, albeit largely unbalanced, took place between the closed ranks of different communities. Yet, what interested the Christians was the knowledge of the Jews, whether it be philosophical, commercial, linguistic, or even magical. Ultimately, we could say that in the Renaissance enthusiasm for Hebrew, Humanism celebrated its ambiguous sort of triumph, whereas in the collective identities of the age, it found only its own, insurmountable limitations.

Translated by James Stuart

4. Pierio Valeriano (Giovanni Pietro Dalle Fosse),
*Hieroglyphica, sive de sacris Aegyptiorum
aliarumque gentium literis commentarii*,
Basileae: per Thomam Guarinum, 1567.
Fondazione Palazzo Bondoni Pastorio,
Castiglione delle Stiviere (cat. 40)

HIEROGLYPHICA,

SIVE DE SACRIS AEGY-
PTIORVM, ALIARVM'QVE GENTIVM

literis Commentarij, Io a n n i s P i e r i i Valeriani Bolzanij Bellunensis,

A' Cælio Avgvstino Curione duobus Libris aucti, &
multis imaginibus illustrati.

L E C T O R I.

Habes in hisce Commentarijs non solùm variarum historiarũ, numismatum, veterumᷓ inscriptionum explicationem, verumetiam præter Aegyptiaca & alia pleraᷓ mystica, tum locorum communium ingentem magna cum oblectatione syluam: tum sacrarum literarum, in quibus haud rarò & Christum ipsum, & Apostolos Prophetasᷓ huiusmodi locutionibus vsos fuisse videmus, exquisitam interpretationem: vt sanè non temerè Pythagoram, Platonem, aliosᷓ summos viros ad Aegyptios doctrinæ gratia profectos intelligas: quippe cùm hieroglyphicè loqui nihil aliud sit, quàm diuinarum humanarumᷓ rerum naturam aperire. Vale, & hoc periucundo iam per Pierium oblato beneficio feliciter fruere.

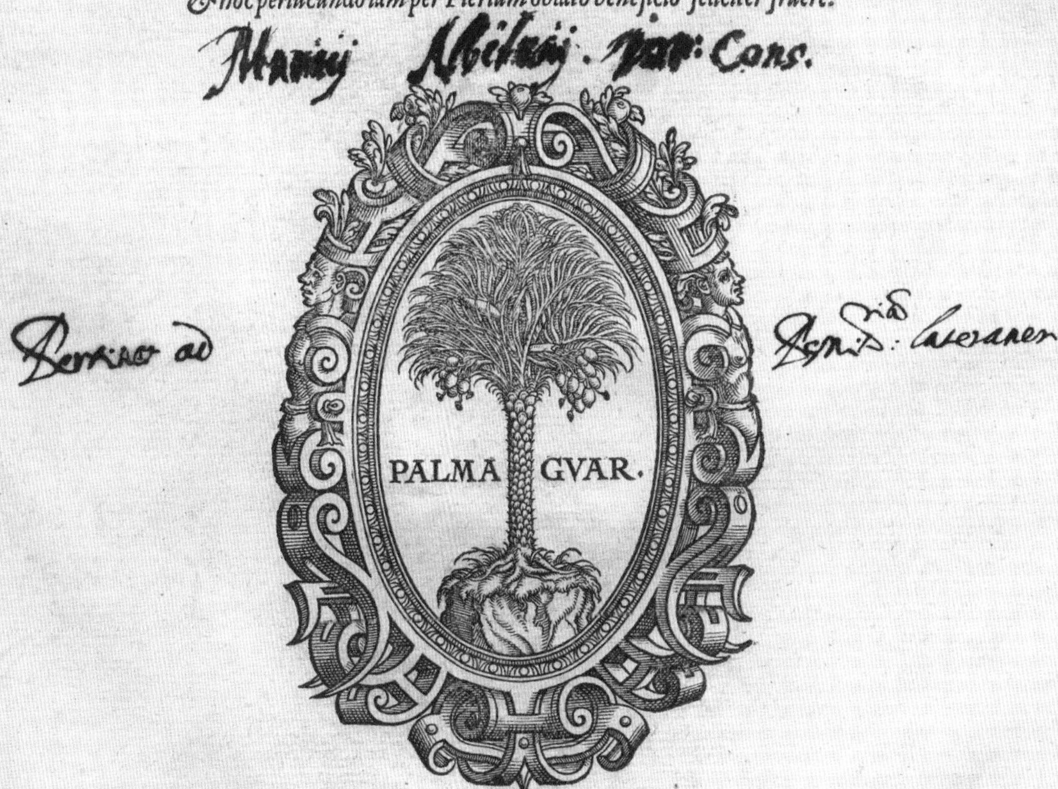

B A S I L E AE,
Per Thomam Guarinum, M. D. LXVII.

Kabbalah and Philosophy: The *Conclusiones* of Giovanni Pico della Mirandola

Raphael Ebgi

The Inspiration of the Muses

The *Conclusiones* composed by the young Giovanni Pico (1463–1494) are perhaps the work that, in philosophical terms, corresponds more than any other to the ideal of peace, harmony, and spiritual reform that animated Italian Humanism. At the same time, it also harbors a flavor of the author's personal restlessness, his appetite for novelty, and a curiosity for the ancient and the different that skirted the heretical. In this tension lies the fascination that this brief overview of fifteenth-century learning continues to hold for its readers.

The *Conclusiones* were printed in Rome by Eucharius Silber on December 7, 1486 when the Count of Mirandola was just twenty-three. The purpose and breadth of the project are immediately apparent from the *prefatio*: the reader will find an account of every field of knowledge, from dialectics, physics and mathematics to astrology, magic, and theology. All this, writes Pico, shall be offered, "quasi per satyram"—in the form of a "medley," we might translate—in which we shall find mixed together nine hundred maxims and theses that include "opinions" of the fathers of the greatest schools of thought together with an eye-opening, and very personal, reinterpretation of them. The latter exercise in exegesis was necessary for revealing the kinship shared, at their root, by all of these schools, or at least such was Pico's hope (Grafton 1999; Busi 2010a; Cacciari 2016).

First up are the medieval Latin authorities, including Albertus Magnus, Thomas Aquinas, and Duns Scotus; then come the representatives of Muslim thought—Averroes, Avicenna, Al-Farabi—and on, forwards in time, to the followers of Aristotle and Plato. Finally, the seekers of knowledge are followed by wise men coming from distant lands and eras: the Pythagoreans, the Chaldean theologians, Hermes Trismegistus.

This climb into the well of the past is mirrored by an inward descent. The vortex that thus leads to an increasingly nascent wisdom is the same that guides each enquirer in the depths of his own mind. As Pico reveals in a letter to his friend Girolamo Benivieni of November 12, 1486, we owe this insight to Pico himself:

> I have preferred to stop at this figure [900] since it is a mystical number. Indeed, if our doctrine on the numbers be true, it is the symbol of the soul that returns to itself, stimulated by the inspiration of the Muses (Dorez 1895, p. 358).

The Muses that make their entrance here are not those of the poets but those of the philosophers. Emerging from the Pythagorean tradition, they unveil their full nobility in the writings of the Neoplatonists—Proclus in particular—where they are revealed as divinities with the power to instill a "frenzy" that is, itself, capable of raising the soul from the abysses of life, and turning it toward itself and the *pura lux* of intelligence (Klutstein 1987, pp. 113–14).

For Pico, however, at the peak of the frenzy, the nine sisters no longer speak their mother tongue of Greek, but revel in a mysterious, exotic argot, given that the last—and thus most remote and authoritative—word in the *Conclusiones* goes to the esteemed representatives of Jewish mysticism.

Thus, we find that the long procession of thinkers and theologians from every nation, to which we are introduced in the *Conclusiones*, ultimately leads to Mount Sinai, where God delivered to Moses the words (*eloquia Dei*) that embodied the true and most profound exposition of the Law, words that were passed down, from generation to generation, to the time of Ezra, whereupon the great body of knowledge was preserved, in written form, in seventy books. This is the tradition known as Kabbalah: those seventy books are

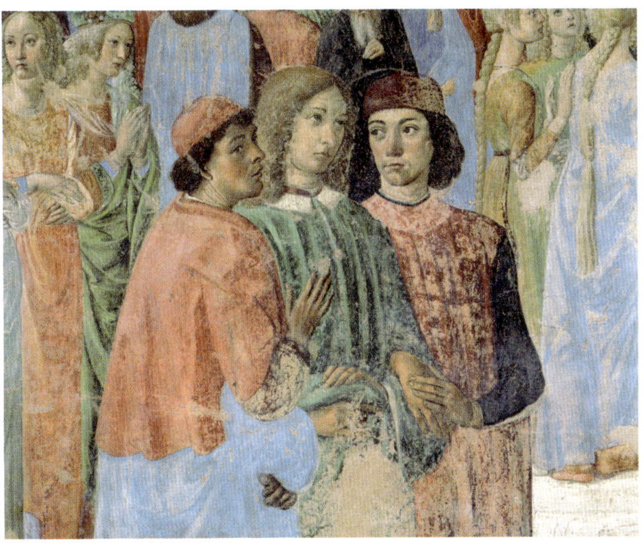

1. Cosimo Rosselli, *The Miracle of the Sacrament*, detail with Pico della Mirandola, Marsilio Ficino, and Angelo Poliziano, 1484–86. Church of Sant'Ambrogio, Florence, Chapel of the Miracle

a rich and unknown continent and he, Giovanni Pico, is the first author in Latin to not only explore them, but also to place them at the summit of the canon of Western learning.

Pico's "discoveries" were to elicit amazement and disbelief on the part of many readers, and condemnation on the part of the Church authorities, who remained entirely unconvinced that the wisdom of the Jews could conserve the greatest mysteries of metaphysics and of the true faith (Busi 2014, pp. 294–306). In his *Apologia* (1487), which he uses to defend his more controversial theses, Pico emphasizes this point: those who know how to read them will find that such texts express a great number of teachings that are in agreement with Christian doctrines (from the Trinity to the incarnation and the divinity of the Messiah); indeed, the mystic exegesis of Scripture they offer is the most sublime and divine there is, so much that, if properly followed, it can lead up "from the Earth to the Heavens, from the senses to the intellect, and from the temporal to the eternal" (Pico della Mirandola 2010b, p. 187).

Though it may appear little more than a young philosopher's *divertissement*, Pico's text marks the dawn of a new discipline that would come to be known as the Christian Kabbalah, in which he remained the principal authority for at least two centuries before the Lutheran theologian and orientalist Christian Knorr von Rosenroth set the discipline on a new path and opened a new chapter in a story still in the writing.

Revealed Kabbalah, philosophical Kabbalah

The interlacing of Christian and mystical Hebrew theology in the writings of Giovanni Pico has been the subject of extensive study. Much work has been done, in particular, in the fields of philology and exegesis in an attempt to better understand the context in which these interests arose (Busi 2009; Bartolucci 2014), from the role played by the converted Jew Flavius Mithridates, not only as a translator but also as an interpreter and exegetist of mystical texts (Wirszubski 1989; Campanini 2008b), to Pico's use of the methods of the Scholastics (Busi 2014) and ideas he found in authors such as Origen to help him frame and decipher the mysteries of the Jewish mystics (Terracciano 2018).

Less attention has been given, however, to the exchange and dialogue that so profoundly characterizes the *Conclusiones*, that between the disciplines of Kabbalah and philosophy (Bacchelli 2001; Gersonide 2009; Andreatta 2014; on this relationship in Pico's *Oratio* see Copenhaver 2002 and 2014). However, we need only read the first of the kabbalistic theses he offers, according to his own interpretation, to understand that this relationship was profound enough, in Pico's mind, to touch the very structure of such mystical thought:

> 11>1: Whatever other Cabalists say, in a first division I distinguish the science of Cabala into the science of *sefirot* and *shemot* [names], as it were into practical and speculative science.
> 11>2: Whatever other Cabalists say, I divide the speculative part of the Cabala [the science of names] four ways, corresponding to the four divisions of philosophy that I generally make. The first is what I call the science of the revolution of the alphabet, corresponding to the part of philosophy that I call universal philosophy ["philosophia catholica," Ed.]. The second, third and fourth is the threefold *merkabah* [chariot], corresponding to the three parts of particular philosophy ["philosophia particularis," Ed.], concerning divine, middle, and sensible natures. (Farmer 1998, pp. 518, 520; brackets in original unless indicated)

For Pico, therefore, the Kabbalah can be expressed in different modes, which—limiting ourselves to the "speculative" part—follow and mirror the "modes" of philosophy. The first of these is the field of knowledge that began with what has been described as the "writing revolution," the art of the combination and "permutation of Hebrew consonants, and numerical equivalents, which play such a large part in mystical speculations" (Busi 2014, p. 299). In a selection of "Latin" kabbalistic pages available to Pico in the difficult script of Mithridates, these games of combination turn out to have a surprising dialectic quality. The artist who succeeds in mastering such techniques, we read, shall become able to distinguish truth from falsehood and good from evil. The author of these reflections was Abraham Abulafia, who in certain passages of his *De secretis legis*—his kabbalistic commentary on Maimonides's *Guide for the Perplexed*—explicitly refers to this dialectical/combinatory art with the term *sirruph* (*idest combinandi*, as translated by Mithridates).

Even more interesting, however, is the text that Mithridates himself inserts, as a sort of explanatory gloss (Wirszubski 1989, p. 101). What Abulafia is describing, he writes, is a "universal science" (*hec scientia universalis*) that is capable of determining the right way to proceed (*modus procedendi*), not only in the divine Kabbalah but in all sciences (*in omnibus scientiis*), and in the examination of all things (*de omnibus considerat*). The young count appears to take these words on faith, citing them virtually word for word in his *Apologia* (Pico della Mirandola 2010b, p. 192), when he finds himself obliged to explain to his accusers that, if nothing else, this art of combination provides "a way to proceed in the sciences" (*modus procedendi in scientiis*).

Leaving the philological notations to one side, what needs to be highlighted here is that—apart from certain differences—for Pico, this technique equates to a form of *ars combinandi* comparable to the *ars Raymundi*, which is to say the special combinatory device comprising concentric wheels of letters and symbols that had been devised by the Catalan philosopher Ramon Llull (Idel 1988; Buzzetta 2011; for a novel analysis of Pico's association of Lullian and kabbalistic methods see Campanini 2015).

These geometric dances of Latin and Hebrew characters, whose movements correspond with one another without quite meshing perfectly, manage to lay the foundations for, and prop up, the structure of what Pico defines as "universal philosophy."

This *philosophia catholica* is flanked by a *philosophia particularis*, which is divided in three parts: metaphysics, physics, and moral philosophy. The "Hebrew" symbol for this trio is the *merkavah*, which signifies the "chariot" that famously appeared to Ezekiel in a vision and that, in the theories of the kabbalists (and of Pico), from one becomes three. As Giulio Busi has noted, the image of a triple "chariot" appears in Joseph Giqatilla's *Ša'are orah* (in relation to the three verses of Exodus from whose letters are derived the seventy-two names of God), while Menahem Recanati formulated a relationship between the three chariots and three different *sefirot* (*tif'eret, ḥesed,* and *gevurah*). However, the final step, by which the triple *merkavah* became equated with the three parts of particular philosophy, appears to be Pico's own discovery (Busi 2014, pp. 299–300).

Beyond these initial intersections of the Jewish world and Western tradition, the question that interests us is this: what is the relationship between the Kabbalah revealed on Mount Sinai, which corresponds to the anagogic reading of the biblical text, and this kabbalistic *scientia*, which speaks with the language of philosophy and proceeds without the crutch of revelation?

The answer is to be found in the *Apologia*, and it is unequivocal: these *qabbalot* are the same in name only. Rather, the speculative Kabbalah, a science by which to investigate

רע אחי · שיהיך דאו כי וואם כתכמה בשבית ביו ימין וביוא שאל ה
מחשבה שביא כבוב פמירןענר נסוף ההשנוע · וחתב שביא
תכמה תמווה לבשין וכבדה ללמרה ונכסוף וכבול והה שנה מועטת ונחוב הכבואס
כם שרעמס לקשין ונבדל ונהשין חה שאי עשטר לבשין ולבול על דיף כחה השאומ
ונקרמות שאם חוברמוף לבציעט קודס בניעט וואמ · ל כתכמה · כי אחף ידעמ
כי בוואם פמכמה כהם ורונשיס נחשאל ונשאלו ונעקשו ונלבכרן · ווה חשאו מרסין בל
ירעעמם ונחשנו שאם במחשה היא השנוחר ונעלוינוף שבכשל נקראופ כפר פניהם
ואחר שבא לדינע כפר נובר עג קצם חיוס שתנמדע לבאור ונקרימע בקרמ ס

רע כי חלופ כפר נתלפף בתרנשוס לל חלכיס כאו שאו בשל
סי שלו מבעל נענמ שאס בעיס · כעב כי פס כפר כבוח ובקר · תכב
תכב בפך · ורעב כי שלו באמוף אונויסו בף כתכואס ירתנק ס ונקרבתס כאו שרעמ
לתשלם · שביא יריך וביא שמאל ובייא רמן לשאס שאא בשל סי ונן שוובל למשלה
וחשאו נעלן כרענה למטה מונע · ונשחיתף ספמיל כלתש כבר תעב יתן וכענף עתף
נאמר כרם כענף שמאל וכענף תעב · האלף שונע · פאלף תעב · האלף כבר פאו לך
כבם · שאו נעו עמיף ורואס וס וופם תעדר לף נראוס לשט חי וופס שונחר וויי בשל
סרכבענם · ואחר שאומר כפרוכרם סוף עב לשט תבף שהוא לשט סנראפ נאחרו
תבר שבועבו לשט הכרם · כלאחר לשבוך הכראו פי · ואחרין לשן רחם כלאחר לרכף עפ
הדעמ אמר שיכר מפעברוג ולבסיף לב שאבר מנערו בשלומף כל דבף שכנוא
לשט מרכבם בלשן רוכב רפ-בף כלאמר ל כרעשפ ס ורכבס · שלותן החרוף הנשאסין
ובשלוע · ונסף כמס נעמ וס הענט שבפתלה אמר כפר ולבסוף ריף כלאמר כפר
המרכבם · נאחר שרברוע כמבוף בשמוף הלן נשוב ונשורו קצם רמה סדי חורי
עלו ואם התכמה בל אמר בשע עגאנ

רע כי לשט כפר שאהרע רנ ב
כבר · ירענמ כי כפר כוא דבר נעלט חשעלס ראש למעלה הראש ונכשי ס
נכבר כונע בראש לעשלא לעג בדבר אחר כלאמר בראש בזכב דמעלם פעלונשוק
וכהכ נעמ יאמר מל בסרד פעלוס כפר · ישעג לף ובל כשעט השאשך מחרין מיום
התעלופו · פך כם דפשל נעמו שיול בשל ילאוכו בקרנשיס · וחס מואר נשאנע סוך
לה · ויבן סוך הדרוען שסובל · וני לוא כרמו וב ד · ונבבן רעמר סוך עמרס ונטוחע
פצא בראשאן וכתף שס מאעורש כמאתנ תצ אש נחצן ברד · וכסופבן סוך שר
השעס פבן סוך וה השעט העגס נמה שבעפנע · ולוס עמר כראשו ונבמצנע נלאוס

both natural and heavenly realities that has been split into four parts, can only be termed such by a process of transumption (*per metalessi*). The important distinction between the revealed Kabbalah and its philosophical namesake appears to be Pico's own invention, even if—on closer examination—it might be seen as an ingenious reworking of a passage in Abulafia's aforementioned *De secretis legis* (Wirszubski 1989, p. 138):

> Therefore, in truth, when you have progressed into the contemplation of the Kabbalah ... you will understand by it not only the secrets of the law, but also those of natural and mathematical things, and universally of all the sciences, be they divine or human, manifest or hidden.

Here we have, then, a Kabbalah that is both the revelation of the secrets of the Torah and the key to unlocking "science"—or rather, "the sciences," a Kabbalah whose scope ranges from the Earth to the Heavens, from the visible to the invisible, and that embraces the human and the divine and holds them together as one. In these words of Abulafia, we can trace one of the most important drivers of the introduction to the West of the Jewish mystical tradition in its guise of philosophical/universal wisdom.

Quidditas/mahut

Even beyond such structural symmetries, for Pico, Kabbalah and philosophy can also be shown to be comparable in terms of their content. In some cases, it is the kabbalists themselves who, by modifying their lexicon and philosophical ideas, produce hybridizations that capture the young count's imagination; in others, it is Pico who constructs the bridge between the two worlds.

One of the most interesting examples of the former process can be found in a passage from an anonymous commentary on the *Ma'arekhet ha-Elohut*, which was translated for Pico by Mithridates and which features a brief but significant reflection on the nature of the divine, taking as its starting point the Hebrew term *belimah*.

As is well known, this word appears in a verse in the Book of Job (26:7), where it is included in the expression *al beli-mah*—translated in the Vulgate as *super nihili*—to indicate the "nothingness" in which God suspends the Earth. The sense of the void is amplified by the inclusion, in the same verse, of the term *tohu*, which occurs in several places in the Bible, notably in the description of the dark desolation of the primordial cosmos in the opening of Genesis.

We encounter the term *belimah* again, in a quite different context, in the *Sefer yetzirah* (a text dating back to the sixth–seventh century that had an enormous influence on the Jewish mystic tradition) where, instead of an abyss of nothingness, it is associated with the ten potencies of the divine. In fact, we find it in the expression *sefirot belimah*, or the indeterminate *sefirot*, an allusion to the nature of these unfathomable realities that, suspended between number and the divine unity, know neither borders nor limitations.

From the *Sefer yetzirah*, the term passes to the *Ma'arekhet*, and to the commentary on it. In the latter case, however, it finds itself in a new setting, no longer a mystical context but one of philosophy—what is more, a philosophy equipped with the vocabulary and theories

2. *Sefer ha-tzeruf* (Book of Permutation), Italy, sixteenth–seventeenth century. Biblioteca Comunale Teresiana, Mantua (cat. 32)

of the Scholastics. After the traditional explanation of *belimah* as a composite of *beli* (*sine*) and *mah* (*quid*), that is, "without anything," the anonymous author of the commentary continues by explaining that the term means nothing other than the impossibility of investigating the essential nature (*quidditas/mahut*) of the divine realities, which are devoid of such essence/determinateness, insofar as we can only actually talk about *quidditas* in relation to the distinct entities (Vatican Library, MS Neofiti 27, fol. 4*r*). Mithridates translates and explains the text as follows (with his explanatory notes in parenthesis):

> <u>Sine aliquo</u> (idest "sine quiditate"). Dictio enim composita est ex *beli* (idest "sine") et *ma* (idest "quiditate"), quasi dicat non est petendum quid sit unaqueque, quia quiditas dicitur de rebus separatis (Vatican Library, MS Vat. ebr. 191, fol. 44*r*)

The passage certainly caught the eye of Pico, who had the occasion to examine it, as demonstrated by the note "*quidditas*" made in his hand in the margin of the cited text. This should not surprise us, given that, in preparing the *Conclusiones*, the young count had for some time been poring over the texts of various medieval authors and annotating their considerations of this important philosophical term (Farmer 1998, pp. 230, 232, 234, 238, 260, 272).

Moreover, it would appear that the ideas raised by this text returned to Pico's attention some years later, when, having completed the *De ente et uno* (1490–91), he found himself engaged in an epistolary dispute with the physician and philosopher Antonio Cittadini of Faenza, a central issue of which was the definition of the nature of the divine.

Here, in order to explain why the Platonists were right when they asserted that we could not describe God as an "entity," Pico turned to the great Scholastics, and especially to Saint Thomas Aquinas. The question is framed on the basis of the distinction between existence and essence. If the existence is concerned with the being of a thing, the essence, Pico specifies, is instead the very thing that, "by more recent authors," is termed *quidditas*: it is concerned not with the *esse* but with the *quid sit* of the thing. In this sense, "essence"/ *quidditas* equates to "entity," and indicates that which makes it possible to outline and delimit any thing within a genre or species, and thus make of it a "definable reality" (*diffinibilis realitas*).

As Aquinas asserts, every thing is therefore composed of existence and essence, except God, who is so simple that he cannot be located in any determined category, and who thus cannot (in the absence of *quidditas*) be an "entity" in the true sense of the term, but *pura existentia*, "pure being," the very being from which every reality, by being part of it, derives its own existence (Pico della Mirandola 2010a, pp. 322–24).

And so it is that the musings of the anonymous kabbalist commentator to the *Ma'arekhet*, and those of Thomas Aquinas in regard to the term *quidditas/mahut*, both lead to the same conclusion, or rather to the recognition of the *no-thingness* of the divine, in other words the status of a divinity that is, for both, *belimah*. The connections and affinities between Jewish mysticism and Latin Scholasticism that this suggests would not have escaped the attention of Pico, by any means, and we would do well to consider them more closely.

Philosophy and mysticism

In closing, then, we must consider the links between philosophy and Kabbalah drawn by Pico himself in the *Conclusiones*. Our first example comes from Conclusion 19.2 (Farmer 1998, p. 294):

I believe that the active intellect that is illuminating only in Themistius is the same as Metatron in the Cabala.

The reference to the Peripatetic doctrine of Themistius (c. 317 – c. 388) is derived from certain passages of his paraphrases of Aristotle's *De anima*, which were published in a Latin translation by Ermolao Barbaro in 1481 and were well known to Pico.

In this text, Themistius follows the parallel, posited by Aristotle, between the separable, impassible intellect and light, reiterating that the *intellectus agens*—which he does not equate to God but to the noblest part of the rational soul—displays the same qualities as the *lux* emitted by the sun. Just as this light is unique, so too is the agent intellect, and just as light is tasked with acting upon vision and potentially visible colors to bring them into actuality, so too is the agent intellect tasked with actualizing the notions and material forms gathered by the various senses and stored in the potential intellect: a process that equates to giving them order and making them intelligible and knowable, in other words, making them take manifest form, like an artist working his medium.

Now, the idea that the agent intellect of the Peripatetic tradition is comparable to the angel Metatron, a figure that winds its way throughout Talmudic literature to emerge as a key figure in Jewish mysticism, is not an invention of Pico's. Indeed, it appears in more than one passage in the aforementioned *De secretis legis*. Consulting the manuscript that contains the Latin version of the text, at folio 342*r*, we find this concise but unequivocal sentence: "*intellectus agens, sive Mattatron*".

A few pages further on, at folio 377*r*, Abulafia elaborates on this concept (Wirszubski 1989, p. 231):

> For this reason it will be necessary for me to mention that the *res*, which guides our intellect from potentiality to actuality, is the intellect that is separated from any material, and which can be expressed in many ways in our language (using numerical equivalents for the letters). Indeed, it is said *hu saro shel ha-'olam*, or rather, "this is the beginning of the world," and "Metatron, prince of the countenances," in Hebrew *Metatron sar ha-panim*; this latter expression has the same numerical value as the former.

This notwithstanding, the specific identification of the kabbalistic "Prince of the World" with the artistic, light-giving intellect of Themistius appears to be an original proposition. It is a paring that was probably suggested to Pico by Themistius's identification of the *intellectus agens* with the most noble part of the human soul and, as we have seen, not with God (in contrast to other authors, see Conclusion 11>2). This is entirely consistent with the value Pico attributes to the figure of Metatron, who in his eyes represents the spiritual intelligence of man. This is an interpretation that he would find confirmed in Enoch's transformation into Metatron, an episode passed down by the "most secret of Hebrew theology" that was the "symbolic" equivalent of the exceptional metamorphosis into angel, or into son of God, that awaits the thinker who, having descended into the inner sanctum of his own mind, becomes one with it (Idel 2014).

Another example of this superposition appears in Conclusion 3>71. This entry relates to a novel fusion of the philosophy of Empedocles and the science of the *sefirot* (Farmer 1998, p. 420):

> By strife and friendship in the soul Empedocles means nothing but the power leading upwards and leading downwards in it, which I believe is proportional in the science of the *sefirot* to eternity and adornment.

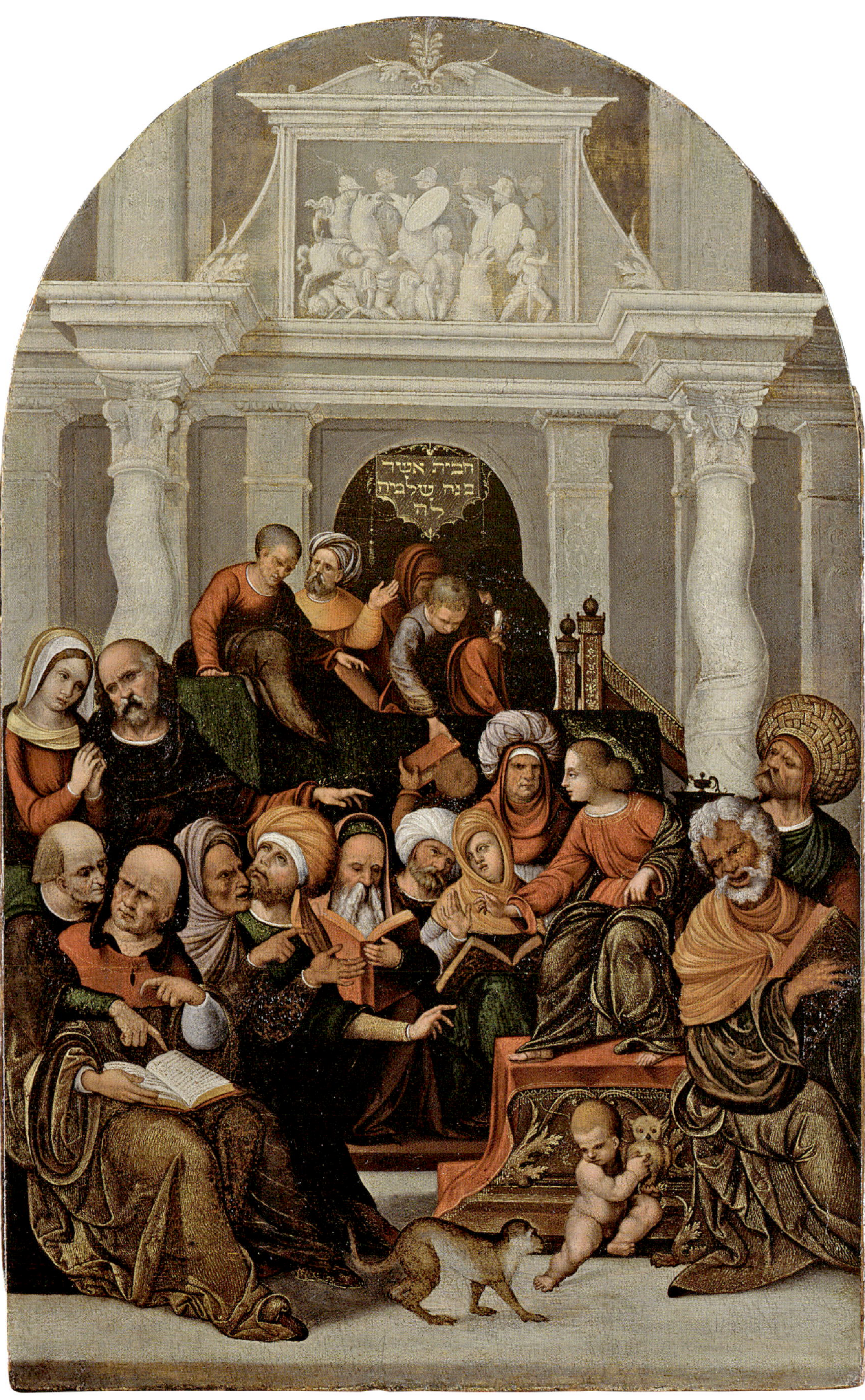

הבית אשר
בנה שלמה
לה׳

The first element we need to underline is that the two principles of love and strife—which in Empedocles indicate the cycle of the unification and division of the cosmos—are here considered in terms of psychological forces. This notion is reinforced in a passage in the *Oratio*, in which Pico explains that when Empedocles speaks of love, he is signifying the force that guides our soul to Heaven, while he uses "strife" to mean the madness that overwhelms the soul and casts it into hell (Pico della Mirandola 2003, pp. 36–39). Pico draws this reading of the Agrigento-born philosopher from the Neoplatonists, who had rendered the Empedoclean doctrine of cosmic cycles as an allegory of the vicissitudes of the soul (namely, the obscure *daimôn* recounted by Empedocles who is exiled from the community of the blessed, and who must undergo numerous incarnations before he can return to his original home) in order to explain it in terms of their own metaphysics, which were based on a distinction between the noetic and sensible worlds, and which provide a framework for the drama of the soul/daimôn, from his "fall" into the world and his return "to the Heavens" (Primavesi 2006).

Where Pico does offer something original, however, is in the relationship he establishes between the lessons of Empedocles and those of the Kabbalah. Indeed, as we read in Conclusion 11>66, in Pico's opinion the Jewish mystics had set out the functions, activities, and properties of the soul according to the model of the *sefirot*, managing to align the soul's ability to turn itself to face the most elevated realms with the seventh *sefirah*, *nezah* (eternity), and its power to address lower realities with *hod* (splendor), the eighth *sefirah* (Farmer 1998, p. 548). In this way, having been dressed in a robe of Neoplatonism, Empedocles is ready to interweave his fortunes with those of the mysterious kabbalists.

What Pico is presenting here is therefore a philosophy that is capable of aligning itself with the wisdom of the Jews according to a scheme that is repeated elsewhere in the text. Consider the Conclusion discussing the parallels between the assembly of the souls on Mount Ida and the congregation of souls at the feet of Mount Sinai at the moment of the promulgation of the Law, which are both taken as symbols—one Neoplatonic, the other kabbalistic—of "the way in which superior things illuminate middle things" (Farmer 1998, p. 438; Bartolucci 2014, p. 59); similarly, we might point to the Conclusion in which Pico sets out a correspondence between the *Ein Sof* and the Night of Orpheus (Ebgi 2013).

This is not merely an exhibition of erudition. The examples mentioned here are vital building blocks in the construction of the *pax philosophica* that the young count is seeking. Indeed, it is only in this game of symmetries that the philosophical and kabbalistic traditions seem to reveal their most authentic message. From this arises the need to know both, to identify similarities and differences between them, and to point toward the common path that they are to follow.

Thus we find that, when stripped of the magic, mystery, and the multiplicious meanings of the Hebrew characters, the wisdom of Jewish mysticism that Pico made available to the Latin-speaking West is revealed as a wisdom that is primed for dialogue with the entire arc of European philosophy and ready to reveal its most ancient roots. These roots were not articulated in concepts and syllogisms produced by our "untiring minds"; rather, they were rendered in symbols and images in which the voice of the divine was still audible to those with the means to hear it (Cacciari 2016, p. LXXI)

Translated by James Stuart

3. Ludovico Mazzolino, *The Twelve-Year-Old Jesus Teaching in the Temple*, c. 1520–21. Gemäldegalerie, Berlin (cat. 42)

Annius (Giovanni Nanni) of Viterbo and His Forgeries
Joanna Weinberg

In 1498, a collection of writings, most of which purported to be the lost works of ancient authors, was published in Rome (*Commentaria* 1498). This handsome folio volume rapidly became a bestseller and its author, the Dominican monk Annius of Viterbo (1452–1502) eventually became "magister sacri palatii," one of the highest offices of the Roman Church. Contained in this work of consummate artifice were writings supposedly compiled by such distinguished authors as Xenophon, Berosus the Chaldean, and Philo the Jew. Framed by commentaries, the forged works gave the appearance of medieval annotated editions of Scripture. Text and commentary, differentiated by the fonts in which they were printed, complemented each other with a perfect uniformity. The central texts of Berosus, Metasthenes, and Philo supplied a complete history of the Middle East from the time of Adam. Thereby, Annius provided his readers with a new universal history, which he narrated through a presentation of a dazzling amalgam of genuine and suppositious sources (Stephens 1979; Grafton 1990; Stephens 2010).

Though the true motivation of the fakes has not yet been totally discerned, there is no question that one of Annius's main aims was to demonstrate the antiquity of Etruria, and in particular, to celebrate his native town of Viterbo, which—so the Annian story goes—had been founded by the giant Noah when he came to Italy after the flood. Noah remained among his favorite descendants, the Etruscans, serving as "pontifex maximus" (a lightly disguised prefiguration of the papacy). Bound up in this show of patriotic pride was the desire to demonstrate that the "veritas Chaldaeorum" (the truth of the Chaldeans) with which Noah had illuminated the West had been wrongly supplanted by the "Graecorum vanitas" (the nonsense of the Greeks). As Weiss put it, Annius wished to "convince the world that his own native place Viterbo had been a cradle of civilization with a history and traditions compared to which even those of Rome paled into insignificance" (Weiss 1962). Written in a conspicuously anti-Greek vein, Annius's syncretistic forgeries, which extolled the ancient wisdom underlying Christian traditions, can be seen as a parallel tradition to the Hermetic writings or the Chaldean oracles, who were similarly popular in the sixteenth century.

Fascination with language and theories about language abounded in the Renaissance, some ideological, some intelligible, and others belonging more or less to the realm of fantasy. These linguistic reflections or discourses mostly related to the antediluvian language that was usually (but not always) identified as Hebrew or Chaldean/Aramaic. Etymology and onomastics sierved Annius's purpose well. His story of Noah as the founder of Western civilization had to be based not only on the chronicles of the so-called reliable ancient witnesses such as Berosus, but also on linguistic evidence. In service of his argument, Annius therefore employed a mixture of Hebrew and Aramaic etymologies. His sources of information, like the forgeries themselves, embraced a strange mixture of the known and the obscure: on occasion, he refers to a certain "Samuel talmudista," whose identity or even existence is not known, or simply to Talmudists or Jews who provided corroboration for his linguistic discoveries (Grafton 2019; Procaccia 1991). Some of his etymologies can be traced back to Jerome's book on the interpretation of Hebrew names, while others can only with considerable contortion be associated with Hebrew or Aramaic. As a Dominican, Annius must have had a good scholastic training which would account for his obsessive interest in the way names function (Ligota 1987). According to his line of reasoning, names would reveal historical truth, especially when the onomastics included a euhemeristic element by which the mythic gods would be reduced to human status. Thus, in retelling the story of the flood, Annius describes the arrival of Noah in Viterbo. Here we find euhemeristic onomastics fully on display with the Annian Berosus referring to the names of the survivors of the flood and Annius himself confirming and corroborating Berosus's information in various passages scattered throughout his carefully composed commentaries: Noah was Janus, a name derived from the word for wine "Iain (*yayin*) because he was the first to discover wine and become drunk"; his wife Tithea, or Aretia, a derivative of the Aramaic word *eretz* which means earth "because she was the mother of all the inhabitants of the world." With her name Noah founded Aretia (Arezzo) in Tuscany. After her death she was called Esta, or Vesta, "a name connected with the word meaning fire (*esh*) because she had become queen of the holy rites and had taught girls how to preserve the eternal fire." Annius does a good job of recycling. The idea of Esta/Vesta is repeated in his forgery of Xenophon entitled *De aequivocis*, where Annius claims Esta is the Aramaic word for fire, citing the corroborating evidence of Ovid's *Fasti* in which Vesta is described as the goddess of the flame. The reference to Arezzo as one of the twelve cities of antiquity founded by Noah/Janus also appears in another Annian forgery, the *Fragmenta Catonis*. Here as in most of his forged texts Annius's purpose is clearly to demonstrate that the Etruscan cities of Italy were not Latin in origin.

Annius's linguistic and historical aberrations had enormous attraction for all kinds of readers. One follower, Pierfrancesco Giambullari, the author of a dialogue on the origins of the Tuscan language, gave Annius's theory of Etruria's distinguished origins its fullest exposition when he asserted that the Tuscan language derived from Etruscan, a branch of Aramaic or Hebrew, and not from Latin (Giambullari 1546). Such a lineage held a strong political significance for Grand Duke Cosimo de' Medici, who could legitimize his new regime in the knowledge that his dominion was inextricably linked with the history of all humanity (Cipriani 1980). Though the authenticity of the Annian writings are called into question in the course of Giambullari's dialogue, the Dominican's influence is not difficult to detect. A list of Italian words that are allegedly derived from Hebrew—"ambasceria" from *baser* (to bring news); "misura" from *mes[h]ura*—certainly yields such an impression. Indeed, one might say that Annius had inspired Giambullari to develop and enhance the Annian stance on Etruscan origins.

Although Annius's discussion about Hebrew/Aramaic had a particular Tuscan flavor, it had its impact beyond Italy. Thus, for example, Guillaume Postel (1510–1581), one of the most engaging orientalists of the sixteenth century, was able to advance Hebraic origins for his native French language. According to Postel, traces of the first language could be detected in all languages, which are all interrelated. Hebrew was certainly given precedence, but French or Gallic was not far down in the hierarchy: the people of Gaul, according to Postel, boasted a great antiquity, for as their name demonstrated, they were saved from the waves (*gallim*) in the time of Noah, their ancient ancestor being Gomer, the eldest son of Japhet. Postel's use of *gallim*, the Hebrew word for waves in order to serve national pride, was simply a French form of the Annian philology.

Giambullari was not the only scholar to question, but also to adopt the Dominican's ancient creations. The German Hebraist and geographer Sebastian Münster (1489–1552) used Annius's writings for his discussion of the peoples of antiquity in his very popular *Cosmographia* (*editio princeps* Basel, 1544). Münster argued against Annius's detractors that the references to Hebrew words, albeit with some occasional lapses, were correct. He claimed that since Berosus had been published at a time when Christians were not expert in Hebrew, it must most certainly be regarded as an authentic work. Münster's approbation must have carried weight—after all, he was one of the foremost Hebraists of the early sixteenth century.

Annius's forgeries belonged as much to the culture of the Renaissance as did the works of Machiavelli, Pomponazzi, and Erasmus (Garin 1967, p. 58). As of the late fifteenth century, any scholar interested in ancient chronology or in the origins of peoples would refer to the Annian "discoveries." True, the texts were submitted to rigorous and scathing denunciation by such critical thinkers as Juan Luis Vives, Melchor Cano, and Joseph Scaliger. Yet, attraction to Annius's stories, which were reprinted at least eighteen times in Latin by 1612, outweighed the power of rational consideration, and most scholars exploited the texts to their full. Jews, too, perused these texts, in particular, that of pseudo-Berosus or Berosus Chaldaeus and pseudo-Philo. The name of Berosus was familiar to readers of ancient sources such as Flavius Josephus and Pliny the Elder. These writers referred to the Babylonian sage Berosus, renowned for his expertise in astrology, who had written a work of history in which certain stories of the Old Testament, particularly that of Noah, were corroborated. The Annian Berosus Chaldaeus embellished and revamped these ancient testimonies. One of the first Jews to read and cite from Annius's Berosus was Obadiah Sforno (Cesena, c. 1475 – Bologna, 1550), rabbi, philosopher, physician, exegete, and teacher of Johannes Reuchlin, the foremost Hebraist of the time (see Campanini's essay in this volume). Sforno's commentary on the Bible ('Ovadyah Sforno 1567) consists of brief explanatory points, often articulated by means of philosophical terminology. The exegete hardly ever refers to sources other than biblical or rabbinic. It is therefore striking that on two occasions in his commentary on Genesis Sforno refers to Berosus the Chaldean whose views concurred with those of the rabbis (Baumgarten 1974). On the verse, "Noah walked with God" (Gen. 6: 9), Sforno writes: "He walked in His ways in order to benefit others and

I CINQVE LIBRI DE LE

ANTICHITA DE BEROSO
SACERDOTE CALDEO.

CON LO COMMENTO DI GIOVANNI
Annio di Viterbo Teologo eccellentißmo.

IL NVMERO DE GLI ALTRI AV=
tori che trattano de la antichità si legge ne la seguen
te pagina . Tradotti hora pur in Italiano
per Pietro Lauro Modonese .

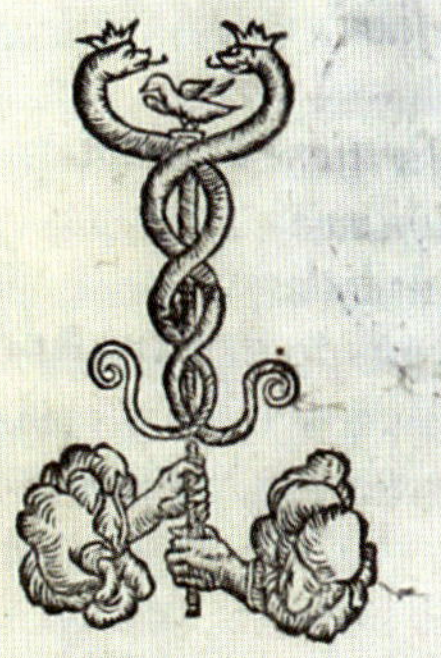

Con Gratia & Priuilegio de l'Illustrißimo
Senato Veneto per anni. X.

In Venetia per Baldissera Constantini. 1 5 5 0.
Al Segno de San Georgio.

1. Annius of Viterbo (Giovanni Nanni), *I cinque libri de le antichità de Beroso sacerdote Caldeo. Con lo commento di Giovanni Annio di Viterbo teologo eccellentissimo*. Venice: Baldissera Constantini, 1550. Fondazione Palazzo Bondoni Pastorio, Castiglione delle Stiviere (cat. 39)

to reprove his contemporaries as our rabbis of blessed memory say and that is what Berosus the Chaldean has written about him." More significant is his use of the Annian Berosus in his comment on Genesis 9: 22: "And Ham, father of Canaan, saw the nakedness of his father." Sforno's comment on this notorious verse clearly demonstrates that he was reading Annius's Berosus. He writes: "He saw the disgraceful act which Canaan his son had done to him, namely castration, as some of our rabbis of blessed memory say. And Berosus the Chaldean wrote that he castrated him by means of magic…" The rabbinic text to which Sforno referred occurs in tractate *Sanhedrin* in the Babylonian Talmud (70a), where it is debated as to whether Ham castrated or sexually abused Noah. There is, however, no reference to magic. This particular detail derived from Annius's narrative: "Ham … finding an opportunity when his father Noah lay drunk, seizing his genitals and softly murmuring a magical incantation sported with his father, rendering him sterile and castrated…"

Annius's additional information about the use of magic in Noah's castration was not a reason for suspecting the authenticity of the story. On the contrary, Sforno seemed to have regarded Berosus's story as a contribution to the rabbinic discussion about the meaning of Scripture and another possible way of understanding the heinous nature of Ham's sin.

Sforno's recourse to Annius's writings in his biblical commentary indicates the extent to which they had penetrated the scholarly republic, whether Jewish or Christian. By the second half of the sixteenth century, another Italian Jew, Azariah de' Rossi, drew heavily from Annius's works in his *Light of the Eyes* (Mantua, 1573–75), a pioneering work on Jewish historiography in which he challenged traditional ideas on chronology and the calendar (Weinberg 1987). Credulous as his contemporaries, de' Rossi translated Annius's Metasthenes and Philo and made thorough use of his Berosus on the grounds that they all shed light on Scripture, one of the reasons he offered for his study of Jewish chronology. Confident in the reliability of the Annian materials—after all, Annius claimed to be publishing "reliable authorities" and even incorporated rules for gauging their reliability into his texts and his own commentaries—de' Rossi applied the relevant data to disprove the rabbinic computations of the duration of the first and second Temples.

Sforno and de' Rossi were not so different from the majority of their Christian contemporaries who were seduced by the "true" and "reliable" authors that Annius had assembled and composed in order to prove his story of the world and its origins.

*2. Degree in medicine awarded to Obadiah
ben Jacob Sforno by the Studio di Ferrara*, April 27,
1501. Archivio di Stato, Ferrara (cat. 11)

FRANCISCVS de Rouelli …

Ariosto and the Representation of Jews in the Literature of Sixteenth-century Ferrara

Gianni Venturi

In the multi-layered concept that emerged at the Este court in Ferrara of an ideal State represented in literary form (among others), what place is reserved for Jewish culture? This is by no means a straightforward question for various historical reasons, but there are also economic and religious factors at work. The Este court's liaisons with different cultures—first and foremost the Arab tradition that paved the way for our own tradition of vernacular poetry—were recorded more or less explicitly both within the context of the court itself and on its behalf, not least in the Boiardo, Ariosto, and Tasso trio of epics. In any case, the presence of Jewish culture and proponents of Judaism, and their place among the sources tapped by the artistic traditions of Este Ferrara is undeniable. Consider, for instance, Garofalo's treatment of the struggle between the modern Christian and ancient Jewish ecclesiae in the celebrated *Allegory of the Old and New Testament* he frescoed at the church of Sant'Andrea (now displayed in the Salon d'Onore at the Palazzo dei Diamanti in Ferrara), the decorations of the chapter room at the church of Santa Rita, where the ceiling frescoes are accompanied by Hebrew script. Turning to the economic activity and political weight carried by the Jewish population of Ferrara, we are presented with a wealth of examples, not least that of Gracia Nasi, alias Gracia Miquez alias Beatriz de Luna (Franceschini 2007; Leoni 2011; see cat. 43 and the essays by Busi and Greco). We have reason, then, to believe that Judaism was an important presence at the Este court, and indeed a decisive cultural wellspring, but that it was not represented proportionally in the literature produced there. This does leave the question of the Jewish community's own publishing activities, and what presence this output had in the context of the city and the surrounding territory. But this is a matter for another time, and another discussion. What is evident is that the varied activities undertaken by Ferrara's Jewish residents extended out from the city to the principality's historic rival, Venice (this relationship being strengthened by the relative freedom Venice granted to Jews) and from there to the courts of the north and the papal territories.

In attempting to understand the role of literature in the construction of the idealized court, we have first to grapple with the idea of the "new Eden." We might say that, following the *Chanson de Roland*, which marked the birth of the romance as a literary form, the epic poems *Orlando Innamorato* (or, as many experts think it would be better to call it, the *Inamoramento de Orlando*) by Matteo Maria Boiardo and *Orlando Furioso* by Ludovico Ariosto succeeded in establishing the paladin Roland/Orlando as a hero for a new, modern age. That they did so is thanks to the cultural policies of the Este family, the rulers of Ferrara, who invested the saga of the Frankish hero and his adventures with a panegyric function, whereby the texts effectively vouch for the family's dynastic pedigree. Adopting a rather innovative approach that demonstrates an understanding of the potential of literature to generate the sort of ideological consensus pursued by other noble courts through the media of visual art and painting, the Este succeeded in creating an imaginary time and space that, because it was modeled on reality, allowed them to transmute that reality into utopia. In doing so, they were able both to marshal a defense of their lineage according to the canons of epic-chivalric poetry, and to recast the role of Biagio Rossetti, the Duke's urban architect, as that of turning Ferrara into a city of Heaven, all as part of a promised Eden whose perfect state will be defended, in very real terms, by the Duke's cannons. In *Orlando Furioso*, the paladin Rinaldo sets sail with the good magician Malagigi in a magical boat that travels at the speed of the *Concorde* of the age, along the River Po, the very real watercourse to which Ferrara owed its prosperity, and to which it entrusted its fate. As the boat is approaching Ferrara, the curious gaze of the knight falls upon a "deserted and neglected" island. Having sought an explanation from the enchanter, who was clearly blessed with powers of divination, he discovers that the island was destined to become Belvedere, the place that would come to epitomize the court of the Prince. This Elysium-cum-Eden, Ariosto tells us, would be brought about through "the diligent efforts of one who, combining knowledge and power with purpose, would so endow the city with dykes and walls that it would stand secure against the world without evoking outside help. The lord who was to effect this would be Alfonso, son of Ercole and father of Ercole (Canto XXXXIII, Octave lix; Ariosto 1974) (prose translation by Guido Waldman, Oxford: Oxford University Press, 2008).

For a more explicit literary testimony of the Jewish presence in Ferrara, we are better served by Ariosto's work as a playwright, specifically the "comedies" on which he lavished much of his energies (exceeded only by his work on his great chivalric epic) and which did so much to generate interest in, and define the forms of, a tradition that blossomed with particular vigor in the Este city: Renaissance theater. As early as the late fifteenth century, the revival of the theatrical form—taking a Classical model but with the novel use of the vernacular (see Boiardo)—had become a mainstay of the life of the Este court. Piggybacking on the liturgical calendar, the arrangement of such spectacles was timed strictly as though to highlight key moments of the holiday, and create a sense of continuous celebration across the twenty-four hours of the day. Through festivities such as these, the power and splendor of the Prince could be magnified. Those who witnessed them would be "transported" to the court represented, whether this be in a pastoral or bucolic setting, a tragic narrative or, most commonly, in the comic-realistic image of a contemporary context involving the city, its neighborhoods and inhabitants—Jews included. To achieve this, Ariosto needed not only to draw on the stories, characters, and activities of his city, but also to locate them within their setting. This would lead directly to the innovation of the

Prologue that "explains" the action and induces the audience to believe in the use of the same scene to represent Ferrara one day, and another city the next, a practice that was still likely to confuse them. Requiring a stable "venue," in addition to using the great halls of the Este residence, he constructed what was (perhaps) the first permanent theater of the early modern period. Following the performance, the spectators would exit into streets and spaces that buzzed with the vibrant life of the city. Among these, skirting the majestic form of the Duomo, was Via dei Sabbioni where the synagogues of Ferrara and the Jewish quarter could be found (and still can). In his comedies (Gareffi 2007; Stefani 2013) Ariosto introduces the Jewish presence as early as the first version of *La Cassaria* (The Coffer), which was drafted first in prose and subsequently in verse. The action takes place in the city of Mytilene, but the allusion to Ferrara is unmistakable. The story follows the adventures of Erofilo and Caridoro, whose respective true loves Eulalia and Corisca are under the control of the procurer Lucrano. Following the counsel of the servant Volpino, Erofilo attempts to negotiate Eulalia's freedom in exchange for a coffer of spun gold belonging to his father, Crisobolo, but the scheme is ruined when his father returns unexpectedly from a journey. Volpino attempts to pin the theft of the coffer on Lucrano, but after it is recovered, the deceit is revealed and Volpino is thrown in jail.

Both versions of the story highlight the figure of the Jewish moneylender.

In prose:

FULCIO: … Borrow the money from someone
EROFILO: From whom?
FULCIO: From the Jew, if there's no-one else who will help you (Ariosto 2007, IV, p. 107)

And in verse:

EROFILO: That you had chosen any other of whom to ask
This thing, that from me not a *carlino*, nor *picciolo*
Can you have.
FULCIO: You are quite poor then;
Find someone to lend it to you.
EROFILO: I have credit with no one
For such a sum.
FULCIO: Let the Jews lend you it
If you have no other friend to which to turn (ibid., p. 255)

La Lena makes a far more explicit reference to the activities of the Ferrara Jews and the profession for which they were best known: money changing and lending.

This comedy, one of the final works composed by Ariosto in 1528—and thus not published in dual prose and verse versions, although it was republished appended with

1. Cosmè Tura and Ambrogio da Milano (?),
Sarcophagus of Prisciano Prisciani, details,
c. 1473–74. Musei Civici di Arte Antica – Palazzo
Schifanoia, Ferrara (cat. 44)

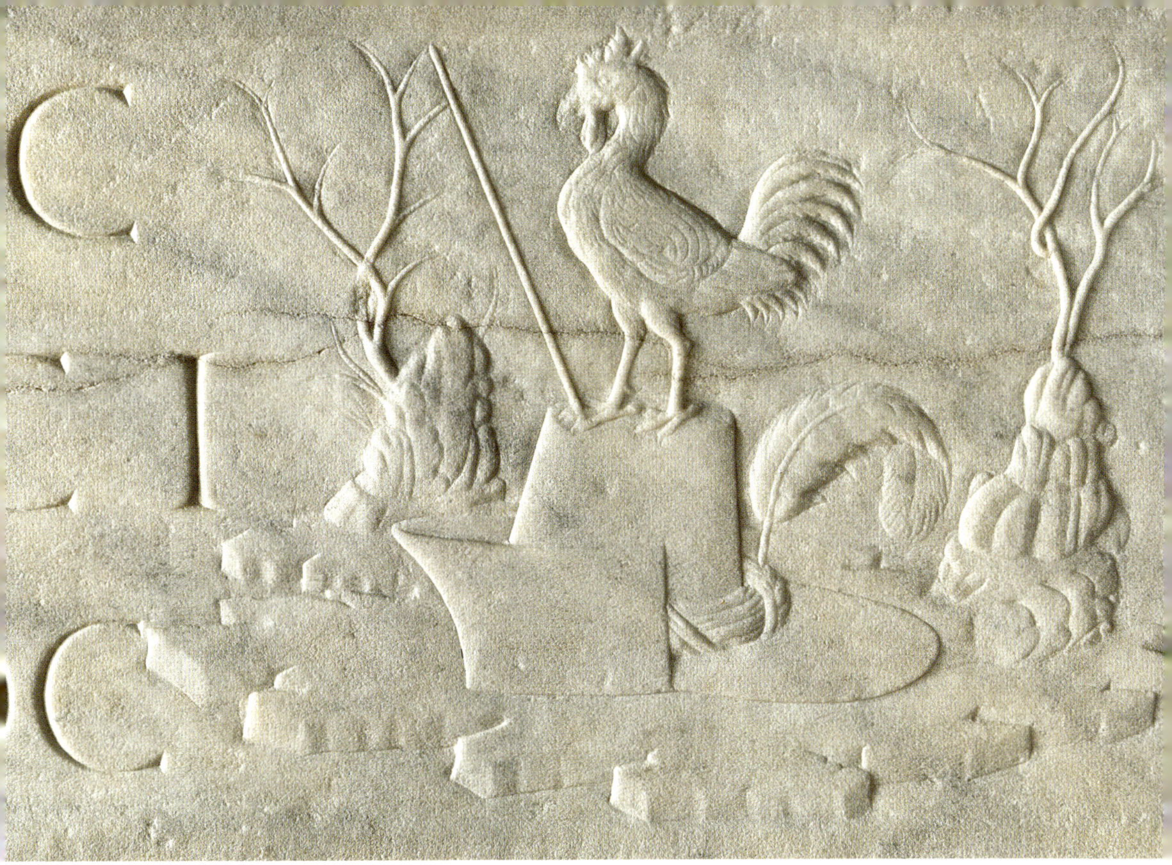

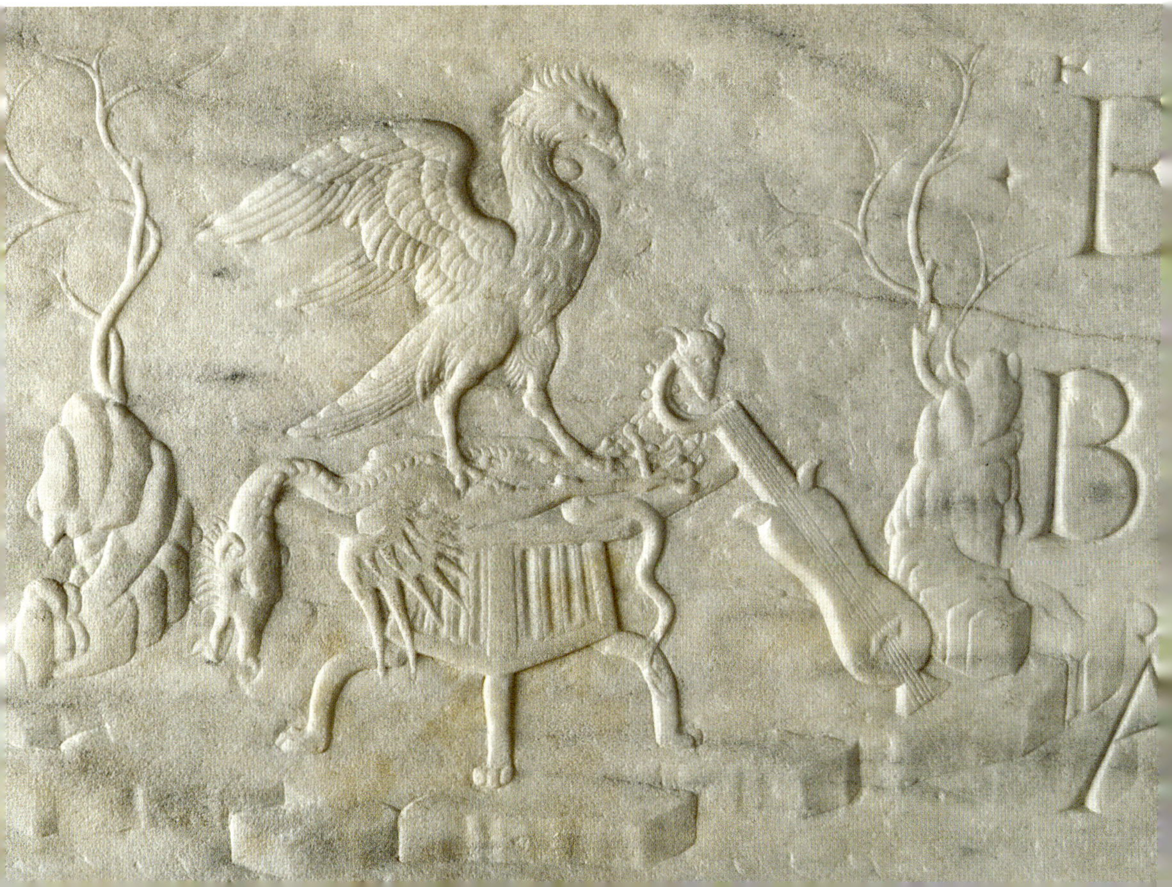

two extra scenes—tells a tale of pimps, harlots, and whorehouses, with the eponymous protagonist at its heart. It was performed in the wood-built theater in Ferrara's Ducal Palace as part of the Carnival celebrations of 1528, as was the author's wish, with the Prologue exceptionally delivered by a member of the ruling family, Francesco d'Este. Among the novelties of *La Lena* is the title page of the *editio princeps* printed in Venice by Melchiorre Sessa some time prior to 1532, which features the woodcut reproduction of Titian's celebrated portrait of the author that was prepared for the 1532 edition of the *Orlando Furioso*.

In Act III, scene VI, in order to redeem the barrel in which the protagonist is hiding, his servant Corbolo makes contact with the Jewish pawnbrokers:

ILARIO: It can't do any harm if I go myself, as well as Corbolo; I can't expect anyone to look after my interests as well as I do myself. But here he is! Well, what have you done?
CORBOLO: I've warned Isaac and Benjamin at the Sabbioni;
now I'm off to the Carri, and the Riva lot will be last (Gareffi, 2007, V, p. 660; translated by C. P. Brand in *Three Renaissance Comedies* 1991, p. 50).

In this case, the Jewish community is invoked with the names of the streets on which they ply their trade: Via dei Sabbioni (now Via Mazzini), the ghetto's principal street, Via Carri, which has retained its name, and Via Riva, at one time Riva Reno, now known as Porta Reno: in each of these places the homonymous loan banks were active (see Graziani Secchieri 2012 and 2017).

In contrast to many other cities, most notably Venice, the places where Jews were permitted to live in Ferrara were scattered throughout the city. This was the case, especially, with the residences of the most important Jewish families. Consider, for instance, where Bassani sites the home of the Finzi-Contini: the most "artistic" street in Ferrara, Corso Ercole d'Este in the new town (where Ariosto himself had his home), at the point where the street once vanished into the countryside, anchored by the crossroads at Palazzo dei Diamanti.

A further issue arises when we consider the comedy that more than any other makes explicit reference to the Jewish population, to the point that it has a Jewish character: *Il Negromante* (The Necromancer). Retaining the verse that was, by then, synonymous with Ariosto's revival of the theatrical form, the second draft presented during the Carnival of 1528 (following the near-fiasco of the first staging) takes as its setting the city of Cremona. This immediately brings to mind the version of *I Suppositi* produced by Ariosto at the behest of Cardinal Innocenzo Cybo, with sets by Raphael, staged in Rome in March 1519 in the presence of Pope Leo X. Even in this earlier work, it is made clear to the audience where the story is set—Ferrara—although, unlike the incipit of *Il Negromante*, in this case the Prologue does not observe the new theatrical convention of simply naming the setting. Instead, it is woven—with evident meta-significance—into the game of traded identities (the "suppositi" of the title), which, we are informed by the Ferrarese ambassador, caused the pontiff to "laugh heartily." Undoubtedly, the most complex working of the passage from one location to another is effected in the Prologue to *Il Negromante*, which refers to the transfer from one city to another and also quotes the passage to Rome on the occasion of the performance of *I Suppositi*:

No more shall you believe you hear of the impossible if it be said that the stones and trees, from one land to another did follow Orpheus; nor shall it appear to you so great a feat if Apollo and Amphion did make the stones climb one atop the other—as do the cockerels mount the hens—and ring with walls Thebes and the city of Priam, had you witnessed the last Carnival [the Roman performance of *I Suppositi*] that Ferrara with its houses and royal residences, its roofs and private and sacred and public places did come, in its entirety, all the way here to Rome, and this city of Cremona has come here before you in deepest winter by a difficult road of mud and harsh mountains: … now it shall not seem so miraculous that Cremona be here, since already you believe that the Necromancer of the fable has had it carried by demons through the air (Gareffi 2007, V, pp. 446–47).

The explanation proffered by the Prologue makes clear reference to an unrealized commission for *Il Negromante* that had come from Rome. Yet, at the same time, it also clarifies the purpose of the relocation.

A first rough draft of *Il Negromante* appeared in 1509, with the first, full version completed in 1520. Ariosto then produced a new, definitive version in 1528. It was first performed in Ferrara between 1528 and 1529, while the story takes place in Cremona.

Is there a reason why it had to be set there? In the first draft, the Prologue focuses on the relocation from Rome to Cremona; in the second, however, the connection is with the previous year's performance of *La Lena* in Ferrara:

Methinks you wish to apprehend the reason that has brought it [Cremona] here: I tell you plainly that I, like one who studies little, cannot perceive those things that do not concern me. If you still wish to find out, there are various stalls and merchants' stores in the square, a number of herbalists where it appears little happens, to which those that want to know the latest like to repair … (Gareffi 2007, V, p. 532).

The city floods into the foreground, with its gathering places including, naturally, those associated with the Jews. Into this world, apparently pulling all the strings, emerges the figure of Master Iachelino, a Jew—dubbed the "Shylock of Cremona"—who is destined to be, by turns, both a perpetrator and a victim of deception. Iachelino is a sort of summary of the socio-economic profile of the Jews as interpreted by Ariosto the writer, but there is also a political aspect to this portrait. By locating the story in Cremona, might he be seeking to avoid slighting the business of Ferrara's Jews?

It cannot be discounted:

NIBBIO: And certainly it is a great faith that Master Iachelino has in himself such that, not knowing how to read or write very well, he passes himself off as a philosopher, an alchemist, a physician, an astrologer, a magician and a conjurer of spirits; and he knows as much of these and of other sciences as the ass and the ox know of how to play the organ; even so, he calls himself *the* Astrologer, just as Virgil is *the* Poet and Aristotle is *the* Philosopher; and with a face more immobile than marble, and with little other industry than chatter and lies, he winds his yarn around men and ties them up in knots; and (aided by the foolishness that is so bountiful in this world) he enjoys the wealth of others, and allows me to enjoy it too … now it is John, now Peter; sometimes he pretends to be Greek, sometimes he comes from Egypt or from Africa. But he is, to tell the truth, Jewish of origin, of those who were expelled from Castile (Gareffi 2007, V, p. 552).

Translated by James Stuart

Christian Thought and the Discovery of the Jewish Tradition in Renaissance Italy: From Expectations of Reform to Suspicions of Heterodoxy

Guido Bartolucci

The attitudes that emerged among Christians during the fifteenth century with regard to the Hebrew language tended to take one of three directions: on the one side, we find an idea passed down in the anti-Jewish treatises of the Middle Ages, that knowledge of works of post-Biblical literature was useful for the purposes of converting Jews; on the other, we find the methods of humanist philology, such as Lorenzo Valla had applied to the Gospels, being used with the Bible's Hebrew texts; and finally, there is a new understanding of Judaism informed by patristic writings in Greek, which were being translated into Latin in those years.

More specifically, the works of Origen and Eusebius of Caesarea (third and fourth centuries AD), which sought to legitimize Christianity in the face of both the Jewish and pagan traditions, had provided a paradigm whereby Christianity was understood to pre-date pagan philosophy and religion, insofar as it was inextricably tied to the Jewish tradition, which was the original custodian of the divine message. In any case, the portrait of Judaism constructed by these writers had two, distinct parts: the ancient, pure, original Judaism of the Patriarchs, and a modern Judaism corrupted by the literal interpretation of the Mosaic Law. The ancientness and, especially, the primogeniture of the Jewish tradition in relation to other modes of thought enabled these authors to argue, in contradiction to their opponents, that not only was Christianity an ancient faith, it being already present in the original teaching received by early men from God (which had been maintained by ancient Judaism), but also that it was superior to any form of pagan thought, since the Greek philosophers themselves (and Plato most of all) had imitated that which the Jewish tradition had preserved. This question of the intimate relationship between Hebrew thought, Christian faith, and pagan philosophy (that of Plato in particular) was picked up by many humanist thinkers in the fifteenth century, whereafter it was harmonized with the traditional, controversialist approach and the new tools of philological enquiry.

The combination of these three visions was to prove fundamental in shaping the attitudes of Christian thinkers in relation to the Jewish tradition. Interest in the Jewish world was no longer (or perhaps, was not only) prompted by the desire to convince Jews of their blindness to the truth. Rather, it afforded a mode through which to reshape the way the Christian tradition itself was understood, at a time—the second half of the fifteenth century—that was marked by religious uncertainty and intense pressure to reform the Church.

It is a trend that is well illustrated by the Florence of Cosimo (1389–1464) and Lorenzo (1449–1492) de' Medici. Here, the foundations of a new, humanistic interest in the Jewish tradition (Bartolucci 2017) were provided by Marsilio Ficino's (1433–1499) translation of the *Corpus Hermeticum* and of Plato's works and the translations of Kabbalah writings championed by Count Giovanni Pico della Mirandola (1463–1494). The contribution of this latter figure was particularly significant. A student of Hebrew himself, having been tutored by converts such as Flavius Mithridates, he had a series of mystical Jewish texts translated (the Kabbalah) that he believed were consistent with the sort of ancient wisdom described by the Church Fathers, and could thus provide a foundation for the central dogmas of the Christian faith (Wirszubski 1989; Busi 2007; see cat. 33 and the essays by Busi, Campanini, and Ebgi in this volume). Pico's objectives, however, were not limited to merely uncovering new knowledge or informing controversies, in the sense of either affirming the philosophical merits of the Jewish tradition or demonstrating the failure of the Jews to recognize the true Messiah. Rather, in his mind, the Kabbalah could provide a key to rethinking the role of both the Roman Church and Christianity itself relative to how they appeared at the end of the fifteenth century. Perhaps inspired by Marsilio Ficino, he sensed that this access to the Jewish tradition (and kabbalistic writings in particular) offered an exclusive pathway (free from the mediation of the Church) to a greater understanding of the original religion, a religion that would undoubtedly prove to be one of Christianity, but shorn of any bond to its historical, worldly institution. In other words, Pico favored the idea that the Jewish tradition could be the means by which to rediscover the hidden truth of the divine message (inevitably an esoteric message transmitted to a restricted circle of the initiated), in open contrast with the tradition whereby the determination of truth remained the preserve of the established Church (Fubini 2016).

These religious and philological interests in Judaism extended into the sixteenth century, where they encountered a new terrain characterized by the gradually weakening unity of European Christianity following the events of 1517. With the Christian world racked by tension and ever-more pressing demands for reform, it is perhaps unsurprising that the new century's first steps in the exploration of Judaism were regarded with suspicion. We need only cite the attacks launched against the work of the German Hebraist Johannes Reuchlin (1455–1522) who, as an heir to the Florentine tradition, was compelled to defend the idea that Jewish texts (Talmud and Kabbalah) could be beneficial to Christian readers from the onslaught of the German Dominicans, who instead held them to be openly blasphemous and dangerous (Parente 1996). All the same, in the early years of the sixteenth century, the study of Hebrew and analysis of the original text of the Old Testament were understood as an important pathway to reforming the Church. In these very years, the lessons of Erasmus of Rotterdam and the idea that a Christian thinker needed to know the three languages of Hebrew, Greek, and Latin were taking hold all over Europe (Burnett 2012).

In Italy, the Medici popes Leo X (1475–1521) and Clement VII (1478–1534) promoted the teaching of Hebrew, supporting the project of Dominican Hebraist Sante Pagnini

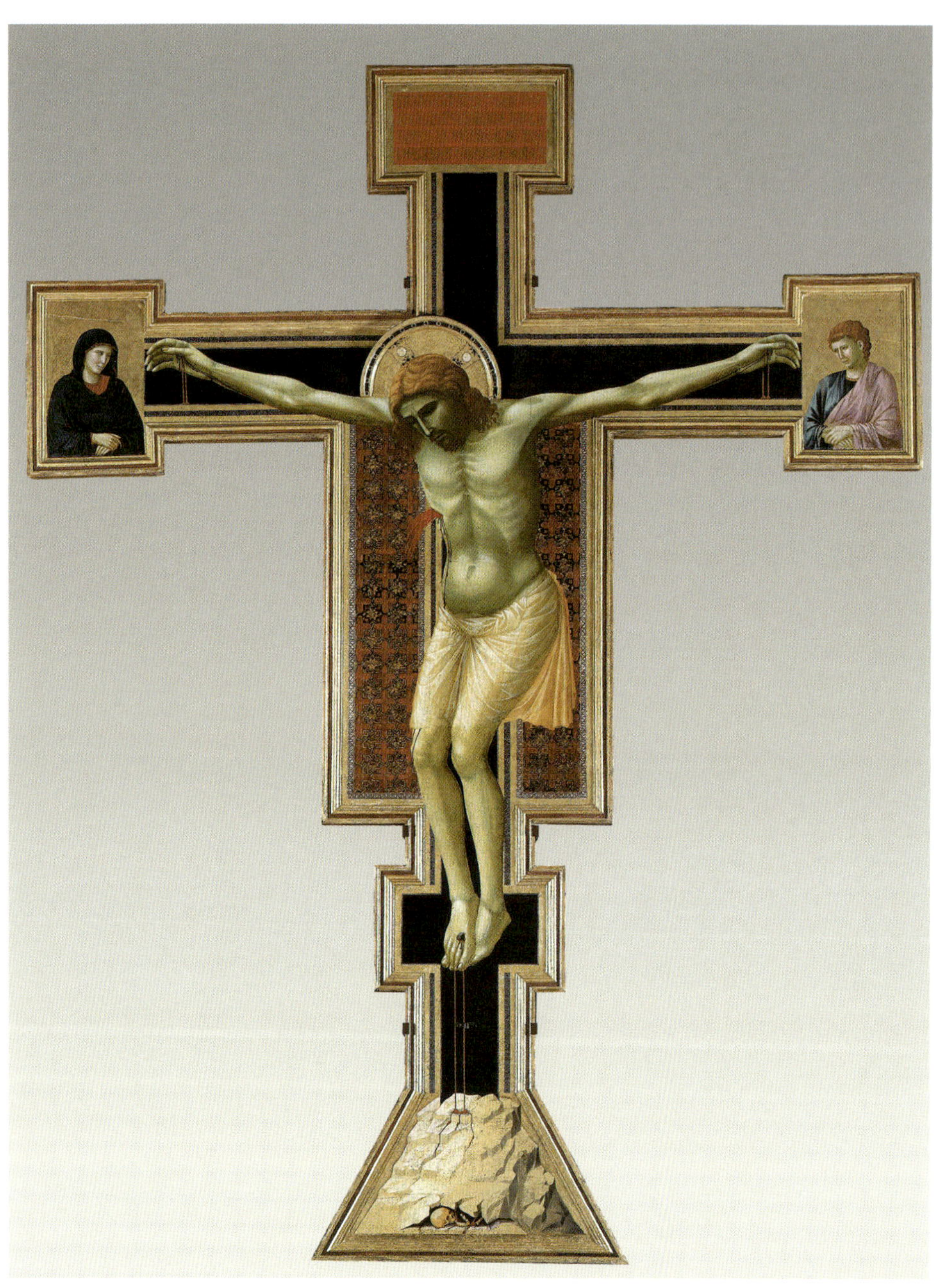

1. Giotto, *Crucifix*, 1290–95. Basilica of Santa
Maria Novella, Florence

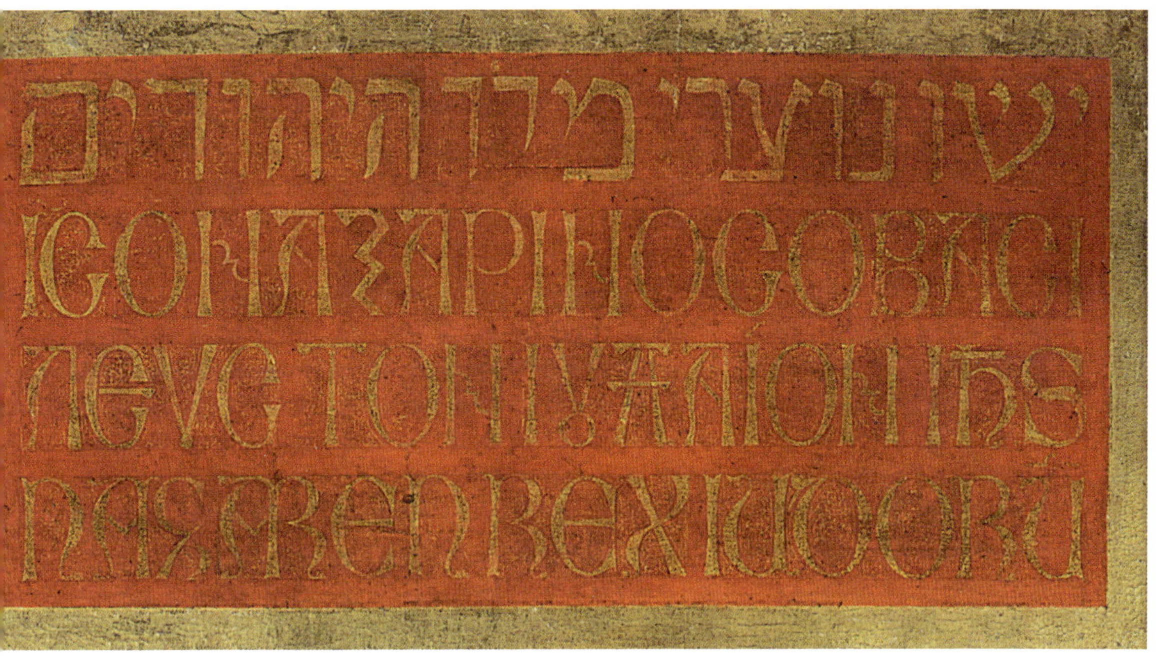

(1470–1541) of retranslating the Bible, and inviting the Calabrian scholar Agazio Guidace-rio (1477–1542) to oversee the teaching of Hebrew between 1520 and 1524. In this early part of the century, in spite of the growing Protestant revolt, knowledge of the Holy Tongue was recognized as an indispensable tool for undertaking a root and branch reform of the Church, as though direct intervention on the words of Scripture (via a better understanding and improved Latin translation of the Hebrew text) would lead to a corresponding improvement in the practices of the Church. The prefaces and letters of dedication in the works of these Hebraists reveal that they were working at the behest of cardinals in Rome, who at that time were contemplating the necessary reform of the Church. Among these were figures such as the future Cardinal of Verona, Carlo Maria Giberti (1495–1543) and the future Bishop of Gubbio, Federico Fregoso (1480–1541), and above all the Prior General of the Augustinian Order, Giles of Viterbo (1469–1532). With Giles, there was a clear philological interest in the Hebrew language, but also that compound of Platonism and Kabbalah that had been such a distinctive motif in the rediscovery of the Jewish tradition in the previous century (see cat. 40 and the essays by Busi and Campanini in this volume). These interests, which Giles indulged with the assistance of Jewish scholars such as Elia Levita, are reflected in his writings, which bear witness to a profound desire for reform in the institutions of the Church at a particularly delicate moment that saw the specter of the Lutheran menace looming within his own order. Albeit he remained faithful to the foundational dogmas of the Roman Church, in manuscripts such as the *Libellus de litteris hebraicis* and the treatise he titled *Scechina*, Giles made use of the kabbalistic background to demonstrate how the Jewish tradition, as Pico had asserted, offered a pathway to the deepest secrets of the Holy Scriptures. What emerges in his writing is therefore not only the possibility of effecting a profound reform of the Church, but also the idea that such a process should be guided by one who has access to this truth, which is to say, by one who through study has attained a state of inner enlightenment (O'Malley 1968). It is notable that the actions of this Roman school, in its various permutations, went beyond the lessons of Erasmus. Where the Flemish humanist—the defense of Reuchlin notwithstanding— had always retained a certain distrust of the rabbinical literature (which he considered a threat), these authors happily added to their knowledge of Judaism using all of the instruments that post-Biblical Jewish literature had to offer, from lexicons, grammars, and commentaries to kabbalistic texts (Friedman 1983, p. 178).

One of the most singular products of this harnessing of the Jewish tradition is the work of the Franciscan friar Francesco Zorzi (1466–1540). Zorzi revived the Platonic-kabbalistic tradition developed in Florence in the latter half of the fifteenth century, using it as the basis for the doctrinal framework of both the *De harmonia mundi*, published in Venice in 1525, and the *In Scripturam Sacram Problemata* of 1536. Zorzi had at his disposal a superb library of kabbalistic writings, which he duly interpreted in the light of the earlier Florentine tradition. The outcome was a sort of introduction to a profoundly spiritualized

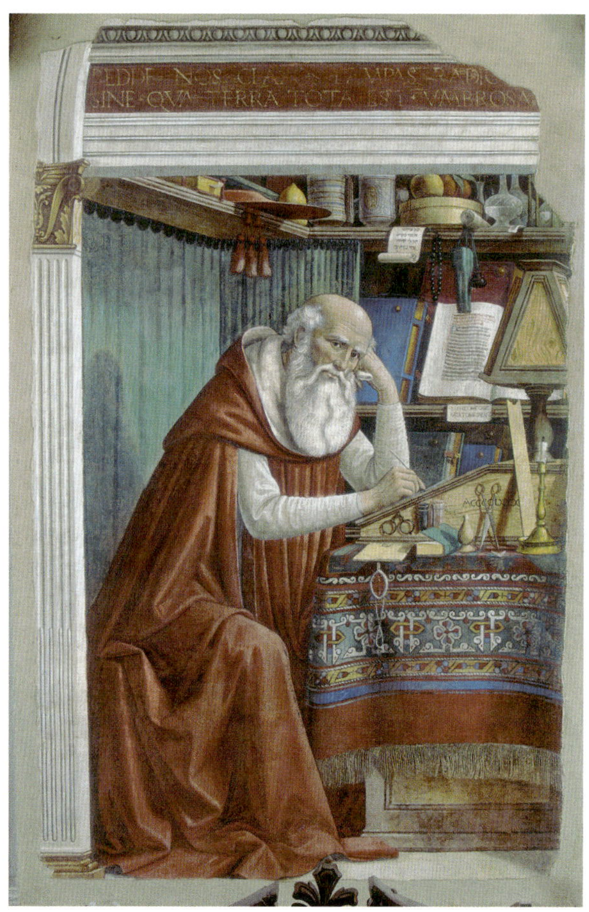

2. Domenico Ghirlandaio, *Saint Jerome in His Study*, c. 1480. Church of Ognissanti, Florence

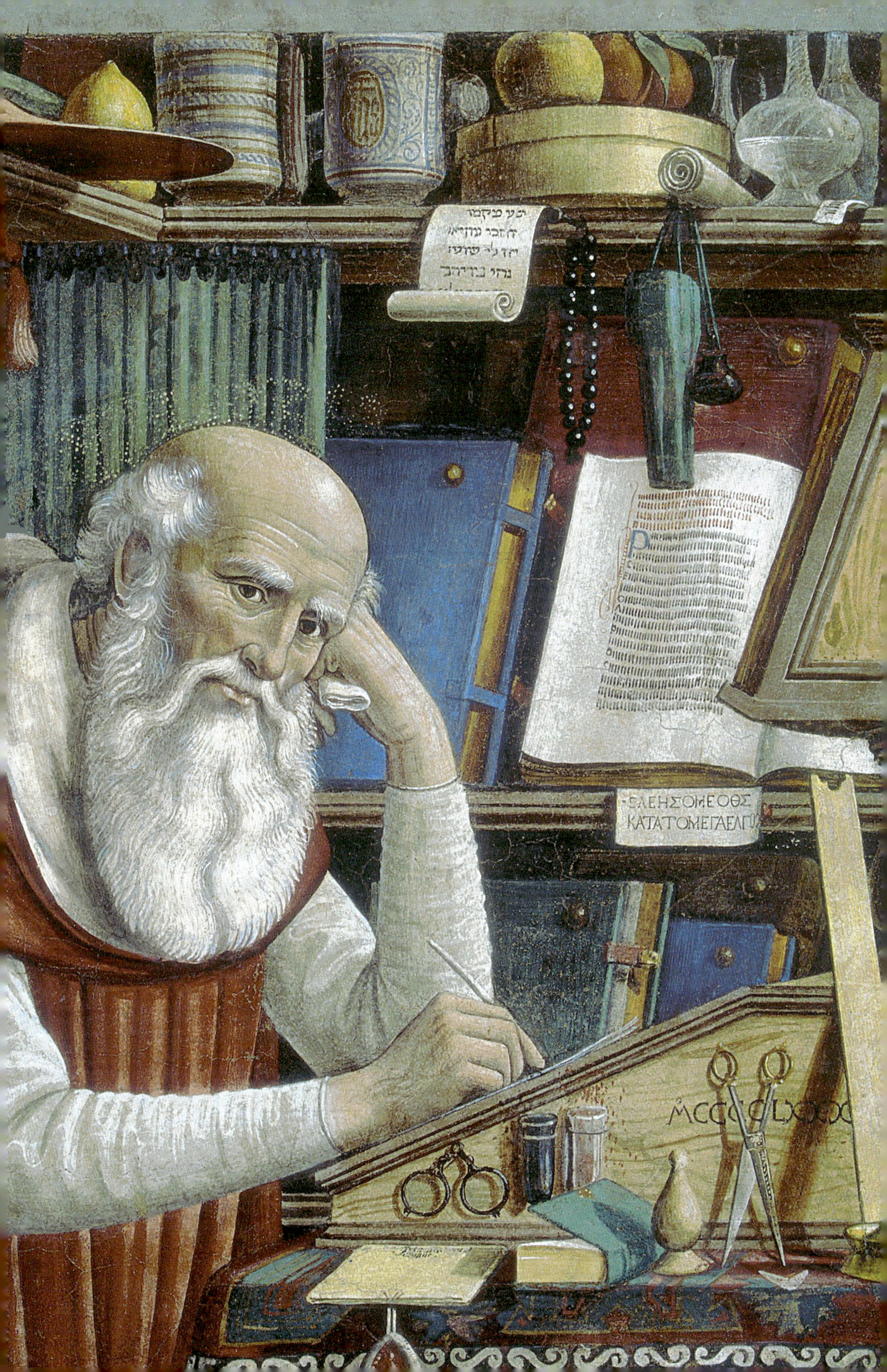

ישע פיקמי
הזבר נגדזאו
יחד לי שועי
נרהי בזיהב
ΕΛΕΗΣΟΜΕΘΣ
ΚΑΤΑΤΟΜΕΓΑΕΛΓΟ
MCCCCLXXXX

version of Christianity in which, for example, the traditional sacraments were interpreted in a deeply symbolic fashion as signifiers of a purely spiritual experience (Vasoli 1988).

And even though the censors only intervened some time later, we know from a number of contemporary letters that concerns about the doctrine developed by Zorzi were serious enough, particularly in reformist circles, for Cardinal Pietro Bembo (1470–1547) to write, in a letter addressed to Federico Fregoso: "And I deem his [Zorzi's] Kabbalah, on which he and I have debated at great length, to be a most suspicious and dangerous thing" (Campanini 2015–16, p. 34).

Alongside these functions, the Jewish tradition was to serve Christian thinkers in yet another fashion. Judaism became the metric by which Christian orthodoxy could be measured in the eyes of the different doctrines. In other words, the Lutheran, Catholic, and Calvinist confessions accused one another of Judaization, that is, of imitating the worst tendencies of the Jewish religion: for the Lutherans, Roman Catholic interpretations of "works" were akin to empty Jewish ritual, while for the Catholics, the doctrine of *sola scriptura* was a variant of Jewish literalism. Accusations such as these fed into the suspicions of heterodoxy harbored in regard to Judaism in general, and specifically, in regard to those who studied or made use of it.

Much like it had in the course of the previous century, in sixteenth-century Italy, the Jewish tradition offered a forum in which lines of theological reflection could be developed that departed from tradition and conceived of a possible renewal of the Church. The religious implications of this process varied hugely according to the different paths taken by the authors involved. There were those, such as Giles of Viterbo, who did not bring traditional dogma into question, but insisted more-or-less forcibly on the need to enter into the most secret meanings of Christian truth in order that the Church might be reformed. Others, such as Zorzi, followed up this same notion with an explicit and radical reconsideration of ecclesiastical authority. These more extreme positions attracted the attention of a number of notable Italian "heretics," such as Celio Secondo Curione (1503–1569) and Francesco Pucci (1543–1597) who found in the writings of the Franciscan friar a model for their own reflections (Vasoli 1988; D'Ascia 1999).

There is no doubt, therefore, that the discovery of the Jewish tradition, such as emerged in the early sixteenth century, had an important role to play in the religious debate around the future of the Church. This relationship with the Jewish tradition became problematic during the long years of the Council of Trent and the troubled process of rebuilding the Roman Church. The gradual confessionalization of this interest in Jewish thought fed into the concern—harbored in many parts of Europe and in Italy, above all— that Judaism represented a threat to the integrity of the Roman Catholic tradition. Perhaps the most visceral manifestation of this suspicion was the burning of the Talmud in 1553 and the stigmatization of Judaism as a threat equal to the other heresies identified around the Italian peninsula.

Translated by James Stuart

3. Teseo Ambrogio Albonesi, *Introductio in Chaldaicam linguam, Syriacam, atque Armenicam, et decem alias linguas*, Papiae: Ioan Maria Simoneta, 1539. Biblioteca Ariostea, Ferrara (cat. 37)

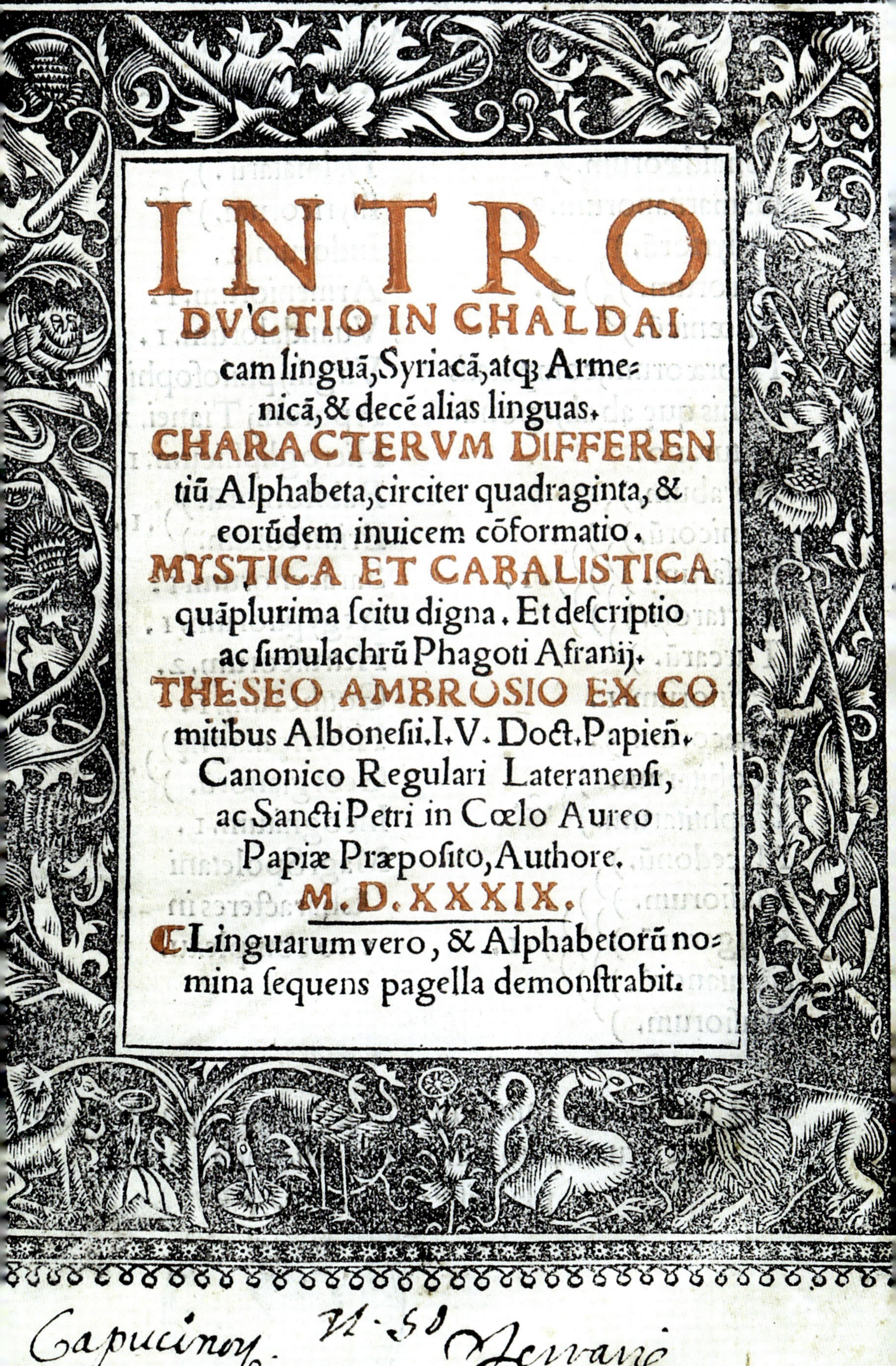

INTRO
DVCTIO IN CHALDAI

cam linguā, Syriacā, atq̄ Arme=
nicā, & decē alias linguas.
CHARACTERVM DIFFEREN
tiū Alphabeta, circiter quadraginta, &
eorūdem inuicem cōformatio.
MYSTICA ET CABALISTICA
quāplurima scitu digna. Et descriptio
ac simulachrū Phagoti Afranij.
THESEO AMBROSIO EX CO
mitibus Albonesii. I. V. Doct. Papien.
Canonico Regulari Lateranensi,
ac Sancti Petri in Cœlo Aureo
Papiæ Præposito, Authore.

M.D.XXXIX.

℃ Linguarum vero, & Alphabetorū no=
mina sequens pagella demonstrabit.

Museum and Exhibition Design
Studio GTRF - Giovanni Tortelli Roberto Frassoni
Architetti Associati

Museum and exhibition design,
map of the route
(GTRF - Giovanni Tortelli Roberto Frassoni
Architetti Associati)

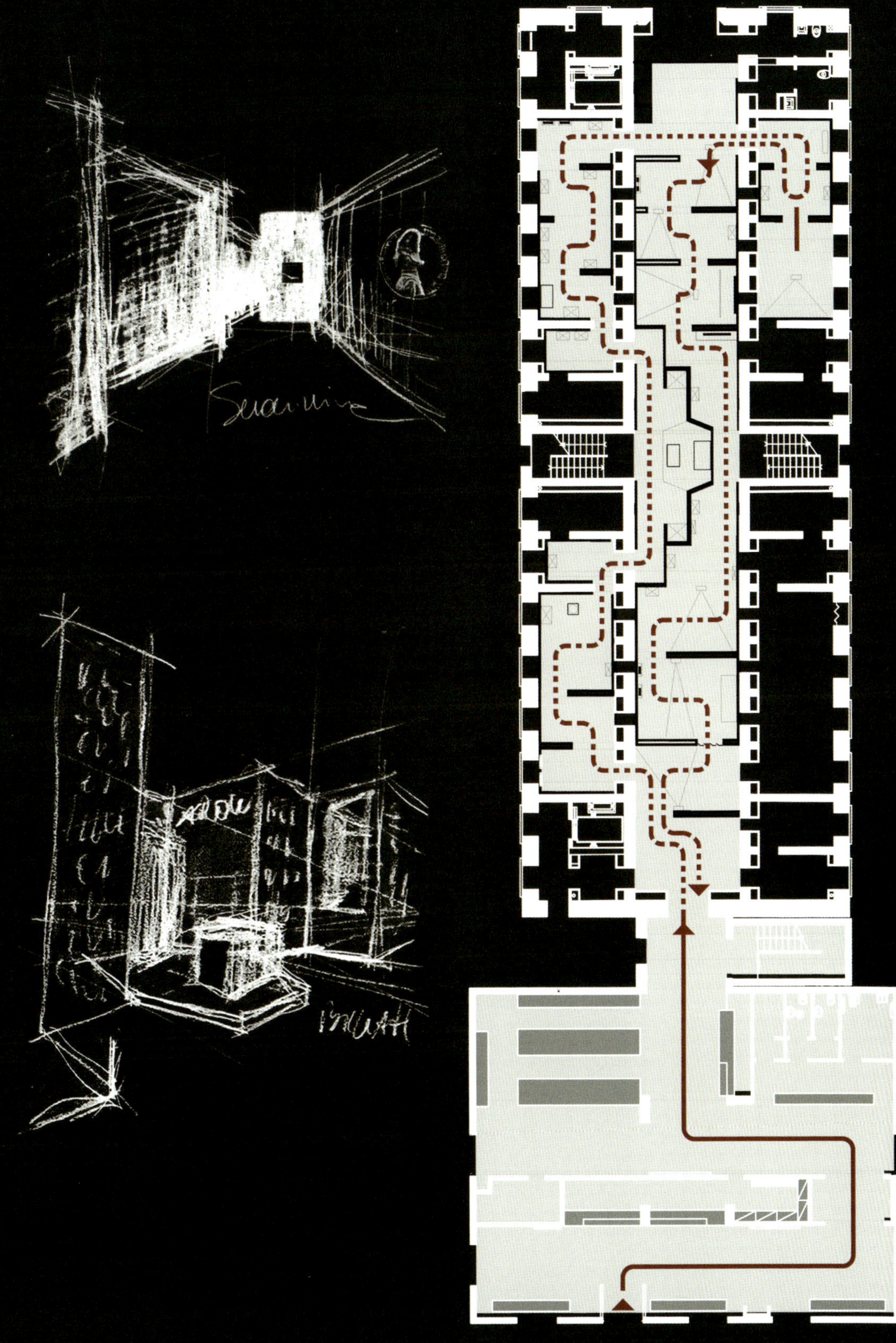

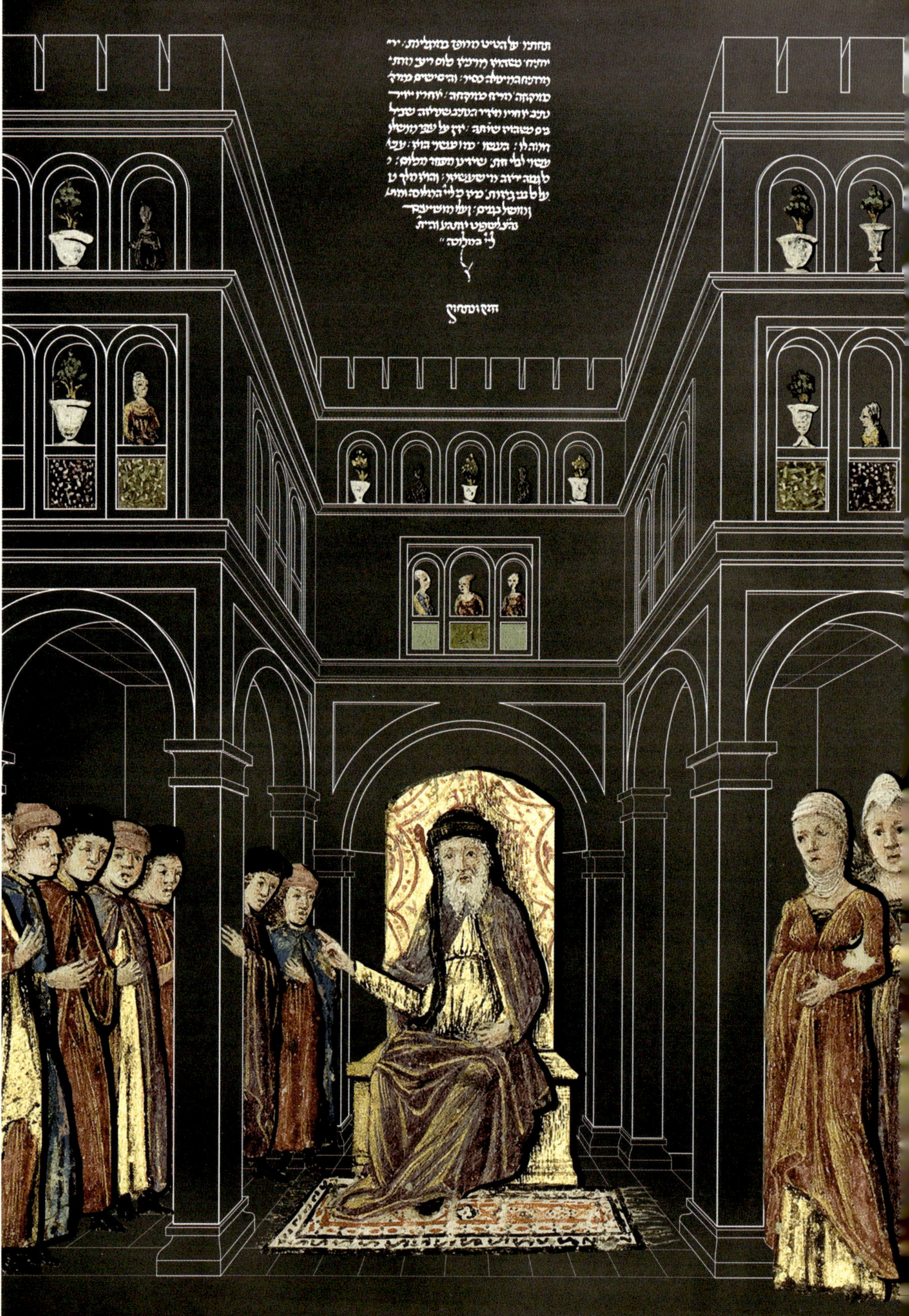

תחתני על הטיט חרוץ כחומר יי
יחיה שבהריו מרכיו כלם ריב וחתי
מרדכ המיעלב כסיר ובסיסים מזרק
כמאזה מרח כמוקחה יוחרין ייזיר
עקב יו חרין מצדי הטעב שעריה שכיל
בם טעבריו שותה יזן על שער חומלו
חוה לו העשו מד ועשרי כויו עכו
עשוי ומי חת שידעו מאחר מלום
לעמה ידיוב מי שעשיאו והיון מלך ט
על ט מב גזית כין כלי הכולה וחו
נוחשל כבים ועל חושיעבר
מעלשפט יותח ועו והיה
לי כחולה
חיים וטובים

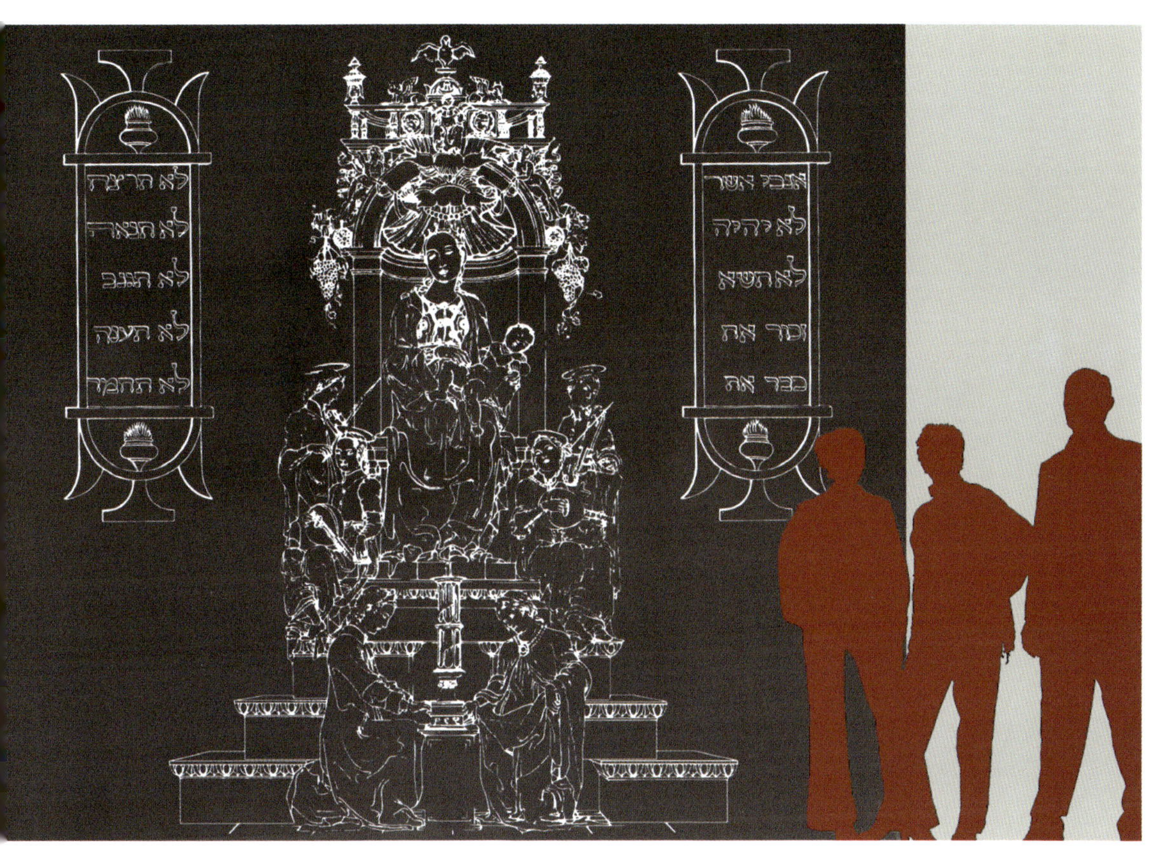

Museum and exhibition design,
introductory background
(GTRF - Giovanni Tortelli Roberto Frassoni
Architetti Associati)

Museum and exhibition design,
the *Madonna Roverella*
(GTRF - Giovanni Tortelli Roberto Frassoni
Architetti Associati)

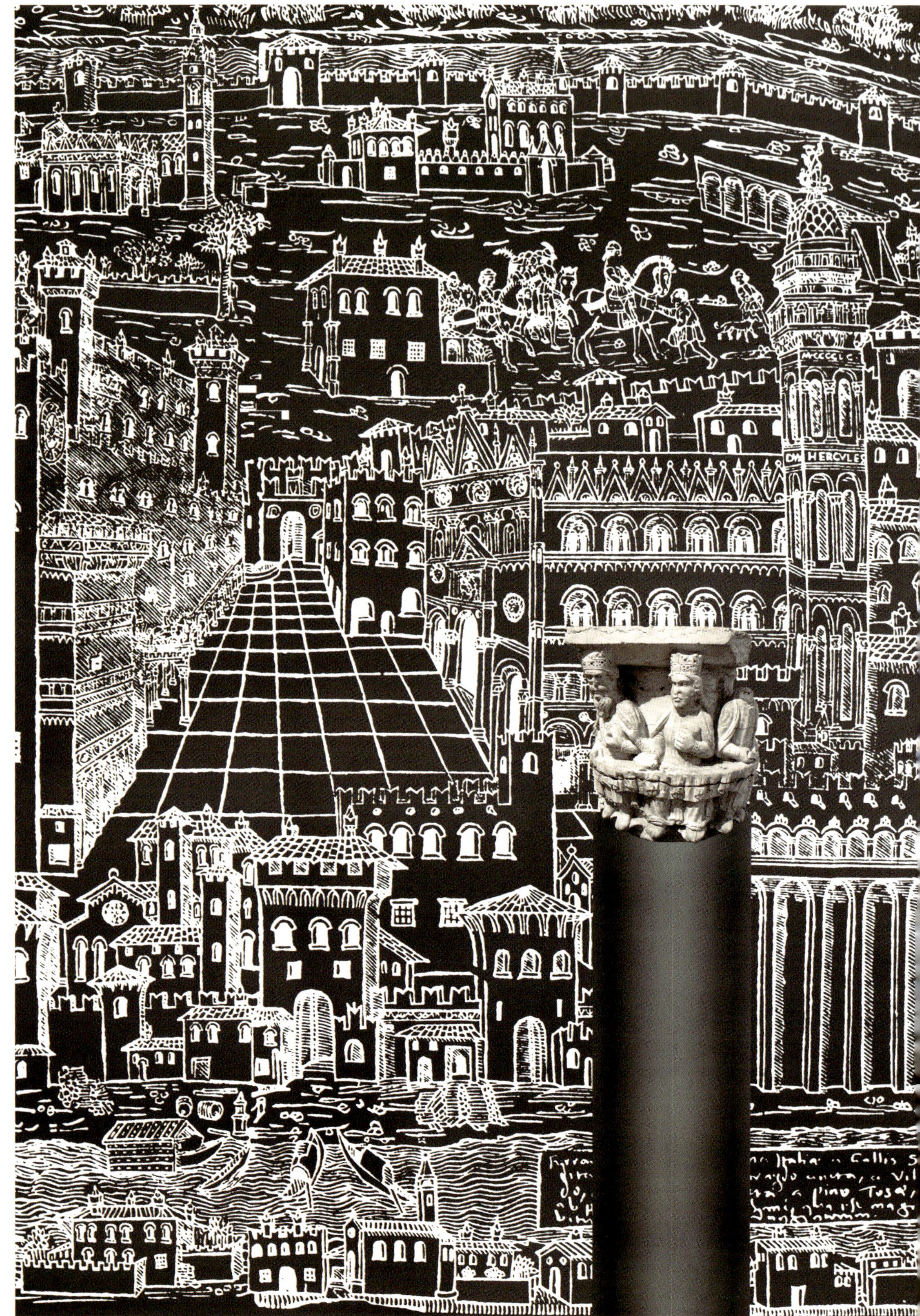
HERCVLE

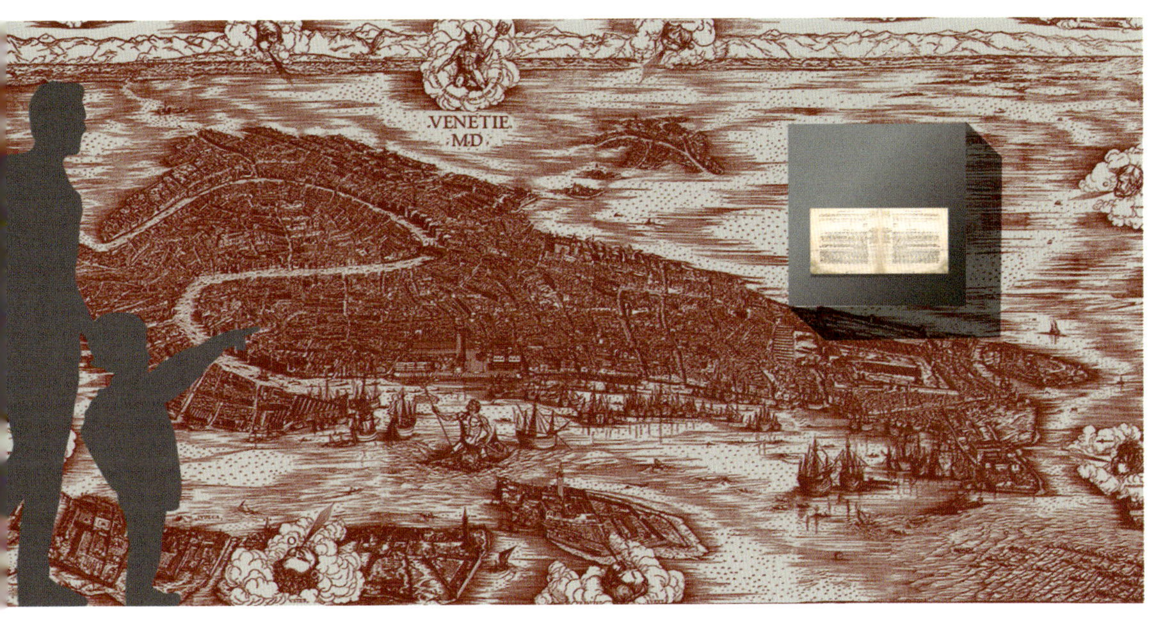

Museum and exhibition design,
Ferrara
(GTRF - Giovanni Tortelli Roberto Frassoni
Architetti Associati)

Museum and exhibition design,
Venice
(GTRF - Giovanni Tortelli Roberto Frassoni
Architetti Associati)

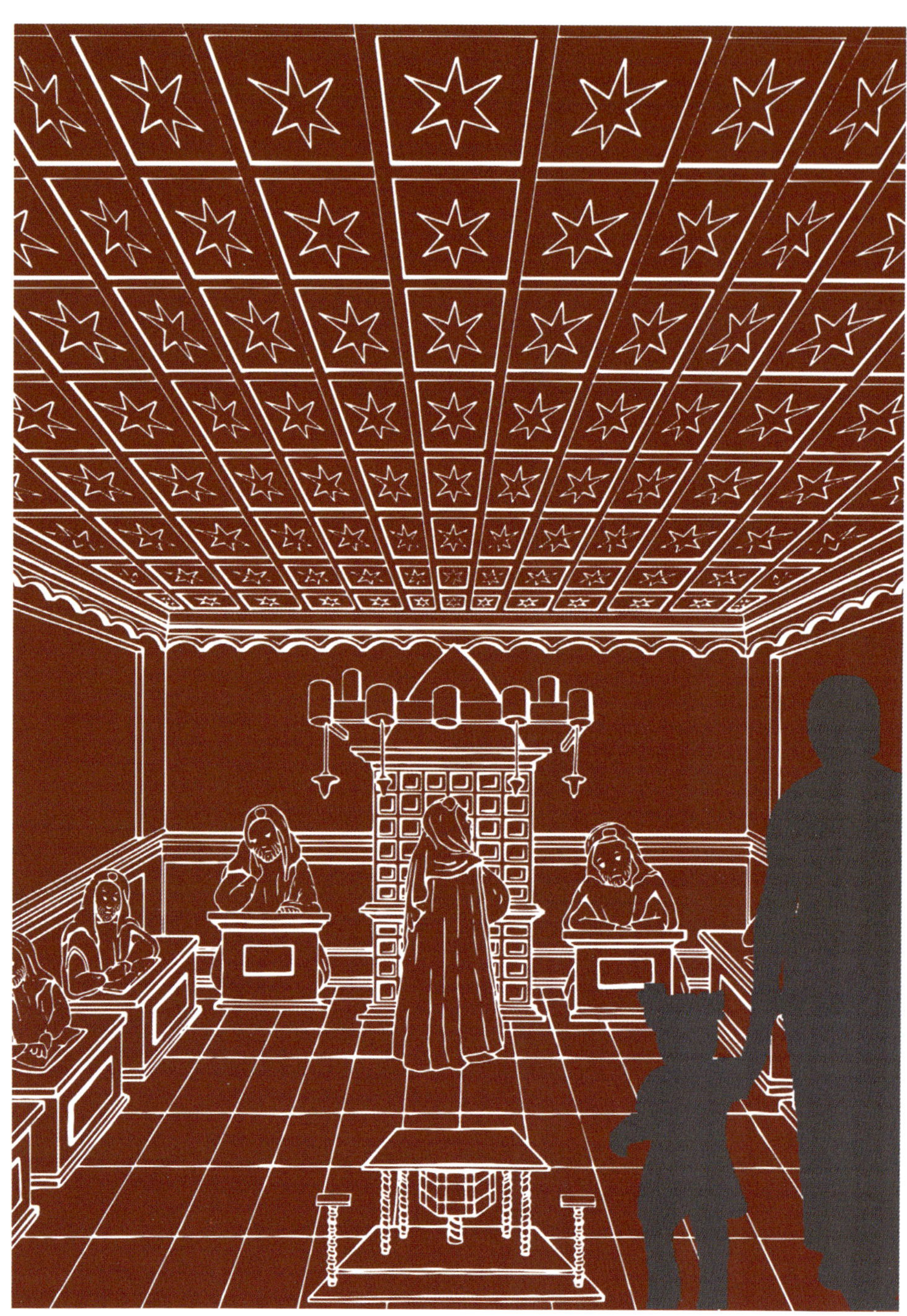

Museum and exhibition design,
inside a synagogue
(GTRF - Giovanni Tortelli Roberto Frassoni
Architetti Associati)

Museum and exhibition design,
medicine
(GTRF - Giovanni Tortelli Roberto Frassoni
Architetti Associati)

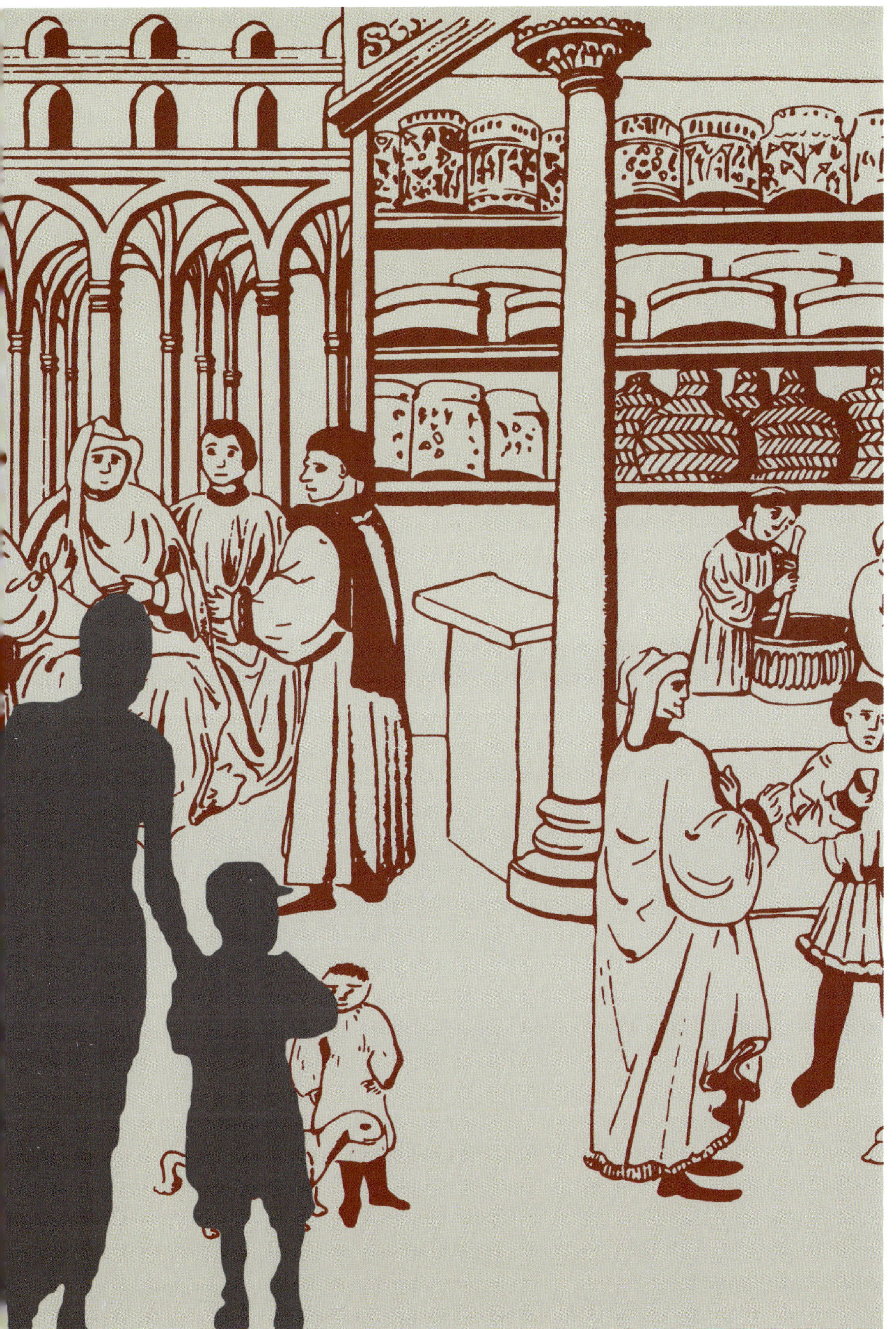

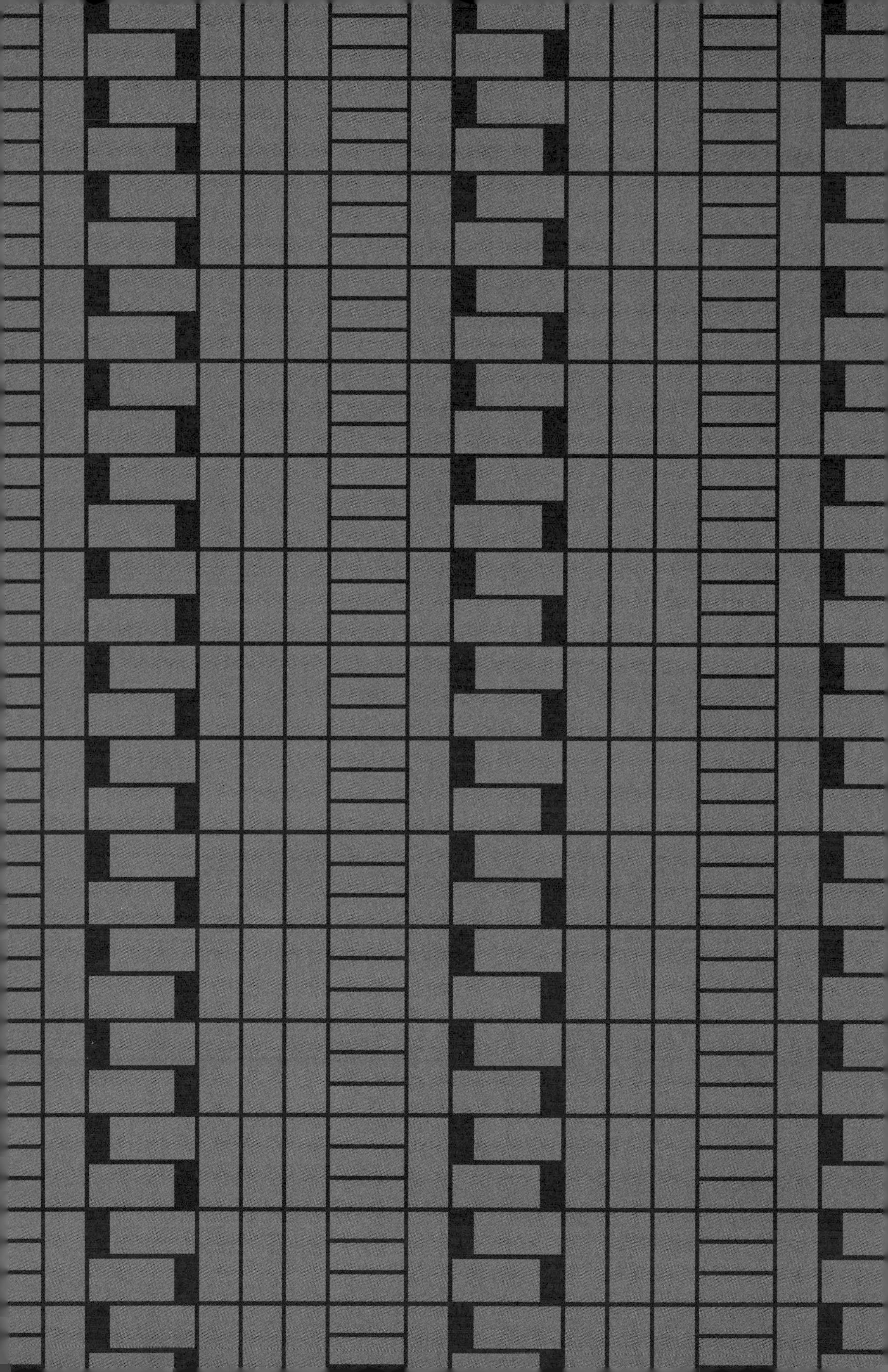

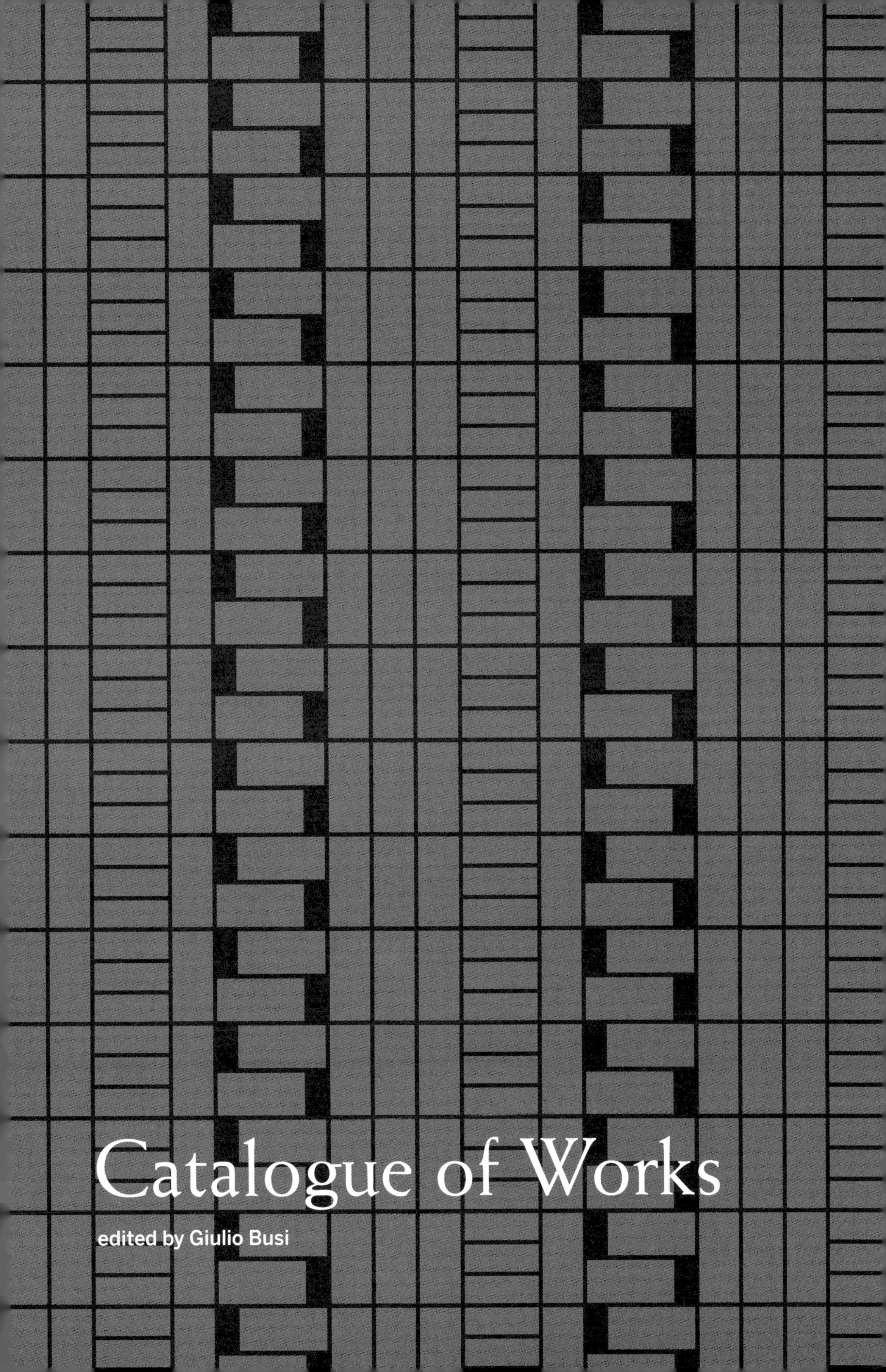

Catalogue of Works
edited by Giulio Busi

1. Ferrara, 1310: Jews and Christians swearing together

The people of Ferrara swear allegiance
to Pope Clement V
Thirteenth–fourteenth century
Parchment manuscript, miscellany
233 fols. (the Ferrara oath features on fols.
127r–147v)
40 × 30 cm
Vatican Library, Vatican City
MS Ott. lat. 2546

Literature: Fontana 1887, pp. 132–33; Colorni 1983, pp. 167–68; Franceschini 2007, p. 30 no. 46; see Sanfilippo 2016, pp. 10–11, 21, 73, 113, 252, 372.

Pope Clement V asked the people of Ferrara to swear an oath of allegiance to him. A total of 3,464 citizens did so. On March 26, 1310 the oath was taken by the inhabitants of the "Centum Vassurarum" district (now Via Centoversuri), which was home to a small Jewish community. The Christians swore on the Gospel, the Jews on the "Law that God gave to Moses on Mount Sinai." Here are their names:

Demelde judeus
Pellegrinus judeus frater Fulchi
Salimbene quondam Bomcambii judeus
Graciadeus
[et] Samuel judeus filii di Salimbene
Bonavancius [et] Benevenutus filii quondam Crescimbene
Jacob quondam Issepi judeus
Bentevegna qui dicitur Rubeus judeus
Salvetus judeus filius dicti Rubei
Fulchus judeus
Liça judeus eius filius
Bonavita judeus filius quondam Exdray
Sabbatynus judeus filius Pauli christiani
Issepo judeus
Sallamon judeus
Jssahac judeus eius filius
Omnes predicti judei et quilibet ipsorum tactis ebraycis scripturis corporaliter per legem quam Deus dedit Moysi in montem Sinay juramentum in formam precedentem prestiterunt. Si Deus eos et quemlibet ipsorum adiuvet et illa lex.

2. The Palace of Herod and the death of John the Baptist

Master of the Baptist Capital, *Capital with the Feast of Herod and Beheading of the Baptist*
Ferrara, c. 1200
Verona stone
56.5 × 53 × 45.5 cm
Museo della Cattedrale, Ferrara
inv. no. MC025

Literature: G. A. Scalabrini, *Acta sacrosanctae Ferrariensis Ecclesiae ab anno 1724 ad 1775*, Biblioteca Comunale Ariostea, Ferrara, MS cl. I 447, ad annum 1736; Venturi 1904, p. 323 and figs. 312–313; Neri Lausanna 1982, pp. 199–228; C. Rapetti, in *Benedetto Antelami* 1990, pp. 374-375, no. 34; Tigler 2007, pp. 71-74; G. Tigler, in *Il Museo della Cattedrale* 2010, pp. 84-89, no. 29.

According to the account given by Giuseppe Antenore Scalabrini (1694–1776), a scholar from Ferrara, the capital came from the Ferrara Cathedral, more specifically from the prothyrum of the Porta dei Mesi, demolished in the second or third decade of the eighteenth century. Scalabrini also describes how he salvaged it and placed it in the cemetery of Santa Maria di Bocche. After being moved from place to place, it is now conserved in the Museo della Cattedrale. The capital is historiated with scenes of the *Feast of Herod*, the *Dance of Salome* and the *Beheading of the Baptist*. The work has been variously attributed to a number of different makers on the basis of comparisons with capitals from the pulpit in the Duomo in Parma and with those from the belfry at the Ghirlandina in Modena (Venturi, 1904 p. 323; Neri Lausanna 1982). According to Tigler (2007, p. 73), certain iconographic and stylistic elements suggest that "the Master of the Baptist Capital trained in Antelami's workshop in the 1180s." Tigler (in *Il Museo della Cattedrale* 2010, p. 86) acknowledges the "architrave of the north door at the Baptistery of Parma as a direct model." The images that feature in the historiated sequence include Herod's palace, the dance of Salome, the banquet, the beheading of the Baptist and a diner flicking through a book, probably a Bible.

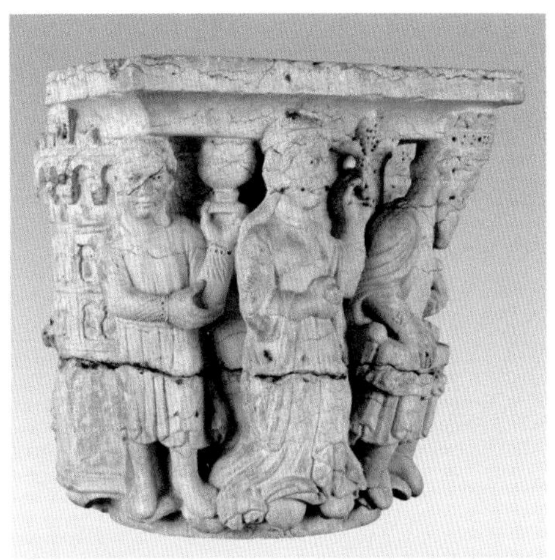

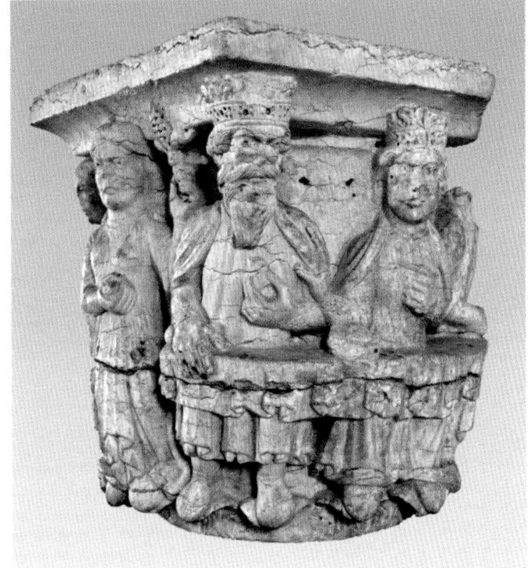

3. Venice, 1516: the birth of the ghetto

Decree for the institution of the Venetian ghetto
dated March 29, 1516
Venice, eighteenth century (copy of the original
document)
Paper register
33 × 21 cm
Archivio di Stato, Venice
Law compilation, envelope 188, fols. 294–295 and
302–303

Literature: Sanudo 1879–1903, vol. 22, cols. 85–88
(transcription of the decree); Bastianello 2016.

The Jews from Venice's mainland territories were admitted to the lagoon city during the threatening advance of the armies of the League of Cambrai, after the Battle of Agnadello on May 14, 1509. Up until then they had only been permitted to stay in the city for a limited time. In 1516, they were confined within a specifically chosen zone in the Cannaregio district. There had previously been a foundry, or "geto," in the area, hence the term "ghetto," later applied to all areas where Jews were forced to reside. Once a place of segregation and a dynamic cultural, religious and financial centre, the Venetian ghetto went on to symbolize the tenacity of the Jewish minority over the following centuries.

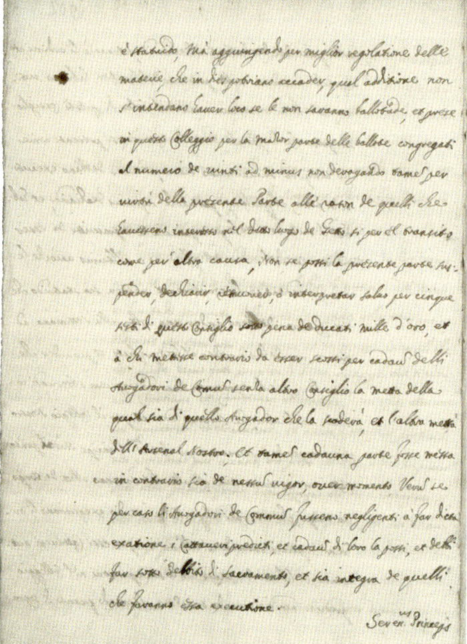

4. The Hebrew Psalter of Parma

Hebrew Bible, Psalms, with vowel-points and accents;
Abraham ibn Ezra, Commentary on the Psalms
Northern Italy (Emilia?), late thirteenth century,
square script and, in another hand, Italian
semi-cursive script
Parchment manuscript, illuminated
226 fols.
130 × 98 cm
Biblioteca Palatina, Parma
MS parm. 1870 (De Rossi 510)

Literature: Tamani 1968, p. 85, no. 97; Metzger 1977;
Tamani 1987, pp. 457–458 no. 7.8:2; *The Parma Psalter*
1996; *Hebrew Manuscripts* 2001, pp. 75–76 no. 371.

This small book, copied in Italy, perhaps in Emilia, in
the last quarter of the thirteenth century, is an outstanding example of mediaeval Hebrew illustration. In
addition to the text of the Psalms, with vowel-points
and accents, the margins feature the commentary by
Abraham ibn Ezra, a Sephardic exegete, poet, philosopher, and scientist. It ought to be impossible to pack
such a limited space with so many fantastic beasts,
turreted cities, Gothic monsters, musical instruments,
voracious lions, shambling dragons and sinuous polychrome tendrils. And yet the anonymous artist, who
decorated 171 sheets of this manuscript, overcame
the challenge with great skill, producing surprisingly
modern inventions. The outlines are elongated and
bent over, clinging like vines around the text. Nor are
the images purely ornamental. They dialogue with the
Psalms, illustrating them, reflecting them and bringing
them to life.

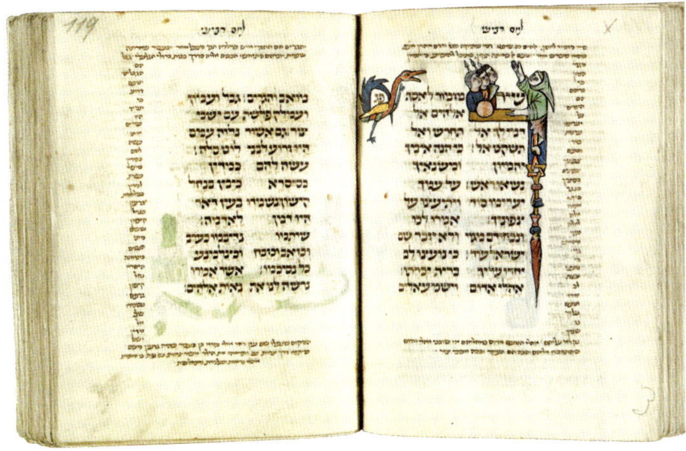

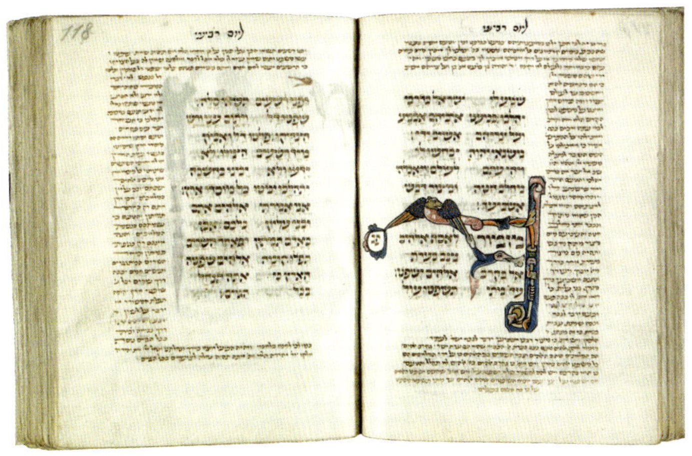

5. An illuminated Code of Law

Isaac Alfasi, *Sefer halakot*, with commentary
Parchment manuscript, illuminated
Northern Italy, c. 1440–80, Ashkenazi square and
semi-cursive script
372 fols.
366 × 267 cm
Biblioteca Palatina, Parma
MS parm. 3273 (De Rossi 134)

Literature: Tamani 1968, p. 98 no. 141; Metzger and
Metzger 1982, p. 86 no. 121, p. 313 no. 224; *Hebrew
Manuscripts* 2001, p. 167 no. 757

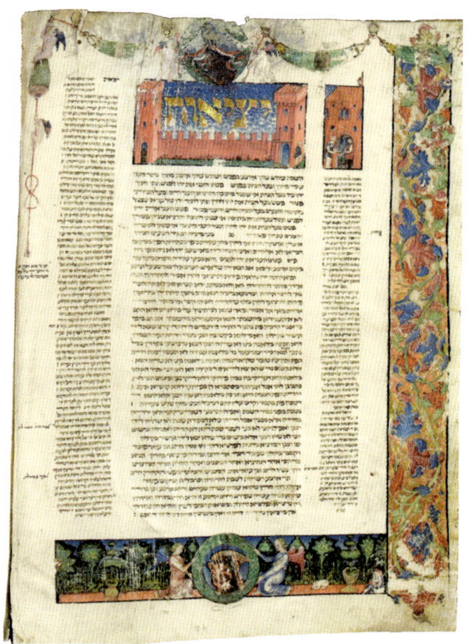

In Judaism, keeping tradition alive means reflecting,
reviving and modernizing. The study of the past is
never an end unto itself, but built upon continuous
comparisons and contemporary reinterpretations.
In this mid-fifteenth-century northern Italian copy
of the *Sefer halakot* (Book of Laws), which also includes some of the author's comments, Isaac Alfasi
(1013–1103), who lived in northern Africa, looks back
at and sums up the legal heritage of the Talmud, bringing it closer to everyday mediaeval usage. In his turn,
the illuminator entrusted with embellishing the manuscript gives the Talmudic laws a very modern setting.
The illustration on fol. 1*v*, with its crenelated walls,
towers, arched doorways, and palace with mullioned
windows, propels us into an urban Renaissance scene.
At the entrance to a sumptuous Jewish mansion, the
two characters interpret the discussion that opens the
tractate *Shabbat* in the Babylonian Talmud (b*Shabbat*
1*v*). The passage questions how a wealthy man can give
charity to the needy, on the threshold of his home,
while still observing the *Shabbat*. One of the figures is
dressed in purple robes and cap, clearly revealing his
wealth, while the other is tattered and afflicted. These
two central characters reflect class differences, the way
in which group solidarity can do away with them, the
integration of certain privileged figures within the city
and the need to question the rules of rabbinical jurisprudence on a daily basis. In short, they paint a picture
of tradition and Judaism in the life and contradictions
of Italian Renaissance society.

6. Silver finials, in exile from Sicily

Pair of *rimmonim* (finials)
Cammarata (Sicily), fifteenth century
Silver, semiprecious stones, coral
32 × 18 × 18 cm each
Palma de Mallorca, Museo de la Catedral
(on display: copy made in 2002, ibid.)

Inscriptions:

תורת יי
עדות יי
פקודי יי
מצות יי
יראת יי
משפט יי
אלו הרמונים קדש ליי
בכנסת יהודי
קמרטא י״צ אמן

The Torah of the Lord
The testimony of the Lord
The commandments of the Lord
The teachings of the Lord
The fear of the Lord
The judgment of the Lord
These *rimmonim* are sacred to the Lord
in the synagogue of the Jews
of Cammarata, may [its] f[ortress] guard it. Amen

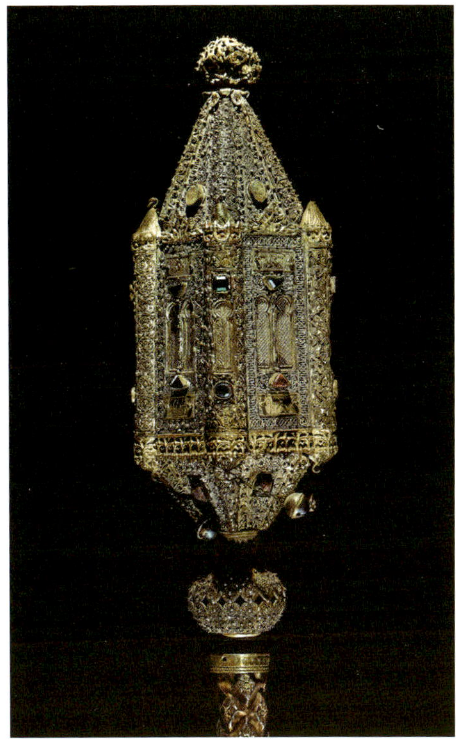

Literature: Cantera-Millás 1956, pp. 389–393 no. 275;
Llompart Moragues 1970; Simonsohn 1999, pp. 514,
517, 529 no. 48 and fig. 305; Bucaria 1996; Bucaria 2002,
p. 380 no. IX; Simonsohn 1997–2010, vol. 18, p. 12279.

Rimmonim (lit. pomegranates) act as finials, placed at
the top of the two sticks around which the Torah scroll
is wrapped for reading in the synagogue. The fact that
the two oldest *rimmonim* known to us today come
from Sicily is a revealing historical coincidence, testi-
fying to the great tradition of that ancient diaspora.
The objects came from the Jewish community living
in the Mazara valley, between Agrigento and Termi-
ni Imerese, until its expulsion in 1492. Their origin is
demonstrated by the Hebrew inscription that embel-
lishes them and that, in addition to a brief reference to
Psalms 18:8–10, includes the following words: "These
rimmonim, sacred to the Lord, [are] in the synagogue
of the Jews of Cammarata, may [its] f[ortress] guard
it. Amen." They were purchased by the Mallorcan
merchant Francesc Puig for 22 gold ducats from the
oppressed Jews who were forced to emigrate. In June
1493 the finials were placed in the Treasury of the Cathedral of Palma de Mallorca, where they are still to
be found today. It seems likely that the items, formerly from the synagogue in Cammarata, were made by
Jewish goldsmiths. Similar finials have been recorded
as being given as collateral to Christians by Jews from
Catania in 1492: "Certain gilded silver knobs, worked
like a castle with enamel on the tips."

7. 1472: the new Holy Ark of Modena

Aron ha-qodesh (Holy Ark)
Modena, 1472
Walnut with wooden inlay in different colors
265 × 130 × 78 cm
Musée d'art et d'histoire du Judaïsme, Paris (on long-term loan from the Musée National du Moyen-âge)
D.98.4.123 (Cl.12237)

Inscriptions:

קדש ליי

כי מציון תצא תורה ודבר ה׳ מירו׳

שלם תורת ה׳ תמימה משיבת נפש עדות ה׳ נמפפהי״מ לב

כסא כבוד מרום מראשון מ׳ מ׳

ארון ברית נעשה לכבוד רם ונ׳

לאלפי חמשה שנת ברכ״י נפשי את ה׳ הללויה

אלחנן רפאל בכמ״ר דניאל תנצב״ה

Sacred to the Lord
For out of Zion shall go forth the law, and the word
 of the Lord from Jerusalem (Is. 2. 3).
The law of the Lord is perfect, restoring the soul; the
 testimony of the Lord is sure, making wise the simple.
 The precepts of the Lord are right, rejoicing the heart
 (Psalm 19. 8-9).
Thou throne of glory, on high from the beginning,
 thou place of our sanctuary (Jer. 17. 12).
Ark of the Covenant, built in honour of Him who is
 elevated and exalted.
In the fifth millennium, in the year (BRKY =[5]232,
 i.e. 1472), Bless the Lord, O my soul. Hallelujah
 (Psalm 104. 35).
Elhanan Raphael, son of the honourable Rabbi Daniel—
 may his soul be safe in the treasure chest of life
 (cf. 1 Sam. 25. 29).

Literature: Klagsbald 1981, pp. 94–96; Klagsbald 1982, p. 13; Bagatin 1990, p. 28; Manni 1993, pp. 46–47; Rodov 2010, pp. 65–98: 72; see Contessa's essay in this volume.

The *aron ha-qodesh* (Holy Ark), in Ashkenazi use, or *hekal* (shrine), in Sephardic use, contains the Torah scrolls used in the synagogue service. This one from Modena, which dates back to 1472, is the oldest known example on wood and offers a rare opportunity to "enter" a Renaissance Jewish liturgical space.

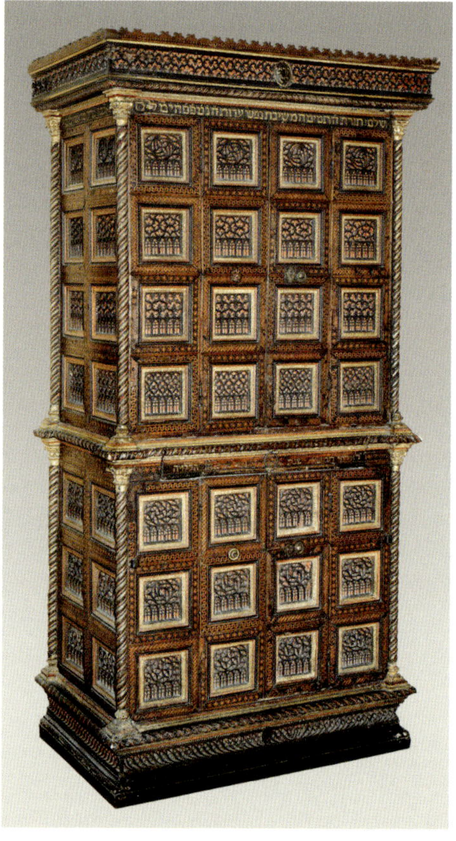

With its solid construction, crowned by a cornice resembling a crenelation, the two-part Modenese ark has a tower-like architectural structure. The four corners are softened by sleek twisted columns, while the surfaces feature frames with *toppo* inlay, which consists of applying filets of wood in different colors in geometric shapes and overlapping layers. The four doors move the central panels vertically: there are sixteen panels on the front of the top section and twelve on the bottom section. Hebrew inscriptions run along the top and in the middle part, with dedicatory and laudatory verses featuring the name of the donor, Elhanan Raphael ben Daniel, and the date. Manni (1993, p. 46) tends toward "a local ascendency, from the Este circle in Modena" and points to Cristoforo Canozi (or Cristoforo Genesini, c. 1420 – before 1490), a master cabinetmaker at the Este court, or at least to his circle.

8. A pulpit for the Torah

Bimah (pulpit)
Northern Italy, c. 1440–75
Walnut with wooden inlay in different colors
(*toppo* technique)
122 × 88.3 × 65.5 cm
Musée d'art et d'histoire du Judaïsme, Paris
(on long-term loan from the Musée National
du Moyen-âge)
D.98.04.124 (Cl. 12238)

Literature: Stenne 1878, pp. 14–15 and plate 2; Metzger
1979 (for the image of a *bimah* in the codex now in
Zurich, Jeselsohn Collection, MS 11); *Savants et croyants* 2018, pp. 239–241 no. 64.

There are very few accounts about the internal arrangement and furnishings of synagogues in Italy between
the fourteenth and fifteenth century. Most of the information available to us derives from codex illuminations and a few rare archive documents. A pulpit,
known as a *bimah* in the Ashkenazi tradition or also as
a *tevah* in the Sephardic tradition, was used to read the
Torah, the central part of the synagogal liturgy. Maimonides, the great philosopher and regulator of the
rabbinic tradition, prescribes that the *bimah* be placed
at the center of the room, so that "he who is reading
the Torah or giving a sermon can stand on it, so that
all the others can hear him." (*Mishneh Torah, Hilkot
tefillah*, 11. 3; see y*Sukkah* V. 1). It is evidently a raised
structure here, while other fifteenth-century sources
describe floor-standing lecterns, used for the collective
study of the sacred text and its liturgical reading (e.g.
Zurich, Jeselsohn Collection, MS 11, fol. 1; Rothschild
Miscellany, fol. 274*v*; British Library Library, MS Add.
14762, fol. 7*v*). The wooden pulpit from northern Italy
has a certain generic resemblance to these depictions
and features a decorative *toppo* inlay. The only infor-

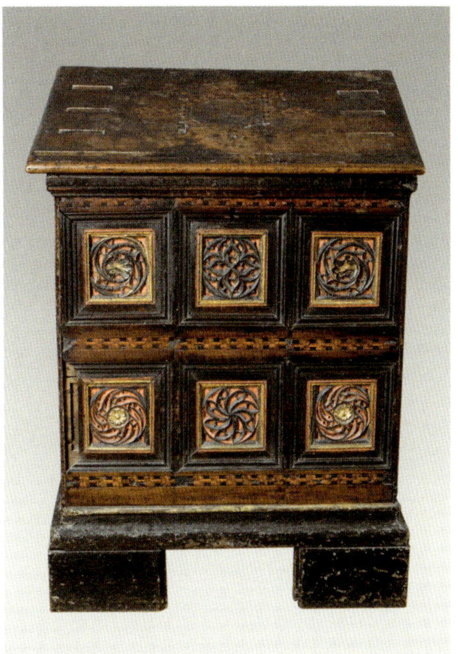

mation we have about the synagogue use of the item,
which is lacking in votive inscriptions or other definite
signs of Jewishness, comes from the catalogue of the
collection of Isaac Strauss (1806–1888), which also
included the *aron ha-qodesh* dated 1472 and originally
from the synagogue of Modena (see cat. 7): "Pupitre
de l'officiant (Théba)." In the catalogue illustration, the
pulpit is topped by an eight-arm candelabrum, which
also features the additional arm or *shammash* (servant)
used for Hanukkah ("Un chandelier en bronze à huit
branches surmonte ce pupitre. Une neuvième branche
mobile est supportée par un lion debout, qui s'appuie
à droite sur un écusson et à la gauche tien une palme").

9. The oldest *Sefer Torah* still in use

Sefer Torah (Torah scroll)
Northern France, c. 1250
Parchment scroll, wooden shafts
61 cm, 104 cm (seventeenth-century shafts)
Jewish community, Vercelli
Scroll 2

Literature: A. Spagnoletto, in *Savants et croyants* 2018, p. 232, no. 60.

The *Sefer Torah* (Torah scroll), used for synagogue readings, comes from the Synagogue of Biella, and was discovered recently, during an inventory of the scrolls conserved by the Jewish Community of Vercelli. Radiocarbon 14 testing indicates a date of 1245–68 and therefore makes this item a rare and priceless testament to material culture and synagogue life during the Middle Ages. It is worth noting a number of specific graphic characteristics, such as the use of *taggin* (crownlets) over certain letters and the modification of the *ductus* of others (such as the *peh lefufah*: that is "wrapped"). These and other aspects indicate the Ashkenazi origin of the scroll and make it possible to ascribe its provenance to northern France. It was probably taken from there to Piedmont on the occasion of the expulsion of the Jews ordered by Charles VI in 1394. Restored after its discovery, the *sefer* has been repaired and rendered suitable for liturgical use once more. It can be said to be the oldest synagogue scroll in the world today that is still owned by a Jewish community and can be used for ritual purposes.

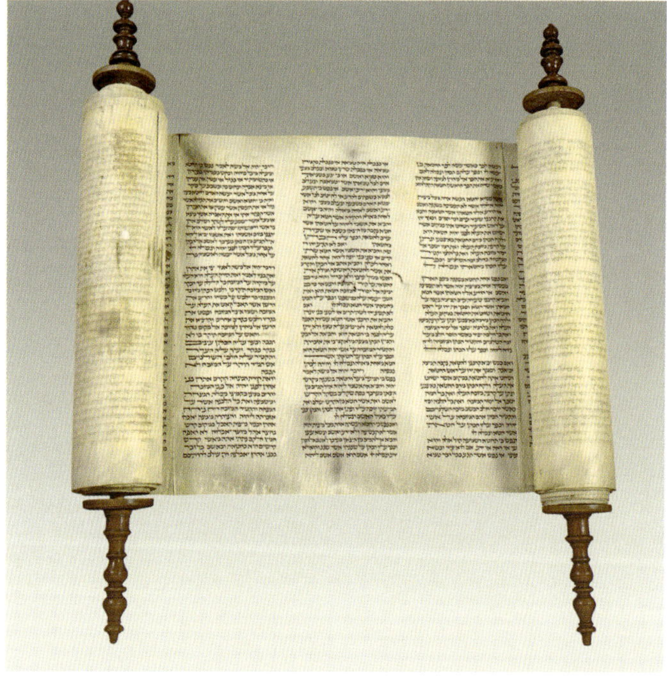

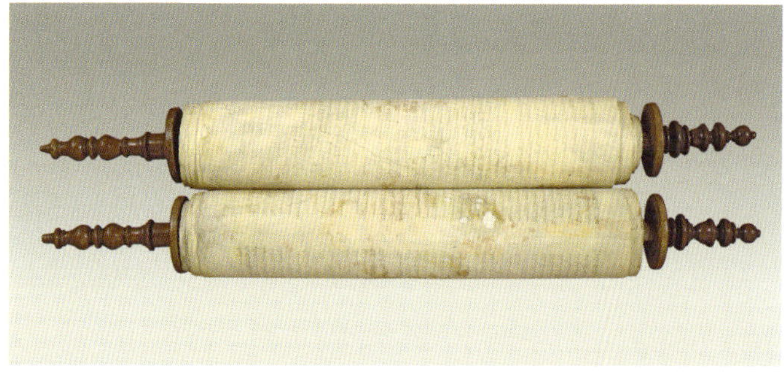

10. Virdimura: Sicilian Jewess and medical expert

Licence to practice medicine, granted
to the Jewess Virdimura
Catania, Sicily, November 7, 1376
Paper register
32 × 23.7 cm
Archivio di Stato, Palermo
Cancelleria reg. 16 (the document regarding
Virdimura is on fol. 57*v*)

Literature: *Codice diplomatico* 1884–88, vol. 1, p. 99; Precopi Lombardo Sparto 1984; Simonsohn 1997–2010, p. 1104 no. 1029.

In 1376, the Jewess Virdimura, wife of the physician Pasquale of Catania, applied to practice medicine, particularly among the poor, who were unable to afford doctors' fees. After being examined by the king's physicians, who found her suitable, Virdimura was authorized to practice medicine throughout the cities and lands of Sicily. Here is the wording of the authorization:

> Novembris ad Catheniam Virdimura Iudea
> Scriptum est per patentes litteras universis officialibus per totam Siciliam constitutis et costituendis ac personis aliis tam presentis quam futuris presentes litteras inspecturis fidelibus suis etc... Cum ad humilem supplicacionem factam noviter excelliencie nostre per Virdimuram iudeam uxorem Pascalis de medico de Cathania iudei servi camere nostre sibi licencia praticandi in sciencia medicine circa curas phisicas corporum humanorum, maxime pauperum quibus dificile censetur in mensa phisicorum et medicorum salaria solucionem vivique [sic] locorum dicti regni nostri Sicilie eo videlicet quod ipsam Virdimuram examinari diligenter fecimur per phisicos nostros in pratica supradicta qui eamdem Virdimuram previa examinacione predicta ac suadente fama laudabili ac experiencia probabili comendarunt et approbarunt esse admictenda in pencione prescripta graciose et benigne duxerimus concedendam, vestre f. m. q. prefatam Virdimuram praticari in huiusmodi sciencie medicine de cetero ubique civitatum terrarum et locorum dicti regni nostri Sicilie vigore presentis gracie nostre ac licencie per nostram serenitatem sibi concesse autem presencium preter condicionis obstaculum permutatis. Datum etc.

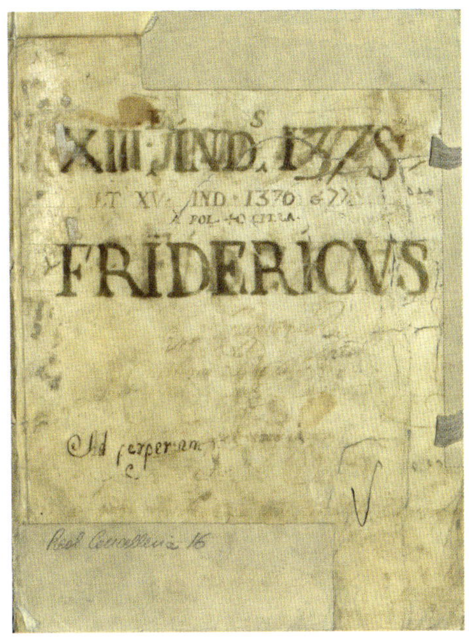

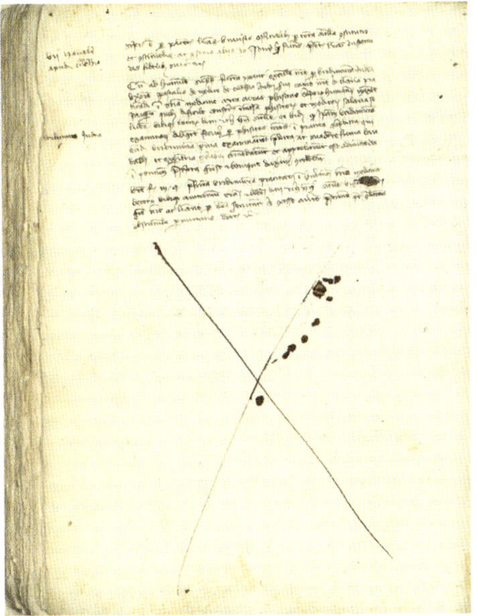

11. Obadiah Sforno graduates in Ferrara

Degree in medicine awarded to Obadiah
ben Jacob Sforno by the Studio di Ferrara
Ferrara, April 27, 1501
Paper register
34 × 25 cm
Notary Tommaso Meleghini, vol. VI, years
1490–1506, fol. 380
Archivio di Stato, Ferrara

Literature: Steinschneider 1878; Pesaro 1880, p. 45;
Colorni 1983, pp. 461–472.

Born in Cesena in around 1475, Obadiah ben Jacob
Sforno subsequently lived in Rome, Ferrara, and Bologna, where he founded a *bet ha-midrash* ("house of
study" or "school"), which he ran until his death in
1550. A leading Jewish figure in the Italy of the first
half of the sixteenth century, he was also a wealthy
banker (Berns 2017) and maintained close links with
the Christian culture of his time. He taught Hebrew
to the renowned Johannes Reuchlin in Rome between
1498 and 1500. In 1501 he was awarded a degree in
medicine from the University of Ferrara, which was
a truly exceptional achievement given how difficult
it was for Jews to be admitted to further education at
the time. The document featured in this exhibition
was fully transcribed by Colorni (1983, pp. 470–27)
and specifies that Sforno had studied "in Rome and
elsewhere" before being examined by the committee
in Ferrara with a "rigoroso ac pertremendo examini."
The degree includes the full dispensation issued by the
bishop of Pesaro, Francesco Oricelli, lieutenant of the
papal legate for the provinces of Bologna, Romagna
and the Exarchate. This dispensation was essential for
a Jew to be awarded a degree despite the canonical regulations.

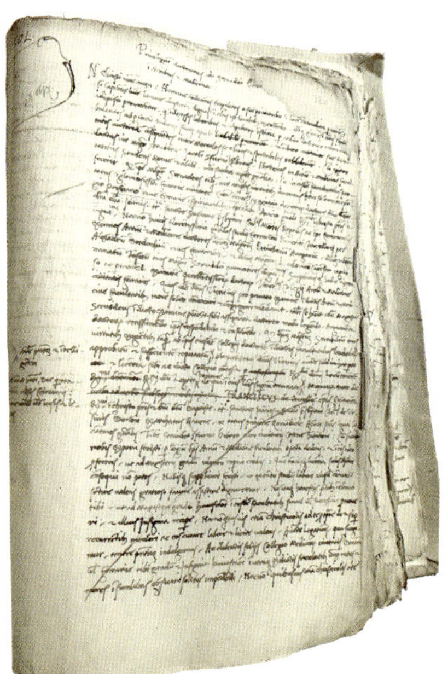

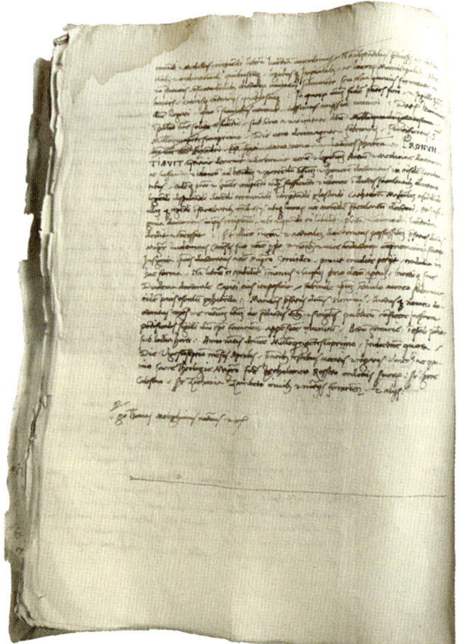

12. Dense iron studs

Safe
Italy, sixteenth century?
Iron safe with wood core
146 × 103 × 55 cm
Jewish community, Ferrara

Literature: *Arte e cultura ebraiche* 1988, no. 111; Tedeschi Falco 1999, p. 22.

Safe comprised of a strong wooden structure covered with wrought iron and extensive studs.

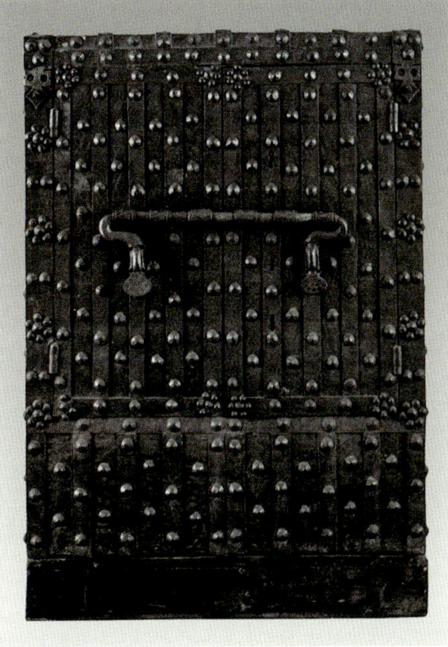

13. Stella Norsa and the Mantua pawnshop

Rental contract for the pawnshop formerly
run by Moses Norsa in Mantua
Mantua, December 17, 1517
Parchment document
35 × 30 cm
Archivio di Stato, Modena
framm. ebraico 351.2

Literature: *I frammenti ebraici* 2012, no. 351.2; Perani 2012b, pp. 120–24.

This sixteenth-century Hebrew contract was reused for the binding of a register of documents dated 1664 and stored at the Archivio di Stato in Modena. The document was detached and identified in 2002.
Stella, widow of the Mantuan pawnbroker Moses Norsa and guardian of their son Solomon Norsa, leased her late husband's pawnbroking business to two Jewish bankers from Mantua, Daniel ben Solomon Ḥazaq [Forti] and Joseph Gallico. This same rental contract was written out in a much more concise form in Latin the following day, December 18, 1517, and is conserved at the Archivio di Stato in Mantua (Archivio Gonzaga, line 3390: Simonsohn 1977, p. 215, note 57; Perani 2012b, pp. 123–24).

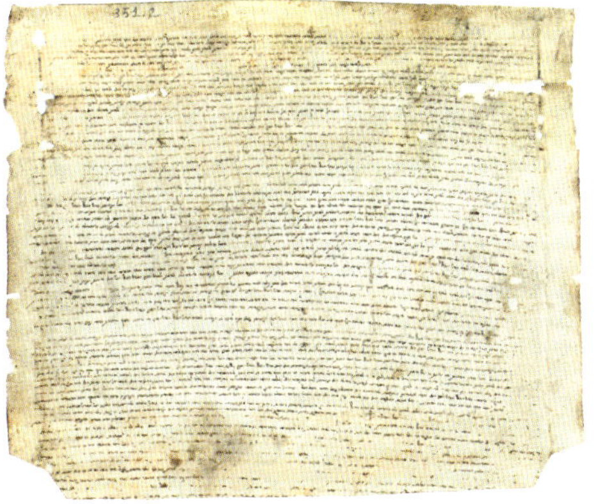

14. Maimonides's codex

Moses Maimonides, *Moreh nevukim*
(Guide for the Perplexed)
Ashkenazi area, 1349
Ashkenazi semi-cursive script. Copyist: Jacob ben
Samuel
Parchment manuscript, illuminated
228 fols.
25.4 × 19.6 cm
MiBAC, Direzione Generale Archivi, Rome

Literature: Metzger 2002; *Il codice Maimonide* 2018.

This manuscript, with its beautiful writing and illuminations, contains the *Moreh nevukim* (Guide for the Perplexed), the influential and difficult philosophical work by Maimonides (d. 1204). As it is often the case with Jewish culture during the Middle Ages, Maimonides drew upon many sources, including the Bible and Greek thinking, theology of Muslim origin, Aristotelianism and rabbinic teachings. Chapter after chapter, the thinker of Iberian origin, whose work was also read and appreciated by Thomas Aquinas, constructs his daringly harmonious blend of faith and reason. Although we do not know the identity of the illuminator, who embellished the volume with illustrations based upon the philosophical text, the copyist, Jacob ben Samuel, who writes in an Ashkenazi hand, signs his name in the poem that contains the copy date, expressed as the year 5109 since Creation according to the Jewish calendar: which corresponds to the year 1349 of the Christian calendar. "The year in which light was transformed into darkness," reads the *colophon*. The darkness referred to here is the darkness brought about by the Black Death, which led to such widespread death and persecution. Accused of having spread the disease deliberately, the Jews were massacred in many different areas of Europe. The first exterminations were carried out in 1348, spreading the following year, particularly in Germany.

Someone brought the book to Italy, perhaps as early as the late fourteenth century, as we can surmise from the ownership inscriptions. A particular aspect of the manuscript on display here is the deed of sale, dated on the 6th day of the month of Shevat in the year [5]276 according to the smaller calculation (= 10 January [1]516). Baruk, son of Joseph Kohen, of blessed memory, sells "this book of the Moreh [nevukim]" to Moses ben Nathanael Norsa. The sale document is rare in itself. However, it is even more significant because it links the volume to the history of the Norsa family, which played a leading part in Jewish financial and cultural life in Mantua and Ferrara between the Renaissance and the modern era. This document offers invaluable evidence of the book collection built up by Moses ben Nathanael Norsa (d. 1519), who owned a library containing many dozens of Hebrew codices (Rothschild 1987, pp. 294–302; Metzger 2002, p. 31; Busi 2018). After remaining in the possession of the same family for five centuries, the codex was acquired by the Direzione Generale Archivi and restored, in 2018, by the Istituto Centrale per il Restauro e la Conservazione del Patrimonio Archivistico e Librario (Rome).

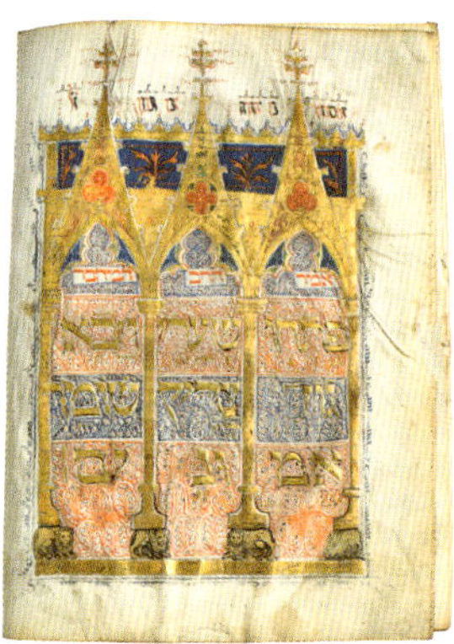
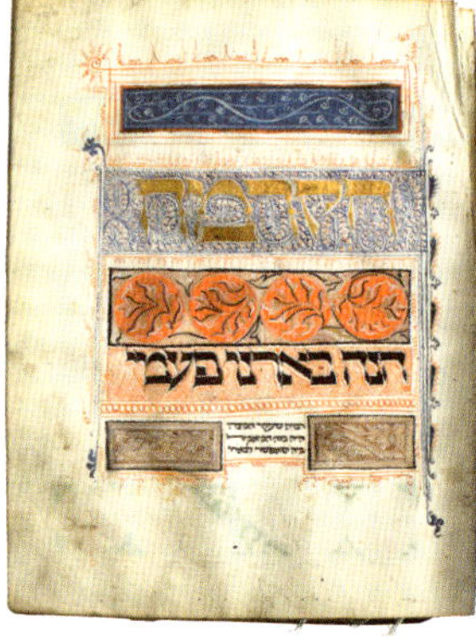
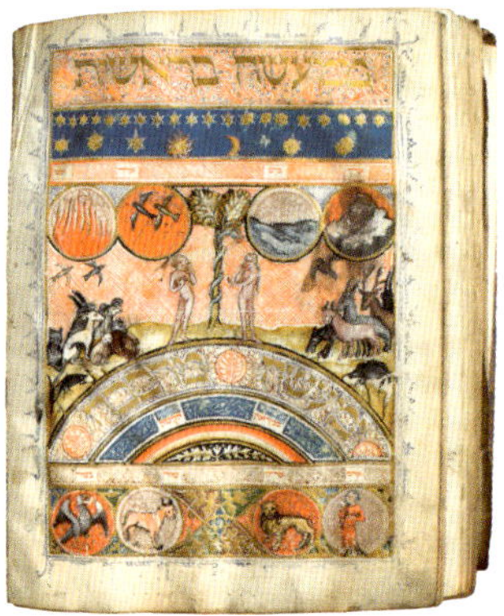

15. Genatano di Ventura and his debtors

List of debtors and inventory of assets belonging to
the banker Genatano di Ventura
Urbino, 1436
Paper register
42 × 29.5 cm
Archivio di Stato, Urbino
Quadra di Pusterla, no. 28 (1436), fols. 132*r*–137*r*

Literature: Luzzatto 1902, p. 33; Veronese 1998, pp.
264, 277.

Archive sources document the presence of Jews in
Urbino from 1407 onwards, although it seems likely
that merchants and lenders had already begun to ar-
rive around thirty years earlier. In the early fifteenth
century the group in Urbino must have comprised
around twenty people, gathered around the family of
the banker Isaia di Maestro Daniele, who lived near
Piazza Maggiore (Veronese 1998, pp. 260–61). Isaia
had obtained a permit (since lost) toward the end of
the fourteenth century and had run the bank alone
until his death in 1416. His children then continued
the lending business together and in partnership
with others. A company that included a lender from
Recanati, Maestro Aliuccio, was founded in Urbino
in 1433. Upon the death of one of the contracting
parties, Genatano di Ventura, the company was dis-
solved and the inventory on display here was drawn
up, comprising over 500 debtors. The sums listed
vary from a few bolognini to the relatively conspicuous figure of 100 ducats, loaned at the annual rate
of 33%.

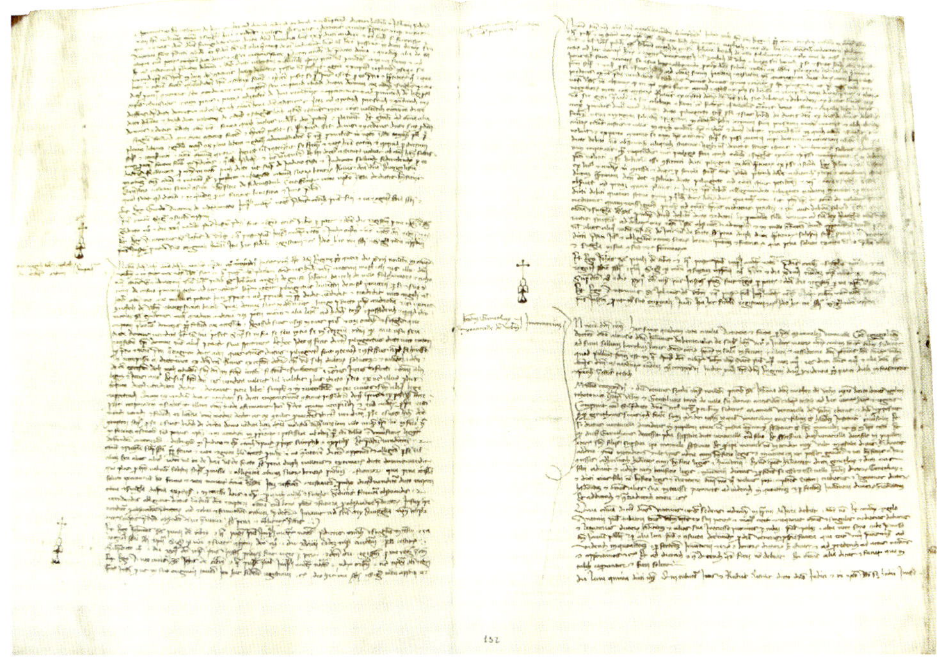

16. Rome, 1287: Hebrew Bible

Hebrew Bible, with vowel-points and accents.
Excerpts from the *Masora parva* and *magna*
Rome, 1287 (*colophon* on fol. 410:
10 Tammuz 5047 [1287])
Italian square script
Parchment manuscript, illuminated
414 fols.
32.3 × 24.3 cm
Vatican Library, Vatican City
MS Vat. ebr. 9

Literature: Mortara Ottolenghi 1974, p. 142, note 6;
Mortara Ottolenghi 1983, pp. 217–18; Metzger and
Metzger 1982, p. 314, note 243; Busi 1990, pp. 86–87
no. III.1.4; *Hebrew Manuscripts* 2008, pp. 5–7

This codex, which comprises the full text of the Hebrew Bible, comes from the great tradition of the
scribes and illuminators active in Rome between the
late thirteenth and early fourteenth century. It features
numerous highly original and elegant illuminations,
incorporating a full mediaeval bestiary populated
by a great variety of creatures ranging from bears to
monkeys, dragons and winged fish. There are five full-
page illustrations, with variations on the symbolism of
the *Etz ḥayyim*, the tree of life, and luxuriant plants.
The numerous ownership and use inscriptions reveal
the great importance and intense use of the volume
from one generation to the next. They include: Joab
ben Jehiel, Elijah ben Judah the Physician, Joseph
ben Shalom (fol. 1), and Solomon ben Joseph Kohen
(fol. 1*v*). Meanwhile, fol. 411 features notes dated October 6 and November 11, 1493 recording the loan of 6
ducats from Immanuel ben Benjamin to Abraham ben
Judah, witnessed by Abraham ben Isaac Provenzali,
with the manuscript as collateral.

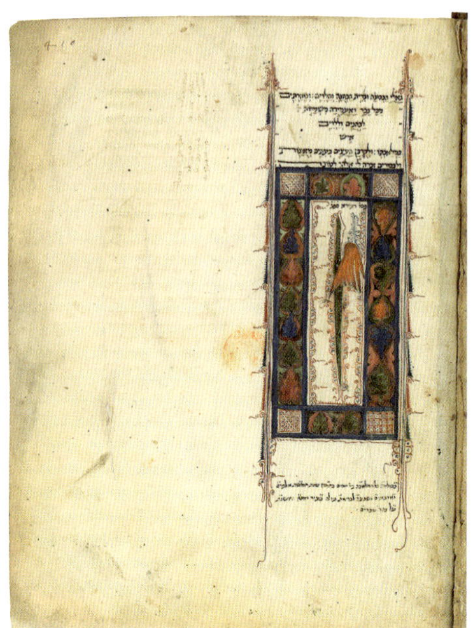

17. Prayers for "many gentlewomen"

Judeo-Italian translation of the *Siddur* for the entire
year (Book of daily prayers)
Fano: Gershom Soncino, 1505
[184] fols.
15.5 × 11 cm
Biblioteca Estense Universitaria, Modena
MS alfa.f.9.1.

Literature: Manzoni 1883–86, 2, pp. 83–85 no. 16;
Habermann 1978, p. 56 no. 23; Tamani 1976, no. 30;
Busi 1987a, p. 126 no. 325 (this exemplar on display);
Busi 1987b, pp. 479–80 no. 8.2:10 (on the second edi-
tion of 1538); Rubin 2017, p. 307

The fact that this translation was primarily intended
for use by Jewish women is confirmed by the introduction to the second edition of the work entitled *Tefillot
latini*, published in Bologna in 1538: "Having been
obliged and requested by many gentlewomen, who
wanted to say their *tefillah latino*, I translated a *siddur*
for the entire year into Latin with the help of God." It
should be noted that, like the rest of the work, the typographic notes are written in Hebrew characters but
in the vernacular (which the translator calls "Latin"),
with Hebrew inserts: "Finished the Siddur for the entire year translated by Rabbi Jacob Israel and printed
by Soncino in Fano in Marḥeshwan [5]266 [October–
November 1505]."

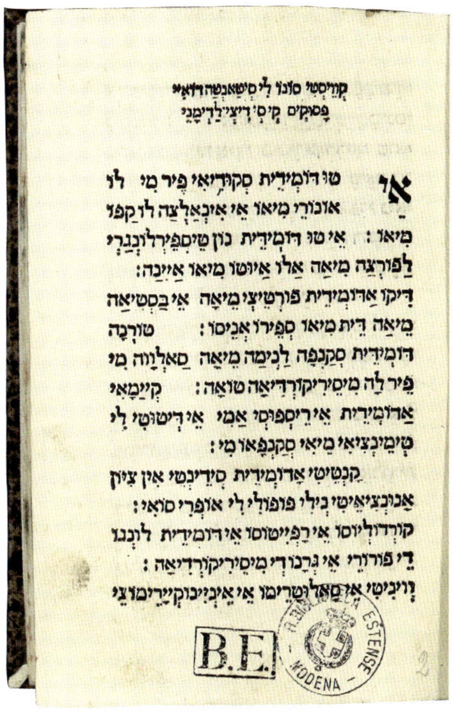

18. The Bible of the Christian Hebraist Giannozzo Manetti

Hebrew Bible, with vowel-points and accents;
Dawid Qimḥi, *Sefer ha-shorashim* (Book of Roots)
Iberian peninsula, fifteenth century
Sephardic square script
Parchment manuscript
470 fols.
27 × 19 cm
Vatican Library, Vatcan City
MS Vat. ebr. 8

Literature: Cassuto 1918, pp. 125–30, 155, 197, 201; Cassuto 1935, p. 45; Cassuto 1956, pp. 10–13; Pasternak 2004; *Hebrew Manuscripts* 2008, p. 5.

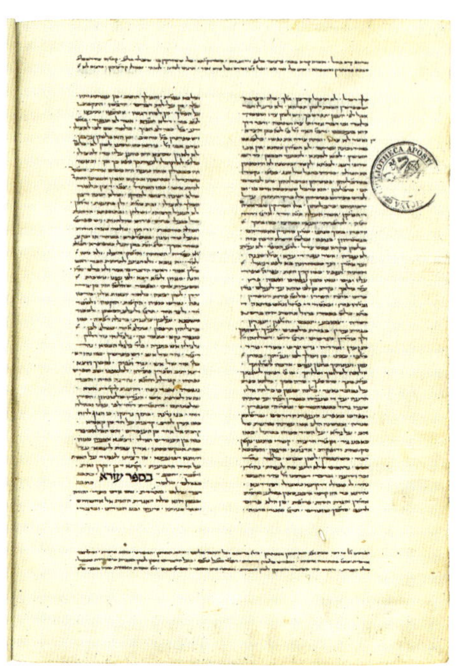

This biblical codex of Iberian origin, which can be dated to the fifteenth century, also contains the *Sefer ha-shorashim* (Book of Roots), a Hebrew dictionary by Dawid Qimḥi. It contains a number of ownership and sale inscriptions that recount a very interesting chapter in the story of Jewish-Christian relations during the Renaissance period. On February 15, 1434 (5194: fol. 1, 465) the codex was acquired by Solomon ben Joseph ha-Kohen, a banker and keen book collector, also known as Salomone di Bonaventura of Prato (or Terracina) in Latin documents. We know that Solomon had serious financial problems in 1441 and was forced to pay a very high fine of 20,000 florins due to irregularities in the management of his affairs (Goldthwaite 2009, pp. 422–23). It was probably after these problems that Solomon lent the codex as collateral, for fourteen soldi, to the humanist Giannozzo Manetti (1396–1450), who used it for his Hebrew studies—as demonstrated by the numerous notes in his hand. On fol. 467r, Manetti noted: "1442, die d[omi]nica xiᵃ nove[m]bris cu[m] Emanuele heb[re]o incepi hebraice." This "Emanuele," teacher of Hebrew studies, has been identified by Cassuto as the Florentine Jewish banker Immanuel ben Abraham from San Miniato. On August 7, 1443 (5203), Solomon ben Joseph went on to sell the manuscript to Manetti for 21 fiorini larghi. This transaction is recorded, in Hebrew, by the vendor on fol. 465 and, in Latin, by the Christian witness Nicola di Bartolo: "I, Nichola di B[ar]tolo di Giovan[n]i di Nichola, was present on August 7, 1443, when Salamone di Bonaventura of P[r]ato received on said day from Gianozo di B[e]rnardo Maneti at his house, 21 florins from our bank, which are for this book, that is this Bible that Gianozo has purchased from Salamone, and so I saw Salamone write the above subscription in his hand, on the said day, year and month."

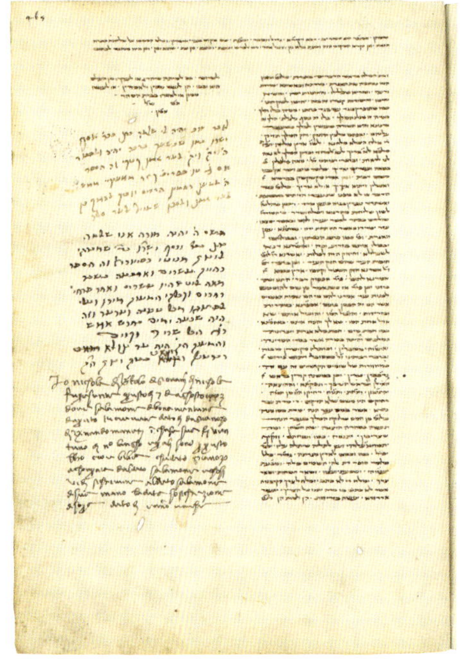

19. An illuminated prayer book

Siddur (Daily prayer book) according to
the Italian or Roman rite
Florence, 1490 (*colophon* on fol. 348*v*)
Italian square and semi-cursive script. Copyist:
Berahiel ben Hezekiah Trabot, for Elijah da Vigevano
[Galli] and Brunetta [daughter of Elijah]
Parchment manuscript, illuminated
360 fols.
12 × 8 cm
Biblioteca Estense Universitaria, Modena
MS alfa.j.9.21

Literature: Berheimer 1960, pp. 26–27 no. 26; Cohen
2006

Elijah from Vigevano, from the Galli family, for whom
this beautiful illuminated manuscript was copied in
Florence in 1490, is known in Latin documents as Elia
di Dattilo (or Dattero), and is mentioned as early as
1469 with business and interests in various Italian
cities (Luzzati 2002; see also Perani's essay in this volume). A wealthy banker, in 1490 Elia gave his daughter Brunetta, for whom the codex was intended, the
sum of 450 florins so that she could marry Jacob ben
Abraham di Consiglio, from the important Toscanella
or da Padova family, resident in Siena (ibid., p. 46: the
notary who registered the deed was Ser Piero da Vin-
ci, Leonardo's father: see cat. 23). On the back of the
first folio, within a typically Florentine floral frame,
is the Galli coat of arms, with a "rooster with a star
and a crescent moon above it" (pp. 366–67), here with
the addition of an ear of corn with a serpent wound
around it.

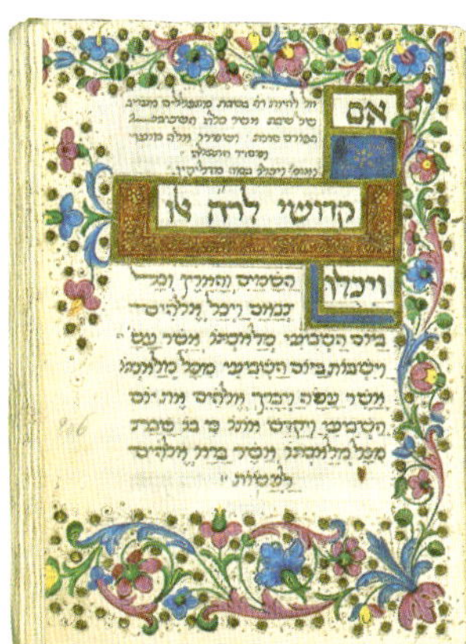
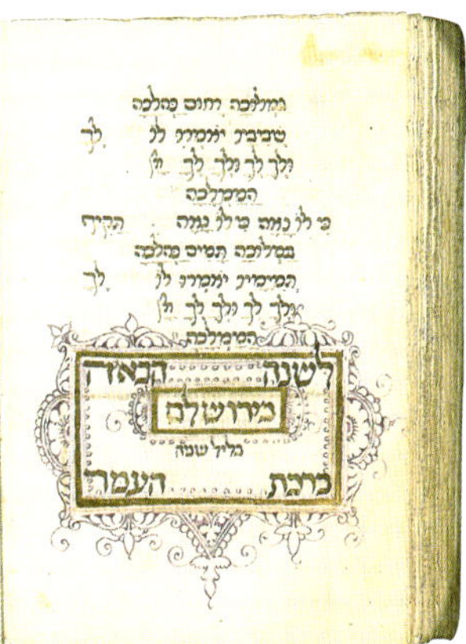
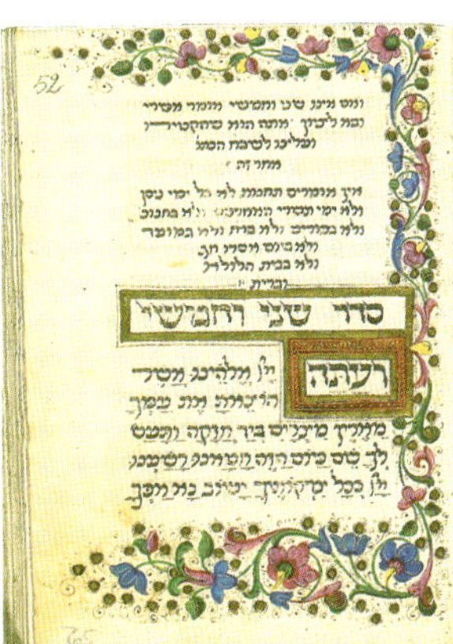
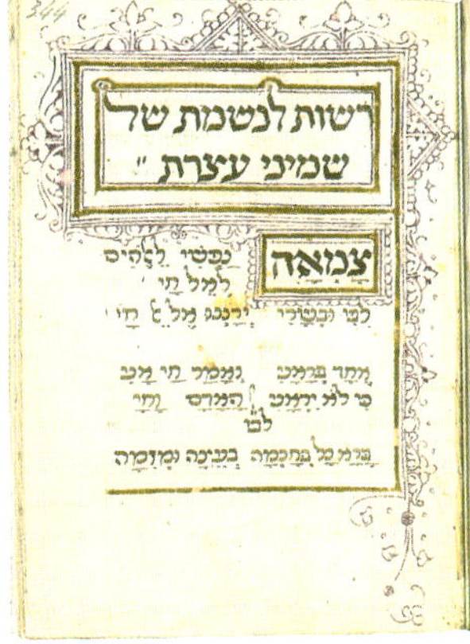
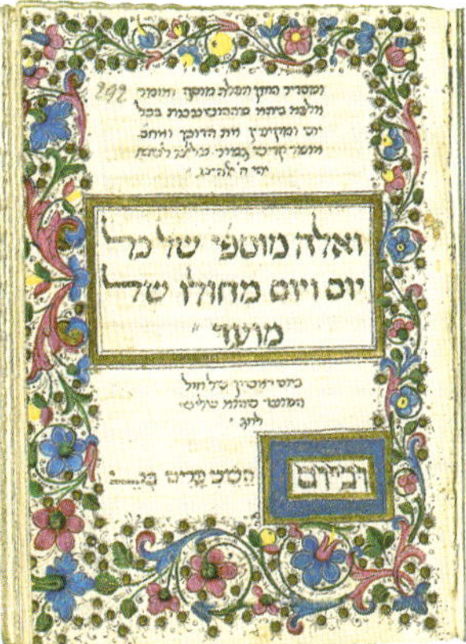
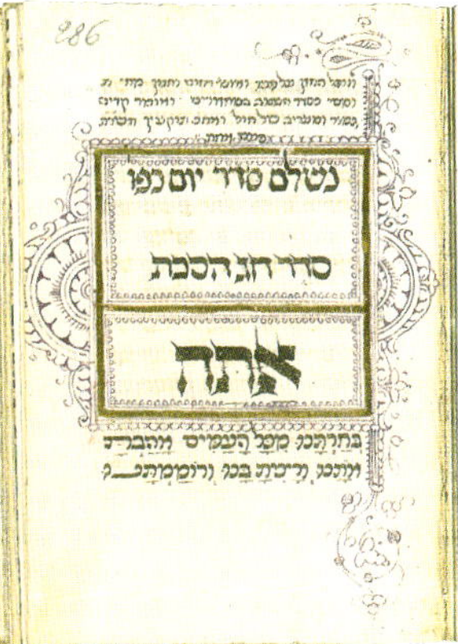

20. Tenson between "Salomone Hebreo" and Giovanni Pellegrino

Miscellany of literary texts from the thirteenth,
fourteenth and fifteenth centuries, defaced
at the beginning and end
Northern Italy, c. 1460–70
Paper manuscript
321 fols.
22 × 15 cm
Biblioteca Comunale, Udine
MS 10 (MS Ottelio)

Literature: Fabris 1909, p. 226; *Inventari* 1930, pp. 12–49; Alfie 2003.

Included in a collection of literary texts ranging from Dante to Petrarch, Cecco Angliolieri and Domenico di Giovanni, known as Il Burchiello, this tenson composed by the poet Giovanni Pellegrino and "Salomone Hebreo" (fols. 252*v*–253*r*) is a rare and as yet little-studied document. The two compositions making up the exchange between the Christian and Jew evidently appeared worthy of transcription to Lunardo da Brissa (Brescia), who compiled the collection in the 1460s. In addition to its poetic qualities, which are not particularly refined, this dialogue in verse offers us an invaluable glimpse of the relations that must have existed between scholars of different faiths in Ferrara and at the Este court. Giovanni Pellegrino di Andrea Arduini, who died in 1466, was initially favored at court before falling into disgrace and being imprisoned for interfering with the succession of Lionello d'Este. He wrote a number of lauds and two autobiographical *frottole* in which he describes the trials and tribulations of his family, devastated by the plague in 1439. In the tenson he addresses his friend Salomone in very complimentary terms, praising his "mature, serious, lofty and lordly" style. While this is of course an appreciation, it also reveals their mutual esteem, as becomes apparent in Salomone's response. Indeed, with equal eloquence Salomone praises Giovanni, whom he describes as an "illustrious Ferrara man" praising "his fine feelings," and by so doing reveals his extensive humanistic reading—Sallust, Valerius Maximus, Lactantius, Augustine. Classical yet also Christian authors, explored but perceived as challenging ("Verse and prose by each gentile, although that study was particularly hostile to me"). We need to ask what this "hostility" entailed: was it simply a question of taste or, more probably, the feeling of entering into a territory that was religiously and culturally different and foreign? As well as documenting an encounter, this Ferrara-based exchange also bears witness to a tension or at least a certain intellectual displacement. It has been suggested that Salomone Hebreo could be identified as Salomone di Manuele Norsa (Solomon ben Immanuel Norsa), who worked in Ferrara as a lender from the first half of the fifteenth century until 1461 (Norsa 1953–69, 6, pp. 12–13; Franceschini 2007, index, ad vocem "Salomone di Manuele da Norcia, lender in the Riva bank"). This identification seems likely and adds further charm to these verses of courteous and complex multiculturalism.

---

*Missiva Ioannis Peregrini ferarensis
ad Salomonem hebreum*

Non dico fra li hebrei ma fra christiani
   qualunque sia, e prima a miser Cino,
   e Guido Cavalcante, el buon sabino,
   miser Colucio, e voi Nestor Pisani
Facio degl'Uberti che passò fra humani,
   el poeta laureato fiorentino
   che in queste rime fece il suo camino
   d'amor scrivendo, in cose alte sop[r]ani
El stile suo quantunque alto e zentile
   fosse amico mio superbo et antico
   non preterisse il tuo per quel ch'io sento
Maturo, grave, alto e signorile,
   e d'ogni vil parlar crudel nemico
   né loro più che io mi fa contento

*Responsiva Salomonis hebrei
ad antedictum*

Gli antiqui gesti ho lecto di romani
   quel da le historie antique, patavino
   Salustio generoso e pelegrino
   Valerio che adoprò le sacre mani
Codici ho lecto non sol di pagani
   ma deli sacri el suo scriver divvino
   l'antiquo Firmiano et Augustino
   e gli devoti grandi de Ambrosiani
Versi anchor prose di cieschun gientile
   ben che quel studio a me sia nemico
   za mai legiendo lor non fui contento
Non che l'ingiegno lor fusse ville
   ma di ti ferarino clario io dico
   che ogn'altro avanza il tuo bel sentimento

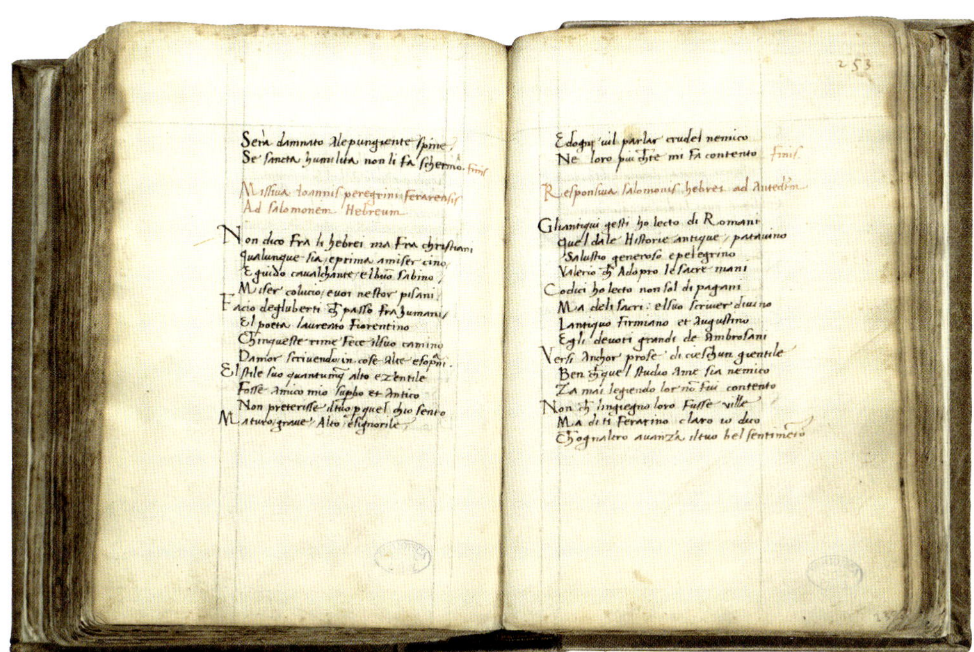

Serà damnato ale pungente spine
Se sancta humilità non li fa schermo. finis

Missiua Ioannis peregrini ferarensis
Ad Salomonem Hebreum

Non dico fra li hebrei ma fra christiani
Qualunque sia, e prima amiser cino
E guido caualchante el buo Sabino
Miser colucio, e uoi nestor pisani
Facio degluberti & passò fra Jumanis
El poeta laurento Fiorentino
Chi in queste rime fece ilsuo camino
D'amor scriuendo in cose alte e sophi.
El stile suo quantunq alto e zentile
Fosse Amico mio Sapho et Antico
Non preterisse d'huo p quel ch'io sento
Maturo, graue, Alto e signorile

Edogni uel parlar crudel nemico
Ne loro piu chte mi fa contento Finis

Responsiua Salomonis hebrei ad Antedim

Gli antiqui gesti ho lecto di Romani
Quel dale Historie antique patauino
Salustio generoso e pelegrino
Valerio ch Adopro le Sacre mani
Codici ho lecto non sol di pagani
Ma deli Sacri: el Suo scriuer diuino
Lantiquo Firmiano et Augustino
Egli deuoti grandi de Ambrosani
Versi Anchor prose di cieschun guentile
Ben ch quel studio Ame sia nemico
Za mai legiendo lor no fui contento
Non ch lingiegno loro fusse ville
Ma di ti Ferarino claro io dico
Ch ogni altro auanza il tuo bel sentimeto

21–22. Male profiles in Eastern costume, perhaps in the Jewish style

Lombard artist
Profile of a man, with turban
Profile of a man, with Jewish-style headgear (?)
c. 1500–12
Oil on panel
46.7 × 46 cm each
Private collection

Literature: Terni De Gregory 1958; Zeri 1978; Zeri 1986.

The two panels, now in a private collection, come from the wooden ceiling decoration removed from a room in the palace of San Martino Gusnago, near Ceresara, in the province of Mantua, built "no later than the 1450s" (Carpeggiani 1973, p. 68; see Dal Prato 1969) for the *condottiero* Francesco Secco (1423–1496), to a design by Luca Fancelli. Secco was accused of treason in 1491 and subsequently fled the city. The building was then requisitioned by the Gonzaga family. According to Zeri's reconstruction (1986, pp. 72–73), the decorative cycle originally comprised forty-four elements: the panels seem to have decorated both sides of the beam that split the original room lengthways and the two walls parallel to it. They were divided into four groups of eleven pieces each, with a three-quarter figure at the center of each group, symmetrically flanked by profiles, perhaps arranged in pairs. Twelve of the panels from San Martino Gusnago are now in the Metropolitan Museum of New York, another six at the Victoria and Albert Museum in London, and a further nine are in various public and private collections, while the remaining panels seem to have been lost. Terni De Gregory (1958, p. 170) comments upon the "markedly Semitic nature" of some of the profiles, attributing this to the fact that the pieces may have been commissioned by Eusebio Malatesta, who was given the palace of San Martino Gusnago by the Marquess of Mantua following Secco's fall from grace. Terni De Gregory, supported in this by Zeri (1978 and 1986), claims that Malatesta—actually the son of Carlo, from the branch of the lords of Pesaro—was a converted Jew, resulting from a longstanding error, still repeated in books today, which was probably due to a misunderstanding by the Mantuan chronicler Andrea Schivenoglia, who wrote "zudeo" (Jew) instead of "zudeso" or "giudice" (judge) (Tamalio 2007). The theory regarding a Jewish patron having been rejected, it is still worth noting the clothing worn by certain figures, which could suggest a generically Eastern inspiration and, in some cases at least, a Jewish one. Indeed, Zeri (1978), when describing panel no. 664–1904 at the Victoria and Albert Museum, identified "the portrait of a rabbi, with the *taled* [e.g. the *tallit*], the ritual striped shawl," going on to add: "but I will write more about this elsewhere, in an essay on Jewish themes in Italian Renaissance painting." Unfortunately, this latter essay never appeared. In the two profiles on display, "Jewishness" could be identified in the turban worn by one of the figures and in the fabric that covers the head of the other, beneath his headgear, with stripes that may also have been inspired by a *tallit*. It is worth noting that the figure with the turban has a parallel in the profile in a wooden panel, probably produced between the late fifteenth and early sixteenth century, and now conserved in the collections of the Banco Popolare di Crema (Ceserani Ermentini 1985, p. 105 no. 20, and 1999). However, there is no real reason to question the date between 1500 and 1512, put forward by Zeri on the basis of the style and clothing. Zeri attributes the works to an anonymous Lombard painter, close to Floriano Ferramola of Brescia, but of superior quality.

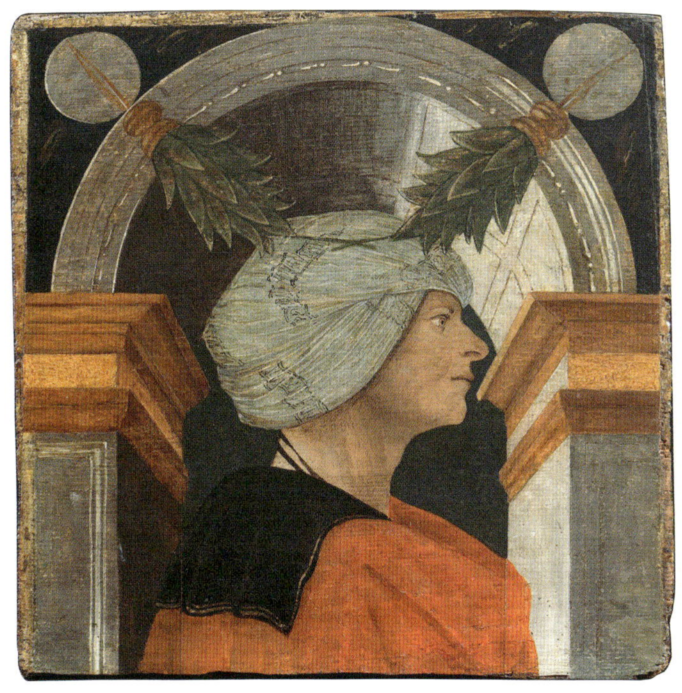

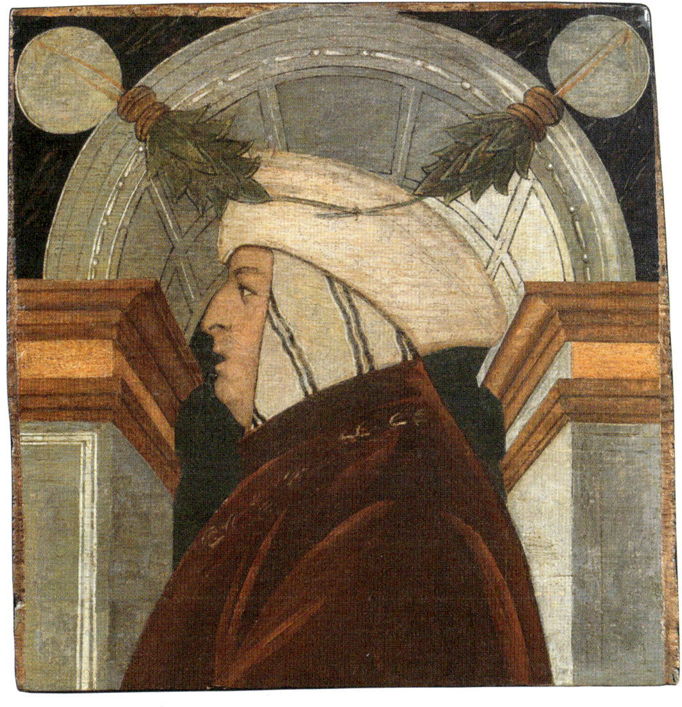

23. A Christian-Jewish dance school

Contract for the establishment of a dance, music
and singing school, between the Jew Joseph of Pesaro
and the Christian Francesco di Domenico
Florence, 1467
Paper document
53 × 31.5 cm
Archivio di Stato, Florence
Notarile Antecosimiano, P. 350, fol. *276v*

Literature: Veronese 1990 and 2013, p. 242; Bryce 2001,
p. 1093.

An exceptional notary for a no less surprising contract.
The notary in question was Ser Piero di Antonio da Vin-
ci, father of the great Leonardo. The agreement, drawn
up by Ser Piero, brings together Joseph of Pesaro and
Francesco di Domenico from Venice—the former a Jew
and the latter a Christian, united by a shared talent. They
are both dance teachers and have decided to go into
business together. It is May 1467 and the company will
last for one year, from June 1, which is long enough to
produce the first results and establish whether it is worth
continuing. They will share the expenses and earnings
and will work together teaching dance, music, and singing to male and female students. They will both bear the
costs of the house that hosts the school. Joseph has a
family background in the business. His father, Moysè or
Musetto, came to Pesaro from Sicily and was employed
as a dance teacher at the city's court. His brother is Guglielmo, famous for parties and choreographies staged
in the most important Italian courts and the author,
in 1463, of a treatise on the art of dance, *De pratica seu
arte tripudii vulgare opusculum* (Guglielmo Ebreo 1993),
dedicated to Galeazzo Maria Sforza. Guglielmo converts
and takes the name Giovanni Ambrosio. Joseph probably keeps faith with his religion right to the very end, to
the annoyance of his brother, who writes the following
words to a very young Lorenzo de' Medici in 1469: "But
if he remains obstinate that he does not want to do this
[become a Christian], I do not want to communicate
with him or have anything to do with him" (McGee
1988; Lacerenza 2010, p. 357). Equal partner, staunch
Jew, dance teacher, ambitious businessman—Joseph of
Pesaro is very much a Renaissance man.

1467, Indictione XV
Item postea dictis anno indictione et die. Actum Florentie in populo Sancti Stephani abbatie florentine presentibus testibus etc. Ser Laurentio Ser Niccolai Diedi notario
florentino et Angelo Ser Allexandri de Chestesio populi
Sancti Michaellis vicedominarum de Florentia. Joseph
olim Moysi ebreus de Pensauro magister tripudiandi ex
parte una et Franciscus olim Dominici de Venetiis etiam
magister tripudiandi ex alia parte omni modo etc. et ex
certa scientia etc. faciunt et firmant inter se infrascriptam
societatem concordiam et conventionem videlizet quod
quilibet dictorum Ioseph et Francisci lucraretur in docendo tripudiare sonare ac cantare teneatur contribuire
[sic] pro dimidie huiusmodi lucri et e converso ita quod
effectus sit quod quid prefati Ioseph et Franciscus lucra-
rentur pro huiusmodi exercitio quilibet eorum debeat
participare pro dimidia et insuper etiam promiserunt ad
invicem concurrere in docendo et tenendo discipulos et
tam mares quam feminae et tam in eorum domo quam
in domo aliena et similiter concurrere quilibet eorum
pro dimidia in solutione pensionis domus quam retine-
rent pro docendo. et predicta omnia intelligantur tam in
civitate comitatu et districtu Florentie quam alibi ubique
locorum. Ita quod prefati Ioseph et Franciscus et quilibet eorum participent de lucro et labore quilibet eorum
pro dimidia et intelligantur predicta omnia ad bonum
et purum intellectum et sine fraude, quam sotietatem
durare voluerunt per unum annum proxime futurum
incipiendum die primo mensis iuni proxime futuri et ut
sequitur finiendam. Que omnie etc. Promiserunt etc. sub
pena florenorum vigintiquinque auri etc. que pena etc.
obligantes etc. renuntiantes etc. quibus per guarantigiam
etc. rogantes etc.

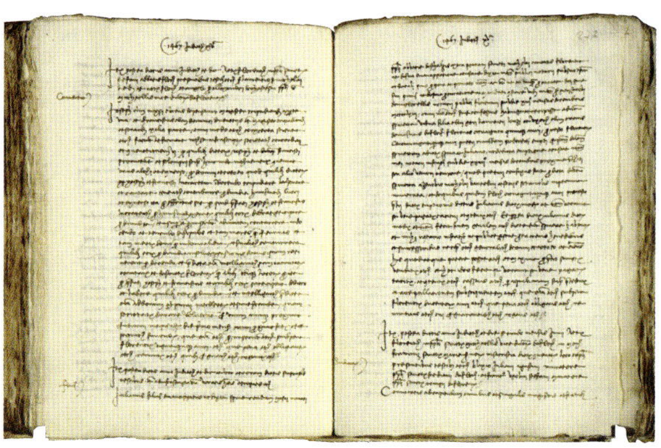

24. The "Martyrdom" of Simon of Trent

Wooden group with the supposed martyrdom
of Simon Unferdorben (Simon of Trent)
Workshop of Daniel Mauch (?)
c. 1500–10
Polychrome carving
81 × 110 × 24 cm
Museo Diocesano Tridentino, Trento
inv. 3016

Literature: *Il Museo diocesano* 1996, pp. 85–86; *Rinascimento e passione* 2008, p. 575; Perini 2012, pp. 160–163

In 1475, the city's Jews were accused of killing Simon Unferdorben, the young son of a Christian tanner, over Easter and using his body for a macabre rite in the synagogue. After a short investigation, fifteen defendants were executed and the child was proclaimed a martyr, becoming an object of worship. There were a number of doubts surrounding the process, even in the Vatican. Indeed, Sixtus IV sent Bishop Battista de' Giudici from Rome to investigate further. After a tug of war with Johannes Hinderbach, the prince-bishop of Trent, who supported the accusation against the Jews, the papal inspector was forced to return to Rome, but he drew up a report that maintained the innocence of the Jews and the irregularity of the case. The trial was effectively conducted in a summary fashion, involving the extensive use of torture. The accused were not permitted to defend themselves and not even the papal inspector managed to obtain a safe-conduct for their lawyers. Despite these initial reservations regarding what was actually a tragic legal farce, the veneration of Simon of Trent, officially permitted in 1588, was only suppressed by the Catholic Church in 1965. The wooden relief on display once featured in the predella of the monumental main altar with doors in the church of Santi Pietro e Paolo in Trento. It depicts the presumed martyrdom of Simon by the Jews, shown in the act of what seems to be an actual sacrifice. It has been attributed to the workshop of the carver Niklaus Weckmann (*Il Museo diocesano* 1996, p. 85) or to that of Daniel Mauch (*Rinascimento e passione* 2008, p. 575), both members of the School of Ulm.

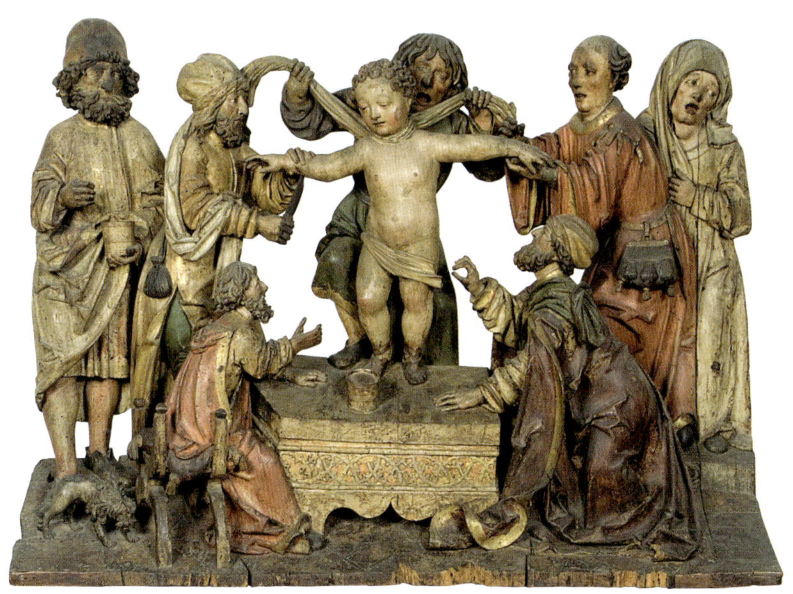

25. Giovanni Tiberino: physician, humanist, agitator

Giovanni Mattia Tiberino, *Passio beati Simonis Tridentini* (Passion of the Blessed Simon of Trento)
c. 1475–1500
Paper manuscript
92 fols.
21.4 × 15 cm
Biblioteca Queriniana, Brescia
MS G IV 10 (Bq²)

Literature: Ferraglio 2002; *I manoscritti datati* 2008, pp. 43–44 no. 62; Bolpagni 2010–11

Born in Chiari, in the province of Brescia, Giovanni Mattia Tiberino (humanistic rendering of the original Tabarino) graduated in Medicine in Ferrara on December 11, 1470 (Zanelli 1904, p. 127; see Sandal 2010, p. 96). He was in Trento from 1473, where he served the prince-bishop Johannes Hinderbach. A young and ambitious humanist physician, Tiberino was handed the greatest opportunity of his life. He and two colleagues were appointed to carry out a post-mortem on the little body of Simon, discovered in a ditch on Easter Sunday 1475 (see cat. 24). It was the beginning of the end for the local Jews, who were immediately accused of murder, imprisoned, tortured, and killed. However, it also marked the start of a brilliant, frenetic and inspired (so to speak) career for Tiberino, whom Hinderbach entrusted with a preeminent role in the "promotion" of the martyrdom. The case of Simon of Trent proved a test bench for new humanistic propaganda and rhetorical conviction strategies and became a real media event, zealously supported by Tiberino. By early April the physician had already written a prose report on the alleged ritual killing, based on his own medical observations and on the statements extracted from the accused, and sent it to the Rectors of Brescia. The account, which features, alongside others, in this codex on display and in another manuscript at the Biblioteca Queriniana, went on to become very well known when it was printed with the title *Passio beati Simonis tridentini* (*Indice generale* 1943–81, vol. 5, no. 9645–9653; Italian translation in Morandini 1989).

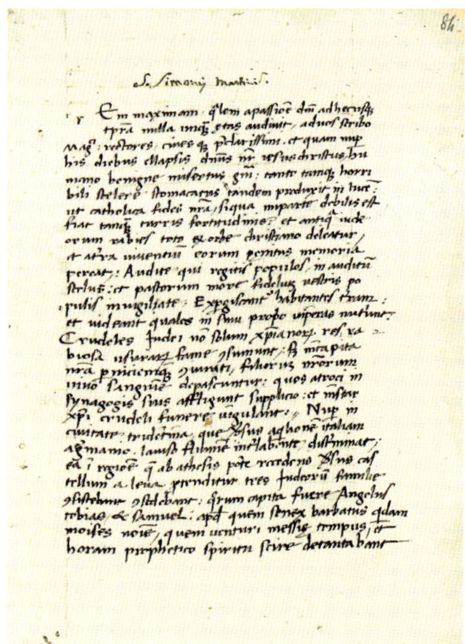
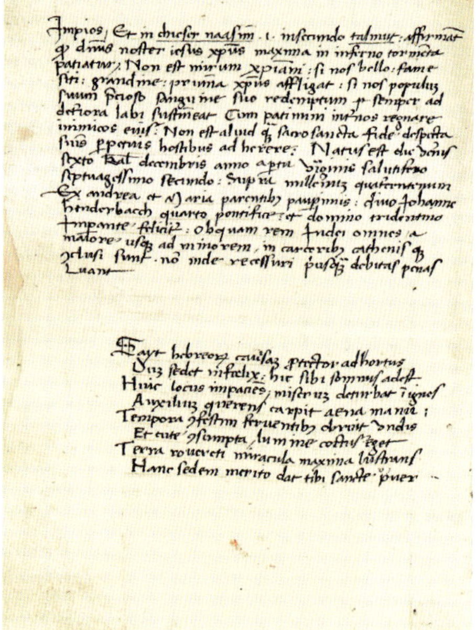

26. The duke wants a yellow identifier for Jews

Decree issued by Duke Ercole I d'Este requiring
Jews to wear a distinctive yellow symbol
Modena, March 13 and 17, 1498
Paper register
20.5 × 22 cm
Archivio di Stato, Modena
Ebrei, 15

Literature: Fabbrici 1987, p. 513 no. 9.3:3

Duke Ercole I orders all the Jews of Modena, Reggio,
Brescello, Castelnovo Parmense (Castelnuovo di Sot-
to, now in the province of Reggio Emilia), and other
Este territories to wear a yellow cap beginning from the
first Sunday after Easter. The draft indicates a yellow
or orange "O" as a symbol, to be worn above the belly
button by everyone, except women and pawnbrokers
with their sons and partners.

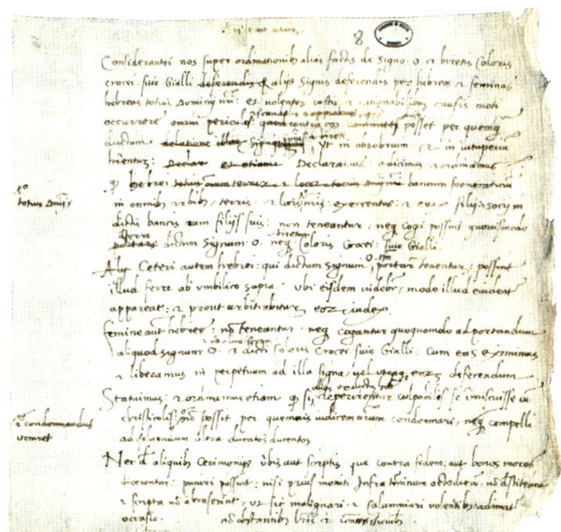

27–28. Elijah and Elisha, Carmelite Hebraists

Stefano di Giovanni, known as Il Sassetta
The Prophet Elijah
The Prophet Elisha
c. 1423–25
Tempera on panel
53 × 20 cm each (cuspidate panels)
Pinacoteca Nazionale, Siena
inv. nos. 95, 87

Literature: Scapecchi 1979; Christiansen, Kanter, and Brandon Strehlke 1989, pp. 78–81; Torriti 1990, pp. 168–74; Ronen 1992, p. 608; Busi and Ebgi 2014, p. LV.

The two cuspidate fragments displayed here come from an altar panel made by Stefano di Giovanni, known as Il Sassetta (d. 1450), for the guild of wool merchants in Siena. It was produced in 1423–25 during the Council, which took place in the Tuscan city from July 1432 to March of the following year. The prophets Elijah and Elisha hold up a scroll, on which their names are written in substantially accurate Hebrew with just two minor errors regarding the position of the vowel sign *pataḥ* in Elisha and the *alef*, instead of *he*, at the end of Elijah. It is worth mentioning that this latter error could suggest the intervention of a learned Jew, who aimed to avoid writing the divine name Yah, included in the correct form Eliyyah, in a painting intended for a Christian setting. The use of the holy language gives an erudite air to the image and is an innovative feature compared to earlier scrolls, generally written in Latin. The two prophets wear the habit of the order of the Carmelites, spiritual patrons of the Sienese wool guild, which adds historical connotations to the two figures, associating them with Old Testament prophetism dear to the Carmelites given their link with Mount Carmel and thus the biblical figures of Elijah and Elisha. Even in this very early example, the use of Hebrew in painting anticipates all the connotations it will maintain throughout the Renaissance, that is to say its exotic nature, added to a complex body of symbols, intensifying the symbolic meanings. In fifteenth-century iconography, the Hebrew alphabet primarily indicated otherness: the outlines of the Semitic letters are immediately perceived as foreign and serve rather to evoke a message than to explain it. The majority of observers, incapable of reading the script, would still be struck by the descriptive yet alienating effect of those letters.

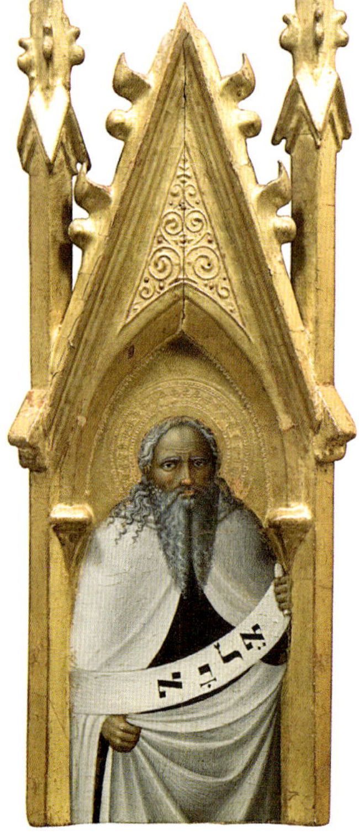

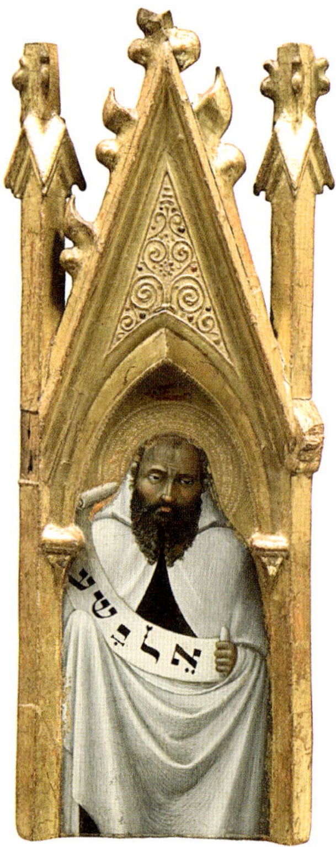

29. A Tree of Life in the Venetian ghetto

Sefirotic tree by Elijah Menahem Halfan,
with the assistance of Abraham Sarfatti
Venice, 1533
Italian semi-cursive script
Parchment
122 × 95 cm
Biblioteca Medicea Laurenziana, Florence
MS Plut. XLIV.18

Literature: Scholem 1933–34 no. 119; Sonne 1934;
Busi 2005; Lelli 2008; Chajes's essay in this volume.

One of the most important kabbalistic parchments of
the Italian sixteenth century was written in Venice in
February 1533. It was produced by Elijah Menahem
Halfan, a physician, rabbi and poet, and a great admir-
er of the kabbalist Solomon Molko.
Born to converted parents, Molko was considered the
prophet of the movement that grew up around the
self-styled messiah David Reubeni. The latter made
his appearance in 1523, proclaiming himself to be
from a royal line and expressing his wish to form an
army to liberate the Land of Israel, thereby also fu-
eling hopes in traditionally conservative Jewish envi-
ronments. Nevertheless, after some initial successes,
the messianic enthusiasm was violently quelled by the
Christian authorities. Reubeni was incarcerated and
probably died in prison, while Molko was burnt at the
stake in Mantua in 1532.
This large Venetian parchment was produced just
a few months after the martyrdom of the messianic
prophet. In the *colophon* of the scroll, Elijah Menahem
Halfan states that he worked together with the "esteemed elder, the wise kabbalist Abraham Sarfatti,
who, around four years ago now, left his family, his

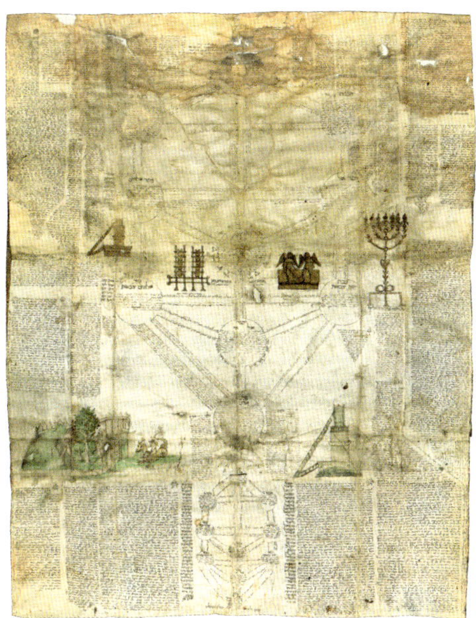

worldly goods and his business affairs to follow the
saint, the divine and pious man, the kabbalist Rabbi
Solomon Molko." The Venetian physician describes
how he hosted him for several days and how he drank
up "his words," for which he "thirsted." Those long discussions led to the idea of creating a tree, "which was
rooted in the earth and whose top reached the heavens,
with the names of the divine angels and with various
vessels, with a twofold aspect (back and front, right
and left), with his minutiae and with his comments, so
as to uncover one palm and cover up two, and it will
remain reserved for the elevated spirits even if they are
still few in number."

30. The mystical encampments of the heavens

Sefirotic tree and comments
Fifteenth century
Parchment
76 × 56 cm
Biblioteca Queriniana, Brescia
MS L._fI.11

Literature: *Biblioteca Queriniana* 2000, p. 217; Caro 2001; Chajes's essay in this volume.

The Sefirotic tree, which occupies most of the parchment, has a clear, imposing and dynamic center. It is the sixth *sefirah*, known as *tiferet*, or beauty. Divine energy radiates in every direction from its core. It is the *sefirah* inscribed with the Tetragrammaton, the ineffable name of God, which corresponds to Jacob and to the "Holy temple in the middle." It is worth noting the long passage entitled *Seder maḥanot smol* (Order of the left encampments), which regards the negative forces of the emanation and is unexpectedly placed on the right side of the parchment with regard to the viewer. Discovered recently, the kabbalistic diagram from the Biblioteca Queriniana contains a comment on the *sefirot* found in other codices (Scholem 1933–34, nos. 76 and 115), predominantly from the Italian area, including a kabbalistic tree, similar to this one, dated 1451 and conserved at the Vatican Library (MS Vat. ebr. 530 III).

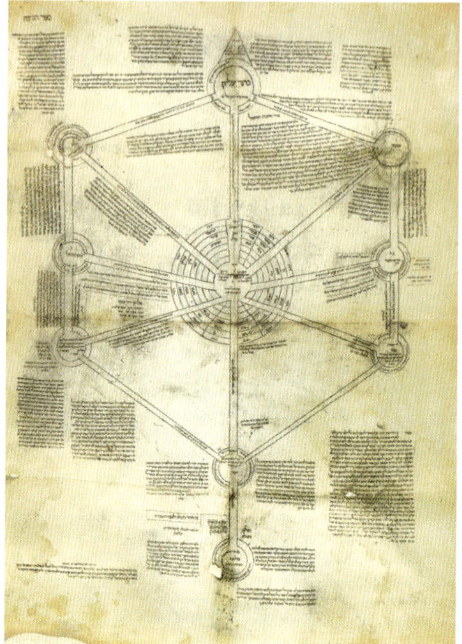

31. (Almost) the whole Kabbalah for Pico

Collection of kabbalistic texts in the Latin translation by Flavius Mithridates for Giovanni Pico della Mirandola
c. 1486–87
Translator and copyist: Flavius Mithridates
(*alias* Guglielmo Raimondo Moncada, *alias* Samuel ben Nissim). With handwritten notes by Giovanni Pico della Mirandola
Paper manuscript
469 fols.
30.3 × 22.2 cm
Vatican Library, Vatican City
MS Vat. ebr. 190

Literature: Wirszubski 1963, pp. 49–65; Wirszubski 1989; *The Great Parchment* 2004; *Hebrew Manuscripts* 2008, pp. 133–34; Menahem Recanati 2008; Busi 2009.

Impatient to learn the secrets of Jewish mysticism, but not yet fluent enough in the holy language, Giovanni Pico commissioned a converted Jew called Flavius Mithridates to translate dozens of texts from the original. The Count of Mirandola had acquired the manuscripts at a very high price, thereby overcoming Jewish reluctance to place such deep mysteries in Christian hands. Mithridates, who was born in Sicily as Samuel ben Nissim, had been baptized as Guglielmo Raimondo Moncada. After moving to Rome and entering papal circles, Samuel/Guglielmo must have had to leave Rome in a hurry, probably due to his involvement in a murder. He moved to Germany, where he taught Greek and Hebrew, before returning to Italy, this time to Florence, under the new identity of Flavius Mithridates, patently in order to escape papal justice. In Florence he frequented Marsilio Ficino and got to know Pico, who commissioned him to carry out the translation, perhaps as early as 1485. A great expert in languages and also well versed in mysticism, Mithridates indulged in falsifications to adapt the meaning of kabbalistic writings in a Christian sense. However, in the Latin versions he produced for Pico, which comprised an extensive library of texts fundamental for understanding the Kabbalah, Mithridates primarily kept to the original, despite adapting it here and there in a Christian sense. Pico used the translations for his *900 Theses*, published in 1486, in which Jewish mysteries play a key part. In 1489, Mitridates, who had moved to Viterbo in the meantime, was arrested upon the orders of Innocent VIII and his books were confiscated. It seems he may have died in prison. Meanwhile, his books, including this one on display, were kept at the Vatican Library from then on.

32. Mystical alphabets

Sefer ha-tzeruf (Book of Permutation)
Italy, sixteenth–seventeenth century
Italian cursive scripts, in several hands
(fols. 48v–130v probably by Ezra Fano)
Paper manuscript
164 fols.
20 × 14.7 cm
Biblioteca Comunale Teresiana, Mantua
MS 151

Literature: Idel 1976, pp. 68–72; Busi 2001, pp. 205–8; Idel 2011, p. 140

A single Hebrew word, *tzeraf*, indicates the alchemical transmutation of metals and the permutation of the letters of the alphabet. Just as the alchemist dissolves the bonds of matter to seek the secret of gold in base metals, so the Jewish exegete transforms the order of letters to discover the deepest sense of the text behind its apparent meaning. Sensibility for language is one of the most distinctive notes of the kabbalistic interpretation, and it is the aspect that has perhaps aroused the most interest in this discipline from the Renaissance onwards, even among non-Jewish scholars. The *Sefer ha-tzeruf* (Book of Permutation) probably dates to the second half of the thirteenth century but the name of its author does not feature in the codices. Modern bibliographers have ascribed it to the great, innovative and much-discussed mystic Abraham Abulafia, to the Castilian kabbalist Joseph ben Abraham Giqatilla (Idel 1976, pp. 68–72), who was a brilliant student of Abulafia, or to another of his followers, who may have lived in Italy (Idel 2011, p. 140).

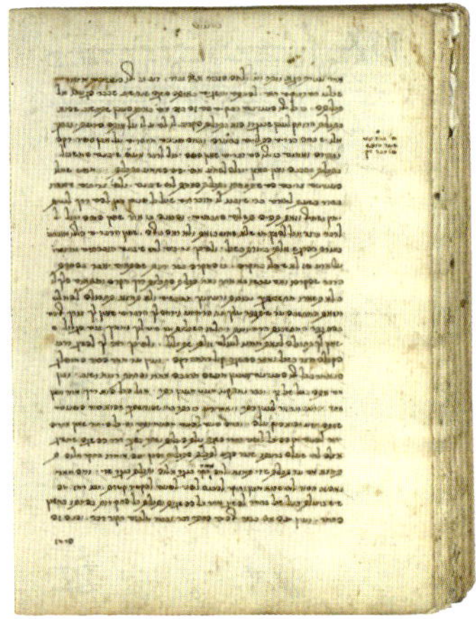
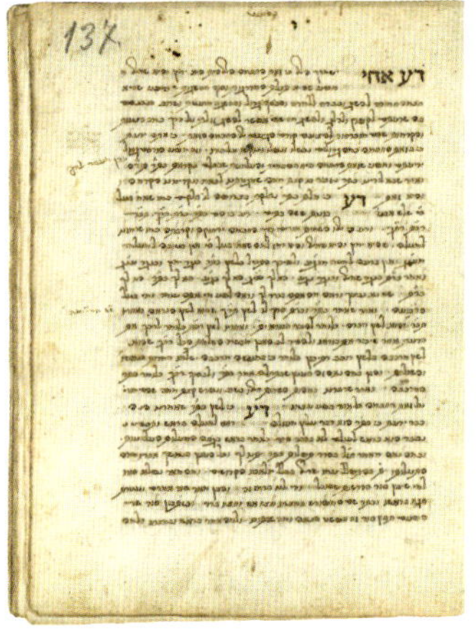
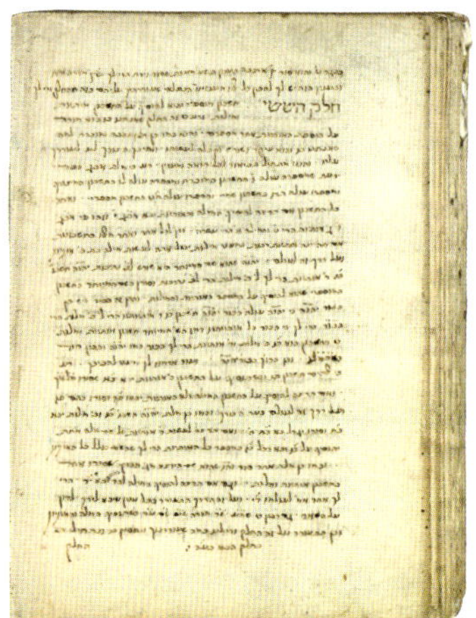
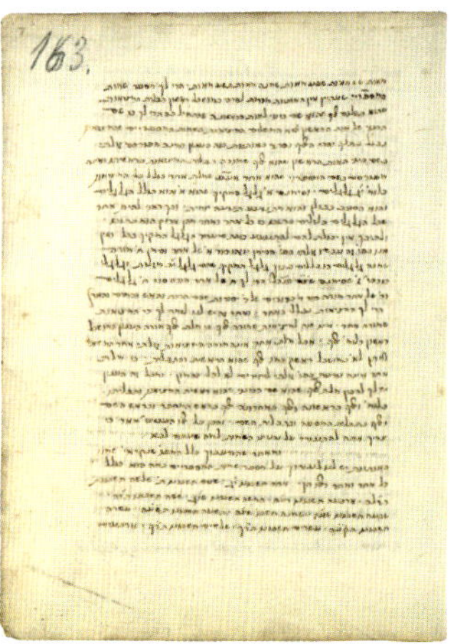

33. Mantegna paints for himself

Andrea Mantegna, *The Holy Family and the Family
of Saint John the Baptist*
Mantua, c. 1504–6
Tempera on canvas
40 × 169 cm
Basilica of Sant'Andrea, Mantua, Chapel
of Saint John the Baptist

Literature: Kristeller 1902; Christiansen 1992: *Mantegna a Mantova* 2006, pp. 112–13 no. 22; Manca 2006, p.
112; Momesso 2008

Around twenty days after the death of Andrea Mantegna on September 13, 1506, his son Filippo wrote
to Marquis Francesco Gonzaga to tell him that the
items left in the great artist's studio included "the two
paintings for his chapel" (Kristeller, 1902, p. 584 no.
190: October 2, 1506). These were evidently the *Holy
Family and the Family of Saint John the Baptist* and the
Baptism of Christ, still to be found today in Mantegna's funerary chapel, in the Basilica of Sant'Andrea
in Mantua. In his will dated 1504, Mantegna himself
expressed his wish to be buried in the chapel devoted to the Baptist, having decided some time before

that he wanted this to be the final resting place for the
members of his family. Despite the detailed documentation, there were some lingering doubts regarding
the autography of the *Holy Family* (and of the *Baptism* as well, given its poor condition) in Sant'Andrea
throughout the nineteenth century and even up until
the 1980s. These were primarily due to the very poor
restoration work carried out in the early nineteenth
century. However, the elegant balance of the composition—which focuses on the two children before
reflecting upon their mothers and then their fathers,
at the edges—with its skillful spanning of the generations, the tender gestures and gazes, are undoubtedly
by the hand of Mantegna (Christiansen 1992). While
Zechariah, to the viewer's right, in his yellow robe and
oriental turban, holds a thurible to indicate his priestly
lineage, Joseph on the left leans on a set square, illustrating his profession as a carpenter. The band around
his head features Hebrew letters, with the word *av*
(meaning "father") at the center. Mantegna adopt-
ed pseudo-Hebrew more than once in his works and
this is the only time he actually used accurate Hebrew,
painting it correctly. This must have been done upon
the suggestion and assistance of a Hebraist, or a Mantuan Jew. A farewell from the "Hebraist" Mantegna on
the eve of his death, paying tribute to the Jewishness of
Joseph and, consequently, of Jesus himself.

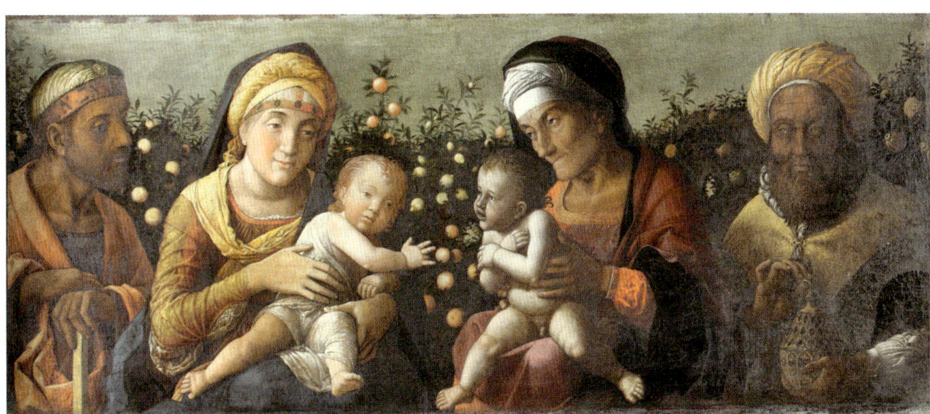

34. A Pentateuch in images

Pentateuch, with captions in Hebrew and the
vernacular, after originals by Moses da Castellazzo
Venice, sixteenth century
Ashkenazi semi-cursive script; Latin script
123 pages
Paper manuscript, illuminated
Formerly Jewish Historical Institute, Warsaw
MS 1164
The National Museum of Italian Judaism and the
Shoah, Ferrara (anastatic reprint: Vienna 1986)

Literature: *Bilder-Pentateuch* 1986; Schubert 1991;
Kogman-Appel 2006

The so-called "Castellazzo Bible" is an illustrated codex,
probably produced in Venice in the 1520s. The manuscript, discovered at the end of World War II in the
cellars of the Gestapo headquarters in Warsaw and then
conserved at the Jewish Historical Institute in the same
city (MS 1164), was sent to a photographic studio in
1980 to be reproduced. It never returned to the library,
having been either lost or stolen. The facsimile edition,
curated by Kurt and Ursula Schubert in 1983–86 and
published in a limited edition of 950 (including the
one on display here), is therefore the only surviving
testimony of the work. Moses da Castellazzo (also: dal
Castellazzo, 1466–1526) was a relatively well-known
painter and draughtsman, as he himself declares in
the printing application submitted to the Venetian
Senate in 1521. In this application, Moses declares
that he has drawn a cycle of biblical illustrations and
intends to have his daughters ("mie fiole") prepare the
woodcut engravings. Permission was granted, but only
two engravings seem to have survived from this cycle.
The manuscript formerly in Warsaw is a copy of the
complete engravings, produced by an artist who was
rather naive in formal terms but very keen to capture
all the details of the original. The Castellazzo Bible is
an important document in early sixteenth-century
Italian Jewish art, with illustrations that expand upon
the words of the Bible through additions taken from
the *midrashim*, rabbinic comments of a predominantly
homiletic nature.

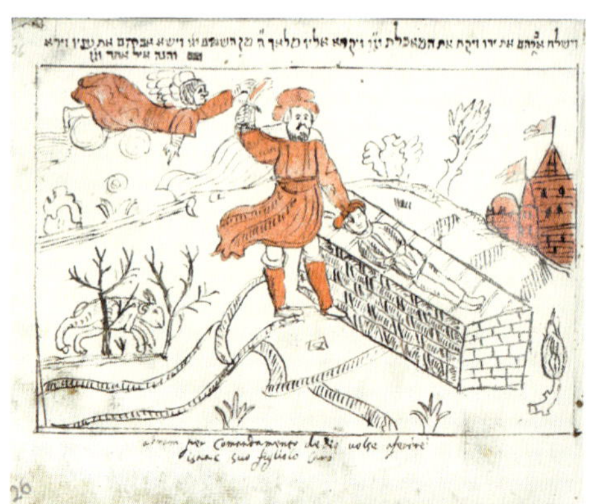

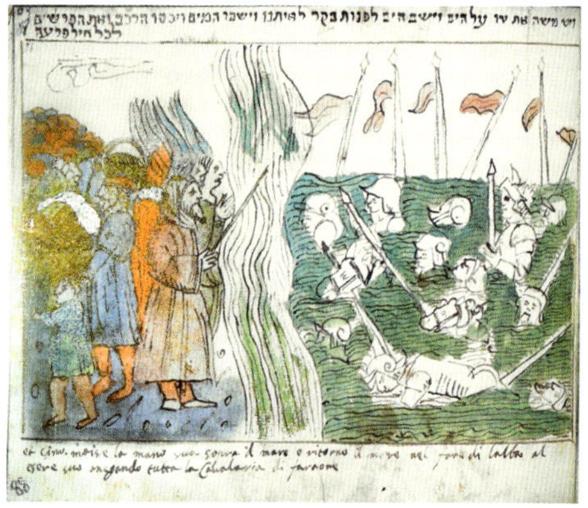

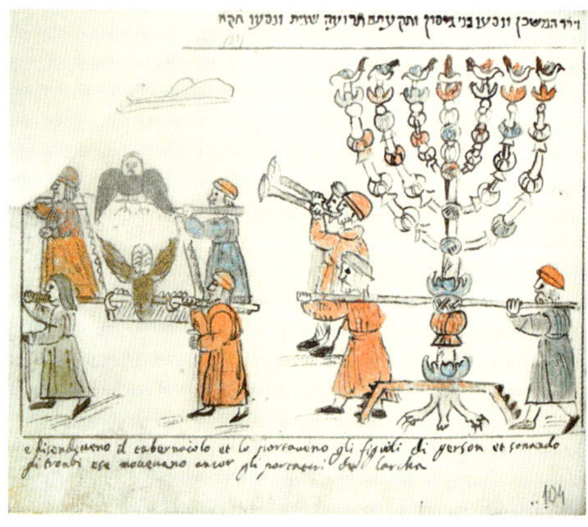

35. Vittore Carpaccio writes in Hebrew

Vittore Carpaccio and workshop
Birth of the Virgin
Venice, c. 1502–7
Oil on canvas
126.8 × 129.1 cm
Accademia Carrara, Bergamo
inv. 731 [155]

Literature: Fortini Brown 1992, pp. 293–94; Ronen 1992, p. 610; Borean 1994; Rossi 1997; Sarfatti 2001, no. 87; *Carpaccio* 2004, pp. 99–103; Busi 2007, pp. 136–39; Busi and Ebgi 2014, pp. XCIX-C.

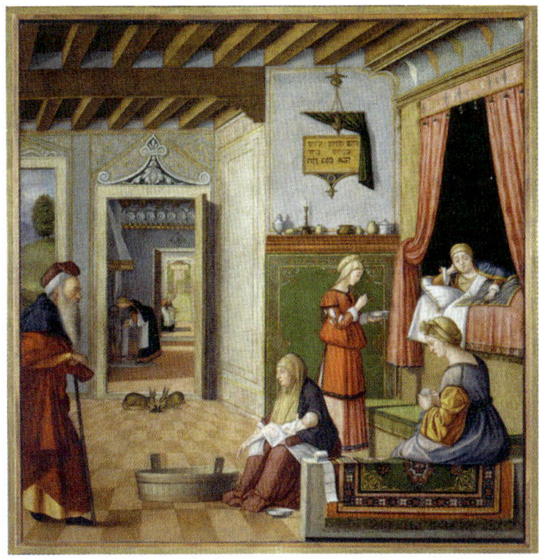

The *Birth of the Virgin*, now at the Accademia Carrara in Bergamo, forms part of a cycle of canvases with stories from the life of Mary, painted by Vittore Carpaccio with the assistance of his workshop for the Venetian Scuola degli Albanesi. In this painting, a Hebrew plaque hangs on the wall next to Anne's bed. A lamp, recalling the synagogal *ner tamid* (eternal lamp), hangs above it, and a short piece of cloth, draped like a curtain, has been slightly drawn aside. The plaque contains the so-called Sanctus, a formula from the Christian liturgy comprised of the conflation of two short biblical verses (Is. 6:3 and Ps. 118:26), which reads: "Qadosh qadosh qadosh ba-marom baruk haba be-shem Yhwh, Santo santo santo in eccelso. Holy, Holy, Holy Lord God of hosts. Blessed is he who comes in the name of the Lord." It is therefore not just a mere erudite feature, but an element that plays a key part in the narrative of the picture, in which the Hebrew yet again reads like a premonition. The words stand out primarily for their similarity to the text of an *Introductio utilissima hebraice discere cupientibus*—that is, very useful introduction for those desiring to learn Hebrew—composed by the Jewish scholar and typographer Gershom Soncino and published anonymously in Venice, in 1501, by the famous Aldus Manutius. Indeed, Soncino had included the Sanctus in Hebrew in his text. However, there is more. The graphic form of the letters is the same as in the *Introductio* and in Carpaccio's painting, just as the Tetragrammaton is written in the same way: the consonants that comprise it are drawn imperfectly so as not to reproduce the writing completely. This creates a kind of optical illusion, making it seem to have been written out in full even though it has not. This measure reveals the Jewish concern not only about not uttering the name of God, but also about not even writing it out in full, so as not to profane its holiness. What is more, this particular way of writing the Tetragrammaton is typical of the *Introductio* and does not seem to appear elsewhere, at least during this period and in this area. If we look closely at Carpaccio's painting, we can glimpse a second piece of writing, carved onto the marble lintel above the door leading into the kitchen in the background. We can see three Latin letters: ISU. Unlike the Hebrew formula, which is clearly legible and written in black ink, the three Latin letters are barely apparent, in a pale tone of sepia, marked out in a hand that seems to have been contracted into a cryptic formula. Nevertheless, it is evident that the painter wants to suggest the word "Iesu" and that we are once again looking at a premonition, a subtle symbol indicating the future outcome of Mary's life. Moreover, this sign also seems to allude to a mystery. The name of Jesus is indicated using the three consonants that designate it in Hebrew, omitting the "e," which is not normally recorded in Hebrew as it is a vowel. The composition of the painting is, therefore, more enigmatic than it appears at first glance and the lintel, in which the name of Jesus is both hinted at and concealed, seems to draw our attention toward a far less evident scene than this domestic interior.

36. Leon, Jew and Platonist

Dialoghi di amore di Leone Hebreo medico,
di nuovo corretti et ristampati
In Venetia, appresso Nicolò Bevilacqua, 1572
246, [2] fol., octavo
14.5 × 9.5 cm
The National Museum of Italian Judaism
and the Shoah, Ferrara

Literature: Leone Ebreo 1929; Dionisotti 1959; Gavrin 2001; Nelson Novoa 2006, 2009, and 2011.

Born in Lisbon in around 1460, the son of Isaac Abravanel, a great Sephardic Jewish statesman and intellectual, Judah Leon Abravanel was an enigmatic and influential figure regarding whom there is still much to learn. His *Dialoghi d'Amore*, printed posthumously in 1535 by the Roman publisher Antonio Blado, enjoyed great success. From the first printing in the early seventeenth century, there were 17 Italian editions, as well as translations into Latin, French (two versions), and Spanish (at least five), with relative reprints. Leone Ebreo is the name that appears in the *Dialoghi*, revealing a philosophical style that never denies his Jewishness, but instead exploits it and furthers it, demonstrating his great theoretical complexity to the educated readers of Italy and Europe. After being forced to leave Portugal, where his father was accused of conspiring against King John II, for Castile, Judah and his family then had to leave Spain too following the expulsion of the Jews decreed in 1492. His first stop was Naples, where the Abravanel family immediately entered into the circle of the rulers Ferdinand I and Alfonso II. However, this good fortune did not last for long. In 1498, they followed Alfonso II to Messina to escape the army of Charles VIII of France. It seems that Leone stayed in Genoa for some time, before going to Puglia and then back to Naples again, when Spanish rule was established. He became personal physician to Viceroy Gonzalo Fernández de Cordoba. Unaffected by the first expulsion of the Jews from Naples in 1510, Leone and his family were still in the city in 1520, when it seems he prevailed upon the court not to introduce measures against the Jews. We have

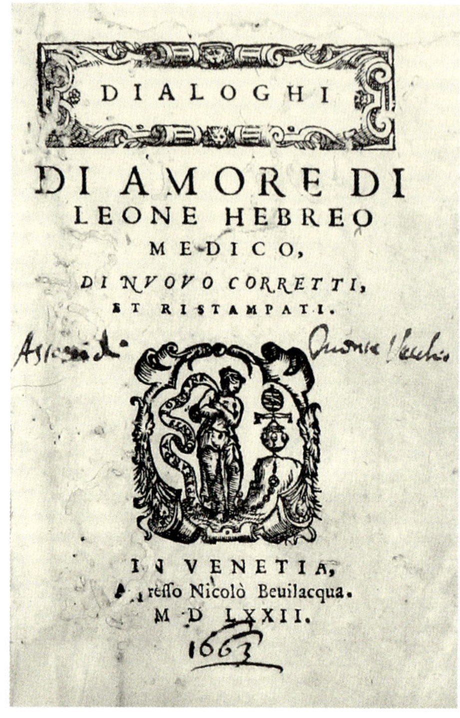

no further news of him after 1521 and it seems likely that he died in the early part of that decade.

What language were the *Dialoghi* written in? Despite extensive research, this question is still open. Some believe they were written in Hebrew, while it has also been suggested that the author wrote them directly in the Italian vernacular interspersed with Spanishisms, Latinisms and some influence of the linguistic koine of central and southern Italy (Gavrin 2001). This first version of the *Dialoghi* dates to around 1510, while the cleaned-up Tuscan-style version of the *editio princeps* was somewhat later. Edited by the Sienese gentleman Mariano Lenzi and dedicated to the writer Aurelia Petrucci (1511–1542), Leone Ebreo's work is about philosophical love. It is of course about platonic love, but also and above all about love of the "willing and knowing" God of Jewish tradition.

37. Teseo Ambrogio Albonesi and the beginnings of Semitic linguistics

Teseo Ambrogio Albonesi
Introductio in Chaldaicam linguam, Syriacam, atque Armenicam, et decem alias linguas
Papiae: Ioan. Maria Simoneta, 1539
215 fols., quarto
20.5 × 14.5 cm
At the author's expense and with his press
Biblioteca Ariostea, Ferrara
L 2.3.22

Literature: Busi 1987a, p. 37 no. 13

The *Introductio in Chaldaicam linguam, Syriacam, atque Armenicam, et decem alias linguas*, produced in Pavia in 1539, is an invaluable document of the birth of the general study of Semitic languages (Contini 1994; Wilkinson 2007, pp. 11–27). However, it would be wrong to expect a strictly philological manual. Teseo Ambrogio Albonesi (1469–1540), of a noble family, who became a Canon Regular of Saint Augustine, was a pioneer and an explorer of traditions as yet to be discovered. He had an enquiring and wandering mind, which explored side issues and slipped down the luxuriant slopes of distractions. It is worth noting that the book is most famous for its description and images of a *phagotus* (fols. 178*v*–179*r*), the instrument built by Afranio degli Albonesi, Teseo's uncle and canon of the Ferrara Cathedral, which was similar to a bagpipe. Teseo's drive for learning was so intense and unstoppable that he even included a diabolical alphabet, the product of the invocations of a certain Ludovico da Spoleto, and meticulously reproduced and commented on by our tireless pansophist (fols. 212*v*–213*v*). Meanwhile, during his research into the Syriac language, Albonesi describes how he also consulted learned Jews, with whom he evidently had friendly relations. The

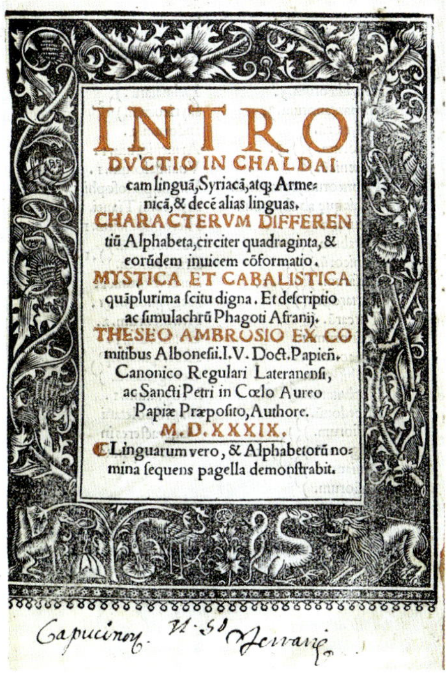

Introductio therefore mentions Abraham de Balmes, physician, philosopher and author of a famous Hebrew grammar, the *Peculium Abrae* (see Campanini's essay in this volume) and relative, so Albonesi tells us (fol. 15*r*), of Giovanni of Spoleto, a converted Jew, who became a Canon of Saint Augustine like Albonesi himself. Another learned Jew, whom our author knew and esteemed, was Joseph ben Samuel Sarfatti (Giuseppe Gallo), son of a famous papal physician. The *Introductio* mentions poems, both in Hebrew and Latin, which Sarfatti had addressed to Albonesi and that he kept in his library (fol. 14*r*; see Busi 2007, pp. 63, 68).

38. The polyglot Psalter of Augustine Giustiniani

Psalterium Hebraeum, Arabicum et Chaldaeum cum tribus Latinis interpraetationibus et glossis
Genuae: Petrus Paulus Porrus, 1516
[200] fols., quarto
32.6 × 23.3 cm
Edition produced and paid for by Augustine Giustiniani
Biblioteca Ariostea, Ferrara
A.2.7.23

Literature: Steinschneider 1852–1860, no. 25; Busi 1987, pp. 71–72 no. 126; Zazzu 1990

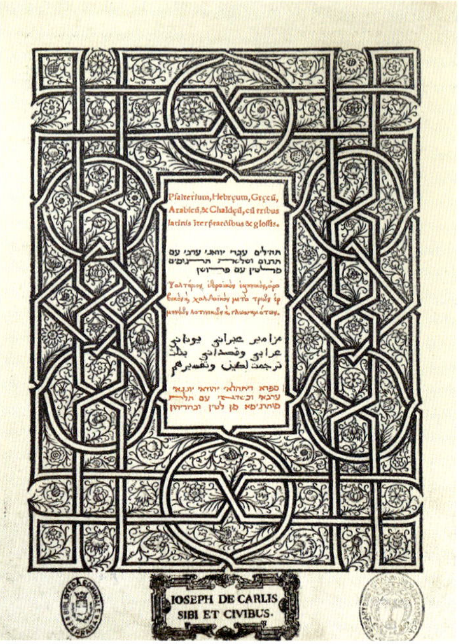

Born into an important wealthy family from Genoa, Pantaleone Giustiniani (1470–1536) rejected his intended mercantile life to become a Dominican monk called Augustine. He acquired enviable knowledge of all things Hebrew, as well as Latin, Greek, and Arabic firstly in Pavia and then during the many years spent in the Bolognese convent of San Domenico. He also moved up the ecclesiastical career ladder at the same time. In 1514 he was appointed bishop of Nebbio, in Corsica, thanks to the support of his cousin, Cardinal Bandinello Sauli. Giustiniani was not only interested in Hebrew for the purpose of studying the Bible. Following in the footsteps of the first Christian kabbalists, Giovanni Pico and Johannes Reuchlin, he believed that the mysterious mystical books conserved by Jews contained ancient teachings that were unknown to Christians and worthy of discovery and commentary. In 1513 he published a *Precatio plena ad Deum omnipotentem composita ex duobus et septuaginta nominibus divinis* in Venice, dedicated to Sauli and replete with interpretations of the Tetragrammaton, the ineffable name of God. Alongside his Judaic speculations, Giustiniani nevertheless sought to avoid the doctrinal suspicions that similar incursions into the Hebrew tradition could arouse in the Christian field. This explains why he condemns the magical proceedings conducted in his time, using divine names, by the messianic prophet Asher Lemmlein (Campanini 2008). The edition of the Psalter, published by Giustiniani at his own expense in 1516, is also packed with kabbalistic references. Conceived as the first part of a comprehensive, polyglot edition of the Bible, which was never completed, Giustiniani's *Psalterium* conceals important extracts from Hebrew texts between the lines of commentary, used for Christian theological purposes to prove that Jesus was the Messiah.

39. Annius of Viterbo, "creative" Hebraist

Annius of Viterbo (Giovanni Nanni), *I cinque libri de le antichità de Beroso sacerdote Caldeo. Con lo commento di Giovanni Annio di Viterbo teologo eccellentissimo*
Venice: for Baldissera Constantini, 1550
[10], 295, [1] fol., octavo
17 × 12.5 cm
Fondazione Palazzo Bondoni Pastorio, Castiglione delle Stiviere

Giovanni Nanni, also known as Annius of Viterbo, was a cultural mediator who ought to have been wise, austere, and a fervent advocate of projects and relations. It cannot be denied that he was erudite, or that he had ambitious plans and excellent relations with people. However, he was anything but austere. There is no point beating about the bush, as his is a well known case in Renaissance studies: he was a real trickster, capable of duping popes, cardinals, dukes, doges, amateurs, and professors. A man able to produce and conceal forged inscriptions, only to reveal them at the right time before the important person in question. One such figure was the pope, when a miraculous discovery of forgeries concocted by the tireless Annius was staged for Alexander VI during his visit to Viterbo in December 1493 (Pedullà 2010; on the unmasking of Annius by sixteenth-century philologists, see Grafton 1990). All this invention, which included real or presumed Hebrew knowledge (Grafton 2019), had just one purpose for Annius. Or in fact two purposes. The first was to establish the antiquity of Viterbo and Italy as a whole, which he claimed to have been founded and populated by Noah and his family, in defiance of every Greek claim to civilization. The second and even more important purpose was to impress people with his knowledge and climb as high up the social ladder as possible. Annius certainly managed to impress the Borgia pope, who appointed him as his trusted theologian. Some say that he also managed to make himself so odious to the pope's son, Cesare Borgia, that he was poisoned by him in 1502. However, what interests us here is the fate of his *opus magnum, Commentaria super opera diversorum auctorum de antiquitatibus*

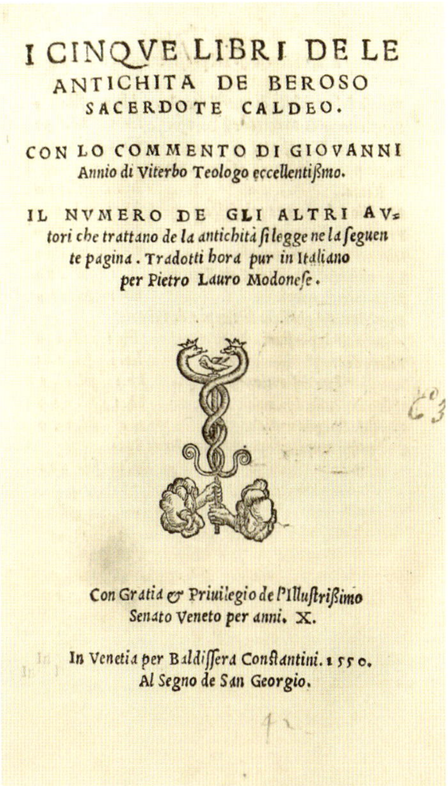

loquentium, commonly called *Antiquitates* (*Commentaria* 1498). The somewhat thinned out translation of part of the work, that is to say the five books of the so-called Berosus Chaldaeus, was printed in Venice again in 1550. This version was produced by Pietro Lauro of Modena, and Baldissera Costantini's dedication to the Venetian nobleman Vittor Girmani does not hold back in its praise of the deceptive work: "A work with so much to commend it in itself, and in the many express declarations regarding the truth of the times, and its very accurate comparison of them, that it is not necessary to spend too much time demonstrating just how praiseworthy it is." Indeed, it is better not to spend any more time on it.

40. The symbolic language of Pierio Valeriano

Pierio Valeriano (Giovanni Pietro Dalle Fosse),
Hieroglyphica, sive de sacris Aegyptiorum aliarumque
gentium literis commentarii
Basileae: per Thomam Guarinum, 1567
[10], 441, [25] fols., folio
32.5 × 22.5 cm
Fondazione Palazzo Bondoni Pastorio,
Castiglione delle Stiviere

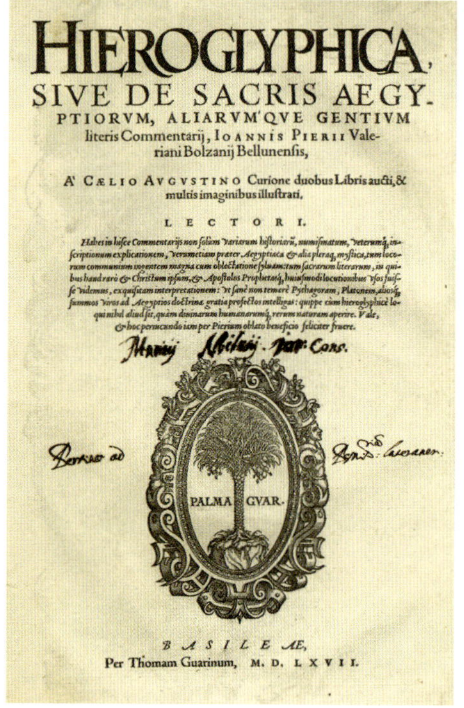

The Renaissance would not have been a truly universal era without seeking a language able to overcome geography, the barriers imposed by customs and temporal limits. Neither Latin nor any other tongue, not even the arcane Hebrew from the creation of the world, could fulfil this role. The most secret Renaissance ambition was to develop a language solely of images, which could bridge the gap between cultures. A silent and potentially infinite language, free to be ignited according to the intellect and sensibility of those whose used it and brought it to life each time. The discovery, in 1419, of the Greek manuscript of the treatise on Egyptian hieroglyphics attributed to Horapollo triggered a real rush of theories, dreams and innovations, which was subsequently intensified by the edition printed by Aldus Manutius in 1505 (see the still fundamental contribution from Giehlow 1915; Gombrich 1972, pp. 123–195). Adapted, guessed at and recreated hieroglyphics were what the humanists preferred when putting together their language of images and suggestions. A language no longer tied to sounds alone, no longer contingent but divine. Giovanni Pietro Dalle Fosse (1477–1558), known by his humanist name Pierio Valeriano, was one of the most important figures in this journey toward a symbolic language, which seemed to emerge from the past but was actually projected toward the future. His *Hieroglyphica* were written for a circle of friends, only circulating in a manuscript edition for some time (Cassiani 2015). The first printed edition in 1556 was followed by the edition on display, published in 1567. Valeriano included various persuasive Hebraic suggestions, and it could not have been otherwise given his close relationship with Cardinal Giles of Viterbo, an expert Hebraist and keen kabbalist (see the essays by Busi, Campanini, and Bartolucci in this volume). As a result, in the *Hieroglyphica* the holy language takes on a creative role and reveals hidden meanings, acting as a source of sapiential images ready to open out in Valeriano's symbolic interpretations.

41. Mazzolino's first *Christ disputing with the Doctors*?

Ludovico Mazzolino, *Christ and the Doctors*
c. 1519
Oil on panel
44 × 34 cm
Galleria Doria Pamphilj, Rome
inv. no. 215

Literature: Zamboni 1968, pp. 54–55 no. 62 (fig. 23); Busi 2007, p. 93

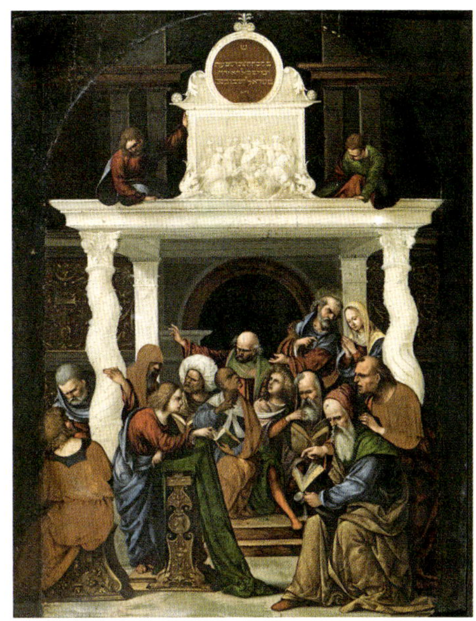

On January 26, 1520, the painter Ludovico (Bigo) Mazzolino (c. 1480 – c. 1528) received a payment from Sigismondo d'Este "for the price of two paintings, one of the Nativity and the other of Christ in the Temple" (Venturi 1889, p. 6; Zamboni 1968, p. 32). It seems likely that the *Christ in the Temple* mentioned in the document is this one on display, which then passed into the hands of Lucrezia d'Este and now belongs to the Galleria Doria Pamphilj. This would make it the oldest of the numerous versions painted by Mazzolino, in his early development of a theme of great symbolic value. "After three days they found him in the temple courts, sitting among the teachers, listening to them and asking them questions" (Luke 2:46). The painting deviates from these words from the Gospel in more than one point. Firstly Jesus is standing instead of sitting, unlike all of the other paintings on the same theme by Mazzolino. What is more, the Gospel clearly sets the temporal frame of the episode involving the Jewish doctors: "Every year Jesus' parents went to Jerusalem for the Festival of the Passover" (Luke 2:41). The writing, in accurate Hebrew, in the tondo at the top of the elaborate architecture, does not mention the Passover, but the Jewish celebration of Sukkot or temporary huts: "Live in temporary shelters for seven days: All native-born Israelites are to live in such shelters" (Lev. 23:42). It is a surprising discrepancy in an artist so attentive to historical detail, therefore raising questions regarding Mazzolino's iconographic and Hebraist sources (Haitovsky 1999, p. 139 recalls the significance of Christ as the new Temple, but this is not enough to explain the temporal contradiction inherent in the scene). It is also worth noting a substantial urbanity in the tense attention of the Jewish doctors, who are more concerned with studying and discussing among themselves than answering the twelve-year-old Jesus. The polemical contrast to the Judaism of the subsequent paintings on the same theme has not yet been explored.

42. Mazzolino and a brighter *Dispute*

Ludovico Mazzolino, *The Twelve-Year-Old Jesus
Teaching in the Temple*
c. 1520–21
Oil on panel
46.8 × 30.4 cm
Gemäldegalerie, Berlin
inv. no. 273

Literature: Zamboni 1968, pp. 37–38 no. 7 (fig. 27);
Busi 2007, pp. 92–93

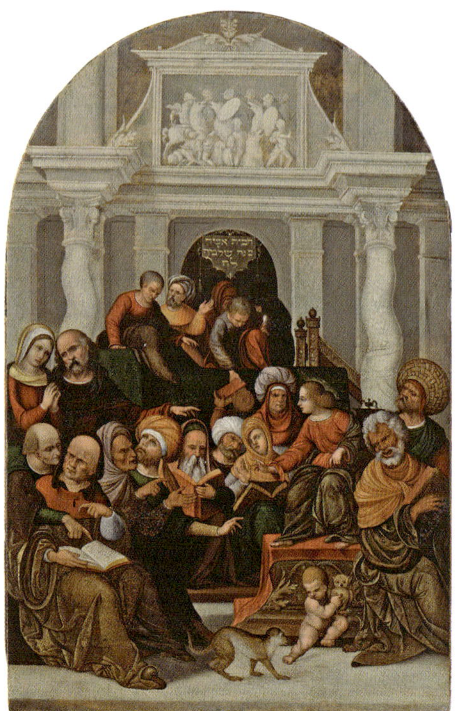

While the architectural structure varies slightly from
that in the Doria Pamphilj painting, the Hebrew inscription in this picture, formerly from the Giustiniani
Collection and now in Berlin, is completely different
and at least seemingly more in keeping with the evangelical context: "The temple that King Solomon built
for the Lord." The phrase is taken, with some omis-
sions, from 1 Kings 6:2, and forms part of the story
of the construction of the ancient Temple of Jerusalem. The expression "for the Lord" is transcribed with
the abbreviation *ha-(Šem)*, suggesting that the idea
came from a Jew who wanted to avoid writing out the
Tetragrammaton in full. As in the case of the *Virgin
and Child Enthroned* by Cosmè Tura (see Greco's essay in this volume), Mazzolino may have spoken with
the learned Abraham Farissol, who was still active in
Ferrara at this date. The doctors seem more perplexed
than in the Doria Pamphilj painting and there is a controversial comparison between the owl, symbol of true
wisdom, protected by Jesus, and the foolish monkey
(Grasso 2008).

43. Ferrara, cradle of the Judeo-Spanish Bible

Biblia en lengua española traduzida palabra por palabra dela verdad Hebrayca por muy excelentes letrados vista y examinada por el officio dela Inquisicion
Ferrara, Abraham Usque, 1553
[8], 400, [1] fols., folio
30 × 20 cm
Biblioteca Ariostea, Ferrara
E 13.8.24

Literature: *Introducción* 1994; *Biblia de Ferrara* 1996

Books can also cross borders. Indeed, they can do so better than anything else, containing displaced and far-removed words and memories, to be read with veneration. The fact that the first translation of the Hebrew Bible into Spanish, "palabra por palabra de la verdad hebrayca por muy excellentes letrados," appeared in Ferrara is in itself an evident trespassing of borders: linguistic limits, first and foremost, then confessional limits, and, even more unusually, gender limits, with a strong female authority. The Ferrara Bible is both a Hebrew-Spanish translation and an exercise in Castilian linguistic pride. It is a version designed for a difficult readership and was produced for the *conversos*, who felt obliged to comply with Christianity but did not feel Christian. What is more, the *Biblia en lengua española* also appealed to many Christians with unorthodox beliefs, attracted by the benevolent protection of Renée of France, wife of Duke Ercole II d'Este. In March 1553, when the Bible was printed by Abraham Usque in Ferrara, the city was still a safe port, not only for Jews fleeing the Inquisition, but also for many protestant intellectuals both from Italy and northern Europe.

The volume features two dedications, according to the exemplar. One "al yllustrísimo y excellentissimo Señor, el Señor Don Hercole de Este el Secundo, quarto Duque de Ferrara" (as in the example on view). The other to "la muy magnifica Señora Doña Gracia Naci." The duke is the local lord, while Gracia Nasi is the patron, or rather the funder and political supporter of Sephardic exiles. It is thanks to her that the Ferrara-based Jewish printing press was able to churn out an enviable number of Hebrew and Ladino editions over the period of a few years. But the real Lord, to cite the editors at the end of their prologue, is another much higher figure, and every care is made to honour him in the text, without profaning his name. "Y hallarán también una .A. con dos puntos, el qual es señal del santo nombre del Señor Tetragrammatón." The Spanish Ferrara Bible of 1553 also "speaks Hebrew."

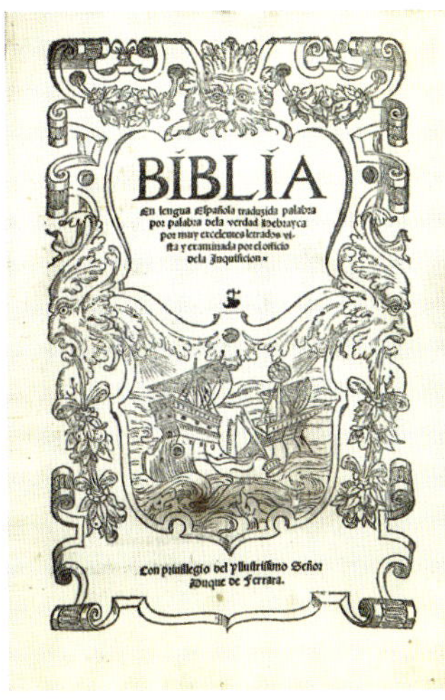

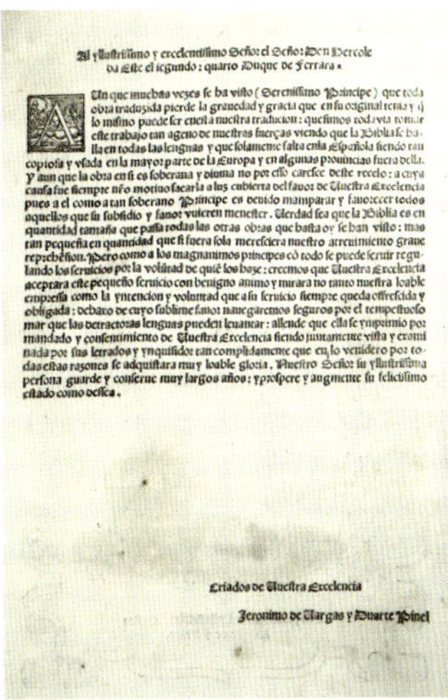

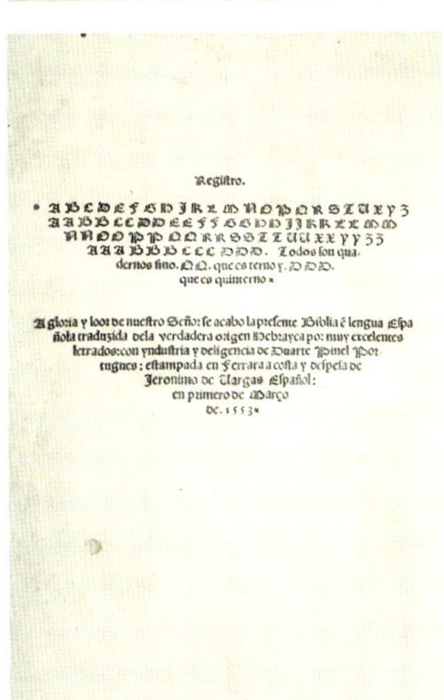

44. Prisciano Prisciani and his cultured sarcophagus

Cosmè Tura and Ambrogio da Milano (?),
Sarcophagus of Prisciano Prisciani
c. 1473–74
Marble
61 × 212 × 73 cm
Musei Civici di Arte Antica – Palazzo Schifanoia, Ferrara

Literature: Stemp 1999; Torboli 2000; Sgarbi 2006, pp. 91, 128–29 (A. Bellandi); Busi 2007, pp. 86–87; Torresi 2007; Toffanello 2010, p. 329; Busi and Ebgi 2014, pp. 86–87

Prisciano Prisciani was a solid man, steward to Duke Borso d'Este and prudent manager of his estates, who worked industriously to further the family fortunes. He enjoyed a few literary pastimes, but only so far as was appropriate for respectable people. He also had an only beloved son, who had many talents, read widely and had a weakness for astrology and esoterism. It would not otherwise be possible to explain why, upon his death, the solid courtier Prisciano Prisciani ended up in a beautiful sarcophagus with evident hermetic ambitions. "Dear to Hermes, favourite of kings" read the Greek words on the stone, and in Latin: "Priscianus Ferrariensis […] Mercurio gratissimus." If there were still any room for doubt regarding the hermetic piety that Pellegrino Prisciani, creator of the artefact, reserved for his father, who died on 18 July, 1473, we simply have to look at the symbols sculpted along the Greek side of the sarcophagus. On the one hand, the cockerel on the hat with visor, embellished with a forward-angled feather, and the caduceus. On the other, the eagle and the dragon on the tripod and a citole or cithara. Seen as a group, this is an esoteric-sapiential apparatus if ever there was one. A pagan-style Renaissance conceived by Pellegrino in honour of Prisciano Prisciani, seeking to remove all references to Christianity. However, it is interesting to note that the two large panels, arranged horizontally along either side of the sarcophagus, reappear in a vertical position on the sides of Mary's throne in the *Virgin and Child Enthroned* by Cosmè Tura, very probably executed a couple of years later, in 1475. These panels demonstrate that Pellegrino Prisciani was also involved in that Hebrew-style throne. It is also an equally clear demonstration that symbols *habent sua fata* in fifteenth-century Ferrara. The same panel, which can only approximately be described as ansate (Longhi described them as "double-horned panels of mosaic intention"), also appears in the *Circumcision*, also from the Roverella altarpiece, now at the Isabella Steward Gardner Museum in Boston, in the tomb in the background of the tapestry of the *Lamentation* attributed to Tura at the Cleveland Museum of Art and on Cosmè Tura's tomb in San Giorgio in Ferrara. This shared iconography has led to Tura himself being put forward as the creator of the sarcophagus (Stemp 1999, p. 215: "Whoever was responsible for its execution, Tura's responsibility for the design of Prisciano Prisciani's tomb seems certain"), perhaps in partnership with the sculptor Ambrogio da Milano (or Ambrogio Bregno from Righeggio, Como, and not, as maintained by A. Bellandi in Sgarbi 2006, p. 128, Ambrogio Barocci; see *Arte e artisti* 1959–64, vol. 1, pp. 21, 29; Angelini 2005; Crescentini 2008; Toffanello 2010, p. 329). Others (Torboli 2000; Torresi 2007), however, have made a comparison with the commemorative medal of Prisciano Prisciani, which his son Pellegrino had engraved by Sperandio Savelli, which features some of the iconography and wording from the sarcophagus, and have suggested that Tura worked in partnership with Savelli.

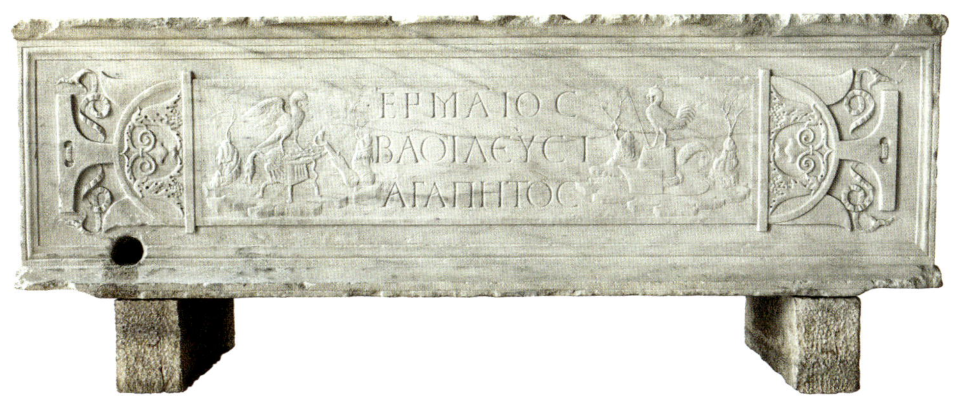

ΕΡΜΑΙΟC
ΒΑCΙΛΕΥCΤ
ΑΓΑΠΗΤΟC

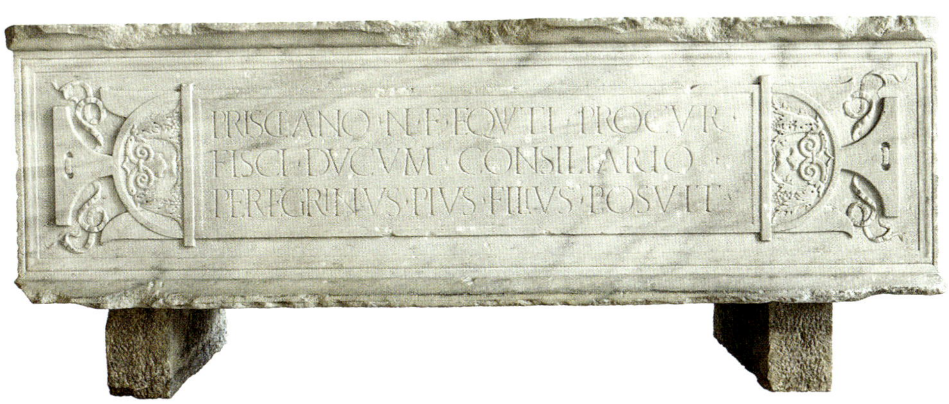

PRISCIANO · N · F · EQVITI · PROCVR ·
FISCI · DVCVM · CONSILIARIO ·
PEREGRINVS · PIVS · FILIVS · POSVIT ·

Bibliography

A Journey 2009
A Journey through Jewish Worlds: Highlights from the Braginsky Collection of Hebrew Manuscripts and Printed Books, ed. by E. Cohen, S. Liberman Mintz, and E. Schrijver, Amsterdam, 2009.

Abel and Leicht 2005
W. von Abel, R. Leicht, *Verzeichnis der Hebraica in der Bibliothek Johannes Reuchlins*, Ostfildern, 2005.

Adelman 1991
H. T. Adelman, "Rabbis and Reality: Public Activities of Jewish Women in Italy During the Renaissance and Catholic Restoration," in *Jewish History*, 5, 1991, pp. 27–40.

Agosti 2005
G. Agosti, *Su Mantegna: I*, Milan, 2005.

Agosti 2008
G. Agosti, "Intorno alla 'Madonna della Vittoria,'" in *Mantegna: 1431–1506*, ed. by G. Agosti, D. Thiébaut, with the assistance of A. Galansino, J. Stoppa, Italian edition revised with the collaboration of A. Canova, A. Mazzotta, Paris–Milan, pp. 297–305.

Alexander-Skipnes 2010
I. Alexander-Skipnes, "'Bound with wond'rous Beauty': Eastern Codices in the Library of Federico da Montefeltro, in *Mediterranean Studies*, 19, 2010, pp. 67–85.

Alfie 2003
F. Alfie, "Giovanni Pellegrino and Salomone: A Fifteenth-Century Tenzone between a Christian Writer and a Jewish Poet," in *Prooftexts*, 23, 2003, pp. 94–109.

Amadei 1954–57
F. Amadei, *Cronaca universale della città di Mantova*, ed. by G. Amadei, E. Marani, G. Praticò, 5 vols., Mantua, 1954–57.

Andrea Mantegna 1992
Andrea Mantegna, ed. by J. Martineau, London and New York 1992.

Andreatta 2014
M. Andreatta, "Filosofia e cabbalà nel Commento al Cantico dei Cantici di Lewi ben Gershom tradotto in latino per Giovanni Pico della Mirandola," in *Giovanni Pico e la cabbalà*, ed. by F. Lelli, Florence, 2014, pp. 69–91.

Angelini 2005
A. Angelini, *Pio II e le arti: La riscoperta dell'antico da Federighi a Michelangelo*, Siena, 2005.

Antoniazzi Villa 1986
A. Antoniazzi Villa, *Un processo contro gli ebrei nella Milano del 1488: crescita e declino della comunità ebraica lombarda alla fine del Medioevo*, Bologna, 1986.

Ariosto 1966
Ludovico Ariosto, *Orlando Furioso*, Turin, 1966.

Ariosto 2007
Ludovico Ariosto, *Le Commedie*, ed. by A. Gareffi, Turin, 2007.

Ariosto 2013
Ludovico Ariosto, *Commedie*, ed. by L. Stefani, 3 vols., Perugia, 2013.

Arte e artisti 1959–1964
Arte e artisti dei laghi lombardi, ed. by E. Arslan, 2 vols., Como, 1959–1964.

Arte e cultura ebraiche 1988
Arte e cultura ebraiche in Emilia-Romagna, Milan and Rome, 1988.

Auerbach 1870
L. Auerbach, *Das jüdische Obligationenrecht*, Berlin, 1870.

Bacchelli 2001
F. Bacchelli, *Giovanni Pico e Pierleone da Spoleto: tra filosofia dell'amore e tradizione cabalistica*, Florence, 2001.

Bagatin 1990
P. L. Bagatin, *L'arte dei Canozi lendinaresi*, Trieste, 1990.

Bahir 2005
The Book of Bahir: Flavius Mithridates' Latin Translation, the Hebrew Text, and an English Version, ed. by S. Campanini, with a foreword by G. Busi, Turin, 2005.

Banchi pubblici 1991
*Banchi pubblici, banchi privati
e monti di pietà nell'Europa
preindustriale: amministrazione,
tecniche operative e ruoli economici*,
Genoa, 1991.

Bandera Bistoletti 1977
S. Bandera Bistoletti, "Persistenze
tardogotiche a Cremona: frate
Nebridio e altri episodi," in
Paragone, 323, 1977, pp. 40–70.

Benedetto Antelami 1990
Benedetto Antelami: Catalogo, ed. by
A. C. Quintavalle, Milano 1990.

Bartolucci 2014
G. Bartolucci, "Marsilio Ficino e
le origini della cabala cristiana," in
Giovanni Pico e la cabbalà, ed. by F.
Lelli, Florence, 2014, pp. 47–67.

Bartolucci 2017
G. Bartolucci, *Vera religio: Marsilio
Ficino e la tradizione ebraica*,
Turin, 2017.

Bato 1956
J. L. Bato, "L'immigrazione degli
Ebrei tedeschi in Italia dal '300 al
'500," in *Scritti in memoria di Sally
Mayer: saggi sull'ebraismo italiano*,
Jerusalem and Milan, 1956, pp.
19–34.

Baumgarten 1974
A. I. Baumgarten, "Sforno and
Berossus," in *Journal of Jewish
Studies*, 25, 1974, pp. 313–15.

Bazzotti 2006
U. Bazzotti, "La chiesa di
Santa Maria della Vittoria e la
pala di Andrea Mantegna," in
*A casa di Andrea Mantegna.
Cultura artistica a Mantova nel
Quattrocento*, ed. by R. Signorini,
D. Sogliani, Cinisello Balsamo,
2006.

Bazzotti 2010
U. Bazzotti, "Aggiornamento
sugli affreschi di Santa Maria
della Vittoria," in *Andrea

Mantegna. Impronta del genio*,
ed. by R. Signorini, V. Rebonato,
S. Tammaccaro, Convegno
internazionale di studi (2006),
Florence, 2010.

Beit-Arié 2003
M. Beit-Arié, *Unveiled Faces of
Medieval Hebrew Books. The
Evolution of Manuscript Production
– Progression or Regression?*
Jerusalem, 2003, pp. 67–81

Beit-Arié 2018
M. Beit-Arié, *Hebrew
Codicology: Historical and
Comparative Typology of Hebrew
Medieval Codices based on the
Documentation of the Extant
Dated Manuscripts in Quantitative
Approach, Preprint internet English
version 0.2+ (November 2018), to
be published by the Israel Academy
of Sciences and Humanities*,
available in English and Hebrew
at http://web.nli.org.il/sites/NLI/
English/collections/manuscripts/
hebrewcodicology/Pages/default.
aspx

Belting-Ihm 1976
C. Belting-Ihm, "'Sub Matris
tutela': Untersuchungen
zur Vorgeschichte der
Schutzmantelmadonna," in
*Abhandlungen der Heidelberger
Akademie der Wissenschaften,
Philologisch-historische Klasse*,
3, Heidelberg, 1976.

Bernardino da Siena 1989
Bernardino da Siena, *Prediche
volgari sul Campo di Siena: 1427*,
ed. by C. Delcorno, 2 vols.,
Milan, 1989.

Bernardino Guslino 2008
Bernardino Guslino, *La vita del
beato Bernardino da Feltre*,
ed. by I. Checcoli, Bologna, 2008.

Bernardino Tomitano da Feltre 1964
*Sermoni del b. Bernardino Tomitano
da Feltre*, ed. by C. Varischi da
Milano, 3 vols., Milan, 1964.

Bernheimer 1960
C. Bernheimer, *Catalogo dei
manoscritti orientali della Biblioteca
estense*, Rome, 1960.

Berns 2017
A. Berns, "Ovadiah Sforno's Last
Will and Testament," in *Journal of
Jewish Studies*, 68, 2017, pp. 1–33.

Bertolotti 2011
M. Bertolotti, "Sette ebrei
sulla forca: Dalla Trinità di
Rubens (1605) alla Madonna
della Vittoria di Mantegna
(1495–6)," in *La fede degli
italiani: per Adriano Prosperi*,
ed. by G. Dall'Olio, A. Malena,
P. Scaramella, vol. 1, Pisa, 2011,
pp. 291–306.

Bianchi 2007
L. Bianchi, "Continuity and Change
in the Aristotelian tradition," in
*The Cambridge Companion to
Renaissance Humanism*, ed. by
J. Hankins, Cambridge, 2007,
pp. 49–71.

Biblia de Ferrara 1996
Biblia de Ferrara, ed. by M. Lazar,
Madrid, 1996.

Biblioteca Queriniana 2000
Biblioteca Queriniana: Brescia,
ed. by A. Pirola, Florence, 2000.

Bilder-Pentateuch 1986
*Bilder-Pentateuch von Moses dal
Castellazzo: Pentateuchus – Venedig
1521: Vollständige Faksimile-
Ausgabe im Original Format des
Codex 1164 aus dem Besitz des
Jüdischen Historischen Instituts
Warschau*, ed. by K. Schubert,
2 vols., Vienna 1986.

Billiani 1895
L. Billiani, *Dei Toscani ed ebrei
prestatori di denaro in Gemona*,
Udine, 1895.

Biondi 1994
A. Biondi, "Gli ebrei e
l'inquisizione negli Stati estensi,"

in *L'inquisizione e gli ebrei in Italia*,
ed. by M. Luzzati, Rome and Bari
1994, pp. 265–85.

Birnbaum 2003
M. D. Birnbaum, *The Long Journey
of Gracia Mendes*, Budapest, 2003.

Bland 1995
K. P. Bland, "Elijah del
Medigo, Unicity of Intellect,
and Immortality of Soul," in
*Proceedings of the American
Academy for Jewish Research*,
61, 1995, pp. 1–22.

Blumenkranz 1960
B. Blumenkranz, *Juifs et chrétiens
dans le monde occidental*, Paris, 1960.

Bode 1902
W. Bode, *Die Italienischen
Hausmöbel der Renaissance*,
Leipzig, 1902.

Bodian 1997
M. Bodian, *Hebrews of the
Portuguese Nation: Conversos
and Community in Early Modern
Amsterdam*, Bloomington, 1997.

Bolpagni 2010–2011
G. Bolpagni, *Giovanni Mattia
Tiberino e la Passio beati Simonis
pueri tridentini: Edizione e
commento*, PhD Dissertation,
Università cattolica del Sacro
Cuore, 2010–11.

Bonfil 1987
R. Bonfil, "Cultura e mistica ebraica,"
in *Gli Ebrei e Venezia*, ed. by G. Cozzi,
Milan, 1987, pp. 478–81.

Bonfil 1988
R. Bonfil, "Change in the Cultural
Patterns of a Jewish Society in
Crisis: Italian Jewry at the Close of
the Sixteenth Century," in *Jewish
History*, 3, 1988, pp. 11–30.

Bonfil 1991
R. Bonfil, *Gli ebrei in Italia
nell'epoca del Rinascimento*,
Florence, 1991.

Bonfil 1992a
R. Bonfil, "The History of the
Spanish and Portuguese Jews in
Italy," in *Moreshet Sepharad:
The Sephardic Legacy*, ed. by
H. Beinart, Jerusalem, 1992,
vol. II, pp. 217–39.

Bonfil 1992b
R. Bonfil, "Chi era Ludovico
Carretto, apostata?" in *E andammo
dove il vento ci spinse: la cacciata
degli ebrei dalla Spagna*, ed. by G. N.
Zazzu, Genoa, 1992, pp. 51–58.

Bonfil 1997
R. Bonfil, "Dubious Crimes
in Sixteenth Century Italy:
Rethinking the Relations between
Jews, Christians, and Conversos in
Pre-Modern Europe," in *The Jews
of Spain and the Expulsion of 1492*,
ed. by M. Lazar and S. Haliczer,
Lancaster, CA, 1997, pp. 299–310.

Bordone 1994
R. Bordone, *L'uomo del banco dei
pegni: "lombardi" e mercato del denaro
nell'Europa medievale*, Turin, 1994.

Borean 1994
L. Borean, "Storie della Vergine
di Carpaccio nella Scuola degli
albanesi," in *Saggi e memorie di
storia dell'arte*, 19, 1994, pp. 23–71.

Botticini and Eckstein 2012
M. Botticini, Z. Eckstein, *I pochi
eletti: il ruolo dell'istruzione nella
storia degli ebrei: 70–1942*, Milan,
2012.

Bourne 2008
M. Bourne, *Francesco II Gonzaga:
the Soldier–Prince as Patron*, Rome,
2008.

Braudel 1953
F. Braudel, *Civiltà e imperi del
Mediterraneo nell'età di Filippo II*
Turin, 1953 (1st French ed. 1949).

Bresc 2001
H. Bresc, *Arabi per lingua, ebrei per
religione*, Messina, 2001.

Brooks 2002
A. A. Broooks, *The Woman who
Defied Kings: The Life and Times
of Doña Gracia Nasi*, S. Paul,
MN, 2002.

Brucker 1971
G. A. Brucker, *The Society of
Renaissance Florence*, New York,
1971.

Bryce 2001
J. Bryce, "Performing for Strangers:
Women, Dance, and Music
in Quattrocento Florence," in
Renaissance Quarterly, 54, 2001, pp.
1074–107.

Bucaria 1996
N. Bucaria, *Sicilia Judaica*, Palermo,
1996.

Budzioch 2016
D. Budzioch, "Italian Origins of
the Decorated Scrolls of Esther," in
*Kwartalnik Historii Zydow / Jewish
History Quarterly*, 257, 2016,
pp. 35–49.

Burke 1987
P. Burke, *The Italian Renaissance:
Culture and Society in Italy*, revised
ed., Princeton 1987 (1st ed. 1972).

Burckhardt 1860
J. Burckhardt, *Die Cultur der
Renaissance in Italien: Ein Versuch*,
Basel, 1860.

Burnett 2012
S. G. Burnett, *Christian Hebraism
in the Reformation Era (1500–
1660): Authors, Books, and the
Transmission of Jewish Learning*,
Leiden, 2012.

Busetto 1983
G. Busetto, ad vocem "Copio Sara,"
in *Dizionario biografico degli italiani*,
vol. 28, Rome, 1983, pp. 582–584.

Busi 1987a
G. Busi, *Edizioni ebraiche del XVI
secolo nelle biblioteche dell'Emilia
Romagna*, Bologna 1987.

Busi 1987b
G. Busi, "Libri a stampa," in *Cultura ebraica in Emilia-Romagna*, ed. by S. M. Bondoni, G. Busi, Rimini, 1987, pp. 465–96.

Busi 1990
G. Busi, *Libri e scrittori nella Roma ebraica del Medioevo*, Rimini, 1990.

Busi 1992
G. Busi, *Il succo dei favi*, Bologna, 1992.

Busi 1996
G. Busi, *Libri ebraici a Mantova: le edizioni del XVII, XVIII e XIX secolo nella Biblioteca della Comunità ebraica*, Fiesole, 1996.

Busi 1997a
G. Busi, "Francesco Zorzi: A Methodical Dreamer," in *The Christian Kabbalah*, ed. by J. Dan, Cambridge, Mass., 1997, pp. 97–125.

Busi 1997b
G. Busi, *Libri ebraici a Mantova: le edizioni del XVI secolo nella Biblioteca della Comunità ebraica*, Fiesole, 1997.

Busi 2001
G. Busi, *Catalogue of the Kabbalistic Manuscripts in the Library of the Jewish Community of Mantua*, Fiesole, 2001.

Busi 2005
G. Busi, *Qabbalah visiva*, Turin, 2005.

Busi 2007
G. Busi, *L'enigma dell'ebraico nel Rinascimento*, Turin, 2007.

Busi 2009
G. Busi, "Toward a New Evaluation of Pico's Kabbalistic Sources," in *Rinascimento*, 48, 2009, pp. 165–83.

Busi 2010a
G. Busi, "Giovanni Pico and the Ideal of Concordia Discourse: Disharmony as a way to Esoteric Wisdom", in *Constructing Tradition: Means and Myths of Transmission in Western Esotericism*, ed. by A. B. Kilcher, Leiden and Boston, 2010, pp. 293–302.

Busi 2010b
G. Busi, *Vera relazione sulla vita e i fatti di Giovanni Pico conte della Mirandola*, Turin, 2010.

Busi 2014
G. Busi, "Qabbalah," in G. Busi, R. Ebgi, *Pico della Mirandola: mito, magia, qabbalah*, Turin, 2014, pp. 294–306.

Busi 2016a
G. Busi, "Editoria ebraica a Venezia: fasti e declino," in *Venezia, gli ebrei e l'Europa*, exh. cat., Venice, 2016.

Busi 2016b
G. Busi, *Lorenzo de' Medici: una vita da Magnifico*, Milan, 2016.

Busi 2017a
G. Busi, "La cultura ebraica a Mantova tra Medio Evo e Umanesimo," in *Lombardia judaica: i secoli aurei di Mantova e un caso emblematico della Shoah milanese*, ed. by G. Busi, E. Finzi, Florence, 2017, pp. 9–38.

Busi 2017b
G. Busi, *Michelangelo: mito e solitudine del Rinascimento*, Milan, 2017.

Busi 2018
G. Busi, "Mosheh ben Netan'el Norsa, a bibliophile banker," in *Il Codice Maimonide e i Norsa: una famiglia ebraica nella Mantova dei Gonzaga*, exh. cat., ed. by C. Farnetti, S. Settis [Italian/English], Rome, 2018, pp. 31–35.

Busi and Campanini 2004
G. Busi, S. Campanini, "Marco Lippomano and Crescas Meir: A Humanistic Dispute in Hebrew," in *Una manna buona per Mantova: Man tov le-Man-Tovah. Studi in onore di Vittore Colorni per il suo 92° compleanno*, ed. by M. Perani, Florence, 2004, pp. 169–202.

Busi and Ebgi 2014
G. Busi, R. Ebgi, *Pico della Mirandola: mito, magia, qabbalah*, Turin, 2014.

Buzzetta 2011
F. Buzzetta, *Aspetti della* magia naturalis *e della* scientia cabalae *nel pensiero di Giovanni Pico della Mirandola (1486–1487)*, PhD Dissertation, Università degli studi di Palermo – École Pratique des Hautes Études, 2011.

Cacciari 2016
M. Cacciari, "Ripensare l'Umanesimo," in *Umanisti Italiani: Pensiero e Destino*, ed. by R. Ebgi, Turin, 2016, pp. VII–CI.

Calabi 2016
D. Calabi, *Il ghetto di Venezia: 500 anni del recinto degli ebrei*, Turin, 2016.

Campanini 1996
S. Campanini, "Un intellettuale ebreo del Rinascimento: 'Ovadyah Sforno e i suoi rapporti con i cristiani," in *Verso l'epilogo di una convivenza: gli ebrei a Bologna nel XVI secolo*, ed. by M. G. Muzzarelli, Florence, 1996, pp. 99–128.

Campanini 1997
S. Campanini, "Peculium Abrae: la grammatica ebraico-latina di Avraham de Balmes," in *Annali di Ca' Foscari*, 36/3, 1997 (Serie orientale 28), pp. 5–49.

Campanini 1999
S. Campanini, "Reuchlins jüdische Lehrer aus Italien," in *Reuchlin und Italien*, ed. by G. Dörner, Stuttgart, 1999, pp. 69–85.

Campanini 2004
S. Campanini, "La radice dolorante:

ebrei e cristiani alla scoperta del giudaismo nel Rinascimento," in *L'interculturalità dell'ebraismo*, ed. by M. Perani, Ravenna, 2004, pp. 234–40.

Campanini 2006
S. Campanini, "Francesco Giorgio's Criticism of the Vulgata: Hebraica Veritas or Mendosa Traductio?", in *Hebrew to Latin – Latin to Hebrew: The Mirroring of two Cultures in the Age of Humanism*, ed. by G. Busi, Turin, 2006, pp. 206–31.

Campanini 2008a
S. Campanini, "A Neglected Source on Asher Lemmlein and Paride da Ceresara: Agostino Giustiniani," in *European Journal of Jewish Studies*, 2, 2008, pp. 89–110.

Campanini 2008b
S. Campanini, "Guglielmo Raimondo Moncada (alias Flavio Mitridate) traduttore di opere Cabbalistiche," in *Guglielmo Raimondo Moncada alias Flavio Mitridate: un ebreo converso siciliano*, ed. by M. Perani, Palermo 2008, pp. 49–88.

Campanini 2012
S. Campanini, "On Abraham's Neck: The Editio Princeps of the Sefer Yetzirah (Mantua 1562) and its Context," in *Rabbi Judah Moscato and the Jewish Intellectual World of Mantua in the 16th–17th Centuries*, ed. by G. Veltri, G. Miletto, Leiden and Boston 2012, pp. 253–78.

Campanini 2014
S. Campanini, "Il commento alle *Conclusiones* cabalisticae nel Cinquecento," in *Giovanni Pico e la cabbalà*, ed. by F. Lelli, Florence, 2014, pp. 167–230.

Campanini 2015
S. Campanini, "Una fonte trascurata del rapporto tra qabbalah e combinatoria lulliana in Pico della Mirandola: il commento

alle preghiere di Yehudah Ibn Malka," in *Studia Lulliana*, 55, 2015, pp. 83–127.

Campanini 2015–16
S. Campanini, "Utriusque Linguae Egregiae Peritus et Prudens: Federico Fregoso cardinale ebraista e l'identità del suo familiaris ebreo 'grandissimo cabalista,'" in *Materia Giudaica*, 20–21, 2015–16, pp. 29–44.

Campanini 2016
S. Campanini, "Elchana Hebraeorum doctor et cabalista: le avventure di un libro e dei suoi lettori," in *Umanesimo e cultura ebraica nel Rinascimento italiano*, ed. by S. U. Baldassarri, F. Lelli, Florence, 2016, pp. 91–114.

Campanini 2018
S. Campanini, "Una lettera in ebraico e una in latino da Matthaeus Adriani a Caspar Amman sul nome di Gesù," in *Bruniana & Campanelliana*, 24, 2018, pp. 25–47.

Cantera and Millás 1956
F. Cantera, J. M. Millás, *Las inscriptiones hebraicas de España*, Madrid, 1956.

Capriotti 2014
G. Capriotti, *Lo scorpione sul petto: iconografia antiebraica tra XV e XVI secolo alla periferia dello Stato pontificio*, Rome, 2014.

Carboni 2008
M. Carboni, *Stato e finanza pubblica in Europa dal Medioevo a oggi: un profilo storico*, Turin, 2008.

Carboni 2014
M. Carboni, *Il credito disciplinato: Il Monte di pietà di Bologna in età barocca*, Bologna, 2014.

Cardillo Di Prima and Scandaliato 2014
L. Cardillo Di Prima, A. Scandaliato, *Flavio Mitridate, i

tre volti del cabbalista*, Palermo, 2014.

Carlebach 2001
E. Carlebach, *Divided Souls: Converts from Judaism in Germany 1500–1750*, New Haven, 2001.

Caro 2001
L. Caro, "Una pergamena cabalistica fra le carte della Biblioteca Queriniana," in *Dalla Libreria del vescovo alla Biblioteca della città: 250 anni di tradizione della cultura a Brescia*, ed. by E. Ferraglio, D. Montanari, Brescia, 2001, pp. 213–22.

Carpaccio 2004
Carpaccio pittore di storie, Venice, 2004.

Carpeggiani 1973
P. Carpeggiani, "Congruenze e parallelismi nell'architettura lombarda della seconda metà del '400: il Filerete e Luca Fancelli," in *Arte Lombarda*, 18, 1973, pp. 53–69.

Cassen 2017
F. Cassen, *Marking the Jews in Renaissance Italy: Politics, Religion, and the Power of Symbols*, Cambridge, 2017.

Cassiani 2015
C. Cassiani, "L'archeologia di un social network: un'ipotesi sui Hiero-glyphica di Pierio Valeriano," in *Roma nel Rinascimento*, 2015, pp. 29–38.

Cassuto 1918
U. Cassuto, *Gli ebrei a Firenze, nell'età del Rinascimento*, Florence, 1918.

Cassuto 1931
U. Cassuto, "Manoscritti e incunaboli ebraici nelle Biblioteche italiane," in *Atti del Primo congresso mondiale delle biblioteche e di bibliografia*, exh. cat., Rome and Venice (June 15–30, 1929), vol. III, Rome, 1931, pp. 68–74.

Cassuto 1935
U. Cassuto, *I manoscritti palatini ebraici della Biblioteca apostolica vaticana e la loro storia*, Vatican City, 1935.

Cassuto 1938
U. Cassuto, *Storia della letteratura ebraica postbiblica*, Florence, 1938 (2nd ed. Rome, 1976).

Cassuto 1956
U. Cassuto, *Codices Vaticani Hebraici: Codices 1–115*, Vatican City, 1956.

Cassuto 1988
D. Cassuto, "A Venetian Parokhet and its Design Origins," in *Jewish Art*, 14, 1988, pp. 35–43.

Cassuto 2004
D. Cassuto, "Aronot qodeš di Mantova in Israele," in *Una manna buona per Mantova: Man tov le-Man-Tovah. Studi in onore di Vittore Colorni per il suo 92° compleanno*, ed. by M. Perani, Florence, 2004, pp. 629–55.

Cassuto 2017
U. Cassuto, "The Destruction of the Rabbinic Academies in South Italy during the Thirteenth Century," English translation from Hebrew by A. Cassuto, D. Cassuto, P. Cassuto, ed. by M. Perani, in *Sefer Yuhasin*, Nuova Serie 5, 2017, pp. 47–70 (1st Hebr. ed. 1942).

Ceccarelli 2003
G. Ceccarelli, *Il gioco e il peccato: Economia e rischio nel tardo Medioevo*, Bologna, 2003.

Ceccarelli 2012
G. Ceccarelli, *Un mercato del rischio: assicurare e farsi assicurare nella Firenze rinascimentale*, Venice, 2012.

Centi 1945
T. M. Centi, "L'attività letteraria di Sante Pagnini (1470–1536) nel campo delle scienze bibliche," in

Archivum Fratrum Praedicatorum, 15, 1945, pp. 5–51.

Ceserani Ermentini 1985
L. Ceserani Ermentini, "Le tavolette da soffitto rinascimentali: la collezione della Banca Popolare di Crema," in *Insula Fulcheria*, 15, 1985, pp. 81–109.

Ceserani Ementini 1999
L. Ceserani Ermentini, *Tavolette rinascimentali: un fenomeno di costume a Crema*, Crema, 1999.

Chajes 2019
J. H. Chajes, "The Kabbalistic Tree", in *The Visualization of Knowledge in the Middle Ages and the Early Modern Period*, ed. by M. Kupfer, A. Cohen, and J. H. Chajes, Turnhout [in press].

Cheles 1986
L. Cheles, *The Studiolo of Urbino: An iconographic Investigation*, Wiesbaden, 1986.

Chester Jordan 1989
W. Chester Jordan, *The French Monarchy and the Jews from Philip Augustus to the Last Capetians*, Philadelphia, 1989.

Chiappini 1967
L. Chiappini, *Gli Estensi*, Milan, 1967.

Christ 1924
K. Christ, *Die Bibliothek Reuchlins in Pforzheim*, Leipzig, 1924.

Christiansen, Kanter, and Brandon Strehlke 1989
K. Christiansen, L. B. Kanter, C. Brandon Strehlke, *La pittura senese nel Rinascimento: 1420–1500*, with an historical essay by M. Ascheri, Siena 1989.

Cipriani 1980
G. Cipriani, *Il mito etrusco nel Rinascimento*, Florence, 1980.

Codice diplomatico 1884–88

Codice diplomatico dei giudei di Sicilia, assembled and published by B. e G. Lagumina, 2 vols., Palermo, 1884–88.

Cohen 2006
E. M. Cohen, "Elia da Vigevano's Prayerbooks of 1490," in *Studia Rosenthaliana*, 38, 2006, pp. 169–77.

Colorni 1983
V. Colorni, *Judaica minora*, Milan, 1983.

Commentaria 1498
Com[m]entaria fratris Ioannis Annii Viterbe[n]sis ordinis p[re]dicator[is] Theologi[a] p[ro]fessoris super opera diversorum auctorum de Antiquitatibus loquentiu[m] confecta finiunt, Romae, Eucharius Silber alias Franck, 1498.

Contessa 2009
A. Contessa, "An Uncommon Representation of the Temple's Implements in a Fifteenth Century Sephardic Bible," in *Ars Judaica*, 5, 2009, pp. 37–58.

Contessa 2013
A. Contessa, "Jewish Book Collection and Patronage in Renaissance Italy," in *Proceedings for the Italia Judaica Jubilee Conference*, ed. by S. Simonsohn, J. Shatzmiller, Leiden and Boston 2013, pp. 37–58.

Contessa 2015
A. Contessa, "L'Aliyah della bellezza: il contributo del Museo di Arte Ebraica Italiana Umberto Nahon allo Stato di Israele," in *La rassegna mensile di Israel*, 2015, pp. 141–69.

Contessa 2016a
A. Contessa, "The Mantua Torah Ark and Lady Consilia Norsa: Jewish Female Patronage in Renaissance Italy," in *Ars Judaica*, 12, 2016, pp. 53–70.

Contessa 2016b
A. Contessa, *The Jewish Court of Venice: The heritage of Jewish Venice 500 years after the establishment of the first ghetto,* Jerusalem, 2016.

Contessa 2017
A. Contessa, *Mantova e Gerusalemme: Arte e cultura ebraica nella città dei Gonzaga,* Florence, 2017.

Contessa 2019
A. Contessa, "Wandering Books: The Migration of Fifteenth Century Sephardic Manuscripts and Their 'New Life' outside Iberia," in *Sephardic Book Art of the Fifteenth Century,* ed. by L. U. Afonso, T. Moita [in press].

Conti 1981
A. Conti, *La miniatura bolognese: scuole e botteghe, 1270–1340,* Bologna, 1981.

Contini 1994
R. Contini, "Gli inizi della linguistica siriaca nell'Europa rinascimentale," in *Rivista degli studi orientali,* 68, 1994, pp. 15–30.

Copenhaver 2002
B. P. Copenhaver, "The Secret of Pico's Oration: Cabala and Renaissance Philosophy," in *Midwest Studies in Philosophy,* 26, 2002, pp. 56–81.

Copenhaver 2014
Pico risorto: Cabbalà e dignità dell'uomo nell'Italia post-unitaria, in *Giovanni Pico e la cabbalà,* ed. by F. Lelli, Florence, 2014, pp. 1–18.

Cortonesi and Palermo 2009
A. Cortonesi, L. Palermo, *La prima espansione economica europea: secoli XI–XV,* Rome, 2009.

Crescentini and Strinati 2008
Andrea Bregno: il senso della forma nella cultura artistica del Rinascimento, ed. by C. Crescentini, C. Strinati, Florence, 2008.

Crescita economica 2017
La crescita economica dell'Occidente medievale: un tema storico non ancora esaurito, Rome, 2017.

Crocifissione 1992
La Crocifissione di Bramantino: storia e restauro, ed. by P. C. Marani, Florence, 1992.

Crouzet-Pavan 2013
E. Crouzet-Pavan, *Renaissances italiennes (1380–1500),* Paris, 2013.

Cultural Intermediaries 2004
Cultural Intermediaries: Jewish Intellectuals in Early Modern Italy, ed. by D. B. Ruderman, G. Veltri, Philadelphia, 2004.

Dahan 1990
G. Dahan, *Les intellectuels chrétiens et les juifs au moyen âge,* Paris, 1990.

Dal castello al palazzo 1997
Dal castello al palazzo: storia e architettura in un'area di confine, Conference Proceedings, Acquafredda and San Martino di Gusnago (1996), ed. by M. Vignoli, [Guidizzolo], 1997.

Dal Prato 1969
P. Dal Prato, "Una concezione di Luca Fancelli: il Palazzo Pastore di San Martino Gusnago," in *Corti e dimore del contado mantovano,* Florence, 1969, pp. 3–11.

Dan 1997
J. Dan, "The Kabbalah of Johannes Reuchlin and its historical Significance," in *The Christian Kabbalah: Jewish Mystical Books and their Christian Interpreters,* ed. by J. Dan, Cambridge, Mass., 1997.

D'Ancona 1914
P. D'Ancona, *La miniatura fiorentina (secoli XI–XVI),* Florence, 1914.

D'Ancona 1969
P. D'Ancona, "Nicolò da Bologna miniaturista del secolo XIV,"

in *Arte Lombarda,* 14, 1969, pp. 1–22.

D'Arco 1857–59
C. D'Arco, *Delle arti e degli artefici di Mantova: notizie illustrate con disegni e documenti,* 2 vols., Mantua, 1857–59.

D'Ascia 1999
L. D'Ascia, "Tra Platonismo e Riforma: Curione, Zwingli e Francesco Zorzi," in *Bibliothèque d'Humanisme et Renaissance,* 61, 1999, pp. 673–99.

Davide 2005
M. Davide, "Il ruolo delle donne nelle comunità ebraiche dell'Italia nord-orientale," in *Ebrei nella Terraferma Veneta del Quattrocento,* Conference Proceedings, Verona (November 14, 2003), ed. by G. M. Varanini, R. C. Müller, Florence, 2005, pp. 31–43.

Davide 2009
M. Davide, *Le presenze "straniere" a Gemona,* in *Gemona nella Patria del Friuli: una società cittadina del Trecento,* Conference Proceedings, Gemona del Friuli (December 5–6, 2008), ed. by P. Cammarosano, Trieste, 2009, pp. 369–417.

Davide 2010
M. Davide, "La pratica testamentaria nelle comunità ebraiche dell'Italia Centro Settentrionale: gli ebrei di origine italiana e gli ebrei askenaziti. Differenze e analogie," in *Volontà tra le pieghe. Testamenti di donne ebree in Italia Settentrionale (secoli XIV–XVI),* in *Margini di libertà: testamenti femminili nel Medioevo,* Conference Proceedings, Verona (October 23–25, 2008), ed. by M. C. Rossi, Caselle di Sommacampagna, 2010, pp. 435–55.

Davide 2012
M. Davide, "Donne e famiglia nella comunità ebraiche del Patriarcato di Aquileia e della Terraferma

Veneta," in *Gli ebrei nell'Italia centro settentrionale fra tardo Medioevo ed età moderna (secoli XV–XVIII)*, ed. by M. Romani, E. Traniello, Rome, 2012, pp. 225–44.

Davide 2016
M. Davide, "Ebrei a Trieste fra Medioevo ed età moderna: vita economica e sociale," in *Gli ebrei nella storia del Friuli Venezia Giulia: una vicenda di lunga durata*, Conference Proceedings, Ferrara (October 12–14, 2015), ed. by M. Davide, P. Ioly Zorattini, Florence, 2016, pp. 181–92.

De Roover 1970
R. De Roover, *Il banco Medici: dalle origini al declino (1397–1494)*, Florence, 1970.

Diario ferrarese 1933
Diario ferrarese dall'anno 1409 sino al 1502 di autori incerti, ed. by G. Pardi, Bologna, 1933.

Dionisotti 1959
C. Dionisotti, "Appunti su Leone Ebreo," in *Italia medievale e umanistica*, 2, 1959, pp. 409–28.

Donesmondi 1612–16
I. Donesmondi, *Dell'historia ecclesiastica di Mantova*, 2 vols., Mantua, 1612–16.

Dorez 1895
L. Dorez, "Lettres inédites de Jean Pic de la Mirandole," in *Giornale storico della letteratura italiana*, 25, 1895, pp. 352–61.

Dorin 2016a
R. Dorin, "'Once the Jews have been Expelled': Intent and Interpretation in Late Medieval Canon Law," in *Law and History Review*, 34, 2016, pp. 335–62.

Dorin 2016b
R. Dorin, "Les maîtres parisiens et les Juifs (fin XIIIe siècle):

perspectives nouvelles sur un dossier d'avis concernant le regimen Iudaeorum," in *Journal des savants*, 2016, pp. 241–82.

Dröge 1987
Ch. Dröge, *Giannozzo Manetti als Denker und Hebraist*, Frankfurt am Main, 1987.

Durissini 1997
D. Durissini, "Credito e presenza ebraica a Trieste," in *Zakhor*, 1, 1997, pp. 2–76.

Ebgi 2013
R. Ebgi, "La mistica notturna nel pensiero di Giovanni Pico della Mirandola," in *Rinascimento*, 53, 2013, pp. 253–68.

Ebrei 2017
Ebrei, una storia italiana: I primi mille anni, ed. by A. Foa, G. Lacerenza, D. Jalla, Milan, 2007.

Ebrei e Sicilia 2002
Ebrei e Sicilia, ed. by N. Bucaria, M. Luzzati, A. Tarantino, Palermo, 2002.

"Ebrei in Italia" 2006
"Ebrei in Italia: arti e mestieri," in *Zakhor: Rivista di Storia degli Ebrei d'Italia*, 9, 2006.

Eliyyah da Genazzano 2002
Eliyyah Hayyim ben Binyamin da Genazzano, *La Lettera preziosa*, ed., transl., and introduction by F. Lelli, Florence, 2002.

Engel 1992
E. Engel, "Abraham ben Mordecai Farissol: Sephardi tradition of Book Making in Northern Italy of the Renaissance Period," in *Jewish Art*, 18, 1992, pp. 148–67.

Engel 2017
M. Engel, *Elijah Del Medigo and Paduan Aristotelianism investigating the Human Intellect*, London and New York, 2017.

Fabbrici 1987
G. Fabbrici, "Gride, bandi, avvisi, notificazioni," in *Cultura ebraica in Emilia-Romagna*, ed. by S. M. Bondoni, G. Busi, Rimini, 1987, pp. 497–545.

Fabris 1909
G. Fabris, "Il codice udinese Ottelio di antiche rime volgari," in *Memorie storiche forogiuliesi*, 5, 1909, pp. p. 33–74, 145–60, 210–35.

Farmer 1998
S. A. Farmer, *Syncretism in the West: Pico's 900 Theses (1486). The Evolution of Traditional Religious and Philosophical Systems*, Tempe, AZ, 1998.

Ferraglio 2002
E. Ferraglio, "Due esemplari bresciani della Passio di Simonino da Trento di Giovanni Mattia Tiberino," in *Civis*, 77, 2002, 26, pp. 91–107.

Flavio Mitridate 2012
Flavio Mitridate mediatore fra culture nel contesto dell'ebraismo siciliano del XV secolo, Conference Proceedings, Caltabellotta (June 30 – July 1, 2008), ed. by M. Perani, G. Corazzol, Palermo, 2012.

Foa 1992
A. Foa, *Ebrei in Europa: dalla peste nera all'emancipazione*, Rome and Bari, 1992.

Foà 2007
S. Foà, ad vocem "Manetti, Giannozzo," in *Dizionario biografico degli italiani*, vol. 68, Rome, 2007, pp. 613–17.

Fontana 1887
B. Fontana, *Documenti vaticani di un plebiscito in Ferrara sul principio del secolo XIV e dell'idea della indipendenza italiana nella mente dei romani pontefici*, Ferrara, 1887.

Formentin 2018
V. Formentin, *Prime manifestazioni del volgare a Venezia*, Rome, 2018.

Fornasari 1993
M. Fornasari, *Il tesoro della città: il Monte di pietà e l'economia bolognese nei secoli 15. e 16.*, Bologna, 1993.

Fortini Brown 1992
P. Fortini Brown, *La pittura nell'età di Carpaccio: i grandi cicli narrativi*, Venezia 1992 (1st English ed. 1988).

Franceschini 2007
A. Franceschini, *Presenza ebraica a Ferrara: testimonianze archivistiche fino al 1492*, ed. by P. Ravenna, Florence, 2007.

Friedenberg 1970
D. M. Friedenberg, *Jewish Medals from the Renaissance to the Fall of Napoleon: 1503–1815*, New York, 1970.

Friedman 1978
Y. Friedman, "An Anatomy of Anti-Semitism: Peter the Venerable's Letter to Louis VII, King of France (1146)," in *Bar-Ilan Studies in History*, 1, 1978, pp. 87–102.

Friedman 1983
J. Friedman, *The Most Ancient Testimony: Sixteenth Century Christian Hebraica in the Age of Renaissance Nostalgia*, Athens, OH, 1983.

Friedman 1988
M. Friedman, "Transplanted Illustrations in Jewish Printed Books," in *Jewish Art*, 14, 1988, pp. 44–55.

Fubini 2016
R. Fubini, "Motivi cabalistico-cristiani nel fregio della villa medicea di Poggio a Caiano: ispirazione e apologia di Giovanni Pico della Mirandola,"

in *Accademia toscana di Scienze e Lettere "La Colombaria. Atti e memorie,"* 81, 2016, pp. 421–55.

Garin 1967
E. Garin, *La cultura del Rinascimento: profilo strorico*, Bari, 1967.

Garzelli 1985
A. Garzelli, *Miniatura fiorentina del Rinascimento (1440–1525): un primo censimento*, Florence, 1985.

Gavrin 2001
B. Gavrin, "The language of Leone Ebreo's Dialoghi d'amore," in *Italia*, 13–15, 2001, pp. 181–210.

Gersonide 2009
Gersonide, *Commento al Cantico dei Cantici nella traduzione ebraico-latina di Flavio Mitridate. Ed. e comm. del ms. Vat. Lat. 4273 (cc. 5r–54r)*, ed. by M. Andreatta, Florence, 2009.

Geschichte der Juden 2002
Geschichte der Juden im Mittelalter von der Nordsee bis zu den Südalpen. Kommentiertes Kartenwerk, ed. by A. Haverkamp, 3 vols., Hannover, 2002.

Gheller 2012
G. Gheller, "Il credito ebraico a Urbino tra Federico da Montefeltro e l'apertura del Monte di Pietà (1444–1470)," in *Gli ebrei nell'Italia centro settentrionale fra tardo Medioevo ed età moderna (secoli XV–XVIII)*, ed. by M. Romani, E. Traniello, Rome, 2012, pp. 245–72.

Giambullari 1546
Pier Francesco Giambullari, *Il Gello*, Florence, 1546.

Giansante 2008
M. Giansante, *L'usuraio onorato: Credito e potere a Bologna in età comunale*, Bologna, 2008.

Giehlow 1915
K. Gielhow, "Die

Hieroglyphenkunde des Humanismus in der Allegorie der Renaissance besonders der Ehrenpforte Kaisers Maximilian I: Ein Versuch," in *Jahrbuch der Kunsthistorischen Sammlungen in Wien*, 32, 1915, pp. 1–232.

Gielhlow 2004
K. Giehlow, *Hieroglyphica: la conoscenza umanistica dei geroglifici nell'allegoria del Rinascimento. Una ipotesi*, Italian ed. by M. Ghelardi, S. Müller, Turin, 2004.

Giovanni Pico e la cabbalà 2014
Giovanni Pico e la cabbalà, ed. by F. Lelli, Florence, 2014.

Giqatilla 2010
Yosef Giqatilla, *The Book of Punctuation: Flavius Mithridates' Latin Translation, the Hebrew Text, and an English Version*, ed. with introduction and notes by A. Martini, Turin, 2010.

Giraldi Cinthio 1597
G. Giraldi Cinthio, *Commentario delle cose di Ferrara et de' principi da Este*, Venezia 1597.

Goldberg 2001
E. L. Goldberg, *Jews and Magic in Medici Florence: The Secret World of Benedetto Blanis*, Toronto, 2001.

Goldthwaite 2009
R. A. Goldthwaite, *The Economy of Renaissance Florence*, Baltimore, 2009.

Gombrich 1972
Symbolic Images: Studies in the Art of the Renaissance, London and New York, 1972.

Grafton 1990
A. Grafton, *Forgers and Critics: Creativity and Duplicity in Western Scholarship*, Princeton, 1990.

Grafton 1999
A. Grafton, *Philologie und prisca sapientia bei Pico della Mirandola,*

in *Wissensbilder: Strategien der Überlieferung*, ed. by U. Raulff, G. Smith, Berlin, 1999, pp. 95–116.

Grafton 2019
A. Grafton, "Annius of Viterbo as a Student of the Jews: The Sources of his Information," in *Literary Forgery in Early Modern Europe, 1450–1800*, ed. by W. Stephens, E. A. Havens, and J. E. Gomez, Baltimore, 2019, pp. 147–69.

Grafton and Weinberg 2011
"I Have Always Loved the Holy Tongue": Isaac Casaubon, the Jews, and a Forgotten Chapter in Renaissance Scholarship, Cambridge, Mass., 2011.

Grailsammer 2007
M. Greilsammer, "Il credito al consumo in Europa: dai 'lombardi' ai Monti di Pietà," in *Commercio e cultura mercantile*, ed. by F. Franceschi, R. Goldthwaite, R.C. Mueller, Treviso, 2007, pp. 591–621.

Graizbord 2004
D. Graizbord, *Souls in Dispute: Converso Identities in Iberia and the Jewish Diaspora, 1580–1700*, Philadelphia, 2004.

Grasso 2008
M. Grasso, ad vocem "Mazzolino, Ludovico," in *Dizionario biografico degli italiani*, vol. 72, Rome, 2008, pp. 681–84.

Grayzel 1933
S. Grayzel, *The Church and the Jews in 13. Century: A Study of their Relations during the Years 1198–1254, based on the Papal Letters and the Conciliar Decrees of the Period*, Philadelphia, 1933.

Graziani Secchieri 2012
L. Graziani Secchieri, "Ebrei italiani, ashkenaziti e sefarditi a Ferrara: un'analisi topografica dell'insediamento e delle sue trasformazioni (secoli XIII–XVI)," in *Gli ebrei nello Stato della Chiesa: insediamenti e mobilità (secoli XIV–XVII)*, ed. by M. Caffiero, A. Esposito, Padua 2012, pp. 163–90.

Graziani Secchieri 2017
L. Graziani Secchieri, "Banchi feneratizi a Ferrara fra tardo Medioevo e prima Età moderna: volàno e specchio di strategie imprenditoriali e familiari a largo raggio," in *I paradigmi della mobilità e delle relazioni: gli ebrei in Italia. In ricordo di Michele Luzzati*, ed. by B. Migliau, Florence, 2017, pp. 47–78.

Greco 2016a
S. Greco, *Kultursoziologie in Italien*, in *Handbuch Kultursoziologie*, ed. by S. Moebius, F. Nungesser, and K. Scherke, vol. I, Wiesbaden, 2016, pp. 1–23.

Greco 2016b
S. Greco, "'Vi servirà di segno': cibo e identità nell'ebraismo," in *Cibo, identità culturale e religione tra antico e contemporaneo: Ebraismo, tradizione classica, Islam e India*, Milan, 2016, pp. 11–40.

Greenblatt 1980
S. Greenblatt, *Renaissance Self-Fashioning: From More to Shakespeare*, Chicago, 1980.

Grévin 2018
B. Grévin, "Editing an illuminated Arabic-Latin Masterwork of the fifteenth Century: Manuscript Vat. Lat.1384 as a Philological Challenge," in *Multilingual and Multigrafic Documents and Manuscripts of East and West*, ed. by A. Mandalà, I. Perez Martin, Piscataway, NJ, 2018, pp. 359–81.

Grunebaum-Ballin 1968
P. Grunebaum-Ballin, *Joseph Naçi duc de Naxos*, Paris and The Hague 1968.

Guglielmo Ebreo 1993
Guglielmo Ebreo of Pesaro, *De pratica seu arte tripudii*, ed., transl., and introduced by B. Sparti, poems transl. by M. Sullivan, Oxford 1993.

Guglielmo Raimondo Moncada 2008
Guglielmo Raimondo Moncada alias Flavio Mitridate: un ebreo converso siciliano, ed. by M. Perani, Palermo 2008.

Gundersheimer 1973
W. Gundersheimer, *Ferrara estense: lo stile del potere*, Ferrara, 1973.

Guttmann 1933
J. Guttmann, *Philosophie des Judentums*, Munich, 1933.

Habermann 1978a
A. M. Habermann, *Studies in the History of Hebrew Printed Books* [in Hebrew], Jerusalem, 1978.

Habermann 1978b
A. M. Habermann, *The Printer Daniel Bomberg and the List of Books published by his Press* [in Hebrew], Zefat, 1978.

Haitovsky 1999
D. Haitovsky, "The Hebrew Inscriptions in Ludovico Mazzolino's Paintings," in *Jewish Studies at the Turn of the Twentieth Century: Proceedings of the 6th EAJS Congress, Toledo, July 1998*, ed. by J. Targarona Borrás, A. Sáenz-Badillos, 2 vols., Leiden, 1999, vol. II, pp. 133–45.

Hebrew Manuscripts 2001
Hebrew Manuscripts in the Biblioteca Palatina in Parma: Catalogue, ed. by B. Richler, paleographical and codicological descriptions by M. Beit-Arié, Jerusalem, 2001.

Hebrew Manuscripts 2008
Hebrew Manuscripts in the Vatican Library: Catalogue, compiled by the Staff of the Institute of Microfilmed

Hebrew Manuscripts, Jewish National and University library, Jerusalem, ed. by B. Richler, palaeographical and codicological descriptions by M. Beit-Arié in collaboration with N. Pasternak, Vatican City 2008.

Hebrew Study 1999
Hebrew Study from Ezra to Ben-Yehuda, ed. by W. Horbury, Edinburgh, 1999.

Herrmann 2003
K. Herrmann, "Ludwig Geiger as the Redactor of Jacob Burckhardt's Die Cultur der Renaissance in Italien," in *Jewish Studies Quarterly*, 10, 2003, pp. 377–400.

Hoffman and Cole 2011
A. Hoffman, P. Cole, *Sacred Trash: The Lost and Found World of the Cairo Genizah*, New York, 2011.

Iakerson 2012
S. Iakerson, "Los primeros impresos hebreos de Sefarad (ca. 1475–1497?) / Early Hebrew Printing in Sepharad (ca. 1475–1497?)," in *Biblias de Sefarad / Bibles of Sepharad*, ed. by F. Javier del Barco, E. Alfonso, Madrid, 2012, pp. 125–47.

Idel 1976
M. Idel, *Abraham Abulafia's Works and Doctrine* [Hebrew/English], PhD Dissertation, The Hebrew University, Jerusalem, 1976.

Idel 1988
M. Idel, "Ramon Lull and Ecstatic Kabbalah: A Preliminary Observation," in *Journal of the Warburg and Courtauld Institutes*, 51, 1988, pp. 170–74.

Idel 2011
M. Idel, *Kabbalah in Italy, 1280–1510: A Survey*, New Haven and London, 2011.

Idel 2014
M. Idel, "The Kabbalistic

Background of the 'Son of God' in Giovanni Pico della Mirandola's Thought," in *Giovanni Pico e la cabbalà*, ed. by F. Lelli, Florence, 2014, pp. 19–45.

I frammenti ebraici 2012
I frammenti ebraici dell'Archivio di Stato di Modena, I, Inventario e catalogo, ed. by M. Perani, L. Baraldi, with the collaboration of E. Sagradini, Florence, 2012.

Il Codice Maimonide 2018
Il Codice Maimonide e i Norsa: una famiglia ebraica nella Mantova dei Gonzaga, exh. cat., ed. by C. Farnetti, S. Settis [Italian/English], Rome, 2018.

Il lateranense 2017
Il lateranense IV: le ragioni di un concilio, LIII International Conference Proceedings, Todi (October 9–12, 2016), Spoleto, 2017.

Il libro miniato 2016
Il libro miniato a Roma nel Duecento. Riflessioni e proposte, ed. by S. Maddalo, E. Ponzi, 2 vols., Rome, 2016.

Il museo della Cattedrale 2010
Il museo della Cattedrale di Ferrara: Catalogo generale, ed. by B. Giovannucci Vigi, G. Sassu, Ferrara, 2010.

Il Museo Diocesano 1996
Il Museo Diocesano Tridentino, ed. by D. Primerano, S. Castri, Trento, 1996.

I manoscritti datati 2008
I manoscritti datati della Biblioteca Queriniana di Brescia, ed. by N. Giovè Marchioli, M. Pantarotto, Florence, 2008.

Indice generale degli incunaboli 1943–81
Indice generale degli incunaboli delle biblioteche d'Italia, 6 vols., Rome, 1943–81.

Introducción 1994
Introducción a la Biblia de Ferrara: Actas del Simposio internacional sobre la Biblia de Ferrara, Sevilla, 25–28 de noviembre de 1991, ed. by I. M. Hassan, with the collaboration of A. L. Berenguer Amador, Madrid, 1994.

Inventari 1930
Inventari dei manoscritti delle biblioteche d'Italia, founded by Prof. G. Mazzatinti, vol. 46: *Udine*, Florence, 1930.

Iogna Prat 1998
D. Iogna Prat, *Ordonner et exclure: Cluny et la société chrétienne face à l'hérésie, au judaïsme et à l'islam*, Paris, 1998.

Ivry 1983
A. Ivry, "Remnants of Jewish Averroism in the Renaissance," in *Jewish Thought in the Sixteenth Century*, ed. by B. D. Cooperman, Cambridge Mass. and London, 1983, pp. 243–65.

Jörg 2008
C. Jörg, *Teure, Hunger, Großes Sterben: Hüngersnöte und Versorgungkrisen in den Städten des Reiches während des 15. Jahrhunderts*, Stuttgart, 2008, pp. 350–62.

Kaplan 1989
Y. Kaplan, *From Christianity to Judaism: The Story of Isaac Orobio de Castro*, Oxford, 1989 [1st Hebrew ed. 1982].

Kaplan 1994
Y. Kaplan, "Wayward New Christians and Stubborn Jews: The Shaping of a Jewish Identity," in *Jewish history*, 8, 1994, pp. 27–41.

Kaplan 1997
Y. Kaplan, "The Self-Definition of the Sephardic Jews of Western Europe and their Relation to the Alien and the Stranger," in *Crisis and*

Creativity in the Sephardic World: 1391–1648, ed. by B. Gampel, New York, 1997, pp. 121–145.

Kaplan 2000
Y. Kaplan, *An Alternative Path to Modernity: The Sephardi Diaspora in Western Europe,* Leiden and Boston, 2000.

Katz 2000
D. E. Katz, "Painting and the Politics of Persecution: Representing the Jew in 15th Century Mantua," in *Art History*, 23, 2000, pp. 474–95.

Kaufmann 1893
D. Kaufmann, "Jacob Mantino: Une page de l'histoire de la Renaissance," in *Revue des études juives*, 27, 1893, pp. 30–60, 207–38.

Keil 2004
M. Keil, "Public Roles of Jewish Women in Fourteenth and Fifteenth-Century Ashkenaz: Business, Community, and Ritual," in *The Jews of Europe in the Middle Ages (Tenth to Fifteenth Centuries): Proceedings of the International Symposium held at Speyer* (October 20–25, 2002), Turnhout, 2004, pp. 317–30.

Keil 2008
M. Keil, "Mobilität und Sittsamkeit: Jüdische Frauen im Wirtschaftsleben des spätmittelalterlichen Aschkenaz," in *Wirtschaftsgeschichte der mittelalterlichen Juden: Fragen und Einschätzungen*, ed. by E. Muller-Luckner, M. Toch, Munich, 2008, pp. 153–80.

Kessler-Mesguich 2013
S. Kessler-Mesguich, *Les études hébraïques en France, de François Tissard à Richard Simon (1508–1680)*, Geneva, 2013.

Klagsbald 1981
V. A. Klagsbald, *Catalogue raisonné de la collection juive du Musée de Cluny*, Paris, 1981.

Klagsbald 1982
V. A. Klagsbald, *Jewish Treasures from Paris: From the Collections of the Cluny Museum and the Consistoire*, Jerusalem, 1982.

Klutstein 1987
I. Klutstein, *Marsilio Ficino et la Théologie Ancienne*, Florence, 1987.

Kogman-Appel 2006
K. Kogman-Appel, "Illuminated Bibles and the Re-written Bible: The Place of Moses dal Castellazzo in Early Modern Book History," in *Ars Judaica*, 2, 2006, pp. 35–52.

Kristeller 1902
P. Kristeller, *Andrea Mantegna*, Berlin and Leipzig, 1902.

Kristeller 1953
P. O. Kristeller, *Il pensiero filosofico di Marsilio Ficino*, Florence, 1953.

Kusman 2013
D. Kusman, *Usuriers publics et banquiers du prince: Le rôle économique des financiers piémontais dans les villes du duché de Brabant (XIIIe–XIVe siècle)*, Turnhout, 2013.

Lacerenza 2002
G. Lacerenza, "Lo spazio dell'ebreo: insediamenti e cultura ebraica a Napoli (secoli XV–XVI)," in *Integrazione ed emarginazione: circuiti e modelli*, ed. by L. Barletta, Naples, 2002, pp. 357–428.

Lacerenza 2010
G. Lacerenza, "Sulla figura del maestro di danza Guglielmo Ebreo da Pesaro, alias Giovanni Ambrosio, e la sua permanenza alla corte di Ferrante d'Aragona," in *Le usate leggiadrie: i cortei, le cerimonie, le feste e il costume nel Mediterraneo tra il XV e XVI secolo*, ed. by G. T. Colesanti, Montella 2010, pp. 355–75.

L'Alba della banca 1982
L'alba della banca: Le origini del sistema bancario tra Medioevo ed età moderna, Rome, 1982.

Lane and Müller 1985
F. C. Lane, R. C. Müller, *Money and Banking in Medieval and Renaissance Venice*, I, *Coins and Moneys of Account*, Baltimore, 1985.

Lauts 1960
J. Lauts, *Die "Madonna della Vittoria,"* Stuttgart, 1960 (1st ed. 1947).

Le Goff 2006
J. Le Goff, *Marchands et banquiers du Moyen Âge*, Paris, 2006.

Lelli 2008
F. Lelli, "L'albero sefirotico di Eliyyà Menahem ben Abba Mari Halfan (Ms. Firenze, Biblioteca Medicea Laurenziana, Plut. 44,18)," in *Rinascimento*, 2008, pp. 271–290.

Leone Ebreo 1929
Leone Ebreo, *Dialoghi d'amore*, with a presentation of the life and work of Leone, bibliography, index to the *Dialoghi*, transmission of the Hebrew texts, documents and notes by C. Gebhardt, Heidelberg, 1929.

Leoni 2011
A. di Leone Leoni, *La Nazione ebraica spagnola e portoghese di Ferrara (1492–1559)*, Florence, 2011.

Lesley 1992
A. Lesley, "Jewish Adaptation of Humanist Concepts in Fifteenth and Sixteenth–Centuries Italy," in *Essential Papers on Jewish Culture in Renaissance and Baroque Italy*, ed. by D. B. Ruderman, New York and London 1992, pp. 45–62.

L'hébreu 1992
L'hébreu au temps de la Renaissance, coord. and ed. by I. Zinguer, Leiden, 1992.

Licata 2017
G. Licata, "Magno in secta

peripatetica: una nuova edizione commentata della lettera di Elia del Medigo a Giovanni Pico della Mirandola (Paris, BNF, ms. lat. 6508)," in *Schede Medievali*, 55, 2017, pp. 103–43.

Lightbown 1986
R. Lightbown, *Mantegna*, Milan, 1986.

Ligota 1987
C. Ligota, "Annius of Viterbo and Historical Method," in *Journal of the Warburg and Courtauld Institutes*, 50, 1987, pp. 44–56.

Linder 1997
A. Linder, *The Jews in the legal Sources of the early Middle Ages*, Detroit and Jerusalem, 1997.

Llompart Moragues 1970
G. Llompart Moragues, "La fecha y circunstancias del arribo de los *rimmonim* de la Catedral de Mallorca," in *Sefarad*, 30, 1970, pp. 48–51.

L'Occaso 2011
S. L'Occaso, *Museo di Palazzo Ducale di Mantova: catalogo generale delle collezioni inventariate. Dipinti fino al XIX secolo*, Mantua, 2011.

Losada 2015
C. Losada, "Powerful Words: St Vincent Ferrer's Preaching and the Jews in Medieval Castile," in *Spoken Word and Social Practice: Orality in Europe (1400–1700)*, ed. by T. V. Cohen, L.K. Twomey, Leiden and Boston, 2015, pp. 206–27.

Lo Studiolo 2015
Lo studiolo del Duca: il ritorno degli uomini illustri alla corte di Urbino, ed. by A. Marchi, Milan, 2015.

Luzzati 1983
M. Luzzati, "Ebrei, chiesa locale, 'principe' e popolo: due episodi di distruzione di immagini sacre alla fine del Quattrocento," in *Quaderni Storici*, 54, 1983, pp. 847–77.

Luzzati 1994
M. Luzzati, "L'insediamento ebraico a Pisa prima del Trecento: conferme e nuove acquisizioni," in *Società, istituzioni, spiritualità: studi in onore di Cinzio Violante*, 2 vols., Spoleto, 1994, vol. I, pp. 509–17.

Luzzati 1996
M. Luzzati, "Banchi e insediamenti ebraici nell'Italia centro-settentrionale fra tardo Medioevo e inizi dell'Età moderna," in *Storia d'Italia: Annali 11, Gli ebrei in Italia*, ed. by C. Vivanti, 2 vols., Torino 1996, vol. I, pp. 173–235.

Luzzati 2002
M. Luzzati, "La circolazione di uomini, donne e capitali ebraici nell'Italia del Quattrocento: un esempio toscano-cremonese," in *Gli ebrei a Cremona: storia di una comunità nel Rinascimento*, Florence, 2002, pp. 33–52.

Luzzatto 1902
G. Luzzatto, *I banchieri ebrei in Urbino nell'età ducale: appunti di storia economica con appendice di documenti*, Padua, 1902.

Luzzatto 1961
G. Luzzatto, *Storia economica di Venezia dall'XI al XVI secolo*, Venice, 1961.

Luzzatto and Ottolenghi 1972
A. Luzzatto, L. Mortara Ottolenghi, *Hebraica Ambrosiana*, Milan, 1972.

Maifreda 2012
G. Maifreda, *From Oikonomia to Political Economy: Constructing Economic Knowledge from the Renaissance to the Scientific Revolution*, Farnham, 2012.

Majarelli and Nicolini 1962
S. Majarelli, U. Nicolini, *Il Monte dei Poveri di Perugia: Periodo delle origini (1462–1474)*, Perugia, 1962.

Manca 2006
J. Manca, *Andrea Mantegna and the Italian Renaissance*, New York, 2006.

Mandalà 2011
G. Mandalà, "Un codice arabo in caratteri ebraici dalla Trapani degli Abbate (Vat. ebr. 358)," in *Sefarad*, 71, 2011, pp. 7–24.

Mandalà 2012
G. Mandalà, "Da Toledo a Palermo: Yishaq ben Šelomoh ibn al-Ahdab in Sicilia (ca. 1395–95–1431)," in *Flavio Mitridate mediatore fra culture nel contesto dell'ebraismo siciliano del XV secolo*, Conference Proceedings, Caltabellotta (June 30 – July 1, 2008), ed. by M. Perani, G. Corazzol, Palermo, 2012, pp. 2–16.

Mandalà and Scandaliato 2015
G. Mandalà, A. Scandaliato, "Origini siciliane e fasti romani di Ferdinando Balami, archiatra pontificio, poeta e traduttore della prima metà del secolo XVI," in *Sefer Yuhasin*, 3, 2015, pp. 125–85.

Manni 1993
G. Manni, *Mobili antichi in Emilia Romagna*, Modena, 1993.

Mantegna 2008
Mantegna: 1431–1506, ed. by G. Agosti, D. Thiébaut, with the assistance of A. Galansino, J. Stoppa, Italian ed. reviewed and updated wih the collaboration of A. Canova, A. Mazzotta, Paris and Milan, 2008.

Mantegna a Mantova 2006
Mantegna a Mantova, ed. by M. Lucco, Milan, 2006.

Manzoni 1883–86
G. Manzoni, *Annali tipografici dei Soncino*, 2 parts, Bologna, 1883–86.

Margoliouth 1909–15
G. Margoliouth, *Catalogue of the Hebrew and Samaritan Manuscripts in the British Museum*, 3 vols., London, 1909–15.

Margonari and Zanca 1973
R. Margonari, A. Zanca, *Il Santuario della Madonna delle Grazie presso Mantova: storia e interpretazione di un raro complesso votivo*, Mantua, 1973.

Mariani Canova 1978
G. Mariani Canova, *Miniature dell'Italia settentrionale nella Fondazione Giorgio Cini*, Venice, 1978.

Mariani Canova 1995
G. Mariani Canova, "Neri da Rimini miniatore," in *Neri da Rimini: il Trecento riminese tra pittura e scrittura*, ed. by A. Emiliani, Milan, 1995, pp. 31–36.

Martin 2004
J. J. Martin, *The Myths of Renaissance Individualism*, Basingstoke, 2004.

Martin 2016
A. von Martin, *Soziologie der Renaissance und weitere Schriften*, ed. by R. Faber, C. Holste, Wiesbaden, 2016 (1st ed. 1932).

Mazzoldi 1961
L. Mazzoldi, *Mantova: la storia*, vol. II, Mantua, 1961.

McGee 1988
T. J. McGee, "Dancing Masters and the Medici Court in the 15th Century," in *Studi musicali*, 17, 1988, pp. 201–24.

Medaglie italiane 1984–85
Medaglie italiane del Rinascimento nel Museo nazionale del Bargello, introduction and entries by J. G. Pollard, 3 vols., Florence, 1984–85.

Melchiorre 2012
M. Melchiorre, *A un cenno del suo dito: Fra Bernardino da Feltre (1439–1494) e gli ebrei*, Milan, 2012.

Melis 1987
F. Melis, *La banca pisana e le origini della banca moderna*, Florence, 1987.

Mell 2017
J. L. Mell, *The Myth of the Medieval Jewish Moneylender*, New York, 2017.

Menahem Recanati 2008
Menahem Recanati, *Commentary on the Daily Prayers: Flavius Mithridates' Latin Translation, the Hebrew Text, and an English Version*, ed. with introduction and notes by G. Corazzol, Turin, 2008.

Mentgen 2008
G. Mentgen, "Netzwerkbeziehungen bedeutender Cividaler Juden in den ersten Hälfte des 14. Jahrhunderts," in *Translokalen Beziehungen der aschkenasischen Juden während des Mittelalters und der frühen Neuzeit in vergleichender Perspektive*, ed. by J. Müller, Hannover, 2008 pp. 147–296.

Metzger 1977
T. Metzger, "Les illustrations d'un psautier hébreu italien de la fin du XIIIe siècle: le ms. Parm. 1870 De Rossi 510 de la Bibliothèque palatine de Parme," in *Cahiers archéologiques*, 26, 1977, pp. 145–62.

Metzger 1979
M. Metzger, "Un mahzor italien enluminé du XVe siècle (Vol. I; Jerusalem, Bibl. Nat. et Univ., Ms. Heb. 8 4450. Vol. II; Jerusalem, coll. Weill)," in *Mitteilungen des Kunsthistorischen Institutes in Florenz*, 20, 1979, pp. 159–96.

Metzger 2002
T. Metzger, "Le manuscrit Norsa: Une copie ashkenaze achevée en 1349 et enluminée du Guide des égarés de Maïmonide," in *Mitteilungen des Kunsthistorischen Institutes in Florenz*, 46, 2002, pp. 1–73.

Metzger and Metzger 1982
M. Metzger, T. Metzger, *La vie juive au Moyen Age*, Fribourg, 1982.

Milani 2017
G. Milani, *L'uomo con la borsa al collo: genealogia e usi di un'immagine infamante medievale*, Rome, 2017.

Milano 1963
A. Milano, *Storia degli ebrei in Italia*, Turin, 1963.

Minervino 1998
F. Minervino in *Corriere della Sera*, March 25, 1998.

Montanari 2001
D. Montanari, *Il credito e la carità: Monti di Pietà delle città lombarde in età moderna*, Milan, 2001.

Montesano 1995
M. Montesano, "Aspetti e conseguenze della predicazione civica di Bernardino da Siena," in *La religion civique à l'époque médiévale et moderne: Chrétienté et Islam*, ed. by A. Vauchez, Rome, 1995, pp. 265–75.

Monti di Pietà 1999
Monti di Pietà e presenza ebraica in Italia, ed. by D. Montanari, Milan, 1999.

Morandini 1989
M. Morandini, "La Passione del beato Simonino," in *Studi in onore di Ugo Vaglia*, Brescia, 1989, pp. 185–90.

Mortara Ottolenghi 1974
L. Mortara Ottolenghi, "Un gruppo di manoscritti ebraici romani del sec. XIII e XIV e la loro decorazione," in *Studi sull'ebraismo italiano in memoria di C. Roth*, Rome, 1974, pp. 141–58.

Mortara Ottolenghi 1983
L. Mortara Ottolenghi, "Miniature ebraiche italiane," in *Italia Judaica*, Rome, 1983, pp. 211–27.

Mortara Ottolenghi 1993–94
L. Mortara Ottolenghi, "Scribes, Patrons and Artist of Italian Illuminated Manuscripts in Hebrew," in *Jewish Art*, 19–20, 1993–94, pp. 86–97.

Mortara Ottolenghi 1997
L. Mortara Ottolenghi, "'Figure e immagini' dal sec. XIII al sec. XIX," in *Storia d'Italia: Annali 11, Gli ebrei in Italia*, ed. by C. Vivanti, 2 vols., Turin, 1997, vol. II, pp. 965–1008.

Möschter 2008
A. Möschter, *Juden im venezianischen Treviso (1389–1509)*, Hannover, 2008.

Moscone 2018
M. Moscone, "The 'Norsa codex' of Maimonide's *Guide for Perplexed*," in *Il Codice Maimonide e i Norsa: una famiglia ebraica nella Mantova dei Gonzaga. Banche libri quadri*, exh. cat. (Archivio di Stato, Rome), ed. by C. Farnetti, S. Settis [Italian/English], Rome, 2018, pp. 36–49.

Mulè 1990
C. Mulè, *Agazio Guidacerio, un umanista catanzarese a Parigi*, Reggio Calabria, 1990.

Mulè 2009
V. Mulè, "Note sulla predicazione del beato Matteo da Girgenti agli ebrei di Sicilia," in *Francescanesimo e cultura nella provincia di Agrigento*, ed. by I. Craparotta, N. Grisanti, Palermo, 2009, pp. 205–16.

Müller 1997
R. C. Müller, *The Venetian Money Market: Banks, Panics and the Public Debt*, Baltimore, 1997.

Münster 1954
L. Münster, "Fu Jacob Mantino lettore effettivo dello Studio di Bologna?" in *La Rassegna Mensile di Israel*, 20, 1954, pp. 310–21.

Muzzarelli 1996
M. G. Muzzarelli, *Gli inganni delle apparenze: disciplina di vesti e ornamenti alla fine del Medioevo*, Turin, 1996.

Muzzarelli 2001
M. G. Muzzarelli, *Il denaro e la salvezza: l'invenzione del Monte di Pietà*, Bologna, 2001.

Muzzarelli 2005
M. G. Muzzarelli, *Pescatori di uomini: predicatori e piazze alla fine del Medioevo*, Bologna, 2005.

Muzzarelli 2015
M. G. Muzzarelli, "The Effects of Bernardino da Feltre's Preaching on the Jews," in *The Jewish-Christian Encounter in Medieval Preaching*, ed. by J. Adams, J. Hanska, New York and London, 2015, pp. 170–94.

Nahon 1970
U. Nahon, *Aronot kodesh we–tashmishe qedushah me–Italyah be-Yisra'el*, Tel Aviv, 1970.

Narkiss 1969
B. Narkiss, *Hebrew Illuminated Manuscripts*, Jerusalem, 1969.

Nashman-Fraiman 2006
S. Nashman-Fraiman, "Joy and Gladness, Happy Festivals for the House of Yehudah: A Unique Parokhet from Alessandra della Paglia," in *Ars Judaica*, 2006, pp. 151–62.

Natan ben Sa'adya Har'ar 2001
Natan ben Sa'adya Har'ar, *Le porte della giustizia: Sha'are Tzedeq*, ed. by M. Idel, Milan, 2001.

Nelson Novoa 2006
J. W. Nelson Novoa, "La pubblicazione dei *Dialoghi d'amore* di Leone Ebreo e l'umanesimo dell'Italia meridionale," in *Itinerari Studi Storici*, 20, 2006, pp. 213–30.

Nelson Novoa 2009
J. W. Nelson Novoa, "Appunti sulla genesi redazionale dei *Dialoghi d'amore* di Leone Ebreo alla luce della critica testuale attuale e la tradizione manoscritta del suo terzo dialogo," in *Quaderni d'italianistica*, 2009, pp. 45–66.

Nelson Novoa 2011
J. W. Nelson Novoa, "Leone Ebreo's Dialoghi d'amore as a Pivotal Document of Jewish-Christian Relations in Renaissance Rome," in *Hebraic Aspects of the Renaissance*, ed. by I. Zinguer, A. Melamed, and Z. Shalev, Leiden and Boston, 2011, pp. 62–79.

Neri Lausanna 1982
E. Neri Lausanna, "L'atelier del Maestro dei Mesi," in *La cattedrale di Ferrara*, Ferrara, 1982, pp. 199–228.

Neubauer 1886–1906
A. Neubauer, *Catalogue of the Hebrew Manuscripts in the Bodleian Library and in the College Libraries of Oxford*, 3 vols., Oxford, 1886–1906.

Norsa 1953–59
P. Norsa, "Una famiglia di banchieri: la famiglia Norsa," in *Bollettino dell'archivio storico del Banco di Napoli*, 6, 1953, pp. 1–79; 13, 1959, pp. 59–191.

Offenberg 1999
A. K. Offenberg, "What do we know about the very first Jewish Printers of Hebrew Books?" in *Studia Rosenthaliana*, 33, 1999, pp. 174–180.

Olivieri 1987
A. Olivieri, "Il medico ebreo a Venezia," in *Gli Ebrei e Venezia*, ed. by G. Cozzi, Milan, 1987, pp. 450–68.

O'Malley 1968
J. W. O'Malley, *Giles of Viterbo on*

Church and Reform: A Study in Renaissance Thought, Leiden, 1968.

Omont 1896
H. Omont, *Journal autobiographique de Jérôme Aléandre*, Paris, 1896.

Ortalli 1996
G. Ortalli, "The Prince and the Playing Cards: The Este Family and the Role of Courts at the Time of the Kartenspiel-Invasion," in *Ludica. Annali di storia e civiltà del gioco*, 2, 1996, pp. 175–205.

'Ovadyah da Bertinoro 1991
'Ovadyah Yare da Bertinoro, *Lettere dalla Terra Santa*, Italian version by G. Busi, Rimini, 1991.

'Ovadyah Sforno 1567
'Ovadyah Sforno, *Be'ur 'al ha-Torah*, Venice, 1567.

Oxford Hanbook 2010
The Oxford Handbook of Judaism and Economics, Oxford, 2010.

Pace 2011
V. Pace, "Storia dell'arte e della miniatura (secoli V–XIV)," in *La Biblioteca Apostolica Vaticana luogo di ricerca al servizio degli studi*, Conference Proceedings, Rome (November 11–13, 2010), ed. by M. Buonocore, A. Piazzoni, Vatican City, 2011, pp. 213–72.

Pacioli 1956
L. Pacioli, *De divina proportione*, Milan, 1956.

Pakter 1979
W. J. Pakter, *De his qui foris sunt: The Teachings of the Medieval Canon and Civil Lawyers concerning the Jews*, Ann Arbor, 1979.

Pakter 1988
W. J. Pakter, *Medieval Canon Law and the Jews*, Ebelsbach, 1988.

Palermo 1997
L. Palermo, *Sviluppo economico e società preindustriali: cicli, strutture e congiunture in Europa dal Medioevo alla prima età moderna*, Rome, 1997.

Palermo 2008
L. Palermo, *La banca e il credito nel medioevo*, Milan, 2008.

Paquier 1900
J. Paquier, *Jérôme Aléandre, de sa naissance à la fin de séjour à Brindes (1480–1529)*, Paris, 1900.

Parente 1996
F. Parente, "La chiesa e il Talmud," in *Storia d'Italia: Annali 11. Gli ebrei in Italia*, ed. by C. Vivanti, 2 vols., Turin, 1996, vol. I, pp. 521–643.

Pasternak 2004
N. Pasternak, "Hebrew Hand-Written Books as Testimonies to Christian-Jewish Contacts in Quattrocento Florence," in *L'interculturalità dell'ebraismo*, Conference Proceedings, Bertinoro and Ravenna (May 26–28, 2003), ed. by M. Perani, Ravenna, 2004, pp. 161–71.

Pedullà 2010
G. Pedullà, "Annio: il falsario di Dio," in *Atlante della letteratura italiana*, vol. I: *Dalle origini al Rinascimento*, Turin, 2010, pp. 596–603.

Perani 1999
M. Perani, "Il reimpiego dei manoscritti ebraici: i frammenti ebraici rinvenuti presso l'Archivio Storico Comunale di Modena e il loro contributo allo studio del giudaismo," in *Le comunità ebraiche a Modena e Carpi*, Conference Proceedings, Modena and Carpi (May 21–22, 1997), ed. by F. Bonilauri, E. Maugeri, Florence, 1999, pp. 67–78.

Perani 2002
M. Perani, "La cultura ebraica a Bologna fra Medioevo e Rinascimento nella testimonianza dei manoscritti," in *La cultura ebraica a Bologna fra Medioevo e Rinascimento*, Conference Proceedings, Bologna (April 9, 2000), ed. by M. Perani, Florence, 2002, pp. 29–70.

Perani 2004
M. Perani, "I manoscritti ebraici come fonte storica," in *Fonti per la storia della società ebraica in Italia dal Tardo-antico al Rinascimento: Una messa a punto*, in *Materia giudaica*, 9, 2004, pp. 79–101.

Perani 2005
M. Perani, "Le firme in giudeo-arabo degli ebrei di Sicilia in atti notarili di Caltabellotta, Polizzi e Sciacca," in *Hebraica Hereditas: studi in onore di Cesare Colafemmina*, ed. by A. Lacerenza, Naples, 2005, pp. 143–234.

Perani 2006
M. Perani, "Tre manoscritti ebraici copiati a Crevalcore tra il XV e il XVI secolo," in *Rassegna storica crevalcorese*, 3, 2006, pp. 8–29.

Perani 2007
M. Perani, "Nuovi dati sul manoscritto Mosca, Guenzburg 786, copiato da Osea Finzi a Crevalcore nel 1505," in *Rassegna storica crevalcorese*, 5, 2007, pp. 8–15.

Perani 2008
M. Perani, "Morte e rinascita dei manoscritti ebraici: il loro riuso come legature e la loro recente riscoperta," in *Studi di storia del Cristianesimo. Per Alba Maria Orselli*, ed. by L. Canetti, M. Caroli, E. Morini, R. Savigni, Ravenna, 2008, pp. 313–36.

Perani 2012a
M. Perani, "I manoscritti ebraici copiati in Sicilia e i loro colophon come testimonianza del background culturale di Flavio Mitridate," in *Flavio Mitridate*

mediatore fra culture nel contesto dell'ebraismo siciliano del XV secolo, Conference Prceedings, Caltabellotta (July 30–1, 2008), ed. by M. Perani, G. Corazzol, Palermo, 2012, pp. 2–16.

Perani 2012b
M. Perani, "Iter Hebraicum Italicum: l'Italia crocevia dei viaggi dei manoscritti ebraici per le rotte e i paesi del Mediterraneo," in *Quod ore cantas corde credas: Studi in onore di Giacomo Baroffio Dahnk*, ed. by L. Scappaticci, Vatican City, 2012, pp. 103–27.

Perani 2015a
M. Perani, "Italia 'paniere' dei manoscritti ebraici e la loro diaspora nel contesto del collezionismo in Europa tra Otto e Novecento, in *Il collezionismo di libri ebraici tra XVII e XIX secolo: Atti del convegno, Torino, 27 marzo 2015*, ed. by C. Pilocane, A. Spagnoletto, Florence, 2015 [2017], pp. 63–91.

Perani 2015b
M. Perani, "Le fonti scritte degli ebrei di Roma nel medioevo," in *Roma e il suo territorio nel Medioevo: le fonti scritte fra tradizione e innovazione*, Conference Proceedings of the Associazione italiana dei Paleografi e Diplomatisti (Rome, September 25–29, 2012), ed. by C. Carbonetti, S. Lucà, and M. Signorini, Spoleto, 2015, pp. 89–123.

Perani 2015c
M. Perani, "I colofoni dei manoscritti ebraici: tipologia, formule e caratteri specifici," in *Colofoni armeni a confronto: le sottoscrizioni dei manoscritti in ambito armeno e nelle altre tradizioni scrittorie del mondo mediterraneo*, Workshop Proceedings, Bologna (October 12–13, 2012), ed. by A. Sirinian, P. Buzi, and G. Shurgaia, Rome, 2015, pp. 347–82.

Perani 2016
M. Perani, "Il libro ebraico a Roma fra XIII e XIV secolo," in *Il libro miniato a Roma nel Duecento. Riflessioni e proposte*, ed. by S. Maddalo, E. Ponzi, 2 vols., Rome, 2016, vol. I, pp. 377–409.

Perani and Grazi 2006
M. Perani, A. Grazi, "La 'scuola' dei copisti ebrei di Otranto (sec. XI): nuove scoperte, in *Materia giudaica*, 9, 2006, pp. 13–41.

Perini 2012
V. Perini, *Il Simonino: geografia di un culto*, with essays by D. Quaglioni and L. Dal Pra, Trento, 2012.

Perles 1884
J. Perles, *Beiträge zur Geschichte der hebräischen und aramäischen Studien*, Munich, 1884.

Pesaro 1880
A. Pesaro, *Appendice alle memorie storiche sulla comunità israelitica ferrarese*, Ferrara, 1880.

Pfeiffer 1975
H. Pfeiffer, *Zur Ikonographie von Raffaels disputa: Egidio da Viterbo und die christlich-platonische Konzeption der Stanza della Segnatura*, Rome, 1975.

Pflaum 1926
H. Pflaum, *Die Idee der Liebe Leone Ebreo: Zwei Abhandlungen zur Geschichte der Philosophie in der Renaissance*, Tübingen, 1926.

Pico della Mirandola 2003
Giovanni Pico della Mirandola, *Discorso sulla dignità dell'uomo*, ed. by F. Bausi, Parma, 2003.

Pico della Mirandola 2010a
Giovanni Pico della Mirandola, *De ente et uno*, ed. by R. Ebgi, with the collaboration of F. Bacchelli, foreword by M. Bertozzi, afterword by M. Cacciari, Milan, 2010.

Pico della Mirandola 2010b
Giovanni Pico della Mirandola, *Apologia: l'autodifesa di Pico di fronte al Tribunale dell'Inquisizione*, ed. by P. E. Fornaciari, Florence, 2010.

Piemontese 2002
A. M. Piemontese, "Codici greco-latino-arabi in Italia fra XI e XV secolo," in *Libri, documenti, epigrafi medievali: possibilità di studi comparativi*, ed. by F. Magistrale, C. Drago, and P. Fioretti, Spoleto, 2002, pp. 445–66.

Poliakov 1974
L. Poliakov, *I banchieri ebrei e la Santa Sede dal XIII al XVIII secolo*, Rome, 1974.

Portioli 1882–84
A. Portioli, "La chiesa e la Madonna della Vittoria di A. Mantegna in Mantova," in *Atti dell'Accademia Virgiliana di Mantova*, 1882–84, pp. 55–79.

Precopi Lombardo and Sparto 1984
A. Precopi Lombardo, [A. Sparto], "Virdimura, dottoressa ebrea del medioevo siciliano," in *La Fardelliana*, 3, 1984, pp. 361–64.

Primavesi 2006
O. Primavesi, "Apollo and Other Gods in Empedocles," in *La costruzione del discorso filosofico nell'età dei Presocratici / The Construction of Philosophical Discourse in the Age of the Presocratics*, Pisa, 2006, pp. 51–77.

Procaccia 1991
M. Procaccia, "Talmudistae Caballarii e Annio," in *Cultura umanistica a Viterbo per il 5. centenario della stampa a Viterbo (1488–1988)* (November 12, 1988), ed. by T. Sampieri, G. Lombardi, Viterbo 1991, pp. 111–21.

Processi del Sant'Uffizio 1987–99
Processi del Sant'Uffizio di Venezia

contro ebrei e giudaizzanti, ed. by P. C. Ioly Zorattini, 14 vols., Florence, 1987–99.

Proto Pisani 2006
R. C. Proto Pisani, *Museo della Collegiata di Sant'Andrea a Empoli*, Florence, 2006.

Pullan 1985
B. Pullan, *Gli ebrei d'Europa e l'inquisizione a Venezia dal 1550 al 1670*, transl. by G. Cengiarotti, Rome, 1985.

Questa 1957
C. Questa, *De duobus codicibus olim Iordani Ursini cardinalis hebraice subscriptis*, Rome, 1957.

Ravà 1903
V. Ravà, "Di due documenti inediti relativi al medico e filosofo ebreo Jacob Mantino," in *Il Vessillo Israelitico*, 51, 1903, pp. 310–13.

Ravid 1976
B. Ravid, "The First Charter of the Jewish Merchants of Venice, 1589," in *Association for Jewish Studies Review*, 1, 1976, pp. 187–222.

Ravid 1987
B. Ravid, "The Religious, Economic and Social Background of the Context of the Establishment of the Ghetti of Venice," in *Gli ebrei e Venezia*, ed. by G. Cozzi, Venice, 1987, pp. 211–60.

Renouard 1834
A. A. Renouard, *Annales de l'imprimerie des Aldes ou Histoire des trois Manuce et de leur éditions*, Paris, 1834 [1st ed. 1825].

Reuchlin 1996
J. Reuchlin, *L'arte cabbalistica (De arte cabalistica)*, ed. by G. Busi, S. Campanini, Florence, 1996.

Richler 1990
B. Richler, *Hebrew Manuscripts: A Treasured Legacy*, Cleveland 1990.

Richler 2013
B. Richler, "Italy, the 'Breadbasket' of Hebrew Manuscripts," in *The Italia Judaica Jubilee Conference*, ed. by S. Simonsohn, J. Shatzmiller, Leiden and Boston 2013, pp. 137–41.

Richler 2014
B. Richler, *Guide to Hebrew Manuscript Collections*, 2nd revised edition, Jerusalem, 2014.

Rinascimento e passione 2008
Rinascimento e passione per l'antico: Andrea Riccio e il suo tempo, ed. by A. Bacchi, L. Giacometti, Trento, 2008.

Rodov 2010
I. Rodov, "Tower-Like Torah Arks: The Tower of Strength and the Architecture of the Messianic Temple," in *Journal of the Warburg and Courtauld Institutes*, 73, 2010, pp. 65–98.

Romano 1990
G. Romano, *Studi sul paesaggio*, Turin, 1990.

Romano 1991–92
D. Romano, "Hispanojudíos traductores del árabe," in *Butlletí de la Reial Acadèmia de Bones Lletres de Barcelona*, 43, 1991–92, pp. 211–32.

Ronen 1992
A. Ronen, "Iscrizioni ebraiche nell'arte italiana del Quattrocento," in *Studi di storia dell'arte sul Medioevo e il Rinascimento nel centenario della nascita di Mario Salmi*, 2 vols., Florence, 1992, vol. 2, pp. 602–24.

Rossi 1997
S. Rossi, "La Nascita della Vergine del pittore umanista Vittore Carpaccio: spunti per un'analisi iconografica ed iconologica," in *Annali di Ca' Foscari*, 35, 1997, pp. 51–81.

Roth 1946
C. Roth, *The History of the Jews of Italy*, Philadelphia, 1946.

Roth 1959
C. Roth, *The Jews in the Renaissance*, Philadelphia, 1959.

Rothschild 1987
J-P. Rothschild, "Quelques listes de livres hébreux dans des manuscrits de la Bibliothèque nationale de Paris," in *Revue d'histoire des textes*, 17, 1987, pp. 291–346.

Rubin 2017
A. D. Rubin, "Judeo-Italian," in *Handbook of Jewish Languages*, revised and updated ed., Leiden and Boston 2017, pp. 297–364.

Ruderman 1981
D. Ruderman, *The World of a Renaissance Jew: The Life and Thought of Abraham ben Mordecai Farissol*, Cincinnati, 1981.

Ruderman 1987
D. B. Ruderman, "The Italian Renaissance and Jewish Thought," in *Renaissance Humanism: Foundations, Forms, and Legacy*, ed. by A. Rabil Jr., vol. 1, Philadelphia, 1987, pp. 382–433.

Ruderman 1995
D. B. Ruderman, *Jewish Thought and Scientific Discovery in Early Modern Europe*, New Haven, 1995.

Ruderman 2010
D. B. Ruderman, *Early Modern Jewry: A New Cultural History*, Princeton and Oxford, 2010.

Rummel 2002
E. Rummel, *The Case against Johann Reuchlin: Social and Religious Controversy in Sixteenth-Century Germany*, Toronto, 2002.

Sabar 1990
S. Sabar, *Bride,* "Heroine and Courtesan: Images of the Jewish

Woman in Hebrew Manuscripts of the Renaissance in Italy," in *Proceedings of the Tenth World Congress of Jewish Studies*, Division D, vol. 11, Jerusalem, 1990, pp. 63–70.

Sabar 2012
S. Sabar, "A New Discovery: The Earliest Illustrated Esther Scroll by Shalom Italia," in *Ars Judaica*, 8, 2012, pp. 121–22.

Sabbatian Heresy 2017
Sabbatian Heresy: Writings on Mysticism, Messianism, and the Origins of Jewish Modernity, ed. by P. Maciejko, Waltham, MA, 2017.

Sandal 2010
E. Sandal in *La Bibliofilía*, 112, 2010, pp. 95–97.

Sanfilippo 2016
C. M. Sanfilippo, *L'onomastica ferrarese del primo Trecento e gli Instrumenta fidelitatis*, Padua, 2016.

Santilli 2017
A. Santilli, "Gli ebrei a Orvieto nella prima metà del Quattrocento," in *Presenze ebraiche in Umbria meridionale dal Medioevo all'Età moderna*, ed. by P. Pellegrini, Foligno, 2017, pp. 81–95.

Sanudo 1879–1903
M. Sanudo, *I Diarii*, Venice, 1879–1903.

Sardi 1566
G. Sardi, *Historie ferraresi*, Ferrara, 1566.

Sarfatti 2001
G. B. Sarfatti, "Hebrew Script in Western Visual Art," in *Italia*, 13–14, 2001, pp. 451–547.

Sarfatti, Pontani, and Zamponi 2001
G. Sarfatti, A. Pontani, and S. Zamponi, "Titulus Crucis," in

Giotto: La croce di Santa Maria Novella, ed. by M. Ciatti, M. Seidel, Florence, 2001, pp. 191–99.

Savants et croyants 2018
Savants et croyants: les juifs d'Europe du nord au moyen âge, ed. by N. Hatot, J. Olszowy-Schlanger, Rouen, 2018.

Scandaliato 2013
A. Scandaliato, "From Sicily to Rome: The Cultural Route of Michele Zumat, Physician and Rabbi in the 16th Century," in *Atti del Convegno Italia Judaica Jubilee Conference* (Tel Aviv University, January 3–5, 2010), Leiden and Boston 2013, pp. 199–210.

Scandalato and Mandalà 2012
A. Scandaliato, G. Mandalà, "Guglielmo Raimondo Moncada e Annio da Viterbo: proposte di identificazione e prospettive di ricerca," in *Flavio Mitridate mediatore tra culture nel contesto dell'ebraismo*, Conference Proceedings, Caltabellotta (June 30 – July 1, 2008), ed. by M. Perani, G. Corazzol, Palermo, 2012, pp. 201–217.

Scapecchi 1979
P. Scapecchi, *La Pala dell'arte della lana del Sassetta*, Siena, 1979.

Schleif 1993
C. Schleif, "Hands that Appoint, Anoint and Ally: Late Medieval Donor Strategies for Appropriating Approbation through Painting," in *Art History*, 16, 1993, pp. 1–13.

Scholem 1933–34
G. Scholem, "An Index to the Commentaries on the Ten Sefirot" [in Hebrew], in *Kirjath sefer*, 10, 1933–34, pp. 494–515.

Schreckenberg 1999
H. Schreckenberg, *Die christlichen Adversus-Judaeos-Texte und ihr*

literarisches und historisches Umfeld (1.–11. Jahrhundert), Frankfurt am Main, 1995 [1st ed. 1982].

Schubert 1991
U. Schubert, "Das mittelalterliche Erbe in der Bilderbibel des Moses dal Castellazzo, Warschau, Jüdisches Historisches Institut, Cod. 1164," in *Die Juden in ihrer mittelalterlichen Umwelt*, ed. by A. Ebenbauer, K. Zatloukal, Vienna 1991 pp. 205–22.

Sed-Rajna 1994
G. Sed-Rajna, *Les manuscrits Hébreux enluminés des Bibliothèques de France*, codicological records and registration records by S. Fellous, Paris, 1994.

Settis 1981
S. Settis, "Artisti e committenti fra Quattro e Cinquecento," in *Annali della Storia d'Italia*, IV: *Intellettuali e potere*, Turin, 1981, pp. 701–61.

Settis 2010
S. Settis, *Artisti e committenti fra Quattro e Cinquecento*, Turin, 2010.

Settis 2018
S. Settis, "Artists and patrons in the 15th and 16th centuries," in *Il Codice Maimonide e i Norsa: una famiglia ebraica nella Mantova dei Gonzaga. Banche libri quadri*, exh. cat. (Archivio di Stato, Rome), ed. by C. Farnetti, S. Settis [Italian/English], Rome, 2018, pp. 7–17.

Sgarbi 2006
V. Sgarbi, *Domenico di Paris e la scultura a Ferrara nel Quattrocento*, entries by A. Bellandi, P. Di Natale, Milan, 2006.

Shulvass 1973
M. Shulvass, *The Jews in the World of the Renaissance*, Leiden, 1973.

Signorini 1996
R. Signorini, "The Creation of Adam: A Detail in Mantegna's

Madonna della Vittoria," in *Journal of the Warburg and Courtauld Institutes*, 69, 1996, pp. 303–4.

Simonsohn 1977
S. Simonsohn, *History of the Jews in the Duchy of Mantua*, Tel Aviv, 1977.

Simonsohn 1982–86
The Jews in the Duchy of Milan, ed. with introduction and notes by S. Simonsohn, 4 vols., Jerusalem, 1982–86.

Simonsohn 1988–91
The Apostolic See and the Jews, ed. by S. Simonsohn, 8 vols., Toronto, 1988–91.

Simonsohn 1997–2010
S. Simonsohn, *The Jews in Sicily*, 18 vols., Leiden and Boston, 1997–2010.

Simonsohn 1999
S. Simonsohn, "Epigrafia ebraica in Sicilia," in *Sicilia Epigraphica*, Pisa, 1999, pp. 509–29.

Simonsohn 2011
S. Simonsohn, *Tra Scilla e Cariddi: storia degli Ebrei in Sicilia*, Florence, 2011.

Sirat 2002
C. Sirat, *Hebrew Manuscripts of the Middle Ages*, Cambridge, 2002.

Sonne 1934
I. Sonne, "I dati biografici contenuti negli scritti di Shelomoh Molco riesaminati alla luce di un nuovo documento," in *Annuario di studi ebraici*, 1, 1934, pp. 187–204.

Sonne 1954
I. Sonne, *Mi-Paulo ha-revi'i 'ad Pius ha-hamishi*, Jerusalem, 1954.

Starrabba 1878
R. Starrabba, "Guglielmo Raimondo Moncada ebreo convertito siciliano del secolo XV,"

in *Archivio Storico Siciliano*, 3, 1878, pp. 15–91.

Steinschneider 1852–60
M. Steinschneider, *Catalogus Librorum Hebraeorum in Bibliotheca Bodleiana*, 2 vols., Berlin, 1852–60.

Steinschneider 1878
M. Steinschneider in *Hebräische Bibliographie*, 18, 1878, pp. 135–36.

Stemp 1999
R. Stemp, "Two Sculptures Designed by Cosmè Tura," in *The Burlington Magazine*, 141, 1999, pp. 208–15, 226–28.

Stenne 1878
G. Stenne, *Description des objets d'art religieux hébraïques exposés dans les galeries du Trocadéro à l'Exposition universelle de 1878: Collection de M. Strauss*, Poissy, 1878.

Stephens 1979
W. Stephens, *Berosus Chaldaeus: Counterfeit and Fictive Authors of thre Early Sixteenth Century*, PhD Dissertation, Cornell University, 1979.

Stephens 2010
W. Stephens, "Annius of Viterbo," in A. Grafton, G. Warren Most, and S. Settis, *The Classical Tradition*, Cambridge, Mass., 2010, pp. 46–47.

Storia di Mantova 2005
Storia di Mantova, ed. by M. A. Romani, vol. 1, Mantua, 2005.

Stow 2007
K. Stow, *Jewish Life in Early Modern Rome: Challenge, Conversion, and Private Life*, Aldershot, 2007.

Stuczynski 2019
C. B. Stuczynski, "From 'Potential' and 'Fuzzy' Jews to 'Non-Jews' / 'Jewish Non-Jews': *Conversos* Living in Iberia and Early Modern

Jewry," in *Connecting Histories: Jews and their Others in Early Modern Europe*, ed. by F. Bregoli, D. Ruderman, Philadelphia, 2019 [in press].

Studemund Halevy 1994–97
M. Studemund Halevy, *Die Sefarden in Hamburg: Zur Geschichte einer Minderheit*, 2 vols., Hamburg, 1994–97.

Tamalio 2007
R. Tamalio, ad vocem "Malatesta, Eusebio," in *Dizionario biografico degli italiani*, vol. 68, Rome, 2007, pp. 33–34.

Tamani 1968
G. Tamani, "Elenco dei manoscritti ebraici miniati e decorati della Palatina di Parma," in *La Bibliofilia*, 70, 1968, pp. 39–134.

Tamani 1976
G. Tamani, "Libri ebraici Soncino nella Biblioteca Palatina di Parma," in *Archivio Storico Province Parmensi*, 28, 1976, pp. 337–52.

Tamani 1987
G. Tamani, "Manoscritti," in *Cultura ebraica in Emilia-Romagna*, ed. by S. M. Bondoni, G. Busi, Rimini, 1987, pp. 415–64.

Tamani 1988
G. Tamani, *Il Canon medicinae di Avicenna nella tradizione ebraica: le miniature del manoscritto 2197 della Biblioteca Universitaria di Bologna*, Padua, 1988.

Tamani 2003
G. Tamani, *Catalogo dei manoscritti filosofici, giuridici e scientifici nella Biblioteca della Comunità ebraica di Mantova*, Fiesole, 2003.

Tedeschi Falco 1999
A. Tedeschi Falco, *Ferrara: Guida alle sinagoghe e al museo*, Venice, 1999.

Terni De Gregory 1958
W. Terni De Gregory, *Pittura artigiana lombarda del Rinascimento*, introduction by E. Arslan, Milan, 1958.

Terracciano 2018
P. Terracciano, "The Origen of Pico's Kabbalah: Esoteric Wisdom and the Dignity of Man," in *Journal of the History of Ideas*, 79, 2018, pp. 343–61.

The Cambridge History 2018
The Cambridge History of Judaism, vol. 6: *The Middle Ages: The Christian World*, ed. by R. Chazan, Cambridge, 2018.

The Gate of Heaven 2012
The Gate of Heaven: The Hebrew Text, Flavius Mithridates' Latin Translation and an English Version, ed. by S. Jurgan, S. Campanini, with a text on Pico della Mirandola by G. Busi, Turin, 2012.

The Great Parchment 2004
The Great Parchment. Flavius Mithridates' Latin Translation, the Hebrew Text and an English Version, ed. by G. Busi, with S. M. Bondoni and S. Campanini, Turin, 2004.

The Hebrew Book 2011
The Hebrew Book in Early Modern Italy, ed. by J. R. Hacker and A. Shear, Philadelphia, 2011.

The Jewish-Christian Encounter 2015
The Jewish-Christian Encounter in Medieval Preaching, ed. by J. Adams and J. Hanska, New York and London, 2015.

The Parma Psalter 1996
The Parma Psalter: A thirteenth-century illuminated Hebrew book of Psalms with a Commentary by Abraham Ibn Ezra, companion volume to the facsimile edition by M. Beit-Arié, T. Metzger, and E. Silver, London, 1996.

Tigler 2007
G. Tigler, "La porta dei Mesi del Duomo di Ferrara e le sue derivazioni ad Arezzo, Fidenza e Traù," in *Il Maestro dei Mesi e il portale meridionale della cattedrale di Ferrara: ipotesi e confronti*, ed. by B. Giovannucci Vigi, G. Sassu, Ferrara, 2007, pp. 71–100.

Tirosh-Rothschild 1991
H. Tirosh-Rothschild, *Between Worlds: The Life and Thoughts of Rabbi David ben Judah Messer Leon*, New York, 1991.

Tirosh-Rothschild 1988
H. Tirosh–Rothschild, "In Defense of Jewish Humanism," in *Jewish History*, 3, 1988, pp. 31–57.

Tirosh-Samuelson 1990
H. Tirosh-Samuelson, "Jewish Culture in Renaissance Italy: A Methodological Survey," in *Italia*, 9/1–2, 1990, pp. 63–96.

Toaff 1987
A. Toaff, "Convergenza sul Veneto di banchieri ebrei romani e tedeschi nel tardo Medioevo," in *Gli ebrei e Venezia*, ed. by G. Cozzi, Milan, 1987, pp. 595–613.

Toaff 1989
A. Toaff, *Il vino e la carne: una comunità ebraica nel Medioevo*, Bologna, 1989.

Toaff 1990
R. Toaff, *La Nazione Ebrea a Livorno e a Pisa (1591–1700)*, Florence, 1990.

Toaff 1991
A. Toaff, "Migrazioni di ebrei tedeschi attraverso i territori triestini e friulani fra XIV e XV secolo," in *Il mondo ebraico: gli ebrei tra Italia Nord-Orientale e Impero Asburgico dal Medioevo all'Età contemporanea*, ed. by G. Todeschini, P. C. Ioly Zorattini, Pordenone, 1991, pp. 3–29.

Toaff 1996
A. Toaff, "'Banchieri' cristiani e 'prestatori' ebrei?" in *Storia d'Italia: Annali 11. Gli ebrei in Italia*, ed. by C. Vivanti, 2 vols., Turin, 1996, vol. 1, pp. 267–87.

Toch 2013
M. Toch, *The Economic History of European Jews: Late Antiquity and Early Middle Ages*, Leiden, 2013.

Todeschini 1989
G. Todeschini, *La ricchezza degli ebrei: merci e denaro nella riflessione ebraica e nella definizione cristiana dell'usura alla fine del Medioevo*, Spoleto, 1989.

Todeschini 1990
G. Todeschini, "Familles juives et chrétiennes en Italie à la fin du Moyen Age: deux modèles de développement économique," in *Annales E. S. C.*, 45, 1990, pp. 787–817.

Todeschini 2002
G. Todeschini, *I mercanti e il tempio*, Bologna, 2002.

Todeschini 2003
G. Todeschini, "Licet in maxima parte adhuc bestiales: la raffigurazione degli Ebrei come non umani in alcuni testi altomedievali," in *Studi Medievali*, 44, 2003, pp. 1135–50.

Todeschini 2007
G. Todeschini, *Visibilmente crudeli: malviventi, persone sospette e gente qualunque dal medioevo all'età moderna*, Bologna, 2007.

Todeschini 2009
G. Todeschini, "'Spiritum non habentes': appunti sulla bestializzazione degli ebrei nell'alto medioevo," in *Dentro e fuori la Sicilia: studi di storia per Vincenzo d'Alessandro*, Rome, 2009, pp. 267–84.

Todeschini 2016
G. Todeschini, *La banca
e il ghetto: una storia italiana*,
Rome, 2016.

Todeschini 2018
G. Todeschini, *Gli ebrei nell'Italia
medievale*, Rome, 2018.

Toffanello 2010
M. Toffanello, *Le arti a Ferrara nel
Quattrocento*, Ferrara, 2010.

Togliani 2009
C. Togliani, *Il principe e l'eremita:
da San Lorenzo in Guidizzolo
a Santa Maria della Vittoria in
Mantova. Uomini, architettura
e territorio fra XV e XVI secolo*,
Mantua, 2009.

Torboli 2000
M. Torboli, "*Nobilissimo sepolcro.
Il sarcofago di Prisciano Prisciani
nella Certosa di Ferrara: fonti e
documenti*," in *Musei ferraresi*,
19, 2000, pp. 57–86.

Torresi 2007
A. P. Torresi, "Tre scultori per
Ercole I: ritratti al Duca di
Bertoldo di Giovanni, Sperandio
mantovano, Guido Mazzoni,"
in *Crocevia estense*, 2007, pp.
189–226.

Torriti 1990
P. Torriti, *La pinacoteca nazionale di
Siena: I dipinti*, Genoa, 1990.

Trivellato 2009
F. Trivellato, *The Familiarity of
Strangers: The Sephardic Diaspora,
Livorno, and cross-cultural Trade
in the Early Modern Period*,
New Haven, 2009.

Trivellato 2016
F. Trivellato, *Il commercio
interculturale: la diaspora sefardita,
Livorno e i traffici globali in età
moderna*, Rome, 2016.

Una Biblia 2014
*Una Biblia a varias voces: estudio

textual de la Biblia Políglota
Complutense*, ed. by I. Carbajosa,
A. García Serrano, Madrid,
2014.

Urbani and Zazzu 1999
R. Urbani, G. N. Zazzu, *The Jews in
Genoa*, 2 vols., Leiden and Boston,
1999.

Vanzan Marchini 1979
N. Vanzan Marchini, "Medici ebrei
e assistenza cristiana nella Venezia
del Cinquecento," in *Rassegna
Mensile d'Israel*, 45, 1979, pp.
139–41.

Vasoli 1988
C. Vasoli, *Filosofia e religione nella
cultura del Rinascimento*, Naples,
1988.

Venezia e le sue lagune 1847
Venezia e le sue lagune, 2 vols.
in 4 tomes, Venice, 1847.

Venezia, gli ebrei 2016
*Venezia, gli ebrei e l'Europa: 1516–
2016*, exh. cat., Venice, 2016.

Venturi 1889
A. Venturi, "L'arte emiliana
del Rinascimento: Ludovico
Mazzolino," in *Rassegna emiliana
di storia, letteratura ed arte*, 2,
1889, pp. 5–14.

Venturi 1904
A. Venturi, *Storia dell'arte italiana*,
III: *Arte romanica*, Milan, 1904.

Venturi 1990
G. Venturi, "Delizia (e altro)," in
*Il Parco del delta del Po: l'ambiente
come laboratorio*, Ferrara, 1990,
pp. 129–39.

Veronese 1990
A. Veronese, "Una societas ebraico-
cristiana in docendo tripudiare
sonare ac cantare nella Florence,
del Quattrocento," in *Guglielmo da
Pesaro e la danza nelle corti italiane
del XV secolo*, ed. by M. Padovan,
Pisa, 1990, pp. 51–57.

Veronese 1998
A. Veronese, "La presenza
ebraica nel ducato di Urbino nel
Quattrocento," in *Italia Judaica:
gli ebrei nello Stato pontificio fino
al Ghetto (1555)*, VI Conference
Proceedings, Rome, 1998, pp.
251–83.

Veronese 2013
A. Veronese, "Interazioni
economiche e sociali tra ebrei e
cristiani con particolare riguardo
all'area mediterranea," in *Religiosità
e civiltà: conoscenze, confronti,
influssi reciproci tra le religioni
(secoli 10–14)*, ed. by G. Andenna,
indexes by E. Filippi, Milan, 2013,
pp. 237–50.

Vespasiano da Bisticci 1892–93
*Vite di uomini illustri del secolo 15,
scritte da Vespasiano da Bisticci,
rivedute sui manoscritti da L. Frati*,
3 vols., Bologna, 1892–93.

Weber 1997–98
A. Weber, "Ark and Curtain:
Monuments for a Jewish Nation
in Exile," in *The Real and Ideal
Jerusalem in Jewish, Christian
and Islamic Art*, ed. by
A. Cohen-Mushlin, B. Kühnel,
in *Jewish Art*, 23–24, 1997–98,
pp. 89–99.

Weil 1963
G. E. Weil, *Élie Lévita humaniste
et massorète (1469–1549)*, Leiden,
1963.

Weingort 1979
A. Weingort, *Interêt et crédit dans
le droit talmudique*, Paris, 1979.

Weingort 1998
A. Weingort, *Responsabilité
et sanction en droit talmudique
et comparé*, Paris, 1998.

Weiss 1962
R. Weiss, "An unknown epigraphic
Tract by Annius of Viterbo," in
*Italian Studies presented to E. R.
Vincent on his Retirement from the*

Chair of Italian at Cambridge, ed. by C.P. Brand, K. Foster, and U. Limentani, Cambridge, 1962, pp. 101–20.

Wilkinson 2007
R. J. Wilkinson, *Orientalism, Aramaic and Kabbalah in the Catholic Reformation: The first Printing of the Syriac New Testament*, Leiden and Boston, 2007.

Winberg 1987
J. Weinberg, "Azariah de' Rossi and the Forgeries of Annius of Viterbo," in *Aspetti della storiografia ebraica*, V Conference Procecdings of ASIG, Rome, 1987, pp. 23–47.

Wirszubski 1963
C. Wirszubski, *Flavius Mithridates: Sermo de Passione Domini*, Jerusalem, 1963.

Wirszubski 1989
C. Wirszubski, *Pico della Mirandola's Encounter with Jewish Mysticism*, Cambridge, Mass. and London, 1989.

Wirtschaftsgeschichte 2008
Wirtschaftsgeschichte der mittelalterlichen Juden: Fragen und Einschätzungen, ed. by E. Muller-Luckner, M. Toch, Munich, 2008.

Yaniv 1989
B. Yaniv, "The Origin of the Two-Column Motif in European Parokhot," in *Jewish Art*, 15, 1989, pp. 26–43.

Yaniv 2009
B. Yaniv, *Ma'ase Rokem: Textile Ceremonial Objects in the Askenazi, Sephardi and Italian Synagogue*, Jerusalem, 2009.

Yerushalmi 1971
Y. H. Yerushalmi, *From Spanish Court to Italian Ghetto: Isaac Cardoso, a Study in Seventeenth Century Marranism and Jewish Apologetics*, New York, 1971.

Zamboni 1968
S. Zamboni, *Ludovico Mazzolino*, Milan, 1968.

Zanelli 1904
A. Zanelli in *Archivio storico lombardo*, 31, 1904, pp. 125–33.

Zazzu 1990
G. N. Zazzu, "La glossa al Salmo XIX nel Salterio Ottaplo di Agaostino Giustiniani," in *Biblische und judaistische Studien. Festschrift für Paolo Sacchi*, ed. by A. Vivian, Frankfurt am Main, 1990, pp. 575–82.

Zeldes 2006
N. Zeldes, "The Last Multi-Cultural Encounter in Medieval Sicily: A Dominican Scholar, an Arabic Inscription, and a Jewish Legend," in *Mediterranean Historical Review*, 21, 2006, pp. 159–91.

Zenarola Pastore 1993
I. Zenarola Pastore, *Gli ebrei a Cividale del Friuli dal XII al XVIII secolo*, Udine, 1993.

Zeri 1978
F. Zeri, review of C. M. Kauffmann, "Victoria and Albert Museum. Catalogue of Foreign Paintings. I: Before 1800," in *Antologia di Belle Arti*, II, 7–8, December 1978, pp. 317–21 (republished in F. Zeri, *Giorno per giorno nella pittura*, Turin, 1998, pp. 189–92).

Zeri 1986
F. Zeri, "Unknown Lombard Painter, first Quarter of the XVI Century," in *The Metropolitan Museum of Art: North Italian School*, with the assistance of E. E. Gardner, New York, 1986, pp. 72–74.

Zonta 2004
M. Zonta, "The Autumn of Medieval Jewish Philosophy: Latin Scholasticism in the late-15th-Century Hebrew philosophical Literature," in *"Herbst des Mittelalters"? Fragen zur Bewertung des 14. und 15. Jahrhunderts*, ed. by J. A. Aertsen, M. Pickave, Berlin and New York 2004, pp. 474–92.

Zonta 2006
M. Zonta, *Hebrew Scholasticism in the Fifteenth Century: A History and Source Book*, Dordrecht, 2006.

Zonta 2011
M. Zonta, "Aristotle's De anima and De generatione et corruptione in the Medieval Hebrew Tradition: New Details regarding Textual History coming from a neglected Manuscript," in *Studies in the History of Culture and Science: A Tribute to Gad Freudenthal*, ed. by R. Fontaine, R. Glasner, R. Leicht, and G. Veltri, Leiden and Boston, 2011, pp. 91–101.

Zorzi 2010
F. Zorzi, *L'armonia del mondo*, ed. by S. Campanini, Milan, 2010.

Photo credits

Album / Oronoz / Mondadori Portfolio
Archivi Alinari, Florence
Archivio di Stato, Venice
Raffaello Bencini / Archivi Alinari, Florence
Biblioteca Comunale Teresiana, Mantova (Prot. n. 0021295
- 28/03/2019)
Rossella Bottini Treves, Vercelli
Courtesy Ministero per i Beni e le Attività Culturali – Polo
museale della Toscana / Photo Archivio della Pinacoteca
Nazionale di Siena
Courtesy Ministero per i Beni e le Attività Culturali /
Archivi Alinari, Florence
Courtesy Fondazione Accademia Carrara, Bergamo
Courtesy Ministero per i Beni e le Attività Culturali –
Biblioteca Medicea Laurenziana, Florence
Courtesy Ministero per i Beni e le Attività Culturali –
Biblioteca Palatina, Parma
Courtesy Ministero per i Beni e le Attività Culturali –
Polo museale della Toscana / Foto Archivio della
Pinacoteca Nazionale di Siena
DeA Picture Library, licensed to Alinari
Diocesi di Mantova / Photo Antonio Lodigiani
Claudio Furin, Ferrara
Galleria Doria Pamphilj, Rome © 2019 Amministrazione
Doria Pamphilj s.r.l.
Luca Gavagna, Le Immagini s.a.s, Ferrara
Iberfoto /Archivi Alinari
Toni Lodigiani, Mantova
Museo della Cattedrale, Ferrara
Photo © Musée du Louvre, Dist. RMN-Grand Palais /
Angèle Dequier
Photo © RMN-Grand Palais (Musée de Cluny – Musée
national du Moyen-Âge) / Jean-Gilles Berizzi
Photo © RMN-Grand Palais (Musée de Cluny – Musée
national du Moyen-Âge) / Gérard Blot / Christian Jean
Photo © RMN-Grand Palais (Musée du Louvre) /
Jean-Gilles Berizzi
Photo © RMN-Grand Palais (Musée d'art et d'histoire
du Judaïsme) / Jean-Gilles Berizzi
Photo © The Israel Museum Jerusalem by Ardon Bar-Hama
SAAS-SIPA (Prot. n. 1304/28.34.01.11/7.1)
Staatliche Museen zu Berlin

Cover Design
Teikna, Claudia Neri

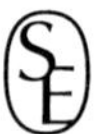

Silvana Editoriale

Direction
Dario Cimorelli

Art Director
Giacomo Merli

Editorial Coordinator
Sergio Di Stefano

Copy Editor
Emanuela Di Lallo

Layout
Annamaria Ardizzi

Translations
Elizabeth Burke, Sarah Elizabeth Cree, Gordon Fisher
for Traduzioni Liquide, Sonia Hill, Susan Scott,
James Stuart, Lauren Sunstein for Scriptum (Rome)

Production Coordinator
Antonio Micelli

Editorial Assistant
Ondina Granato

Photo Editors
Alessandra Olivari, Silvia Sala

Press Office
Lidia Masolini, press@silvanaeditoriale.it

All reproduction and translation rights
reserved for all countries
© 2019 Silvana Editoriale S.p.A.,
Cinisello Balsamo, Milano
© Museo Nazionale dell'Ebraismo Italiano e della Shoah,
Ferrara

Available through ARTBOOK | D.A.P.
155 Sixth Avenue, 2nd Floor, New York, N.Y. 10013
Tel: (212) 627-1999 Fax: (212) 627-9484

Silvana Editoriale S.p.A.
via dei Lavoratori, 78
20092 Cinisello Balsamo, Milano
tel. 02 453 951 01
fax 02 453 951 51
www.silvanaeditoriale.it

Reproductions, printing and binding
in Italy
Printed by Grafiche Lang S.r.l., Genova
April 2019

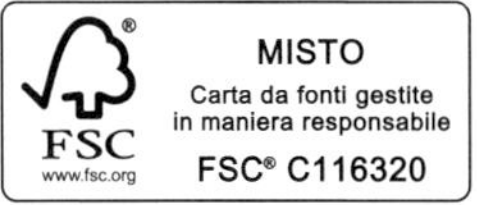